The ACT Has Changed!
We Have You Covered.

Recently, there have been a few changes to the ACT test. None of these changes are extreme, and each practice test in this book is still the perfect tool for you to improve your skills.

Below is a list of ACT updates, and after the updates you will find brand-new, supplemental practice material. We encourage you to use the supplemental material throughout your preparation process. In other words, do not do all the supplemental material immediately. We've given you six new writing prompts; use these prompts as a replacement for the prompts found at the end of each practice test. We have also provided you with two new "dual passage" reading passages. You may complete these any time you'd like. In addition, Test 3 contains a dual passage.

Most importantly, the list of strategies, or "rules" as we call them, found at the beginning of this book, should be used by you as you learn how to raise your ACT score. Our strategies are simple, clear, and direct; simply put, they work! Do yourself and your ACT score a favor; learn our strategies and use them each time you take an ACT.

ACT UPDATES

English

There are almost no changes to the English portion of the ACT, and the six practice tests in this book are completely aligned to the types of questions ACT asks. In the past, the percentages of types of questions ACT asked on English were extremely firm. Now, ACT provides a range of percentages for English. The table below shows these percentages.

Percentage of Topics Tests on ACT English	
Punctuation	10–15%
Grammar and Usage	15–20%
Sentence Structure	20–25%
Strategy	15–20%
Organization	10–15%
Style	15–20%

HW tst 4 p 2

Math

There are only minor changes to the math portion of the ACT. Again, the six practice tests in this book are completely aligned to the types of questions ACT asks. Like the English sections, the percentages of types of questions ACT asked on the math section in the past were extremely firm. Now, ACT provides a range of percentages for math. This table shows these percentages.

Percentage of Topics Tests on ACT English	
Pre-Algebra	20–25%
Elementary Algebra	15–20%
Intermediate Algebra	15–20%
Coordinate Geometry	15–20%
Plane Geometry	20–25%
Trigonometry	5–10%

Reading

The only change to the reading portion of the ACT is the likelihood of being presented with a "dual passage." A "dual passage" can show up in any of the four sections of reading. This new type of passage, if presented, gives you two shorter reading samples, labeled Passage A and Passage B. When and if this occurs on your test, don't panic. Use the reading strategies we provided and trust yourself. It is more effective to read Passage A and immediately answer the corresponding questions and then read Passage B and answer the remaining questions.

Note: We have provided you with two new "dual passage" reading samples for practice. We recommend that you complete these two new passages at some point during your preparation process. Be sure to time yourself! Most reading passages should be completed in 8–9 minutes.

Science

The only change in this section is that students could see either six or seven passages. In the past, science was always presented with exactly seven passages, but that seems to be changing. The good news here is that most students prefer a science test with only six passages instead of seven. Having less data to sort through can be an advantage. Be sure to review and learn our strategies before starting out.

Writing

The ACT Writing has completely changed. The Writing section is still optional, but we encourage most students to take it as many universities now require the score.

The new Writing is scored on a scale 1–36, but the Writing score does not factor into the overall composite score. Each essay is evaluated in four areas: Ideas and Analysis, Development and Support, Organization, and Language Use. These four areas are scored on a 1–6 scale; those scores are then added together and multiplied by 1.5, resulting in the overall score of 1–36.

The ACT Writing will be administered about 5 minutes after the end of the ACT Science test. During the writing test, you will have 40 minutes to plan and write an analytical essay in response to a prompt. Although there is no length requirement, higher-scoring essays tend to be at least 1.5–2 pages long, and while you should spend more time writing than you should spend on planning, you should definitely make time to determine your position and examples before beginning.

If you have taken any older practice tests, or have been studying before, be aware that the writing test has changed. Older material may not reflect these changes. Here is a brief rundown of the changes:

You now have 40 minutes in which to plan and write, instead of 30. The real reason for the time change is there is more initial material to evaluate and address in the prompt.

- **The prompt no longer involves "picking a side."** The "old" ACT Writing presented you with a proposed "new rule" involving teenagers (e.g., requiring a certain GPA in order to get a driver's license, or getting rid of music class so the money could be used for better science equipment) and asked you to write an essay that was "for it" or "against it." Although this type of prompt lent itself much more closely to the traditional "Introduction, Three Points, Conclusion" template you probably learned in school, there was concern that it was testing skill at *debating* more than it was testing skill at *writing* (after all, arguing for/against a position is only *one type* of writing, not *all* writing), and so it was changed.
- **You are now provided with three other people's opinions/perspectives (i.e., "some quotes") that you have to address.** This may sound more complex, but it really is not. The general idea is that the new ACT Writing is more like a conversation than a debate. The new ACT Writing will tell you about an issue in society; give you several ways of thinking about that issue; and then ask you to state your own perspective on that issue. You may also partially agree with one of the other perspectives or totally agree. In any case, you are asked to address the other three perspectives within your essay. You do not have to mention them directly, but make sure the reader knows that you are referring to them. In addition, make sure your essay includes strong examples which support your view.

Note: We have provided you with six brand-new Writing prompts for practice. One of these prompts also has a set of pre-written essays for your consideration. Please use these new prompts in place of the "old" prompts currently attached to each of the six practice tests.

NEW PRACTICE MATERIAL FOR READING AND WRITING

The New Social Studies

For generations, high-school Social Studies curricula and textbooks have been arranged chronologically. The class starts the year's studying at a specific point in history (e.g., the American Revolution) and moves forward in time until the last unit (e.g., the Vietnam War). Recently some U.S. states have reorganized the curricula so that Social Studies classes are divided into different units by topic—such as "Immigration" or "Women's Rights"—rather than starting in the past and advancing chronologically. Proponents of the new method argue that it gives students a better sense of how important issues of the past relate to their own lives. Opponents point out that it weakens students' grasp of when important events happened—how long ago, and in what order.

Read and carefully consider these perspectives. Each suggests a particular way of approaching the debate surrounding the new Social Studies curriculum.

Perspective One	Perspective Two	Perspective Three
Students these days are not well informed about history! Ask one how long ago Columbus sailed to the New World, or whether the Civil War or World War II came first, and he'll have no idea. Knowing *when* things happened is the whole point of history, so if students don't know that, then what *do* they know?	It's true that the new methods don't place as much emphasis on memorizing dates, but some things are more important than that. When the curriculum starts in the distant past and moves forward, students fail to make meaningful connections between events which are related but not in the same time period. Students have the ability to put events in their perspective periods even if they are not taught chronologically.	History needs to be taught with a sense of chronology, but that doesn't mean multicultural perspectives and role models need to be excluded until the textbook reaches the recent past. Why not move chronologically but bring in related concepts when they are relevant?

ESSAY TASK

Write a unified, coherent essay in which you evaluate multiple perspectives on the topic of the new Social Studies curriculum. In your essay, be sure to:

- analyze and evaluate the perspectives given
- state and develop your own perspective on the issue
- explain the relationship between your perspective and those given

Your perspective may be in full agreement with any of the others, in partial agreement, or wholly different. Whatever the case, support your ideas with logical reasoning and detailed, persuasive examples.

Red Meat in School

Recent scientific studies have revealed that all processed meats, and all red (mammalian) meats even if unprocessed, are *carcinogenic*, or cancer-causing. Many processed-meat meals, such as hamburger or chicken nuggets, are staples of public-school cafeteria food. Today, many people argue that red and processed meats in school lunches should be eliminated, or at least that the frequency with which they are served should be significantly curtailed. While it is true that it takes many years of eating a diet very heavy in red and/or processed meats to cause cancer, some make the point that it is incumbent upon the nation's schools to set a good example and assist in the development of lifelong healthy habits.

Read and carefully consider these perspectives. Each suggests a particular way of approaching the debate surrounding red and processed meats in school lunches.

Perspective One	Perspective Two	Perspective Three
If red meat and processed meat cause cancer, then they shouldn't be served in schools. I don't care how long it takes for cancer to develop. It takes a long time to get cancer from smoking, yet there is still a federal law banning smoking on school grounds.	The students have to eat something during the school day. The cost of replacing all processed meats with fresh and healthy options would be enormous. People complain about processed meat now, but if their taxes were raised to cover the cost of providing better lunches, they'd complain about that too.	Scientists go back and forth a lot about which foods are supposedly bad for you. While I'm sure processed meat may not be the healthiest food, there has only been one study that says it causes cancer. We should reduce the frequency with which it is served to be on the safe side, but there is no need to eliminate it entirely.

ESSAY TASK

Write a unified, coherent essay in which you evaluate multiple perspectives on the topic of red and processed meats in school lunches. In your essay, be sure to:

- analyze and evaluate the perspectives given
- state and develop your own perspective on the issue
- explain the relationship between your perspective and those given

Your perspective may be in full agreement with any of the others, in partial agreement, or wholly different. Whatever the case, support your ideas with logical reasoning and detailed, persuasive examples.

Updating Standardized Tests

It seems as though every few years, one of the major standardized tests is changing its format, eliminating one section or type of question and adding others. Often, the reason given by the testing organization is that the old format was "biased" in favor of students with a particular innate ability, whereas performance on the new format can more easily be improved via diligent study by students of all kinds. Some educators, however, don't see why it is any more "fair" to reward excessive preparation and schools "teaching to the test" than it is to reward natural ability.

Read and carefully consider these perspectives. Each suggests a particular way of approaching the debate surrounding contemporary changes made to standardized tests.

Perspective One	Perspective Two	Perspective Three
Students go to school to learn, so what's the point of measuring a skill that cannot be learned by everyone? Standardized tests should be crafted to reflect how much effort students are willing to put in preparation, rather than inborn skills. Effort is what will end up mattering more, both in college and in life.	When we talk about students "preparing" for standardized tests, what we are really talking about is private tutoring. Why should the tests be changed to reward the students whose families can afford that? Students from disadvantaged backgrounds who happened to possess certain natural abilities would get a shot at a better future because of the old tests, and now that happens less.	No matter what material or types of questions appear on a standardized test, the students who are naturally bright are going to perform well, and the people who did poorly are always going to complain that the test was not fair. These changes are just about the testing companies trying to improve their image; these changes will not make a significant difference in performance.

ESSAY TASK

Write a unified, coherent essay in which you evaluate multiple perspectives on the topic of changes being made to standardized tests. In your essay, be sure to:

- analyze and evaluate the perspectives given
- state and develop your own perspective on the issue
- explain the relationship between your perspective and those given

Your perspective may be in full agreement with any of the others, in partial agreement, or wholly different. Whatever the case, support your ideas with logical reasoning and detailed, persuasive examples.

Religious Holidays for All

Even though the First Amendment to the U.S. Constitution forbids the government from endorsing a particular religion, it's no secret that the public-school calendar in the United States was designed with Christianity in mind: "Winter Break" coincides with Christmas and "Spring Break" with Easter. Some years ago, the important Jewish holidays of Yom Kippur and Rosh Hashanah became days off from school as well. As America becomes even more multicultural, many people argue that there should be school holidays that accommodate other religions. Some districts have already changed their calendars to this effect, such as in New York City, where schools are now closed on the Muslim holiday of Eid.

Read and carefully consider these perspectives. Each suggests a particular way of approaching the debate surrounding additional school holidays to accommodate religious observance.

Perspective One	Perspective Two	Perspective Three
Public schools are run by the government, and the Constitution says that the government cannot endorse religion, so case closed. Rather than adding holidays to accommodate other religions, we should change the existing calendar so that *no* religious holidays mandate a day off from school.	It is already the case that members of minority religions are excused from school in observance of religious holidays. I don't think more than that needs to be done. Why should school be closed for *everyone* on a particular religious holiday if only a few students from that religion attend that school?	We could easily have days off from school to accommodate *every* holiday in *every* religion if we eliminated summer break, or at least made it much shorter. Educators already think a three-month summer vacation is a bad idea because students forget so much, so why not kill two birds with one stone?

ESSAY TASK

Write a unified, coherent essay in which you evaluate multiple perspectives on the topic of additional school holidays to accommodate religious observance. In your essay, be sure to:

- analyze and evaluate the perspectives given
- state and develop your own perspective on the issue
- explain the relationship between your perspective and those given

Your perspective may be in full agreement with any of the others, in partial agreement, or wholly different. Whatever the case, support your ideas with logical reasoning and detailed, persuasive examples.

The Rhetoric of Obesity

Although the causes are still feverishly debated, nobody can deny that the obesity epidemic is on the rise in the United States. If current trends continue unabated, statistics indicate that roughly two-thirds of American adults will be clinically obese in just another few decades. While medical professionals, and many private citizens as well, consider this a major public-health crisis that needs to be checked by almost any means necessary, others see discrimination against the obese as an equally pressing problem and stress the need for sensitivity and respect. They counsel us to remember that the desire to combat obesity must not degenerate into "shaming" those who are unable to lose weight.

Read and carefully consider these perspectives. Each suggests a particular way of approaching the debate surrounding the American obesity epidemic.

Perspective One	Perspective Two	Perspective Three
It is a scientific fact that being obese is terrible for one's health, and it should not be considered "shaming" or "prejudice" to state a fact. Obesity is an illness. We have campaigns to stop many diseases. Why is obesity any different?	Americans are unhealthy in a number of ways. Obesity seems to be the only health concern that enrages those who are not obese. This so-called "concern" about obesity has nothing to do with improving people's health—rather, it's just about pressuring people to conform to the body type that society tells us is attractive.	People have the right to be obese if they want to, but they don't have the right to lie. Some people who claim to be standing up for the obese are doing so by spreading lies about how it isn't actually unhealthy or how it's not scientifically possible to lose weight. There's a difference between making choices that only hurt yourself and trying to drag others down with you by spreading disinformation.

ESSAY TASK

Write a unified, coherent essay in which you evaluate multiple perspectives on the topic of the American obesity epidemic. In your essay, be sure to:

- analyze and evaluate the perspectives given
- state and develop your own perspective on the issue
- explain the relationship between your perspective and those given

Your perspective may be in full agreement with any of the others, in partial agreement, or wholly different. Whatever the case, support your ideas with logical reasoning and detailed, persuasive examples.

Mandatory Voting

Voting is an essential component of democracy, but many people who live in democracies don't vote. These days, in the United States, approximately 60% of the people who are eligible to vote in a presidential election do so. Voter turnout hasn't exceeded 60% since the election of 1968. Some political analysts argue that voting should be mandatory, as this would result in elections that accurately mirror the true will of the people. Others, however, point out that citizens should have the right to not vote at all if they don't like either candidate.

Read and carefully consider these perspectives. Each suggests a particular way of approaching the debate surrounding mandatory voting.

Perspective One	Perspective Two	Perspective Three
The right to vote inherently implies the right not to do so. The reason so many Americans do not vote is because the political parties keep nominating unimpressive candidates. If people were forced to vote, then the candidates would get even worse!	The reason voter turnout in the U.S. is low is not because people do not want to vote, but rather because a number of people do not have the opportunity. For example, the poorest Americans, may work too many jobs to have time to get to the polling place, or have no way to get there. If voting were mandatory, then it would be the government's responsibility to make sure everybody has the means to vote.	The reasons many Americans do not vote is because they know they live in states where their vote won't make a difference. The electoral college, wherein candidates win states that are worth a certain amount of electoral votes, is an outdated system. Before we start talking about taking away people's right not to vote, we should let presidential elections be decided by the popular vote and see if that helps turnout.

ESSAY TASK

Write a unified, coherent essay in which you evaluate multiple perspectives on the topic of mandatory voting. In your essay, be sure to:

- **analyze and evaluate the perspectives given**
- **state and develop your own perspective on the issue**
- **explain the relationship between your perspective and those given**

Your perspective may be in full agreement with any of the others, in partial agreement, or wholly different. Whatever the case, support your ideas with logical reasoning and detailed, persuasive examples.

Sample Essays for Writing Prompt, "Mandatory Voting"

HIGH-SCORING (5/6 RANGE) ESSAY SAMPLE

This is a difficult subject for me to analyze, but the reason why I find it difficult is the same as the reason why I find it so interesting: namely, the fact that I agree with all three perspectives. I don't merely mean that I can understand or that I have sympathy for the viewpoints presented, but rather that all three of the people who voiced their opinions on this issue are, as far as I can tell, stating facts. I agree with Perspective One that American citizens have the right not to vote, as the right to vote itself inherently implies the right not to do so. I think it almost goes without saying that Perspective Two is right about the fact that, in every presidential election, there are many people who end up not voting but wish that they had been able to do so. And I know for a fact that Perspective Three is right when he suggests that many people don't bother voting because it is a forgone conclusion which candidate is going to win their home state, because I personally heard many people give this as their reason for not voting in the most recent election.

Even though I agree with all three of the presented perspectives, however, I had no trouble making up my mind on this issue. If the right to vote is inviolable, and the right not to vote is necessarily implied by the right to vote, then this means the right not to vote is inviolable as well. While Perspective Two is doubtlessly correct that mandatory voting would yield many desirable results, such as a reduction in the disenfranchisement of the working poor, the fact that mandatory voting would be unconstitutional (as far as I can see, anyway) means that the option is simply off the table. It's pointless to talk about how much good could be done by violating people's rights if we agree—as I hope we do—that those rights cannot and must not be violated.

Although mandatory voting is off the table as far as I am concerned, I still believe we must try and think of other ways to address the legitimate problems brought up in Perspectives Two and Three. In a way, Perspective Two has already voiced another possible solution to the problem herself: she says that "If voting were mandatory, then it would be the government's responsibility to make sure everybody has the chance to vote." Well, it seems to me that if the government could take on this responsibility as a result of mandatory voting, it could still choose to take it on without voting being made mandatory. There's no real reason, for example, why Election Day has to keep being a single day forever—all voting taking place on one day is just a custom, not a right. Why not have an Election Week instead? Everyone would surely be able to find a chance to go vote if they had a whole week to do so, no matter how busy they are. Or if the idea is that every citizen over 18 would be responsible for sending back a personalized ballot electronically, we could simply add an option indicating "no vote" in addition to the names of the candidates—that way, everyone's right to not vote would be preserved, even though everyone would receive a ballot and have the guaranteed opportunity to vote if they want to.

As for Perspective Three's idea that the electoral college should be abolished and presidential elections decided by popular vote alone, I'm not so sure. As I've already explained, I agree with him that this system is a reason why a lot of people don't vote, and that voter turnout would go up if we got rid of it. However, there are other factors to consider besides raising turnout. The reason why we have the electoral college in the first place is so presidential candidates are obliged to try and appeal to all areas of the country, instead of just trying to be as popular as possible in the parts of the country with the biggest populations. The ten most populous U.S. states have more people in them than the other 40 states combined, so if presidential elections were decided by popular vote alone, then there's a chance that the candidates would just try to appeal to those 10 states and ignore the rest of the country, and nobody wants that. I think the solution here is to remember that we cast votes for other offices besides the president on election day—congresspeople and local politicians matter too, and the electoral college has nothing to do with them. If we could educate people to be more civic-minded, then they would come out to the ballot box on Election Day, even if it is the case that one presidential candidate already has their state "in the bag."

And so, while I am firmly against the idea of mandatory voting, I am glad that this is a debate people are having. I don't think mandatory voting has a chance of ever happening in the United States, but encouraging people to talk about it is a flashy way of encouraging them to confront various other important issues. Hopefully, as a result, we will find other, constitutionally acceptable ways of solving these.

MID-SCORING (3/4 RANGE) ESSAY SAMPLE

Having been presented with three perspectives on the topic of mandatory voting in the United States, I will now analyze them and also give my own perspective on this important issue. I believe that Perspective One is definitely right where it says that the reason some people don't vote is because they do not like either of the candidates. Although, even if they don't especially like either of them, you probably still think one of them is at least a little bit worse than the other. So mandatory voting wouldn't really be violating your rights, because all you have to do is vote for the other person besides the one you think is worse.

Also, it is true what Perspective Two says that many people want to vote but do not have time on election day. For example, maybe you have one job all day but then go to a second job and when you get out of that job the polls are closed, or even if you have only one job, maybe you are a single parent and nobody can babysit your kids long enough for you to go to your job and also vote afterwards. Speaking of which, why do kids get off from school on election day when they are too young to vote anyway? I am glad to have a day off from school, but if we want more grown-ups to vote, then the law should be that grown-ups get off from work on election day but kids still have to go to school, so that way if there are people who don't vote because they can't get a babysitter, they could vote when their kids are in school.

The Perspective Three person says that lots of people don't vote because they know it won't matter because they know already who is going to win the states they live in, but how does he know this is why people don't vote? I bet there are lots of other more popular reasons why people don't vote. Anyway, let's say if there are a lot of people who don't vote because of this reason, then I would say they should not be so sure. After all, if everyone said it didn't matter because they know who is going to win their state and stayed home, then that person might not end up winning the state at all. Besides, a lot of states are always close. And Barack Obama who is a Democrat, won a lot of states that the Republicans has won a bunch of times in a row before that. Maybe the Republicans in those states stayed home because they thought the Republican was definitely going to win the state, but they were wrong, so people should be careful when they think that.

In conclusion, mandatory voting does not really violate your rights because all you have to do is vote for the person you hate less than the other person, because at the end of the day somebody has to win and you can at least say it is better than if it was the other person.

LOW-SCORING (1/2 RANGE) ESSAY SAMPLE

Voting is an essential of democracy but, many people who live in the democracies they don't vote. This is because the last time 60% voter was eligible was in 1968. Some politics analysis that voting should be mandatory, because the reason is the true will of the people. Others point is that the citizens they are right to not vote because they do not like either candidate.

For example, Perspective One says that to this day in age the candidates are unimpressed and they would get even worst if people were forced to vote. I do not agree and believe about this because he has no proof that this is going to be the truth. Even if we forced people to vote, the candidates who are the people who are running, they are still going to be trying to win. They are not going too all of the sudden be bad on purpose or something since they are still trying to win against the other guy. Just because people have to vote, and that doesn't mean they have to vote for them.

Moreover, Perspective Two says that a lot of people don't not want to vote, on the other hand it is because they can't, and the reason being is that they do not have time to vote even though they want to. They say it should be the government responsible to making sure that everybody gets a chance to vote, and I am definitely in agreement with this all the way. The government is always telling us to vote, so how come they aren't seem to be making sure that we vote? They are the government they can do anything.

Also, the Perspective Three says that people don't vote because they have to go to college instead, in which it is an outdated system that is not as popular as it used to be and should be popular instead. He says we should find a way to make voting popular before we take away people's right to vote or not vote. I agree with this that we should make voting popular, because as it said in the passage people only vote half of the time.

For my conclusion I think that it would definitely be a good idea if everybody was voting. The reason being that the candidates are going to try to win still no matter what, they government should make sure that we vote, and to vote it should be more popular. Thank you very much for reading my opinions that I wrote about voting.

Essay Response

EXPLANATION OF HIGH-SCORING (5/6 RANGE) ESSAY

> **Note:** *Although this high-scoring essay is written in the first-person (using "I"), it is not necessarily always better to do this. Students should write in whichever voice they feel most comfortable using. However, many students who prefer to use the first-person are under the mistaken impression that they are not allowed to do so on the ACT, as their teachers do not allow the first-person in essays for class. This book therefore presents an example of a strong essay using the first-person, the voice in which most students find it easier to incorporate relevant examples and support into their essays, as it allows them to directly cite personal experience. Students should always remember that the ACT is not school, and that the particular preferences of their English teachers in school do not necessarily apply to the test, although certain universal rules, such as those of grammar, obviously still do.*

While writing in an engaged, confident voice that wastes no time with filler (such as restating the prompt), this student jumps right in by making a complex point: namely, the fact that all three perspectives can simultaneously be true, and merely emphasize different aspects of the issue rather than directly contradicting one another. This immediately establishes that the student fully understands both the nature of the issue and all three perspectives (remember that the longer prompt means that the ACT Writing test is also, to some extent, a reading-comprehension test as well).

Stylistically, the student's prose is mature, rather than sounding like something a nervous student was forced to write under pressure for school or a test. His sentence structure is varied and usually complex, and the sentences are long without sounding rambling or padded. The sentences are long because the student is analyzing complex ideas and making fine distinctions using many qualifying statements and comparisons, and he never sounds as though he is merely trying to make his sentences "long for the sake of long" to fill up space. Though he uses advanced vocabulary words such as *inviolable* and *disenfranchisement*, it sounds as though these words come naturally to him, rather than as if he has simply memorized random big words and is inserting them into sentences willy-nilly. He maintains a sophisticated tone, but the attempt to do so never causes him to misuse words or make grammatical errors.

By doing things such as appealing to the readers as equals at the end of Paragraph Two and demonstrating knowledge of the U.S. political system beyond what the prompt explains in Paragraph Four, he makes himself sound like a mature and engaged young adult, rather than like a kid who is "faking it." All of his examples and suggestions are actually intelligent and well reasoned, in addition to demonstrating a firm grasp of the issue and the prompt. From beginning to end, the writer seeks to present himself as someone who is on the same "level" as both the voices from the Three Perspectives and the readers themselves, and he succeeds at doing so.

EXPLANATION OF MID-SCORING (3/4 RANGE) ESSAY

Though this student's prose is mechanically correct and comprehensible, the "vibe" that this essay gives off is still that of a young person who is not used to writing without being forced to do so for school: the essay opens with the classic "kid" move of announcing that it is an essay being written on demand in response to a prompt ("I will now...").

The transitions, although clear argumentatively, are still "marked" by the employment of awkward transition words and phrases typically unseen outside of teenagers' writing (e.g., *anyway, also, for example, I bet*). Sentences are typically shaky and rambling in structure, even though they are seldom technically incorrect (a notable exception is the fragment in the third sentence of the opening paragraph). The student even explicitly embraces the identity of a child by referring to himself and his peers as *kids* and to others as *grown-ups*. The response to the Third Perspective that opens Paragraph Three is the infamous weak move of simply saying "How does he know?" instead of coming up with an actual counterargument.

The one-sentence final paragraph telegraphs the fact that the student ran out of time, and it pulls the "kid" move of beginning with the words *in conclusion*. Even more troublingly, it restates his worst point: the idea that mandatory voting would not violate citizens' rights simply because they could look at it in a positive way. This betrays a simplistic and immature understanding of what rights are and what would or would not constitute a violation of them.

EXPLANATION OF LOW-SCORING (1/2 RANGE) ESSAY

From the very beginning, it is immediately clear to any reader that this essay is going to be terrible. He uses grammatically incorrect sentences with misplaced commas (e.g., after *but*, rather than before it) and unnecessary/redundant pronouns ("the citizens they are right...").

The student opens by randomly cobbling together long phrases from the prompt, some of which he does not even appear to understand (the "60%" figure is about voter turnout in 1968, not eligibility).

The writer misuses common phrases (e.g., "to this day in age" instead of "in this day and age") and employs word forms that are incorrect in context (e.g., *unimpressed* for *unimpressive, even worst* for *even worse*). He also regularly adds unnecessary padding to sentences that serves no purpose other than to make them longer (e.g., "I do not agree and believe…"). He confuses homophones such as *to/too,* and his prose contains many examples of fragments, run-ons, and comma splices.

Most problematically, the writer appears not to understand all of the presented perspectives or even the issue itself. He seems to think that the term "electoral college" from Perspective Three has something to do with students going to college, and he closes by ignoring the main issue, simply saying "it would definitely be a good idea if everybody was voting" instead of addressing the proposed matter of legally *mandatory* voting.

Reading Exercises: Dual Passages

Passage II

SOCIAL SCIENCE: Passage A is adapted from "Meditation XVII" by John Donne (1624). Passage B is adapted from "Ubuntu" by Kevin Hurt, from the blog *Edumacation: Lessons in Teaching and Coaching* (2010).

Passage A by John Donne

Perchance he for whom this bell tolls may be so ill, as that he knows not it tolls for him; and perchance I may think myself so much better than I am, as that they who are about me, and see my state, may have caused it to toll for me, and I know not that.

All mankind is of one author, and is one volume; when one man dies, one chapter is not torn out of the book, but translated into a better language; and every chapter must be so translated; God employs several translators; some pieces are translated by age, some by sickness, some by war, some by justice; but God's hand is in every translation, and his hand shall bind up all our scattered leaves again for that library where every book shall lie open to one another.

Who casts not up his eye to the sun when it rises? Who takes off his eye from a comet when that breaks out? Who bends not his ear to any bell which upon any occasion rings? Who can remove it from that bell which is passing a piece of himself out of this world?

No man is an island, entire of itself; every man is a piece of the continent, a part of the main. If a clod be washed away by the sea, Europe is the less, as well as if a promontory were, as well as if a manor of thy friend's or of thine own were: any man's death diminishes me, because I am involved in mankind, and therefore never send to know for whom the bells tolls; it tolls for thee.

Tribulation is treasure in the nature of it, but it is not current money in the use of it, except we get nearer and nearer our home, heaven, by it. Another man may be sick too, and sick to death, and this affliction may lie in his bowels, as gold in a mine, and be of no use to him; but this bell, that tells me of his affliction, digs out and applies that gold to me: if by this consideration of another's danger I take mine own into contemplation, and so secure myself, by making my recourse to my God, who is our only security.

Passage B by Kevin Hurt

A Zulu maxim provides perhaps the simplest definition of Ubuntu: *umuntu ngumuntu ngabantu,* which means "a person is a person through other persons." It is a philosophical belief that being human means recognizing and respecting the humanity of others. As Archbishop Desmond Tutu said, "It is the essence of being human. It speaks of the fact that my humanity is caught up and is inextricably bound up in yours. I am human because I belong."

A person with Ubuntu is welcoming, hospitable, warm and generous, willing to share. Such people are open and available to others, willing to be vulnerable, affirming of others, do not feel threatened that others are able and good, for they have a proper self-assurance that comes from knowing that they belong in a greater whole. They know that they are diminished when others are humiliated, diminished when others are oppressed, diminished when others are treated as if they were less than who they are. When we truly believe in the concept of Ubuntu, we realize that when someone else is degraded, then we ourselves are degraded. This leads us to a point where we are enacting justice on behalf of others.

Ubuntu does not mean that people should not enrich themselves. The question is, are you going to do so in order to enable the community around you to be able to improve? Ubuntu puts our own personal gains in a larger context—the context of something greater than ourselves, some transcendent cause. Our own personal gains, whether mental gains (such as education) or physical gains (such as money), inevitably benefit the greater community and make it a better place for everyone.

Respecting our humanity and the humanity of others should always be the primary motive for any action. Wealth, while useful for advancing the good of the community, should never be valued above preserving the humanity of another person. For example, even something as simple as an insult degrades the humanity of someone else, and given the opportunity to make money by insulting someone, we should always say no to the money, because that person's dignity is more valuable to us.

Questions 11–14 ask about Passage A

11. The passage opens by repeatedly mentioning a bell because:
    A. a bell has been ringing in the author's town, and he is trying to figure out why.
    B. the bell represents some nameless deed about which the author feels guilty.
    C. the bell represents each human being's eventual and unknowable fate.
    D. the bell is ringing to observe the death of a specific person who was close to the author.

12. As it is used in line 18, the word *tribulation* most nearly means:
    F. affliction.
    G. nature.
    H. wealth.
    J. ringing.

13. The passage references "this bell, that tells me of his affliction" (line 21) to suggest that:

    A. people should be grateful that trouble has befallen someone else and spared them.

    B. an opportunity to show sympathy to another should be regarded as a treasure.

    C. the author is speculating whether he may be about to inherit money.

    D. in small communities, everyone is too concerned with everyone else's business.

14. The fourth paragraph (lines 13–17) mentions Europe in order to:

    F. compare it to the community of mankind.

    G. suggest that concepts of fellowship are more advanced there than in other regions.

    H. warn that it will be in trouble if the author's ideas are not taken seriously.

    J. suggest that there is less concern for morality there than in other parts of the world.

Questions 15–17 ask about Passage B

15. The author's attitude towards the Ubuntu philosophy is partially based on the opinion that:

    A. it will help people to become educated and therefore successful in their careers.

    B. it is the best method of eliminating prejudice in the author's particular culture.

    C. it can prevent any one person from becoming wealthy to a degree that is unfair.

    D. it spiritually enriches the practitioner, as well as encouraging good to others.

16. As it is used in line 24, the word *maxim* most nearly means:

    F. translation.

    G. statute.

    H. proverb.

    J. warning.

17. The quotation from Desmond Tutu most nearly suggests that:

    A. the Zulu concept of Ubuntu is quite ancient.

    B. Ubuntu is equally applicable to all cultures.

    C. cultures that respect their ancestors are more moral than those that do not.

    D. wise people seek out the advice of others before making important decisions.

Questions 18-20 ask about both Passages

18. One of the most obvious differences between the two passages is that:

    F. Passage A explicitly ties its thesis to religion, whereas Passage B does not.

    G. Passage A uses no quotations, whereas Passage B quotes multiple famous people.

    H. Passage B does not literally discuss making money, whereas Passage A does so.

    J. One of the passages analyzes a specific part of the world, and the other the whole world.

19. Which of the following methods of support do both authors use to convey their ideas?
    A. rhetorical questions.
    B. allusions to great literature.
    C. appraisals of the essence of humanity.
    D. long sarcastic metaphors.

20. Which of the following famous expressions is most nearly in line with the central thesis of *both* passages?
    F. "To thine own self be true."
    G. "A thing of beauty is a joy forever."
    H. "Fools rush in where angels fear to tread."
    J. "He ain't heavy; he's my brother."

Passage III

HUMANITIES: Passage A is adapted from "A Defence of Poetry" by Percy Bysshe Shelley (1821). Passage B is adapted from "The Poetics of Disobedience" by Alice Notley (1998).

Passage A by Percy Bysshe Shelley

A poem is the very image of life expressed in its eternal truth. There is this difference between a story and a poem, that a story is a catalogue of detached facts, which have no other connection than time, place, circumstance, cause and effect; the other is the creation of actions according to the unchangeable forms of human nature, which is itself the image of all other minds. Time, which destroys the beauty and the use of the story of particular facts, stripped of the poetry which should invest them, augments that of poetry, and forever develops new and wonderful applications of the eternal truth which it contains.

The functions of the poetical faculty are twofold: by one it creates new materials of knowledge, and power, and pleasure; by the other it engenders in the mind a desire to reproduce and arrange them according to a certain rhythm and order which may be called the beautiful and the good. The cultivation of poetry is never more to be desired than at periods when, from an excess of the selfish and calculating principle, the accumulation of the materials of external life exceed the quantity of the power of assimilating them to the internal laws of human nature. Poetry is the record of the best and happiest moments of the happiest and best minds.

The most unfailing herald, companion, and follower of the awakening of a great people to work a beneficial change in opinion or institution, is poetry. At such periods there is an accumulation of the power of communicating and receiving intense and impassioned conceptions respecting man and nature. The person in whom this power resides, may often, as far as regards many portions of their nature, have little apparent correspondence with that spirit of good of which they are the ministers. But even whilst they deny, they are yet compelled to serve that power which is seated on the throne of their own soul.

It is impossible to read the compositions of the most celebrated writers without being startled with the electric life which burns within their words. They measure the circumference and sound the depths of human nature with a comprehensive and all-penetrating spirit, and they are themselves perhaps the most sincerely astonished at its manifestations; for it is less their spirit than the spirit of the age. Poets are the hierophants of an unapprehended inspiration; the mirrors of the gigantic shadows which futurity casts upon the present; the words which express what they understand not; the trumpets which sing to battle, and feel not what they inspire; the influence which is moved not, but moves. Poets are the unacknowledged legislators of the world.

Passage B by Alice Notley

For a long time I've seen my job as bound up with the necessity of noncompliance with pressures, dictates, atmospheres of society at large, my own past practices as well. For a long time—well in fact since the beginning, since I learned how to be a poet inside the more rebellious wing of poetry. Learning itself meant a kind of disobedience, so like most words the Dis word, the Dis form, cannot be worshipped either—that would be an obedience anyway. I've spoken in other places of the problems, too, of subjects that hadn't been broached much in poetry and of how it seemed one had to disobey the past and the practices of literary males in order to talk about what was going on most literarily around one.

It seems as if one must disobey everyone else in order to see at all. This is a persistent feeling in a poet, but staying alert to all the ways one is coerced into denying experience, sense, and reason is a huge task. I recently completed a very long poem called *Disobedience* but I didn't realize that disobeying was what I was doing, what perhaps I'd always been doing until the beginning of the end of it, though the tone throughout was one of rejection of everything I was supposed to be or to affirm.

It's possible that my biggest act of disobedience has consistently, since I was an adolescent, been against the idea that all truth comes from books, really other people's books. I hate the fact that whatever I say or write, someone reading or listening will try to find something out of their reading I "sound like." 'You sound just like...,' 'you remind me of...,' 'have you read...?' I've been trying to train myself for thirty or forty years not to believe anything anyone tells me. It's necessary to maintain a state of disobedience against... everything.

Questions 21–24 ask about Passage A

21. The passage characterizes poetry as being all of the following EXCEPT:
    A. produced by special and advanced people.
    B. an accurate source of scientific information.
    C. true for all time.
    D. a valuable corrective to society.

22. As it is used in line 9, the word *faculty* most nearly means:
F. easiness.
G. staff.
H. goal.
J. ability.

23. The passage cites "the selfish and calculating principle" (line 13) as an example of:
A. something that keeps the work of inferior poets from being truly great and immortal.
B. a character flaw that even the greatest poets seek to cover up in themselves.
C. a socially influenced human tendency that makes poetry immediately necessary.
D. a reason why certain politically powerful individuals pretend to dislike poetry.

24. The passage closes by suggesting that poets:
F. have a much greater influence on the course of human civilization than most people realize.
G. are on rare occasions even imbued with the ability to predict the future.
H. are generally less emotionally affected by their own work than other people are.
J. may have had a hand in starting wars from time to time in history.

Questions 25–27 ask about Passage B

25. The author characterizes disobedience as being all of the following EXCEPT:
A. a healthy way of taking people's opinions.
B. an attitude that she even applies to poetry.
C. the title of her own most famous work.
D. something that must itself be disobeyed.

26. In the context of the passage, the phrases that appear in quotation marks in the final paragraph function as examples of:
F. "pressures, dictates, atmospheres of society" (line 35).
G. "subjects that hadn't been broached much in poetry" (lines 39–40).
H. "all the ways one is coerced into denying experience" (lines 44–45).
J. "my biggest act of disobedience" (line 49).

27. Based on the passage, the author seems to regard her duty as a poet as involving:
A. protest against traditional concept of ethics and justice.
B. preventing her mode of expression from becoming contaminated.
C. questioning whether writing poetry is a morally acceptable way of making a living.
D. preventing male poets of the past from being taught so frequently in schools.

Questions 28–30 ask about both Passages

28. One of the most obvious differences between the two passages is that:
    - **F.** Passage B regards society with skepticism, whereas Passage A is in agreement with most of society's opinions.
    - **G.** Only Passage A makes reference to any of the author's own poetical works.
    - **H.** Only Passage B attempts to explain the essential difference between poetry and fiction.
    - **J.** Passage A sees poetry as serving something objective, whereas Passage B sees it as a totally subjective matter.

29. Which of the following does *neither* of the two passages contain?
    - **A.** an opinion about whether poetry should be read in books or heard aloud.
    - **B.** a characterization of what poets themselves are like as people.
    - **C.** an assertion that poets speak for someone or something other than themselves.
    - **D.** a reference to the types of poetical subjects the author favors in his or her work.

30. Despite their many differences, which of the following is something about which the two passages *agree*?
    - **F.** The idea that only a certain rare type of person is able to write poetry well.
    - **G.** The fact that poetry ideally performs a necessary moral duty for society.
    - **H.** The suggestion that writing poetry the right way will make one a happier person.
    - **J.** The assertion that the poetry of the past is less valuable than the poetry of the present.

PASSAGE II: SOCIAL SCIENCE (DONNE/HART)

11. **C**	14. **F**	17. **B**	20. **J**
12. **F**	15. **D**	18. **F**	
13. **B**	16. **H**	19. **C**	

PASSAGE III: HUMANITIES (SHELLEY/NOTLEY)

21. **B**	24. **F**	27. **B**	30. **G**
22. **J**	25. **C**	28. **J**	
23. **C**	26. **F**	29. **A**	

PASSAGE II: SOCIAL SCIENCE (DONNE/HURT)

11. **(C) is the correct answer** because the first and fourth paragraphs establish that the bell (like "Europe" and other things) is a metaphor. The references to God and the future in the second and final paragraphs establish that the concern is fate or unknowable future troubles.

    (A) and (D) are incorrect because the bell does not literally exist. It is a metaphor.

    (B) is incorrect because the author never speaks of himself in any specific way, just as an example of a living human—so there is no reason to believe he himself has done some specific thing wrong.

12. **(F) is the correct answer** because *Tribulation* means *troubles* (as in "trials and tribulations"). The word *affliction,* which appears several times subsequently in the paragraph, is clearly being used to signify the same idea.
(G) is incorrect because the fact that the sentence refers to the *nature* of *tribulation* does not necessarily signify that *tribulation* means *nature.*
(H) is incorrect because the metaphorical *gold* that is repeatedly mentioned in this paragraph is not sufficient to signify that *tribulation* is a synonym for *wealth.*
(J) is incorrect because, although a *bell* is repeatedly brought up as a prominent metaphor in the passage, that does not necessarily mean that *tribulation* means *ringing.*

13. **(B) is the correct answer** because ironically, *gold* serves as a metaphor for another person's troubles (rather than something good, as you'd expect). What's good about these troubles is that they remind someone else (the author) that we are all connected, and so are *gold* in that sense.
(A) is incorrect because the passage advocates a sense of sympathy and community throughout, rather than *schadenfreude* (being spitefully glad for someone else's misfortune).
(C) is incorrect because the *gold* mentioned here is a metaphor, not literal gold.
(D) is incorrect because, while this may be true generally, this passage is about being humble and sympathetic, rather than nosy.

14. **(F) is the correct answer** because the idea in this metaphor is that any one person's death diminishes the human race, just as the loss of land would make a continent smaller.
(G) is incorrect because *Europe* here just stands in for the concept of a landmass in a metaphor—the passage does not actually compare Europe to other places.
(H) is incorrect because the passage contains no specific warnings or predictions about the future of any one culture or place—it just gives advice to people as individuals.
(J) is incorrect because *Europe* here just stands in for the concept of a landmass in a metaphor—the passage does not actually compare Europe to other places.

15. **(D) is the correct answer** because as is often the case on the ACT Reading, this broad and positive answer contains nothing that is falsified by the text.
(A) is incorrect because the passage never refers to academic education, and does not necessarily advocate the pursuit of career success (though it does not oppose it either).
(B) is incorrect because there is nothing in the passage about prejudice—don't *assume* that's what it is about just because the philosophy being discussed is of African origin.
(C) is incorrect because, while the passage says that people should not take advantage of others in order to become wealthy, it never says that wealth is bad in and of itself.

16. **(H) is the correct answer** because m*axim* and *proverb* are rough synonyms both indicating a phrase that espouses a "philosophical belief," a phrase that appears shortly thereafter.
(F) is incorrect because, although the *maxim* included here has indeed been *translated,* that doesn't mean that *maxim* means *translation.*
(G) is incorrect because a *statute* is more like a law or rule, as opposed to a principle or piece of advice.

(J) is incorrect because it can plainly be seen that the *maxim* in question ("A person is a person through other persons") is *not* an example of a *warning*—so how could *maxim* mean *warning*?

17. **(B) is the correct answer** because if Tutu thinks Ubuntu is "the essence of being human," then obviously that must imply that it is applicable to all human cultures.
(A) is incorrect because there is no indication in the passage of how old the concept of Ubuntu is—just because it is Zulu, that doesn't necessarily mean it is ancient.
(C) is incorrect because the passage never makes any mention whatsoever of ancestors, with respect to their veneration or otherwise.
(D) is incorrect because, while this may be true, the passage never brings it up—there is nothing in it about wisdom or about asking for advice.

18. **(F) is the correct answer** because Passage A makes mention of God several times, and Passage B never explicitly does so.
(G) is incorrect because, while it is true that Passage A uses no quotations, Passage B only quotes *one* famous person (Desmond Tutu), not *multiple* famous people.
(H) is incorrect because it is the other way around—Passage B discusses making money, not Passage A.
(J) is incorrect because *both* passages concern all of humanity, and *neither* only discusses one specific part of the world.

19. **(C) is the correct answer** because both passages are attempts to characterize what it truly means to be human (*appraisals* means *characterizations*).
(A) is incorrect because only Passage A uses rhetorical questions.
(B) is incorrect because neither passage contains any allusions to literature (even if you were afraid that there were some literary allusions you just didn't get, you should still have been able to eliminate this choice based on the fact that Choice C is correct, and they can't *both* be correct).
(D) is incorrect because, while metaphors abound in both passages, neither of the passages is ever sarcastic.

20. **(J) is the correct answer** because as can be intuited even if you've never heard it, the expression "He ain't heavy; he's my brother" indicates that it is no burden to care for others—exactly the point of both passages.
(F) is incorrect because both passages are about concern for others, not only for yourself.
(G) is incorrect because neither passage ever brings up appreciation for beautiful things.
(H) is incorrect because the passages are about being charitable and sympathetic, not about being cautious.

PASSAGE III: HUMANITIES (SHELLEY/NOTLEY)

21. **(B) is the correct answer** because the passage never brings up science, and never discusses poetry as a source of factual information.
(A) is incorrect because the passage characterizes poetry as being produced by a special type of people in lines 15–16.

(C) is incorrect because the passage characterizes poetry as containing eternal truth in line 7.

(D) is incorrect because the passage characterizes poetry as changing the opinions of society for the better in lines 17–18.

22. **(J) is the correct answer** because the "poetical *faculty*" is the *ability* to write poetry.

    (F) is incorrect because *faculty* does not mean *easiness*—if you picked this answer, you were probably confusing it with *facility*.

    (G) is incorrect because, while *staff* is a synonym for *faculty* when we are talking about teachers, the word *faculty* can mean other things too.

    (H) is incorrect because, though this section of the passage does concern the *goals* and results of poetry, in context the word *faculty* is not used as a synonym for *goal*.

23. **(C) is the correct answer** because the passage mentions how poetry is "to be desired" at such times—i.e., that it can ameliorate the bad influence of selfishness.

    (A) and (B) are incorrect because this section of the passage is talking about why people in general should *read* poetry, rather than saying anything specifically about people who *write* it.

    (D) is incorrect because this section of the passage is talking about why people in general should read poetry, rather than saying anything about specific people who oppose it, be they politicians or anyone else.

24. **(F) is the correct answer** because Shelley's famous closing phrase "Poets are the unacknowledged legislators of the world" concerns poetry's influence on society—*legislators* means "lawmakers," and *unacknowledged* means "not openly admitted or known."

    (G) is incorrect because the phrase about "the gigantic shadows which futurity casts" means that poetry helps *shape* the future, not that it literally *predicts* the future.

    (H) is incorrect because it is the *trumpets* themselves that "feel not," and the *influence* itself that "is moved not" in these metaphors, rather than poets themselves.

    (J) is incorrect because "the trumpets which sing to battle" is a metaphor about calls to action, not about anything to do with actual wars.

25. **(C) is the correct answer** because the author mentions disobedience merely as a "very long poem" that she "recently completed"—there is no indication that it is her *most famous* work.

    (A) is incorrect because the author talks about "disobeying" people's opinions in lines 51–54.

    (B) is incorrect because the author talks about "disobeying" poetry itself in lines 34–35, 40–41, and 49–50.

    (D) is incorrect because the author even talks about *disobeying disobedience*, in lines 37–39.

26. **(F) is the correct answer** because the quoted snippets of conversation in these lines represent poetry fans trying to characterize the author, something that she regards as pressure coming from society.

(G) is incorrect because the quoted snippets of conversation in these lines represent poetry fans trying to characterize the author, not other poets suggesting subjects.
(H) is incorrect because the quoted snippets of conversation in these lines represent poetry fans characterizing the author's work, not denying her experience.
(J) is incorrect because the quoted snippets of conversation in these lines represent poetry fans characterizing the author's work, not an act of disobedience on the part of the author herself.

27. **(B) is the correct answer** because throughout the passage, the author discusses wanting to prevent her own poetic voice (i.e., her "mode of expression") from being influenced (or "contaminated") by tradition and society.
(A) is incorrect because, while the author discusses protesting many traditional ideas, nothing about "ethics and justice" is among them.
(C) is incorrect because, while the author wants *her own* poetry to be as moral as possible, she never questions whether poetry *itself* is somehow inherently immoral.
(D) is incorrect because, while the author discusses her rebellion against a male-dominated tradition, she never mentions anything about school curricula one way or the other.

28. **(J) is the correct answer** because Passage A sees poets as serving and channeling some ultimate truth that exists outside themselves (in lines 22–24, for example), whereas the author of Passage B talks only about her own "experience."
(F) is incorrect because *both* passages are highly skeptical of society and in disagreement with majority opinion with respect to many things, not *just* Passage B.
(G) is incorrect because it's the other way around—the author of Passage B makes reference to her own works, but the author of Passage A does not.
(H) is incorrect because it's the other way around—the author of Passage A explains the difference between poetry and fiction, but the author of Passage B does not.

29. **(A) is the correct answer** because nothing about reading poetry in books versus hearing it read aloud appears in either passage.
(B) is incorrect because Passage A contains several characterizations about what poets themselves are like as people, for example in lines 15–16.
(C) is incorrect because Passage A contains several suggestions that poets speak for something other than themselves, for example in lines 22–24 and lines 29–31.
(D) is incorrect because the author of Passage B makes mention of the sorts of subjects on which she chooses to concentrate, in lines 39–42.

30. **(G) is the correct answer** because despite their differences, both Shelley and Notley agree that poetry can change society for the better, at least when it is done well.
(F) is incorrect because only Passage A argues this.
(H) is incorrect because neither passage argues this (Passage A suggests that the best poets are happy, but not necessarily that writing poetry *caused* them to be happy).
(J) is incorrect because neither of the two passages suggests this.

BARRON'S

6 ACT®

PRACTICE TESTS

Second Edition

Patsy J. Prince, M.Ed.
James D. Giovannini

About the Authors

James D. Giovannini and Patsy J. Prince, owners and founders of Academic Tutoring Centers, located in the Chicago area, have been providing high-quality ACT test prep services for more than 25 years. Together, they have established a premier tutoring and test prep business. Over the years, Patsy and Jim, along with their dedicated staff of tutors, have enabled students to reach their maximum score on the ACT.

We wish to dedicate this book to our spouses and our children. Thank you for your unconditional love and support. The assistance of many others made this book possible. Thanks to Christopher Cook, Pauline Alford, Bernard O'Connor, Joseph Newton, Dan Siegfried, Jason Wake, and Mary Netzky for their written contributions. Thanks to Russell Mallen and Kimberly Savini for editing the many sections of this book. Finally, we wish to thank the faculty and staff of Academic Tutoring Centers for their support. We could not have produced this book without your help.

All inquiries should be addressed to:
Barron's Educational Series, Inc.
250 Wireless Boulevard
Hauppauge, New York 11788
www.barronseduc.com

ISBN: 978-1-4380-0494-5
ISSN 2163-3339

Printed in the United States of America

9 8

Contents

Introductory Words

We know this must be a stressful time in your life: balancing schoolwork, family, friends, sports, jobs, AND college admission! Whew...that's a mouthful. This book has been created with your busy life in mind.

The ACT is a five-section test: English, Mathematics, Reading, Science, and Writing. This book covers all these areas. As we created this book, we made a point of reviewing and teaching only material presented on this high-stakes test.

The ACT is unlike any test you have ever taken. It requires a new way of thinking. Look at it this way: in your English or math class, you would need a minimum of 70% to earn the lowest possible C. However, on the ACT, 70% correct would turn into a score of about 25. (The ACT is scored 1–36. You will learn more about scoring in a minute.) While a 25 might or might not be your goal, it is considered above the national average. What does all this mean? It means you can get a lot of questions wrong on the ACT and still get a good score. The key is to never give up while taking the test.

The rules and strategies that follow have been used successfully by students over the past years. They are the perfect tool to help you reach your maximum score. Use this book and ACE THE ACT!

About the ACT

FORMAT

The ACT test consists of four multiple-choice sections plus an optional writing exercise. Here's the breakdown:

Section	Time	No. of Questions
English	45 minutes	75
Math	60 minutes	60
Reading	35 minutes	40
Science	35 minutes	40
Writing (optional)	30 minutes	1 essay

SCORING

The four multiple-choice sections (English, Math, Reading, and Science) are scored on a scale from 1 to 36; the more questions you answer correctly, the higher your score will be. You will receive an individual score for each subject test, as well as a *composite* score. Your composite score is found by averaging your four subject test scores—that is, adding them all together and dividing the sum by 4—rounding up at .5 or above.

For example, let's say you took a practice test and received the following scores:

English: 26
Math: 21
Reading: 24
Science: 24

Your composite score would be 24. (Added together, these scores total 95. Divide that value by 4, and you get 23.75. Because 23.75 has a decimal value greater than or equal to .5, you round up to 24.)

When colleges speak of ACT scores or list the median ACT score of their student bodies, they are referring to composite scores.

The only aspect of the ACT not scored from 1 to 36 is the Writing section. Every essay is read by two essay graders, who each give the writing sample a score ranging from 1 to 6. These scores are added together, resulting in a Writing score ranging from 2 to 12. Students will also receive a combined English/Writing score (on a scale of 1–36), drawing one-third from your Writing score and two-thirds from your English score.

PRACTICE TESTS

The best way to prepare for the ACT is to take several full-length practice tests. Once you have reviewed all of the skills presented in this book and learned our proven strategies, you can truly begin to measure your progress as a test taker. Do not expect to reach your score goals on the first practice test. **It takes time to familiarize yourself with the ACT.** As you move through the various practice tests, always keep one goal in mind—**steady progress.**

Though scale scores (explained earlier) are certainly important, the most helpful tool to measure your progress is actually your raw score on each subject test. In other words, on each successive practice test, your goal should always be to answer more questions correctly than you did on the previous test. Always think of how many questions you answer correctly, because in most cases, for every one question you get right on the Reading and Science sections, your scale scores go up by a full point; on the English and Math sections, you get 1 scale point for every two questions you answer correctly. Keep track of your scores on the sheets provided after each practice test, and push yourself to answer at least one more question correctly per section as you move through the tests. If you can reach this very modest goal, **by the time you finish working through this book you will have raised your composite score by 3 points!**

You might think that one little question doesn't matter, but nothing could be further from the truth. Getting one or two more questions right might just help you get into the college of your dreams! Since there is no penalty for incorrect answers, be sure you answer every question. Do not leave blanks.

Monitoring Time

We will discuss pacing for each section in the strategies for that particular section. To succeed on this test, both during practice and on the actual test, you need to be responsible for keeping track of time. Practice pacing yourself so that you are not surprised during the actual ACT.

Suggestion for timekeeping: Use a digital watch on both the practice tests and on the actual test. Be sure it has a stopwatch feature and does not beep. If you must use a watch with a sweeping second hand, set it to noon before you begin each test. It is far easier to gauge your time from this setting.

Regardless of which type of watch you choose, **the most important thing is that you use the same watch for the practice tests and for the actual ACT.**

Building Endurance

The ACT is nearly 4 hours long. Your ultimate goal should be to complete at least one full practice test in one sitting before the actual test. Begin to build endurance by doing at least two sections together (e.g., English then Math or Reading then Science). Additionally, the ACT is always given in the morning, so it is a good idea to do at least some of your practicing in the morning (especially if you are not a "morning person!").

English Rules

The ACT English test is possibly the easiest section for you to make vast skill and score improvements.

HIGHLIGHTS

- 5 passages, each with 15 questions
- 75 questions total
- 45 minutes
- Answer *every* question

DO'S AND DON'TS

- **DO** know the difference between a sentence and a fragment. A sentence has a subject and a verb and expresses a complete thought.
  Fragment: *She, acting like an infant, crying and whining.*
  Sentence: *I swim.*
- **DO** pick the clearest, most concise way of stating something. SHORTEST IS BEST, as long as you have a complete sentence.
- **DO** read to the very end of a sentence before answering a question. This way you will be sure that you pick an answer that creates a complete sentence.
- **DO** test the "DELETE the underlined portion" choice first: it is the correct answer about 50 percent of the time. Remember, though, that means it is a wrong answer 50 percent of the time as well, so choose DELETE when the underlined portion is repetitive or does not fit the main idea of the passage.
- **DO** be cautious when considering any answer with the word *being* in it, as it is seldom correct.
- **DO** look for wrong answers. Wrong answers are often much easier to find than right ones. Unless the right answer comes to you immediately, **ELIMINATE WRONG ANSWERS!**
- **DON'T** jump from question to question.
- **DON'T** be afraid to pick NO CHANGE. It is typically correct as often as any other answer.

PACING AND PRACTICING

- You have 45 minutes to complete the five English passages—that's 9 minutes per passage.
- Here's a tip for practicing your pacing: Draw a box at the end of each section. Under each box write in multiples of 9 (9, 18, 27, 36, and 45). Don't forget, you only have 45 minutes. As you take the exam, time yourself and write in the actual time it took you to finish each passage. This will help you know whether you need to speed up or slow down.
- The sections do <u>not</u> get more difficult as you go, so it is better to finish even if you have to make a few guesses along the way.
- It takes practice to get used to the English section. If you apply the rules and strategies while taking the practice tests, you will be fully prepared for the actual test.

PUNCTUATION

Commas

There are six comma rules to learn for the ACT.

1. Commas are used to mark the end of an introductory clause and are followed by a complete sentence. Introductory clauses often begin with words such as *although, when, while, since, if,* and *because*. (Yes. The word *because* can start a sentence!)

   EXAMPLE: *When it stops raining, Mark is going to wash his car.*

   EXAMPLE: *Although I'd love to go to the movie with you, I need to study for the ACT.*

   Please notice that each clause is followed by a comma and then a complete sentence. Also, the subject of the sentence must be mentioned immediately after the comma in order for it to make sense.

   EXAMPLE: *Feeling very sad, she felt a tear run down her cheek.*

   This is correct because it is clear that "she" was feeling very sad. If the sentence were written, "Feeling very sad, a tear ran down her cheek" it would be incorrect. A tear cannot feel sad!

2. Commas are used to set off nonrestrictive clauses/appositives (phrases that interrupt the flow of the sentence).

   EXAMPLE: *Jim, a champion swimmer, hoped to make the Olympic team.*

   To check for interruptions, remove the words between the commas. If the remaining portion is a complete sentence and the meaning is not changed, then the commas are correct. If not, then test another answer. Be sure to read the whole sentence! Words such as *however*, *for example*, *for instance*, and *though* are usually surrounded by commas.

3. Commas are used to separate two or more adjectives preceding a noun.

   EXAMPLE: *The ACT is not a stressful, difficult test.*

   However, do not use a comma if the first word is an adverb describing an adjective.

   EXAMPLE: *The man wore a bright blue sweater.* (*Bright* describes the type of blue.)

4. Commas separate more than two words in a series.

   EXAMPLE: *I bought eggs, cheese, milk, and butter at the store.*

   (The last comma after "milk" is optional, though the ACT tends to leave it in.)

5. A comma before a conjunction can be used to separate two complete sentences. (Conjunction words are *and*, *but*, *or*, *so*.)

   EXAMPLE: *The palm trees blew softly in the wind, and the hot sun beat down from the sky.*

   Do not use a comma without the conjunction to separate two complete sentences!

   EXAMPLE: *The palm trees blew softly in the wind, the hot sun beat down from the sky.*

6. A comma can be used at the end of a sentence followed by an afterthought.

   EXAMPLE: *The football game was a massacre, 49 to 0.*

Other comma tips:

- When in doubt, leave the comma out!
- Just because you pause when reading a sentence does not mean the sentence requires a comma.
- If all four answer choices are identically worded and three of the four answer choices contain commas in various places, the correct answer is likely to be the one that omits the commas.

Dash

There are two dash rules used on the ACT.

1. The dash, like the comma, is used to mark an interruption.

   EXAMPLE: *The Chicago Marathon—a race of endurance, strength, and skill—is difficult to complete.*

   Two dashes or two commas can be used interchangeably; however, never use one of each.

2. The dash can also be used to stress a word or phrase at the end of a sentence.

   EXAMPLE: *Roxann's hair is unlike anyone else's in the family—thick and dark.*

Colon

There are three colon rules for the ACT.

1. The colon is used **after a complete sentence** followed by a summary list.

   EXAMPLE: *I have many hobbies: golfing, rock climbing, sailing, and windsurfing.*

   Complete sentence + COLON + list

2. The colon is also used at the end of a complete sentence followed by an afterthought.

   EXAMPLE: *Japan has a high literacy rate: 99 percent.*

   Complete sentence + COLON + afterthought

3. The colon is also used to separate two complete sentences when the second sentence explains or restates an idea in the first.

   EXAMPLE: *These seat covers are the most durable kind: they are reinforced with double stitching and covered with a heavy plastic coating.*

   Complete sentence + COLON + explanation

Semicolon

There are two semicolon rules to know for the ACT.

1. The semicolon is used to separate complete sentences.

   EXAMPLE: *Harris practiced diligently for the ACT; he wanted to maximize his score.*

2. The semicolon is also used before a coordinating adverb (*however, therefore, since*) to separate two sentences.

   EXAMPLE: *I enjoy living in a small community; however, the neighbors are often too nosy.*

Apostrophe

An apostrophe is used to show ownership.

1. If there is one owner, use *'s*.

   EXAMPLE: *Patsy's car is brand new.*

2. If there is more than one owner, use *s'*.

   EXAMPLE: *Ten boys' bikes were stolen.*

3. Words that are plural without adding the *s* form the possessive by adding *'s*.

   EXAMPLE: *Women's, men's, people's, children's*

GRAMMAR

Possessives

One owner = *'s*
More than one owner = *s'*

Words that are plural without adding *s* like women, men, or people: use '*s*.

EXAMPLE: *I went into the men's locker room to change into my bathing suit.*

It's = it is
Its = one owner
Its' = THIS IS NOT A WORD, but ACT gives it as an answer choice—NEVER choose it!

Their = more than one owner
They're = they are
There = location

Subject-Verb Agreement

Always check for agreement. Within a sentence, a singular subject must be followed by a singular verb and a plural subject must be followed by a plural verb.

EXAMPLE: *The stack of books is on the floor.*
The subject here is "stack," which is singular, so the verb *is* is correct.

BE CAREFUL! Verbs are not made plural just by putting an *s* on the end. If you want a singular verb, put the word *he* or *she* in front of it and make sure it works. If you want a plural verb, put the word *they* in front of it and make sure it works.

EXAMPLE: *He sits*
They sit.

One of the ACT's most common questions begins with a singular subject and is followed by several prepositional phrases with plural nouns and then a verb. This verb MUST be singular so as to agree with the sentence's singular subject.

EXAMPLE: *The color of the glass in the panes of glass in the windows of the nearby house is actually a reflection of the sun's rays.*

Though there are multiple nouns in the prepositional phrase above, the subject in this sentence is in fact *color*. You must therefore use the singular verb *is*.

Subject-Pronoun Agreement

Within a sentence a singular subject must be followed by a singular pronoun, and a plural subject must be followed by a plural pronoun.

EXAMPLE: *Each of the boys took his seat on the bus.*

Since the subject is "each of the boys" it is singular. *His* is a singular pronoun.

Parallel Phrasing

Express ideas in a consistent, grammatical way. Phrases or words in a series must be in the same form.

DO THIS: *I like to run, bike, and swim.*
NOT THIS: I like to run, biking, and swimming.

Transitions

If all answers except one have a transition, read the sentence before to see whether you really need a transition.

A. Consequently, the dog
B. Therefore, the dog
C. *The dog*
D. For example, the dog

If all answers contain transitions…

1. Look for two transitions that have similar meanings.
2. Eliminate the two with similar meanings.
3. Look at the sentence before and after the transition to determine how the sentences should be linked. One of the two remaining answers should clearly be the better choice.

> ACT English scores are broken down into two categories: (1) usage and mechanics (previously covered), and (2) rhetorical skills. It is imperative that you learn the different types of rhetorical questions that the ACT tends to ask. Be sure to look for (and underline) the clue in the question. With a little practice, you will master these question types!

Math Rules

The ACT Math test covers most areas of high school mathematics. Regardless of your math level or proficiency, you will achieve your maximum potential score by completing the practice tests in this book.

HIGHLIGHTS

- 60 multiple-choice questions
- 60 minutes
- No penalty for guessing; answer **every** question
- Questions increase in difficulty throughout the test
- The TI-83 and TI-84 calculators are allowed on the test. The TI-89 is **not** allowed.

Content Area	Percentage of Test	Typical Number of Questions
Pre-Algebra	23%	14
Elementary Algebra	17%	10
Intermediate Algebra	15%	9
Coordinate Geometry	15%	9
Plane Geometry	23%	14
Trigonometry	7%	4
Total	100%	60

The Math test is the only section of the ACT arranged in order of difficulty; generally speaking, you will find significantly easier questions toward the beginning of the test and more difficult questions toward the end. (This is not to say, of course, that you will never find a "tough" question on the first half or an "easy" question at the end.) Knowing that the test is laid out in this way can help you tremendously as you work through the section on test day. For instance, if one of the first questions seems extremely complicated, you are probably overthinking it; if the answer to one of the last 10 questions appears extremely obvious and straightforward, it likely is not the correct answer.

While there is no precise point where the Math section jumps from easy to difficult questions, a good rule of thumb is that typically the first 30 questions cover the more basic skill sets, and the last 30 questions test more advanced topics. You might find that you are entirely unfamiliar with some of the advanced topics, and that's okay! If you have never taken an advanced algebra or a trigonometry class, you are not expected to know the answers to these questions. **Remember: You can still receive an excellent score on the ACT Math section without any knowledge of these advanced skills!**

DO'S AND DON'TS

- **DO** use your test booklet! Often a quick sketch will help you solve the problem. If a diagram is already provided, begin by marking all known information.
- **DO** work backwards. This is especially true when there are variables in the question and numbers in the answer choices. For these questions, use the "**Plug and Chug**" strategy: Plug answer choices back into the problem to find the correct solution to the problem.
- **DO** use the "**Plug in C Strategy**" when working backwards: all ACT math answers are listed in numerical order, either smallest to largest or vice versa. Therefore, when possible, plug in choice C (or H). If it is not the right answer, it will be immediately clear whether a larger or smaller answer choice would have led you to the correct answer. If you need a larger number, you can immediately eliminate choices A and B; if you need a smaller one, you can eliminate D and E. By using this method, you can eliminate three choices by checking only one!
- **DO** read the question first on long word problems. Previewing the actual question helps you eliminate unnecessary words and information.
- **DO** assign the variable(s) a number and evaluate the problem accordingly if a question has variables in the answer choices. Plug in an easy number to work with, like 2 or 3. (Beware of using zero or 1—they are more trouble than they are worth!)
- **DO** be sure to **answer the question being asked!** One of the most commonly made mistakes on the ACT is also one of the most avoidable. A good way to avoid this scenario is to underline the part of the question that directly poses the question (e.g., "What is the value of x?"). That way, after you finish solving the problem, you can quickly glance back at the part of the question that you have underlined and double check that you are answering the right question (i.e., circling the answer that corresponds to the value of x, rather than the value of y).
- **DO** assume that diagrams are drawn to scale if you don't know where to start on a problem or cannot find the answer mathematically, and estimate lengths and angle measures from the diagram.
- **DO** look for wrong answers in addition to correct ones, and use **process of elimination**. Even if you do not find the answer, guessing after eliminating three answer choices will increase your probability of guessing correctly from 20 percent to 50 percent!
- **DO** start the test with your calculator in degree mode. To put a TI-83 or TI-84 in degree mode, first press the "MODE" button, located directly to the right of the yellow "2nd" button. Once in the "MODE" screen, look to the third line down. It will say "Radian" and "Degree." Make

sure "Degree" is highlighted. If it is not, place the cursor on "Degree" and press the "ENTER" button. "Degree" should now be highlighted, and your calculator will be in degree mode.

- **DO** be alert for charts/graphs that apply to more than one question.
- **DON'T** spend too much time on any one question.

PACING AND PRACTICING

Sixty minutes to answer 60 questions corresponds to 1 minute per question. However, you should limit yourself to 25 minutes for the first 30 questions, and save the extra time to work through the more difficult questions on the second half of the test.

Remember, DO NOT leave any answers blank! However, on the practice tests it is helpful to mark which questions you guessed on, so you can see which math concepts you might need to review again.

Reading Rules

To be successful on the Reading test, you must be an **active reader**. This means being able to determine main ideas, evaluate supporting details, and arrive at appropriate conclusions. Don't let your mind wander; stay focused on what the passage is saying.

Completing the practice tests in this book will enable you to improve your reading proficiency. The reading tests/passages in this book reflect the word count of actual ACT test passages.

HIGHLIGHTS

- 35 minutes
- 4 reading passages, each with 10 questions

Passage 1: Prose Fiction

- This passage is a story.
- The first paragraph will indicate who (the character or characters) and what about that person.
- Use the **CAPS** strategy by identifying: **C**haracters, **A**ttitudes, **P**roblems (or issues), and **S**olutions (or ending). Know each character's personality traits and to whom they are related in the passage.

Passage 2: Social Science

- This passage is informative.
- Read the first paragraph carefully for the author's purpose. To determine the author's purpose, ask yourself, "Why did the author write this?" or "What is the one main thing the author wants me to know after reading this passage?"
- Pay close attention to the first sentence or two of each paragraph and to the last paragraph, particularly the last sentence because it often restates the main idea.

Passage 3: Humanities

- This passage is often a narrative but sometimes resembles a social science passage.
- While reading, focus on the author/narrator's attitudes toward the subject of the passage.
- If it's a narrative, use the **CAPS** strategy.
- If it's informative, use the **TD** strategy.

Passage 4: Natural Science

- This passage is also informative, so use the **TD** strategy.
- Read the passage for the big picture focusing on the first and last paragraphs for the thesis.
- Don't spend too much time learning details; read for location of information.

TEST-TAKING STRATEGIES

1. Questions about a passage usually follow one main idea. The author wrote the passage for a reason; once you figure out the point that the author is trying to make, you will be well on your way to answering questions correctly.

   Placing a star (*) next to the main points helps you to focus and locate important information as you read. Main points are key ideas in the passage.
2. On the prose fiction and (sometimes) the humanities passages, use the **CAPS** strategy: look for **C**haracters, **A**ttitudes, **P**roblems, and **S**olutions. There is always an issue (the problem) in the passage, so identify it! Every prose fiction passage will also have a conclusion or resolution, even if it's not a final one.
3. On the nonfiction passages—social science, natural science, and (sometimes) humanities—focus on the TD: thesis and details. Be sure to read the first two paragraphs carefully, as they generally contain the author's purpose, thesis, or main idea. The rest of the passage contains details that support the author's main idea. You do not need to memorize them all on your initial read. If you can simply pick out the author's important supporting details (each paragraph generally corresponds to one major detail), you will be in great shape as you move on to the questions.
4. Each student will approach the ACT Reading test slightly differently. No two brains are identical; therefore, no two strategies are identical. However, for most students there is a definitive reading strategy that produces the highest possible ACT reading score, and it's very simple.

   Step 1: <u>Read the entire passage quickly but actively, seeking out the most important information.</u> Place a star in the margin next to significant information. When you finish reading the passage, you should be able to mentally answer the CAPS or TD questions! If you cannot do this easily, you were not actively reading! (Reading the passage should take between 4 and 5 minutes.)

   Step 2: <u>Answer the questions.</u> Be sure to read ALL FOUR answer choices, using the process of elimination, BEFORE looking back to the passage. (Answering questions should take about 4–5 minutes.) Do not keep looking back. Keep moving.

No matter what, you must complete each passage in LESS THAN 9 MINUTES! In order to reach your maximum reading score, it is imperative that you get to all four passages. Remember, it is possible to get some answers wrong on the ACT and still achieve a great score.

An alternative strategy that works for some students is to actively read only the first and last paragraphs while skimming the body of the passage and then answering the questions as described above.

You waste precious time by reading the questions first. On a rare occasion, this strategy will work, but for 99 percent of students it does not help with comprehension or with earning a high reading score.

5. Although the content of the passages changes from test to test, the types of questions do not. If you know how to answer each type of question, you will be in good shape.

- **Main Idea or Author's Purpose**
  Look for a general, vague, or broad answer.
- **Inferential**
  Make an assumption based on what you read; don't bother looking back.
- **Tone**
  Usually positive; look for a "nice" answer.
- **Detail**
  If the question includes "the passage states" or "the passage indicates," the answer is in the passage. When referring to line numbers, read before and after the lines given. However, be sure to still read all the answer choices before looking back in order to save valuable time.
- **Vocabulary Words**
  You must look back for context: read the lines before and after for clues as to meaning and then plug in words.
- **"Except" or "Not" Questions**
  Answer as if they are true/false questions.

DO'S AND DON'TS

- **DO** read all choices and try to eliminate some before looking back. It is acceptable to look back as long as you first use the process of elimination. If you do look back, you must do so very quickly!
- **DO** be consistent with theme; questions often repeat themselves.
- **DO** be careful on questions with specific line references. When looking back in the passage, make sure to read a few lines before and after the given line reference for context.
- **DO** look at the title of the passage for social science, humanities, and natural science. It can often give you a clear hint as to what the passage is primarily about.
- **DO** match ideas from the passage to the questions.
- **DO** choose moderate words such as *sometimes*, *tend to be*, and *likely*.
- **DON'T** look back for the answer without reading all choices and eliminating wrong answers first.
- **DON'T** just match words, match ideas. Be sure your selection answers the question.
- **DON'T** choose answers containing definitive words such as *always*, *never*, *only*, and *alone*.

PACING AND PRACTICING

- You have approximately **9 minutes** per passage. Always spend more time answering questions (e.g., 5 minutes) than reading the passage (e.g., 4 minutes).

- You can speed up your reading by using an index card or pencil to help you focus. Be sure to place a star next to key ideas.
- It is better to make educated guesses throughout the test than to guess on an entire passage. Remember, each passage contains easy, medium, and difficult questions. If you spend too much time on the truly difficult questions early on, you might run out of time and end up missing some easy questions because you never got to them. You want to get to all questions if possible.
- Try the following to practice your pacing: Draw a box at the end of each reading passage. Under the first box, write in 8–9. Under the second, write in 17–18. Under the third, 26–27, and under the fourth, write in 35. With 35 minutes to complete four passages, you actually get 8 minutes and 45 seconds per passage, so try your best to complete each passage in less than 9 minutes! You MUST be finished in 35 minutes. As you take the practice exams, time yourself and write in the actual time you take to finish. This will give you a strong idea of where you need to speed up or slow down.

> Remember: To get a good score on the Reading test, you must finish it—even if you have to guess along the way!

Science Rules

For most students, the ACT Science Reasoning test appears to be the most difficult of the four, but with a little practice, it becomes fairly straightforward. This is the point in the test where many students lose focus. *Do not let this happen!*

HIGHLIGHTS

- The Science section is not arranged in order of difficulty. Each passage contains a difficult question or two, so it is important not to spend too much time on challenging questions. If necessary, make an educated guess and move on.
- The Science section is really a reasoning or logic test. You do not need to have prior knowledge of the subject matter, though sometimes it is helpful.
- Think of the Science section as a puzzle or riddle that you have to figure out.
- The focus is on interpreting data and information and making logical conclusions.
- It is important to be FLEXIBLE and to be able to SHIFT GEARS in the Science section. In other words, if one method doesn't work, try another. If looking at one piece of information doesn't help you, look in a different place.
- With all of the information put in front of you and only 35 minutes to answer all of the questions, the Science section can seem overwhelming. The most important thing you can do to conserve time is orient yourself. Use the headings on charts and graphs the same way you would at the grocery store, and the ACT Science Reasoning test can be as straightforward as buying a loaf of bread.
- The Science section contains three distinct types of passages.

  1. **Data representation.** Each of the three data representation passages has 5 questions.
  2. **Research summaries.** Each of the three research summaries passages has 6 questions.
  3. **Conflicting viewpoints** (1 passage) with 7 questions.

The conflicting viewpoints passage is unique and is not usually accompanied by charts and graphs. Instead, it involves interpreting data. It can fall anywhere in the test, but you will easily recognize it because it will consist of a brief introduction to the topic followed by two to four sections (e.g., Scientist 1, Scientist 2...or The Dust Theory, The Dirt Theory, The Rock Theory) written in paragraph form. It is the only Science passage with 7 questions. It may look like you need to read everything but you do not!

In many ways, the conflicting viewpoints passage is similar to the passages in the Reading section: It is essential that you determine the MAIN IDEA of each view.

REMEMBER

"Conflicting viewpoints" is called that for a reason. Though they will discuss the same general topic, the views must oppose each other in some fundamental way. Once you have figured out each view's main idea and where the views disagree, you will be in great shape on the questions.

Follow these steps on the conflicting viewpoints passage:

1. Skim the introductory paragraph.
2. Then read enough of each viewpoint to determine the main idea of each one. (The main idea can usually be found in the first two sentences of each viewpoint.)
3. Then go straight to the questions. Look back when you need to, using as much logic as possible.
4. There are two basic types of questions. The first is a simple word match—just look for the words in the passages. The second asks you to define the viewpoint. These may seem more difficult but they should revolve around the first two sentences of each viewpoint that you read.
5. Questions often ask about one of the viewpoints but list answer choices that correspond to the other(s). Look to eliminate these extraneous answer choices first.

- In general, there are three types of questions on the Science section:

1. **PATTERNS AND TRENDS** For this type of question, you need to find the answer based on the data. Focus on investigating the information *directionally* (e.g., Does the pressure increase or decrease when velocity increases? When exposed to more sunlight, do the plants flower more frequently, less frequently, or is there no relationship?).
2. **HYPOTHESIS** This question involves yes/no or true/false answers. These questions can be best tackled by a "plug and chug" method. Try out each answer as you go through them.
3. **LOGIC** These questions are designed to challenge your thinking. You should focus on connecting the information. If the question talks about the *design* of the experiment, you may need to read a little bit.

ACT science questions can also be thought of as either navigation or manipulation questions.

Navigation. Within each passage there are typically three questions that you can answer simply by locating (navigating) the necessary information in a chart or graph.

Manipulation. There are approximately two per passage. These questions involve three steps: first you must locate the appropriate information and then you must use the data in some way to find the correct answer and decide if you need additional information from the reading.

TEST-TAKING STRATEGIES

1. For most of the passages, your first step should be to skim the introduction. Look at the data, reading the labels and headings quickly. Your goal is to just get a general idea of where everything is. DO NOT WORRY IF YOU DON'T UNDERSTAND WHAT'S GOING ON. It may be confusing, but there isn't enough time to try to completely comprehend each experiment.
2. Your focus then becomes the questions. Read through the first question and underline key words. DO NOT go straight to the data yet.
3. Next, match the information in the question to the appropriate chart/graph(s). BE SURE THAT YOU ARE LOOKING AT THE CORRECT GRAPH OR CHART! **Then, work backward from the answers.** Use the process of elimination to help you determine the true answer. Almost every question refers to a data table even though the question might not specifically mention that table. *Use the answers as a guide to locate the correct table.*
4. Think simply and linearly! Try not to overthink—the answers are usually simpler than you realize.
5. If you are not able to find the answer using just the charts and graphs, then you may have to go to the text. Sometimes italicized words can be helpful. If the question states "based on the information," you should look at the text. The introductory passage may have some information to help you.

DO'S AND DON'TS

- **DO** focus on the charts and graphs. You may have to use data from two sources to answer the question.
- **DO** pretend that you are shopping at an unfamiliar grocery store. Use the headings on the tables, charts, and graphs to help you!
- **DO** look for patterns, trends, and directions. If there is an obvious pattern, such as a column of numbers increasing or decreasing, it might be helpful to draw an arrow showing that trend.
- **DO** write in the test booklet. Circling and underlining both help prevent careless errors.
- **DO** work backward from each answer—using process of elimination. (Check each answer to see if it is true. There should only be one true answer).
- **DON'T** let the wording of the questions confuse you. Break them down; underline key words. There is often more information in the questions than you actually need to answer.

PACING AND PRACTICING

- With seven passages and 35 minutes, you have essentially 5 minutes per passage; however, some will take a minute less while others may take a minute more. Try to use pacing boxes during practice.
- Don't rush; just be conscious of your time from the beginning.
- If you can't figure out a question, **make your best guess and move on.** You will not have enough time to dwell on questions, and it is better to guess on one or two than to not even make it to an entire passage.
- If you find yourself struggling with finishing, complete the conflicting views passage last. (Be careful on your answer sheet!)
- Don't panic as you begin to practice. It may take you longer at first! You *will* get the hang of it!

Writing Rules

The ACT Writing section will be administered about 5 minutes after the end of the Science section. During the 30-minute ACT Writing test, you will be asked to plan and write a persuasive essay in response to a prompt. Although there is no length requirement, **higher-scoring essays tend to consist of four or five paragraphs that take up about two pages of writing.**

THE PROMPT/ESSAY ESSENTIALS

Writing prompts from past tests have typically addressed an aspect of the high school experience.

The ACT writing prompt will look like this:

> Some high schools in the United States have considered dropping music and art courses. Proponents of this change believe that budget cuts demand that time, money, and resources should be directed to "core" subjects like reading and math. Others insist that music and art courses are invaluable because they instill in students a lifelong appreciation for the arts. In your opinion, should music and art courses be cut from high school programs?
>
> In your essay, take a position on this question. You may write about either one of the two points of view given, or you may present a different point of view on this question. Use specific reasons and examples to support your position.

The second paragraph is of interest for several reasons:

- It is the universal ACT writing prompt. No matter what scenario you are asked to consider, this information will follow.
- It asks that you **TAKE A POSITION**. All too often, students think they can get by with a survey of multiple positions, or a position-less essay that omits any semblance of a thesis. No matter how completely indifferent you feel toward the issue or how reluctant you feel about taking a stand one way or another, the single most important aspect of the Writing section is crafting a clear thesis statement.
- It also presents three options: side with one of the two views or take your own position. Unless you are suddenly struck by a creative alternative to the two extremes, stick with one of the two already outlined for you. This choice leaves less room for muddy thinking.
- It also calls for **SPECIFIC REASONS AND EXAMPLES**. Remember that even if your thoughts seem obvious, you need to prove them. General statements do not provide proof. For example, if you are arguing for keeping funding for the arts (based on the above prompt), you might make the statement that classes in the arts provide a much-needed break in an academic day. While you would assume that any grader would know exactly what you mean, you still need to provide reasons why arts classes provide a much-needed break.

OVERALL APPROACH: THE "BOW" STRATEGY

Brainstorm

Think about the question. Ask yourself about what will answer it best. Are there facts, emotions, descriptions, examples, statistics, or expressions that can help you explain your ideas? Write down key words that remind you of those ideas. This process should be completed in about 1 to 2 minutes. The target is to create a thesis.

Organize

Take the ideas in the thesis and put them in an order that is effective. Consider strength of support when ordering body paragraphs. You may want to order the body from strongest to weakest or from weakest to strongest. It depends on the impact you want to have on the reader. This process should be accomplished in approximately 2 to 3 minutes. The target is to organize thoughts into a cohesive presentation in outline form using key words and short phrases.

Write

Write the paper. Put the ideas organized in key word outline form onto paper in full sentences. Remember, sentences express complete thoughts. Paragraphs are composed of complete thoughts to express main ideas. Paragraphs begin with clear topic sentences, which are the building blocks of a strong thesis. The outline helps with what you want to say; punctuation and grammar help with how to say it. There should be about 20 to 25 minutes to write the paper legibly. The target is for the reader to discern the cohesive logical expression of thought.

PLAN AHEAD: DEVELOP A TEMPLATE OR BRIEF OUTLINE

For more effective time management during the test, develop a template for your essay by planning many of its components beforehand. If these decisions about structure are made in advance, you will have more time to develop your examples. The following is an example of a possible template:

First: Make a two-column table (one column for each postion) and fill in anything that you can think of that would support either side. Whichever column has more items in it after 2 to 3 minutes is the side you take.

Second: Write an introduction consisting of a few sentences and ending with a statement of your side. If introductions are difficult for you, use some of the opposing ideas that you listed. In other words, briefly give the opposite view first; just be sure to discuss the opposite view again in your supporting paragraphs. **In order to get a high score, you must also incorporate the counterargument (something about the other side) somewhere in the essay!**

Third: Body Paragraph 1: Take the first item from your chart and support it with SPECIFIC REASONS AND EXAMPLES.

Body Paragraph 2: Take the second item from your chart and support it with SPECIFIC REASONS AND EXAMPLES.

Body Paragraph 3: Take the third item from your chart and support it with SPECIFIC REASONS AND EXAMPLES.

Alternate approach:

Paragraph 1: Take a few of the items from your chart that support your side and support them with SPECIFIC REASONS AND EXAMPLES.

Paragraph 2: State one thing about the other side (that's your counterargument!). You can even get this from the prompt. Then write about a compromise that still supports your side. For example: If you are arguing for keeping the arts in schools, you could write, "It is true that school budgets are tight, and schools need to be sure that they have enough funds to support the core curriculum, but eliminating the arts entirely is not the solution. Instead, a solution might be for schools to cut back on the variety or number of classes in the arts, but still have students take one course per semester. Additionally, schools could do fund-raising events for arts classes or look for outside arts organizations that are willing to provide arts programs for the school. For example, a local artist could be asked to volunteer to spend the day speaking with students or a local dance troop could perform during an all-school assembly."

Fourth: Write a brief conclusion consisting of a few sentences that summarize your side. Do not bring up new information in the conclusion!

SCORING

Two readers will evaluate your essay and each person will then assign it a score from 1 to 6. If, by chance, these two scorers disagree by more than 1 point, a third reader will step in and resolve the discrepancy. Performance on the essay will not affect the English, Math, Reading, Science, or composite scores. You will receive two additional scores on your score sheet—a combined English/Writing score (1–36) and a Writing test subscore (2–12). Neither of these scores will affect your composite score!

Answer Sheet

PRACTICE TEST 1

Directions: Mark one answer only for each question. Make the mark dark. Erase completely any mark made in error. (Additional or stray marks will be counted as mistakes.)

English Test

1	A B C D	21	A B C D	41	A B C D	61	A B C D
2	F G H J	22	F G H J	42	F G H J	62	F G H J
3	A B C D	23	A B C D	43	A B C D	63	A B C D
4	F G H J	24	F G H J	44	F G H J	64	F G H J
5	A B C D	25	A B C D	45	A B C D	65	A B C D
6	F G H J	26	F G H J	46	F G H J	66	F G H J
7	A B C D	27	A B C D	47	A B C D	67	A B C D
8	F G H J	28	F G H J	48	F G H J	68	F G H J
9	A B C D	29	A B C D	49	A B C D	69	A B C D
10	F G H J	30	F G H J	50	F G H J	70	F G H J
11	A B C D	31	A B C D	51	A B C D	71	A B C D
12	F G H J	32	F G H J	52	F G H J	72	F G H J
13	A B C D	33	A B C D	53	A B C D	73	A B C D
14	F G H J	34	F G H J	54	F G H J	74	F G H J
15	A B C D	35	A B C D	55	A B C D	75	A B C D
16	F G H J	36	F G H J	56	F G H J		
17	A B C D	37	A B C D	57	A B C D		
18	F G H J	38	F G H J	58	F G H J		
19	A B C D	39	A B C D	59	A B C D		
20	F G H J	40	F G H J	60	F G H J		

Math Test

1	A B C D E	16	F G H J K	31	A B C D E	46	F G H J K
2	F G H J K	17	A B C D E	32	F G H J K	47	A B C D E
3	A B C D E	18	F G H J K	33	A B C D E	48	F G H J K
4	F G H J K	19	A B C D E	34	F G H J K	49	A B C D E
5	A B C D E	20	F G H J K	35	A B C D E	50	F G H J K
6	F G H J K	21	A B C D E	36	F G H J K	51	A B C D E
7	A B C D E	22	F G H J K	37	A B C D E	52	F G H J K
8	F G H J K	23	A B C D E	38	F G H J K	53	A B C D E
9	A B C D E	24	F G H J K	39	A B C D E	54	F G H J K
10	F G H J K	25	A B C D E	40	F G H J K	55	A B C D E
11	A B C D E	26	F G H J K	41	A B C D E	56	F G H J K
12	F G H J K	27	A B C D E	42	F G H J K	57	A B C D E
13	A B C D E	28	F G H J K	43	A B C D E	58	F G H J K
14	F G H J K	29	A B C D E	44	F G H J K	59	A B C D E
15	A B C D E	30	F G H J K	45	A B C D E	60	F G H J K

Answer Sheet

PRACTICE TEST 1

Reading Test

1 A B C D	11 A B C D	21 A B C D	31 A B C D
2 F G H J	12 F G H J	22 F G H J	32 F G H J
3 A B C D	13 A B C D	23 A B C D	33 A B C D
4 F G H J	14 F G H J	24 F G H J	34 F G H J
5 A B C D	15 A B C D	25 A B C D	35 A B C D
6 F G H J	16 F G H J	26 F G H J	36 F G H J
7 A B C D	17 A B C D	27 A B C D	37 A B C D
8 F G H J	18 F G H J	28 F G H J	38 F G H J
9 A B C D	19 A B C D	29 A B C D	39 A B C D
10 F G H J	20 F G H J	30 F G H J	40 F G H J

Science Test

1 A B C D	11 A B C D	21 A B C D	31 A B C D
2 F G H J	12 F G H J	22 F G H J	32 F G H J
3 A B C D	13 A B C D	23 A B C D	33 A B C D
4 F G H J	14 F G H J	24 F G H J	34 F G H J
5 A B C D	15 A B C D	25 A B C D	35 A B C D
6 F G H J	16 F G H J	26 F G H J	36 F G H J
7 A B C D	17 A B C D	27 A B C D	37 A B C D
8 F G H J	18 F G H J	28 F G H J	38 F G H J
9 A B C D	19 A B C D	29 A B C D	39 A B C D
10 F G H J	20 F G H J	30 F G H J	40 F G H J

Practice Test 1

ENGLISH TEST

45 MINUTES—75 QUESTIONS

Directions: In the five passages that follow, certain words and phrases are underlined and numbered. In the right-hand column, you will find alternatives for the underlined part. In most cases, you are to choose the one that best expresses the idea, makes the statement appropriate for standard written English, or is worded most consistently with the style and tone of the passage as a whole. If you think the original version is best, choose "NO CHANGE." In some cases, you will find in the right-hand column a question about the underlined part. You are to choose the best answer to the question.

You will also find questions about a section of the passage, or about the passage as a whole. These questions do not refer to an underlined portion of the passage, but rather are identified by a number or numbers in a box.

For each question, choose the alternative you consider best and fill in the corresponding oval on your answer document. Read each passage through once before you begin to answer the questions that accompany it. For many of the questions, you must read several sentences beyond the question to determine the answer. Be sure that you have read far enough ahead each time you choose an alternative.

Passage I

No Place I'd Rather Be

[1]

I started taking group skating lessons when I was four. I progressed through various levels rapidly and gave my first ice performance at age seven, soon I started (1) winning local and regional competitions. I began seriously training when I was nine years old. Mom and I would wake up at four o'clock in the morning, six days a week. I'd skate for five hours. Then I'd go to school.

1. **A.** NO CHANGE
   B. seven. Soon I started
   C. seven, soon I was
   D. seven. Soon I had

GO ON TO THE NEXT PAGE.

[2]

Saying good-bye to my family, and friends made me homesick before I even left, but I knew deep down that I had to leave and train full-time in Canada to give my dreams a chance at reality. I went to compete in the Olympic Games in 1992. No one, not my coach or even my family, ever talked to me about giving up. In fact, I wouldn't even allow myself to think about it. I thought my thoughts would jinx me. Yet, I went with the attitude that I wanted to enjoy the Olympic spirit. [6]

[3]

My practice sessions felt great leading up to the competition. Finally, the day arrived. I remember stepping onto the ice and thinking, *I can't do this*. How am I going to keep myself from freaking out? I took a deep breath and begun a solid performance that placed me first going into the finals.

[4]

When medals were awarded, I found myself on the top step, the gold hanging around my neck and

2. **F.** NO CHANGE
   G. family, and, friends
   H. family and friends,
   J. family and friends

3. Which of the following alternatives to the underlined portion would NOT be acceptable?
   A. even left yet I knew
   B. even left. I knew
   C. even left; I knew
   D. even left; however, I knew

4. Given that all of the choices are true, which one provides information that is most relevant at this point in the essay?
   F. NO CHANGE
   G. all the hard work required
   H. the joy of competing in the Olympics
   J. winning a gold medal

5. **A.** NO CHANGE
   B. Nevertheless, I
   C. However, I
   D. I

6. Which of the following statements, if added at the beginning of Paragraph 2, would most effectively introduce readers to the information presented in the paragraph?
   F. I had always wanted to move away from home, so when the opportunity presented itself, I jumped.
   G. Knowing that it was time to leave my childhood behind, I followed my coach's advice and randomly moved to Canada.
   H. Twenty-four hours after graduating from high school, I moved to Canada.
   J. There was only one road to success, and hanging around my hometown waiting to be discovered wasn't it.

7. **A.** NO CHANGE
   B. begin
   C. began
   D. had begun

8. **F.** NO CHANGE
   G. top step the gold, hanging
   H. top, step the gold hanging
   J. top step the gold hanging

Americas national anthem[9] playing. Words can't describe the overwhelming mixture of emotions I felt.

[5]

[1] Two days later, I was the first of the final six skaters on the cold, but shimmering ice[10]. [2] My long performance started well, but I slipped while completing one of my easiest triple jumps, and my hand touched the ice. [3] I didn't want to make two mistakes in a row, so next I did a jump with just two spins to play it safe. [4] Usually jumps have three spins. [5] As I neared the end, I had one more jump, the triple Lutz. [6] Okay, this is it. [7] You have to do this, I told myself. [8] I landed perfectly. [11]

[6]

Why is ice so popular?[12] Frozen water can be so painfully hard and oh so cold—just as life can be. Ice doesn't care who skates across its surface. It doesn't care who loses balance and falls on its[13] slippery back. Still, when the lights go on and the crowd roars its welcome, there's no place I'd rather be.

9. **A.** NO CHANGE
   B. Americas national anthem's
   C. Americas' national anthem
   D. America's national anthem

10. **F.** NO CHANGE
    G. cold yet shimmering, ice
    H. cold, shimmering, ice
    J. cold, shimmering ice

11. Which of the following sentences in this paragraph is LEAST relevant to the purpose of describing the narrator's actions, and therefore, could be deleted?
    A. Sentence 3
    B. Sentence 4
    C. Sentence 5
    D. Sentence 7

12. Which of the following choices best introduces this paragraph?
    F. NO CHANGE
    G. There are so many reasons to love ice.
    H. How can anyone love ice?
    J. Ice has been around forever.

13. **A.** NO CHANGE
    B. it's
    C. their
    D. there

Questions 14 and 15 ask about the preceding passage as a whole.

14. For the sake of the logic and coherence of this essay, Paragraph 5 should be placed:
    F. where it is now.
    G. after Paragraph 3.
    H. before Paragraph 1.
    J. after Paragraph 6.

GO ON TO THE NEXT PAGE.

15. Suppose the writer's goal had been to write a brief essay about a significant event in her life. Would this essay successfully accomplish that goal?
  A. Yes, because it focuses on a specific time in the narrator's life and goes into detail about winning an Olympic gold medal.
  B. Yes, because it details every event that indirectly led to an important achievement in the narrator's life.
  C. No, because it is more of a persuasive essay motivating the readers to pursue their dreams, even if it means personal sacrifice.
  D. No, because the narrator mentions several events and doesn't go into much detail about any one event.

Passage II

A Journey on Cane River

Growing up, I knew for an absolute fact that no one on the planet was stronger than my mother. So when she told me stories of people she admired growing up, I paid attention. She was clearly in awe of her grandmother, Emily. She described [16] her grandmother as iron-willed and devilish, physically beautiful and demanding of beauty from others, determined to make her farmhouse in central Louisiana a fun place to be on Sundays when family gathered, and fanatical and unforgiving about the responsibilities generated from family ties. On one hand, Emily was refined, graceful, elegant, [17] soft-spoken, and classy. On the other, she was a woman from the backwoods of Louisiana, possibly born a slave, unapologetic about dipping snuff, who buzzed on her homemade muscadine wine each and every day.

Emily intrigued me, and the puzzle [18] of this woman simmered on the back burner of my conscious mind for

16. **F.** NO CHANGE
  G. She describes
  H. Describing
  J. Because she described

17. **A.** NO CHANGE
  B. Emily was, refined, graceful, elegant,
  C. Emily was refined, and graceful and elegant
  D. Emily was; refined, graceful, elegant,

18. **F.** NO CHANGE
  G. intrigued me, and, the puzzle
  H. intrigued me and, the puzzle
  J. intrigued me and the puzzle,

decades, undoubtedly activating questions about who I was as well. [19]

Hooked, I traced my mother's line to a place in Louisiana called Cane River, a unique area that before the Civil War housed one of the largest and wealthiest collections of free people of color in the United States. [20]

I decided to hire a specialist on Cane River culture; a genealogist to [21] find my great-grandmother Emily's grandmother.

In a collection of ten thousand unindexed local records written in poor preserved [22] Creole French, she found the bill of sale for my great-great-great-great-grandmother Elisabeth, whom was [23] sold in 1850 in Cane River, Louisiana, for eight hundred dollars.

One day, [24] I had no choice. I had to write their story and document their lives—my history. They were, [25] after all, real flesh-and-blood people. I pieced their lives

19. Which of the following alternatives to the underlined portion would be LEAST acceptable?
   A. prompting
   B. halting
   C. stirring
   D. triggering

20. If the writer were to delete the underlined portion from the sentence, the paragraph would primarily lose:
   F. details that emphasize the historical importance of the geographical location.
   G. a comparison of this location with the rest of the state of Louisiana.
   H. information that explains the narrator's reasons for wanting to explore the Cane River.
   J. nothing at all, since these geographical details are irrelevant to the paragraph.

21. **A.** NO CHANGE
   B. culture a genealogist, to
   C. culture—a genealogist—to
   D. culture a genealogist

22. **F.** NO CHANGE
   G. poorly preserved
   H. preserved poorly
   J. preserved poor

23. **A.** NO CHANGE
   B. whom
   C. who have
   D. who was

24. Given that all choices are true, which one provides the best transition between paragraphs?
   F. NO CHANGE
   G. Sooner or later,
   H. At this point,
   J. However,

25. **A.** NO CHANGE
   B. They are,
   C. I am,
   D. We could be,

together as best I could, re-creating what life must have been like for them during the 1800s and 1900s. [26]

<u>Resulting with</u>[27] *Cane River*, a novelized account covering one hundred years in America's history and following four generations of Creole slave women in Cane River, <u>Louisiana. As they</u>[28] struggled to keep their families intact through the dark days of slavery, the Civil War, Reconstruction, and the pre-civil rights era of Jim Crow South. <u>The book ended up on Oprah's book list and made the *New York Times* Bestseller list.</u>[29]

26. The writer is considering adding the following phrase to the preceding sentence, after the word *could*:

    from over a thousand documents uncovered in my years of research.

    Should the writer make this addition?

    F. Yes, because it emphasizes how much work the writer had to do in order to complete the book.
    G. Yes, because it provides details that prove that *Cane River* is a fictional novel.
    H. No, because the information is unnecessary and detracts from the main idea of the sentence.
    J. No, because the phrase fails to specify the precise number of documents examined.

27. **A.** NO CHANGE
    B. The result was
    C. Having the result of
    D. Results were

28. **F.** NO CHANGE
    G. Louisiana when they
    H. Louisiana, they
    J. Louisiana, who

29. Given that all of the choices are true, which one best concludes this essay by tying this paragraph to the essay's introduction?

    A. NO CHANGE
    B. I had always wanted to write a book, and was proud of my accomplishment.
    C. Finally I, along with the rest of the world, had an idea of who Emily really was.
    D. This was the first book published about Creole slave women.

Question 30 asks about the preceding passage as a whole.

30. Suppose the writer's goal had been to describe the personal benefits of writing a book. Does this essay successfully accomplish that goal?

    F. Yes, the author explains how writing *Cane River* made her a better person.
    G. Yes, the author discusses why she wanted to write a book and then details the many steps involved.
    H. No, because it focuses instead on biographical information about the author's family.
    J. No, the essay fails to provide enough information about what the author gained from the experience of writing the book.

Passage III

Illinois Prairies

There are different kinds of prairies in Illinois depending on the moisture gradient and soil type. The different kinds of prairie wildflowers, are often (31) associated with these different moisture gradients and soil types. As an ecological habitat, grasses and herbaceous wildflowers, rather than trees and shrubs, or areas with more or less permanent water, dominated (32) prairies.

[33] High quality prairies are interesting and colorful places to visit during the growing season because they demonstrate high biodiversity. (34)

Black soil prairie was the dominant type of prairie in central and northern Illinois, until (35) it was almost totally destroyed by agricultural development during the 19th century. The landscape of such prairies is rather flat. A high-quality black soil prairie has lots of wildflowers in

31. A. NO CHANGE
B. wildflowers are often
C. wildflowers often
D. wildflowers: often

32. F. NO CHANGE
G. dominates
H. dominating
J. dominate

33. At this point in the opening paragraph, the writer is considering adding the following true statement:

In Iowa, six different types of coneflowers sway in summer breezes.

Should the writer make this addition here?

A. Yes, because it helps establish that the essay is set in the Midwest.
B. Yes, because it helps reinforce the main idea of the paragraph.
C. No, because it does not make clear whether coneflowers grow in every state.
D. No, because it distracts from the main focus of the paragraph.

34. The writer is considering deleting the underlined portion from the sentence. Should the phrase be kept or deleted?

F. Kept, because it provides supporting details that reinforce the main idea of the sentence.
G. Kept, because it establishes that prairies contain more biodiversity than any other habitat.
H. Deleted, because it has already been established earlier in the paragraph that prairies have low biodiversity.
J. Deleted, because it draws attention away from the different types of prairies.

35. A. NO CHANGE
B. Illinois,
C. Illinois: until
D. Illinois. Until

GO ON TO THE NEXT PAGE.

bloom from late spring until the middle of fall. Today, small remnants of original black soil prairie can be found in pioneer <u>cemeteries or at construction sites.</u> 36

[1] Gravel and dolomite prairies were never very common in Illinois, and can be found primarily in northern Illinois. [2] Gravel and dolomite prairies can be rather flat, or slightly hilly. [3] <u>Yet,</u> 37 the original gravel and dolomite prairies have been largely destroyed by modern development. [4] They tend to be rather dry and well drained. [5] More recently, such prairies have been found along the gravelly ballast of railroads, where they probably did not formerly exist. [38] [6] In this case, they are degraded <u>and often contain flora</u> 39 from Western states. [40]

Hill prairies occur primarily along the Illinois and Mississippi <u>Rivers, hill</u> 41 prairies are very dry and exposed to prevailing winds from the south or west. The wild-

36. Given that all choices are grammatically correct, which one best establishes that black soil prairies are difficult to find today?
    F. NO CHANGE
    G. cemeteries or along old railroads.
    H. cemeteries, state parks, and surrounding farmland.
    J. cemeteries and in many neighborhoods.

37. **A.** NO CHANGE
    B. However,
    C. Unfortunately,
    D. Accordingly,

38. The writer is considering deleting the phrase "where they probably did not formerly exist" from the preceding sentence (and placing a period after the word *railroads*). Should the phrase be kept or deleted?
    F. Kept, because the information helps to establish the rampant proliferation of gravel and dolomite prairies in Illinois.
    G. Kept, because it strengthens the paragraph's focus on the unchanging landscape of prairies.
    H. Deleted, because it is not relevant to the description of gravel and dolomite prairies found in Illinois.
    J. Deleted, because the speculation is inconsistent with the claim made earlier in the paragraph that the prairies have been largely destroyed.

39. **A.** NO CHANGE
    B. and many bird species migrate to them
    C. consisting of a mix of native grasses and flowers and flora
    D. and are of particular interest to tourists

40. For the sake of the logic and coherence of this paragraph, Sentence 4 should be placed:
    F. where it is now.
    G. before Sentence 1.
    H. before Sentence 3.
    J. before Sentence 6.

41. **A.** NO CHANGE
    B. rivers. Hill
    C. rivers hill
    D. rivers; hill,

flowers of hill prairies are similar to those who are found (42) in the drier areas of gravel and dolomite prairies. Some species that are found in hill prairies is typical (43) of western areas.

Sand prairies can be moist mesic or dry and (44) their landscape is either flat or slightly hilly. They usually occur near current or former bodies of water. Their vegetation is sparser than that of black soil prairies. (45)

42. **F.** NO CHANGE
    G. which are finding
    H. if found
    J. that can be found

43. **A.** NO CHANGE
    B. are more typical
    C. typify
    D. are more usual

44. **F.** NO CHANGE
    G. moist mesic, or dry; and
    H. moist: mesic or dry, and
    J. moist, mesic, or dry, and

45. Given that all of the choices are true, which best concludes the paragraph with a colorful image that relates to the description of a sand prairie?
    A. NO CHANGE
    B. Vegetation includes woody shrubs, wildflowers, and native prairie grasses.
    C. The spectacular vegetation includes the vibrant hues of purple spiderwort, orange butterfly weed, and yellow goldenrod.
    D. More than sixty colorful species of wildflowers have been identified as being native to sand prairies.

Passage IV

Money Monkeys

The mountainous regions of northern Japan renowned (46) not only for their beauty but also for their hot springs, known as *onsen*. Created naturally by the same volcanic activity that formed the Japanese islands initially, (47) the springs are not only relaxing but believed to be therapeutic, due to the high mineral content of their waters.

[1] At many onsen, native populations of Japanese Macaques, a gray, pink-faced monkey species famed for the (48) intelligence, make a habit of dipping in them as well. [2] For the most part, the monkeys are well mannered and cause no problems for humans. [3] Tourists

46. **F.** NO CHANGE
    G. renown
    H. are renowned
    J. have been renown

47. Which of the following alternatives to the underlined portion would NOT be acceptable?
    A. later,
    B. themselves,
    C. on which they sit,
    D. DELETE the underlined portion (but preserve the comma).

48. **F.** NO CHANGE
    G. it's
    H. its
    J. they're

GO ON TO THE NEXT PAGE.

are always especially entertained by them, and so the monkeys are gladly tolerated by the operators of the various springs. [4] Humans are not the only creatures who enjoy bathing in the springs. [49]

At one onsen however, the clever apes are causing an amusing problem. Visitors to this particular location encourage strongly to keep their cars locked and their wallets and purses hidden, because the monkeys are out to get their money! After years of observing humans in line at the gift and snack shops, the macaques at this onsen have deduced that certain special objects namely paper money and coins can be exchanged for food. In short order, the hungry simians were sneaking into unlocked cars, grabbing money, and trotting over to the shops to purchase themselves a snack.

At first, the flabbergasted employees didn't know what to do. After all, the monkeys were waiting politely in line and paying for their purchases, just like the human customers, so there was no real reason not to accept their business. Meanwhile, however, someone pointed out that there was no possible way a monkey

49. For the sake of the logic and coherence of this paragraph, Sentence 4 should be placed:
A. where it is now.
B. before Sentence 1.
C. before Sentence 2.
D. before Sentence 3.

50. **F.** NO CHANGE
G. onsen, however the
H. onsen, however, the
J. onsen—however, the

51. **A.** NO CHANGE
B. are strong with encouragement
C. being strongly encouraged
D. are strongly encouraged

52. Which of the following alternatives to the underlined portion would be LEAST acceptable?
F. wanting
G. seeking
H. after
J. pilfering

53. **A.** NO CHANGE
B. objects—namely, paper money and coins—can be exchanged
C. objects, namely, paper money—and coins—can be exchanged
D. objects, namely paper money and coins—can be exchanged

54. If the writer were to delete the underlined portion, the paragraph would primarily lose:
F. an explanation of the fact that the employees at this onsen were particularly inexperienced.
G. further detail about the cleverness of this species of monkey.
H. emphasis on the extremely bizarre nature of the situation.
J. foreshadowing of the fact that things are not going to turn out well for the monkeys.

55. **A.** NO CHANGE
B. Additionally,
C. Eventually,
D. Although

1 ■ ■ ■ ■ ■ ■ ■ ■ ■ 1

could get money <u>other than</u> [56] stealing it from a human. So now, when a cash-carrying macaque steps into line, special monkey-specific security guards are on hand to chase him <u>out in the hopes that</u> [57] this will eliminate the monkey's motive for theft.

I suppose that makes sense, but <u>I'm disappointedly personable.</u> [58] I'm not much of a traveler, but if there was one thing that could <u>have motivated me to fly</u> [59] halfway around the world, it's the possibility of seeing a monkey with a wad of bills in his paw waiting in line to buy a bag of chips. [60]

56. Which of the following alternatives to the underlined portion would be LEAST acceptable?
    - **F.** would be
    - **G.** except for
    - **H.** besides
    - **J.** outside of

57. **A.** NO CHANGE
    - **B.** out, in the hopes that
    - **C.** out in the hopes, that
    - **D.** out, in the hopes, that

58. **F.** NO CHANGE
    - **G.** I disappoint people.
    - **H.** personally I'm disappointed.
    - **J.** I'm personally disappointed.

59. **A.** NO CHANGE
    - **B.** motivate me flying
    - **C.** be motivating me flying
    - **D.** be motivating me to fly

60. At this point, the writer is considering adding the following true statement:

    Although I'm not even sure monkeys like chips, so I suppose I shouldn't buy my ticket just yet.

    Should the writer make this addition here?
    - **F.** Yes, because it provides the necessary information that the author is a cautious person.
    - **G.** Yes, because this is a question about monkeys that is important for the reader to consider.
    - **H.** No, because the previous sentence already effectively and humorously ended the passage.
    - **J.** No, because the tone of the sentence is inconsistent with that of the rest of the passage.

Passage V

The Birth of Surrealism

Joan Miró was a Catalan painter, sculptor, and ceramicist born in Barcelona, Spain, in 1893. <u>His work has been interpreted with international acclaim, earning a reputation</u> [61] as Surrealism, a sandbox for the subconscious mind, a re-creation of the childlike, and a manifestation of Catalan pride. In numerous interviews

61. **A.** NO CHANGE
    - **B.** He has earned international acclaim, his work
    - **C.** Interpreted as having earned international acclaim, his work is seen
    - **D.** Earning international acclaim, his work has been interpreted

GO ON TO THE NEXT PAGE.

dating from the 1930s onwards, Miró <u>expressing</u> [62] contempt for conventional painting methods as a way of supporting bourgeoise society, and famously declared an "assassination of painting" in favor of <u>utilizing common traditional methods of blending colors.</u> [63]

<u>Born to the family of a goldsmith and watchmaker, the young Miró was drawn toward the arts community</u> [64] that was gathering in Montparnasse and in 1920 moved to Paris. There, under the influence of the poets and <u>writers, developing</u> [65] his unique style: organic forms and flattened picture planes drawn with a sharp line. Generally thought of as a Surrealist because of his interest in automatism and the use of sexual symbols, Miró was influenced in <u>varying</u> [66] degrees by Surrealism and Dada, yet he rejected membership in any artistic movement in the interwar European years. Andre <u>Breton, the founder of Surrealism described</u> [67] him as "the most Surrealist of us all."

<u>Miró often received inspiration for his paintings in visions,</u> [68] and thus, with Andre Masson, represented the

62. F. NO CHANGE
G. expressed
H. had express
J. were to express

63. Which choice best illustrates Miró's contempt for conventional painting and helps explain the "assassination of painting" mentioned earlier in the sentence?
A. NO CHANGE
B. applying works of art by famous Renaissance painters.
C. boycotting painting as an art form and turning to sculpting instead.
D. rejecting the visual elements of established painting.

64. F. NO CHANGE
G. Miró was drawn to the arts community, born to the family of a goldsmith and watchmaker
H. The arts community, born to the family of a goldsmith and watchmaker, the young Miró was drawn to
J. The young Miró was drawn to the family of a goldsmith and watchmaker, born to the arts community

65. A. NO CHANGE
B. writers. He developed
C. writers, he developed
D. writers develops

66. F. NO CHANGE
G. variety
H. different and varying
J. various, multiple

67. A. NO CHANGE
B. Breton the founder of Surrealism, described
C. Breton: the founder of Surrealism, describe
D. Breton, the founder of Surrealism, described

68. At this point in the essay, the writer wants to highlight the influence that Miró had on painting as an art form. Given that all of the choices are true, which one would best accomplish that purpose?
F. NO CHANGE
G. Miró greatly disliked all bourgeoise art, especially Cubism,
H. Miró was the first artist to develop automatic drawing as a way to undo previous established techniques in painting,
J. Miró worked heavily in ceramics in the last phase of his career,

beginning of Surrealism as an art movement. <u>However,</u>[69] Miró chose not to become an official member of the Surrealists in order to be free to experiment with other artistic styles without compromising his position within the group. He pursued his own interests in the art <u>world, ranges</u>[70] from automatic drawing and Surrealism to Expressionism and Color Field painting.

In his final decades, Miró <u>were to accelerate</u>[71] his work in different media and produced hundreds of ceramics, including the *Wall of the Moon* and *Wall of the Sun*. He also made temporary window paintings (on glass) for an exhibit. In the last years of his life Miró wrote his most radical and least <u>known ideas: explored</u>[72] the possibilities of gas sculpture and four-dimensional painting.

He died bedridden, at his home in Palma, Mallorca, on December 25, 1983. He suffered from heart disease, and <u>visits</u>[73] a clinic for respiratory problems two weeks before his death. Many of his pieces are exhibited today in the Fundació Joan Miró in Barcelona and the U.S. National Gallery in <u>Washington, D.C. he is buried nearby</u>[74] at the Montjuïc cemetery. Today, his paintings sell for between $250,000 and $17 <u>million, that</u>[75] was the auction price for the *La Caresse des Etoiles* on May 6, 2008, and is the highest amount paid for one of Miró's works to date.

69. **A.** NO CHANGE
B. Consequently,
C. Furthermore,
D. Thus,

70. **F.** NO CHANGE
G. world, ranging
H. world which ranges
J. world and range

71. **A.** NO CHANGE
B. is accelerating
C. accelerates
D. accelerated

72. **F.** NO CHANGE
G. known ideas exploring—
H. known ideas. He explored
J. known ideas, he explored

73. **A.** NO CHANGE
B. had visited
C. visiting
D. were to visit

74. **F.** NO CHANGE
G. Washington D.C. he is buried nearby,
H. Washington, D.C., he is buried, nearby
J. Washington, D.C.; he is buried nearby

75. **A.** NO CHANGE
B. million and that
C. million, which
D. million which

STOP

If there is still time remaining, check your answers to this section.

2 △ △ △ △ △ △ △ △ 2

MATHEMATICS TEST

60 MINUTES—60 QUESTIONS

Directions: Solve each problem, choose the correct answer, and then fill in the corresponding oval on your answer document.

Do not linger over problems that take too much time. Solve as many as you can; then return to the others in the time you have left for this test.

You are permitted to use a calculator on this test. You may use your calculator for any problems you choose, but some of the problems may best be done without using a calculator.

Note: Unless otherwise stated, all of the following should be assumed.

1. Illustrative figures are NOT necessarily drawn to scale.
2. Geometric figures lie in a plane.
3. The word *line* indicates a straight line.
4. The word *average* indicates arithmetic mean.

DO YOUR FIGURING HERE.

1. If $x = 3$, then $x^2 + 2x - 12 = ?$

   A. –3
   B. 0
   C. 3
   D. 6
   E. 21

2. If $3(2x - 1) = 11x + 27$, then $x = ?$

   F. –6
   G. –2
   H. 2
   J. 6
   K. 7

3. To make space for new merchandise, a clothing store offered a 15% discount on all current stock. What is the sale price of a jacket that regularly sells for $42?

   A. $6.30
   B. $8.40
   C. $35.70
   D. $37.80
   E. $41.85

2 △ △ △ △ △ △ △ △ 2

DO YOUR FIGURING HERE.

4. In the figure below, line m is parallel to line n. One angle formed with transversal line t measures 60°, as shown. What is the degree measure of $\angle a$?

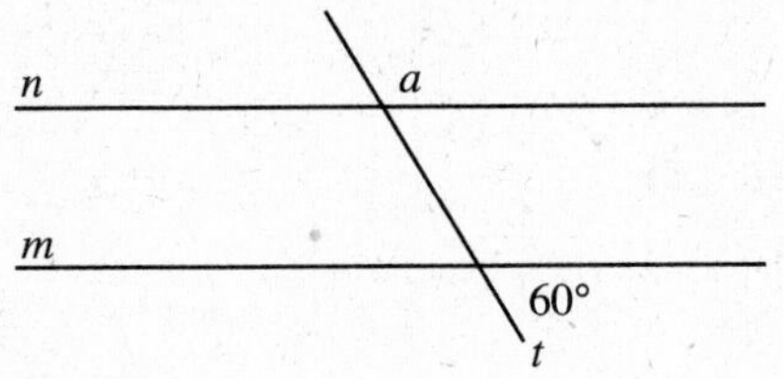

F. 30°
G. 60°
H. 90°
J. 120°
K. Cannot be determined

5. If $x = 3$, $y = 5$, and $w = 4$, what is the value of $xw^3 + \frac{3w}{2} - x^2y$?

A. 9.0
B. 12.0
C. 79.5
D. 153.0
E. 1,689.0

6. For all x, $(3x - 5)(4x + 3) = ?$

F. $12x^2 - 15$
G. $12x^2 + 11x - 15$
H. $12x^2 - 11x - 15$
J. $12x^2 + 29x - 15$
K. $12x^2 - 29x - 15$

7. $|5 - 8| - |9 - 3| = ?$

A. −9
B. −3
C. 1
D. 3
E. 9

8. $(5\sqrt{3})^2 = ?$

F. 15
G. $10\sqrt{6}$
H. 45
J. $34 + 10\sqrt{3}$
K. 75

GO ON TO THE NEXT PAGE.

2 △ △ △ △ △ △ △ △ 2

DO YOUR FIGURING HERE.

9. A carpet company uses the following formula for estimating the number of square feet, A, of carpeting needed for a room x feet by y feet, containing a stairway w feet by z feet, with n stairs:

$$A = xy + w[z(2n - 1) + 2n]$$

What is the company's estimate for the number of square feet of carpeting needed for a room that is 15 feet by 18 feet, containing a stairway that is 6 feet by 6 feet with 8 stairs?

A. 826
B. 894
C. 906
D. 1,086
E. 1,636

10. An urn contains 7 blue balls, 5 white balls, and 3 red balls. What is the probability that the first ball drawn at random from the urn will NOT be red?

F. $\frac{7}{45}$

G. $\frac{1}{5}$

H. $\frac{1}{3}$

J. $\frac{7}{15}$

K. $\frac{4}{5}$

11. A certain watch costs $100, and a certain pearl necklace costs $300. If the cost of the watch increases by 5% and the cost of the pearl necklace decreases by 10%, what will be the sum of their new costs?

A. $375
B. $385
C. $395
D. $405
E. $415

2 △ △ △ △ △ △ △ △ 2

DO YOUR FIGURING HERE.

12. In the figure below, $\overline{CA}$ is tangent to circle O at point T. If $\overline{AT} = 6$ units, $\overline{CT} = 8$ units, and $\overline{CO} = 10$ units, how many units long is the radius of the circle?

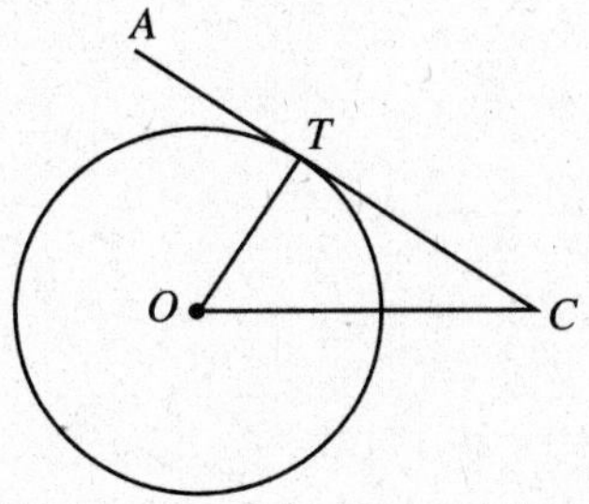

F. 2
G. 5
H. 6
J. 8
K. 10

13. If $A = BC$, $B = x$, and $C = yz$, then $AB = ?$

A. $xyzx$
B. $yzxy$
C. $zxyz$
D. $xyyz$
E. xyz

14. Which of the following inequalities specifies precisely the real values of x that are solutions to the inequality $-5 < -3x - 7$?

F. $x < 4$

G. $x < -\frac{2}{3}$

H. $x > -\frac{2}{3}$

J. $x < \frac{2}{3}$

K. $x > 4$

15. What is the slope of the line determined by the equation $y - \frac{1}{3}x + \frac{3}{5} = 0$?

A. 3
B. 1

C. $\frac{1}{3}$

D. $-\frac{3}{5}$

E. -3

2 △ △ △ △ △ △ △ △ 2

DO YOUR FIGURING HERE.

16. Which of the following expresses the equation $4x - 2y = 12$ in slope-intercept form?

    F. $x = \frac{1}{2}y + 3$

    G. $x = -\frac{1}{2}y + 3$

    H. $y = 2x - 6$

    J. $y = -2x + 6$

    K. $y = -2x - 6$

17. Which of the following values for a in the equation $3x + 3a - 5 = 5x - a$ causes the solution for x to be 6?

    A. –8.5
    B. –4.25
    C. 4.25
    D. 8.5
    E. 13.25

18. The centers of 3 identically sized circles lie on the diameter of a larger circle, as shown in the figure below. Each of the 4 circles is tangent to 2 other circles, as shown. If the circumference of each small circle is 8π inches, what is the circumference of the largest circle, in inches?

    F. 16π
    G. 24π
    H. 48π
    J. 64π
    K. 144π

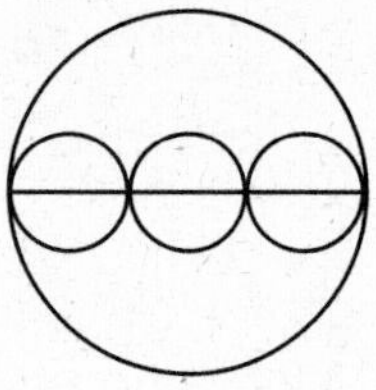

19. A recipe calls for cooking a turkey 1 hour for every 3 pounds it weighs. How long should a 19-pound turkey cook?

    A. 6 hours and 15 minutes
    B. 6 hours and 20 minutes
    C. 6 hours and 30 minutes
    D. 6 hours and $33\frac{1}{3}$ minutes
    E. 6 hours and 40 minutes

DO YOUR FIGURING HERE.

20. Line t intersects parallel lines m and n. Angle measures are as shown in the figure below. What is the degree measure of $\angle a$?

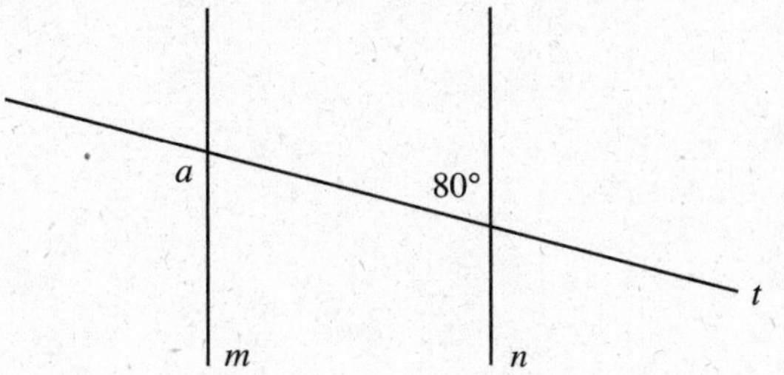

F. 10°
G. 80°
H. 90°
J. 100°
K. 110°

21. A photocopy machine enlarges a small triangle to produce a larger, similar triangle, as shown below. If the lengths of the sides, in inches, are as marked on the figure, and the triangles are similarly oriented, what is the value of x in inches?

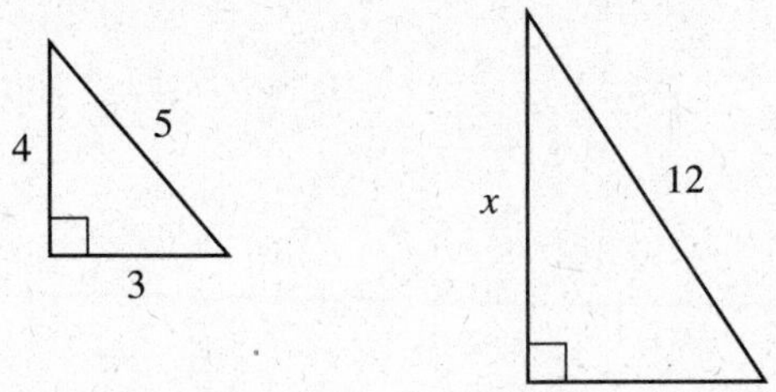

A. $7\frac{1}{5}$

B. 9

C. $9\frac{1}{2}$

D. $9\frac{3}{5}$

E. 11

22. If the lengths of adjacent sides of a rectangular playground have measures of $4x - 3$ and $2x^2 + 7$ units, respectively, then which of the following expressions represents the area, in square units, of the playground?

F. $2x^2 + 4x + 4$
G. $4x^2 + 8x + 8$
H. $8x^3 - 21$
J. $8x^3 - 6x^2 + 28x - 21$
K. $8x^3 + 6x^2 + 28x + 21$

Practice Test 1

2 △ △ △ △ △ △ △ △ 2

DO YOUR FIGURING HERE.

23. Which of the following is a prime factorization of 2,100?

A. $2 \cdot 3 \cdot 5 \cdot 7$
B. $2^2 \cdot 3 \cdot 5^2 \cdot 7$
C. $2^2 \cdot 3 \cdot 5 \cdot 35$
D. $2^2 \cdot 5^2 \cdot 21$
E. $2^2 \cdot 550$

24. After Jean spent 90% of her vacation money, $100 remained. How much vacation money did she originally have?

F. $111
G. $191
H. $900
J. $1,000
K. $1,111

25. Which of the following is a simplified version of $\frac{2x+1}{x} - \frac{x-3}{5x}$ whenever $x \neq 0$?

A. $9x + 2$
B. $9x^2 + 2x$
C. $\frac{-(x-4)}{4x}$
D. $\frac{9x+8}{5x}$
E. $\frac{9x^2+8x}{5x^2}$

26. If $2x^2 - x - 15 = 0$, what are the 2 possible values for x?

F. -5 and $\frac{3}{2}$
G. -3 and $\frac{2}{5}$
H. -3 and $\frac{5}{2}$
J. 3 and $-\frac{5}{2}$
K. 5 and $-\frac{3}{2}$

27. All angles in the figure shown below are right angles. If each side has a length of 4 centimeters, what is the area of the figure in square centimeters?

A. 32
B. 40
C. 44
D. 48
E. 80

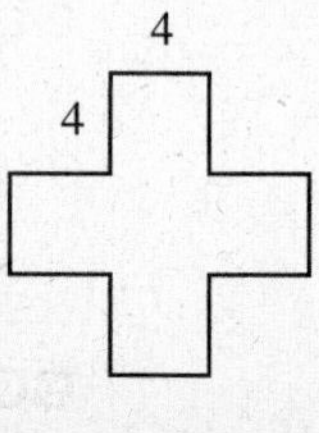

2 △ △ △ △ △ △ △ △ 2

DO YOUR FIGURING HERE.

28. If M, located at $(-1, 2)$, is the midpoint of $\overline{AB}$, and the coordinates of A are $(2, 9)$, what are the coordinates of B?

F. $(-5, 16)$
G. $(-4, -5)$
H. $(0.5, 5.5)$
J. $(4, -5)$
K. $(5, 16)$

29. In the figure below, lengths in units and angle measures in degrees are as marked. How many units long is $\overline{BC}$?

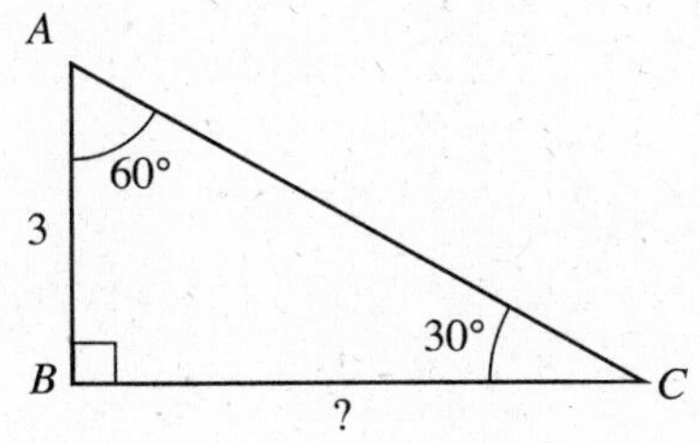

A. 3
B. $3\sqrt{2}$
C. $3\sqrt{3}$
D. 6
E. $3\sqrt{5}$

30. To increase the mean of 5 numbers by 3, by how much would the sum of the 5 numbers need to increase?

F. 3
G. 6
H. 9
J. 15
K. 18

31. Josh pounded a stake into the ground. When he attached a leash to both the stake and his dog's collar, the dog could walk 12 feet from the stake in any direction. Using 3.14 for π, what is the approximate area of the lawn, in square feet, that the dog could roam while tied to the stake?

A. 38
B. 75
C. 151
D. 377
E. 452

GO ON TO THE NEXT PAGE.

DO YOUR FIGURING HERE.

32. Television screen sizes are determined by the diagonal length of the rectangular screen. Chad recently changed from watching a television with a 19-inch screen to a television with a similarly shaped 32-inch screen. If a car on the 19-inch screen appeared 12 inches long, how long, to the nearest inch, would the same car appear on the 32-inch screen?

F. 16
G. 18
H. 20
J. 22
K. 24

33. In the figure below, *ABCD* is a square. Points are connected on each pair of adjacent sides of *ABCD* to form 4 congruent right triangles, as shown below. Each of these triangles has one leg that is twice as long as the other leg. If the area of the shaded region is 25 square feet, what is the area of square *ABCD* in square feet?

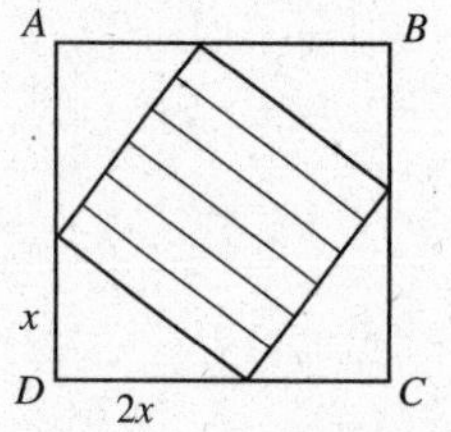

A. 225
B. 112.5
C. 56.25
D. 45
E. 27

34. A surveyor took and recorded the measurements shown in the figure below. If the surveyor wants to use these 3 measurements to calculate the length of the pond, which of the following would he find to be the most useful?

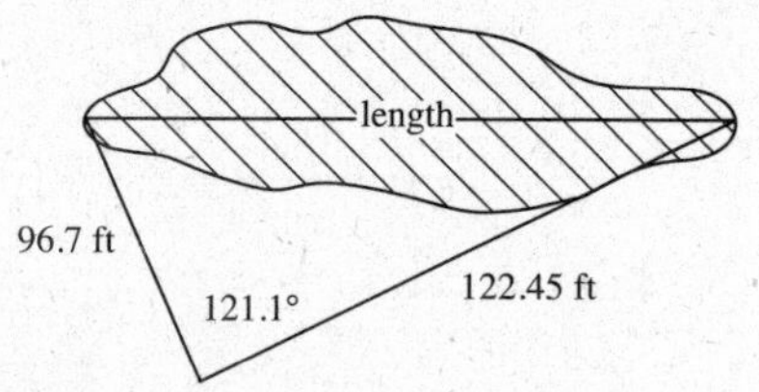

F. The Pythagorean Theorem
G. The ratios for the side lengths of 30°–60°–90° triangles
H. The ratios for the side lengths of 45°–45°–90° triangles
J. The law of cosines, which states that for any $\triangle ABC$, where a is the length of the side opposite $\angle A$, b is the length of the side opposite $\angle B$, and c is the length of the side opposite $\angle C$, $a^2 = b^2 + c^2 - 2bc[\cos(\angle A)]$
K. The law of sines, which states that the ratio between the length of the side opposite an angle and the sine of that angle is the same for all of the interior angles in the same triangle.

2 △ △ △ △ △ △ △ △ 2

DO YOUR FIGURING HERE.

35. Which of the following is the graph of the equation $y = \frac{4x - 2x^2}{x}$ in the standard (x, y) coordinate plane?

A.
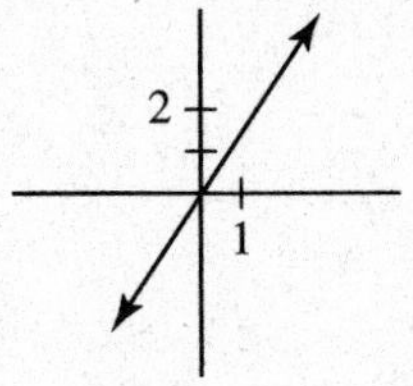

B.
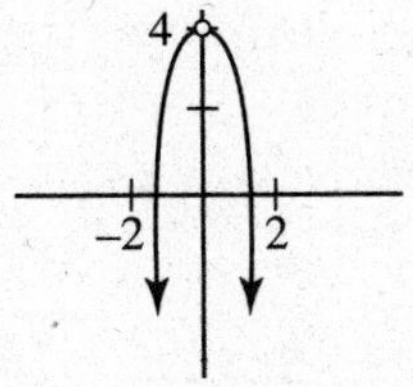

C.
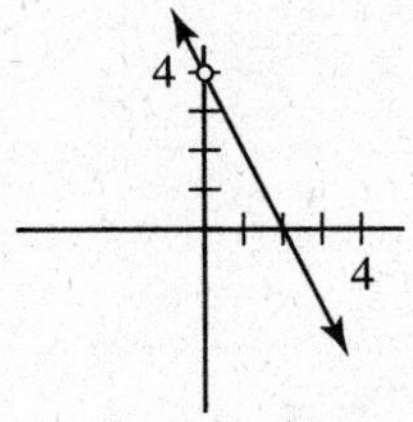

D.
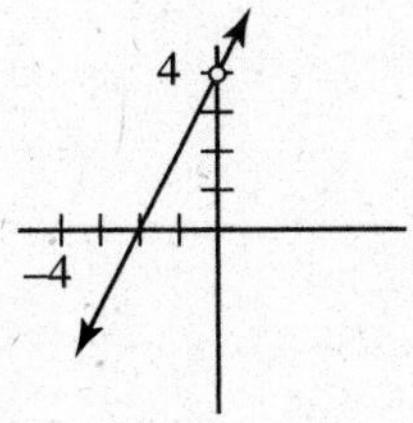

E.
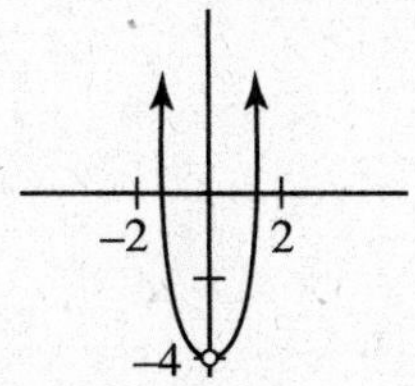

36. A line in a plane separates the plane into how many sets of points that do not contain the line?

F. 0
G. 1
H. 2
J. 3
K. Cannot be determined

2 △ △ △ △ △ △ △ △ 2

DO YOUR FIGURING HERE.

37. What is the maximum number of distinct diagonals that can be drawn in the hexagon shown below?

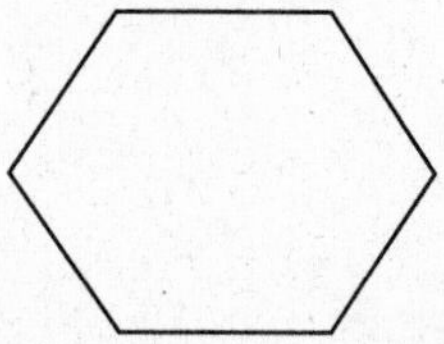

A. 12
B. 9
C. 6
D. 5
E. 4

38. In the standard (x, y) coordinate plane, the center of a circle lies in quadrant III. If the circle is tangent to the x-axis and the y-axis, which of the following is an equation for the circle?

F. $(x + 4)^2 + (y + 4)^2 = 4$
G. $(x - 4)^2 + (y - 4)^2 = 4$
H. $x^2 + (y - 4)^2 = 16$
J. $(x + 4)^2 + (y + 4)^2 = 16$
K. $(x + 4)^2 + (y - 4)^2 = 16$

39. How must $-\frac{3}{5}, -\frac{4}{7}, -\frac{5}{6},$ and $-\frac{8}{9}$ be arranged so that they are listed in increasing order?

A. $-\frac{8}{9} < -\frac{5}{6} < -\frac{3}{5} < -\frac{4}{7}$

B. $-\frac{8}{9} < -\frac{5}{6} < -\frac{4}{7} < -\frac{3}{5}$

C. $-\frac{4}{7} < -\frac{3}{5} < -\frac{5}{6} < -\frac{8}{9}$

D. $-\frac{3}{5} < -\frac{4}{7} < -\frac{5}{6} < -\frac{8}{9}$

E. $-\frac{5}{6} < -\frac{8}{9} < -\frac{3}{5} < -\frac{4}{7}$

40. The perimeter of an elliptical billiard table is to be covered with red velvet. The perimeter of an ellipse is given by the formula $p = \frac{\pi}{2}\sqrt{2(l^2 + w^2)}$, where l is the length and w is the width, as shown in the diagram below. If the length is 4 feet and the width is 3 feet, what is the outside perimeter of the ellipse in feet?

F. $\frac{5}{2}\pi\sqrt{2}$

G. $\frac{\pi}{2}(4\sqrt{2} + 3)$

H. $\frac{7}{2}\pi\sqrt{2}$

J. $(4\pi + 3)\sqrt{2}$

K. $5\pi\sqrt{2}$

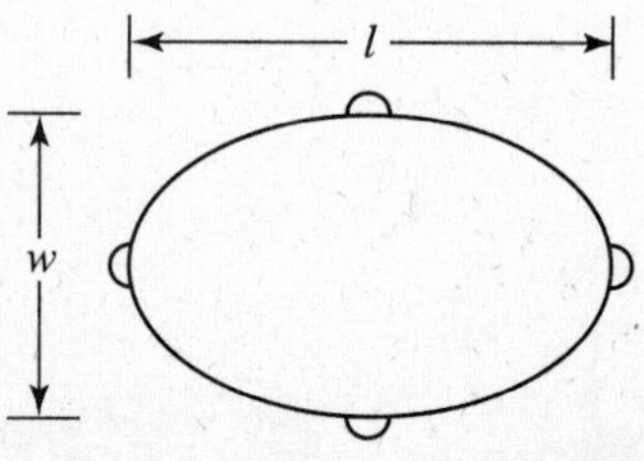

2 △ △ △ △ △ △ △ △ 2

DO YOUR FIGURING HERE.

41. If $\frac{A}{28}+\frac{B}{126}=\frac{9A+2B}{x}$, and A, B, and x are integers greater than 1, what must x equal?

    A. 11
    B. 154
    C. 252
    D. 1,134
    E. 3,528

42. Which one of the following expresses the number of meters that a contestant must travel in a 5-lap race around a circular track with a radius of R meters?

    F. $5R$
    G. $5\pi R$
    H. $5\pi R^2$
    J. $6R$
    K. $10\pi R$

43. In $\triangle ABC$, shown below, the measure of $\angle B$ is 40°, the measure of $\angle C$ is 35°, and $\overline{AB}$ is 27 units long. Which one of the following is an expression of the length, in units, of $\overline{BC}$?

    (Note: The law of sines states that for any triangle, the ratio between the sine of an angle and the length of the side opposite that angle is the same for all of the interior angles in the triangle.)

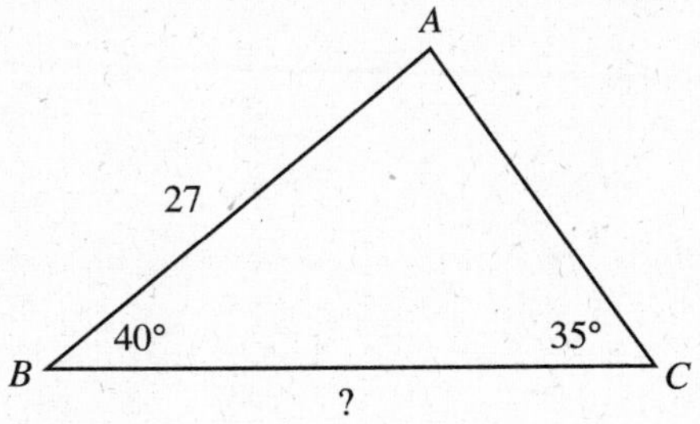

A. $\frac{27(\sin 105°)}{\sin 40°}$

B. $\frac{27(\sin 105°)}{\sin 35°}$

C. $\frac{27(\sin 75°)}{\sin 40°}$

D. $\frac{27(\sin 40°)}{\sin 105°}$

E. $\frac{27(\sin 35°)}{\sin 75°}$

GO ON TO THE NEXT PAGE.

2 △ △ △ △ △ △ △ △ 2

DO YOUR FIGURING HERE.

Use the following information to answer questions 44–45.

Kaylee is planning to purchase a car. She will need to borrow some of the money and has a chart, shown below, that will help her to approximate her monthly payment. The chart gives the approximate monthly payment per $1,000 borrowed.

Monthly payment per $1,000 borrowed for various annual rates and various numbers of payments.			
Annual Interest Rate	Number of Monthly Payments		
	36	48	60
5%	$29.97	$23.03	$18.87
6%	$30.42	$23.49	$19.33
8%	$31.34	$24.41	$20.28
10%	$32.27	$25.36	$21.24
12%	$33.22	$26.34	$22.24

44. Kaylee found a used car that she is thinking about purchasing. The list price is $8,785. She calculates that she will need to borrow $6,500. Approximately what would her monthly payment be if she borrowed the money for 36 months at an annual interest rate of 10%?

F. $164.84
G. $171.21
H. $209.76
J. $234.72
K. $283.81

45. A local dealership is having an end-of-the-model-year clearance sale and is offering 5% annual interest on new-car loans for 36, 48, or 60 months. The maximum amount that Kaylee can budget for her monthly car payment is $300. Of the following loan amounts, which one represents the maximum amount that Kaylee can borrow at 5% annual interest while staying within her budget?

A. $10,000
B. $13,000
C. $14,000
D. $15,000
E. $20,000

DO YOUR FIGURING HERE.

46. For $i^2 = -1$, $(5 - i)^2 = ?$

    F. 24
    G. 26
    H. $24 - 5i$
    J. $24 - 10i$
    K. $26 + 10i$

47. If x and y are integers such that $y > 12$ and $2x + y = 19$, which of the following is the solution set for x?

    A. $x \geq 4$
    B. $x \geq 3$
    C. $x \leq 4$
    D. $x \leq 3$
    E. $x \leq 0$

48. If $pq^3t^4 > 0$, which of the following products must be positive?

    F. pq
    G. pt
    H. qt
    J. pqt
    K. pq^2

49. If $\log_3 81 = x + 1$, then $x = ?$

    A. 3
    B. 4
    C. 5
    D. 6
    E. 243

50. In $\triangle RST$ below, $\angle S$ is a right angle, $\overline{RT} = 7$ units, and $\overline{TS} = 2$ units. What does $\csc \angle T$ equal?

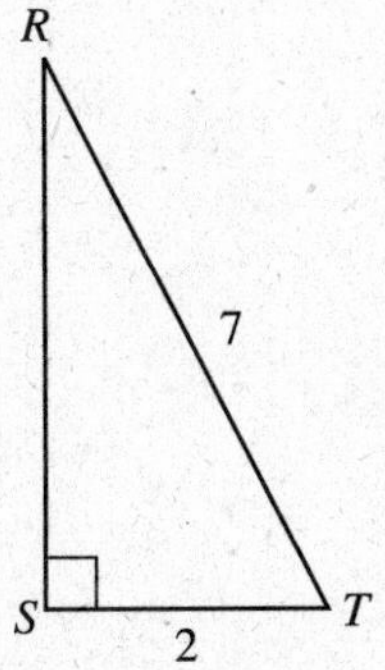

F. $\frac{2\sqrt{5}}{15}$

G. $\frac{3\sqrt{5}}{7}$

H. $\frac{7\sqrt{5}}{15}$

J. $\frac{3\sqrt{5}}{2}$

K. $\frac{7}{2}$

2 △ △ △ △ △ △ △ △ 2

51. A flight instructor charges \$75 per lesson, plus an additional fee for the use of his plane. The charge for the use of his plane varies directly with the cube root of the time the plane is used. If a lesson plus 27 minutes of plane usage costs \$120, what is the total amount charged for a lesson involving 64 minutes of plane usage?

A. \$195
B. \$180
C. \$157
D. \$135
E. \$60

DO YOUR FIGURING HERE.

52. In $\triangle ABD$ shown below, C is on $\overline{BD}$, $\overline{AC} \perp \overline{BD}$, the length of $\overline{AD}$ is 6 inches, the length of $\overline{BD}$ is 10 inches, and $\sin d = 0.8$. What is the area of $\triangle ABD$ in square inches?

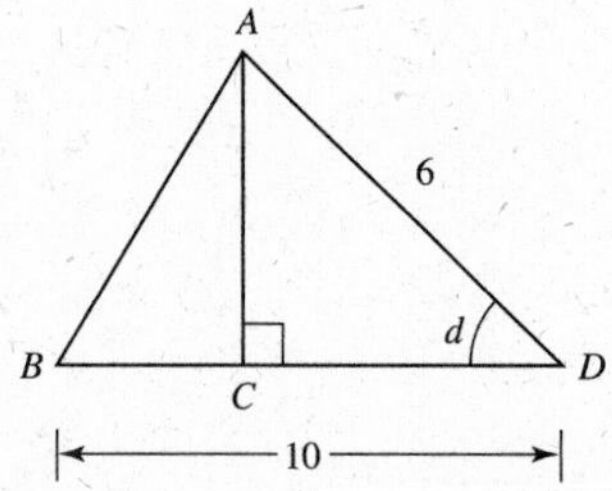

F. 6
G. 12
H. 24
J. 30
K. 60

53. For real numbers x and y, when is the equation $|2x+3y| = |2x-3y|$ true?

A. Never
B. Always
C. Only when $2x = 3y$
D. Only when $x = 0$ and $y = 0$
E. Only when $x = 0$ or $y = 0$

54. In the figure below, all line segments that intersect are perpendicular. Using only the segments and vertices in the figure, how many distinct rectangles are there with areas less than the area of $ADLI$?

(Note: If 2 rectangles have all four vertices in common, then they are not distinct.)

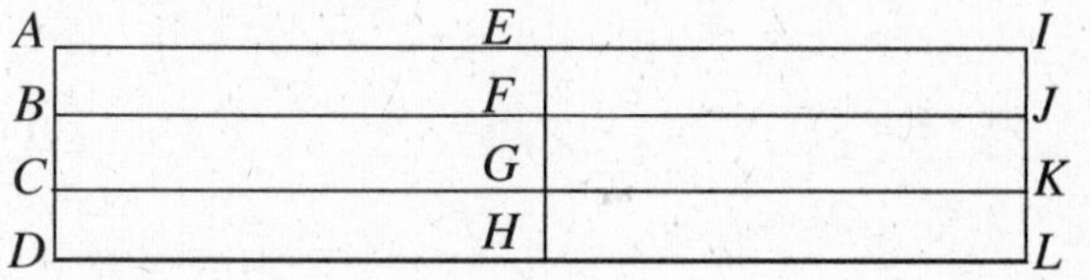

F. 7
G. 8
H. 17
J. 18
K. 19

2 △ △ △ △ △ △ △ △ 2

DO YOUR FIGURING HERE.

55. For some real number A, the graph of $y = (A + 3)x + 5$ in the standard (x, y) coordinate plane passes through the point (3, 11). What is the slope of this line?

A. –5
B. –2
C. –1
D. 2
E. $5\frac{1}{3}$

56. In the figure below, $\overline{BCF}$ is a line segment and all distances are given in inches. What is the ratio of the area of quadrilateral $RBCS$ to the area of quadrilateral $SCFT$?

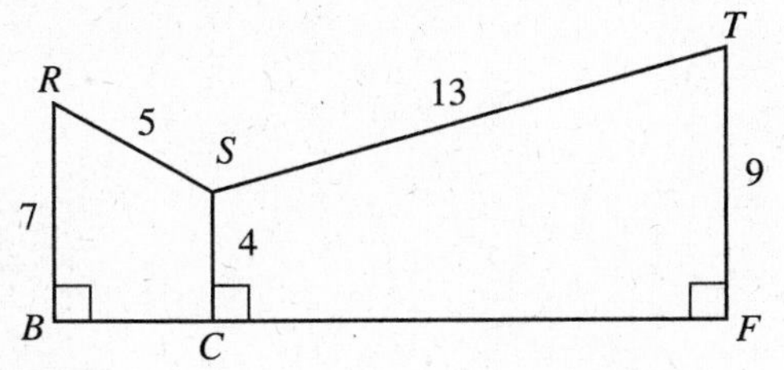

F. 9:7
G. 7:9
H. 11:13
J. 11:39
K. 11:50

57. When graphed in the standard (x, y) coordinate plane, the graphs of $y = x^2 - 5$ and $y = x + 1$ intersect at which of the following points?

A. (–3, 2) and (2, 3)
B. (–3, 4) and (2, –1)
C. (3, –4) and (–2, 1)
D. (3, 4) and (–2, –1)
E. The graphs do not intersect.

58. In septagon $ABCDEFG$ shown below, $\angle A = 115°$ and $\angle G = 70°$. What is the sum of the measures of the other 5 interior angles?

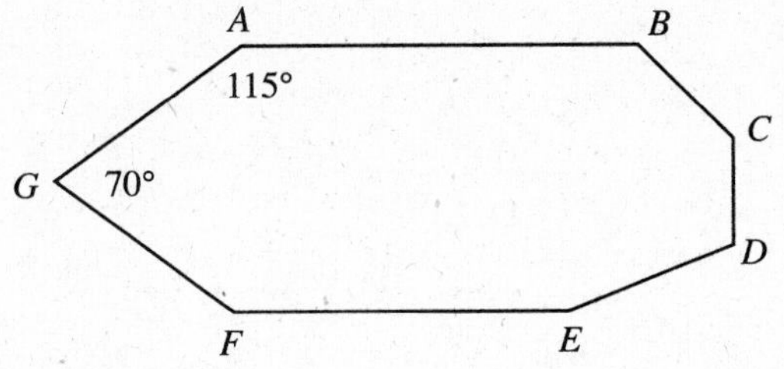

F. 585°
G. 595°
H. 655°
J. 690°
K. 715°

2 △ △ △ △ △ △ △ △ 2

DO YOUR FIGURING HERE.

59. For all real numbers x and y such that the product of y and 4 is x, which of the following expressions represents the sum of y and 4 in terms of x?

A. $x + 4$
B. $4x + 4$
C. $4(x + 4)$
D. $\frac{x+4}{4}$
E. $\frac{x+16}{4}$

60. What is $\cos \frac{7\pi}{12}$ given that $\frac{7\pi}{12} = \frac{\pi}{3} + \frac{\pi}{4}$ and that $\cos(A+B) = \cos A(\cos B) - \sin A(\sin B)$?

(Note: You may use the following table of values.)

θ	$\sin\theta$	$\cos\theta$
$\frac{\pi}{6}$	$\frac{1}{2}$	$\frac{\sqrt{3}}{2}$
$\frac{\pi}{4}$	$\frac{\sqrt{2}}{2}$	$\frac{\sqrt{2}}{2}$
$\frac{\pi}{3}$	$\frac{\sqrt{3}}{2}$	$\frac{1}{2}$

F. $\frac{\sqrt{2}-\sqrt{6}}{4}$
G. $-\frac{1}{4}$
H. $\frac{\sqrt{2}-\sqrt{3}}{4}$
J. 0.999
K. $\frac{1+\sqrt{2}}{2}$

STOP

If there is still time remaining, check your answers to this section.

Turn page for the Reading Test

READING TEST

35 MINUTES—40 QUESTIONS

Directions: There are four passages in this test. Each passage is followed by several questions. After reading a passage, choose the best answer to each question and fill in the corresponding oval on your answer document. You may refer to the passages as often as necessary.

Passage I—Prose Fiction

This passage is adapted from the short story *The First Sense* by Nadine Gordimer (©2006).

She has never felt any resentment that he became a musician and she didn't. Could hardly call her amateur flute playing a vocation. She sits at a computer in a city-government office earning a salary that has at least provided regularly for their basic needs.

She found when she was still an adolescent that her father, with his sports shop and the beguiling heartiness that is a qualification for that business, and her mother, with her groupies exchanging talk of female maladies, did not have in their comprehension what it was that she wanted to do.

A school outing at sixteen had taken her to a concert where she heard, coming out of a slim tube held to human lips, the call of the flute. The teacher who had arranged the cultural event was understanding enough to put the girl in touch with a musical youth group in the city. She babysat on weekends to pay for the hire of a flute, and began to attempt to learn how to produce with her own breath and fingers something of what she had heard.

He was among the Youth Players. His instrument was the very antithesis of the flute. The sounds he drew from the overgrown violin between his knees: the complaining moo of a sick cow, the rasp of a blunt saw. "Excuse me!" he would say, with a clownish lift of the eyebrows and a down-twisted mouth. Within a year, his exceptional talent had been recognized by the professional musicians who coached these young people.

They played together when alone, to amuse themselves and secretly imagine that they were already in concert performance, the low, powerful cadence coming from the golden-brown body of the cello making her flute voice sound, by contrast, more like that of a squeaking mouse. In time, she reached a certain level of minor accomplishment. He couldn't deceive her and let her suffer the disillusions of persisting with a career that was not open to her level of performance. "You'll still have the pleasure of playing the instrument you love best." She would always remember what she said: "The cello is the instrument I love best."

Sometimes she fell asleep to the low tender tones of what had become his voice, the voice of that big curved instrument, sharing the intimacy that was hers. At concerts, when his solo part came, she did not realize that she was smiling in recognition, that his was a voice she would have recognized anywhere. She was aware that, without a particular ability of her own, she was privileged enough to have an interesting life, and a remarkably talented man whose milieu was also hers.

He began to absent himself from her at unexplained times or for obligations that he must have known she knew didn't exist. She had suggestions for relaxation: a film or a dinner. He was not enthusiastic. "Next week, next week." He took the revered cello out of its solitude in the case and played, to himself, to her—well, she was in the room those evenings. It was his voice, that glorious voice of his cello, saying something different, speaking not to her but to some other. The voice of the cello doesn't lie.

She waited for him to speak. About what had happened. To trust the long confidence between them. He never did. And she did not ask, because she was also afraid that what had happened, once admitted, would be irrevocably real.

One night, he got up in the dark, took the cello out of its bed, and played. She woke to the voice, saying something passionately angry in its deepest bass. She knew that the affair was over. She felt a pull of sadness—for him. For herself, nothing. By never confronting him she had stunned herself.

3 3

1. If the fourth paragraph (lines 20–27) were omitted from the passage, the reader would not know:

   A. that he played the violin.
   B. how the couple met.
   C. that he became a famous musician.
   D. that he was an angry person.

2. Which of the following best describes what the first paragraph reveals about her character?

   F. She has a rewarding and high-paying career.
   G. She earns money playing a flute.
   H. She is generous and pragmatic.
   J. She regrets not becoming a musician.

3. Which of the following can most reasonably be inferred from the passage about her parents' feelings about music?

   A. They are accomplished musicians.
   B. They do not have a capacity for music themselves, but support her interest.
   C. They are opposed to her becoming a musician.
   D. They didn't understand why she would want to pursue a career in music.

4. In lines 38–39 the statement "The cello is the instrument I love best" most nearly communicates what?

   F. She would rather play the cello than play the flute.
   G. She will stop playing the flute so that she can play the cello.
   H. She never really loved playing the flute.
   J. She loves him more than she loves playing the flute.

5. The main conflict in this passage can best be described as:

   A. both he and she want to become famous musicians, but only one of them is able.
   B. challenges she faces as the girlfriend of a famous musician.
   C. tension created when he starts distancing himself from her.
   D. her need to choose between the flute and the cello.

6. It can reasonably be inferred from the passage that she views him as:

   F. a competent competitor.
   G. a teacher and a mentor.
   H. someone whose responsibility it is to entertain her.
   J. a talented musician whose opinion she respects.

7. In lines 57–58 the statement "The voice of the cello doesn't lie" mostly means:

   A. that she can tell something is wrong because of the music he plays.
   B. the cello is telling her what is bothering him.
   C. he is using music to communicate his love for her.
   D. he is playing the cello in order to demonstrate its power to deliver a message to her.

8. Which of the following statements describing how she feels about his musical ability is most clearly supported by the passage?

   F. She respects him, but gets annoyed at how often he is out of town playing concerts.
   G. She is jealous that he is so much better than she is.
   H. She loves listening to him play, and enjoys the life of a musician's partner.
   J. She is proud of his success and takes advantage of the opportunities that brings for her to play the flute.

9. The main purpose of the sixth paragraph (lines 40–48) is to:

   A. illustrate his success.
   B. show how intimate their relationship is.
   C. explain why she gets upset when he leaves her.
   D. tell the reader more about his voice.

10. Why didn't he encourage her to pursue a career as a musician?

    F. He didn't want the competition.
    G. He was jealous of her abilities.
    H. He wanted her to earn steady money for them.
    J. He didn't think she was talented enough.

Passage II—Social Science

This passage is adapted from "The Disappearing Computer" by Bill Gates, which appeared in *The World in 2003 (The Economist)* (©2002 by The Economist).

A few years from now, the average home entertainment system might not look much different than it does today. But it will probably have an Internet connection that enables it to download and play digital music and video, display album artwork and song titles on the television, and even interrupt your listening if an important message arrives. It will have a central processor, disk storage, graphics hardware and some kind of intuitive user interface. Add a wireless mouse and keyboard, and this home entertainment system will start looking a lot like a personal computer. Will people buy and use these systems in large numbers? Absolutely. Will they think of them as computers? Probably not.

According to Gartner Dataquest, an American research firm, the world computer industry shipped its one billionth PC in 2002, and another billion more are expected to be built in the next six years. Add to this the exploding number of embedded computers—the kind found in mobile phones, gas pumps and retail point-of-sale systems—which are fast approaching the power and complexity of desktop PCs. On one estimate, people in the United States already interact with about 150 embedded systems every day, whether they know it or not. These systems, which use up to 90 percent of the microprocessors produced today, will inevitably take on more PC-like characteristics, and will be able to communicate seamlessly with their traditional PC counterparts. They will also become amazingly ubiquitous. In 2001, according to the Semiconductor Industry Association, the world microchip industry produced around 60 million transistors for every man, woman and child on earth. That number will rise to one billion by 2010.

At the same time, the general-purpose PC as we know it today will continue to play an important, and increasingly central, role in most people's lives, but it will be at the center of a wide range of intelligent devices that most people wouldn't think of as "computers" today. This scenario is in sharp contrast to the computers of just a few years ago—back in the pre-Internet age—which were still mostly passive appliances that sat in the corner of the den or living room. Back then, people used their PCs for little more than writing letters and documents, playing games or managing their family finances.

But today we are truly in a digital decade, in which the intelligence of the PC is finding its way into all kinds of devices, transforming them from passive appliances into far more significant and indispensable tools for everyday life. Many of the core technologies of computing-processing power, storage capacity, graphics capabilities and network connectivity are all continuing to advance at a pace that matches or even exceeds Moore's Law (which famously, and correctly, predicted that the number of transistors on a computer chip would double every two years).

As people find more ways to incorporate these inexpensive, flexible and infinitely customizable devices into their lives, the computers themselves will gradually "disappear" into the fabric of our lives. We are still a long way from a world full of disembodied intelligent machines, but the computing experience of the coming decade will be so seamless and intuitive that, increasingly, we will barely notice it. At the same time, computing will become widespread enough that we will take it for granted—just as most people in the developed world today trust the telephone service.

The pervasiveness and near-invisibility of computing will be helped along by new technologies such as cheap, flexible displays, fingernail-sized chips capable of storing terabytes of data, or inductively powered computers that rely on heat and motion from their environment to run without batteries.

The economics of computing will also bring change. Decreasing costs will make it easy for electronics manufacturers to include PC-like intelligence and connectivity in even the most mundane devices.

All this will lead to a fundamental change in the way we perceive computers. Using one will become like using electricity when you turn on a light. Computers, like electricity, will play a role in almost everything you do, but computing itself will no longer be a discrete experience. We will be focused on what we can do with computers, not on the devices themselves. They will be all around us, essential to almost every part of our lives, but they will effectively have "disappeared."

11. This passage is best described as being:
   A. an analysis of how computers are vanishing from everyday use in society.
   B. an argument in support of introducing more computer-friendly products.
   C. an examination of the changing roles computers have in people's lives.
   D. a thorough evaluation of the benefits and drawbacks of using computers.

12. The author uses all of the following sources of evidence to support his claims EXCEPT:
   F. research data gathered by professionals.
   G. the opinion of a scientist.
   H. statistics provided by industry experts.
   J. reference to a famous mathematical prediction.

13. The word *ubiquitous*, as used in line 28, most likely means:
   A. small.
   B. difficult to find.
   C. inexpensive.
   D. ever-present.

14. According to the passage, new technologies and decreasing costs of electronics will lead directly to an increase in all of the following EXCEPT:
   F. interconnectivity among objects.
   G. the presence of computer intelligence in everyday objects.
   H. the amount of power and batteries that will be required to run computers.
   J. computers being involved in most aspects of life.

15. Which of the following best describes how the author predicts people will perceive computers in the future?
   A. Computers will be so much a part of everyday life that people will hardly notice them.
   B. Computers will have disappeared from people's lives.
   C. People will be afraid of how invasive computers have become and will use them less.
   D. Computers will be everywhere and people will be very aware of using them constantly and will become dependent on them.

16. The word *disappeared* used in line 84 most likely refers to the idea that:
   F. people will no longer use computers.
   G. computers will be so embedded in people's everyday lives that they won't even notice them anymore.
   H. computers will become invisible.
   J. computers will become so small and will be inside so many other objects that people will not be able to see them anymore.

17. All of the following are identified in the passage as parts of a future entertainment system EXCEPT:
   A. a satellite.
   B. graphics hardware.
   C. a wireless keyboard.
   D. an Internet connection.

18. The author refers to computers of the past as "passive appliances" (line 40) because:
   F. they were indispensable tools for everyday life.
   G. they were incapable of complex tasks.
   H. they remained in one location.
   J. people only used them occasionally for specific tasks.

19. The main point of the second paragraph (lines 14–32) can best be summarized as:
   A. there are more microchips than people.
   B. microprocessors are being produced more quickly than we can use them.
   C. both the number of and uses for microprocessors is rapidly increasing.
   D. there is more need for microprocessors than for personal computers.

20. In the first paragraph, the author suggests that all of the following are core technologies EXCEPT:
   F. storage capacity.
   G. power profiles.
   H. graphics capabilities.
   J. network connectivity.

GO ON TO THE NEXT PAGE.

Passage III—Humanities

This passage is adapted from the article "The Trouble with Frida Kahlo" by Stephanie Mencimer, which appeared in *Washington Monthly* (©2002 Washington Monthly).

Never has a woman with a mustache been so revered, or so marketed, as Frida Kahlo. Like a female Che Guevara, she has become a cottage industry. Feminists might celebrate Kahlo's ascent to greatness—if only her fame were related to her art. Instead, her fans are largely drawn by the story of her life, for which her paintings are often presented as simple illustration. Fridamaniacs are inspired by Kahlo's tragic tale of physical suffering—polio at six, grisly accident at 18—and fascinated with her glamorous friends and lovers. But, like a game of telephone, the more Kahlo's story has been told, the more it has been distorted, omitting uncomfortable details that show her to be a far more complex and flawed figure than the movies suggest. This elevation of the artist over the art diminishes the public understanding of Kahlo's place in history and overshadows the deeper and more disturbing truths in her work.

Until the 1970s there were almost no "great" women artists. As the feminist movement gathered steam, women sought to rectify that problem. Historically, women's limited opportunities meant there were few women artists to begin with, and even fewer whose work had been collected and could be definitively attributed to them. Once scholars did identify significant women artists, they had to demonstrate that those artists met the male standards for admission to the canon—i.e., they had to suffer and be mostly ignored during their lifetimes. It was also helpful if the emerging female artists were beautiful and had glamorous friends.

Kahlo made a perfect candidate. As if her bodily injuries weren't compelling enough, Kahlo's drama was enhanced by what she referred to as the second accident in her life: Diego Riverá, the famous Mexican muralist to whom she was married for 25 years. Rivera was a notorious womanizer, a habit he did not abandon after marrying Kahlo. Both Kahlo and Rivera were active in the Communist Party and Mexican politics. Kahlo's paintings often reflect her tumultuous relationship with Rivera, as well as the anguish of her ever-deteriorating health. Between the time of her accident and her death, Kahlo had more than 30 surgeries, and a gangrenous leg was eventually amputated. She dramatized the pain in her paintings, while carefully cultivating a self-image as a "heroic sufferer."

While Kahlo's work never attracted the attention her husband's did, it did win some critical acclaim. Eventually, though, her failing health left her addicted to painkillers and alcohol. She continued to paint, but the addiction destroyed the controlled, delicate brushwork that had characterized her best work. In 1954, suffering from pneumonia, Kahlo went to a Communist march. Four days later, she died in what may or may not have been a suicide.

If the focus of the art business must be on biography, that biography should at least include the artists' warts. Many of Kahlo's surgeries may have been unnecessary. She also made several suicide attempts and spent much of her adult life addicted to drugs and alcohol. More importantly, though, Kahlo's Communism, now treated as somehow sort of quaint, led her to embrace some unforgivable political positions. Less scandalous but worth noting is that Kahlo despised the very gringos who now champion her work, and her art reflects her obvious disdain for the United States.

Neglecting the dark side of the artist's narrative deprives the public of a full appreciation of the art. Without knowing that by 1953 Kahlo was so strung out that she could barely pick up a paintbrush, how can the public possibly know why some of her late work is so bad? Which is the really tragic part of Kahlo's story. Because when you sweep away the sideshow, ignore the overwrought analysis, and take a hard look at what she painted, much of it is extraordinary. Her paintings tap into sex and violence, life and death, in original and profound ways. So while women might celebrate Kahlo's success, it may be that real progress has come when a woman can be remembered both as a great artist and as a despicable cur.

21. The author implies that Kahlo is famous primarily because of her:

A. exceptionally liberal paintings.
B. dramatic life full of intrigue and suffering.
C. marriage to Diego Rivera.
D. being one of the first female artists.

22. Frida Kahlo's story was compared to "a game of telephone" (line 11) because:

F. just like a message passed over the phone, the details of her life have been told accurately.
G. people are purposely leaving out important pieces of her history.
H. her story has been passed on verbally from person to person.
J. over time the story has become distorted and parts have been omitted.

23. The author states that all of the following contributed to the lack of great female artists prior to 1970 EXCEPT:

A. the scarce number of female artists.
B. scholars' difficulty identifying great female artists.
C. higher standards for admission to the canon.
D. the small number of female artists' works that had been collected.

24. The author's tone in this passage can best be described as:

F. persuasive.
G. informative.
H. sarcastic.
J. humorous.

25. Based on the information presented in the passage, the quality of Kahlo's painting began to decline because of:

A. her injuries.
B. catching pneumonia.
C. her addiction to painkillers and alcohol.
D. her tumultuous marriage to Rivera.

26. In the context of lines 54–64, the phrase "the artists' warts" (line 55) most nearly means:

F. Kahlo's poorer paintings.
G. the imperfections in Kahlo's appearance.
H. Kahlo's highest achievements.
J. the less pleasant parts of Kahlo's life.

27. According to the passage, all of the following are true about Kahlo's paintings EXCEPT:

A. they reflect her complicated relationship with Rivera.
B. they dramatized the pain from her surgeries.
C. they were all forms of self-portraits.
D. they portray concepts in unique and profound ways.

28. The author's purpose in writing this passage can best be summarized as:

F. to discuss how the movies and Fridamaniacs are distorting the story of Kahlo's life.
G. to convince women to embrace both the dark and light side of Kahlo's life when choosing to celebrate her success.
H. to provide hidden details of Kahlo's life, hoping that people will realize she is not worthy of such high acclaim.
J. to explain why some of Kahlo's later work is so bad.

29. What would the author probably say is the most tragic thing about Kahlo's story?

A. That Rivera remained unfaithful even after their marriage
B. That Kahlo died so young, and wasn't able to create more paintings
C. The grisly accident when she was 18
D. That people don't realize how extraordinary her work is because they are more caught up in the sordid details of her life

30. What is the "sideshow" the author refers to in line 71?

F. The dramatic details of Kahlo's life
G. The critical acclaim Kahlo has received
H. The Fridamaniacs who idolize Kahlo
J. Kahlo's addictions

GO ON TO THE NEXT PAGE.

Passage IV—Natural Science

This passage is adapted from "The Truth Behind Lightsaber Technology" by Matt Gluesenkamp (©2010 General Electric).

There are a lot of myths and legends about lasers that Hollywood has generated or perpetuated over the years, but perhaps the most well-known instance of "lasers" in cinema are the lightsabers from the *Star Wars* saga. I put quotes around "lasers" because the way lightsabers behave in these movies is quite a bit different from the way lasers behave in real life.

In the *Star Wars* universe, lightsabers are typically custom-built by Jedi and Sith warriors, and all have several common elements. Each has a power source, a lightsaber crystal, one or more focusing crystals, and a stabilizing emitter system. The power source is typically a diatium power cell, often with a capacity of several megawatt-hours. The lightsaber crystal converts the power cell's energy into a plasma that is then passed through and directed by the focusing crystals. Finally, the emitter system stabilizes the plasma into a blade shape using a mix of power modulation and magnetic field containment.

Did that make sense to anyone? No? Good, then I'm not alone. Science fiction is typically a blend of materials or physical laws that exist and some that don't. Although real-life battery technology is coming along great, we are a long way off from creating handheld batteries with capacities like the ones found in the lightsaber's diatium power cell. Perhaps the key lies in discovering this fictional "diatium" material? And although crystals do have many useful optical and piezoelectric properties, I don't know of one that could magically create plasma from electricity. (However, I read that the crystals must be "attuned to the Force" by a Jedi or Sith in a meditation ritual that can take days, so maybe we should start there.)

Where the explanations of lightsaber technology get really convoluted is when they start talking about how the blade is shaped and contained. Magnetic fields are currently used to contain plasmas, but they are generated by machinery that must also surround it—generating such a magnetic envelope from a single, unidirectional source would likely require some new laws of physics. There are no crystals that can "direct" a plasma.

In fact, a plasma being "directed" by a crystal lens doesn't even make any physical sense. A plasma is really just an ionized gas—a gas in which the electrons have been stripped from their atomic nuclei. We see plasmas all the time. They make up and are emitted from every star, like our solar wind and solar flares. The interaction of the solar wind with Earth's magnetic field produces the *aurora borealis*, or northern lights—another form of plasma. Plasmas are also the stuff of every spark and lightning bolt.

Plasmas can be created by bringing gases up to a high energy level. The higher the energy, the more atoms will be stripped of their electrons, and the better quality plasma we will have. It's completely possible that one could create a plasma by producing a large enough voltage difference—as with lightning—or a powerful enough laser focus. However, enormous amounts of energy are required with either of these approaches, and it would be extremely difficult to control the plasma's shape. An electrical arc can have wild shifts in direction, and it can hardly be controlled without being surrounded by magnets. A laser will go in a straight line... but, of course, it doesn't stop. A laser-based lightsaber would require a block or a couple of mirrors floating in midair, moving in sync with the hilt, which is largely impossible. On top of that, they would certainly melt in the presence of such a plasma anyway. Furthermore, all of this says nothing about what the actual quality of the plasma would be and how reliably or quickly it would cut through objects.

So it seems quite impossible to create a lightsaber, as seen in the *Star Wars* films, using existing technologies, materials, and physical laws. But given the enthusiasm of *Star Wars* superfans out there, I wouldn't be surprised if people are trying.

31. The author of this passage would most likely agree with which of the following statements?

A. The authors who invented science-fiction never intended for it to depict things like lightsabers.
B. Science-fiction films can give people inaccurate ideas about the world that really surrounds them.
C. One should "never say never," because anything might be possible someday.
D. The content of science-fiction films should be more carefully regulated by the government.

32. The main point of the fifth paragraph (lines 42–51) is that:

F. real-life crystals are not nearly powerful enough to direct plasma at high temperatures.
G. studying lightning would be the logical first step in the construction of a lightsaber.
H. the commonness of plasmas in the real world is a good sign for lightsaber technology.
J. the idea of plasma having a predetermined "shape" is inherently absurd.

33. According to the passage, which of the following is an example of a plasma, either real or fictional?

A. The *aurora borealis*
B. A wild electrical arc
C. Earth's magnetic field
D. Diatium crystals

34. As it is used in line 35, the word *convoluted* most nearly means:

F. possible.
G. precise.
H. interesting.
J. confusing.

35. If a new crystal were discovered that might make plasma-lightsaber technology possible, how would the author most likely feel about this discovery?

A. Embarrassed and angry at having been proven wrong
B. Excited that his lifelong dream of owning a lightsaber might be about to come true
C. Interested in the new opportunities promised by such a discovery
D. Concerned that such a discovery will detract from the seriousness of the scientific profession

36. The main purpose of the third paragraph (lines 20–33) is to:

F. establish that the author is not in fact an expert in the type of science being discussed.
G. explain in a humorous fashion that the official explanation of lightsabers borders on nonsense.
H. remind the reader of the important difference between science fiction and fantasy.
J. express disdain for the silliness of the *Star Wars* film series.

37. According to the passage, which of the following would be LEAST likely to be involved in a real-life lightsaber?

A. Crystals
B. Batteries
C. Magnetic fields
D. An ionized gas

38. Which of the following statements about plasmas is accurate, according to information in the passage?

F. They can be directed by magnetic fields
G. They are rarely visible to the naked eye
H. They are typically slow moving
J. They nearly always take up large amounts of space

39. Which of the following is true about the author's attitude toward the *Star Wars* films?

A. Even by Hollywood standards, they are exceptionally inaccurate in their presentation of science
B. They have an adoring fan base that retains hope in fanciful scientific ideas despite the odds
C. They insult their audience by depicting wildly unfeasible technology with little explanation
D. They have indirectly helped society by making generations of people more enthusiastic about science

40. Which of the following is NOT mentioned in the passage as an obstacle to the creation of a real lightsaber?

F. The difficulty of developing a sufficiently compact power source
G. The practical impossibility of containing a plasma field in a way that renders it small and portable
H. The likelihood that such "blades" would just pass through each other, making dueling impossible
J. The difficulty of controlling a plasma's shape

STOP

If there is still time remaining, check your answers to this section.

SCIENCE TEST

35 MINUTES—40 QUESTIONS

Directions: There are seven passages in this test. Each passage is followed by several questions. After reading a passage, choose the best answer to each question and fill in the corresponding oval on your answer document. You may refer to the passages as often as necessary.

You are NOT permitted to use a calculator on this test.

Passage I

Astronomers have found over 400 planets orbiting stars. The discovered planets have a variety of compositions, masses, and orbits. Despite the variety, the universal rules of physics and chemistry allow scientists to broadly categorize these planets into just a few types: Gas Giant, Carbon Orb, Water World, and Rocky Earth. Table 1 shows the composition of the various planet types and typical mass ranges relative to Earth.

Table 1

Planet Classification	Composition	Stars Orbited by Planet Type	Mass Range (Earth = 1)
Gas Giant	Hydrogen/helium Rock	OGLE TR 132 Gliese 777	250–1000
Carbon Orb	Iron/nickel/carbon Diamond Carbon monoxide Silicon carbide	PSR 1257	.5–25
Water	Silicates Iron Water	Gliese 581	.5–25
Rocky Earth	Silicate Nickel (molten and solid) Rock	Kepler 11 HD 69830	.5–25

Table 2 shows a sampling of planets orbiting various stars described in Table 1. These planets are merely numbered 1–7. Table 2 details the masses and orbital radii of the planets.

Table 2

Planet	Star That the Planet Orbits	Planet Mass (Earth Mass = 1)	Orbital Radius (Earth Orbit =1)
1	Gliese 777	500	4.0
2	Gliese 581	20	2.0
3	Gliese 581	10	4.0
4	Kepler 11	15	3.5
5	OGLE TR 132	315	.35
6	HD 69830	15	.5
7	PSR 1257	4	.25

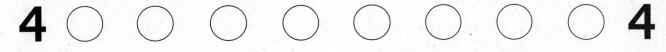

1. The data in Table 1 and Table 2 support which of the following statements?

   A. Gas Giant planets have the largest orbital radii.
   B. Orbital radius is directly related to mass.
   C. Orbital radius is inversely related to mass.
   D. The data does not support a correlation between mass and orbital radius.

2. According to Table 1 and Table 2, which of the following stars has the most massive Gas Giant planet orbiting it?

   F. Gliese 777
   G. OGLE TR 132
   H. PSR 1257
   J. Gliese 581

3. If a new planet were discovered, with a mass of 325, an orbital radius of 1.5, and a composition of mostly hydrogen, what would be its most likely classification?

   A. Carbon Orb
   B. Water
   C. Rocky Earth
   D. Gas Giant

4. All of the following are true about the star Gliese 581 EXCEPT:

   F. Gliese 581 has multiple planets orbiting it.
   G. Gliese 581 has the most massive planet orbiting it.
   H. Gliese 581 has planets orbiting it that are classified as water.
   J. Gliese 581 has only planets with masses less than 50 Earth masses orbiting it.

5. The Rocky Earth planets in Table 2 have what in common?

   A. Their masses are less than 20 Earth masses.
   B. They are only found in deep space.
   C. Hydrogen is a major component of the crust.
   D. Their orbits are all less than 1 Earth radius.

4 ◯ ◯ ◯ ◯ ◯ ◯ ◯ ◯ 4

Passage II

A group of researchers studied the greenhouse gas (GHG) and energy savings associated with rigid plastic foam sheathing used to insulate single-family housing. The results show the typical annual energy savings for a single house in the United States. Table 1 displays energy savings for various temperature zones, whereas Table 2 shows GHGs avoided.

Table 1

Energy Savings (in million BTUs)	Zone 1 (colder)	Zone 3	Zone 5 (warmer)	U.S. Average
Natural gas	4.2	2.7	0.9	2.37
Petroleum	0.04	0.02	0.22	0.04
Coal	0.81	0.98	0.93	0.76
Hydropower	0.06	0.02	0.03	0.06
Nuclear	0.26	0.26	0.19	0.25
Other	0.03	0.02	0.23	0.03
Total annual	5.41	4.01	2.50	3.51

Table 2

GHGs (in pounds)	Zone 1 (colder)	Zone 3	Zone 5 (warmer)	U.S. Average
Carbon dioxide	609	608	606	599
Methane	101	101	101	101
Nitrous oxide	4.5	4.5	4.5	4.5
HCFC-141b	588	588	588	588
HCFC-142b	1511	1511	1511	1511
Total	2813	2812	2811	2803

There is an initial use of energy and GHG released when the insulation is installed, but large savings result from the use of the product over time. After the "payback" time expires, there is a net savings in energy and GHG emissions for as long as the insulation is in place. Figure 1 displays the payback time in years for energy savings and GHGs avoided.

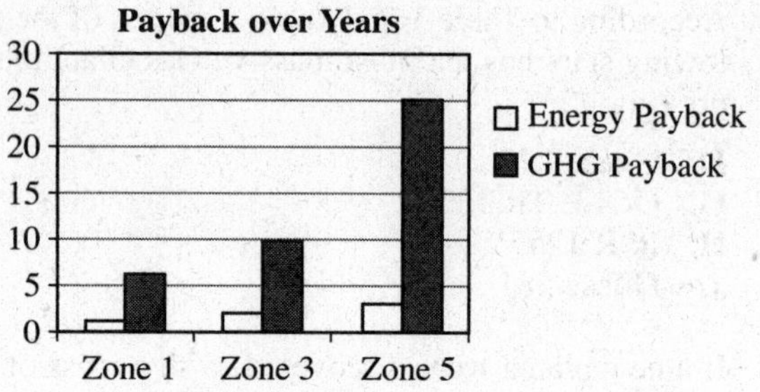

Figure 1

6. Foam sheathing proved to create the highest energy savings in Zone 5 for what type of energy?

   F. Coal
   G. Nuclear
   H. Natural Gas
   J. Petroleum

7. According to the data presented in Table 1 and Table 2, which of the following is true?

   A. Foam sheathing prevents more HCFC-141b than HCFC-142b from entering the atmosphere.
   B. The yearly energy savings vary more by zone than the yearly GHGs avoided.
   C. The warmer the zone, the less the energy savings from petroleum.
   D. The U.S. average for GHGs avoided is greatest for carbon dioxide.

8. According to Figure 1, the GHG payback for Zone 3 is approximately:

   F. 12 years.
   G. 2 years.
   H. 13 years.
   J. 9 years.

9. According to Table 1, what zone and fuel combination yield the greatest energy savings after 1 year?

   A. Nuclear in Zone 1
   B. HCFC-142b in Zone 3
   C. Coal in Zone 5
   D. Natural gas in Zone 1

10. Ten years after installing rigid plastic foam sheathing in Zone 3, which of the following is true?

   F. The customer will have produced fewer GHGs, but will not yet have saved money on energy.
   G. The customer will have saved money on energy, but will not yet have produced fewer GHGs.
   H. The customer will have neither saved money on energy nor produced fewer GHGs.
   J. The customer will have both saved money on energy and produced fewer GHGs.

11. Based on the data in Table 1, which of the following lists the fuels that yielded the highest average energy savings, in decreasing order?

   A. Natural gas, coal, and nuclear
   B. Hydropower, nuclear, and other
   C. Coal, natural gas, and nuclear
   D. Nuclear, petroleum, and coal

---

4 ○ ○ ○ ○ ○ ○ ○ ○ 4

Passage III

Ohm's law states that V = I × R and WRC/L where V = voltage, I = current, R = resistance, C = cross-sectional area of the wire, W = resistivity of the wire, and L = length of the wire. Using the circuit pictured in Figure 1, a student performed two experiments.

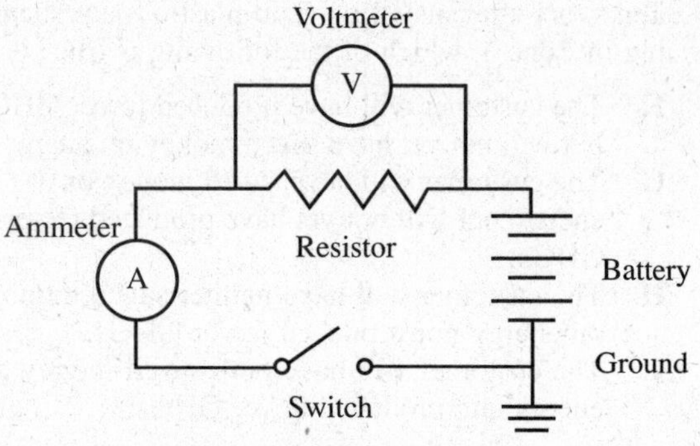

Figure 1

Experiment 1

A 5 V battery was used and the resistance was varied. Table 1 displays the results.

Table 1

Trial	Resistance (ohms)	Current (amperes)
1	2	2.5
2	4	1.25
3	10	0.5
4	20	0.25

Experiment 2

A battery of 1 volt was used and three different wires, each with the same resistivity and length, were used to complete the circuit. Table 2 shows the results and Figure 2 shows the relationship between the diameter of the wire and the measured resistance of each wire.

Table 2

Trial	Diameter (mm)	Resistance (ohms)	Current (amperes)
1	0.22	5.11	0.21
2	0.41	1.51	0.70
3	0.68	0.56	1.84
4	1.04	.20	4.91

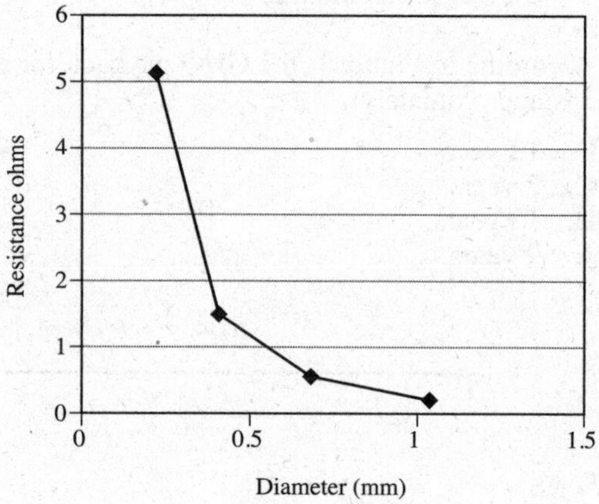

Figure 2

4 ○ ○ ○ ○ ○ ○ ○ ○ 4

12. In Table 1, what is true about the relationship between current and resistance?

 F. As resistance increased, current increased.
 G. As resistance increased, current was unchanged.
 H. As resistance increased, current decreased.
 J. There is no relationship between current and resistance.

13. Based on Table 2 or Figure 2, it could be determined that a wire with a diameter of .5 mm would have a resistance close to:

 A. 2.6 ohms.
 B. 1.0 ohms.
 C. .5 ohms.
 D. .25 ohms.

14. In Experiment 2, which of the following factors was varied?

 F. Voltage of the battery
 G. Diameter of the wire
 H. Length of the wire
 J. The material of the wire

15. The following hypothesis was put forth prior to the experiments: Current is inversely related to resistance. An inverse relationship implies that when one quantity increases, the other decreases. Do Tables 1 and 2 support this hypothesis?

 A. No. Experiment 1 contradicts the hypothesis and shows a direct relationship between current and resistance. The current increases with the resistance.
 B. No. Experiment 2 contradicts the hypothesis and shows a direct relationship between current and resistance. The current increases with resistance.
 C. Yes. The results of both experiments show an inverse relationship between current and resistance. When the resistance increases, current decreases.
 D. No. Neither experiment shows any relationship between current and resistance.

16. Using the circuit in Figure 1 and the results of both experiments, which of the following conditions would result in the largest current?

 F. 5-volt battery, .5-mm wire
 G. 5-volt battery, .25-mm wire
 H. 2.5-volt battery, .5-mm wire
 J. 2-volt battery, .25-mm wire

17. Consider a circuit like that in Figure 1. Based on Experiment 2, which of the following will produce a current of about 5 amperes (assume the wire used is the same wire in Experiment 2)?

 A. 0.22 mm; 5.11 ohms
 B. 0.41 mm; 1.51 ohms
 C. 1.04 mm; 0.20 ohms
 D. 1.04 mm; 0.56 ohms

Passage IV

Scientists tested a new method of titration, called atomic absorption inhibition titration (AAIT). They ran a series of experiments to determine if AAIT could be used successfully to determine the presence of phosphate, silicate, and sulfate in river and waste water. AAIT involves continually adding magnesium to a stirred sample solution while monitoring the solution for magnesium absorption.

Experiment 1

The scientists conducted an experiment to determine the effect of sulfate on titration of phosphate. Four trials were conducted, varying the concentration of both the sulfate and the magnesium used for the titration. Table 1 displays the results of the AAIT for solutions containing phosphate and sulfate and varying concentrations of magnesium.

Table 1

Trial	PO_4 ppm	SO_4 ppm	Mg		
			2.5 ppm	4.0 ppm	4.5 ppm
1	10	0	0.556	0	0
2	10	5	0.527	0.297	0.244
3	10	10	0.551	0.321	0.263
4	10	15	0.538	0.366	0.289

Experiment 2

Analysis of water from the Milwaukee River was performed. Solutions containing phosphate and sulfate were analyzed using AAIT. Titrations were performed on river water, river water plus the addition of phosphate, and standardized phosphate solution. The endpoint was noted for each trial when the titration reached the conditions under which only silicate would be detected. Table 2 shows the data collected, in ml.

Table 2

Trial	PO_4	River Water	River Water + PO_4
1	0.73	1.50	2.24
2	0.59	1.23	1.80
3	0.50	1.08	1.60
4	0.51	1.05	1.61
5	0.57	1.29	1.84

Experiment 3

Scientists created artificial waste water by adding phosphate, silicate, and sulfate to water and then conducting AAIT to simultaneously determine how much of each substance was in the water. Four titrations were conducted. Table 3 displays the results.

Table 3

Trial	Added μ/ml			Found μ/ml		
	PO_4	SO_4	SiO_2	PO_4	SO_4	SiO_2
1	3.00	20.00	1.50	3.04	20.50	1.44
2	2.00	20.00	1.50	1.56	20.30	1.60
3	2.00	20.00	4.00	2.38	20.30	3.48
4	5.00	20.00	10.00	9.56	20.00	7.30

18. According to the data in Table 2, which trial resulted in the most silicate being detected in river water?

    F. Trial 1
    G. Trial 2
    H. Trial 3
    J. Trial 4

19. Based on the information presented in Table 3, which trial resulted in less PO_4 being found than was initially added?

    A. Trial 1
    B. Trial 2
    C. Trial 3
    D. Trial 4

20. Before conducting Experiment 1, the scientists hypothesized that the higher the concentration of Mg used, the more Mg that would be absorbed. Do the results of the experiment support the hypothesis?

    F. Yes. For each trial as the concentration of Mg used increased from 2.5 to 4.5 ppm, more Mg was absorbed.
    G. Yes. Table 1 shows that the most Mg absorbed was during Trial 1 and with an Mg concentration of 2.5 ppm.
    H. No. The opposite has been shown to be the case. For each trial as the Mg concentration increased, the amount of Mg absorbed decreased.
    J. No. There is not a clear relationship between the Mg concentration and the amount of Mg absorbed.

21. Based on the results of Experiment 2, what type of solution was found to reach the endpoint with the least amount of solution?

    A. Phosphate and sulfate
    B. Standardized phosphate solution
    C. River water
    D. River water plus phosphate

22. The data in Table 1 supports which of the following statements?

    F. The titrations done using Mg with a concentration of 4.0 ppm resulted in the most Mg being absorbed.
    G. The titrations done using Mg with a concentration of 2.5 ppm resulted in the least Mg being absorbed.
    H. With a Mg concentration of 4.5 ppm, as the titrations included more concentrated SO_4, less Mg was absorbed.
    J. With a Mg concentration of 4.5 ppm, as the titrations included more concentrated SO_4, more Mg was absorbed.

Passage V

More than 5 percent of Americans have asthma, a chronic disease that affects the airways and lungs, causing shortness of breath, wheezing, and sometimes death. In the United States, rates for asthma have steadily increased, nearly doubling during the past 20 years. There is no cure for asthma. Two researchers discuss factors that cause individuals to develop asthma.

Researcher 1

There has long been an association between the allergen *Dermatophagoides pteronyssinus* (dust mites) and asthma. Evidence for a causal relationship has been supported by bronchial challenge studies and avoidance experiments. Studies have shown that exposure in the child's own house was the primary determinant of sensitization. Research from around the world has provided evidence about other indoor allergens, specifically cats, dogs, and the German cockroach. These studies showed that perennial exposure to allergens was an important cause of inflammation in the lungs and associated nonspecific bronchial hyperreactivity. Children are being exposed to more perennial allergens now than ever before. Houses are built more tightly and are better insulated and have more furnishings and fitted carpets. In addition, children are spending more time indoors. This increased exposure to allergens, including dust mites, has led to increased sensitization, and more cases of asthma.

Since assays for total serum IgE (immunoglobulin E) became available, it has been clear that patients with asthma have, on average, higher total IgE than patients with hay fever or no allergy. Recent work on patients hospitalized for asthma has suggested that the interaction between rhinovirus and allergy occurs predominantly among patients with total IgE > 200 IU/ml. Thus, the different properties of allergens could influence both the prevalence and severity of asthma.

Researcher 2

It is widely accepted that air pollution exacerbates asthma. For example, when traffic controls were put in place during the 1996 Summer Olympic Games in Atlanta, Georgia, morning peak traffic counts declined by 23 percent. This in turn lowered ozone (O_3) concentrations by 13 percent, carbon monoxide (CO) by 19 percent, and nitrogen dioxide (NO_2) by 7 percent. Associated with these declines in ambient air pollution were drops in Medicaid-related emergency room visits and hospitalizations for asthma (down 42 percent), asthma-related care for health maintenance organizations (down 44 percent), and citywide hospitalizations for asthma (down 19 percent). Despite such striking relationships between exposure to air pollution and asthma aggravation, air pollution has not been regarded as a cause of the disease. Increasingly, however, recent studies have been suggesting that air pollution may, indeed, be a cause of asthma.

The Children's Health Study (CHS) followed 3,535 children with no lifetime history of asthma for five years. During that period 265 reported a new physician diagnosis of asthma. Analysis of CHS data has shown that children living in communities with high ozone levels developed asthma more often than those in less polluted areas. The hypothesis that ozone might cause asthma is reinforced by a study of 3,091 nonsmoking adults aged 27 to 87 years who were followed for 15 years. The results of this study showed that 3.2 percent of the men and 4.3 percent of the women reported new doctor-diagnosed asthma. The researchers concluded that there was a connection between ozone concentration and development of asthma.

23. If ozone levels decrease nationwide, Researcher 2 would expect to see what change in asthma rates?

    A. An increase in the prevalence of asthma
    B. A decrease in the prevalence of asthma
    C. No change in the prevalence of asthma
    D. First a decrease and then an increase in the prevalence of asthma

24. Researcher 1 would agree with which of the following statements:

    F. Asthma rates are lower in rural areas.
    G. Men are more likely to have asthma than women.
    H. People who have pets are more likely to have asthma.
    J. Asthma rates are related to the quality of air.

25. Researcher 1 would most likely agree with which of the following statements about IgE?

    A. People who have IgE levels of 400 IU/ml have a high chance of having severe asthma.
    B. People who have IgE levels of 100 IU/ml have a high chance of having severe asthma.
    C. Most people who have asthma have low levels of IgE; less than 200 IU/ml.
    D. There has been no connection made between IgE levels and the prevalence of asthma.

26. If the prevalence of asthma in the United States continues to increase, Researcher 1 would likely cite which of the following as a solution to the problem?

    F. People need to spend less time outside.
    G. Houses need to be better insulated.
    H. People need to be given supplements to increase their IgE levels.
    J. Fans need to be added to houses to allow more circulation and to bring more outside air into the house.

27. Researchers 1 and 2 would both agree with which of the following statements?

    A. Asthma rates are likely to decline over the next 20 years.
    B. Air pollution and high IgE levels are the two leading causes of asthma.
    C. Women are more likely to develop asthma than men.
    D. Measures can be taken to lower a person's risk of developing asthma.

28. If Researcher 2 is correct, which of the following graphs would best represent the relationship between CO concentrations and cases of asthma?

    F.

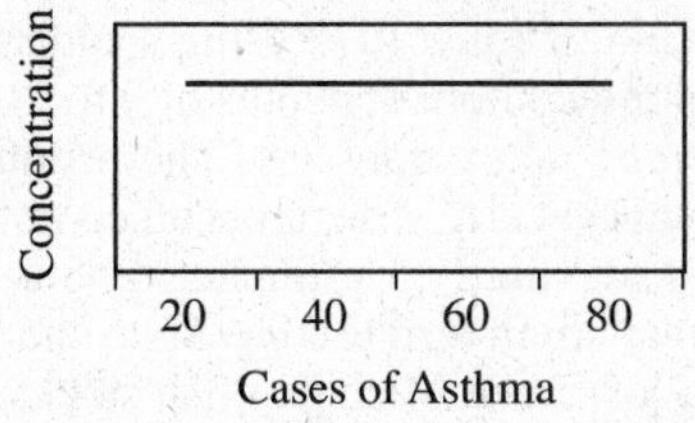

    G.

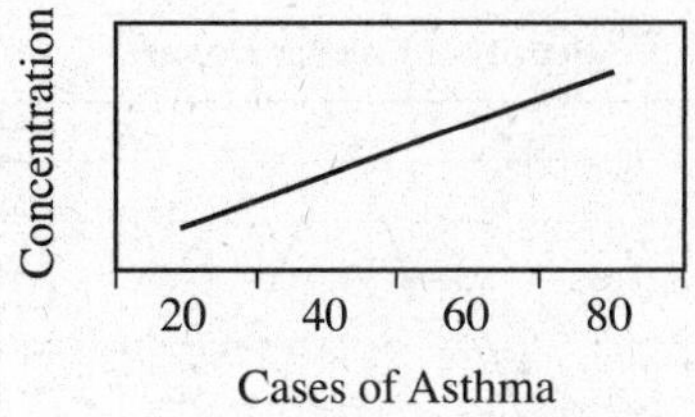

    H.

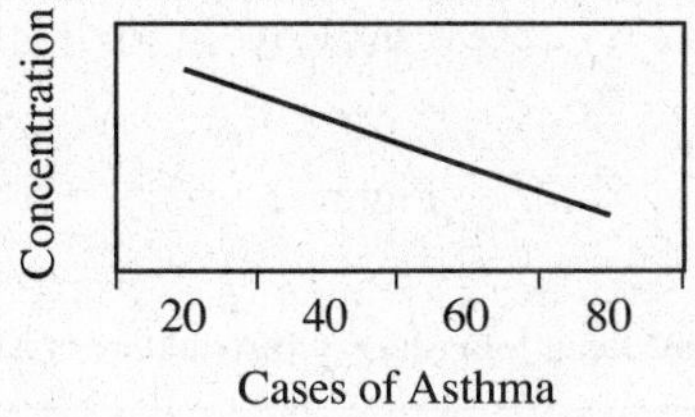

    J.

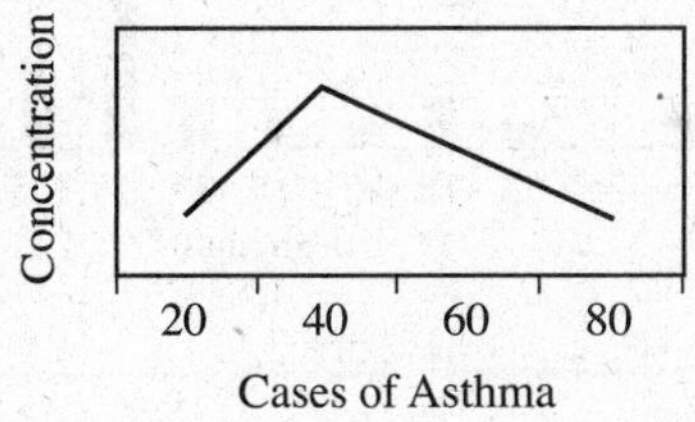

29. Researcher 2 would most likely agree with which of the following statements regarding the prevalence of asthma 20 years ago?

    A. There was a higher prevalence of asthma 20 years ago because there was less pollution.
    B. There was a lower prevalence of asthma 20 years ago because there were higher ozone levels and less pollution.
    C. There was a lower prevalence of asthma 20 years ago because there was less pollution and lower ozone levels.
    D. There was a lower prevalence of asthma 20 years ago because people spent more time outside.

Passage VI

The Great Lakes Science Center (GLSC) has conducted lakewide surveys of the fish community in Lake Michigan each fall since 1973 using standard 12 m bottom trawls along contour at depths of 9 to 110 m at each of seven to nine index transects. The resulting data on relative abundance, size structure, and condition of individual fishes are used to estimate various population parameters that are in turn used by state and tribal agencies in managing Lake Michigan fish stocks.

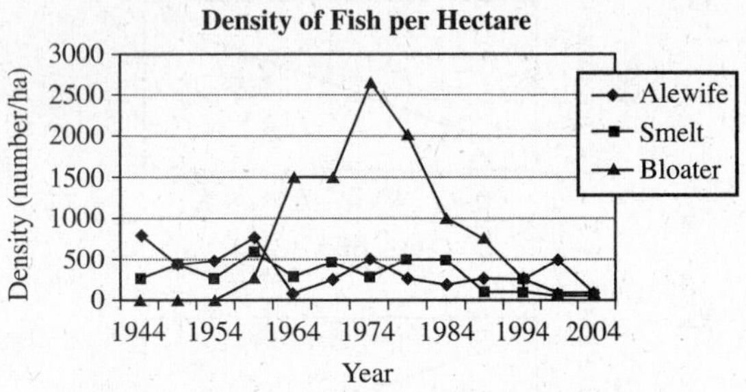

Figure 1

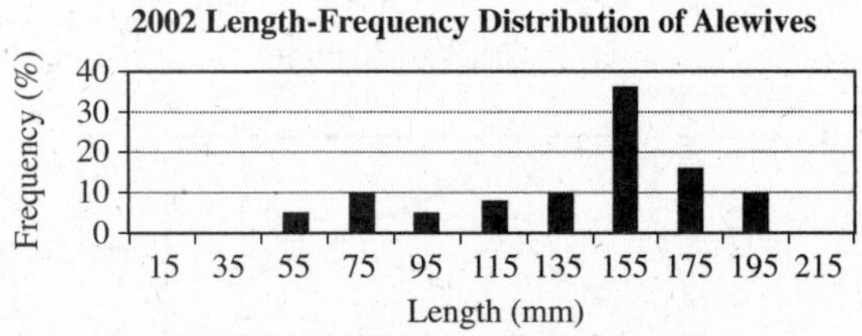

Figure 2

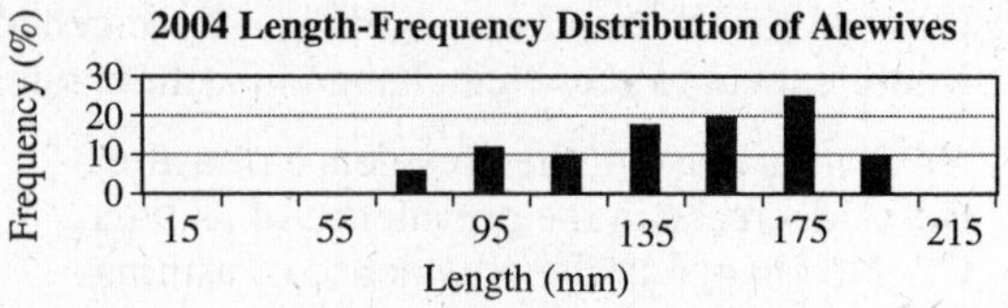

Figure 3

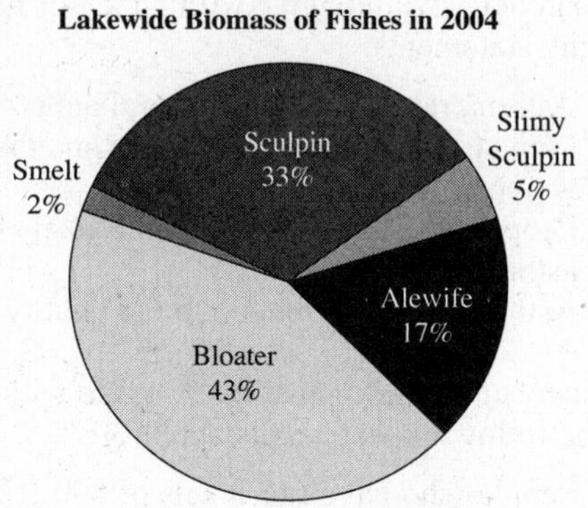

Figure 4

30. According to Figure 1, which species of fish was most prevalent in 1954?

    F. Alewife
    G. Smelt
    H. Bloater
    J. Smelt and bloater

31. Based on the information in Figure 4, which of the following statements is true?

    A. There were more smelt than sculpin in 2004.
    B. There were more bloater than sculpin in 2004.
    C. There were more alewife than bloater in 2004.
    D. There were more slimy sculpin than alewife in 2004.

32. According to Figure 2 and Figure 3, which of the following is NOT true about the size of alewives?

    F. There were more 175-mm alewives in 2004 than in 2002.
    G. There were fewer 75-mm alewives in 2004 than in 2002.
    H. There were fewer 115-mm alewives in 2002 than in 2004.
    J. There were more 155-mm alewives in 2004 than in 2002.

33. Considering the fact that the older an alewife fish, the longer it is, and using the data in Figures 2 and 3, which of the following can be deduced about alewife fish populations in 2002 and 2004?

    A. In 2004 there were more young alewives than in 2002.
    B. In 2004 there were more adult alewives than in 2002.
    C. In 2004 the fish were, on average, younger than in 2002.
    D. In 2004 the greatest percentages of fish were young.

34. Scientists at the GLSC have hypothesized that the bloater population may be cycling in abundance, within a period of about 30 years. Does the data in Figure 1 support this hypothesis?

    F. No. The population of bloater fish has decreased since 1973.
    G. No. In 2004 there were more bloater fish than any other species.
    H. Yes. The density of bloater fish steadily increased before 1973 and then decreased from 1973 to 2003.
    J. Yes. In 2004 there were more bloater fish than any other species.

Passage VII

Pertussis, commonly known as whooping cough, is a highly infectious disease of the respiratory tract caused by bacteria. The disease spreads by direct contact with secretions from the nose or throat of an infected person, or by breathing in the air when an infected person coughs. Pertussis most easily passes between people in the initial stage of illness, but it can be spread at any time during the course of the illness. Figure 1 depicts the course of pertussis from exposure to recovery.

<table>
<tr><td colspan="6">Incubation Period
5–21 days</td><td colspan="4">Catarrhal Stage
1–2 weeks</td></tr>
<tr><td colspan="2">Weeks: –3</td><td colspan="2">–2</td><td colspan="2">–1</td><td colspan="2">0 + 1
(onset)</td><td colspan="2">2</td></tr>
<tr><td colspan="2">Maximum incubation period 21 days</td><td colspan="4">Average incubation period 7–10 days</td><td colspan="4">*Communicability*
Cold symptoms: rhinorrhea, anorexia, conjunctivitis, lacrimation, malaise, sneezing, and low-grade fever</td></tr>
<tr><td colspan="6">Paroxysmal Stage
1–6 weeks</td><td colspan="4">Convalescent Stage
2–3 weeks</td></tr>
<tr><td>3</td><td>4</td><td>5</td><td>6</td><td>7</td><td>8</td><td>9</td><td>10</td><td>11</td><td>12</td></tr>
<tr><td colspan="6">Paroxysmal cough, vomiting, cyanosis</td><td colspan="4" rowspan="2">Coughing</td></tr>
<tr><td colspan="3">Communicability ends after 5 days of antibiotics</td><td colspan="3">Communicability ends 3 weeks after onset of cough if no antibiotics taken</td></tr>
</table>

Figure 1

The number of reported cases of pertussis from 1974 through 2004 is depicted in Figure 2.

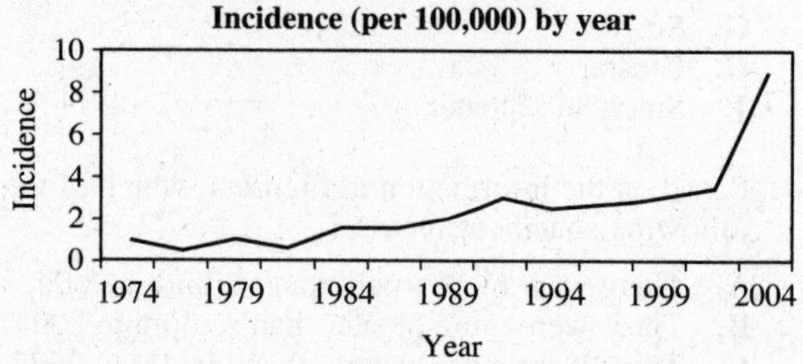

Figure 2

The number of reported cases of pertussis in 2004 by age group is shown in Figure 3.

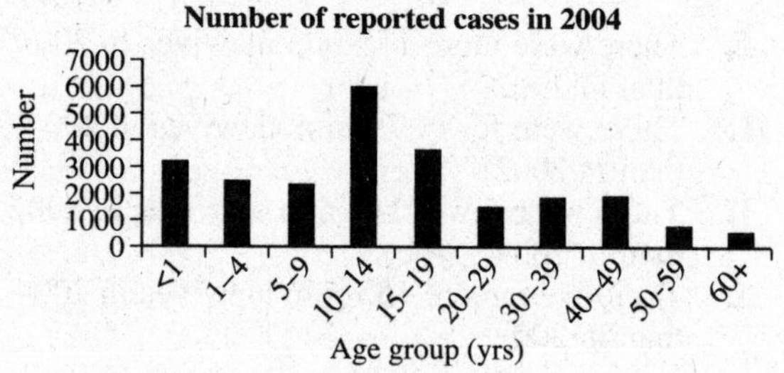

Figure 3

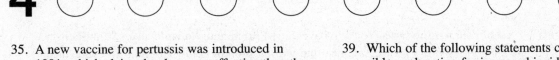

35. A new vaccine for pertussis was introduced in 1991, which claimed to be more effective than the previous vaccine. Does the data in Figure 2 support this claim?

A. No. Rates of pertussis increased after 1991.
B. No. Rates of pertussis remained the same after 1991.
C. Yes. Rates of pertussis decreased after 1991.
D. Yes. Rates of pertussis increased after 1991.

36. If a person was experiencing a cough, was medicated, and was still contagious, he or she would be in what stage of the disease?

F. Incubation
G. Catarrhal
H. Paroxysmal
J. Convalescent

37. What is the maximum number of weeks that pertussis can be transmitted?

A. 1
B. 3
C. 8
D. 12

38. Doctors hypothesized that because of their immature immune systems young children are the most susceptible to pertussis. Does the data from 2004, in Figure 3, support this theory?

F. No. Pertussis mostly affects the elderly.
G. No. Ten- to fourteen-year-olds were the most likely to contract pertussis.
H. Yes. Infants had the highest rate of pertussis.
J. Yes. Seven thousand young children contracted pertussis.

39. Which of the following statements could be a plausible explanation for increased incidence of pertussis?

A. Fewer infants are being vaccinated for pertussis, and are therefore contracting the disease.
B. Regulations on reporting pertussis are more lax now, so the numbers are inaccurate.
C. There are more blood transfusions performed now, increasing people's risks of contracting pertussis.
D. Vaccine immunity wanes after 5–10 years, so more young adults are succumbing to pertussis.

40. Which of the following statements about pertussis is NOT true?

F. The disease has an incubation period ranging from 1 to 3 weeks.
G. Symptoms are similar to those of a common cold.
H. The disease is a virus that cannot be treated with antibiotics.
J. Pertussis can be communicated via particles left in the air after a person coughs.

STOP

If there is still time remaining, check your answers to this section.

WRITING PROMPT

Directions: This is a test of your writing skills. You will have thirty (30) minutes to write an essay in English. Before you begin planning and writing your essay, read the writing prompt below carefully to understand exactly what you are being asked to do. Your essay will be evaluated on the evidence it provides of your ability to express judgments by taking a position on the issue in the writing prompt; to maintain a focus on the topic throughout the essay; to develop a position by using logical reasoning and by supporting your ideas; to organize ideas in a logical way; and to use language clearly and effectively according to the conventions of standard written English.

You may use the unlined page to plan your essay. This page will not be scored. You must write your essay in pencil on the lined pages provided. Your writing on those lined pages will be scored. You may not need all the pages, but to ensure you have enough room to finish, do NOT skip lines. You may write corrections or additions neatly between the lines of your essay, but do NOT write in the margins of the lined pages. Illegible essays cannot be scored, so you must write (or print) clearly.

If you finish before time is called, you may review your work. Lay your pencil down immediately when time is called.

Your local public library has come under criticism for allowing patrons under the age of eighteen to check out books that are considered unacceptable. The books are either explicit, describe graphic violence, or use questionable language. These critics argue that minors should not be given access to explicit materials. Other people think that public libraries have no business denying anyone access to any materials, and parents should be the ones to control what books their children can and cannot read. In your opinion, should public libraries place restrictions on which books patrons under the age of eighteen can check out?

In your essay, take a position on this question. You may write about either one of the two points of view given, or you may present a different point of view on this question. Use specific reasons and examples to support your position.

Use this page to *plan* your essay.

Begin WRITING TEST here.

If you need more space, continue on the next page.

WRITING TEST

STOP

Answer Key

PRACTICE TEST 1

English Test

1. B	16. F	31. B	46. H	61. D
2. J	17. A	32. J	47. A	62. G
3. A	18. F	33. D	48. H	63. D
4. J	19. B	34. F	49. B	64. F
5. D	20. F	35. A	50. H	65. C
6. H	21. C	36. G	51. D	66. F
7. C	22. G	37. C	52. F	67. D
8. F	23. D	38. J	53. B	68. H
9. D	24. H	39. A	54. H	69. A
10. J	25. A	40. H	55. C	70. G
11. B	26. F	41. B	56. F	71. D
12. H	27. B	42. J	57. B	72. H
13. A	28. J	43. B	58. H	73. B
14. G	29. C	44. J	59. A	74. J
15. A	30. J	45. C	60. H	75. C

Math Test

1. C	13. A	25. D	37. B	49. A
2. F	14. G	26. J	38. J	50. H
3. C	15. C	27. E	39. A	51. D
4. J	16. H	28. G	40. F	52. H
5. D	17. C	29. C	41. C	53. E
6. H	18. G	30. J	42. K	54. H
7. B	19. B	31. E	43. B	55. D
8. K	20. J	32. H	44. H	56. J
9. C	21. D	33. D	45. D	57. D
10. K	22. J	34. J	46. J	58. K
11. A	23. B	35. C	47. D	59. E
12. H	24. J	36. H	48. F	60. F

Answer Key

PRACTICE TEST 1

Reading Test

1. B	9. B	17. A	25. C	33. A
2. H	10. J	18. J	26. J	34. J
3. D	11. C	19. C	27. C	35. C
4. J	12. G	20. G	28. G	36. G
5. C	13. D	21. B	29. D	37. A
6. J	14. H	22. J	30. F	38. F
7. A	15. A	23. C	31. B	39. B
8. H	16. G	24. F	32. J	40. H

Science Test

1. D	9. D	17. C	25. A	33. B
2. F	10. J	18. F	26. J	34. H
3. D	11. A	19. B	27. D	35. A
4. G	12. H	20. H	28. G	36. H
5. A	13. B	21. B	29. C	37. C
6. F	14. G	22. J	30. F	38. G
7. B	15. C	23. B	31. B	39. D
8. J	16. F	24. H	32. J	40. H

HOW TO SCORE YOUR PRACTICE TEST

Step 1: Add up the number correct for each section and write that number in the blank under the Raw Score column on the Score Conversion Table. (Your goal is to get more questions correct on each subsequent practice test.)

Step 2: Using the Score Conversion Chart, find your scale score for each section and write it down. Then add up all four sections and divide by 4 to find your overall composite score. (Composite scores are rounded up at .5 or higher.)

Score Conversion Table

Section	Raw Score	Scaled Score
English	(out of 75)	____ / 36
Math	(out of 60)	____ / 36
Reading	(out of 40)	____ / 36
Science	(out of 40)	____ / 36
		Add and divide by 4
Overall Composite =		____ / 36

Score Conversion Chart

	Number Correct				
ACT Score*	English Section	Mathematics Section	Reading Section	Science Section	ACT Score*
36	75	60	40	40	**36**
35	74	59	39	39	**35**
34	73	58	38	38	**34**
33	72	57	37	—	**33**
32	71	56	36	37	**32**
31	70	54–55	35	36	**31**
30	69	53	34	35	**30**
29	67–68	51–52	33	34	**29**
28	65–66	49–50	32	33	**28**
27	64	46–48	31	31–32	**27**
26	62–63	44–45	30	30	**26**
25	60–61	41–43	29	28–29	**25**
24	58–59	39–40	27–28	25–27	**24**
23	55–57	37–38	25–26	24	**23**
22	53–54	35–36	23–24	22–23	**22**
21	50–52	33–34	22	20–21	**21**
20	47–49	31–32	21	18–19	**20**
19	44–46	28–30	19–20	17	**19**
18	42–43	25–27	18	15–16	**18**
17	40–41	22–24	17	14	**17**

Continued

Score Conversion Chart *(Continued)*

ACT Score*	Number Correct: English Section	Mathematics Section	Reading Section	Science Section	ACT Score*
16	37–39	19–21	16	13	16
15	34–36	15–17	15	12	15
14	31–33	11–14	13–14	11	14
13	29–30	09–10	12	10	13
12	27–28	07–08	10–11	09	12
11	25–26	06	08–09	08	11
10	23–24	05	07	07	10
9	21–22	04	06	05–06	9
8	18–20	03	05	—	8
7	15–17	—	—	04	7
6	12–14	02	04	03	6
5	09–11	—	03	02	5
4	07–08	01	02	—	4
3	05–06	—	—	01	3
2	03–04	—	01	—	2
1	00–02	00	00	00	1

**These scores are based on student trials rather than national norms.*

SCORING YOUR ESSAY

As mentioned earlier in this text, two readers will evaluate your essay and each person will then assign it a score from 1 to 6. If, by chance, these two scorers disagree by more than 1 point, a third reader will step in and resolve the discrepancy. Performance on the essay will not affect your English, math, reading, science, or composite scores. You will receive two additional scores on your score sheet—a combined English/writing score (1–36) and a writing test subscore (1–12). Neither of these scores will affect your composite score!

The sample essay that follows reflects higher-level writing. It meets the criteria that ACT has put forth for essays that demonstrate effective writing skills.

- It takes a definite position.
- It addresses and expands on the counterargument.
- It has details that support the topic sentences and is well organized.
- It is not repetitive, and while there may be errors, they do not interfere with the competence of the essay.
- It is consistent and well balanced.
- The essay has a clear introduction and a conclusion that is not just a summary but ends with a significant thought.
- The vocabulary demonstrates good use of language and the sentence structure is varied.

Answer Explanations: English Test

1. **(B)** This choice correctly separates two grammatically correct independent clauses into two sentences with a period.
2. **(J)** No comma is necessary. The narrator is saying goodbye to *both* her family and her friends, so the conjunction should not be preceded by a comma—both *family* and *friends* are objects of the preposition *to*. Furthermore, *saying goodbye to my family and friends* acts as one single noun phrase (with *saying* acting as a gerund noun), so no comma is needed between it and the verb *made* (you do not need a comma between the subject and the verb, no matter how long the subject is).
3. **(A)** This is a run-on sentence. Two independent clauses are mashed together with no punctuation. The fact that the conjunction *yet* is present does not make any difference (although the sentence would be correct if there was a comma before *yet*).
4. **(J)** The subsequent sentences mention being afraid to "jinx" something. This implies that the narrator is trying not to think about a desirable outcome, for fear that it will not come true. The idea of winning a gold medal is the only one of the choices that involves a desirable outcome that may or may not happen and is therefore vulnerable to being "jinxed."
5. **(D)** As a general rule, when three of the choices open with a transition word and one does not, the one without a transition word is correct (except in the case of the "*although* trick," where removing *although* would result in a comma splice). Choice D is a correct and comprehensible independent clause, so why mess with it? Besides, none of the proposed transition words makes sense in context.
6. **(H)** This choice explains that the narrator moved to Canada and adds the interesting detail that she did so only 24 hours after graduating, without adding any further details or implications that are unsupported by the text.
7. **(C)** Like the rest of the passage, this sentence is in the past tense (as indicated by the past-tense verb *took*, which appears earlier in the sentence). *I began* is the correct past-tense form.
8. **(F)** This choice correctly presents an independent clause followed by a dependent "afterthought" clause, with the two clauses separated by a comma.
9. **(D)** The national anthem belongs to America, and so the noun *America* needs to be possessive: *America's national anthem.*
10. **(J)** This choice correctly separates multiple adjectives with a comma.
11. **(B)** The phrase *Usually jumps have three spins* does not describe the narrator's actions and is not necessary in order to understand the actions mentioned elsewhere in the paragraph, as the fact that jumps usually have three spins is implied by the phrase *a jump with <u>just</u> two spins* in the preceding sentence.
12. **(H)** The cold, unfeeling qualities of ice described in the subsequent sentences render the idea that anyone would love it is unexpected or ironic. Therefore, the rhetorical question, *How can anyone love ice?* is the best introduction.
13. **(A)** *Its* is the possessive form, with no apostrophe.
14. **(G)** Paragraph 3 describes the narrator waiting to perform, and paragraph 4 describes the medal ceremony. Therefore, paragraph 5, which describes the narrator's performance, should go in between them.
15. **(A)** The essay centers around the narrator's winning an Olympic gold medal. This certainly qualifies as a "significant event," and none of the details mentioned in choice A are wrong or irrelevant.
16. **(F)** Although the sentence is long, the last several clauses concerning the grandmother's qualities are essentially a list; they are not going to affect the grammar of the beginning of the sentence. We need the first few words here to form an independent clause, and one that is in the past tense, like the rest of the passage: only *She described her grandmother* accomplishes this.
17. **(A)** This choice correctly inserts commas after each item in the list of adjectives, and refrains from inserting any unnecessary commas elsewhere.
18. **(F)** In this choice, two independent clauses are correctly joined with a comma + conjunction (*and*). The fact that the first clause is short and the second is long does not matter; they are both independent clauses.
19. **(B)** The idea we need here is a synonym for *activating*, something like *starting* or *spurring*. The other choices are all synonymous with that idea, but *halting* (which means *stopping*) is the opposite and so the LEAST acceptable.
20. **(F)** The only information contained in the underlined portion deals with who lived in that area before the Civil War. Therefore, the underlined portion contains *details that emphasize the historical importance* of the area.

21. **(C)** The phrase *a genealogist* is a "lift-out" appositive clause containing extra information, inserted in the middle of a single independent clause. It needs to be set off with something, and the only choice that works is a pair of dashes (a pair of commas would also be correct, but is not one of the choices).

22. **(G)** What we are supposed to have here is an adverb modifying an adjective that is modifying a noun: *poorly* (adverb) *preserved* (adjective) *Creole French* (noun phrase).

23. **(D)** The pronoun *who* is used here to introduce a clause containing further information, and *was* is used as part of a passive-voice phrase: *Elisabeth, who was sold.*

24. **(H)** The narrator means to say that *immediately* after finding out this new information, she felt uncontrollably compelled to write her family's history. Of the choices, only *At this point* refers to the *specific moment* in question.

25. **(A)** Both the preceding sentence ("their lives") and the rest of this sentence ("people") demonstrate that we are talking about more than one person. As the people we are talking about have long since passed away, we need the past-tense plural form *They were*.

26. **(F)** The fact that over a thousand documents were used is valuable information, as it demonstrates how hard the author worked and how thorough the resulting account must be.

27. **(B)** Although the sentence is long, everything after the comma is an "afterthought" clause containing extra information, so the part before the comma needs to be an independent clause. Of the choices, only *The result was Cane River* is a grammatically correct independent clause.

28. **(J)** Although some may be made nervous by the fact that this choice results in a very long sentence, it is the only correct one. It combines an independent clause (ending at *Louisiana*) with a dependent clause containing extra information, and separates the two with a comma.

29. **(C)** The beginning of the essay was about the author's great-grandmother Emily. Since this is the only one of the choices that is about her, it is the only one that "ties in" to the beginning.

30. **(J)** Although it may safely be assumed that the experience of writing *Cane River* was personally enriching for the author, the essay is not primarily about the author's feelings or why writing a book is personally beneficial in general. Nothing specific to this effect is said.

31. **(B)** Assuming that they are right next to each other, as they are here, no punctuation is necessary between the subject of a sentence and the main verb. *The different kinds of prairie wildflowers* is our noun phrase (technically, the subject is *kinds*, and *of prairie wildflowers* is a prepositional phrase, but this doesn't make a difference here), and the main verb is *are*.

32. **(J)** This section of the passage is in the present tense, and the subject phrase is *grasses and herbaceous wildflowers*, so the correct form for the main verb is *dominate* (present-tense plural).

33. **(D)** Coneflowers, and how many types there are, are not mentioned anywhere else in this paragraph or the entire passage. The passage is about prairies, not specific types of flowers. Therefore, this sentence would distract from the main idea.

34. **(F)** The entire passage so far has been about the diverse flora found on prairies. The reader would expect that the assertion that prairies are "interesting and colorful" would have something to do with biodiversity.

35. **(A)** This choice correctly results in an independent clause followed by a dependent clause, with the two clauses separated by a comma.

36. **(G)** Old railroads are the rarest of the four environments offered as choices, and so this choice best establishes that black soil prairies are difficult to find today.

37. **(C)** The implication of the sentence in the context of the paragraph is that it is regrettable that the original prairies have been destroyed. Therefore, *Unfortunately* is the appropriate introductory word.

38. **(J)** The main idea of the paragraph concerns the depletion of gravel prairies, and so a guess that some of these prairies are probably new seems out of place.

39. **(A)** Since the noun *they* performs both the verb *are* and the verb *contain*, no comma is necessary after *degraded*. Furthermore, the information presented in this choice is the most relevant to the paragraph. (In this question, the right and wrong answers are determined by a combination of grammatical and stylistic factors—the test does not do this often, but it does happen, so watch out for it!)

40. **(H)** The antecedent of the pronoun *they* is the noun phrase *gravel and dolomite prairies*. Therefore, sentence 4 should come right after a sentence that makes this apparent. It should also not come between sentences 3 and 5, as sentence 5 is clearly supposed to immediately follow sentence 3. And it makes sense that sentence 4 should be next

to sentence 2, as both concern the physical characteristics of gravel and dolomite prairies. Of the choices, only H (which places sentence 4 between sentences 2 and 3) resolves all of these issues.

41. **(B)** This choice correctly separates two independent clauses into two separate sentences by use of a period.

42. **(J)** This choice correctly uses *that* (with no comma) to attach a grammatically correct essential/limiting clause to the pronoun *those*.

43. **(B)** The subject noun *species* is plural here (although the singular form is identical), and so the plural verb *are* is necessary.

44. **(J)** The adjectives *moist*, *mesic*, and *dry* constitute a list of three different things that sand prairies can be. Therefore, commas are necessary after *moist* and *mesic*. (Although the comma before the conjunction that separates the final two items in a list is optional when the conjunction is *and*, it is mandatory when the conjunction is *or*!) The word *dry* ends one independent clause, which then needs to be joined to the subsequent one via a comma + conjunction, and so a comma is also necessary after *dry*.

45. **(C)** The question asks for a "colorful image," and choice C offers us the most vivid and specific image: *purple spiderwort, orange butterfly weed, and yellow goldenrod*.

46. **(H)** *Renowned* means "widely known" (by others). The correct construction would be to say that the regions *are renowned* for their beauty. Also, the subject, "regions," is plural so you need the plural verb "are."

47. **(A)** If the springs are on the islands, then the springs couldn't have been formed before the islands were. So *later* makes no sense in context.

48. **(H)** Species is singular, and so we need the singular (gender–neutral) possessive pronoun *its* here.

49. **(B)** The sentence in question foreshadows the presence of monkeys, and so could only be used *before* the monkeys are specifically introduced. After that, we would already know about the monkeys.

50. **(H)** *However* is set off with a pair of commas when it is inserted into the middle of a single independent clause.

51. **(D)** The visitors *are encouraged* by others; other people are doing the encouraging to the visitors. The addition of the adverb *strongly* provides additional information.

52. **(F)** *"Are wanting" their money* is an extremely awkward construction in English. It is simply not something we would say.

53. **(B)** The pair of dashes should set off the portion of the sentence that "interrupts" the main independent clause. If that phrase were taken out, the words around it would form a complete correct independent clause. (Parentheses would also be correct, but are not one of the choices.)

54. **(H)** This sentence merely serves to emphasize how weird the situation is, and does not do too much more than that. (Sometimes the least ambitious answer choice is the safe bet.)

55. **(C)** Someone pointed this out *later*, or *after a while*, or *in due time*—in other words, *eventually*.

56. **(F)** *There was no possible way a monkey could get money would be stealing it* does not make sense. (Remember, read the *whole* sentence, not just the part around the underline!)

57. **(B)** This choice correctly precedes an afterthought clause with a single comma.

58. **(H)** *Personally I'm disappointed* is the preferred construction, with *personally* coming before the first-person contraction *I'm*.

59. **(A)** This choice correctly presents the hypothetical *could have motivated me* with the infinitive *to fly*.

60. **(H)** The previous sentence already eloquently ends the passage. The additional aside about whether monkeys like chips is less funny, and also doesn't make much sense, since the author has already established that the monkey problem has been taken care of.

61. **(D)** This choice correctly presents an independent clause (the end of which is a list) preceded by a dependent modifying clause. Because the modifying clause refers to Miró's work, the independent clause correctly begins with "his work" (otherwise it would be a misplaced modifier).

62. **(G)** The sentence, like the rest of the passage, is in the past tense, and the regular past-tense form *expressed* is all that is needed here.

63. **(D)** Even if you don't know what "visual elements" traditional painting involved, this choice clearly refers to Miró *rejecting* something about *established painting*, and so demonstrates his contempt for conventional painting, as the question requests.

64. **(F)** This is the only grammatically correct choice that says what you mean to say: that Miró was *born* to a goldsmith and watchmaker, and that he was *drawn* to the arts community.

65. **(C)** This choice correctly presents an independent clause (*He developed his unique style*) preceded by a dependent clause containing extra information, and followed by a colon and description.

66. **(F)** *Varying* here is correctly used as an adjective to modify *degrees* (*varying degrees* basically means "many ways").

67. **(D)** *The founder of surrealism* is a "lift-out" appositive clause that gives extra information about Andre Breton, and as such, it is set off with a pair of commas.

68. **(H)** Only this choice makes reference to a specific influential technique that Miró developed, thereby demonstrating his importance in the history of painting.

69. **(A)** The fact that Miró chose not to become an official Surrealist is surprising in light of the fact that he helped start the movement, and so the appropriate transition word is *However*, which is used to introduce contrasting information. (It also helps to notice that the other three choices are basically interchangeable.)

70. **(G)** This choice correctly results in an independent clause followed by a dependent participial modifier clause containing extra information.

71. **(D)** The passage is in the past tense, and the regular past-tense form *accelerated* is all we need here.

72. **(H)** This choice correctly makes two independent clauses into two separate sentences, separated by a period.

73. **(B)** The past perfect (the "past of the past") form *had visited* is correct here (the normal past tense would also work, but is not one of the choices).

74. **(J)** This choice correctly presents two independent clauses separated with a semicolon.

75. **(C)** This choice correctly presents a nonessential *which* clause preceded by a comma.

Answer Explanations: Math Test

1. **(C)** Substituting $x = 3$ into the equation $x^2 + 2x - 12$ gives $(3)^2 + 2(3) - 12 = 9 + 6 - 12 = 3$

2. **(F)** $3(2x - 1) = 11x + 27 \rightarrow 6x - 3 = 11x + 27 \rightarrow -5x = 30 \rightarrow x = -6$.

3. **(C)** 15% of \$42 is $0.15 \cdot 42 =$ \$6.30. This answer is the amount the \$42 jacket is discounted, so to find the discounted price take \$42 – \$6.30 = \$35.70.

4. **(J)** $\angle a$ is a same-side exterior angle to the given angle, which is supplementary to 60°. Therefore, $m\angle a = 180 - 60 = 120°$.

5. **(D)** Substituting $x = 3$, $y = 5$, and $w = 4$ into the given expression yields $(3)(4)^3 + \frac{3(4)}{2} - (3)^2(5) =$ $(3)(64) + 6 - 45 = 192 + 6 - 45 = 153$.

6. **(H)** Distributing the given expression gives $(3x - 5)(4x + 3) = 12x^2 + 9x - 20x - 15$. Combining like terms gives $12x^2 - 11x - 15$.

7. **(B)** $|5 - 8| - |9 - 3| = |-3| - |6| = 3 - 6 = -3$. Remember when evaluating absolute values to simplify inside the absolute value first, then take the absolute value of the resulting number.

8. **(K)** $(5\sqrt{3})^2 = 5\sqrt{3} \cdot 5\sqrt{3} = 25\sqrt{9}$. Evaluating the square root gives $25 \cdot 3 = 75$. Also, your calculator could get this answer by plugging the given expression into it.

9. **(C)** Despite all the words in the problem, it just boils down to plugging the numbers into the proper variables and evaluating. Plugging $x = 15$, $y = 18$, $w = 6$, $z = 6$, and $n = 8$ into the formula gives $A = (15)(18) + (6)[6(2 \cdot 8 - 1) + 2 \cdot 8]$. Evaluating using the order of operations gives $A = 270 + 6[90 + 16] = 270 + 636 = 906$.

10. **(K)** To calculate probability use the formula $P = \frac{\textit{number of successful outcomes}}{\textit{total number of outcomes}} = \frac{7+5}{15} = \frac{12}{15}$. Simplifying the fraction gives $\frac{4}{5}$.

11. **(A)** The watch increases by 5%, which is an increase of $100 \cdot 0.05 =$ \$5 making the new price of the watch 100 + 5 = \$105. The necklace decreases by 10%, which is a decrease of $300 \cdot .10 =$ \$30 making the new price 300 – 30 = \$270. Adding these two prices together gives the sum of the costs as \$105 + \$270 = \$375.

12. **(H)** The triangle in the figure is a right triangle given that $\overline{CA}$ is tangent to the circle and $\overline{OT}$ is a radius (all tangents to circles are perpendicular to the radius of the circle at the point of tangency). Using this along with the facts

Practice Test 1

$\overline{TC} = 8$ and $\overline{OC} = 10$ we can set up the Pythagorean Theorem to calculate the leg $\overline{OT}$ as $a^2 + b^2 = c^2 \rightarrow 8^2 + x^2 = 10^2 \rightarrow 64 + x^2 = 100$. Solving for x gives $x^2 = 36 \rightarrow x = 6$. It is also a Pythagorean triple: 6, 8, 10 (3, 4, 5).

13. **(A)** We are asked to find AB and by looking at the answer choices, we want our answer in terms of x, y, and z. First substituting BC in for A we get $AB = (BC)B$. Now substituting x in for B and yz in for C we get $(BC)B = (xyz)x$, which equals $xyzx$.

14. **(G)** Solving an inequality is almost identical to solving an equation except if you multiply or divide by a negative number you have to switch the direction of the inequality. Solving this inequality for x we get $-5 < -3x - 7 \rightarrow 2 < -3x \rightarrow -\frac{2}{3} > x$, which is equivalent to $x < -\frac{2}{3}$.

15. **(C)** To find the slope of a linear equation, first get it in the form $y = mx + b$ where m represents the slope of the line and b represents the y-intercept. Solving for y in the given equation we get $y - \frac{1}{3}x + \frac{3}{5} = 0 \rightarrow y = \frac{1}{3}x - \frac{3}{5}$ so the slope of the line is $m = \frac{1}{3}$.

16. **(H)** The slope-intercept form is $y = mx + b$. Solving the given equation for y gives $4x - 2y = 12 \rightarrow -2y = -4x + 12$. Dividing both sides by -2 gives $y = 2x - 6$.

17. **(C)** If the solution for x is 6, then we can substitute 6 into the equation for x and solve for a. Plugging 6 in for x gives $3(6) + 3a - 5 = 5(6) - a$. Solving the equation for a gives $18 + 3a - 5 = 30 - a \rightarrow 13 + 3a = 30 - a \rightarrow 4a = 17$. Dividing both sides by 4 gives $a = 4.25$.

18. **(G)** The formula for the circumference of a circle is $C = \pi d$ where d is the diameter of the circle. Using the formula, we can find the diameter of each of the smaller circles by substituting 8π for C and solving for d: $8\pi = \pi d \rightarrow 8 = d$. Therefore the diameter of each of the small circles is 8 inches. The large circle's diameter is equivalent to all 3 of the smaller circles' diameters combined, which is $8 + 8 + 8 = 24$ inches. Now, using the formula again to find the circumference of a circle with $d = 24$ we get $C = \pi(24) = 24\pi$.

19. **(B)** The length of time needed to cook the turkey is proportional to the weight of the turkey. In other words, $\frac{time}{weight} = \frac{time}{weight}$. Plugging in 1 hour for time, 3 pounds for the weight and 19 pounds for the other weight gives: $\frac{1}{3} = \frac{x}{19}$. Cross multiplying gives $1(19) = 3(x)$. Solving for x gives $x = 6\frac{1}{3}$ hours. One-third of an hour is $\frac{1}{3}(60) = 20$ minutes, so the answer is 6 hours and 20 minutes.

20. **(J)** Lines m and n are parallel, which makes $\angle a$ supplementary to the given angle of 80°. Calculating $\angle a$ we get $m\angle a = 180 - 80 = 100°$.

21. **(D)** The problem states the triangles are similar so the corresponding parts are proportional. Setting up the ratio as $\frac{\textit{big left side}}{\textit{big hypotenuse}} = \frac{\textit{little left side}}{\textit{little hypotenuse}}$ we get $\frac{x}{12} = \frac{4}{5}$. Cross multiplying and solving for x gives $5x = 4(12) \rightarrow x = 9.6$ or $x = 9\frac{3}{5}$.

22. **(J)** To find the area of a rectangle use the formula $A = L \cdot W$. The problem states the length and width are $4x - 3$ and $2x^2 + 7$. Substituting these expressions in for L and W in the formula gives $A = (4x - 3) \cdot (2x^2 + 7)$. Multiplying the expressions together gives $A = 8x^3 + 28x - 6x^2 - 21$. Rewriting in standard form gives $A = 8x^3 - 6x^2 + 28x - 21$.

23. **(B)** Building a prime factor tree for 2,100 gives the prime factorization as $2 \cdot 2 \cdot 3 \cdot 5 \cdot 5 \cdot 7 = 2^2 \cdot 3 \cdot 5^2 \cdot 7$.

24. **(J)** If Jean spent 90% of her vacation money, the percent that remained equals $100 - 90 = 10\%$. Setting up a proportion we get $\frac{\%\ \textit{remained}}{\textit{total}\ \%} = \frac{\textit{amount remained}}{\textit{total amount}} \rightarrow \frac{10}{100} = \frac{100}{x}$. Cross multiplying and solving for x we get $10x = 10{,}000 \rightarrow x = 1{,}000$.

25. **(D)** To add two fractions we must first start with a common denominator. Multiplying the first fraction by $\frac{5}{5}$ gives $\frac{5}{5} \cdot \frac{2x+1}{x} - \frac{x-3}{5x} = \frac{5(2x+1)}{5x} - \frac{x-3}{5x} = \frac{10x+5}{5x} - \frac{x-3}{5x}$. Combining the numerators together gives $\frac{10x + 5 - (x - 3)}{5x} = \frac{9x + 8}{5x}$.

26. **(J)** Factoring the equation gives $(2x + 5)(x - 3) = 0$. Setting each factor equal to zero and solving gives $2x + 5 = 0 \rightarrow x = -\frac{5}{2}$ and $x - 3 = 0 \rightarrow x = 3$. Keep in mind there are several ways to solve this problem. You could also plug it into the quadratic formula if factoring is not your strength.

27. **(E)** The figure is made up of 5 congruent squares. Each square has side length 4. To find the area of one square, use the formula $A = s^2$. Plugging in 4 for s gives $A = (4)^2 = 16$. Since there are 5 squares, the total area is $5 \cdot 16 = 80$.

28. **(G)** Midpoint problems require knowing the midpoint formula: $midpoint = \left(\frac{x_1 + x_2}{2}, \frac{y_1 + y_2}{2}\right)$. Since we are given the midpoint and one endpoint, use (x, y) for the unknown endpoint B. Plugging these values into the formula gives $(-1, 2) = \left(\frac{x+2}{2}, \frac{y+9}{2}\right)$. Solving for x and y gives $\frac{x+2}{2} = -1 \rightarrow x = -4$ and $\frac{y+9}{2} = 2 \rightarrow y = -5$. Therefore, the coordinates of B are $(-4, -5)$. If formulas and equations are not your strength, you could also solve this problem by drawing an accurate picture, estimating the location of B, and eliminating incorrect answers.

29. **(C)** The given triangle is a 30°-60°-90° right triangle. Using 30°-60°-90° ratios of x, $x\sqrt{3}$, $2x$, we get $x = 3$. The question asks us to find $\overline{BC}$, the side opposite the 60° angle, which has the value $x\sqrt{3}$. Plugging in 3 for x gives $\overline{BC} = 3\sqrt{3}$.

30. **(J)** To increase the mean of 5 numbers by 3, each number must be increased by 3. Increasing each of 5 numbers by 3 gives a total increase of $3 + 3 + 3 + 3 + 3 = 15$.

31. **(E)** The area the dog is able to roam is the shape of a circle with radius equal to the length of the leash, 12 feet. To find the area of a circle use the formula $A = \pi r^2$. Plugging in 12 for the radius gives $A = \pi(12)^2 = 144\pi$. Using 3.14 for pi gives $144(3.14) \approx 452.16 \approx 452$.

32. **(H)** Setting up a proportion gives $\frac{\textit{original tv size}}{\textit{original car size}} = \frac{\textit{new tv size}}{\textit{new car size}} = \frac{19}{12} = \frac{32}{x}$. Solving for x gives $19x = 12(32) \rightarrow x \approx 20.21 \approx 20$.

33. **(D)** The little white triangles in the figure are all right triangles with legs x and $2x$. Since the shaded square has area 25 square feet, each side of the square has measure 5 feet making the hypotenuse of the right triangles each 5. Setting up Pythagorean Theorem we get $a^2 + b^2 = c^2 \rightarrow x^2 + (2x)^2 = 5^2$. Solving for x we get $x^2 + 4x^2 = 25 \rightarrow 5x^2 = 25 \rightarrow x = \sqrt{5}$. To find the area of square $ABCD$ we first need to know the length of one side. Each side is made of $x + 2x$, which equals $3x$. Substituting for x gives each side of square $ABCD$ equals $3\sqrt{5}$. Now, to find the area, square the length of the side of $ABCD$ to get $(3\sqrt{5})^2 = 45$. This is quite a lengthy problem, but using your eye to approximate the area could help eliminate 3 of the 5 answers giving you a 50% chance of guessing and saving several minutes of computations.

34. **(J)** For non-right triangles, when presented with SAS (side-angle-side), always use the law of cosines. This problem can also be done by eliminating wrong answers. The given triangle has an angle measuring 121.1°, which means it cannot be a right triangle. This eliminates choices F, G, and H. To distinguish between the law of cosines and the law of sines, use this general rule of thumb: given AAS, SSA, or ASA use the law of sines. Use the law of cosines with SSS or SAS.

35. **(C)** The given equation will simplify by dividing the numerator and the denominator by x giving $y = 4 - 2x$. Graph the linear equation with y-intercept 4 and slope -2 to get choice C as the correct answer. Also, this problem could have been solved using a graphing calculator as long as parentheses are put around the numerator. Remember, since x was divided out, a hole will remain when $x = 0$.

36. **(H)** Dividing a plane using a single line splits the plane into two parts: one part left of the line, the other part right of the line. Therefore, there are two sets of points, the points to the left and the points to the right.

37. **(B)** To calculate the number of diagonals in a given polygon, use the formula $D = \frac{n(n-3)}{2}$ where n represents the number of sides of the polygon. Substituting 6 for n gives $D = \frac{6(6-3)}{2} = 9$.

38. **(J)** Using the circle formula $(x - h)^2 + (y - k)^2 = r^2$, the center of circle J is at $(-4, -4)$ putting it in the third quadrant and the radius is $\sqrt{16} = 4$ meaning it just touches the x-axis and y-axis from the center.

39. **(A)** Converting each of the fractions to decimals gives $-\frac{3}{5} = -0.6, -\frac{4}{7} \approx -0.57, -\frac{5}{6} \approx -.83, -\frac{8}{9} \approx -.89$. Order

the decimals from least to greatest to get $-0.89 < -0.83 < -0.6 < -0.57$, then substitute the fractions back in to get $-\frac{8}{9} < -\frac{5}{6} < -\frac{3}{5} < -\frac{4}{7}$.

40. **(F)** Substituting $L = 4$ and $W = 3$ into the formula gives $p = \frac{\pi}{2}\sqrt{2(4^2 + 3^2)} = \frac{\pi}{2}\sqrt{50}$. Simplifying the square root gives $\frac{\pi}{2} \cdot \sqrt{25} \cdot \sqrt{2} = \frac{\pi}{2} \cdot 5 \cdot \sqrt{2} = \frac{5}{2}\pi\sqrt{2}$.

41. **(C)** x is the common denominator you get when combining the two given fractions. The least common denominator of 28 and 126 is 252 because $28 \cdot 9 = 252$ and $126 \cdot 2 = 252$. Therefore, $x = 252$.

42. **(K)** The circumference of a circle is calculated using the formula $C = 2\pi r$. Substituting R for the radius gives $C = 2\pi R$. Since the runner needs to run 5 laps, multiply the circumference by 5 to get $2\pi R \cdot 5 = 10\pi R$.

43. **(B)** Setting up the law of sines we get $\frac{\sin A}{a} = \frac{\sin C}{c} \rightarrow \frac{\sin(105)}{x} = \frac{\sin(35)}{27}$. Angle A is calculated from $180 - (40 + 35) = 105$. Cross multiplying and solving for x gives $27 \cdot \sin(105) = x \cdot \sin(35) \rightarrow x = \frac{27\sin(105)}{\sin(35)}$.

44. **(H)** The chart shows the payment for a 36-month loan at 10% is \$32.27 per \$1,000 borrowed. Setting up a proportion for the \$6,500 Kaylee needs to borrow gives $\frac{32.27}{1000} = \frac{x}{6500}$. Cross multiplying and solving for x gives $1000x = 32.27(6500) \rightarrow x \approx 209.76$.

45. **(D)** The cheapest loan payment of Kaylee's options is the 60-month loan at 5%, which is \$18.87 per \$1,000 borrowed. Setting up a proportion along with Kaylee's \$300 maximum payment amount gives $\frac{18.87}{1000} = \frac{300}{x}$. Cross multiply and solve for x to get $18.87x = 300(1000) \rightarrow x \approx \$15{,}898.25$ so the maximum Kaylee can borrow of the given amounts is \$15,000.

46. **(J)** $(5 - i)^2 = (5 - i)(5 - i)$. Distributing the expression gives $25 - 5i - 5i + i^2$. Recall that $i^2 = -1$, so the expression becomes $25 - 5i - 5i + (-1)$. Combining like terms gives $24 - 10i$.

47. **(D)** Solving the second equation for y gives $y = 19 - 2x$. Substituting this expression into the inequality for y gives $19 - 2x > 12$. Solve the inequality for x to get $-2x > -7 \rightarrow x < 3.5$. Since the solution for x must be an integer, the inequality becomes $x \le 3$.

48. **(F)** For the product of pq^3t^4 to be greater than zero it must be positive. The only way the product of three expressions can be positive is if each is positive or if exactly two are negative and the other is positive. Since t^4 is always positive, p and q^3 must either both be positive or both be negative; either way, the product of pq must be positive.

49. **(A)** $3^4 = 81$; therefore, $\log_3 81 = 4$. The equation then becomes $4 = x + 1$. Solve for x to get $x = 3$.

50. **(H)** Using the Pythagorean Theorem to find the missing side of the triangle we get $a^2 + b^2 = c^2 \rightarrow 2^2 + x^2 = 7^2 \rightarrow 4 + x^2 = 49 \rightarrow x^2 = 45$. Taking the square root of both sides of the equation and simplifying the radical gives $x = \sqrt{45} = \sqrt{9} \cdot \sqrt{5} = 3\sqrt{5}$. Recall $\csc T = \frac{hypotenuse}{opposite} = \frac{7}{3\sqrt{5}}$. Rationalizing the denominator gives $\frac{7}{3\sqrt{5}} \cdot \frac{\sqrt{5}}{\sqrt{5}} = \frac{7\sqrt{5}}{15}$.

51. **(D)** Setting up an equation for the total charge by the flight instructor gives $C = 75 + k\sqrt[3]{t}$ where C is the cost of the flight, k is the constant of variation, and t is time. Substituting 27 for time and \$120 for cost yields the equation $120 = 75 + k\sqrt[3]{27}$. Solving for k gives $120 = 75 + 3k \rightarrow 45 = 3k \rightarrow k = 15$. Now that we know the constant of variation, use it along with $t = 64$ to find the cost of a 64-minute lesson: $C = 75 + 15\sqrt[3]{64} = 75 + 15(4) = \$135$.

52. **(H)** The ratio for the sine of an angle is $\sin d = \frac{opposite}{hypotenuse} = \frac{\overline{AC}}{6}$. Setting this ratio equal to the ratio given in the problem gives the new equation: $\frac{\overline{AC}}{6} = 0.8$. Solve for $\overline{AC}$ to get $\overline{AC} = 4.8$. Now that we know the height of the triangle, calculate the area using the formula $A = \frac{1}{2}bh = \frac{1}{2}(10)(4.8) = 24$.

53. **(E)** Sometimes the best way to find the right answer is to plug in values and eliminate wrong answers. Starting with $x = 1$ and $y = 1$, we get $|2(1) + 3(1)| = |2(1) - 3(1)| \rightarrow |5| = |-1| \rightarrow 5 = 1$. This is not true, which eliminates choices B and C. Next, substitute $x = 0$ and $y = 1$ to get $|2(0) + 3(1)| = |2(0) - 3(1)| \rightarrow |3| = |-3| \rightarrow 3 = 3$, which is a true statement eliminating choices A and D leaving E as the correct answer.

54. **(H)** There is no simple trick to this problem; we just have to count all the rectangles. A good strategy is to start with the smallest rectangles and work our way up. There are 6 small rectangles, 7 rectangles composed of 2 small rectangles, 2 rectangles composed of 3 small rectangles, and 2 rectangles composed of 4 small rectangles, making a total of 17 rectangles with area less than that of rectangle *ADLI*.

55. **(D)** Substituting the given point for x and y into the equation and solving for A gives $11 = (A + 3)(3) + 5 \rightarrow 11 = 3A + 9 + 5 \rightarrow 11 = 3A + 14 \rightarrow A = -1$. Now to find the slope we need to get the equation into $y = mx + b$ form. Substituting $A = -1$ we get $y = 2x + 5$, so the slope is 2.

56. **(J)** To find the area of a trapezoid we need to know the heights of each of the trapezoids. Draw a strategic line parallel to $\overline{BF}$ to make two special 3-4-5 and 5-12-13 right triangles at the top of the figure. Now that we know the heights of the two trapezoids are 4 and 12, we can use the area of a trapezoid formula: $A = \frac{1}{2}(b1 + b2) \cdot h$.

The area of the smaller trapezoid is $A = \frac{1}{2}(7 + 4) \cdot 4 = 22$. The area of the larger trapezoid is $A = \frac{1}{2}(9 + 4) \cdot 12 = 78$.

The ratio of the two trapezoids is now $\frac{22}{78} = \frac{11}{39} \rightarrow 11{:}39$.

57. **(D)** Substituting $x + 1$ for y in the first equation gives $x + 1 = x^2 - 5$. Solving for x gives $x^2 - x - 6 = 0$. Factor to get $(x - 3)(x + 2) = 0$. Solve for x: $x - 3 = 0 \rightarrow x = 3$ and $x + 2 = 0 \rightarrow x = -2$. Substitute these values back into either equation for x to solve for y. Solving for y we get $y = (3) + 1 \rightarrow y = 4$ and $y = (-2) + 1 \rightarrow y = -1$ so the two points of intersection are $(3, 4)$ and $(-2, -1)$.

58. **(K)** To find the sum of the interior angles of a septagon, use the formula $(n - 2) \cdot 180$. Substituting 7 for n gives $(7 - 2) \cdot 180 = 900$. Since two of the angles have measures 70° and 115° the remaining angles have a sum of $900 - (70 + 115) = 715°$.

59. **(E)** "The product of y and 4 is x" can be represented as the equation $y \cdot 4 = x$. Solving for y gives $y = \frac{x}{4}$. The question asks to find the "sum of y and 4 in terms of x." Writing this as an expression we get $y + 4$. Substitute $\frac{x}{4}$ for y to get $\frac{x}{4} + 4$. Add the two fractions to get $\frac{x}{4} + \frac{16}{4} = \frac{x+16}{4}$.

60. **(F)** $\cos\frac{7\pi}{12} = \cos\left(\frac{\pi}{3} + \frac{\pi}{4}\right)$. Using the given formula the expression becomes

$\cos\left(\frac{\pi}{3}\right) \cdot \cos\left(\frac{\pi}{4}\right) - \sin\left(\frac{\pi}{3}\right) \cdot \sin\left(\frac{\pi}{4}\right)$. Substituting the values from the chart gives $\frac{1}{2} \cdot \frac{\sqrt{2}}{2} - \frac{\sqrt{3}}{2} \cdot \frac{\sqrt{2}}{2}$

$= \frac{\sqrt{2}}{4} - \frac{\sqrt{6}}{4} = \frac{\sqrt{2} - \sqrt{6}}{4}$. You can also ignore the chart, set your calculator in radian mode and get the decimal answer, $-.2588$. You would then evaluate all the possible answers as decimals and also arrive at choice F as correct.

Answer Explanations: Reading Test

1. **(B)** The fourth paragraph reveals that the narrator met her boyfriend when he was one of the Youth Players that she had gone to see on a school outing, and describes her earliest memories of him. Though it does not explicitly depict their meeting, this is still how she first learned of his existence.

2. **(H)** The last sentence of the first paragraph establishes that the narrator works an office job to pay the bills for both herself and her boyfriend, so that her boyfriend can pursue his music. This means she is *generous* (because she supports him) and *pragmatic* (which means that she is a logical person who does what is necessary to achieve specific goals).

3. **(D)** Paragraph 2, which concerns the narrator's parents, states that they "did not have in their comprehension what it was that she wanted to do." Choice D simply paraphrases this without adding anything further, and so cannot possibly be wrong.

4. **(J)** The narrator's boyfriend is a cellist, and so when the narrator says "the cello is the instrument I love best," she means that she loves him and his playing more than her own comparatively meager musical talent. This is the only one of the four choices where what the narrator says works as a metaphor, whereas the other three are very similar literal paraphrases of one another. (As in so many places on the ACT, "which of these things is not like the others" is a very good strategy here!)

5. **(C)** Although it does not become clear until the last three paragraphs, the main conflict concerns the tension and emotional distance between the narrator and her boyfriend. Everything else serves merely as background to underscore this.

6. **(J)** Although saying that the narrator views her boyfriend as a *talented musician whose opinion she respects* does not tell the whole story, there is certainly nothing in it that is incorrect. (Remember, on the ACT Reading, the right answer is just the one with nothing wrong in it!)

7. **(A)** Although all of the answer choices seem very similar, there are important differences between them, and the line in question most nearly means that *she can tell something is wrong because of the music he plays*. The point of the paragraph is that his feelings are revealed through his music despite his efforts to conceal them.

8. **(H)** It is most directly established in paragraph 6 (lines 40–48) that the narrator loves listening to her boyfriend play the cello and enjoys the life of a musician's partner.

9. **(B)** The descriptions in paragraph 6 of the narrator falling asleep to the sound of her boyfriend's playing and smiling unconsciously at his solos are evidence of emotional intimacy. This is all that choice B suggests, and so it is the right answer.

10. **(J)** Lines 34–36 establish that the narrator's boyfriend was honest with her about the fact that her talents would not be sufficient for her to make a living by playing the flute.

11. **(C)** The main idea of the passage is that computer technology is steadily being incorporated into more and more things that are not themselves computers. This can be simply paraphrased as "the changing roles computers have in people's lives," and choice C doesn't assert anything beyond this.

12. **(G)** Nowhere in the passage does the *opinion of a scientist* appear (a clue to this would be the fact that the author never incorporates a single proper name or direct quote).

13. **(D)** *Ubiquitous* means "ever-present" (or "all over the place"). The subsequent sentence deals with the sheer number of transistors and embedded systems being produced, and so it should have been possible to intuit this.

14. **(H)** The passage never hints that more *power and batteries* will be required to run computers, and is in fact explicitly contradicted in lines 69–71, so all of the answer choices are correct EXCEPT this one. And regardless of the passage, the suggestion that computers in the future would need "more batteries" probably sounded funny to you. (It is always a good idea to <u>remember real life</u> on the ACT Reading; although outside knowledge is never necessary, it can reliably be used to eliminate wrong answers!)

15. **(A)** The statement "Computers will be so much a part of everyday life that people will hardly notice them" is essentially a paraphrase of the main idea of the passage, which is stated most directly in the final sentence (lines 82–84). Remembering the right answers to questions 11, 13, and 14 would also be a big help here.

16. **(G)** Yet again, the correct answer is a paraphrase of the main idea: that computers will be so omnipresent that people will hardly notice them. (You may have thought that the fact that choice G is nearly identical to the correct answer on question 15 meant it was a trick, but this is not how the ACT Reading typically works: the main idea is the main idea, and several right answers on a given passage will more or less be paraphrases of the main idea!)

17. **(A)** The *future entertainment system* is described in paragraph 1, and nothing about a satellite is mentioned. All of the other choices are mentioned EXCEPT this one.

18. **(J)** The subsequent sentence describes how people used to use computers *occasionally for specific tasks*. This is what the author means by *passive appliances*, since it stands in sharp contrast to today's interactive devices that are at the center of so many modern activities, as described throughout the passage.

19. **(C)** Lines 16–23 establish that the number of uses for microprocessors is increasing, and lines 27–31 establish that the number of microprocessors themselves is also dramatically increasing. This is overwhelmingly the main focus and "point" of paragraph 2.

20. **(G)** All of the choices are mentioned (although not always word-for-word) in paragraph 1 EXCEPT *power profiles*.

21. **(B)** The main focus of the passage is on Kahlo's life, and the closing sentence of the first paragraph makes reference to the *elevation of the artist over the art* (line 15). (The first and last sentences of the first and last paragraphs are <u>always</u> good places to look when answering "main idea" questions!)

22. **(J)** The author's point in comparing Kahlo's story to *a game of telephone* is that it has been changed in the telling to suit the priorities and biases of the tellers. Choice J is the nearest paraphrase of this idea.

23. **(C)** Lines 25–26 establish that the standards applied to women for admission to the canon were the same as those used for men. All the answer choices identify phenomena that contributed to the lack of great female artists prior to 1970 EXCEPT this one.

24. **(F)** The author is presenting and supporting an argument; the point of the passage is to *persuade* people that it is short-sighted to selectively edit Kahlo's biography and to focus more on that biography than on her work. The last sentence of the first paragraph and the first and last sentences of the last paragraph all present assertions that the author is trying to support.

25. **(C)** Lines 48–50 establish that the quality of Kahlo's work severely declined due to her abuse of alcohol and painkillers.

26. **(J)** *Warts* in line 55 is a metaphor for *the less pleasant parts of Kahlo's life*. The expression "warts and all" means to describe someone fully, including their negative qualities. The sentence avowedly concerns *biography*, and the rest of the paragraph concentrates on Kahlo's personal flaws.

27. **(C)** The passage never says anything about *any* of Kahlo's paintings being self-portraits, and certainly does not imply that *all* of them were. All of the answer choices are true EXCEPT this one.

28. **(G)** The purpose of the passage is to convince Kahlo enthusiasts—specifically feminist women—to acknowledge a more complete picture of the artist's life. The last sentence of the first paragraph, the first sentence of the last paragraph, and the last sentence of the last paragraph are all paraphrases of this exhortation.

29. **(D)** The first paragraph, and especially its last sentence, establish that the author thinks people are paying far too much attention to Kahlo's life and not enough to her work. In the last paragraph, line 70 explicitly states that *the really tragic part of Kahlo's story* is how much her biography overshadows her work. The other three answer choices are all biographical details, and focusing on them is exactly what the author says people should *not* do. (As with many places on the ACT, "which of these things is not like the others" is a good strategy here!)

30. **(F)** If the author thinks it should be *swept away*, then we know that the *sideshow* must refer to all the things the author wants people to pay *less* attention to: the dramatic details of Kahlo's life.

31. **(B)** Although he doesn't seem especially angry about it or necessarily want things to be any different, the author would clearly agree with the simple fact that science-fiction films can misinform people about how certain principles work in real life. (Well, don't they?) The last sentence of paragraph 1 and the first few sentences of paragraph 3 make this pretty clear.

32. **(J)** The author opens the paragraph by deriding the idea of a plasma's being "directed" (that's why it's in quotation marks), before going on to explain that this is because a plasma is basically a gas.

33. **(A)** Lines 49–50 explicitly state that the *aurora borealis*, or "northern lights," is composed of plasma.

34. **(J)** *Convoluted* means "hard to follow or make sense of," and if one is speaking casually, then *confusing* works as a synonym (remember, the author's point here is that the explanation makes no sense).

35. **(C)** The author doesn't seem especially emotionally invested in this debate one way or the other (he is simply calmly analyzing the issue), and so it is probably best to say that he would simply be "interested" in the new opportunities in the quest for real lightsabers.

36. **(G)** The author opens the paragraph with a joke about how the explanation in the previous paragraph made no sense, and goes on to mock the idea of compact crystal batteries powerful enough to generate plasma, as well as the fact that even the writers of the extended *Star Wars* universe themselves seem to know how ridiculous this is, since they bothered to specify that the crystals must, in effect, be rendered magical by the mystical Jedi and Sith warriors in some sort of meditation ritual.

37. **(A)** The author spends lines 31–45 mocking the idea that crystals could play any role whatsoever in the generation, direction, or containment of plasma.

38. **(F)** The passage establishes repeatedly in lines 55–63 that plasmas can indeed be contained by magnetic fields.

39. **(B)** The author closes the paragraph by stating that enthusiastic *Star Wars* "superfans" will probably never abandon the quest for a real lightsaber.

40. **(H)** Although the idea that laser or plasma "blades" would just pass through each other like the beams of two flashlights has often been suggested as an obstacle to real lightsabers, this particular passage never brings this up.

Answer Explanations: Science Test

1. **(D)** If there were a correlation one way or the other between mass and orbital distance, then the planets in Table 2 would be getting either consistently larger or smaller as the orbital distances increase. But they're not: there are large and small planets all over the place. For example, the two largest planets have orbital distances of 4.0 and .35, whereas the two smallest planets have orbital distances of 4.0 and .25. Therefore, there is no correlation between mass and orbital distance.
2. **(F)** By looking at Table 1, we know that the answer has to be either OGLE TR 132 or Gliese 777, because those are the two stars with Gas Giants orbiting them. Next, we look at Table 2 and see that the planet orbiting Gliese 777 (500 Earth masses) is bigger than the planet orbiting OGLE TR 132 (315 Earth masses).
3. **(D)** Table 1 establishes the only planet type with a mass over 250 Earth masses and composed of hydrogen is a Gas Giant.
4. **(G)** Table 1 shows the planets orbiting Gliese 581 are Water type with a mass range of .5–25 Earth masses. Also, Table 2 shows the most massive planet is orbiting Gliese 777. Therefore, the statement is NOT true and must be correct.
5. **(A)** Every planet shown in Table 2 has a mass less than 20 Earth masses. The Kepler 11 planet has a mass of 15 and the HD 6980 planet has a mass of 15.
6. **(F)** All you have to do here is go to Figure 1, look at the (vertical) column for Zone 5, and find the biggest number. The biggest number is 0.93, which is in the (horizontal) column for coal.
7. **(B)** The numbers across zones vary more in Table 1 (energy savings) than they do in Table 2 (GHGs avoided). In Table 2, the numbers for all three zones are often identical, and are still very close even when they are not identical.
8. **(J)** In Figure 1, the black bar representing GHG payback for Zone 3 stops just under the line representing 10 years, and so 9 years is clearly the closest of the answer choices.
9. **(D)** All the question is asking is "Which box in Table 1 has the highest number in it, not counting averages and totals?" The highest number is 4.2, representing the savings for natural gas in Zone 1.
10. **(J)** The bars in Figure 1 represent how long it takes to profit from the installation of plastic foam insulation. Since both the white and black bars in Zone 3 have "run out" by the 10-year mark, this means that at that point the customer will have both saved on energy costs and produced fewer pounds of GHGs.
11. **(A)** In Table 1, the three highest numbers in the U.S. Average column, starting with the highest and decreasing, are for natural gas (2.37), coal (0.76), and nuclear (0.25).
12. **(H)** In Table 1, the numbers in the Resistance column get bigger trial by trial, and the numbers in the Current column get smaller trial by trial. Therefore, as the resistance increased, the current decreased.
13. **(B)** This is a simple "Go Up, Hit Line, Go Over" question. In Figure 2, a diameter of 0.5 mm would be a little less than halfway between .41 and .68 mm. Moving upward from this point to the black line, we hit it somewhere around the line representing a resistance of 1 ohm. (The answer can also be gotten by looking at Table 2 and doing math, but getting it from Figure 2 is easier.)
14. **(G)** In Experiment 2, the student uses three different wires of varying diameters.
15. **(C)** Both Table 1 and Table 2 show current decreasing as resistance increases, and vice versa. Remembering the answer to question 12 would be a big help here. (It is often the case on the ACT Science that two questions in the same passage will be closely related!)
16. **(F)** $V = IR$ from the opening paragraph and Experiment 2 establishes that the largest diameter will allow the greatest current. Therefore, the largest voltage from the choices and the largest diameter would be 5 volts and a .5-mm diameter.
17. **(C)** We know from Table 2 that as diameter increases and resistance decreases the current increases. The current closest to 5 amperes is 4.91 amperes; therefore, we need a diameter of 1.04 mm and a resistance of 0.20 ohms.
18. **(F)** This is correct because of the data presented in Table 2. The third column has the heading "River Water." The largest number in that column is the first one, 1.50. The first row represents Trial 1.

19. **(B)** This is correct because of the data presented in Table 3. To find the correct answer, the values for the columns with the headings PO_4 must be compared—the one on the left side of the table under "Added μg/ml" and the one on the right side of the table under "Found μg/ml." For Trial 2 the amount under "Found μg/ml" is 1.56, whereas the number under "Added μg/ml" is 2.00.

20. **(H)** This is correct because of the data presented in Table 1. Compare the values in the three columns under the heading "Mg." For every trial the value under the concentration 2.5 ppm is the highest, whereas the value under the concentration 4.0 ppm is in the middle, and the value under the concentration 4.5 ppm is the lowest.

21. **(B)** This is correct because of the data presented in Table 2. Find the smallest number in the table. It is 0.50, found in the column for PO_4 and the row for Trial 3, making this the correct answer.

22. **(J)** This is correct because of the data presented in Table 1. For Trials 1–4, each subsequent trial used a higher concentration of SO_4. Compare this to the values in the column with the heading "4.5 ppm" to see that as the SO_4 concentration increased, the amount of Mg absorbed also increased.

23. **(B)** In the third sentence of her first paragraph, Researcher 2 mentions ozone as one of the air pollutants that had their concentrations lowered by a decrease in traffic, which also led to a decrease in asthma-related emergencies. Therefore, she would expect a decrease in ozone levels to lead to a decrease in the prevalence of asthma.

24. **(H)** Researcher 1 thinks that asthma is caused by allergens, and mentions dogs and cats as being among these allergens in the middle of her first paragraph. Therefore, she would view pet owners as more likely to have asthma.

25. **(A)** In her second paragraph, Researcher 1 states that high IgE levels and asthma are positively correlated, and that a "high" IgE level is considered to be one above 200 IU/ml. Therefore, she would regard someone with an IgE level of 400 IU/ml as being significantly at risk for asthma.

26. **(J)** In her first paragraph, Researcher 1 names indoor allergens as a cause of asthma, and suggests that less exposure to outside air increased the detrimental effects of these allergens (*Houses are built more tightly and are better insulated*). Therefore, she would expect *more circulation* and *more outside air* to lessen the prevalence of asthma.

27. **(D)** Researcher 1 blames asthma on indoor allergens, and Researcher 2 blames asthma on air pollution. Since these are both things that people can do something about, both researchers would agree that *measures can be taken to lower a person's risk of developing asthma.*

28. **(G)** Researcher 2 names CO as one of the air pollutants linked to high rates of asthma-related emergencies. Therefore, she would expect CO concentration and asthma rates to increase concurrently. Only choice G depicts a graph where CO and cases of asthma increase together, as indicated by the line going steadily upward from left to right.

29. **(C)** Researcher 2 regards air pollution (of which high ozone levels are a component) as a cause of asthma. Therefore, she would expect asthma rates to have been lower 20 years ago when there was less air pollution (including lower ozone levels).

30. **(F)** Right above the point on the x-axis (horizontal) of Figure 1 that indicates 1954, the line that is the highest (just above 500) is the one with diamonds on it, representing alewives.

31. **(B)** Figure 4 indicates that, in 2004, bloaters comprised 43% of the fish population of Lake Michigan, and sculpin 33%. So there were indeed more bloaters than sculpin.

32. **(J)** The 155-mm bar in the 2002 graph (Figure 2) is almost up to the 40% mark, clearly higher than the 155-mm bar in the 2004 graph (Figure 3), which is not even up to the 20% mark. Therefore, there were *not* more 155-mm alewives in 2004 than in 2002, and so choice J is the statement that is NOT true.

33. **(B)** The question states that alewives get increasingly longer with age. Since Figure 3 (representing 2004) shows us more long and fewer short alewives than does Figure 2 (representing 2002), it would appear that Lake Michigan had more adult alewives in 2004 than in 2002. You may have also noticed that the other three choices all say the same thing. (As with many questions on the ACT, "which of these things is not like the others" is a good strategy here!)

34. **(H)** Figure 1 shows that the density of bloater fish (triangle line) increased steadily up until about 1973, and then decreased steadily from that point until around 2003. Although it is not conclusive proof, these data are consistent with the idea that the bloater population fluctuates according to a 60-year cycle.

35. **(A)** If the new vaccine introduced in 1991 had really been more effective, then rates of pertussis would have dropped thereafter, but instead they increased (the line starts going upward). Therefore, the data in Figure 2 do not support this claim.

36. **(H)** According to Figure 1, the only stage in which someone would have a cough *and* be contagious is the paroxysmal stage. Although Figure 1 establishes that medication can significantly shorten the period of time that one is contagious, the fact that the person in the question is medicated is superfluous information. (Questions on the ACT Science frequently provide more information than is necessary to answer the question!)
37. **(C)** Figure 1 states that the two stages in which a patient is contagious are the catarrhal and the paroxysmal. It also shows that the maximum amount of time the catarrhal stage can last is 2 weeks, and that the maximum amount of time the paroxysmal stage can last is 6 weeks. Therefore, the maximum amount of time a patient can be contagious is 8 weeks.
38. **(G)** The highest bars in Figure 3 are the ones representing the 10–14 and 15–19 age groups, and so Figure 3 does not support the idea that young children are the most susceptible to pertussis.
39. **(D)** The claim that vaccine immunity wanes after 5–10 years is consistent with the data in Figure 3, which indicates the greatest numbers of pertussis cases are in children ages 10–19.
40. **(H)** Figure 1 states that antibiotics make a big difference in how long pertussis communicability lasts. Therefore, the assertion that pertussis cannot be treated with antibiotics is the one that is NOT true.

Writing Sample

Intellectual curiosity is a hallmark of human nature, and the freedom to explore that curiosity in whatever ways one sees fit has always been a cherished American value. In some other cultures, young people are taught simply to obey, but in this country the young are encouraged to think for themselves. This is why adults and schools are always encouraging young people to read, read, read. For as far back as I can remember, I've been exposed to rhetoric about how books could open new doors and take me to new worlds. But now I hear that some of my fellow citizens are criticizing libraries for allowing people under 18 to check out books containing violence, bad language, or explicit content. On some level, I can understand where these people are coming from, but I am here to deliver the good news that their fears are unfounded. For one thing, a young person would have to be pretty smart in the first place to even know about the objectionable books, so the kids who are not mature enough to handle those books wouldn't even know about them. Secondly, even if a kid who was immature somehow got wind of some spicy book full of inappropriate content, he's not going to bother to read it for that reason alone when he can find much worse on the internet. And even if, for the sake of argument, we imagine that young people are checking out age-inappropriate library books left and right, people have the right to read whatever they like in this country. America has always been opposed to censorship, because the people who founded this nation knew that censorship is a Pandora's Box, and that things can quickly get out of hand once it is opened.

It is undeniable that there are many brilliant and influential works that contain mature elements. There are lots of bawdy jokes in the works of Shakespeare, there is tons of graphic violence in the Bible, and most famous writers have been using words that are considered bad language since the early 20th century. In fact, I can hardly think of one work of great literature that doesn't contain something that someone might find objectionable. That is simply the nature of art. In my experience, however, anyone who is actually studious enough to sit down and read great literature is also mature enough to handle the content properly. It's not the young people who read too much that we need to worry about—it is the young people who don't read enough! While I can't deny that some of my peers would not be able to deal with mature content properly, this is a moot point because these kids wouldn't even know what books to find it in. Anyone who thinks that teenagers are going to come streaming into libraries and start a riot just because a bad word appears near the end of "The Catcher in the Rye" is delusional. We read that book in school and the bad students still didn't read it, so why would they go get it from the library of their own free will just because there is a bad word? I guarantee you that any of the things people are worried about young people seeing in books, they already saw and heard in movies long before they were old enough to read the books. Far from making a rule against it, I think that making young people aware of the mature content in great literature would be the best thing we could do for them! If that's what it takes to get them to read, then so be it.

Maybe the people in favor of this rule believe that some teenagers are so determined to find inappropriate material of some kind that they would just flip through the great books looking for bad words and such without even reading them. Well, I suppose I can't deny that some of my peers really are that immature and that obsessed with finding inappropriate material. But what I can tell you for certain is that the library is the last place they would go looking for it. Nowadays, nearly every kid has a computer with internet access right in his or her room. Every teenager I know, including myself, had already seen and read more inappropriate things on the internet by the age of twelve than you could probably find in any book in the library. Immature people are in the habit of taking the path of least resistance, so I guarantee you that the number of adolescents who are going to ride their bikes all the way to the library just to find a book with some sex or bad words in it is exactly zero. Maybe there were kids who did this years ago, but times have changed. There is absolutely no reason to ruin things for those young people who genuinely want to read great works for the right reasons. I am barely seventeen, and if I were suddenly not allowed to get books by Ernest Hemingway or James Joyce from the library just because some other people my age can't handle them, I would be furious. All you'd be doing is forcing me to spend money on those books at a bookstore, since bookstores don't have such restrictions. What is the sense in punishing the bright students by preventing them from reading for free?

I feel strongly that people should not be criticizing the library for letting young people check out whatever books they want. The kids who are not mature enough to read them will not know about the books in the first place, no immature kid who just wants to see scandalous things will bother to go to the library instead of the Internet, and America was founded on the principle that people have a right to read whatever they like and censorship is a road to nowhere.

Answer Sheet

PRACTICE TEST 2

Directions: Mark one answer only for each question. Make the mark dark. Erase completely any mark made in error. (Additional or stray marks will be counted as mistakes.)

English Test

1 A B C D	21 A B C D	41 A B C D	61 A B C D
2 F G H J	22 F G H J	42 F G H J	62 F G H J
3 A B C D	23 A B C D	43 A B C D	63 A B C D
4 F G H J	24 F G H J	44 F G H J	64 F G H J
5 A B C D	25 A B C D	45 A B C D	65 A B C D
6 F G H J	26 F G H J	46 F G H J	66 F G H J
7 A B C D	27 A B C D	47 A B C D	67 A B C D
8 F G H J	28 F G H J	48 F G H J	68 F G H J
9 A B C D	29 A B C D	49 A B C D	69 A B C D
10 F G H J	30 F G H J	50 F G H J	70 F G H J
11 A B C D	31 A B C D	51 A B C D	71 A B C D
12 F G H J	32 F G H J	52 F G H J	72 F G H J
13 A B C D	33 A B C D	53 A B C D	73 A B C D
14 F G H J	34 F G H J	54 F G H J	74 F G H J
15 A B C D	35 A B C D	55 A B C D	75 A B C D
16 F G H J	36 F G H J	56 F G H J	
17 A B C D	37 A B C D	57 A B C D	
18 F G H J	38 F G H J	58 F G H J	
19 A B C D	39 A B C D	59 A B C D	
20 F G H J	40 F G H J	60 F G H J	

Math Test

1 A B C D E	16 F G H J K	31 A B C D E	46 F G H J K
2 F G H J K	17 A B C D E	32 F G H J K	47 A B C D E
3 A B C D E	18 F G H J K	33 A B C D E	48 F G H J K
4 F G H J K	19 A B C D E	34 F G H J K	49 A B C D E
5 A B C D E	20 F G H J K	35 A B C D E	50 F G H J K
6 F G H J K	21 A B C D E	36 F G H J K	51 A B C D E
7 A B C D E	22 F G H J K	37 A B C D E	52 F G H J K
8 F G H J K	23 A B C D E	38 F G H J K	53 A B C D E
9 A B C D E	24 F G H J K	39 A B C D E	54 F G H J K
10 F G H J K	25 A B C D E	40 F G H J K	55 A B C D E
11 A B C D E	26 F G H J K	41 A B C D E	56 F G H J K
12 F G H J K	27 A B C D E	42 F G H J K	57 A B C D E
13 A B C D E	28 F G H J K	43 A B C D E	58 F G H J K
14 F G H J K	29 A B C D E	44 F G H J K	59 A B C D E
15 A B C D E	30 F G H J K	45 A B C D E	60 F G H J K

Answer Sheet

PRACTICE TEST 2

Reading Test

1 Ⓐ Ⓑ Ⓒ Ⓓ	11 Ⓐ Ⓑ Ⓒ Ⓓ	21 Ⓐ Ⓑ Ⓒ Ⓓ	31 Ⓐ Ⓑ Ⓒ Ⓓ
2 Ⓕ Ⓖ Ⓗ Ⓙ	12 Ⓕ Ⓖ Ⓗ Ⓙ	22 Ⓕ Ⓖ Ⓗ Ⓙ	32 Ⓕ Ⓖ Ⓗ Ⓙ
3 Ⓐ Ⓑ Ⓒ Ⓓ	13 Ⓐ Ⓑ Ⓒ Ⓓ	23 Ⓐ Ⓑ Ⓒ Ⓓ	33 Ⓐ Ⓑ Ⓒ Ⓓ
4 Ⓕ Ⓖ Ⓗ Ⓙ	14 Ⓕ Ⓖ Ⓗ Ⓙ	24 Ⓕ Ⓖ Ⓗ Ⓙ	34 Ⓕ Ⓖ Ⓗ Ⓙ
5 Ⓐ Ⓑ Ⓒ Ⓓ	15 Ⓐ Ⓑ Ⓒ Ⓓ	25 Ⓐ Ⓑ Ⓒ Ⓓ	35 Ⓐ Ⓑ Ⓒ Ⓓ
6 Ⓕ Ⓖ Ⓗ Ⓙ	16 Ⓕ Ⓖ Ⓗ Ⓙ	26 Ⓕ Ⓖ Ⓗ Ⓙ	36 Ⓕ Ⓖ Ⓗ Ⓙ
7 Ⓐ Ⓑ Ⓒ Ⓓ	17 Ⓐ Ⓑ Ⓒ Ⓓ	27 Ⓐ Ⓑ Ⓒ Ⓓ	37 Ⓐ Ⓑ Ⓒ Ⓓ
8 Ⓕ Ⓖ Ⓗ Ⓙ	18 Ⓕ Ⓖ Ⓗ Ⓙ	28 Ⓕ Ⓖ Ⓗ Ⓙ	38 Ⓕ Ⓖ Ⓗ Ⓙ
9 Ⓐ Ⓑ Ⓒ Ⓓ	19 Ⓐ Ⓑ Ⓒ Ⓓ	29 Ⓐ Ⓑ Ⓒ Ⓓ	39 Ⓐ Ⓑ Ⓒ Ⓓ
10 Ⓕ Ⓖ Ⓗ Ⓙ	20 Ⓕ Ⓖ Ⓗ Ⓙ	30 Ⓕ Ⓖ Ⓗ Ⓙ	40 Ⓕ Ⓖ Ⓗ Ⓙ

Science Test

1 Ⓐ Ⓑ Ⓒ Ⓓ	11 Ⓐ Ⓑ Ⓒ Ⓓ	21 Ⓐ Ⓑ Ⓒ Ⓓ	31 Ⓐ Ⓑ Ⓒ Ⓓ
2 Ⓕ Ⓖ Ⓗ Ⓙ	12 Ⓕ Ⓖ Ⓗ Ⓙ	22 Ⓕ Ⓖ Ⓗ Ⓙ	32 Ⓕ Ⓖ Ⓗ Ⓙ
3 Ⓐ Ⓑ Ⓒ Ⓓ	13 Ⓐ Ⓑ Ⓒ Ⓓ	23 Ⓐ Ⓑ Ⓒ Ⓓ	33 Ⓐ Ⓑ Ⓒ Ⓓ
4 Ⓕ Ⓖ Ⓗ Ⓙ	14 Ⓕ Ⓖ Ⓗ Ⓙ	24 Ⓕ Ⓖ Ⓗ Ⓙ	34 Ⓕ Ⓖ Ⓗ Ⓙ
5 Ⓐ Ⓑ Ⓒ Ⓓ	15 Ⓐ Ⓑ Ⓒ Ⓓ	25 Ⓐ Ⓑ Ⓒ Ⓓ	35 Ⓐ Ⓑ Ⓒ Ⓓ
6 Ⓕ Ⓖ Ⓗ Ⓙ	16 Ⓕ Ⓖ Ⓗ Ⓙ	26 Ⓕ Ⓖ Ⓗ Ⓙ	36 Ⓕ Ⓖ Ⓗ Ⓙ
7 Ⓐ Ⓑ Ⓒ Ⓓ	17 Ⓐ Ⓑ Ⓒ Ⓓ	27 Ⓐ Ⓑ Ⓒ Ⓓ	37 Ⓐ Ⓑ Ⓒ Ⓓ
8 Ⓕ Ⓖ Ⓗ Ⓙ	18 Ⓕ Ⓖ Ⓗ Ⓙ	28 Ⓕ Ⓖ Ⓗ Ⓙ	38 Ⓕ Ⓖ Ⓗ Ⓙ
9 Ⓐ Ⓑ Ⓒ Ⓓ	19 Ⓐ Ⓑ Ⓒ Ⓓ	29 Ⓐ Ⓑ Ⓒ Ⓓ	39 Ⓐ Ⓑ Ⓒ Ⓓ
10 Ⓕ Ⓖ Ⓗ Ⓙ	20 Ⓕ Ⓖ Ⓗ Ⓙ	30 Ⓕ Ⓖ Ⓗ Ⓙ	40 Ⓕ Ⓖ Ⓗ Ⓙ

Practice Test 2

ENGLISH TEST

45 MINUTES—75 QUESTIONS

Directions: In the five passages that follow, certain words and phrases are underlined and numbered. In the right-hand column, you will find alternatives for the underlined part. In most cases, you are to choose the one that best expresses the idea, makes the statement appropriate for standard written English, or is worded most consistently with the style and tone of the passage as a whole. If you think the original version is best, choose "NO CHANGE." In some cases, you will find in the right-hand column a question about the underlined part. You are to choose the best answer to the question.

You will also find questions about a section of the passage, or about the passage as a whole. These questions do not refer to an underlined portion of the passage, but rather are identified by a number or numbers in a box.

For each question, choose the alternative you consider best and fill in the corresponding oval on your answer document. Read each passage through once before you begin to answer the questions that accompany it. For many of the questions, you must read several sentences beyond the question to determine the answer. Be sure that you have read far enough ahead each time you choose an alternative.

Passage I

Why I Ride a Bicycle

I waited thirty-two years before I rode a bicycle for the first time, down a tree-lined street in Toronto. I had barely sat on one before, so there were a few false starts as my boyfriend Stephen called [1] out instructions beside me. But then I found I was moving. And since I, more than most objects, seem to obey Newton's first law of motion—an object in motion will remain in motion until acted upon by an external force—off I went, whizzing downhill, weaving like a drunk, and smiled [2] idiotically. I didn't stop until three blocks later; where [3] a car was speeding toward the intersection. I'd not yet learned to brake, so I just dropped both feet to the ground

1. **A.** NO CHANGE
   B. boyfriend, Stephen called
   C. boyfriend Stephen, called
   D. boyfriend, called

2. **F.** NO CHANGE
   G. smiling
   H. had been smiling
   J. smiles

3. **A.** NO CHANGE
   B. later. Where
   C. later, where
   D. later, and—when

GO ON TO THE NEXT PAGE.

inelegantly. Then I got back on the bicycle and did the whole thing again.

I don't know why I'd never learned to ride before, a rite of passage that most people <u>understand</u> [4] somewhere around age six. Clearly, not all middle-class parents in India teach <u>they're</u> [5] children to ride bicycles. Mine certainly didn't. I had singing lessons and, briefly, dancing lessons. I had math tutors and physics tutors. I even had swimming lessons but no bicycles.

It's strange to come to this mysterious activity as an adult. Most people my age <u>are riding</u> [6] for so long they give little thought to an act that is nothing short of miraculous. But getting on a bike for the first time at thirty-three reveals the triumph of physics and human will that is cycling. Five hundred years ago, someone (the tireless Leonardo da Vinci, it was thought) drew a sketch of what was meant to be the <u>world's first bicycle,</u> [7] though both sketch and artist are now disputed. [8] Since then we've had the "walking machine" (Baron von Drais of Sauerbrun's wooden two-wheeled contraption without pedals, designed to aid walkers—a bicycle even I could have ridden), velocipedes, ordinaries, and high-wheel tricycles. <u>They are all results</u> [9] of engineering and machine-age design, but also of something more intangible.

4. **F.** NO CHANGE
   G. experience
   H. practice
   J. need

5. **A.** NO CHANGE
   B. there
   C. their
   D. one's

6. **F.** NO CHANGE
   G. rode
   H. had ridden
   J. have been riding

7. **A.** NO CHANGE
   B. worlds first bicycle
   C. world's first bicycle
   D. worlds first bicycle,

8. The writer is considering adding the following true statement:

   The sketch was done in pencil and charcoal.

   Should the writer make this addition here?
   F. Yes, because it helps support the idea that bicycles have an important place in history.
   G. Yes, because it provides necessary insight into the variety of bicycles that exist.
   H. No, because it is not relevant to the narrative at this point in the essay.
   J. No, because this information has already been presented elsewhere in the essay.

9. Given that all of the choices are true, which one most strongly reinforces the writer's attitude that bicycles are amazing inventions?
   A. Each is a marvel
   B. They are debacles
   C. Each is a creation
   D. Each is a product

1 ■ ■ ■ ■ ■ ■ ■ ■ 1

The saying that to ride on a bicycle is to balance upon two tubes of rubber and wire, connected by a frame, and to propel them forward with no more than a little foot power and the conviction that you can. We think bicycles carry us forward, but they don't, we carry them. It is largely human will that keep bicycle and rider in motion, as well as that law of Newton's, that it can be adapted into an exhortation: move, because if you are moving, you will keep moving. [15]

10. Which choice provides the most concise and stylistically effective wording here?
  - **F.** NO CHANGE
  - **G.** Operating a bicycle one can say
  - **H.** A person riding a bicycle
  - **J.** To operate a bicycle

11. Which of the following alternatives to the underlined portion would be LEAST acceptable?
  - **A.** NO CHANGE
  - **B.** on top of
  - **C.** atop
  - **D.** on which

12. **F.** NO CHANGE
  - **G.** don't we must carry
  - **H.** don't: we carry
  - **J.** don't, we are carrying

13. **A.** NO CHANGE
  - **B.** by keeping
  - **C.** keeps
  - **D.** kept

14. **F.** NO CHANGE
  - **G.** Newton's Law, which can
  - **H.** Newton's Law which is
  - **J.** Newton's Law and that can

15. The writer is considering concluding the essay with the following statement:

    How much of our lives are lived like this?

    Should the writer end the essay with this statement?
  - **A.** Yes, because it adds to the writer's persuasive goal of convincing the reader to learn to ride a bicycle.
  - **B.** Yes, because it sums up the main points of the essay in a memorable way.
  - **C.** No, because it does not have a meaningful connection to the topic of this essay.
  - **D.** No, because it conflicts with the overall tone and message of this essay.

Passage II

I Give Update

Everyone talks about how social networking sites like Facebook have brought us together and aloud us to connect with friends 24 hours a day. To some people, however, this "connecting" is more complicated than it looks. Sometimes I'll stare at that blank status-update

16. **F.** NO CHANGE
  - **G.** have brought to us
  - **H.** has brought to us
  - **J.** has brought us

17. **A.** NO CHANGE
  - **B.** aloud us too
  - **C.** allowed us to
  - **D.** allowed us too

GO ON TO THE NEXT PAGE.

box for half an hour trying to think of what to type, and usually I just give up without typing anything. <u>This strikes me as odd,</u> [18] considering that I'm a professional writer. Back in school, the other kids used to beg me for help with their English papers, so why am I suddenly the only one who <u>can't remember most of the grammatical rules?</u> [19]

<u>I've always hated computers</u>. [20] After all, other people's status updates aren't especially brilliant or interesting, and nobody seems to mind. Sometimes, they don't even make sense. "Sitting in Starbucks LOL?" What the heck is up with that? Are you really sitting in a Starbucks, laughing out loud? Doesn't <u>everyone think you're</u> [21] insane?

It feels like I'm the only <u>one has</u> [22] figured out that "social networking" is really just a big competition for attention, with success measured in the number of comments other people leave on your updates. <u>Theirs</u> [23] nothing wrong with competition, but some people have such a big advantage in this one that it's not even fun to play. A pretty girl can type "Bought a new swimsuit today!" and get 35 comments in about six minutes. I'm just as interested in pretty <u>girls swimsuits</u> [24] as the next guy, but come on. I didn't get 35 comments when I announced that my first book was being published. Maybe I should have announced it from a Starbucks, in which I was laughing out loud.

18. Which of the following choices would provide the most logical opening to this sentence?
    F. NO CHANGE
    G. My life has always been like this,
    H. I have everybody fooled,
    J. Nobody is very interested in what I have to say anyway,

19. Which of the following choices would provide the most logical conclusion to this sentence?
    A. NO CHANGE
    B. spends most of his time online?
    C. cares about what other people think?
    D. can't think of anything to say?

20. Given that all of the choices are true, which one would make the most logical opening for this paragraph?
    F. NO CHANGE
    G. Maybe I'm overthinking this.
    H. Obviously, there are more productive things I could be doing with my time.
    J. As everyone knows nowadays, Facebook was developed by Mark Zuckerberg at Harvard in 2003.

21. **A.** NO CHANGE
    B. everyone thinks you're
    C. everyone think your
    D. everyone thinks your

22. **F.** NO CHANGE
    G. one had
    H. one whose
    J. one who's

23. **A.** NO CHANGE
    B. Theres
    C. There's
    D. Their's

24. **F.** NO CHANGE
    G. girl's swimsuits
    H. girls' swimsuits
    J. girl's swimsuit's

Practice Test 2

It's all so depressing.[25]

Being depressed[26] would at least give me something to type, if not for the fact that depressing status updates are looked down upon. Social networking isn't just about attention; it's also[27] about making other people think, which you're having more fun there then.[28] I'm starting to wonder how many status updates are even true. Did that person really just have "the best day ever" or just get back from "the best party ever," or does he just want everyone to think he did? It would certainly be ironic if a program designed to help us connect with friends has instead forced us to spend all our[29] time lying to them. I've spent so much time thinking about this, I could probably write a book. Unfortunately, nobody would care, so I think instead I'll just go buy a swimsuit.

25. **A.** NO CHANGE
    B. Its' also
    C. Its all so
    D. Its also

26. **F.** NO CHANGE
    G. It is depressed
    H. It is depressing
    J. I am depressed

27. Which of the following alternatives to the underlined portion would NOT be acceptable?
    A. attention. It is also
    B. attention, you see, it's also
    C. attention, you see; it's also
    D. attention—it's also

28. **F.** NO CHANGE
    G. think that your having more fun than there.
    H. think, which your having more fun then theirs.
    J. think that you're having more fun than they are.

29. **A.** NO CHANGE
    B. is
    C. are
    D. hour

Question 30 asks about the preceding passage as a whole.

30. Suppose the writer's goal had been to write a brief essay arguing in favor of increased legal regulation of people's online behavior. Would this essay fulfill that goal?
    F. Yes, because the author established that other people's online behavior lowers his self-esteem, which constitutes cyberbullying.
    G. Yes, because the author clearly doesn't like the way people act on social networking sites, which logically means he must want it to be illegal.
    H. No, because the author does not sound angry, and therefore this cannot be an argumentative essay.
    J. No, because the essay never mentions legal regulations or implies that the government needs to get involved in the matter.

Passage III

The Rodeo

I could hear their whispers as we begun [31] cantering around the rodeo grounds after our number was called. "I can't believe she's riding that horse in this competition. Look at him!" Monte snorted as if he heard their collective voices in the wind. Yet his head was up, proud as ever and [32] so was mine, hearing a stronger, unwavering voice.

If the truth were told, he [33] wasn't the most beautiful horse in the world. [34]

Naturally, [35] Monte had learned a grace that could only have come from sheer spirit and determination.

[1]"No way! No way!" [2] My butt firmly in the saddle, my back straight, and the reins held just right, we smoothly turned into the barrels. [3] Western equitation had been [36] as unfamiliar to Monte and me as five forks in a place setting at an upscale restaurant. [4] The voices in the wind followed us as Monte galloped faster around the ring. [5] Far from the bareback rides across the desert we had cherished over the years,

31. **A.** NO CHANGE
    B. beginning
    C. begin
    D. began

32. **F.** NO CHANGE
    G. up, proud as ever, and
    H. up proud as ever, and
    J. up proud as ever and

33. **A.** NO CHANGE
    B. were, told he
    C. were told; he
    D. were told he,

34. At this point, the writer is considering adding the following sentence:

    His huge workhorse body and thoroughbred legs made him appear clumsy and out of proportion.

    Would this be a relevant addition to make here?

    F. Yes, because it provides clarity about why Monte is so graceful.
    G. Yes, because it adds details relevant to the focus of the paragraph.
    H. No, because it provides a digression that leads the paragraph away from its primary focus.
    J. No, because the information is already provided elsewhere in the passage.

35. **A.** NO CHANGE
    B. In fact,
    C. Meanwhile,
    D. Yet

36. **F.** NO CHANGE
    G. is
    H. will be
    J. has been

1 ■ ■ ■ ■ ■ ■ ■ ■ 1

we had learned (37) the rules and were making believers out of the crowd. [6] Monte, now almost on his side, was racing around the barrels as gracefully as if he had wings touched by angels, not grazing even one barrel. (38) [39]

I patted Monte's neck (40) as we cantered out of the ring and suddenly I didn't see or hear anyone accepting (41) my family. "No one will hurt your spirit but you," my grandfather's (42) voice echoed (43) in the gentle wind that kissed my cheeks and my spirit. Monte looked so proud when he and me (44) won first place.

37. Which of the following alternatives to the underlined portion would be LEAST acceptable?
   A. NO CHANGE
   B. beat
   C. mastered
   D. grasped

38. If the writer were to delete the underlined portion, placing a period after the word *angels*, the paragraph would primarily lose:
   F. an emphasis on how quickly Monte raced.
   G. information about how Monte was judged.
   H. an explanation for how Monte raced gracefully.
   J. an unnecessary detail.

39. For the sake of the logic and coherence of this paragraph, Sentence 4 should be placed:
   A. where it is now.
   B. before Sentence 2.
   C. after Sentence 2.
   D. after Sentence 6.

40. Given that all of the choices are true, which one most effectively introduces the action in this paragraph while suggesting the writer's nervousness?
   F. NO CHANGE
   G. I proudly held up my head
   H. I dropped the reins
   J. I glanced anxiously at the crowd

41. **A.** NO CHANGE
   B. accept for
   C. except for
   D. excepting

42. **F.** NO CHANGE
   G. grandfathers
   H. grandfathers'
   J. grandfather

43. **A.** NO CHANGE
   B. will echo
   C. echoing
   D. echoes

44. **F.** NO CHANGE
   G. he and I
   H. him and me
   J. him and I

Practice Test 2

GO ON TO THE NEXT PAGE.

Question 45 asks about the preceding passage as a whole.

45. Suppose that one of the writer's goals had been to illustrate that spirit and determination are just as important as inborn ability. Would this essay fulfill this goal?
   A. Yes, because Monte was a beautiful racehorse who helped the writer overcome her challenges.
   B. Yes, because the writer was able to win the race riding Monte, even though Monte wasn't born with grace.
   C. No, because the essay doesn't address inborn abilities.
   D. No, because neither Monte nor the writer demonstrated spirit and determination.

Passage IV

Not in Our Stars

I guess I can't blame people <u>from</u> [46] thousands of years ago for believing in astrology—there was simply <u>no way for them to now</u> [47] any better. But it's honestly incredible to me that, after all the knowledge science has given us about how the universe really works, there are still millions of people who eagerly read their horoscopes in the paper every morning and actually expect <u>them</u> [48] to mean anything. [49]

46. Which of the following alternatives to the underlined portion would be LEAST acceptable?
   F. in which
   G. who lived
   H. all those
   J. DELETE the underlined portion.

47. **A.** NO CHANGE
   B. know way for them to now
   C. no way for them to know
   D. now way for them to no

48. **F.** NO CHANGE
   G. it
   H. themselves
   J. DELETE the underlined portion.

49. At this point, the writer is considering adding the following sentence:

   > Just imagine if a newspaper ever accidentally printed the horoscopes under the wrong signs—people would be so confused, watching things happen to the wrong people all day!

   Should the writer add this sentence here?
   A. Yes, because it is a humorous way of illustrating the fact that horoscopes are meaningless.
   B. Yes, because this is something that might actually happen, and people deserve to be warned.
   C. No, because it is disrespectful to people who work in graphic design for newspapers.
   D. No, because it does not offer definitive proof that horoscopes do not accurately predict the future.

Even when I was little, I didn't believe in horoscopes. [50] We're all familiar with the twelve signs of the zodiac and the traits of people supposedly personally [51] born under different signs: a Pisces is emotional, a Taurus is stubborn, an Aquarius is clever. The problem, of course, is that these vague qualities can appear to apply to anyone. Who isn't emotional or stubborn at times? And all people *think* they're clever—even when they aren't! If only astrology made claims which were [52] a little more specific, we might be rid of it by now. For example, if "the stars" predicted that all Sagittarians would be left-handed, or that all Libras would have 20/20 vision, we would be able to test these claims, and astrology would fail. But since the only "test" involves people who *want* to believe in it decide [53] whether to apply broad compliments like "brave" or "insightful" to their friends and them, [54] astrology probably won't be going away anytime soon.

I can see how people centuries ago would be thinking [55] it was logical for heavenly bodies to "influence" events on Earth, but the funny part is that the math is all wrong. All of the star charts on which astrology is based were drawn up when people still thought that the Earth, rather than the sun, was at the center of the solar system. Plus, as Einstein figured out

50. Which of the following would make for the most logical opening to this paragraph?
    - **F.** NO CHANGE
    - **G.** Modern astronomy first became distinct from astrology in the second century.
    - **H.** I do have a few friends who believe in astrology, which has led to some amusing arguments.
    - **J.** I'm sure I don't need to explain what astrology is.

51. **A.** NO CHANGE
    - **B.** personality traits of people supposed to be
    - **C.** people's traits supposedly personally
    - **D.** supposed personality traits of people

52. **F.** NO CHANGE
    - **G.** claims, which were
    - **H.** claims that were
    - **J.** claims, that were

53. **A.** NO CHANGE
    - **B.** deciding
    - **C.** to decide
    - **D.** and decided

54. **F.** NO CHANGE
    - **G.** their friends and they,
    - **H.** their friends, and themselves,
    - **J.** themselves and their friends,

55. **A.** NO CHANGE
    - **B.** could've thought
    - **C.** should have thought
    - **D.** might of thought

Practice Test 2

anyway [56], the stars' apparent positions aren't really where they are, because the light they emit is bent by gravity before it reaches our eyes. So even if astrology were true, it would be full of mistakes! Luckily for astrologers, it's [57] all a bunch of nonsense, so nobody ever noticed.

I'm not ready for astrology to go away just yet, however, I [58] always enjoy meeting people who believe in it at a party. Once someone brings it up, I know it's only a matter of time before he or she asks me what my sign is, and my answer is always the same. "Well, you've been talking to me all night," I replied [59].

"Shouldn't you be able to tell?" [60]

56. The best placement for the underlined portion would be:
- **F.** where it is now.
- **G.** after the word *are* (but before the comma).
- **H.** after the word *emit*.
- **J.** after the word *gravity*.

57. **A.** NO CHANGE
- **B.** astrologers are
- **C.** astrologers, and
- **D.** astrologers, and it's

58. **F.** NO CHANGE
- **G.** yet, however I
- **H.** yet, however; I
- **J.** yet—however—I

59. **A.** NO CHANGE
- **B.** I'll reply.
- **C.** and I replied.
- **D.** and replied:

60. The writer is considering concluding the essay with the following statement:

> At the end of the day, though, I don't think anything annoys me as much as going into a bookstore and seeing all the space they waste with books on astrology.

Should the writer end the essay with this statement?
- **F.** Yes, because it is logical for a writer to end an essay with a reference to bookstores.
- **G.** Yes, because unnecessary books are a waste of trees and therefore bad for the environment.
- **H.** No, because this is an essay about people's superstitions, not how bookstores are arranged.
- **J.** No, because the previous sentence makes for a much more pointed and memorable ending.

Passage V

Gut Feelings

Intuitions or gut feelings, [61] are sudden, strong judgments whose origin they can't [62] immediately explain. Although they seem to emerge from an

61. **A.** NO CHANGE
- **B.** Intuitions, or gut feelings
- **C.** Intuitions, or gut feelings,
- **D.** Intuitions or gut feelings

62. **F.** NO CHANGE
- **G.** you can't
- **H.** people won't
- **J.** one doesn't

obscure inner force, they actually begin with a perception of something outside—a facial expression, a tone of voice, or a visual inconsistency so fleeting you're not even aware you <u>had noticed</u> [63] it.

63. **A.** NO CHANGE
B. notice
C. felt
D. feel

<u>Think of them</u> [64] as rapid cognition or condensed reasoning that takes advantage of the brain's built-in shortcuts. Or think of intuition as an unconscious associative process. [65]

64. **F.** NO CHANGE
G. Think of intuition
H. Think on it
J. Thinking of them

65. At this point, the writer is considering adding the following sentence:

> Long dismissed as magical or beneath the dignity of science, intuition appears to consist of fast mental operations.

Would this be a relevant addition to make here?
A. Yes, because it provides a needed transition between sentences.
B. Yes, because it finally provides the official definition of *intuition*.
C. No, because it contradicts the idea expressed in the following sentence.
D. No, because it provides a digression that leads the paragraph away from its primary focus.

<u>The best explanation psychologists now offer is</u> [66] that intuition is a mental matching game. The brain <u>takes in a situation, doing a very quick search</u> [67] of its files, and then finds its best analogy among the stored sprawl of memories and knowledge. Based on that <u>analogy, you</u> [68] ascribe meaning to the situation in front of you. A doctor might simply glance at a pallid young woman complaining of fatigue and shortness of breath and immediately intuit <u>one</u> [69] suffers from anemia.

66. Which phrase best introduces the sentence?
F. NO CHANGE
G. The only thing we know for sure is
H. The only possible explanation is
J. Psychologists now believe

67. **A.** NO CHANGE
B. takes in a situation, does a very quick search
C. took in a situation, doing a very quick search
D. take in a situation, does a very quick search

68. **F.** NO CHANGE
G. analogy: you
H. analogy—you
J. analogy; you

69. **A.** NO CHANGE
B. she
C. he
D. her

Practice Test 2

Experience is encoded in our brains as a web of fact and feeling. [70] When a new experience calls up a similar pattern, it doesn't unleash just stored knowledge but also an emotional state of mind and a predisposition to respond by it [71] in a certain way.

While endless reasoning in the absence of intuitions is unproductive, some people champion the other extreme—"going with the gut" at all times. [72]

Accordingly, [73] intuition is best used as the first step in solving a problem or deciding what to do. The more experience you have in a particular domain, the more reliable your intuitions, because they haven't been used many times before [74]. But even in your area of expertise, it's wisest to test out your hunches—you could easily have latched on to the wrong detail and pulled up the wrong web of associations in your brain. So pay attention to your intuition, because the information you received [75] is valid. But it's important to balance this with reason so that you don't make an error of judgment in an impulsive moment.

70. Which choice best illustrates how information is stored in our brains?
F. NO CHANGE
G. Everything we do is stored in our brain.
H. Experience is processed by our brain.
J. Our brain remembers all of our experiences.

71. **A.** NO CHANGE
B. respond
C. have responded
D. be responding

72. The writer is considering deleting this sentence. Should the sentence be kept or deleted?
F. Kept, because it is relevant to the discussion of where intuitions come from.
G. Kept, because it provides a useful introduction to the paragraph.
H. Deleted, because it contradicts the idea that people should pay attention to their intuitions.
J. Deleted, because it is stylistically inconsistent with the rest of the essay.

73. **A.** NO CHANGE
B. Also,
C. For instance,
D. But

74. Which phrase best supports the idea presented in this sentence?
F. NO CHANGE
G. because you haven't formed many situational analogies.
H. because they arise out of the richest array of collected patterns of experience.
J. because you should trust your unconscious mind.

75. **A.** NO CHANGE
B. have received
C. will be receiving
D. receive

STOP

If there is still time remaining, check your answers to this section.

2 △ △ △ △ △ △ △ △ 2

MATHEMATICS TEST

Directions: Solve each problem, choose the correct answer, and then fill in the corresponding oval on your answer document.

Do not linger over problems that take too much time. Solve as many as you can; then return to the others in the time you have left for this test.

You are permitted to use a calculator on this test. You may use your calculator for any problems you choose, but some of the problems may best be done without using a calculator.

Note: Unless otherwise stated, all of the following should be assumed.

1. Illustrative figures are NOT necessarily drawn to scale.
2. Geometric figures lie in a plane.
3. The word *line* indicates a straight line.
4. The word *average* indicates arithmetic mean.

DO YOUR FIGURING HERE.

1. What is the value of the expression $(y - x)^3$ when $x = 5$ and $y = 1$?

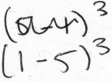

   A. -64
   B. -4
   C. 4
   D. 16
   E. 64

2. What is the smallest positive integer that is divisible by 3, divisible by 5, and divisible by 6 (with no remainders)?

   F. 15
   G. 30
   H. 60
   J. 90
   K. 180

3. If $[-s + h(t \cdot 3 - w)]r = 1$, then which of the following variables CANNOT equal 0?

   A. h
   B. r
   C. s
   D. t
   E. w

Practice Test 2

GO ON TO THE NEXT PAGE.

DO YOUR FIGURING HERE.

4. In a certain school district, exactly 30% of the students come from families that have only one child. If there are 7,340 students in the district, how many do NOT come from families with only one child?

   F. 220
   G. 514
   H. 2,202
   J. 5,138
   K. 7,120

5. For all $x < 3$, $(3 - 2x)^2 = ?$

   A. x^2
   B. $9 - x^2$
   C. $9 + x^2$
   D. $9 - 10x - 4x^2$
   E. $9 - 12x + 4x^2$

6. What is the slope-intercept form of the equation $3y + 2x = 24$?

   F. $y = -\frac{2x}{3} + 8$
   G. $y = -\frac{3x}{2} + 12$
   H. $3 = 2m + b$
   J. $m = 2b + 24$
   K. $y = 2x + 24$

7. What is the slope of a line perpendicular to the line $3x + 2y = 19$?

   A. $-\frac{3}{2}$
   B. $-\frac{2}{3}$
   C. $\frac{2}{3}$
   D. $\frac{3}{2}$
   E. 3

DO YOUR FIGURING HERE.

8. The volume of a cone is given by the formula $V = \frac{\pi}{3}r^2h$, where r is the radius of the base of the cone and h is the height of the cone. What is the volume, in cubic centimeters, of a cone with a height of 8 cm that has a base with a radius of 3 cm?

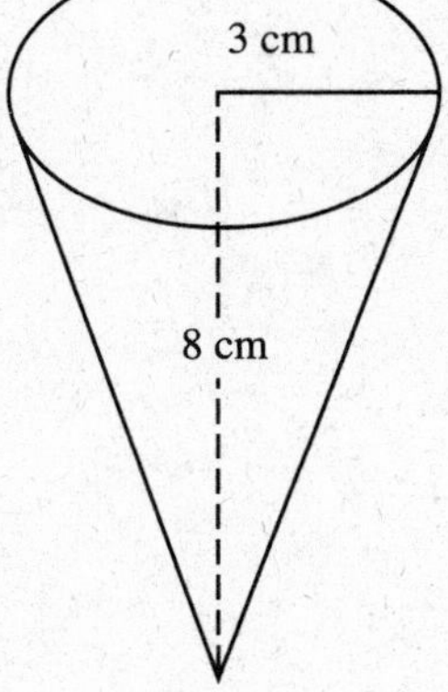

F. 72π
G. 48π
H. 24π
J. 12π
K. 8π

9. Given that m and n are parallel lines, t is a transversal crossing both m and n, and m $\angle b = 100°$, what is the measure of $\angle e$?

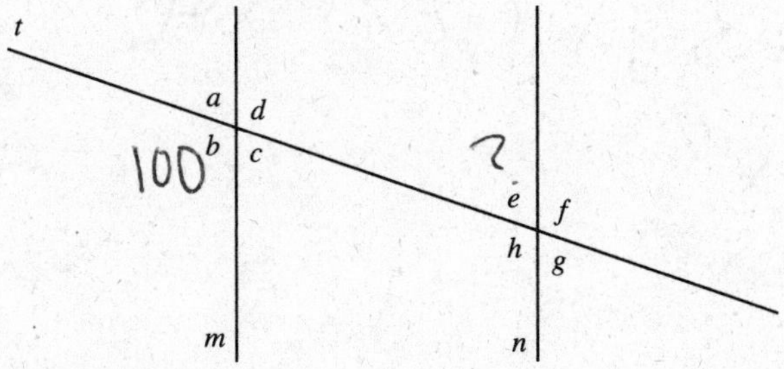

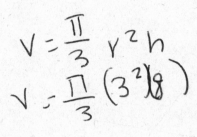

A. 40°
B. 50°
C. 80°
D. 100°
E. 120°

DO YOUR FIGURING HERE.

10. In the figure below, 3 lines intersect at the indicated angles.

What is the degree measure of $\angle x$?

F. 35°
G. 52.5°
H. 65°
J. 70°
K. 75°

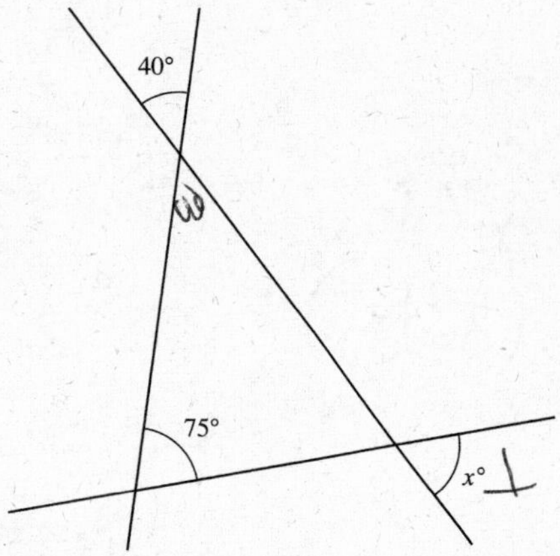

11. Find two arithmetic means between 11 and 26 such that the difference between consecutive numbers is the same:

11, _____, _____, 26

A. 14, 18
B. 15, 20
C. 16, 21
D. 17, 23
E. 18, 24

12. For all real numbers x and y, $(2x + 3y)^2$ = ?

F. $6x^2y^2$
G. $4x^2 + 6y^2$
H. $4x^2 + 9y^2$
J. $4x^2 + 6xy + 6y^2$
K. $4x^2 + 12xy + 9y^2$

13. In a certain town in New Hampshire, there are 7,695 registered voters, 60% of whom are Democrats. How many of the town's registered voters are Democrats?

A. 513
B. 2,565
C. 3,078
D. 4,617
E. 7,695

2 △ △ △ △ △ △ △ △ 2

DO YOUR FIGURING HERE.

14. Which of the following lines has the same graph as the line $2x - y = 12$?

F. $6x + 3y = 36$
G. $4x + 2y = 24$
H. $4x - 2y = 12$
J. $4x - 4y = 24$
K. $-6x + 3y = -36$

15. When $\frac{1}{3}w + \frac{2}{5}w = 1$, what is the value of w?

A. $\frac{1}{11}$
B. $\frac{3}{8}$
C. $\frac{11}{15}$
D. $\frac{15}{11}$
E. $\frac{8}{3}$

16. In the figure below, $\overline{AB}$ and $\overline{CD}$ bisect each other at E. The measure of $\angle CAE$ is 80° and the measure of $\angle BDE$ is 60°. What is the measure of $\angle CEA$?

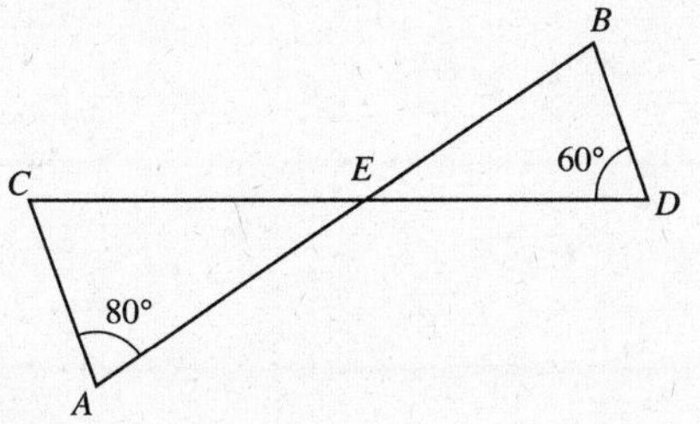

F. 10°
G. 30°
H. 40°
J. 60°
K. Cannot be determined

17. Given that $A = (3, 2)$ and $B = (15, 8)$ in the standard (x, y) coordinate plane, what is the distance from A to B?

A. $5\sqrt{2}$
B. 8
C. $4\sqrt{10}$
D. $6\sqrt{5}$
E. 18

Practice Test 2

GO ON TO THE NEXT PAGE.

2 △ △ △ △ △ △ △ △ 2

DO YOUR FIGURING HERE.

18. For all real numbers a, b, and c such that $a < b$ and $c > 0$, which of the following inequalities, if any, must be true?

    F. $a < c$
    G. $b < c$
    H. $a > c$
    J. $b > c$
    K. None of the above inequalities must be true.

19. A deli offers 4 types of sandwich meat, 3 kinds of cheese, and 5 bread varieties. When you order a sandwich at the deli, you are allowed to choose 1 meat, 1 cheese, and 1 type of bread. How many different sandwich combinations are possible at the deli?

    A. 3
    B. 12
    C. 15
    D. 30
    E. 60

20. At a certain company, 240 of the employees are women and the remaining 160 are men. What percentage of the company's workers are women?

    F. 25%
    G. $33\frac{1}{3}\%$
    H. 40%
    J. 60%
    K. $66\frac{2}{3}\%$

21. Alana leaves home to drive to college. She drives 200 miles in 4 hours before stopping for gas. She then drives 10 miles per hour faster than she did on the first part of her trip, and arrives at her dorm in 3 hours. How many miles did she drive in total?

    A. 200
    B. 300
    C. 350
    D. 380
    E. 430

22. If the monthly payment, M dollars, on a house that costs P dollars is given by the formula $M = \frac{P}{200} - .0008P + 40$, what is the monthly payment, to the nearest dollar, on a house that costs $200,000?

    F. $868
    G. $880
    H. $960
    J. $1,060
    K. $1,200

Practice Test 2

2 △ △ △ △ △ △ △ △ 2

DO YOUR FIGURING HERE.

23. What is the sum of the prime factors of the number 330?

A. 6
B. 19
C. 21
D. 22
E. 43

24. In the standard (x, y) coordinate plane, a line passes through the points $(1, -2)$ and $(5, 10)$. At which of the following points does the line cross the y-axis?

F. $(-8, 0)$
G. $(-5, 0)$
H. $(0, 0)$
J. $(0, -5)$
K. $(0, -8)$

25. For all positive a, b, and c, $\dfrac{2^{-1}a^{-3}b^7c^2}{(5a)^2b^{-1}c^7} = ?$

A. $\dfrac{2b^6}{5a^2c^5}$

B. $\dfrac{2b^8c^9}{2a^5}$

C. $\dfrac{2b^8c^9}{25a^5}$

D. $\dfrac{b^8}{10a^5c^5}$

E. $\dfrac{b^8}{50a^5c^5}$

26. One endpoint of a diameter of a circle with center $(2, -3)$ has coordinates at $(5, -2)$ in the standard (x, y) plane. What are the coordinates of the other endpoint of the diameter?

F. $(2 - \sqrt{10}, -3 - \sqrt{10})$
G. $(-1, -4)$
H. $(0, -4)$
J. $(2 + \sqrt{10}, -3 + \sqrt{10})$
K. $(8, -1)$

27. Payton ran $1\frac{2}{3}$ miles on Monday, $2\frac{1}{5}$ miles on Tuesday, and $1\frac{7}{8}$ miles on Wednesday. What is the median distance that he ran?

A. 7.200 miles
B. 5.742 miles
C. 1.914 miles
D. 1.875 miles
E. None of these.

GO ON TO THE NEXT PAGE.

Practice Test 2

2 △ △ △ △ △ △ △ △ 2

DO YOUR FIGURING HERE.

28. If $6x^2 + x - c = (cx - 1)(3x + 2)$, what is the value of c?

    F. –2
    G. –1
    H. 2
    J. 3
    K. 6

29. What is the y-coordinate of the point of intersection of the lines $y = 3x - 7$ and $y = 5x + 5$ in the standard (x, y) coordinate plane?

    A. –25
    B. –11
    C. –6
    D. 6
    E. 11

30. What is the area, in square inches, of the figure shown below?

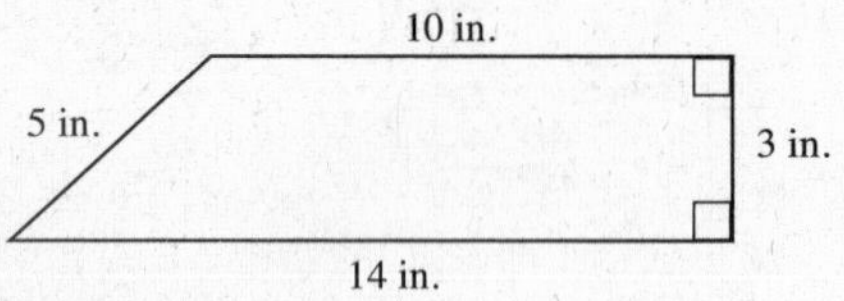

    F. 24
    G. 32
    H. 36
    J. 42
    K. 72

31. What is the solution set for the inequality $6 - 4(x - 2) > 4x + 5$?

    A. $x < -\frac{7}{8}$
    B. $x < -\frac{1}{4}$
    C. $x < \frac{9}{8}$
    D. $x > -\frac{7}{8}$
    E. $x > \frac{9}{8}$

32. For the circle whose standard equation is $(x - 1)^2 + (y + 2)^2 = 8$, the center and radius are:

    F. center = (–1, 2); radius = $2\sqrt{2}$.
    G. center = (–1, 2); radius = 4.
    H. center = (0, 0); radius = 4.
    J. center = (1, –2); radius = $2\sqrt{2}$.
    K. center = (1, –2); radius = 4.

2 △ △ △ △ △ △ △ △ 2

DO YOUR FIGURING HERE.

33. Parallelogram $RSTU$ is shown below, with $\overline{UA} = 4$ inches, $\overline{AS} = 7$ inches, and $\overline{ST} = 5$ inches. What is the area of $RSTU$ in square inches?

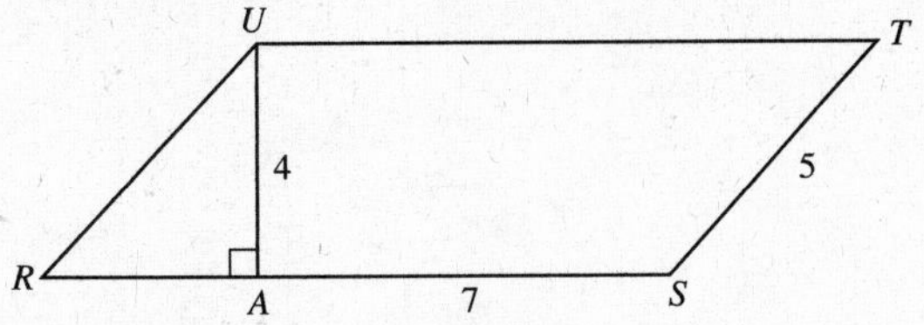

A. 16
B. 20
C. 28
D. 35
E. 40

34. If the lengths of the sides of the triangle below are shown in inches, how many inches long is side $\overline{AB}$?

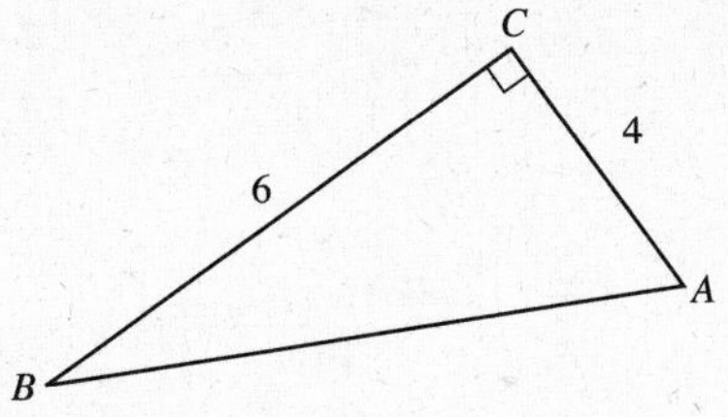

F. $2\sqrt{13}$
G. 10
H. $4\sqrt{13}$
J. 26
K. 42

35. Which of the following is the equation for a circle with diameter $\overline{AB}$, given that $A = (4, 2)$ and $B = (8, -4)$?

A. $x^2 + y^2 = 13$
B. $x^2 + y^2 = 26$
C. $(x - 6)^2 + (y + 1)^2 = 13$
D. $(x + 6)^2 + (y - 1)^2 = 13$
E. $(x - 6)^2 + (y + 1)^2 = 26$

36. Which of the following comprises all of the values of x for which $\frac{2}{3}x - \frac{1}{2} < \frac{1}{2}x + \frac{2}{3}$?

F. $x < 1$

G. $x < \frac{7}{6}$

H. $x < 7$

J. $x > \frac{7}{3}$

K. $x > 7$

2 △ △ △ △ △ △ △ △ 2

DO YOUR FIGURING HERE.

37. A guide wire for a telephone tower makes an angle of 50° with the level ground and is 14 meters from the base of the tower. How many meters long is the guide wire?

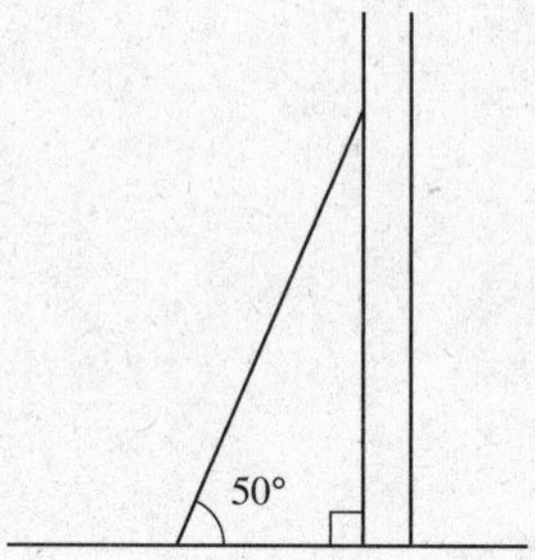

A. 3.80
B. 13.50
C. 16.68
D. 21.78
E. 22.58

38. For all $x^2 \neq 9$, $\frac{(x-3)^2}{x^2-9}$ is equivalent to:

F. –1
G. $\frac{1}{2}$
H. 1
J. $\frac{1}{x+3}$
K. $\frac{x-3}{x+3}$

39. In the standard (x, y) coordinate plane, the midpoint of $\overline{AB}$ is (5, 7) and A is located at (2, 3). If the coordinates of B are (x, y), what is the value of $(x + y)$?

A. 19
B. 17
C. 11
D. 8.5
E. 8

40. If the solutions to the equation $(x + a)(x + b) = 0$ are $x = 8$ and $x = -\frac{3}{2}$, then $a + b = ?$

F. –13
G. –12
H. –6.5
J. 6.5
K. 12

Practice Test 2

2 △ △ △ △ △ △ △ △ 2

DO YOUR FIGURING HERE.

41. In the figure below, all line segments intersect at right angles, and all measurements are given in inches. What is the perimeter of the figure in inches?

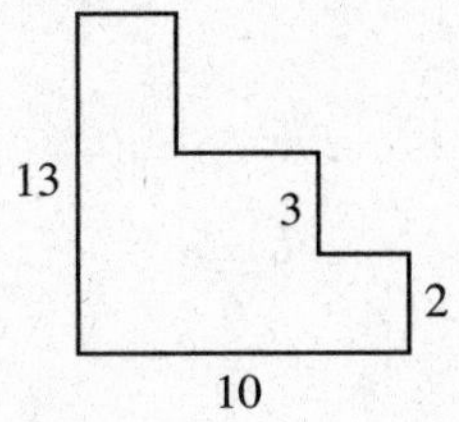

A. 23
B. 28
C. 46
D. 130
E. Cannot be determined

42. If cot θ = P, which of the following expressions must also equal P?

F. tan θ
G. csc θ – 1
H. sin θ – cos θ
J. $\frac{\sin \theta}{\cos \theta}$
K. $\frac{\cos \theta}{\sin \theta}$

43. A line in the standard (x, y) coordinate plane contains the points (5, 9) and (8, 3). What is the x-intercept of this line?

A. 19
B. $\frac{19}{2}$
C. 0
D. –2
E. $-\frac{19}{2}$

44. Each side of a given cube is a square with an area of 729 square inches. What is the volume of the cube in cubic inches?

F. 3^3
G. 3^9
H. 3^{12}
J. 3^{18}
K. 3^{64}

Practice Test 2

GO ON TO THE NEXT PAGE.

2 △ △ △ △ △ △ △ 2

DO YOUR FIGURING HERE.

45. If p and q are positive integers, and $6pq^4$ and $12p^2q^2$ have a greatest common factor of 1,050, then which of the following is a possible value for the sum of p and q?

A. 6
B. 8
C. 12
D. 35
E. 42

46. In the figure shown below, $\triangle ABC$ is a right triangle, $\overline{AB}$ is 8 inches long, and $\overline{BC}$ is 10 inches long. What is the area, in square inches, of square $ACDE$?

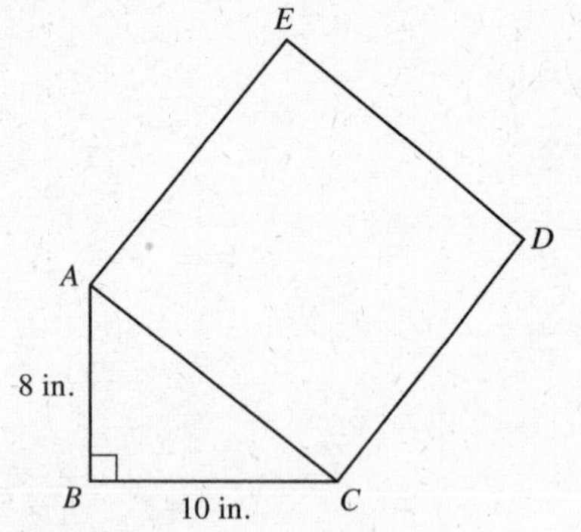

F. $2\sqrt{41}$
G. $\sqrt{164}$
H. 36
J. $8\sqrt{41}$
K. 164

47. In the standard coordinate plane, what is the distance between the points (5, 7) and (13, 11)?

A. 80
B. 12
C. $\sqrt{80}$
D. 8
E. $\sqrt{8}$

48. What value must be added to $9x^2 - 30x$ in order to *complete the square* (that is, make it a perfect square trinomial)?

F. –5
G. 5
H. 9
J. 25
K. 45

Practice Test 2

2 △ △ △ △ △ △ △ △ 2

DO YOUR FIGURING HERE.

49. A circle in the standard (x, y) coordinate plane is tangent to the x-axis at $-a$, and tangent to the y-axis at a, with $a > 0$. The radius of the circle is 4 units. What is the equation of the circle?

A. $x^2 + y^2 = 4$
B. $x^2 + y^2 = 16$
C. $(x - 4)^2 + (y - 4)^2 = 4$
D. $(x + 4)^2 + (y + 4)^2 = 16$
E. $(x + 4)^2 + (y - 4)^2 = 16$

50. Compared to the graph of $y = \sin x$, the graph of $y = 2\sin(4x)$ has:

F. 8 times the amplitude and the same period.
G. 2 times the amplitude and 4 times the period.
H. 2 times the amplitude and $\frac{1}{4}$ the period.
J. $\frac{1}{2}$ the amplitude and 4 times the period.
K. $\frac{1}{2}$ the amplitude and $\frac{1}{4}$ the period.

51. Which of the following is the solution set for x such that $3x - 9 \geq -3(9 - x)$?

A. The empty set
B. The set containing only zero
C. The set of negative numbers
D. The set of positive numbers
E. The set of real numbers

52. In the figure below, square $ABCD$ has a side length of 6 inches, and squares $AEFG$ and $CHIJ$ each have a side length of 1 inch. What is the area, in square inches, of the shaded pentagon $DGFIJ$?

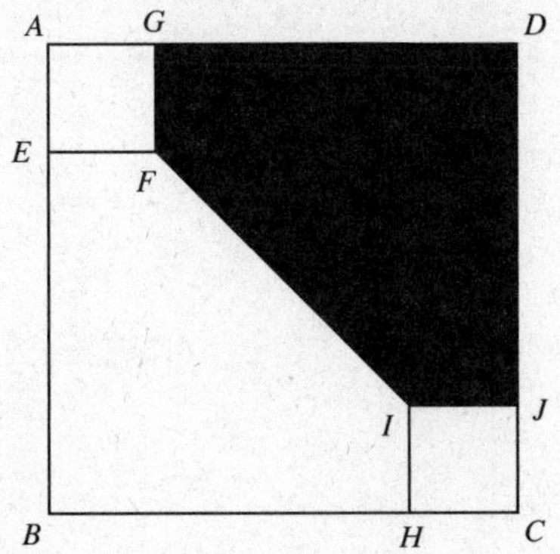

F. 9
G. 12.5
H. 17
J. 18
K. 20.5

Practice Test 2

GO ON TO THE NEXT PAGE.

DO YOUR FIGURING HERE.

53. Let the operation # be defined for the set of real numbers by:

$$x \# y = \frac{x + y}{3}.$$

Which of the following statements are true for all real numbers x, y, and z?

I. $x \# y = y \# x$
II. $(x \# y) \# z = x \# (y \# z)$
III. $0 \# x = 0$

A. I only
B. II only
C. III only
D. I and III only
E. II and III only

54. If $x^2 - 36a^2 = 5ax$, what are the two solutions for x in terms of a?

F. $-4a$ and $-9a$
G. $-4a$ and $9a$
H. $-3a$ and $12a$
J. $3a$ and $-12a$
K. $4a$ and $-9a$

55. For all values of θ over which sin θ and cos θ are nonzero, $\frac{\sqrt{1-\cos^2\theta}}{\sin^2\theta} \cdot \cos\theta = ?$

A. 1
B. $\tan\theta$
C. $\cot\theta$
D. $\sec\theta$
E. $\csc\theta$

56. If $\log_a x = p$, $\log_a y = q$, and $\log_a z = t$, then $\log_a\left(\frac{x^2y^3}{\sqrt{z}}\right)$ is equivalent to:

F. $p^2q^3 - \sqrt{z}$
G. $\frac{p^2q^3}{\sqrt{z}}$
H. $2p + 3q + \frac{1}{2}t$
J. $2p + 3q - \frac{1}{2}t$
K. $2p + 3q - t^{\frac{1}{2}}$

57. What is the solution set for the equation $|-x| = x$?

A. All real numbers
B. $x \geq 0$
C. $x \leq 0$
D. Only $x = 0$
E. Only $x = -1$

2 △ △ △ △ △ △ △ △ 2

DO YOUR FIGURING HERE.

58. For which of the following values of a will there be exactly one real solution to the equation $2x^2 - ax + 8 = 0$?

F. $2\sqrt{3}$
G. 4
H. $4\sqrt{3}$
J. 6
K. 8

59. If $x = 3t + 4$ and $y = 5 - t$, then which of the following equations expresses y in terms of x?

A. $y = \frac{19 - x}{3}$
B. $y = \frac{1 - x}{3}$
C. $y = 9 - x$
D. $y = x + 9$
E. $y = x - 1$

60. In the circle below, radius $\overline{OA}$ has a length of 10 meters, and central angle $\angle AOB$ measures 30°. What is the area, in square meters, of shaded sector AOB?

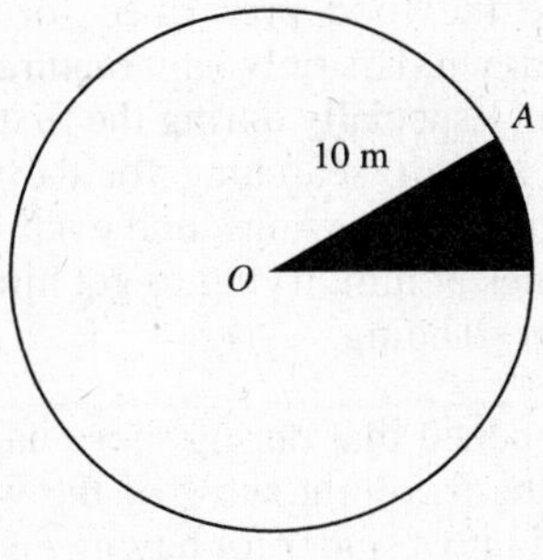

F. $\frac{5\pi}{6}$
G. $\frac{5\pi}{3}$
H. $\frac{10\pi}{3}$
J. $\frac{25\pi}{6}$
K. $\frac{25\pi}{3}$

STOP

If there is still time remaining, check your answers to this section.

READING TEST

35 MINUTES—40 QUESTIONS

Directions: There are four passages in this test. Each passage is followed by several questions. After reading a passage, choose the best answer to each question and fill in the corresponding oval on your answer document. You may refer to the passages as often as necessary.

Passage I—Prose Fiction

This passage is adapted from the short story "A Very Old Man With Enormous Wings" by Gabriel Garcia Márquez (© 1971 by Gabriel Garcia Márquez).

The light was so weak at noon that when Pelayo was coming back to the house, it was hard for him to see what it was that was moving and groaning in the rear of the courtyard. He had to go very close to see that it was an old man lying face down in the mud, who, in spite of his tremendous efforts, couldn't get up, impeded by his enormous wings.

Pelayo ran to get Elisenda, his wife, who was putting compresses on the sick child, and he took her to the rear of the courtyard. They both looked at the fallen body with a mute stupor. There were only a few faded hairs left on his bald skull and very few teeth in his mouth, and his pitiful condition took away any sense of grandeur he might have had. And yet, they called in a neighbor woman who knew everything about life and death to see him, and all she needed was one look.

"He's an angel," she told them. "He must have been coming for the child, but the poor fellow is so old that the rain knocked him down."

On the following day everyone knew that a flesh-and-blood angel was held captive in Pelayo's house. With the first light of dawn, they found the whole neighborhood in front of the chicken coop having fun with the angel, tossing him things to eat through the openings in the wire.

The news of the captive angel spread with such rapidity that after a few hours the courtyard had the bustle of a marketplace and they had to call in troops with fixed bayonets to disperse the mob that was about to knock the house down. Elisenda, her spine all twisted from sweeping up so much marketplace trash, then got the idea of fencing in the yard and charging five cents admission to see the angel.

The curious came from far away. The most unfortunate invalids on earth came in search of health: a poor woman who since childhood has been counting her heartbeats and had run out of numbers; a Portuguese man who couldn't sleep because the noise of the stars disturbed him; a sleepwalker who got up at night to undo the things he had done while awake; and many others with less serious ailments. Pelayo and Elisenda were happy with fatigue, for in less than a week they had crammed their rooms with money and the line of pilgrims waiting their turn to enter still reached beyond the horizon.

The angel was the only one who took no part in his own act. He spent his time trying to get comfortable in his borrowed nest, befuddled by the heat of the oil lamps and sacramental candles that had been placed along the wire. At first they tried to make him eat some mothballs, which, according to the wisdom of the wise neighbor woman, were the food prescribed for angels. But he turned them down. His only supernatural virtue seemed to be patience. Especially during the first days, when the hens pecked at him, searching for the stellar parasites that proliferated in his wings, and even the most merciful threw stones at him, trying to get him to rise so they could see him standing.

It so happened that during those days there arrived in the town the traveling show of the woman who had been changed into a spider for having disobeyed her parents. The admission to see her was not only less than the admission to see the angel, but people were permitted to ask her all manner of questions and to examine her up and down. While still practically a child she had sneaked out of her parents' house to go to a dance, and while she was coming back through the woods after having danced all night without permission, a fearful thunderclap rent the sky in two and through the crack came the lightning bolt of brimstone that changed her into a spider. A spectacle like that, with such a fearful lesson, was bound to defeat that of a haughty angel who scarcely deigned to look at mortals. Pelayo's courtyard went back to being as empty as during the time it had rained for three days and crabs walked through the bedrooms.

With the money they saved they built a two-story mansion with iron bars on the windows so that angels wouldn't get in. Pelayo also set up a rabbit warren close to town and gave up his job as a bailiff for good, and Elisenda bought some satin pumps with high heels and many dresses of iridescent silk, the kind worn on Sunday by the most desirable women in those times.

3 3

One morning Elisenda was cutting some bunches of onions for lunch when a wind that seemed to come from the high seas blew into the kitchen. Then she went to the window and caught the angel in his first attempts at flight. He was on the point of knocking the shed down with the ungainly flapping that slipped on the light and couldn't get a grip on the air. But he did manage to gain altitude. Elisenda let out a sigh of relief, for herself and for him, when she watched him pass over the last houses. She kept watching him even when she was through cutting the onions, until it was no longer possible for her to see him, because then he was no longer an annoyance in her life but an imaginary dot on the horizon of the sea.

1. The inhabitants of the town in which the story takes place are depicted as:
   A. proud and stubborn people who are always arguing about religion.
   B. laid-back people who react to odd events with less surprise than one might expect.
   C. wise people who are always constructing elaborate theories about the universe.
   D. devious people who will do anything to make money.

2. The "neighbor woman" believes that the angel is a(an):
   F. angel of death.
   G. angel of good fortune.
   H. warrior angel.
   J. angel who can predict the future.

3. All of the following are described in detail EXCEPT:
   A. the ailments of the invalids.
   B. the girl who disobeyed her parents.
   C. the clothes bought by Elisenda.
   D. the crabs brought by the rainstorm.

4. The character of the angel can best be described as
   F. wise and loving.
   G. powerful but unforgiving.
   H. baffling and mysterious.
   J. pessimistic but determined.

5. Elisenda's idea to start charging people admission to see the angel is a(an):
   A. disrespectful decision motivated by greed.
   B. understandable decision motivated by necessity.
   C. risky decision motivated by poor business sense.
   D. weak decision motivated by her tendency to be influenced by others.

6. When they first encounter him, the townspeople treat the angel as if he is a(an):
   F. animal.
   G. impostor.
   H. impartial judge.
   J. bad omen.

7. All of the following are reasons why people became more interested in the spider girl than they had been in the angel EXCEPT:
   A. it is more obvious what moral they are supposed to learn from her.
   B. she is more willing to interact with her audience.
   C. she has been officially approved by local religious authorities.
   D. it is less expensive to see her.

8. Which of the following phrases indicates that the appearance of the angel is regarded as a somewhat normal occurrence?
   F. "They both looked at the fallen body with a mute stupor." (lines 10–11)
   G. "The most unfortunate invalids on earth came in search of health." (lines 33–34)
   H. "The angel was the only one who took no part in his own act." (lines 44–45)
   J. "they built a two-story mansion with iron bars on the windows so that angels wouldn't get in." (lines 74–76)

9. At the beginning of the story, Pelayo is employed as a(an):
   A. farmer.
   B. fisherman.
   C. bailiff.
   D. architect.

10. The main point of the last paragraph is that after the departure of the angel, Elisenda feels:
    F. remorseful about how poorly the townspeople treated the angel.
    G. frightened about what the angel might do if he ever comes back.
    H. optimistic about the new lifestyle that was made possible for her by the angel.
    J. unburdened now that she doesn't have to worry about the angel anymore.

Passage II—Social Science

This passage is adapted from the essay "Are Academics Different?" by Stanley Fish (©2009 Stanley Fish).

Last week's column about Denis Rancourt, a University of Ottawa professor who is facing dismissal for awarding A-plus grades to his students on the first day of class and for turning the physics course he had been assigned into a course on political activism, drew mostly negative comments.

It may be outlandish because it is so theatrical, but one could argue that Rancourt carries out to its logical extreme a form of behavior many display in less dramatic ways. What links Rancourt and these milder versions of academic acting-out is a conviction that academic freedom confers on professors the right to order (or disorder) the workplace in any way they see fit, irrespective of the requirements of the university that employs them. The response many would make to this accusation is that a teacher's responsibility is to the ideals of truth and justice and not to the parochial rules of an institution in thrall to intellectual, economic and political orthodoxies.

It would be hard to imagine another field of endeavor in which employees believe that being attentive to their employer's goals and wishes is tantamount to a moral crime. But this is what many (not all) academics believe, and if pressed they will support their belief by invoking a form of academic exceptionalism, the idea that while colleges and universities may bear some of the marks of places of employment—workdays, promotions, salaries, vacations, meetings, etc.—they are really places in which something much more rarefied than a mere job goes on.

An understanding of academic freedom as a right unbound by the conditions of employment goes hand in hand with, and is indeed derived from, an understanding of higher education as something more than a job to be performed; rather it is a calling to be taken up and followed wherever it may lead, even if it leads to a flouting of the norms that happen to be in place in the bureaucratic spaces that house (but do not define) this exalted enterprise. If that's the kind of work you think yourself to be doing, it follows that you would think yourself free to pursue it unconstrained by external impositions.

The alternative is to understand academic freedom as a much more earthbound thing, as a freedom tailored to and constrained by the requirements of a particular job. Statements like this are likely to provoke the objection that academe should not be a Business or a Corporation. But that is a fake issue. Saying that higher education has a job to do (and that the norms and standards of that job should control professorial behavior) is not the same as saying that its job is business. It is just to say that it is a job and not a sacred vocation, and that while it may differ in many ways from other jobs—there is no discernible product and projects may remain uncompleted for years without negative consequences for researchers—its configurations can still be ascertained (it is not something ineffable) and serve as the basis of both expectations and discipline.

So these are the two conceptions of academic freedom that are in play: academic freedom as the freedom to do the academic job (understood by reference to university norms and requirements); and academic freedom as the freedom to chart your own way, to go boldly where no man or woman has gone before, constrained only by your inner sense of what is right and true.

That of course is the key question. Are academics different, and if so, in what ways, and to what extent do the differences legitimate a degree of freedom not enjoyed by the members of other professions? Chief Judge Wilkinson finds ample evidence in the record to persuade him that "academic speech" is a matter of "public concern" and so rises to the level of constitutional notice. What exactly would the public's interest in academic speech be? One answer is provided by law professor J. Peter Byrne who argues that a constitutional right of academic freedom exists "not for the benefit of the professors themselves but for the good of society." Why? Because it is only in universities that a certain kind of speech—"serious and communal, seeking to improve the understanding"—flourishes.

Now I have my elitist moments, but this is a bit much. Only professors, we're being told, do real thinking; other people accept whatever they hear on TV and retail popular (but uninformed) wisdom on street corners. Thus while there is no reason to extend special protections in the workplace to non-academic speech—which is worthless—there is a good reason to extend them to the incomparably finer utterances of the professorial class.

It should be possible to acknowledge the distinctiveness without making academic work into a holy mission taken up by a superior race of beings. Free inquiry means free in relation to the goals of the enterprise, not free in the sense of being answerable to nothing. Those who would defend academic freedom would do well to remove the halo it often wears. Stay away from big abstractions and remain tethered to work on the ground. If you say, "This is the job and if we are to do it properly, these conditions must be in place," you'll get a better hearing than you would if you say, "We're professors and you're not, so leave us alone to do what we like."

11. The main point that the author seeks to make in the essay is that the limits of academic freedom should be dictated by the:
    A. ideals of truth and justice.
    B. beliefs of students' parents.
    C. terms of the course being taught.
    D. U.S. Constitution.

12. The author's opinion about the story of Denis Rancourt is that it is:
    F. typical of the sorts of abuses perpetrated by the average professor nowadays.
    G. an extreme example that nevertheless raises an interesting question.
    H. the first and last time that any professor will be able to get away with such behavior.
    J. probably not what actually happened.

13. The author can best be characterized as a:
    A. public intellectual analyzing an academic concept.
    B. judge justifying a legal ruling.
    C. professor arguing for a greater amount of freedom.
    D. former student complaining about his experiences at college.

14. The author mentions "workdays, promotions, salaries, vacations, meetings" (lines 27–28) because they are:
    F. things about academia of which most outsiders are unaware.
    G. among the reasons that most professors choose to go into teaching.
    H. the things that make academic jobs different from other jobs.
    J. some things that academic jobs have in common with other jobs.

15. The tone and purpose of paragraph 4 (lines 31–41) can best be characterized as:
    A. a dispassionate attempt to logically support the author's own definition of academic freedom.
    B. an explanation of how people used to think about academia, before all the problems started.
    C. a sarcastic explanation of thinking of those who believe in academic exceptionalism.
    D. the author's best guess about what the reader probably believes.

16. The author quotes law professor J. Peter Byrne in the second half of paragraph 7 (lines 73–79) because:
    F. Byrne's ideas closely match his own.
    G. he is about to explain why he finds Byrne's ideas absurd.
    H. Byrne is a friend of Denis Rancourt's who can shed light on what really happened.
    J. Byrne is explaining why the laws that started the whole problem were passed in the first place.

17. As it is used in line 56, *ineffable* most nearly means:
    A. unproductive.
    B. inexpressible.
    C. self-reliant.
    D. traditional.

18. The viewpoint on the duties and rights of professors with which the author *disagrees* can best be summed up in the term:
    F. political orthodoxy.
    G. free inquiry.
    H. academic freedom.
    J. academic exceptionalism.

19. The author believes that professors should refrain from doing all of the following EXCEPT:
    A. assigning grades on the first day of class.
    B. suddenly changing the subject matter of a particular course.
    C. believing that as professors they should have absolute freedom.
    D. taking years to complete projects.

20. Based on the passage, it is most likely that the author would define *academic freedom* as the:
    F. amount of leeway professors require in order to fulfill their duties.
    G. protection of professorial speech for the good of society.
    H. freedom to ascertain the configurations of academia.
    J. idea that academic work is not a mere job, but a calling taken up by superior beings.

Passage III—Humanities

This passage is adapted from the essay "My Father's Suitcase" by Orhan Pamuk (©2006 Orhan Pamuk).

Two years before my father died, he gave me a small suitcase filled with his manuscripts and notebooks. Assuming his usual jocular, mocking air, he told me that he wanted me to read them after he was gone, by which he meant after his death.

"Just take a look," he said, slightly embarrassed. "See if there's anything in there that you can use. Maybe after I'm gone you can make a selection and publish it." We were in my study, surrounded by books. My father was searching for a place to set down the suitcase, wandering around like a man who wished to rid himself of a painful burden. In the end, he deposited it quietly, unobtrusively, in a corner.

For several days after that, I walked back and forth past the suitcase without ever actually touching it. I knew what was inside some of the notebooks it held. I had seen my father writing in them. In his youth, he had wanted to be an Istanbul poet, but he had not wanted to live the sort of life that came with writing poetry in a poor country where there were few readers.

The first thing that kept me away from my father's suitcase was, of course, a fear that I might not like what I read. Because my father understood this, he had taken the precaution of acting as if he did not take the contents of the case seriously. By this time, I had been working as a writer for twenty-five years, and his failure to take literature seriously pained me. But my real fear—the crucial thing that I did not wish to discover—was that my father might be a good writer. If great literature emerged from my father's suitcase, I would have to acknowledge that inside my father there existed a man entirely different from the one I knew. This was a frightening possibility. Even at my advanced age, I wanted my father to be my father and my father only—not a writer.

A writer is someone who spends years patiently trying to discover the second being inside him, and the world that makes him who he is. To write is to transform that inward gaze into words, to study the worlds into which we pass when we retire into ourselves, and to do so with patience, obstinacy, and joy. As I sit at my table, for days, months, years, slowly adding words to empty pages, I feel as if I were bringing into being that other person inside me, in the same way that one might build a bridge or a dome, stone by stone.

I was afraid of opening my father's suitcase and reading his notebooks because I knew that he would never have tolerated the difficulties that I had tolerated, that it was not solitude he loved but mixing with friends, crowds, company. I would have to remember that my father enjoyed being alone with his books and his thoughts—and not pay too much attention to the literary quality of his writing. But as I gazed so anxiously at the suitcase he had bequeathed to me I also felt that this was the very thing I would not be able to do.

In fact, I was angry at my father because he had not led a life like mine—because he had never quarreled with his life, and had spent it happily laughing with his friends and his loved ones. But part of me also knew that I was not so much "angry" as "jealous," and this, too, made me uneasy. What is happiness? Is happiness believing that you live a deep life in your lonely room? Or is happiness leading a comfortable life in society, believing in the same things as everyone else, or, at least, acting as if you did? Is it happiness or unhappiness to go through life writing in secret, while seeming to be in harmony with all that surrounds you?

On some deeper level, I was able to become a writer because my father, in his youth, had also wished to be one. I would have to read him with tolerance—to seek to understand what he had written in those hotel rooms. It was with these hopeful thoughts that I walked over to the suitcase, which was still sitting where my father had left it. Using all my will power, I read through a few manuscripts and notebooks. What had my father written about? I recall a few views from the windows of Paris hotels, a few poems, paradoxes, analyses…

A week after he left me his suitcase, my father paid me another visit; as always, he brought me a bar of chocolate (he had forgotten that I was forty-eight years old). As always, we chatted and laughed about life, politics, and family gossip. A moment arrived when my father's gaze drifted to the corner where he had left his suitcase, and he saw that I had moved it. We looked each other in the eye. There followed a pressing silence. I did not tell him that I had opened the suitcase and tried to read its contents; instead, I looked away. But he understood. Just as I understood that he had understood. Because my father was a happy, easygoing man who had faith in himself, he smiled at me the way he always did. And, as he left the house, he repeated all the lovely and encouraging things he always said to me, like a father.

As always, I watched him leave, envying his happiness, his carefree and unflappable temperament. But I remember that on that day there was also a flash of joy inside me that made me ashamed. It was prompted by the thought that maybe I wasn't as comfortable in life as he was, maybe I had not led as happy or footloose a life as he had, but at least I had devoted mine to writing. I was ashamed to be thinking such things at my father's expense—of all people, my father, who had never been a source of pain to me, who had left me free. All this should remind us that writing and literature are intimately linked to a void at the center of our lives, to our feelings of happiness and guilt.

21. The author of the passage would most strongly agree with which of the following statements?

A. Happiness can only be found through others.
B. The paths that children take can be predicted by anyone who knows their parents well.
C. Good writing is actually the opposite of what has traditionally been viewed as "great literature."
D. Writing is largely a solitary endeavor.

22. All of the following are reasons why the author is afraid to open the suitcase and read its contents EXCEPT:

F. he fears that he will come to see his father as a writer, rather than as just his father.
G. he suspects that the notebooks might contain painful secrets about his parents' relationship.
H. he suspects that his father's writing will force him to examine his own ideas about happiness.
J. he is afraid that his father's writing will be very good.

23. In the context of the passage, the statement "he had forgotten that I was forty-eight years old" (lines 80–81) suggests that the:

A. author's father is becoming absent-minded in his old age.
B. author's father was absent for most of his childhood.
C. author's father still treats him like a child in some small ways.
D. author may have been adopted.

24. When the author says that his father "would never have tolerated the difficulties that I had tolerated" (lines 46–47), he means that his father:

F. prioritized making money when he was a younger man.
G. could not have endured the solitude that real writing demands.
H. tended toward orthodoxy in his political and religious opinions.
J. fled their native country rather than trying to improve it from within.

25. As it is used in lines 12–13, *unobtrusively* most nearly means:

A. inconspicuously.
B. rudely.
C. painfully.
D. ashamedly.

26. The author mentions feeling all of the following emotions concerning his father EXCEPT:

F. anger.
G. joy.
H. jealousy.
J. suspicion.

27. The main point of paragraph 7 (lines 55–66) is that:

A. the author is jealous of his father for being able to make friends so easily wherever he goes.
B. happiness means being in harmony with all that surrounds you.
C. it is unclear whether the author's approach to life or his father's is ultimately more satisfying.
D. there is really no such thing as true happiness.

28. Writing, according to the author, is a lifelong process of discovering:

F. an alternate version of oneself.
G. one's relationship to one's native country.
H. one's true feelings about one's family.
J. the true nature of happiness.

29. When the author's father was young, he aspired to write:

A. novels.
B. poetry.
C. plays.
D. comedy.

30. The point of the last paragraph (lines 94–106) is that:

F. the author did not realize until that day that his father truly loved him.
G. the author is ashamed of his father.
H. writing draws on negative emotions as well as positive ones.
J. the author has finally decided to have children of his own.

Passage IV—Natural Science

This passage is adapted from *The Selfish Gene* by Richard Dawkins (©1976 Oxford University Press).

Most of what is unusual about man can be summed up in one word: "culture." I use the word not in its snobbish sense, but as a scientist uses it. Cultural transmission is analogous to genetic transmission in that, although basically conservative, it can give rise to a form of evolution. Geoffrey Chaucer could not hold a conversation with a modern Englishman, even though they are linked to each other by an unbroken chain of some twenty generations of Englishmen, each of whom could speak to his immediate neighbors in the chain as a son speaks to his father. Language seems to "evolve" by non-genetic means, and at a rate which is orders of magnitude faster than genetic evolution.

As an enthusiastic Darwinian, I have been dissatisfied with explanations that my fellow-enthusiasts have offered for human behavior. They have tried to look for "biological advantages" in various attributes of human civilization. These ideas are plausible as far as they go, but I find that they do not begin to square up to the formidable challenge of explaining culture, cultural evolution, and the immense differences between human cultures around the world. I think we have got to start again and go right back to first principles. The argument I shall advance is that, for an understanding of the evolution of modern man, we must begin by throwing out the gene as the sole basis of our ideas on evolution.

What, after all, is so special about genes? The answer is that they are replicators. But do we have to go to distant worlds to find other kinds of replicators and other kinds of evolution? I think that a new kind of replicator has recently emerged on this very planet. It is staring us in the face. It is still in its infancy, still drifting clumsily about in its primeval soup, but already it is achieving evolutionary change at a rate that leaves the old gene panting far behind.

The new soup is the soup of human culture. We need a name for the new replicator, a noun that conveys the idea of a unit of cultural transmission, or a unit of *imitation*. "Mimeme" comes from a suitable Greek root, but I want a monosyllable that sounds a bit like "gene." I hope my classicist friends will forgive me if I abbreviate "mimeme" to *meme*. Examples of memes are tunes, ideas, catch-phrases, clothes fashions, ways of making pots or of building arches. Just as genes propagate themselves in the gene pool by leaping from body to body, so memes propagate themselves in the meme pool by leaping from brain to brain. If a scientist hears, or reads about, a good idea, he passes it on to his colleagues and students. He mentions it in his articles and his lectures. If the idea catches on, it can be said to propagate itself, spreading from brain to brain.

Imitation, in the broad sense, is how memes *can* replicate. But just as not all genes that can replicate do so successfully, so some memes are more successful in the meme-pool than others. The longevity of any one copy of a meme is probably relatively unimportant, as it is for any one copy of a gene. The copy of the tune "Auld Lang Syne" that exists in my brain will last only for the rest of my life. But I expect there will be copies of the same tune on paper and in people's brains for centuries to come. If the meme is a scientific idea, its spread will depend on how acceptable it is to the population of individual scientists; a rough measure of its survival value could be obtained by counting the number of times it is referred to in successive years in scientific journals. If it is a popular tune, its spread through the meme pool may be gauged by the number of people heard whistling it in the streets. If it is a style of women's shoe, the population memeticist may use sales statistics from shoe shops.

Some memes, like some genes, achieve brilliant short-term success in spreading rapidly, but do not last long in the meme pool. Popular songs and stiletto heels are examples. Others may continue to propagate themselves for thousands of years, usually because of the great potential permanence of written records.

When we die there are two things we can leave behind us: genes and memes. We were built as gene machines, created to pass on our genes. But that aspect of us will be forgotten in three generations. Your child, even your grandchild, may bear a resemblance to you, perhaps in facial features, in a talent for music, in the color of her hair. But as each generation passes, the contribution of your genes is halved. It does not take long to reach negligible proportions. We should not seek immortality in reproduction.

But if you contribute to the world's culture, if you have a good idea, compose a tune, invent a sparking plug, write a poem, it may live on, intact, long after your genes have dissolved in the common pool. Socrates may or may not have a gene or two alive in the world today, but who cares? The meme-complexes of Socrates, Leonardo, Copernicus and Marconi are still going strong.

3 3

31. The author's motivation in writing the passage is his belief that:

    A. genes actually have nothing to do with human evolution.
    B. genetics does not sufficiently explain human culture.
    C. culture is too obsessed with trivial things like fashion and pop songs.
    D. humans are too concerned with seeking immortality.

32. When the author says that he uses the word *culture* "not in its snobbish sense, but as a scientist uses it" (lines 2–3), he means that he:

    F. plans to honestly admit what aspects of culture he really likes, rather than pretending he only likes the critically respected things.
    G. does not believe that there is really such a thing as culture at all.
    H. thinks that culture can be completely explained by Darwinian evolution.
    J. does not distinguish between "good" and "bad" culture, but refers merely to the facts of human civilization.

33. The author argues that all of the following would constitute examples of *memes* EXCEPT:

    A. a word.
    B. a piece of music.
    C. a particular hair color.
    D. a fashion item.

34. According to the author, one thing that genes and memes have in common is that they are both:

    F. examples of replicators.
    G. still only unproven theories rather than facts.
    H. ideas that people in the future will only know about because of written records.
    J. capable of inspiring great art.

35. The author mentions Geoffrey Chaucer in the first paragraph as an example of:

    A. a pioneer in the field of mimetics.
    B. one of the first major poets to write in English.
    C. someone who would not have understood modern science, even though he was a genius for his time.
    D. a speaker of English as it existed twenty generations ago.

36. As it is used in lines 45, 47, 51, and 75, the word *propagate* most nearly means:

    F. multiply.
    G. change.
    H. prove.
    J. conceal.

37. According to the passage, the word *memes* was invented by:

    A. the ancient Greeks.
    B. friends of the author.
    C. the author's former teacher.
    D. the author himself.

38. The author states that "[t]he copy of the tune 'Auld Lang Syne' that exists in my brain will last only for the rest of my life" (lines 58–60) in order to demonstrate that:

    F. no two people's brains are alike.
    G. memories do not survive death.
    H. no one copy of an idea is vital, as long as the idea survives.
    J. he is older than he imagines most of his readers will be, and accordingly has memories of older songs.

39. According to the author, the "survival value" of a meme is expressed by:

    A. how widespread the meme itself becomes.
    B. how it contributes to the survival of the people who have memories of it.
    C. whether it makes the people who have memories of it into better people or worse people.
    D. whether scientists believe that it is true or false.

40. The author mentions "Socrates, Leonardo, Copernicus and Marconi" in the closing paragraph because they are:

    F. people whose genes have become extremely widespread.
    G. people whose ideas have become extremely influential.
    H. the four most complex thinkers in the history of science.
    J. the people who made the biggest contributions to the field of memetics.

STOP

If there is still time remaining, check your answers to this section.

SCIENCE TEST

35 MINUTES—40 QUESTIONS

Directions: There are seven passages in this test. Each passage is followed by several questions. After reading a passage, choose the best answer to each question and fill in the corresponding oval on your answer document. You may refer to the passages as often as necessary.

You are NOT permitted to use a calculator on this test.

Passage I

Scientists examined several ingredients commonly used as active agents in sunscreen. The goal of the study was to determine which ingredients are most effective at blocking harmful UV rays.

Scientists used PABA, oxybenzone, octyl salicylate, and a broad-spectrum commercial sunscreen (SPF 45). The samples were exposed to sunlight with wavelengths ranging from 240 to 440 nm. The percent transmittance of UV rays at each wavelength was recorded. The data was collected manually using a spectrophotometer. The results, in 20-nm increments, are shown in Table 1.

Table 1

nm	PABA	Oxybenzone	Octyl Salicylate	Commercial Sunscreen
240	38.2	15.7	12.7	15.2
260	2.9	19.2	83.5	24.5
280	1.7	3.2	33.1	4.2
300	9	4.2	3	1.5
320	82.9	6	10.8	2.5
340	99.2	9.7	93.5	25.5
360	100	45.3	100	67.6
380	100	92.6	100	96.8
400	100	100	100	99.8
420	100	100	100	100
440	100	100	100	100

Figure 1 displays the intensity of sunlight across the spectrum.

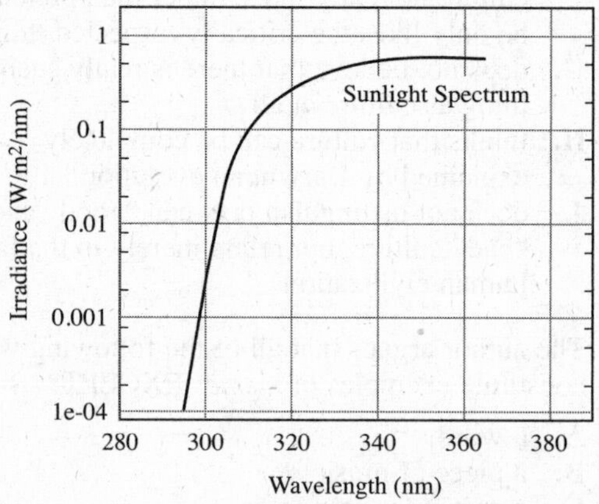

Figure 1

In 1975, Thomas B. Fitzpatrick, MD, Ph.D., of Harvard Medical School, developed a classification system for skin type. This system was based on a person's complexion and responses to sun exposure. Table 2 lists the skin types and their characteristics.

Table 2

Skin Type	Color	Reaction to UVA	Reaction to Sun
Type I	Very fair skin tone	Very sensitive	Always burns easily, never tans
Type II	Fair skin tone	Very sensitive	Usually burns easily, tans with difficulty
Type III	Fair to medium skin tone	Sensitive	Burns moderately, tans gradually
Type IV	Medium skin tone	Moderately sensitive	Rarely burns, always tans well
Type V	Olive or dark skin tone	Minimally sensitive	Very rarely burns, tans very easily
Type VI	Very dark skin tone	Least sensitive	Never burns, deeply pigmented

4 ○ ○ ○ ○ ○ ○ ○ ○ 4

1. According to Table 1, which substance had the highest percent transmittance of UV rays for sunlight with a wavelength of 260 nm?

   A. Octyl salicylate
   B. PABA
   C. Oxybenzone
   D. Commercial sunscreen

2. Based on the information in Figure 1, sunlight is most intense at which of the following wavelengths?

   F. 290 nm
   G. 300 nm
   H. 320 nm
   J. 340 nm

3. A person with fair skin tone, whose skin burns but also tans slowly, likely has which of the following skin types?

   A. Type I
   B. Type II
   C. Type III
   D. Type IV

4. Experts state that anyone whose skin is sensitive or very sensitive to UVA should always wear sunscreen. According to Table 2, people with which skin types should always wear sunscreen?

   F. Types I and II
   G. Types I, II, and III
   H. Types II, III, and IV
   J. Types V and VI

5. In sunlight with an irradiance of 0.01 W/m2/nm, oxybenzone would be expected to have a UV ray percent transmittance of:

   A. 3.8
   B. 5
   C. 9.7
   D. 100

Passage II

The most common type of red-green color perception defect is caused by a mutation on the X chromosome. X-linked red color blindness is a recessive trait. The eggs of the mother will contain either a normal X chromosome (X^R) or an X chromosome with the mutation (X^r) causing red-green color blindness. The sperm of the father will contain the normal X chromosome, the X chromosome with the mutation, or the Y chromosome. Females *heterozygous* (one normal gene, one mutated gene) for this trait have normal vision. The color perception defect manifests itself in females only when it is inherited from both parents. By contrast, males inherit their sole X chromosome from their mothers, and become red-green color blind when this one X chromosome has the color perception defect.

Genotype refers to the combination of alleles that an individual has for a gene. Table 1 lists the possible genotypes for red-green color perception and their corresponding effects on vision.

Table 1

Female Genotype	Vision
$X^R X^R$	normal
$X^R X^r$	normal, carrier
$X^r X^r$	red-green color blind
Male Genotype	**Vision**
$X^R Y$	normal
$X^r Y$	red-green color blind

Students interviewed members of the Allen family to investigate the inheritance of red-green color blindness. Figure 1 displays the family tree of the Allen family.

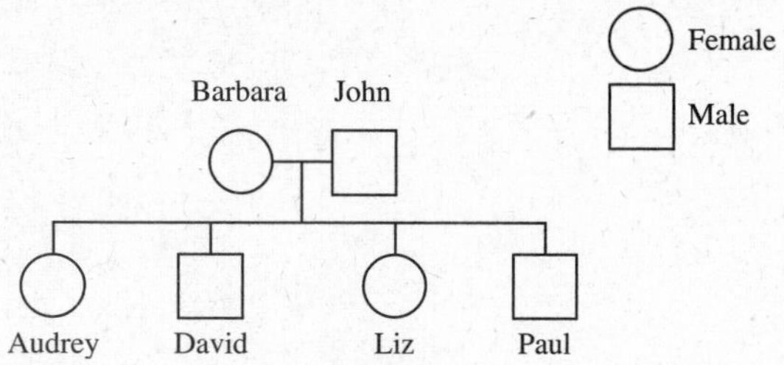

Figure 1

Study 1

Students interviewed Barbara and John and learned that Barbara is red-green color blind, while John is not. Based on this information, the students deduced that their four children have the following genotypes:

Females:	$X^R X^r$
Males:	$X^r Y$

Figure 2

Study 2

Students assumed that Liz would have children with a man who has normal vision, and using a Punnett square calculated all of the possible genotypes for their children:

$X^R X^R$	$X^R Y^r$
$X^R X^r$	$X^r Y$

Figure 3

Study 3

Students assumed that David would have children with a woman who has red-green color blindness, and using a Punnett square calculated all of the possible genotypes for their children:

$X^r X^r$	$X^r Y$

Figure 4

4 ○ ○ ○ ○ ○ ○ ○ ○ 4

6. A female who has normal vision but is a carrier of red-green color blindness must have which of the following genotypes?

   F. $X^R X^R$
   G. $X^R X^r$
   H. $X^r X^r$
   J. $X^R Y$

7. For a couple to produce only red-green color-blind children, regardless of the child's sex, they would need to have which of the following pairs of genotypes?

   A. $X^R X^R$ and $X^r Y$
   B. $X^r X^r$ and $X^R Y$
   C. $X^R X^r$ and $X^r Y$
   D. $X^r X^r$ and $X^r Y$

8. All of the male offspring exhibited red-green color blindness in Studies:

   F. 1 and 3.
   G. 1, 2, and 3.
   H. 2 and 3.
   J. 1 and 2.

9. Suppose that Barbara and John have 4 daughters. According to the information in Study 1 and the passage, how many of their daughters will manifest the color blind defect?

   A. 0
   B. 1
   C. 2
   D. 4

10. The ratio of Barbara and John's offspring with normal vision to offspring with red-green color blindness is:

   F. 1:2
   G. 2:1
   H. 1:1
   J. 3:1

11. Barbara's parents could have had which of the following pairs of genotypes?

   A. $X^r X^r$ and $X^R Y$
   B. $X^R X^r$ and $X^r Y$
   C. $X^R X^R$ and $X^r Y$
   D. $X^R X^R$ and $X^R Y$

Passage III

Crude oil contains many different types of carbons. Different carbon chain lengths have different boiling points, so they can be separated using *distillation*—the process of boiling and then condensing a liquid in order to separate and purify its components (see Figure 1).

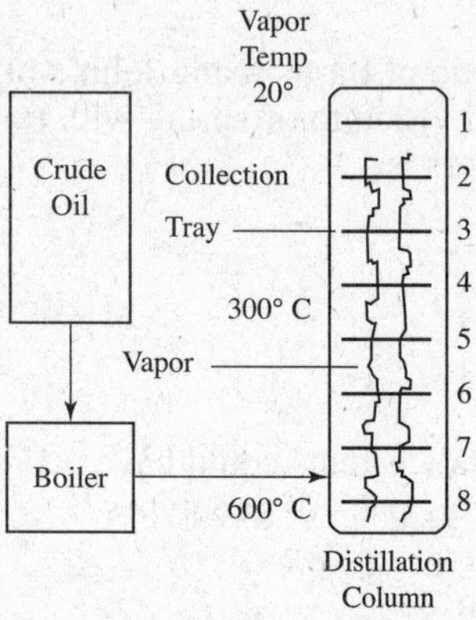

Figure 1

Crude oil is put into a boiler. The boiler is connected to a distillation column filled with collection trays. As the heated oil boils, the vapors released enter the distillation column and rise to the top. When a substance in the vapor reaches a height where the temperature of the column is equal to that substance's boiling point, it will condense to form a liquid. The liquid is gathered on the collection trays.

Experiment 1

Students determined the boiling points of various components of crude oil by recording the temperature of the vapor at various heights in the distillation column, then determining which component was collected in each of the eight collection trays. See Table 1 and Table 2.

Table 1

Boiling Point	Tray #
20°C	1
40°C	2
120°C	3
200°C	4
350°C	5
400°C	6
500°C	7
600°C	8

Table 2

Crude Oil Component	Tray #
Gas	1
Naphtha	2
Gasoline	3
Kerosene	4
Diesel	5
Lubricating oil	6
Heavy gas oil	7
Residual oil	8

The students distilled one barrel of crude oil. Figure 2 shows the breakdown of that barrel, in terms of which components were collected.

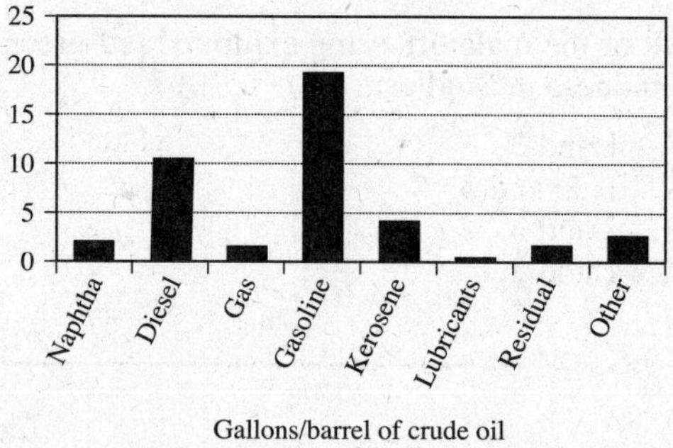

Figure 2

Experiment 2

Students determined the number of carbons in each component of crude oil and recorded the data in Table 3.

Table 3

Crude Oil Component	# of Carbons
Diesel	12+
Gas	1–4
Gasoline	5–12
Heavy gas oil	20–70
Kerosene	10–18
Lubricating oil	20–50
Naphtha	5–9
Residual oil	70+

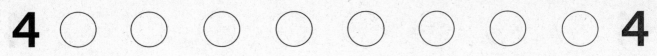

4 ○ ○ ○ ○ ○ ○ ○ ○ 4

12. Based on the results of Experiment 1, the boiling temperature of Naphtha is:
    - **F.** 20°C
    - **G.** 40°C
    - **H.** 120°C
    - **J.** 200°C

13. According to the results of Experiment 1, one barrel of crude oil contains about how many gallons of diesel?
    - **A.** 2
    - **B.** 6
    - **C.** 11
    - **D.** 29

14. One of the students hypothesized that the components of crude oil with the highest boiling points would be collected at the top of the distillation column. Do the results of Experiment 1 support the student's claim?
    - **F.** No. As the vapor rose in the distillation column, the temperature cooled, so the components with the lowest boiling points were collected at the top of the column.
    - **G.** No. There was no correlation between boiling point and location in the distillation column.
    - **H.** Yes. Gasoline and diesel had the highest boiling points, and they were collected in the top two trays.
    - **J.** Yes. The lower the collection tray was in the distillation column, the lower the component's boiling point.

15. A scientist claimed that the more carbons a substance has, the higher its boiling point will be. Do the results of Experiment 1 and Experiment 2 support this claim?
    - **A.** No. There is no relationship between the number of carbons and the boiling point.
    - **B.** No. Diesel has more carbons than gasoline, yet its boiling point is lower.
    - **C.** Yes. Residual oil has the most carbons and the lowest boiling point, whereas gas has the fewest carbons and the highest boiling point.
    - **D.** Yes. Residual oil has the most carbons and the highest boiling point, whereas gas has the fewest carbons and the lowest boiling point.

16. Which of the following components of crude oil has the highest boiling point?
    - **F.** Naphtha
    - **G.** Kerosene
    - **H.** Heavy gas oil
    - **J.** Diesel

17. The data in Table 1 and Figure 2 support which of the following?
    - **A.** Components with the highest boiling points are collected in greatest quantity.
    - **B.** Components with the lowest boiling points are collected in greatest quantity.
    - **C.** Components with medium boiling points are collected in greatest quantity.
    - **D.** Components with higher boiling points are collected in the same quantities as those with medium boiling points.

Practice Test 2

GO ON TO THE NEXT PAGE.

4 ○ ○ ○ ○ ○ ○ ○ ○ 4

Passage IV

Solubility refers to the ability of one substance, the solute, to dissolve in another (the *solvent*). The balance of molecules between the solvent and the solute determines the solubility of one substance in another. Factors such as temperature and pressure will alter this balance, thus changing the solubility.

Experiments to determine the solubility of methane and carbon dioxide in polyamide (PA-11) were performed in the temperature range 50–90°C, and the pressure range 50–150 atm for methane and 20–40 atm for carbon dioxide. Table 1 displays the solubility (sol) of methane in PA-11. Table 2 shows the solubility (sol) of carbon dioxide in PA-11.

$$\text{Solubility} = (g \text{ gas}/g \text{ PA-11}) \times 10^3$$

Table 1—Methane

T = 50°C		T = 70°C		T = 90°C	
Pressure (atm)	Sol	Pressure (atm)	Sol	Pressure (atm)	Sol
51.2	3.18	55.3	2.61	53.1	2.38
107.2	4.51	104.0	4.97	106.5	5.14
156.6	3.45	158.1	5.33	144.4	6.52

Table 2—Carbon Dioxide

T = 50°C		T = 70°C		T = 90°C	
Pressure (atm)	Sol	Pressure (atm)	Sol	Pressure (atm)	Sol
22.1	12.8	20.3	11.8	20	6.93
31.1	18.9	26.4	14.3	30.4	12.0
39.8	23.1	37.5	18.7	42.4	14.0

Figure 1 shows the pressurization cycle for methane at 100 atm and 50°C. The mass gain divided by the net polyamide mass determines the solubility of the gas.

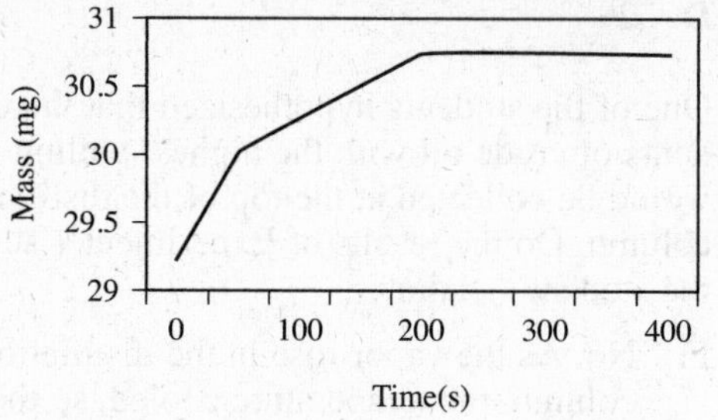

Figure 1

Practice Test 2

18. Which of the following substances did NOT become more soluble as pressure increased?

F. Methane at 70°C
G. Methane at 50°C
H. Carbon dioxide at 50°C
J. Carbon dioxide at 90°C

19. According to Table 2, at which temperature was carbon dioxide the most soluble under pressure of 31.1 atm?

A. 50°C
B. 70°C
C. 90°C
D. 100°C

20. Figure 1 supports which of the following claims about polyamide mass gain over time?

F. The polyamide steadily gained mass.
G. The polyamide lost mass over time.
H. The polyamide gained mass at first, and then lost mass.
J. The polyamide quickly gained mass and then leveled off.

21. If the experiment was repeated at a temperature of 90°C and a pressure of 80 atm, the solubility of methane would be closest to:

A. 2.61 atm.
B. 3.75 atm.
C. 5.08 atm.
D. 14.0 atm.

22. Based on the results shown in Table 2, which of the following conclusions can be drawn regarding the relationship between pressure and solubility?

F. Solubility increases with pressure only above 70°C.
G. As pressure increases, solubility decreases.
H. As pressure increases, so does solubility.
J. There is no correlation between pressure and solubility.

23. In this experiment, which substance functioned as the *solvent*?

A. Methane
B. Carbon dioxide
C. Mass
D. Polyamide

4 ○ ○ ○ ○ ○ ○ ○ ○ 4

Passage V

As shown in Figures 1 and 2, the composition of soil varies by zone. Scientists wanted to determine which types of prairie plants grew best in which zones. To accomplish this, they visited prairies in Zone 3 and in Zone 4 and determined average plant height and root depth (see Table 1). They also looked at several 1-acre plots in both Zone 3 and Zone 4, and recorded the average number of each type of plant found (see Figure 3).

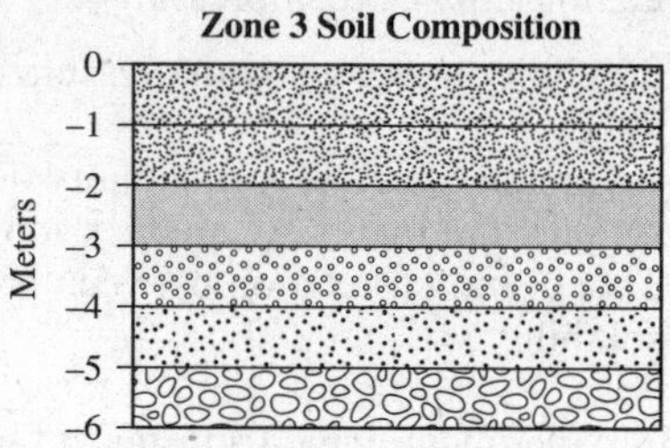

Figure 1

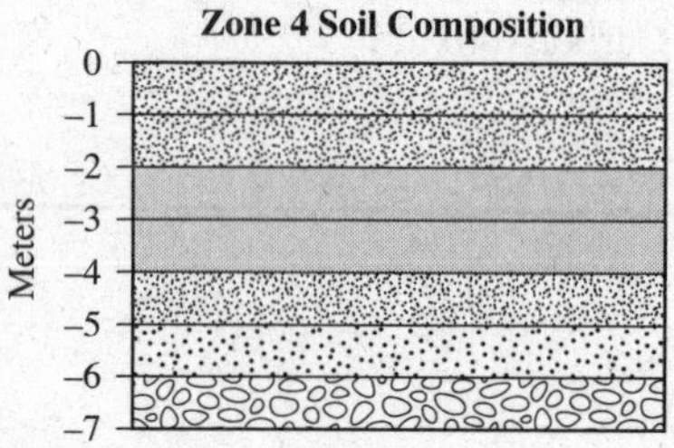

Figure 2

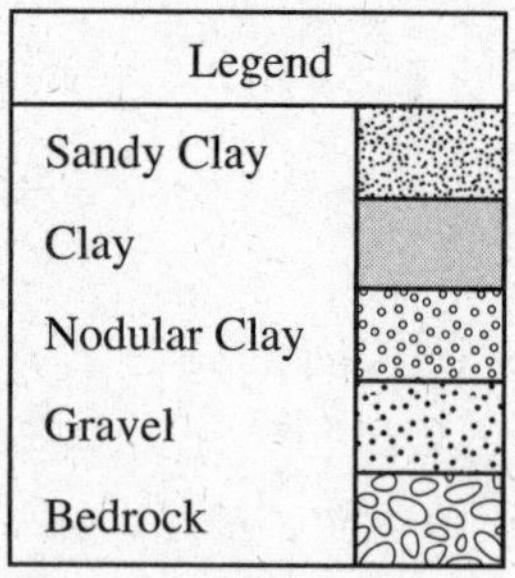

Table 1

Plant Name	Root Depth (m)	Plant Height (m)
Aster	2.4	0.5
Big Blue Stem	3.0	2.1
Compass Plant	5.0	2.4
Goldenrod	2.2	1.0
Indian Grass	2.8	2.3
Kentucky Blue Grass	0.1	0.1
Lead Plant	4.5	0.8
Purple Coneflower	1.8	1.5

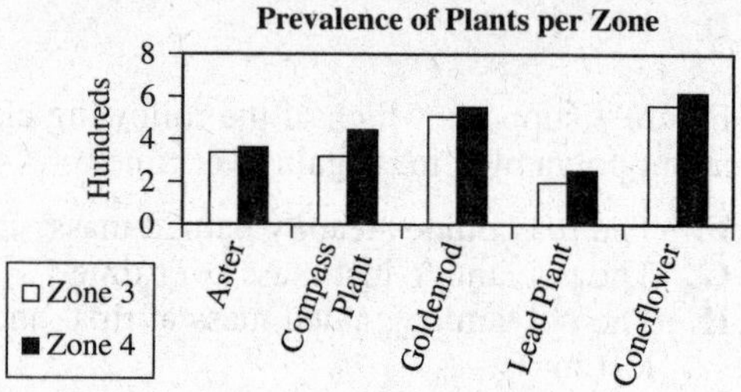

Figure 3

24. In which zone is clay found at a depth of –3.5m?

    F. Zone 3
    G. Zone 4
    H. Zones 3 and 4
    J. Neither Zone 3 nor 4

25. Of the prairie plants studied, which had the tallest average plant height?

    A. Aster
    B. Kentucky Blue Grass
    C. Indian Grass
    D. Compass Plant

26. Based on the data in Figure 3, which of the following can be concluded about the prevalence of plants per zone?

    F. The prairie plants studied grow more easily in Zone 4.
    G. The prairie plants studied grow more easily in Zone 3.
    H. The prairie plants studied grow equally well in Zone 3 and Zone 4.
    J. No conclusion can be drawn about the prevalence of plant growth per zone.

27. A plant growing in which zone would have roots that reach clay first?

    A. Zone 3
    B. Zone 4
    C. None of the plants studied have roots that would reach clay.
    D. Plants in Zone 3 and Zone 4 would reach clay at the same depth.

28. The average Lead Plant growing in Zone 3 would have roots that, at their deepest point, reach down to which of the following soil layers?

    F. Sandy clay
    G. Clay
    H. Gravel
    J. Bedrock

Passage VI

Ever since Darwin proposed his theory of natural selection in 1859, biologists have regarded the gene as the sole unit of inheritance, and the discovery of DNA in the twentieth century only served to reinforce this view, known as "hard inheritance." The idea that environmental factors could produce heritable changes in an organism without altering the organism's DNA (as occurs in gene mutation due to radiation exposure, for example), known as "soft inheritance," had long been written off as an impossibility. "Inheritance of acquired traits" became a biological fallacy associated with pre-Darwinians like Jean-Baptiste Lamarck and fanatical Soviet scientists like Trofim Lysenko. But the very recent discovery of what has been termed *epigenetics*—biological mechanisms that leave DNA unchanged but can alter the ways in which individual genes express themselves—has opened the door on the possibility of "soft inheritance" once again, although many biologists remain skeptical.

Scientist 1

Although study of the so-called "epigenome" is worthwhile and possesses the potential to answer questions about a host of problems from diabetes to cancer, it would be premature to call true "soft inheritance" a reality, at least in animal species. Isolated situations in which environmental factors could affect an organism's immediate descendants—a mother with a zinc deficiency producing children and grandchildren with weakened immune systems, for example—had already been documented without anyone ever suggesting that there was more to heritability than the gene. Immediate successive generations may exhibit observable effects, but the bloodline always reverts to the true expression of its DNA. A map with dust on it may be hard to read, but the information on the map remains unchanged, and it is simply a matter of how long it takes for a strong wind to blow away the dust.

Scientist 2

Someone who is determined never to see "true soft inheritance" will never see it, but that doesn't change the fact that it occurs, and indeed has been occurring all along without our realizing it. Epigenetic mechanisms may not alter DNA, but they possess the ability to turn genes "on" or "off" for the duration of an organism's bloodline, at least until such time as the genes are affected by another epigenetic mechanism. There is already compelling evidence, for example, that tobacco smoking poses risks not only to the individual smoker, but to all of his or her descendants. Imagine a three-way light bulb with three possible brightness settings being put into a three-way lamp on which one of the settings is broken. The fact that the bulb still possesses three settings is immaterial if it is permanently set into a broken lamp. It will continue to "express itself" in a limited way. And the same thing can happen to a gene. If environmental factors can permanently alter the way in which an unaltered gene expresses itself down along a bloodline, resulting in observable effects in the members of that bloodline, then what can we possibly call this other than true soft inheritance?

4 ○ ○ ○ ○ ○ ○ ○ ○ 4

29. According to the information in the passage, which of the following might constitute an example of true soft inheritance?

    A. inherited gene damage due to a parent's heavy radiation exposure
    B. a susceptibility to diabetes as the result of a malnourished grandparent
    C. a left-handed parent producing predominantly left-handed offspring
    D. a parent who loves books teaching her children to love books

30. Who first proposed the theory of epigenetics?

    F. Charles Darwin
    G. Trofim Lysenko
    H. Scientist 2
    J. The information is not included in the passage.

31. In the offspring of which of the following organisms might Scientist 1 currently be willing to concede the documented existence of true soft inheritance?

    A. a rhinoceros
    B. a radiation-exposed human being
    C. an apple tree
    D. a zinc-deficient human being

32. Scientist 2 would most likely *disagree* with the suggestion that genes:

    F. are the primary units of inheritance.
    G. act in isolation to produce traits.
    H. possess the ability to express themselves.
    J. are made up of stretches of DNA.

33. Scientist 1 would be most likely to predict that any ill effects on the grandchildren of a tobacco smoker:

    A. have nothing to do with the epigenome.
    B. are probably psychological rather than biological in origin.
    C. must be the result of tobacco use having altered the smoker's DNA.
    D. will cease to be expressed in the bloodline given enough time.

34. *Histones* are proteins that attach themselves to sequences of DNA and can alter the expression of genes depending on whether they are *acetylated* or *methylated*. Given this information, it would appear that *histones* are analogous to the:

    F. sole unit of inheritance.
    G. zinc-deficient mother mentioned by Scientist 1.
    H. map mentioned by Scientist 1.
    J. lamp mentioned by Scientist 2.

35. A study of what would be most likely to resolve the disagreement between Scientist 1 and Scientist 2?

    A. the length of time that epigenetic mechanisms tend to remain in a bloodline
    B. the unpublished work of Jean-Baptiste Lamarck
    C. a comparison of cancer rates among identical twins
    D. the inner workings of three-way light bulbs

Passage VII

Figure 1 shows the average sleep pattern of a child, Figure 2 shows the average sleep pattern of a young adult, and Figure 3 shows the average sleep pattern of an elderly person. At Stage 0, the person is awake. As sleep moves from Stage 1 to Stage 4, it grows progressively deeper. REM sleep, commonly associated with dreaming, is predominant in the final third of a sleep cycle.

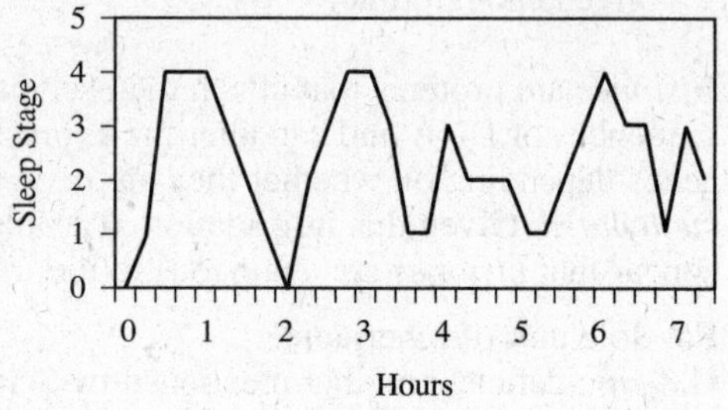

Figure 1

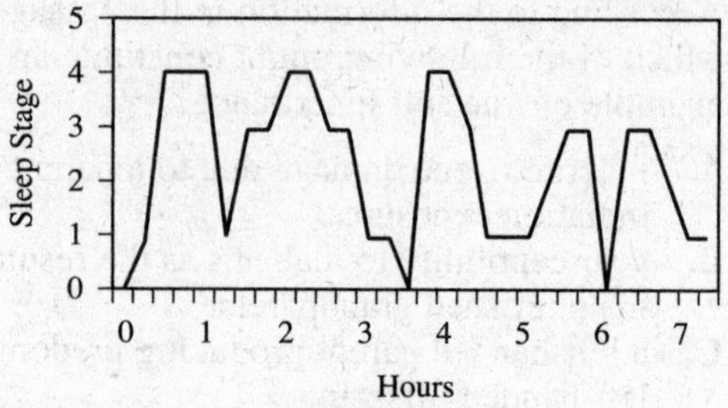

Figure 2

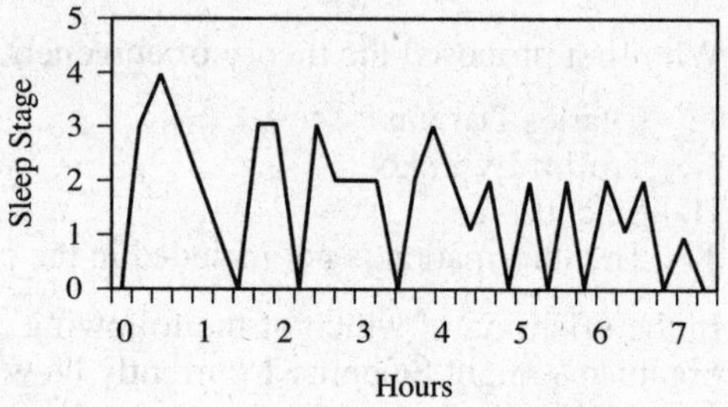

Figure 3

36. According to Figure 2, a young adult who has been asleep for 5 hours will most likely be in which sleep stage?

    F. Stage 0
    G. Stage 1
    H. Stage 3
    J. Stage 5

37. Based on the information in the passage, a child will wake up how many times during a 7-hour stretch of sleep?

    A. 7
    B. 2
    C. 1
    D. 0

38. Based on the data presented in Figures 1, 2, and 3, which of the following conclusions can be properly drawn?

    F. As people age, they wake up more frequently during the night.
    G. As people age, they wake up less frequently during the night.
    H. As people age, they spend more time in deep sleep.
    J. As people age, they spend more consecutive time in each sleep stage.

39. Based on the information in the passage and in Figure 2, at which of the following hours into a sleep interval will a young adult be most likely to experience REM sleep?

    A. 0
    B. 1
    C. 2
    D. 7

40. At which of the following hours of sleep will a child most likely be in the deepest sleep?

    F. 2
    G. 3
    H. 5
    J. 7

STOP

If there is still time remaining, check your answers to this section.

WRITING PROMPT

Directions: This is a test of your writing skills. You will have thirty (30) minutes to write an essay in English. Before you begin planning and writing your essay, read the writing prompt below carefully to understand exactly what you are being asked to do. Your essay will be evaluated on the evidence it provides of your ability to express judgments by taking a position on the issue in the writing prompt; to maintain a focus on the topic throughout the essay; to develop a position by using logical reasoning and by supporting your ideas; to organize ideas in a logical way; and to use language clearly and effectively according to the conventions of standard written English.

You may use the unlined page to plan your essay. This page will not be scored. You must write your essay in pencil on the lined pages provided. Your writing on those lined pages will be scored. You may not need all the pages, but to ensure you have enough room to finish, do NOT skip lines. You may write corrections or additions neatly between the lines of your essay, but do NOT write in the margins of the lined pages. Illegible essays cannot be scored, so you must write (or print) clearly.

If you finish before time is called, you may review your work. Lay your pencil down immediately when time is called.

The need for a long summer vacation has been questioned by a group of parents. These parents would like students to attend school all year long, with several short vacation breaks at different times during the year. This group believes that children forget too much of what they have learned over the long summer break. Other people think that students need the long summer vacation to decompress from the school year and to participate in various extracurricular activities. In your opinion, should schools abandon long summer vacations and adopt a year-round calendar?

In your essay, take a position on this question. You may write about either one of the two points of view given, or you may present a different point of view on this question. Use specific reasons and examples to support your position.

Use this page to *plan* your essay.

Begin WRITING TEST here.

If you need more space, continue on the next page.

WRITING TEST

Answer Key

PRACTICE TEST 2

English Test

1. A	16. F	31. D	46. F	61. C
2. G	17. C	32. G	47. C	62. G
3. C	18. F	33. A	48. F	63. B
4. G	19. D	34. G	49. A	64. G
5. C	20. G	35. D	50. J	65. A
6. J	21. A	36. F	51. D	66. J
7. A	22. J	37. B	52. H	67. B
8. H	23. C	38. H	53. B	68. F
9. A	24. H	39. B	54. J	69. B
10. J	25. A	40. J	55. B	70. F
11. D	26. F	41. C	56. G	71. B
12. H	27. B	42. F	57. A	72. G
13. C	28. J	43. A	58. H	73. D
14. G	29. A	44. G	59. B	74. H
15. C	30. J	45. B	60. J	75. D

Math Test

1. A	13. D	25. E	37. D	49. E
2. G	14. K	26. G	38. K	50. H
3. B	15. D	27. D	39. A	51. E
4. J	16. H	28. H	40. H	52. H
5. E	17. D	29. A	41. C	53. A
6. F	18. K	30. H	42. K	54. G
7. C	19. E	31. C	43. B	55. C
8. H	20. J	32. J	44. G	56. J
9. C	21. D	33. E	45. C	57. B
10. H	22. G	34. F	46. K	58. K
11. C	23. C	35. C	47. C	59. A
12. K	24. J	36. H	48. J	60. K

Answer Key

PRACTICE TEST 2

Reading Test

1. B	9. C	17. B	25. A	33. C
2. F	10. J	18. J	26. J	34. F
3. D	11. C	19. D	27. C	35. D
4. H	12. G	20. F	28. F	36. F
5. B	13. A	21. D	29. B	37. D
6. F	14. J	22. G	30. H	38. H
7. C	15. C	23. C	31. B	39. A
8. J	16. G	24. G	32. J	40. G

Science Test

1. A	9. A	17. C	25. D	33. D
2. J	10. H	18. G	26. F	34. J
3. C	11. B	19. A	27. D	35. A
4. G	12. G	20. J	28. H	36. G
5. B	13. C	21. B	29. B	37. C
6. G	14. F	22. H	30. J	38. F
7. D	15. D	23. D	31. C	39. D
8. F	16. H	24. G	32. G	40. G

HOW TO SCORE YOUR PRACTICE TEST

Step 1: Add up the number correct for each section and write that number in the blank under the Raw Score column on the Score Conversion Table. (Your goal is to get more questions correct on each subsequent practice test.)

Step 2: Using the Score Conversion Chart, find your scale score for each section and write it down. Then add up all four sections and divide by 4 to find your overall composite score. (Composite scores are rounded up at .5 or higher.)

Score Conversion Table

Section	Raw Score	Scaled Score
English	(out of 75)	____ / 36
Math	(out of 60)	____ / 36
Reading	(out of 40)	____ / 36
Science	(out of 40)	____ / 36
		Add and divide by 4
Overall Composite =		____ / 36

Score Conversion Chart

	Number Correct				
ACT Score*	English Section	Mathematics Section	Reading Section	Science Section	ACT Score*
36	75	60	40	40	**36**
35	74	59	39	39	**35**
34	73	58	38	38	**34**
33	72	57	37	—	**33**
32	71	56	36	37	**32**
31	70	54–55	35	36	**31**
30	69	53	34	35	**30**
29	67–68	51–52	33	34	**29**
28	65–66	49–50	32	33	**28**
27	64	46–48	31	31–32	**27**
26	62–63	44–45	30	30	**26**
25	60–61	41–43	29	28–29	**25**
24	58–59	39–40	27–28	25–27	**24**
23	55–57	37–38	25–26	24	**23**
22	53–54	35–36	23–24	22–23	**22**
21	50–52	33–34	22	20–21	**21**
20	47–49	31–32	21	18–19	**20**
19	44–46	28–30	19–20	17	**19**
18	42–43	25–27	18	15–16	**18**
17	40–41	22–24	17	14	**17**

Continued

Score Conversion Chart *(Continued)*

	Number Correct				
ACT Score*	English Section	Mathematics Section	Reading Section	Science Section	ACT Score*
16	37–39	19–21	16	13	**16**
15	34–36	15–17	15	12	**15**
14	31–33	11–14	13–14	11	**14**
13	29–30	09–10	12	10	**13**
12	27–28	07–08	10–11	09	**12**
11	25–26	06	08–09	08	**11**
10	23–24	05	07	07	**10**
9	21–22	04	06	05–06	**9**
8	18–20	03	05	—	**8**
7	15–17	—	—	04	**7**
6	12–14	02	04	03	**6**
5	09–11	—	03	02	**5**
4	07–08	01	02	—	**4**
3	05–06	—	—	01	**3**
2	03–04	—	01	—	**2**
1	00–02	00	00	00	**1**

**These scores are based on student trials rather than national norms.*

SCORING YOUR ESSAY

As mentioned earlier in this text, two readers will evaluate your essay and each person will then assign it a score from 1 to 6. If, by chance, these two scorers disagree by more than 1 point, a third reader will step in and resolve the discrepancy. Performance on the essay will not affect your English, math, reading, science, or composite scores. You will receive two additional scores on your score sheet—a combined English/writing score (1–36) and a writing test subscore (1–12). Neither of these scores will affect your composite score!

The sample essay that follows reflects higher-level writing. It meets the criteria that ACT has put forth for essays that demonstrate effective writing skills.

- It takes a definite position.
- It addresses and expands on the counterargument.
- It has details that support the topic sentences and is well organized.
- It is not repetitive, and while there may be errors, they do not interfere with the competence of the essay.
- It is consistent and well balanced.
- The essay has a clear introduction and a conclusion that is not just a summary but ends with a significant thought.
- The vocabulary demonstrates good use of language and the sentence structure is varied.

Answer Explanations: English Test

1. **(A)** Although it would also be correct to turn the name *Stephen* into an appositive clause set off with commas on both sides (since you could take out the name and it would still be a complete sentence), when the appositive clause is *just the person's name and nothing else* it is fine to leave out the commas. (For example, you could write *My friend Adam has a car* without having to put commas before and after *Adam*.) But remember, *only one* comma in this situation is wrong; you have to either have two or none.
2. **(G)** This is a parallel phrasing question. The end of the sentence presents a list of three actions, and the previous two verbs (*whizzing* and *weaving*) are in the progressive tense (meaning they end in *-ing*, to signify an ongoing action), so this verb has to be too.
3. **(C)** The first clause is an independent one, and then the clause beginning with the relative pronoun *where* is a dependent descriptive one, and so all we need is a comma. Although the second clause would be an independent one if you got rid of the *where*, with the *where* it is not. (Remember, when you see that two of the choices are a semicolon and a period, it is almost always the case that they cancel each other out and the right answer is a comma!)
4. **(G)** A *rite of passage* is an event or ceremony you go through that changes you in some important way and makes you part of something. So *experience* would be the right verb here, because you *go through* it.
5. **(C)** The third-person plural possessive pronoun is spelled *their*. You can remember that this is the possessive one because it contains the word *heir* (as in a person who eventually *possesses* something), and distinguish it from the other spellings by memorizing the sentence *They're in there with their bear*.
6. **(J)** What we need here is *have been riding*, which is in the present perfect continuous tense. That sounds complicated, but all it means is that someone is currently in the state of having been doing something for a long time—in other words, the verb needs to include both the present *and* the past, and choice J is the only option that does. (Remember, you don't need to know what tenses are *called* to get tense questions right!)
7. **(A)** *How many* worlds are there here? One. And does it *possess* something? Yes (the first bicycle). So what we need is the singular possessive *world's*. The sentence is an independent clause up through the word *bicycle*, and the clause beginning with though is an "afterthought clause" that adds extra information, so it needs to be preceded by a comma.
8. **(H)** The essay is about the narrator and her relationship to bicycles, not about da Vinci or the history of bicycles themselves, and so specifics about da Vinci's bicycle sketch are unnecessary and distracting.
9. **(A)** The question asks for the phrase that reinforces the idea that bicycles are *amazing inventions*, and so you want the one that is extremely complimentary. The best choice is A, which refers to bicycles as a *marvel*.
10. **(J)** Since the underlined part is followed by *is*, we know that the right answer has to be a noun phrase, because it will function as the subject of the sentence. The infinitive form of a verb represents a concept, and so can work like a noun (as in *To err is human*). It also matches the infinitive *to balance* that comes after the *is*, and so obeys the rule of parallel phrasing. That is pretty complicated, but hopefully the wrong answers all "sounded strange," even if you couldn't explain why. (Remember, when in doubt on the ACT English, always go with the shortest answer, as long as it makes a complete sentence and doesn't sound strange!)
11. **(D)** All of the choices are prepositions or prepositional phrases that simply mean "on" and can be used in its place, except for *on which*, which would be used to introduce extra information and would precede the thing that is on something else: *The dog, on which there were fleas, was brown.*
12. **(H)** Every answer choice involves how to separate two independent clauses. A colon can be used to separate two independent clauses, although it does not always have to.
13. **(C)** The earlier *is* establishes that the sentence is in the present tense, and *human will* is singular. So what we need here is the present third-person singular form of the verb, which is *keeps*.
14. **(G)** This is the only choice that efficiently completes the preceding independent clause and appropriately introduces the subsequent dependent clause with a comma and *which*.
15. **(C)** The proposed sentence doesn't have anything directly to do with the subject of the essay, and the previous sentence conveyed a much more forceful "sense of an ending."
16. **(F)** The plural verb *have* agrees with the plural noun *sites*. *Like* acts as a preposition here, and the prepositional phrase *like Facebook* must be "jumped over." As the pronoun *us* is the object of *have*, there is no reason to add the preposition *to* (no object is being brought *to* us; rather, *we* are being brought together).

17. **(C)** What we need here is the adjective *allowed*, which means "permitted" (rather than the adverb *aloud*, which means "out loud"), and the preposition *to*, which introduces infinitives (rather than the adverb *too*, which means "also").

18. **(F)** The fact that the author is a professional writer means that he would find it odd or ironic that he is having more trouble writing something simple than nonwriters are having.

19. **(D)** The preceding paragraph has been about how the author has difficulty thinking of Facebook status updates. Although being good at writing English papers involves many different skills, the one that is relevant in context is the ability to think of things to say.

20. **(G)** The subsequent sentences joke about how no one cares that other people's status updates are boring, and yet the author is still agonizing over making his perfect. Therefore, *Maybe I'm overthinking this* is a logical opening.

21. **(A)** We need the contraction *you're* here ("you are"), rather than the possessive pronoun *your*. Additionally, although normally *thinks* would be required by the noun *everyone* (which is singular, despite the fact that it refers to many people), the fact that this is a question beginning with *doesn't* changes things. It's "everyone *thinks*," but "everyone does/doesn't *think*." That may sound complicated, but it's easy if you just remain calm and think about what *sounds* right.

22. **(J)** The author is calling himself the only one *who has* figured this out, and *who's* is a contraction for "who has" (or "who is").

23. **(C)** What we need here is the contraction *there's*, for "there is" ("There is nothing wrong with…").

24. **(H)** We are talking about girls in general, and so we need the plural possessive *girls'* (with the apostrophe after the *s*). *Swimsuits* is not possessive, and does not need an apostrophe anywhere.

25. **(A)** The author means to say *It's* ("it is") *all* (meaning the "whole situation") *so* (as in "very") *depressing*. This is the only one of the choices that presents a comprehensible sentence. ("It's also depressing" would also be a comprehensible sentence, but it is not one of the choices.)

26. **(F)** *Being* is a gerund here, and *being depressed* is the subject clause of the sentence. None of the other choices make sense. (Remember, just because the test tries to trick you with *being* a lot, that doesn't mean that it's *never* the right answer!)

27. **(B)** This is a comma splice, albeit a comma splice in disguise. The clauses before and after "you see" are both independent clauses, and putting "you see" between them doesn't change this. Remember, you can't fix a comma splice by just inserting *any* words—the words you add have to render one of the independent clauses dependent! The other choices are all correct, but this one is NOT acceptable.

28. **(J)** The clause is an essential one (it is not "extra") and so we need to begin it with *that*, not with comma + *which*. Furthermore, we need the contraction *you're* ("you are"), not the possessive pronoun *your*. We also need the comparative conjunction *than*, rather than the time-related adverb *then*. Finally, we need the pronoun + verb *they are*, rather than the possessive pronoun *theirs* or adverb/pronoun *there*. That sounds complicated, but the clause we're trying to construct here is perfectly straightforward: "making people think *that you're* having more fun *than they are*." None of the other choices make even a little bit of sense.

29. **(A)** What we need here is the possessive pronoun *our*.

30. **(J)** An argument that something should be legally regulated would have to mention the law or the government at some point, and this passage does not.

31. **(D)** The other verb phrases in the sentence (*could hear, was called*) establish that it is in the past tense. Therefore, the past tense form *we began* is what is needed.

32. **(G)** The descriptive phrase *proud as ever* is an "extra" clause providing additional information that could be lifted out of the sentence. Therefore, it should be set off with commas on both sides.

33. **(A)** *He wasn't the most beautiful horse in the world* is an independent clause, and *If the truth were told* is a dependent introductory clause that needs to be followed by a comma.

34. **(G)** As the preceding and subsequent sentences indicate, the paragraph is about how Monte is a fine horse despite not being beautiful. This sentence offers a physical description of the ways in which he is not beautiful, and so it is relevant and necessary here. Furthermore, without it the paragraph would only have two sentences and seem bizarrely short, further indicating that you are probably supposed to include it.

35. **(D)** The information in this sentence stands in opposition or contrast to the information contained in the previous sentence. Therefore, the appropriate transition phrase is *Yet*, which implies contrast or counterpoint; the other choices do not. (As with so many places on the ACT, "which of these things is not like the others" is a very good strategy here!)

36. **(F)** The idea is that once upon a time Western equitation was unfamiliar to them, but it is not now. Therefore, what is needed is the past perfect tense *had been*. The regular past tense might be acceptable too, but it is not one of the choices; the past perfect is the only type of past tense that is an option.

37. **(B)** All of the answers are synonyms for *learned* or *understood* except for *beat*, which means "overcome." Therefore, *beat* is the LEAST acceptable alternative to the underlined portion. An athlete might say that they beat their competition, but not that they beat the *rules* of the sport themselves. (As with so many places on the ACT, "which of these things is not like the others" is a very good strategy here!)

38. **(H)** The fact that Monte did not touch any of the barrels provides more specific information about the nature of his graceful racing; it explains that he was not just good, but perfect.

39. **(B)** This sentence concerns the portion of the race *before* the narrator and Monte entered the barrels. Therefore, it needs to come before sentence 2, where they enter the barrels.

40. **(J)** The question asks for a phrase that suggests the narrator's nervousness. Only choice J, which includes the word *anxiously*, does so. The others all make her seem satisfied and confident. (Remember, even when it seems obvious what a question on the ACT English is asking for, always carefully read the little directions in their entirety, because they usually give a fairly big hint!)

41. **(C)** What you need here is a phrase that means *besides*, and *except for* is the only one of the choices that does.

42. **(F)** *How many* grandfathers are we talking about? One. And does he *possess* anything? Yes (his voice). So what we need is the singular possessive, which is *grandfather's*. It is just that simple.

43. **(A)** The story is in the past tense, and the past tense verb *kissed* in the same sentence reminds us of this. The form we need here is the past tense *echoed*.

44. **(G)** The underlined portion is followed by the verb *won*, which means that the pronouns in the underlined portion are performing a verb. Therefore, they should both be in the subjective case, which means what we need is *he and I* (you wouldn't say *him won* or *me won*; you would say *he won* and *I won*).

45. **(B)** The point of the story is that Monte was able to win the race even though he wasn't a natural-born athlete. This successfully fulfills the question's requirement about spirit and determination being just as important as inborn ability.

46. **(F)** The phrase "people *in which* thousands of years ago" makes no sense. It would mean that "thousands of years ago" is a subject phrase that *did* something *inside* people. All of the other choices make sense.

47. **(C)** This choice correctly uses *no* (i.e., "not any") and *know* (i.e., "to understand").

48. **(F)** This choice correctly uses the plural pronoun *them* to stand in for the plural noun *horoscopes*.

49. **(A)** The phrase is indeed humorous, and does indeed illustrate the fact that horoscopes are meaningless (i.e., they are so vague that there would be no way to know they are wrong, even if they had been misprinted).

50. **(J)** The next sentence continues the idea that the reader already knows what astrology is ("We're all familiar with....").

51. **(D)** This results in a comprehensible sentence with the clauses in the right order. The *supposed personality traits* are what we're all familiar with, and these traits allegedly belong to *people* (who were) born under certain signs.

52. **(H)** The issue is *essential* versus *nonessential* clauses. We already know that astrology makes claims; the issue is whether it makes sufficiently specific claims. Therefore, the part about whether the claims are specific is not "extra," but essential, and should be introduced with *that* (and no comma).

53. **(B)** The so-called test involves *people* (who are) *deciding*. The test involves *people deciding whether to apply* terms. The present progressive *-ing* form is necessary, as this is an *ongoing* state. This is easy to see if you just "jump over" the extra descriptive clause *who want to believe*.

54. **(J)** The people in question are self-applying the terms, and so the reflexive *themselves* is needed, rather than the nominative *they* or objective *them*. Since the preposition *to* extends to both objects, no comma before the conjunction is necessary. Though it is a polite convention to name oneself after others, it is not a grammatical rule, and so the fact that *themselves* comes before *their friends* is not enough to make this choice wrong, especially in light of the serious errors in the other choices.

55. **(B)** *Could've* is a contraction of *could have*, and so makes perfect sense in context.

56. **(G)** *Anyway* (here acting like "in the first place") makes the most sense after *are*: "the stars' apparent positions aren't really where they are *in the first place*."

57. **(A)** *It's all a bunch of nonsense* is the main independent clause. *Luckily for astrologers* is a dependent introductory clause followed by a comma, and *so nobody ever noticed* is a dependent clause preceded by a comma.

58. **(H)** The semicolon correctly separates two independent clauses. This is a deliberate trick question. Although *however* is typically inserted into the middle of a single independent clause and set off with a pair of commas, it can also appear as the first word of an independent clause (meaning "on the other hand") or the last word of an independent clause (meaning "though" or "despite this"), set off with a single comma. In this sentence, an independent clause that *happens to end* with *however* is followed by a semicolon and a second independent clause. Although this would hardly ever happen in real life because it's so confusing, it is technically grammatically correct, and so the ACT English does it occasionally to trick you. If you see *however* set off with two commas, make sure that a *single* independent clause exists *around* it—not one on each side.

59. **(B)** As the preceding sentence implies ("my answer is always the same"), this describes a *habitual* practice, and so the future tense ("I'll reply") is used.

60. **(J)** In addition to being funny and memorable, the previous sentence sums up what the entire final paragraph was about. Adding the bit about bookstores would be a weaker ending and randomly introduces a new idea.

61. **(C)** The subject of the sentence is *Intuitions* and the verb is *are*. The phrase *or gut feelings* is extra information that can be lifted out of the sentence, and so should be set off with commas.

62. **(G)** Although there has been no indication of this so far, by the end of the subsequent sentence it is established that the passage is written in the second person. Therefore, what we need here is *you can't*. (Remember, person and tense questions on the ACT English <u>frequently</u> necessitate reading ahead, especially when they appear early in a passage!)

63. **(B)** The passage is in the present tense, as indicated in this sentence by the verbs *emerge* and *begin*, and by the contraction *you're* ("you are"). And the antecedent of *it* is *visual inconsistency*, which you would *notice* rather than *feel*. Therefore, what we need is the second-person present tense form *notice*.

64. **(G)** As the first sentence of the first paragraph establishes, what is being referred to here is *intuition*. You must be clear. "It" has no reference.

65. **(A)** The proposed sentence explains that intuition is now acknowledged by science, and therefore provides a needed transition between the previous sentence and the following one, which involves psychologists studying intuition.

66. **(J)** *Psychologists now believe* is the most direct way of saying what you want to say here. (Remember, on the ACT English, when a question presents alternate ways of arranging a phrase, and the question does not ask for something specific such as "the most vivid description," the right answer is <u>almost always</u> the shortest one as long as it results in a complete sentence!)

67. **(B)** The rule of parallel phrasing dictates that the other verbs in the series need to match the third-person singular present tense form *finds* (which is in that form because the sentence is in the present tense and the subject is *brain*). Therefore, the forms we need for the other verbs are *takes* and *does*.

68. **(F)** *You ascribe meaning to the situation in front of you* is the independent clause, and *Based on that analogy* is the introductory dependent clause. They should be separated with a comma.

69. **(B)** The antecedent of the pronoun is the *young woman*, and so the pronoun needed here is *she*.

70. **(F)** The question asks for the best illustration of how information is stored in our brain; only choice A, which includes the phrase *as a web of fact and feeling*, offers an *illustration* of this.

71. **(B)** The sentence is in the present tense, and there is no indication that we need anything other than the simplest form of the infinitive: a new experience unleashes a predisposition *to respond*.

72. **(G)** The sentence provides a useful introduction to the closing paragraph by contextualizing intuition alongside another means of arriving at knowledge. You would also do well to notice that, regardless of how you answer question 73, the subsequent sentence is going to begin with a transition phrase that suggests it is not the first sentence of the paragraph (which means you are supposed to keep this one).

73. **(D)** The sentence suggests a third option different from the two explored in the previous sentence. A simple *But* is the most effective transition phrase. (Remember, although you may have been told in grade school not to begin a sentence with a conjunction such as *and* or *but*, it is actually acceptable to begin a sentence with a conjunction under certain circumstances, and so <u>an answer choice on the ACT English cannot be eliminated solely because it begins a sentence with a conjunction!</u>)

74. **(H)** The question asks for a phrase supporting the idea that intuitions are reliable in an area where one is experienced. Only choice H, which points out that such intuitions *arise out of the richest array of collected patterns of experience*, gets the job done.

75. **(D)** The sentence, along with the rest of the passage, is in the present tense. There is no indication that anything other than the regular present tense *receive* is what is needed here.

Answer Explanations: Math Test

1. **(A)** $(1 - 5)^3 = (-4)^3 = -64$.
2. **(G)** 30 is divisible by 3, 5, and 6. It is the lowest common multiple.
3. **(B)** If $r = 0$, $[-s + h(t \cdot 3 - w)](0) = 0$, not 1.
4. **(J)** If 30% come from families that have only one child, then 70% come from families that do not have one child. 70% of 7,340 = .70(7,340) = 5,138.
5. **(E)** $(3 - 2x)^2 = (3 - 2x)(3 - 2x) = 9 - 6x - 6x + 4x^2$. Combining like terms gives $9 - 12x + 4x^2$. Incidentally, this is true for all x, not just for $x < 3$.
6. **(F)** $3y + 2x = 24$ is $3y = -2x + 24$ when we subtract $2x$ from both sides. Finally, dividing each term by 3 gives $y = \frac{-2}{3}x + 8$.
7. **(C)** The equation $3x + 2y = 19$ is equivalent to $y = \frac{-3}{2}x + \frac{19}{2}$. The slopes of perpendicular lines are opposite reciprocals. Therefore, the slope would be $\frac{2}{3}$.
8. **(H)** $V = \frac{\pi}{3}(3)^2(8) = \frac{\pi}{3}(9)(8) = 24\pi$.
9. **(C)** $\measuredangle b \cong \measuredangle d$ by vertical angles. $\measuredangle d$ and $\measuredangle e$ are supplementary because they are interior angles on the same side of the transversal. Since $m\measuredangle l = m\measuredangle b = 100°$, $m\measuredangle e = 80°$.
10. **(H)** In the diagram $m\measuredangle 1 = 40°$ by vertical angles. Then $m\measuredangle 2 = 65°$, since the angles of a triangle add to 180°. By vertical angles $x = 65$.

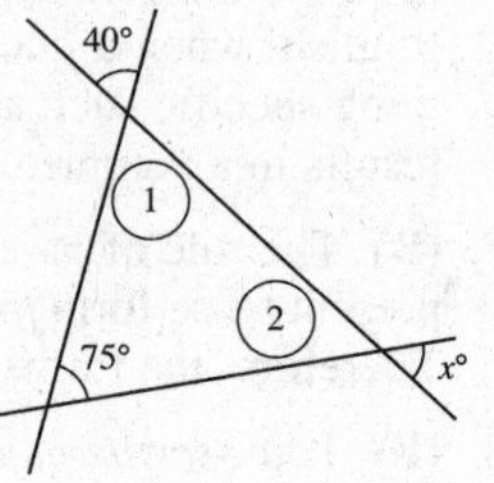

11. **(C)** 11, 16, 21, 26 is an arithmetic sequence with a common difference equal to 5.
12. **(K)** $(2x + 3y)^2$ means $(2x + 3y)(2x + 3y) = 2x(2x) + 2x(3y) + 3y(2x) + (3y)(3y)$. This simplifies to $4x^2 + 6xy + 6xy + 9y^2$ and finally to $4x^2 + 12xy + 9y^2$.
13. **(D)** 60% are Democrats translates to (.60)(7695) = 4617. This problem can also be done by using the proportion: $\frac{60}{100} = \frac{x}{7695}$.
14. **(K)** $-6x + 3y = -36$ is (-3) times $2x - y = 12$. If an equation is a nonzero multiple of another equation, their graphs are equal. Another way would be to put $2x - y = 12$ in slope-intercept form $y = 2x - 12$. We now know the slope is 2 and the y-intercept is (-12). Then $-6x + 3y = -36 \Rightarrow 3y = 6x - 36$ and $y = 2x - 12$.
15. **(D)** $\frac{1}{3}w + \frac{2}{5}w = 1$ equals $\frac{5}{15}w + \frac{6}{15}w = 1$ when we get a common denominator. (You could also add $\frac{1}{3} + \frac{2}{5}$ on your calculator.) Combining like terms we have $\frac{11}{15}w = 1$. Either multiply by $\frac{15}{11}$ or divide by $\frac{11}{15}$.

$$\frac{15}{11} \cdot \frac{11}{15}w = \frac{15(1)}{11} \cdot w = \frac{15}{11}.$$

16. **(H)** $\Delta CEA \cong \Delta DEB$. To see this we have $\overline{CE} \cong \overline{DE}$ and $\overline{AE} \cong \overline{BE}$ and $\measuredangle CEA \cong \measuredangle DEB$. The segments are congruent since $\overline{AB}$ and $\overline{CD}$ bisect each other. The angles are vertical angles. So the triangles are congruent by SAS. By CPCTC, $\measuredangle C \cong \measuredangle D$. That means $m\measuredangle C = 60°$. In ΔCEA we have a 60° and an 80° angle, so the third angle ($\measuredangle CEA$) must be 40°.

17. **(D)** The distance formula is $\sqrt{(x_2 - x_1)^2 + (y_2 - y_1)^2}$. For $A(3, 2)$ and $B(15, 8)$, we have $\sqrt{(15-3)^2 + (8-2)^2} = \sqrt{144 + 36} = \sqrt{180} = \sqrt{36}\sqrt{5} = 6\sqrt{5}$.

18. **(K)** Although we are not told that a and b are positive, we can use positive values to help us eliminate incorrect choices. Let $a = 2$ and $b = 3$. And c can be any number greater than zero. Now we can eliminate answers. We see that F, G, H, and J can be eliminated, which leaves K. So K must be correct because the others cannot be correct.

19. **(E)** This problem is done by using the fundamental counting principle that if Event 1 can be done in M ways and Event 2 can be done in N ways, then the total number of ways that we can do both events is M(N). Applying this we have (4)(3)(5) = 60 ways of choosing meat, cheese, and bread.

20. **(J)** There are 400 employees (240 women + 160 men). The percentage who are women can be found by $\frac{\text{number of women}}{\text{total number}} \times 100$. This equals $\frac{240}{400} \times 100 = 60\%$.

21. **(D)** We will use the equation $d = rt$, where d = distance, r = rate, and t = time. $200 = (4)r$, which gives $r = 50$ mph before stopping for gas. She then drives 10 mph faster for 3 hours. 50 + 10 = 60 mph. $d = 60(3) = 180$ miles. The total number of miles equals 200 + 180 = 380 miles.

22. **(G)** We are given the formula $M = \frac{P}{200} - .0008P + 40$ where M is the monthly payment and P is the cost of the house. Since the house costs \$200,000, $P = 200{,}000$ and $M = \frac{200{,}000}{200} - .0008(200{,}000) + 40$. $M = \$880$.

23. **(C)** The prime factorization of 330 is 2(3)(5)(11). The sum is 2 + 3 + 5 + 11 = 21.

24. **(J)** If you sketch the points and draw the line that contains the two points, it appears that it crosses the y-axis at –5. Mathematically, the slope of the line is $\frac{10-(-2)}{5-1} = \frac{12}{4} = 3$. Using $y = mx + b$ and the point (5, 10), we have $10 = 3(5) + b$. Thus $b = -5$. The y-intercept is –5, so the point is (0, –5).

25. **(E)** $\frac{2^{-1}a^{-3}b^7c^2}{(5a)^2b^{-1}c^7}$ can be rewritten as $\frac{2^{-1}a^{-3}b^7c^2}{25a^2b^{-1}c^7}$ by squaring (5a). Then as $\frac{b \cdot b^7c^2}{2 \cdot 25a^2a^3c^7}$ by getting rid of negative exponents. And finally, $\frac{b^8}{50a^5c^5}$.

26. **(G)** The center of the circle is the midpoint of any diameter. Thus if we say the other endpoint is (a, b) and use the midpoint formula we have $\left(\frac{a+5}{2}, \frac{b+-2}{2}\right) = (2, -3)$. The x-coordinates must be equal. $\frac{a+5}{2} = 2 \Rightarrow a + 5 = 4$, so $a = -1$. There is only one answer choice with $x = -1$ so we really don't need to find y. But $\frac{b-2}{2} = -3 \Rightarrow b - 2 = -6$ so $b = -4$.

27. **(D)** The median is the middle number when arranged in order. When arranged from least to greatest we have $1\frac{2}{3}$, $1\frac{7}{8}$, and $2\frac{1}{5}$. Thus the median is $1\frac{7}{8}$ • $1\frac{7}{8}$ is 1.875 as a decimal.

28. **(H)** If we FOIL $(cx - 1)(3x + 2)$ we have $3cx^2 + 2cx - 3x - 2$. Putting this back into the equation, the result is $6x^2 + x - c = 3cx^2 + (2c - 3)x - 2$. For this to be true for all x, we equate the coefficients of x^2 and x and the constant terms. This gives us $6 = 3c$, $1 = 2c - 3$, and $-c = -2$, and $c = 2$.

29. **(A)** This can be solved easily by the substitution method. $5x + 5 = 3x - 7$ is equivalent to $2x = -12$. Therefore $x = -6$. But we were asked for the y-coordinate. Using the equation $y = 3x - 7$ and substituting (–6) for x we find that $y = 3(-6) - 7 = -25$.

30. **(H)** The figure is a trapezoid. The area formula is $A = \frac{h(b_1 + b_2)}{2}$, where h is the height and b_1 and b_2 are the bases. $A = \frac{3(10+14)}{2} = \frac{72}{2} = 36$.

31. **(C)** $6 - 4(x - 2) > 4x + 5$ is equivalent to $6 - 4x + 8 > 4x + 5$. $14 - 4x > 4x + 5$ is equivalent to $-8x > -9$. Now we divide by (-8). When dividing an inequality by a negative number, the inequality sign must be flipped. The answer then is $x < \frac{9}{8}$.

32. **(J)** The equation of a circle with center (H, K) and radius R is $(x - H)^2 + (y - K)^2 = R^2$. Thus for $(x - 1)^2 + (y + 2)^2 = 8$ the center is $(1, -2)$ and $R^2 = 8$. $R = \sqrt{8} = 2\sqrt{2}$.

33. **(E)** The area of a parallelogram is base times height. The base is $\overline{RS}$, so we must find RA. UR is 5 since opposite sides of a parallelogram are congruent. Either by the Pythagorean Theorem or by a 3 – 4 – 5 right triangle, $RA = 3$. So $RS = 3 + 7 = 10$. Height of $UA = 4$. $A = 10(4) = 40$.

34. **(F)** We have a right triangle and are given the lengths of two sides. Therefore, we use the Pythagorean Theorem: $a^2 + b^2 = c^2$. $6^2 + 4^2 = c^2 \Rightarrow c^2 = 52$. Taking square roots gives us $c = \sqrt{52} = 2\sqrt{13}$.

35. **(C)** The center of the circle is the midpoint of the diameter and the radius is one-half the length of the diameter $\overline{AB}$. For A (4, 2) and B (8, –4), the midpoint is $\left(\frac{4+8}{2}, \frac{2+-4}{2}\right) = (6, -1)$. This is the center.

$AB = \sqrt{(8-4)^2+(-4-2)^2} = \sqrt{16+36} = \sqrt{52} = 2\sqrt{3}$. The radius is $\frac{2\sqrt{13}}{2} = \sqrt{13}$. Substituting into the equation of a circle that is $(x - h)^2 + (y - k)^2 = r^2$ yields $(x - 6)^2 + (y + 1)^2 = (\sqrt{13})^2$.

36. **(H)** If we multiply both sides of the inequality by 6 (the lowest common denominator), we get an inequality with no fractions. $4x - 3 < 3x + 4$, which is equivalent to $x < 7$.

37. **(D)** For this problem we have a right triangle shown with x (the hypotenuse) representing the length of the guide wire and 14 representing the base. Since $\cos 50° = \frac{\text{adj}}{\text{hyp}}$, we have $\cos 50° = \frac{14}{x}$. So $x = \frac{14}{\cos 50°}$, which is 21.78 (to the nearest hundredth).

38. **(K)** $x^2 - 9 = (x - 3)(x + 3)$. This gives $\frac{(x-3)(x-3)}{(x-3)(x+3)} = \frac{x-3}{x+3}$. Another method that will work on a problem such as this is to pick a value for x such that $x^2 \neq 9$. Say $x = 2$. Then $\frac{(2-3)^2}{2^2-9} = \frac{1}{-5} = \frac{-1}{5}$. Now put $x = 2$ in for x in the answer choices and see which one equals $\frac{-1}{5}$. Only choice K yields this value.

39. **(A)** We know the midpoint is (5, 7) and A (2, 3) with B (x, y) as endpoints. By the midpoint formula $\left(\frac{x+2}{2}, \frac{y+3}{2}\right) = (5, 7)$. Thus $\frac{x+2}{2}$ must equal 5 and $\frac{y+3}{2}$ must equal 7. Solving these two equations $\frac{x+2}{2} = 5$ and $\frac{y+3}{2} = 7$, we get $x = 8$ and $y = 11$. Therefore $x + y = 19$.

40. **(H)** $(x + a)(x + b) = x^2 + (a + b)x + ab$. Since the solutions are $x = 8$ and $x = \frac{-3}{2}$, we have $(x - 8)(x - \frac{-3}{2}) = 0$. This multiplies to $x^2 - 8x + \frac{3}{2}x - 12 = 0$ and simplifies to $x^2 - 6.5x - 12 = 0$. Therefore $a + b = -6.5$. Or we could use the theorem that says for quadratic equations of the type $x^2 + Bx + C = 0$ that the sum of the solutions equals $(-B)$. Therefore, $8 + \frac{-3}{2} = -B \Rightarrow 6.5 = -B$ or $B = -6.5$.

41. **(C)** We do not have enough information to find the lengths of the three horizontal segments but we know their sum is 10. The missing vertical segment is 8. So the perimeter is $10 + 13 + 10 + 8 + 3 + 2 = 46$. If we make a rectangle out of the figure, the perimeter is the same as the perimeter of the original figure. So the perimeter of the figure is $13 + 10 + 13 + 10 = 46$.

42. **(K)** $\cot\theta = \dfrac{\cos\theta}{\sin\theta} = P$. We could also make a right triangle with θ as one of the acute angles. Write P as $\dfrac{P}{1}$.

$\cot\theta = \dfrac{adj}{opp}$. (Remember that $\cot\theta = \dfrac{1}{\tan\theta}$). $\cos\theta = \dfrac{P}{\sqrt{P^2+1}}$ and $\sin\theta = \dfrac{1}{\sqrt{P^2+1}}$.

$\dfrac{\cos\theta}{\sin\theta} = \dfrac{P}{\sqrt{P^2+1}} \div \dfrac{1}{\sqrt{P^2+1}} = \dfrac{P}{\sqrt{P^2+1}} \cdot \dfrac{\sqrt{P^2+1}}{1} = \dfrac{P}{1}$.

43. **(B)** The slope of the line is $\dfrac{3-9}{8-5} = \dfrac{-6}{3} = -2$. From $y = mx + b$ and the point (5, 9), we have $9 = -2(5) + b$. Therefore, $b = 19$. The equation of the line is $y = -2x + 19$. To find the x-intercept, let $y = 0$. $0 = -2x + 19$ and $x = \dfrac{19}{2}$. For a problem with coordinates, we can often find the answer from a sketch. Clearly, the x-intercept cannot be zero or negative. That leaves only A 19 and B $\dfrac{19}{2}$. 19 is not a reasonable answer.

44. **(G)** If a square has an area of 729, the length of a side is $\sqrt{729} = 27 = 3^3$. The volume of a cube is s^3, where s is the length of a side. Thus, in this problem $V = (3^3)^3 = 3^9$.

45. **(C)** The GCF of $6pq^4$ and $12p^2q^2$ is $6pq^2$. Thus $6pq^2 = 1{,}050$ or $pq^2 = 175$. It asks for a possible value of p and q. One way of finding p and q, is to find the prime factorization of 175. It is $7(5)^2$. Comparing pq^2 to $7(5)^2$, we see that $p = 7$ and $q = 5$. So $p + q = 7 + 5 = 12$.

46. **(K)** $AC = \sqrt{164}$. We get this value by using the Pythagorean Theorem on $\triangle ABC$. $8^2 + 10^2 = (AC)^2$, $(AC)^2 = 64 + 100 = 164$. Taking square roots leaves $AC = \sqrt{164}$. $\overline{AC}$ is a side of square $ACDE$. Therefore, the area of square $ACDE$ is $(\sqrt{164})^2 = 164$. You could also get this value by taking $\sqrt{164}$ on your calculator and squaring the answer.

47. **(C)** The distance between two points formula is $\sqrt{(x_2-x_1)^2+(y_2-y_1)^2}$. In this case $\sqrt{(13-5)^2+(11-7)^2} = \sqrt{8^2+4^2} = \sqrt{64+16} = \sqrt{80}$.

48. **(J)** A perfect square trinomial will factor to a binomial squared: $(x + y)^2 = x^2 + 2xy + y^2$. This tells us that the number to be added must be a perfect square. If we add 9, it would have to factor to $(3x - 3)^2$. But this equals $9x^2 - 18x + 9$, and we need $(-30x)$. Adding 25, we have $9x^2 - 30x + 25 = (3x - 5)^2$.

49. **(E)** From the data given in the problem, we can conclude that the center of the circle is $(-a, a)$. Since the radius of the circle is 4, a must equal 4. Therefore, the center is (–4, 4). The formula for a circle with center (h, K) and radius r is $(x - h)^2 + (y - K)^2 = r^2$. Substituting in the formula, we get $(x + 4)^2 + (y - 4)^2 = 16$.

50. **(H)** In the equation $y = A\sin Bx$, the amplitude is $|A|$ and the period is $\dfrac{2\pi}{|B|}$. From $y = \sin x$ to $y = 2\sin(4x)$, the amplitude increases from 1 to 2 and the period decreases from $\dfrac{2\pi}{1} = 2\pi$ to $\dfrac{2\pi}{4} = \dfrac{1}{2}\pi$.

51. **(E)** Doing the algebra $3x - 9 \geq -3(9 - x)$ is equivalent to $3x - 9 \geq -27 + 3x$. Subtracting $3x$ from both sides leaves $-9 \geq -27$. This is true and since there is no x in the inequality, it is true for all real numbers.

52. **(H)** Extend $\overline{GF}$ and $\overline{IJ}$ to intersect at a new point P. $GDJP$ is a square with side length of 5. Its area $= 5^2 = 25$. The area of the shaded pentagon equals the area of $GDJP$ minus the area of $\triangle FIP$. Area of $\triangle FIP = \dfrac{1}{2}(4)(4) = 8$. Therefore the area of pentagon $DGFIJ$ is $25 - 8 = 17$.

53. **(A)** $x \# y = \dfrac{x+y}{3}$ and $y \# x = \dfrac{y+x}{3}$, therefore $x \# y = y \# x$. Thus I is true.

54. **(G)** This is a quadratic equation. To solve, we must get one side equal to zero. So we come up with $x^2 - 5ax - 36a^2 = 0$. This factors to $(x - 9a)(x + 4a) = 0$. Now we use the zero product property and set each factor equal to zero.

$$x - 9a = 0 \qquad x + 4a = 0$$

$$x = 9a \qquad x = -4a$$

55. **(C)** To simplify this we will use the identity $\sin^2\theta + \cos^2\theta = 1$. From this we have $1 - \cos^2\theta = \sin^2\theta$. Substituting we now have $\dfrac{\sqrt{\sin^2\theta}}{\sin^2\theta} \cdot \cos\theta = \dfrac{\sin\theta}{\sin^2\theta} \cdot \cos\theta$. This simplifies to $\dfrac{\cos\theta}{\sin\theta}$, which is the cot θ.

56. **(J)** By multiplication and division properties of logarithms, $\log_a\left(\frac{x^2y^3}{\sqrt{z}}\right) = \log_a x^2 + \log_a y^3 - \log_a \sqrt{z}$. By power rule, $\log_a x^2 + \log_a y^3 - \log_a z^{\frac{1}{2}}$ equals $2\log_a x + 3\log_a y - \frac{1}{2}\log_a z = 2p + 3q - \frac{1}{2}t$. So (J) is the correct answer.

57. **(B)** We know that the absolute value of a number is non-negative. Since $|-x| = x$, x must be non-negative, which means $x \geq 0$. Mathematically, $|x| = x$ if $x \geq 0$ and $|x| = -x$ if $x \leq 0$. We could also substitute numbers in for x.

58. **(K)** When a quadratic equation has exactly one real solution, the discriminate "$b^2 - 4ac$" must equal zero. This gives us the equation $(-a)^2 - 4(2)(8) = 0$ OR $a^2 - 64 = 0$ OR $a^2 = 64$. Taking the square root we get $a = \pm 8$. We could also plug 8 (or another number) into the equation. $2x^2 - 8x + 8 = 0 \Rightarrow 2(x^2 - 4x + 4) = 0$. $2(x-2)^2 = 0$.

59. **(A)** Because all the possible answers only contain x and y, we want to eliminate t. Solve $y = 5 - t$ for t and substitute into the other equation. $t = 5 - y$, so $x = 3(5 - y) + 4 \Rightarrow x = 15 - 3y + 4$. Solving for y, we first combine the 15 and 4. $x = 19 - 3y \Rightarrow x - 19 = -3y$. Multiply both sides by (–1) to get $19 - x = 3y$. Divide by (3) and $y = \frac{19-x}{3}$. If you had solved the other equation for t, the work would look like this: $t = \frac{x-4}{3}$ and $y = 5 - \frac{x-4}{3} \Rightarrow y = \frac{15}{3} - \frac{x-4}{3}$ and $y = \frac{15-(x-4)}{3} = \frac{15-x+4}{3} = \frac{19-x}{3}$.

60. **(K)** To find the area of a sector we use this formula: $\frac{\text{central angle}}{360}$(area of circle). Substituting the given values, we get $\frac{30}{360}(\pi(10)^2)$. Simplify to get $\frac{25\pi}{3}$.

Answer Explanations: Reading Test

1. **(B)** The cavalier reaction of the townspeople to the angel in lines 21–24, as well as Elisenda's casual reaction to his departure at the end, establish that the appearance of an angel was not a terribly big deal to these people. In other words, they are *laid-back* and *react with less surprise* than others would to such things.

2. **(F)** In light of the child's illness (line 9), it is safe to assume that when the neighbor woman says the angel was "coming for the child" (line 18), she means that he is an angel of death.

3. **(D)** The crabs from the rainstorm are mentioned in line 73, but only mentioned, and not described.

4. **(H)** This angel never really does much of anything. We know basically nothing about him other than the fact that he has wings. He may not even be an angel, for all anyone knows. Therefore, the only possible answer is that he is *baffling and mysterious*.

5. **(B)** Right before she gets the idea to charge admission, we are told that Elisenda is practically crippled from the hard work she is compelled to do (lines 29–32). We are supposed to feel pity for her, and regard her idea to charge admission as *understandable and motivated by necessity*.

6. **(F)** In line 24, the first reaction of the townspeople to the angel involves *tossing him things to eat through ... the wire*. This is clearly supposed to mirror the behavior of humans toward an *animal* at the zoo.

7. **(C)** Nowhere is it stated or implied that the spider girl had the approval of any religious authority of any kind.

8. **(J)** Building a mansion with bars to keep out angels implies that Pelayo and Elisenda considered it likely that more angels would show up someday—that is, that the appearance of angels is *somewhat normal*.

9. **(C)** The question is structured in a tricky way: it refers to *the beginning of the story*, but the fact that Pelayo had been employed as a *bailiff* is not mentioned until line 77.

10. **(J)** Elisenda's sigh of relief (line 88) and the statement that the angel was no longer an annoyance in her life (line 92) both imply that she feels unburdened by not having to deal with him anymore. (Remember, on a question like this, you have to look at the *emotion words*!)

11. **(C)** In lines 43–45, the author makes it clear that he sees academic freedom as *a freedom tailored to and constrained by the requirements of a particular job*. The overall tone of the passage is *critical* of people like the professor in the first paragraph who completely disregarded the stated purpose of the course he was teaching.

12. **(G)** Lines 7–10 (*It may be outlandish*... [but it is] *a form of behavior many display in less dramatic ways*) establish that the author realizes the Rancourt example is extreme, but represents a way of thinking that is common in less extreme forms, and so raises the issue subsequently addressed in the passage.

13. **(A)** The passage is an analysis of an academic concept ("academic freedom"). Regardless of whether you know that the author is a public intellectual (which basically means "popular philosopher"), nothing in the passage conflicts with this idea, whereas the other three choices all have elements contradicted by the passage.

14. **(J)** The author introduces that list by saying that *colleges and universities may bear some of the marks of places of employment* (lines 26–27); hence, these are things that academic jobs have in common with normal jobs.

15. **(C)** In this paragraph, the author is analyzing the probable origin of his opponents' viewpoint. Phrases like "rather it is a calling" (line 35) and "this exalted enterprise" (lines 38–39) are clearly sarcastic in context.

16. **(G)** The first sentence of the subsequent paragraph (lines 80–81) make it clear that the author finds Byrne's opinion ludicrous ("but this is a bit much").

17. **(B)** If the fact that the academic mission's *configurations can be ascertained* (i.e., that its boundaries can be figured out) means that the task is not *ineffable*, then *ineffable* must mean something like "un-figure-out-able," or *inexpressible*.

18. **(J)** The author uses the phrase *academic exceptionalism* (line 25) to describe the notion that academics are special and don't have to play by the same rules as everyone else—exactly the viewpoint with which the author spends the entire passage *disagreeing*.

19. **(D)** The author mentions professors taking years to complete research projects (lines 54–55) as an example of a legitimate, noncontroversial way that academic jobs are different from other ones. It is a definition of academic freedom that he agrees with, rather than one he is decrying.

20. **(F)** When the author states that academic freedom should be more narrowly defined, as *a freedom tailored to and constrained by the requirements of a particular job* (lines 43–45), this is his expression of his own belief that academic freedom should be limited to the amount of freedom required for professors to do the job that they are supposed to be doing (as opposed to just letting them do whatever they want).

21. **(D)** In lines 35–40, the author characterizes a writer as someone who tries to *discover the second being inside him*, who tries to *transform that inward gaze into words*, and who studies *the worlds into which we pass when we retire into ourselves*. These phrases clearly characterize writing as a solitary activity.

22. **(G)** The author never mentions anything at all about his parents' relationship, and certainly doesn't hint that the suitcase might hold painful secrets about it.

23. **(C)** Since the author says this in response to his father's having brought him a candy bar, it is clear in context that he is merely making a joke about how his father still sees him as a child in some ways—that is, his father has not *really* forgotten his age.

24. **(G)** Immediately after this statement, the author goes on to say that his father was a very social man who disliked solitude and loved company—that is, he could not have endured the solitude that is necessary in order to be a real writer.

25. **(A)** The fact that the author's father put the suitcase quietly in a corner implies that he is depositing it shyly and without fanfare: *unobtrusively* means "inconspicuously."

26. **(J)** The author never mentions being *suspicious* of his father about anything, for any reason.

27. **(C)** The series of rhetorical questions that ends the paragraph makes it clear that the point is ultimately about the true source of happiness.

28. **(F)** Lines 35–40 establish that, according to the author, writing is a long process of self-discovery.

29. **(B)** It is mentioned in lines 17–18 that the author's father had wanted to write poetry as a young man.

30. **(H)** The linkage of opposites in the final paragraph (*a flash of joy inside me that made me ashamed ... our feelings of happiness and guilt*) establishes that the author sees writing as wrapped up in both positive and negative emotions.

31. **(B)** The first paragraph establishes something to do with "culture" as our topic, and the end of the second and beginning of the third paragraphs (lines 25–31) establish that the author feels that something besides genes is necessary to explain culture.

32. **(J)** The remainder of the first paragraph (as well as the passage itself) establishes that the author's goal is to dispassionately analyze the means by which culture changes—that is, he is using the word *culture* to mean everything about society, rather than to distinguish between the good and bad things about it.

33. **(C)** A hair color is not an *idea* (though a hair*style* is), and thus could not succeed or fail as a meme.

34. **(F)** Lines 29–43 explain that, just as genes are replicators of DNA, memes are replicators of ideas.

35. **(D)** Chaucer is mentioned merely as an example of someone who spoke English as it existed twenty generations ago (lines 6–11).

36. **(F)** It is clear in all four contexts that *propagate* means something like "spread," or *multiply* (in the sense that living beings *multiply* by reproduction).

37. **(D)** Lines 37-43 establish that the author is making up the word *meme* himself ("*if I abbreviate 'mimeme' to meme*").

38. **(H)** In the sentence immediately following, the author explains that other copies of the same tune will continue to exist on paper or in other people's brains—that is, no one copy of an idea is the "real" one, as long as the idea continues to exist somewhere.

39. **(A)** The examples in lines 67–71 (immediately following the term *survival value*) all concern possible ways to measure how widespread a particular concept has become.

40. **(G)** When the author says that their *meme-complexes ... are still going strong* (lines 93–95), he means that the ideas these people came up with are continuing to thrive after their deaths.

Answer Explanations: Science Test

1. **(A)** All this question is asking you to do is look at Table 1 and find the biggest number in the (horizontal) 260 nm row. The biggest number in that row by a wide margin is 83.5, which falls in the (vertical) Octyl Salicylate column. The fact that the numbers represent *percent transmittance of UV rays* is explained in the text, rather than in Table 1 itself, but this is the only thing Table 1 measures, and the question tells you that the answer is in Table 1.

2. **(J)** This is a simple "Go Up, Hit Line, Go Over" question. The black line in Figure 1 is higher at the point on the *x*-axis (horizontal) representing a wavelength of 340 nm than it is at the points representing any of the other choices. Since the line in Figure 1 only increases (it goes up and up but never down), another reliable method of getting the answer would be to just look at the choices and pick the highest number.

3. **(C)** The question asks about someone whose skin *burns but also tans slowly*. "Gradually" is a synonym for "slowly," and so the question is likely asking about Skin Type III, which Table 2 says *Burns moderately, tans gradually*. Although the person *could possibly* have Skin Type II, the question is clearly indicating Skin Type III as the preferable answer.

4. **(G)** All you have to do here is look at Table 2 and list all the skin types identified as *sensitive* or *very sensitive*. Skin Types I and II are identified as *very sensitive*, and Skin Type III is identified as *sensitive*. You probably also already know from real life that sunscreen should be worn by pale people, and so the answer is going to be the people on the paler half of the table. (Remember, although the ACT Science does not require real-life knowledge, the questions are always accurate, and so any real-life knowledge you happen to have can be useful!)

5. **(B)** This is one of those questions that require looking in two places. Figure 1 establishes that sunlight with an irradiance of 0.01 W/m2/nm would have a wavelength of *a little more than* 300 nm (because the black line at the 0.01 point on the *y*-axis is a little past the 300 point on the *x*-axis). Then you look in Table 1 and see that the percent transmittance for oxybenzone at a wavelength of 300 nm would be 4.2, and so the answer is *a little more than* 4.2, in other words 5%.

6. **(G)** Table 1 establishes that a female who has normal vision but is a carrier of red-green color blindness would have one normal X chromosome and one mutated X chromosome. (It is also entirely possible to figure this out without Table 1, assuming you knew that women have two X chromosomes and a bit about how heritability works.)

7. **(D)** For a couple to be assured of producing only red-green color-blind children, both parents would have to be red-green color blind. The genotypes in choice D represent a red-green color-blind female and a red-green color-blind male.

8. **(F)** The top right corner of the Punnett square in Figure 3 (Study 2) represents a male with normal vision. All of the males represented in Figures 2 and 4 (in Studies 1 and 3) are red-green color blind.

9. **(A)** The information in the passage states that the defect appears in women only when both parents possess the gene.

10. **(H)** Study 1 establishes that all of Barbara and John's male children are red-green color blind, while none of their female children are (though they all carry the mutated gene). Figure 1 establishes that Barbara and John have two girls and two boys; that is, they have an equal number of red-green color-blind children and children with normal vision, for a ratio of 1:1 (2:2 reduced).

11. **(B)** A red-green color-blind female would have to have had a red-green color-blind father and a mother who was either red-green color-blind herself or a carrier. Only choice B presents one of these options (red-green color-blind father and carrier mother).

12. **(G)** This is one of those questions that requires you to look in two places. Table 2 indicates that naphtha is in Tray 2, and Table 1 indicates that the boiling point of whatever is in Tray 2 is 40°C.

13. **(C)** In Figure 2, the bar representing diesel goes up to 11, indicating 11 gallons of diesel per barrel of crude oil.

14. **(F)** This question involves looking in <u>three</u> places, but still is not really that hard (technically, getting the right answer only requires looking in two places, but eliminating some of the wrong answers requires looking in three). Figure 1 establishes that the trays are arranged from 1 to 8 from the top to the bottom of the Distillation Column, Table 2 indicates which substances are in which trays, and Table 1 indicates their boiling points. All together, these data indicate that the substances with the lowest boiling points are at the top of the column, and so the student's hypothesis is wrong (it is not necessary to understand the explanation in choice F about the rising vapor and all that, only to see that the substances with the lowest boiling points are on top).

15. **(D)** A comparison of Table 3 with Tables 1 and 2 establishes that the greater the number of carbons in a substance, the higher the boiling point, in decreasing order from residual oil to gas.

16. **(H)** Tables 1 and 2 establish that heavy gas oil has a boiling point of 500°C, higher than that of any of the components except residual oil, which is not one of the choices.

17. **(C)** Components with medium boiling points on Table 1 in a range of 120 to 350 degrees correspond to the gasoline, kerosene, and diesel on Figure 2, which are collected in greatest quantity.

18. **(G)** Table 1 indicates that the solubility of methane at 50°C *increases and then decreases* as pressure is increased. All of the other choices involve substances that steadily increased in solubility as pressure increased, but NOT this one.

19. **(A)** At 50°C, the solubility is 18.9.

20. **(J)** The line in Figure 1 climbs until about the 200-second mark and then levels off. It is not necessary to understand the paragraph above Figure 1 in order to answer the question: all you need to know is that the graph is measuring an increase in the PA-11 mass over time.

21. **(B)** In Table 1, we see that the solubility of methane at 90°C and 53.1 atm is 2.38. At a pressure of 106.5, the solubility is 5.14. Since 3.75 is halfway between 2.38 and 5.14 and 80 is roughly halfway between 53.1 and 106.5, the best answer is 3.75.

22. **(H)** Table 2 establishes that the solubility of carbon dioxide increases as pressure increases, at all three temperatures.

23. **(D)** The first paragraph states that the *solvent* is the substance that another substance is being dissolved in. The second paragraph states that methane and carbon dioxide are being dissolved in polyamide. Therefore, polyamide is the solvent and carbon dioxide and methane are the solutes.

24. **(G)** The key indicates that white bars represent clay. In Figure 2 (but not Figure 1) the bar representing the depth between 3 and 4 meters is white. Clay is found at a depth of 3.5 m in Zone 4 and only in Zone 4.

25. **(D)** All this question is asking you to do is find the biggest number in the right-hand column in Table 1 (Plant Height in meters). The biggest number in that column is 2.4, for the Compass Plant.

26. **(F)** In Figure 3, the black bars representing the number of plants per zone in Zone 4 are higher than the white bars representing the number of plants per zone in Zone 3 for every type of plant studied. Therefore, all the plants studied grow more easily in Zone 4.

27. **(D)** In both Figure 1 and Figure 2, the highest white bar (indicating clay) represents a depth between 2 and 3 meters. Therefore, the roots of plants in Zone 3 and Zone 4 would hit clay at the same time (i.e., the clay is equally far down in both places).

28. **(H)** This is one of those questions that require you to look in two places. Table 1 indicates that Lead Plants have roots that go 4.5 m deep, and then Figure 1 indicates that a depth of 4.5 m in Zone 3 would be in a gravel layer (gray shading).

29. **(B)** Nutrition or the lack thereof is an environmental factor, and does not alter an individual's DNA, so if ill effects due to a grandparent's malnutrition are turning up in grandchildren, then this would be an example of "soft inheritance."

30. **(J)** The passage does not say who proposed the theory of epigenetics. It only mentions that the discovery was "very recent."

31. **(C)** Scientist 1 states that it would be premature to acknowledge true soft inheritance *in animal species*. This implies that she might be willing to concede its existence in plant species (as many otherwise skeptical biologists indeed do). An apple tree is the only one of the choices that is a plant.

32. **(G)** A believer in epigenetic soft inheritance would disagree with the idea than genes *act in isolation* to produce traits. In other words, he or she would believe that an organism's expressed traits are the result partly of genes and partly of other factors.

33. **(D)** Scientist 1 dismisses apparent evidence for epigenetic theory by arguing that the inherited acquired traits would work themselves out of the bloodline in time ("the bloodline always reverts to the true expression of its DNA," and the map and wind analogy).

34. **(J)** If *histones* are the modules through which genes express themselves, and Scientist 2 figures genes (i.e., "sequences of DNA") as light bulbs, then it follows that histones would be analogous to the lamp.

35. **(A)** Scientist 1's defense against all epigenetic arguments is to imply that all apparently epigenetic effects are only temporary. And Scientist 2 appears to have no proof so far that they are not. Only a conclusive study of how long the "altered expression" of a gene truly lasts (which would take a pretty long time) can settle the matter for good.

36. **(G)** This is a simple "Go Up, Hit Line, Go Over" question. In Figure 2, right above the 5-hour mark on the *x*-axis (horizontal), the line representing sleep stages is at a height of around 1 on the *y*-axis (vertical).

37. **(C)** The line in Figure 1, which represents the sleep pattern of a child, hits the bottom of the graph (Stage 0, or being awake) only once. The 0 at the left of the graph is not included because this represents the beginning of sleep.

38. **(F)** The subjects of the figures get increasingly older, and the line in Figure 3 hits bottom more than the lines in the other figures do. Therefore, the conclusion that people wake up more frequently as they age is supported by the data. Remember, each touch at the bottom is stage 0 and stage 0 indicates awake.

39. **(D)** The introductory paragraph states that REM sleep is associated with the final third of a sleep cycle. Of the answer choices, only the 7-hour mark is in the final third of the sleep cycle depicted in Figure 2, which represents a young adult (although since the passage states that REM sleep occurs in the final third of a sleep cycle for everyone, it wouldn't matter which figure you looked at).

40. **(G)** The introduction says sleep gets deeper as it moves from Stage 1 to Stage 4.

Writing Sample

Close your eyes and start thinking about the most fun times you have ever had in your life. Now, how many of those times took place over summer vacation when you were not in school? I believe a lot of them—maybe even all of them. But, unbelievably, there are some people who think there should be no such thing as summer vacation anymore! These individuals claim that students forget too much from the previous year over summer vacation, and that summer vacation should be broken up into a bunch of smaller vacations scattered throughout the year. This is a terrible idea for the following reasons: the abolishment of summer break will cause new generations of kids to lose their link with America's past, it will cause kids to grow up and mature less effectively, and it will damage families by reducing the amount of quality time they can spend together.

Summer vacation has always been a part of America's culture. It started years ago when everybody was a farmer, because in the summer the parents needed the kids to be at home helping with all the farm work that went on at that time. Contributing to the family was so important that there was no school for three months. Thus, it became celebrated in our culture in many different ways. Just think of all the classic movies that are set over summer vacation, and all the popular songs that mention summer vacation. Everything from Beach Boys songs to the "Friday the 13th" horror film series will not make any sense anymore. Of course, it is not always valuable to keep something the way it is purely for the sake of tradition, but in some cases the place that a certain tradition holds in people's hearts is more important than a few minor flaws it might have, and summer vacation is one of those cases.

Our culture revolves around advancing into higher and higher grades in school. When you are a fifth-grader, fourth-graders look like babies to you, and then the next year fifth-graders look like babies to you when you are a sixth-grader. It is that very feeling that makes kids proud to be maturing and taking on new responsibilities. But what you may not realize is that summer vacation is responsible for that. Imagine how weird it would be if on Friday you were in fifth grade and then all of a sudden on Monday you were in junior high! You would probably have a nervous breakdown. Kids need those three months to process things and start to think about themselves in new ways. Although we don't admit it to adults, by the end of summer vacation kids even start to miss school a little bit. Being away from it for three months helps us appreciate everything great about school, like friends, sports, and even academics. Although we may forget a few things, because we are well-rested and enthusiastic, it's like riding a bike: a quick review and we are ready to move on to new challenges. And when you walk back through those doors in September, it's like you're a whole new person, one who is suddenly tall enough to reach that good water fountain in the south hall that is always super-cold.

Most importantly, getting rid of summer vacation runs the risk of destroying the American family as we know it. I know that all my best memories of being around my parents and my little sister are from the vacations we would take in the summer. When we were all just in the house going through our respective daily grinds, we would get on each other's nerves. Many parents don't get summer vacation, but still often plan their vacation time for the summer because their kids are already off then. You might say that there will still be vacations throughout the year, but having that big block of three months gives parents more room to plan things. Plus, smaller vacations might not provide enough time for families to spend quality time together.

Summer vacation is important. It is an American tradition that has been woven into the fabric of our culture through film and song. It provides down time that is psychologically valuable for stressed-out kids trying to mature as best they can. And it is the best possible time for the family bonding that kids need to grow up to be rational adults who would never do anything like getting rid of summer vacation.

Answer Sheet

PRACTICE TEST 3

Directions: Mark one answer only for each question. Make the mark dark. Erase completely any mark made in error. (Additional or stray marks will be counted as mistakes.)

English Test

1 A B C D	21 A B C D	41 A B C D	61 A B C D
2 F G H J	22 F G H J	42 F G H J	62 F G H J
3 A B C D	23 A B C D	43 A B C D	63 A B C D
4 F G H J	24 F G H J	44 F G H J	64 F G H J
5 A B C D	25 A B C D	45 A B C D	65 A B C D
6 F G H J	26 F G H J	46 F G H J	66 F G H J
7 A B C D	27 A B C D	47 A B C D	67 A B C D
8 F G H J	28 F G H J	48 F G H J	68 F G H J
9 A B C D	29 A B C D	49 A B C D	69 A B C D
10 F G H J	30 F G H J	50 F G H J	70 F G H J
11 A B C D	31 A B C D	51 A B C D	71 A B C D
12 F G H J	32 F G H J	52 F G H J	72 F G H J
13 A B C D	33 A B C D	53 A B C D	73 A B C D
14 F G H J	34 F G H J	54 F G H J	74 F G H J
15 A B C D	35 A B C D	55 A B C D	75 A B C D
16 F G H J	36 F G H J	56 F G H J	
17 A B C D	37 A B C D	57 A B C D	
18 F G H J	38 F G H J	58 F G H J	
19 A B C D	39 A B C D	59 A B C D	
20 F G H J	40 F G H J	60 F G H J	

Math Test

1 A B C D E	16 F G H J K	31 A B C D E	46 F G H J K
2 F G H J K	17 A B C D E	32 F G H J K	47 A B C D E
3 A B C D E	18 F G H J K	33 A B C D E	48 F G H J K
4 F G H J K	19 A B C D E	34 F G H J K	49 A B C D E
5 A B C D E	20 F G H J K	35 A B C D E	50 F G H J K
6 F G H J K	21 A B C D E	36 F G H J K	51 A B C D E
7 A B C D E	22 F G H J K	37 A B C D E	52 F G H J K
8 F G H J K	23 A B C D E	38 F G H J K	53 A B C D E
9 A B C D E	24 F G H J K	39 A B C D E	54 F G H J K
10 F G H J K	25 A B C D E	40 F G H J K	55 A B C D E
11 A B C D E	26 F G H J K	41 A B C D E	56 F G H J K
12 F G H J K	27 A B C D E	42 F G H J K	57 A B C D E
13 A B C D E	28 F G H J K	43 A B C D E	58 F G H J K
14 F G H J K	29 A B C D E	44 F G H J K	59 A B C D E
15 A B C D E	30 F G H J K	45 A B C D E	60 F G H J K

Answer Sheet

PRACTICE TEST 3

Reading Test

1 Ⓐ Ⓑ Ⓒ Ⓓ	11 Ⓐ Ⓑ Ⓒ Ⓓ	21 Ⓐ Ⓑ Ⓒ Ⓓ	31 Ⓐ Ⓑ Ⓒ Ⓓ
2 Ⓕ Ⓖ Ⓗ Ⓙ	12 Ⓕ Ⓖ Ⓗ Ⓙ	22 Ⓕ Ⓖ Ⓗ Ⓙ	32 Ⓕ Ⓖ Ⓗ Ⓙ
3 Ⓐ Ⓑ Ⓒ Ⓓ	13 Ⓐ Ⓑ Ⓒ Ⓓ	23 Ⓐ Ⓑ Ⓒ Ⓓ	33 Ⓐ Ⓑ Ⓒ Ⓓ
4 Ⓕ Ⓖ Ⓗ Ⓙ	14 Ⓕ Ⓖ Ⓗ Ⓙ	24 Ⓕ Ⓖ Ⓗ Ⓙ	34 Ⓕ Ⓖ Ⓗ Ⓙ
5 Ⓐ Ⓑ Ⓒ Ⓓ	15 Ⓐ Ⓑ Ⓒ Ⓓ	25 Ⓐ Ⓑ Ⓒ Ⓓ	35 Ⓐ Ⓑ Ⓒ Ⓓ
6 Ⓕ Ⓖ Ⓗ Ⓙ	16 Ⓕ Ⓖ Ⓗ Ⓙ	26 Ⓕ Ⓖ Ⓗ Ⓙ	36 Ⓕ Ⓖ Ⓗ Ⓙ
7 Ⓐ Ⓑ Ⓒ Ⓓ	17 Ⓐ Ⓑ Ⓒ Ⓓ	27 Ⓐ Ⓑ Ⓒ Ⓓ	37 Ⓐ Ⓑ Ⓒ Ⓓ
8 Ⓕ Ⓖ Ⓗ Ⓙ	18 Ⓕ Ⓖ Ⓗ Ⓙ	28 Ⓕ Ⓖ Ⓗ Ⓙ	38 Ⓕ Ⓖ Ⓗ Ⓙ
9 Ⓐ Ⓑ Ⓒ Ⓓ	19 Ⓐ Ⓑ Ⓒ Ⓓ	29 Ⓐ Ⓑ Ⓒ Ⓓ	39 Ⓐ Ⓑ Ⓒ Ⓓ
10 Ⓕ Ⓖ Ⓗ Ⓙ	20 Ⓕ Ⓖ Ⓗ Ⓙ	30 Ⓕ Ⓖ Ⓗ Ⓙ	40 Ⓕ Ⓖ Ⓗ Ⓙ

Science Test

1 Ⓐ Ⓑ Ⓒ Ⓓ	11 Ⓐ Ⓑ Ⓒ Ⓓ	21 Ⓐ Ⓑ Ⓒ Ⓓ	31 Ⓐ Ⓑ Ⓒ Ⓓ
2 Ⓕ Ⓖ Ⓗ Ⓙ	12 Ⓕ Ⓖ Ⓗ Ⓙ	22 Ⓕ Ⓖ Ⓗ Ⓙ	32 Ⓕ Ⓖ Ⓗ Ⓙ
3 Ⓐ Ⓑ Ⓒ Ⓓ	13 Ⓐ Ⓑ Ⓒ Ⓓ	23 Ⓐ Ⓑ Ⓒ Ⓓ	33 Ⓐ Ⓑ Ⓒ Ⓓ
4 Ⓕ Ⓖ Ⓗ Ⓙ	14 Ⓕ Ⓖ Ⓗ Ⓙ	24 Ⓕ Ⓖ Ⓗ Ⓙ	34 Ⓕ Ⓖ Ⓗ Ⓙ
5 Ⓐ Ⓑ Ⓒ Ⓓ	15 Ⓐ Ⓑ Ⓒ Ⓓ	25 Ⓐ Ⓑ Ⓒ Ⓓ	35 Ⓐ Ⓑ Ⓒ Ⓓ
6 Ⓕ Ⓖ Ⓗ Ⓙ	16 Ⓕ Ⓖ Ⓗ Ⓙ	26 Ⓕ Ⓖ Ⓗ Ⓙ	36 Ⓕ Ⓖ Ⓗ Ⓙ
7 Ⓐ Ⓑ Ⓒ Ⓓ	17 Ⓐ Ⓑ Ⓒ Ⓓ	27 Ⓐ Ⓑ Ⓒ Ⓓ	37 Ⓐ Ⓑ Ⓒ Ⓓ
8 Ⓕ Ⓖ Ⓗ Ⓙ	18 Ⓕ Ⓖ Ⓗ Ⓙ	28 Ⓕ Ⓖ Ⓗ Ⓙ	38 Ⓕ Ⓖ Ⓗ Ⓙ
9 Ⓐ Ⓑ Ⓒ Ⓓ	19 Ⓐ Ⓑ Ⓒ Ⓓ	29 Ⓐ Ⓑ Ⓒ Ⓓ	39 Ⓐ Ⓑ Ⓒ Ⓓ
10 Ⓕ Ⓖ Ⓗ Ⓙ	20 Ⓕ Ⓖ Ⓗ Ⓙ	30 Ⓕ Ⓖ Ⓗ Ⓙ	40 Ⓕ Ⓖ Ⓗ Ⓙ

Practice Test 3

ENGLISH TEST

45 MINUTES—75 QUESTIONS

Directions: In the five passages that follow, certain words and phrases are underlined and numbered. In the right-hand column, you will find alternatives for the underlined part. In most cases, you are to choose the one that best expresses the idea, makes the statement appropriate for standard written English, or is worded most consistently with the style and tone of the passage as a whole. If you think the original version is best, choose "NO CHANGE." In some cases, you will find in the right-hand column a question about the underlined part. You are to choose the best answer to the question.

You will also find questions about a section of the passage, or about the passage as a whole. These questions do not refer to an underlined portion of the passage, but rather are identified by a number or numbers in a box.

For each question, choose the alternative you consider best and fill in the corresponding oval on your answer document. Read each passage through once before you begin to answer the questions that accompany it. For many of the questions, you must read several sentences beyond the question to determine the answer. Be sure that you have read far enough ahead each time you choose an alternative.

Passage I

The Real Johnny B. Goode?

No one person invented rock and roll single-handedly, but for years both _critics, and fans have agreed that_ (1) no individual is due more credit than Chuck Berry. The singer, songwriter, and guitarist behind such rock classics as "Maybelline" and "Johnny B. Goode" _was a major influence_ (2) on everything from the songwriting of the Beatles to the guitar playing of Jimi Hendrix.

He sold millions of records and in 1986 _among_ (3) the first class of inductees into the Rock and Roll Hall of Fame. But in 2000, the music world was shocked when Berry was sued by an old piano player of his, Johnnie

1. **A.** NO CHANGE
   B. critics and fans have agreed, that
   C. critics, and fans have agreed, that
   D. critics and fans have agreed that

2. **F.** NO CHANGE
   G. were a major influence
   H. were major influences
   J. have had a major influence

3. **A.** NO CHANGE
   B. was
   C. was among
   D. would have been among

1 ■ ■ ■ ■ ■ ■ ■ ■ 1

<u>Johnson claimed</u> [4] it was really he who had composed the music for nearly all of Berry's hits.

Could the great Chuck Berry <u>is</u> [5] a fraud, and the virtually unknown Johnson the true force behind the songs that shaped rock and roll? It seemed <u>distracting</u> [6] at first, but eventually even the biggest Berry fans had to admit that certain details seemed <u>to corroborate</u> [7] Johnson's story. The band that became the Chuck Berry Trio in 1955 was originally the Johnnie Johnson Trio, and Berry, a struggling local musician, had joined as a last-minute addition <u>when a member fell ill before a St. Louis gig in 1953</u> [8].

<u>Although</u> [9] Berry claimed sole responsibility for the many hits that soon followed, his gift for composition mysteriously dried up after he stopped working with Johnson. Berry was jailed in 1959 over shady goings-on at a nightclub he owned, and his only Top Ten hits after his 1963 release <u>was</u> [10] a silly novelty record called "My Ding-a-Ling" and a tune called "No Particular Place to Go," which was clearly just the Berry classic "School Days" with new lyrics. Even lifelong Berry fan Bruce Springsteen <u>from remarking</u> [11] years earlier that their songs were written in unusual keys for a guitar

4. **F.** NO CHANGE
   G. Johnson, claimed
   H. Johnson, claiming
   J. Johnson, who claimed

5. **A.** NO CHANGE
   B. be
   C. possibly was
   D. DELETE the underlined portion.

6. Which word or phrase best emphasizes the shocking nature of the allegations?
   F. NO CHANGE
   G. silly
   H. unthinkable
   J. impossible to determine

7. Which of the following alternatives to the underlined portion would be **LEAST** acceptable:
   A. to prove
   B. to verify
   C. to confirm
   D. to dispute

8. If the writer were to delete the underlined portion, the paragraph would primarily lose:
   F. an instance of foreshadowing.
   G. an explanation of why the type of music Berry played was popular in the South.
   H. a reminder of how cruel the music business can be.
   J. evidence of how close Berry came to not being a rock star at all.

9. **A.** NO CHANGE
   B. Since
   C. On the other hand,
   D. DELETE the underlined portion.

10. **F.** NO CHANGE
    G. had
    H. were
    J. being

11. **A.** NO CHANGE
    B. had remarked
    C. did remark
    D. would remark

player—keys more commonly found in songs composed on piano. [12]

Why had Johnnie not spoken up at the time? Tragically, Johnson was plagued by alcoholism for most of his life, and took little notice of what went on outside the studio. He also knew far less about things like rights and royalties than did the more educated and business-savvy Berry. [13]

A judge dismissed the suit because too much time had elapsed <u>until the songs in question were written,</u> [14] and Johnnie Johnson passed away in 2005, so the world will never know exactly who wrote what in all those immortal songs. Johnson never claimed he wrote them alone, however, and Chuck Berry still deserves his legendary status even if all he did was pen the lyrics and play the guitar—but maybe the name of Johnnie Johnson should be no less famous than his.

12. At this point, the writer is considering adding the following true statement:

    Berry had been in trouble with the law many times before, so allegations that he had cheated a former partner were hardly inconsistent with his character.

    Should the writer make this addition here?

    F. Yes, as it provides relevant information.
    G. Yes, because it proves Berry is a fraud.
    H. No, because only Berry's talent is the issue, and not his character.
    J. No, because it doesn't specify every crime of which Berry was accused.

13. Given that all the following statements are true, which one, if added here, would most effectively conclude the paragraph and support information given in the preceding sentence?

    A. As far as Johnson knew, what he was paid for his time at the end of a session was fair.
    B. Many African-American musicians of that era never received the money they deserved.
    C. Of course, how music publishing works has changed a great deal since the 1950s.
    D. Later rock stars were even more educated, a notable example being Mick Jagger.

14. **F.** NO CHANGE
    G. between the writing of most of the songs,
    H. since the writing of the songs in question,
    J. before any more songs could be written,

Question .15 asks about the preceding passage as a whole.

15. Suppose the author had intended to write an essay about how celebrities are almost never really the people we think they are. Would this essay fulfill that goal?

    A. Yes, because it makes a strong case that one of the greatest rock stars of all time did not write his own songs.
    B. Yes, because the essay just confirms what most people already suspected anyway.
    C. No, because the essay deals only with Chuck Berry, and not celebrities in general.
    D. No, because the concept of "celebrities" did not exist yet in the 1950s.

GO ON TO THE NEXT PAGE.

Passage II

Stealing *Mona Lisa*

It is the world's most famous painting, <u>and endlessly</u> [16] admired, analyzed, <u>parodied</u> [17] for over 500 years. You'd think that any sane thief would set his sights on a less ambitious target. But in 1911, Leonardo da Vinci's masterpiece, the *Mona Lisa*, <u>was stolen, and it remained missing</u> [18] for two years.

Vincenzo Perrugia was an Italian immigrant who had worked at France's famous Louvre museum for barely a month, <u>but this was</u> [19] enough time for him to formulate a daring plan. Knowing that the museum would be closed for restorations on August 21, he hid inside at closing the night before. The following day, <u>Peruggia tried his hardest to keep calm</u> [20] until he found himself alone in the gallery where the *Mona Lisa* hung.

He quickly snatched it <u>off</u> [21] the wall and absconded into a stairwell, where he smashed the frame, then rolled up the painting and hid it in his smock.

<u>He found</u> [22] the door at the bottom of the stairs locked, he smashed the knob and calmly reported the broken lock to a custodian on his way out of the building.

16. **F.** NO CHANGE
    G. endlessly
    H. it was endlessly
    J. that has been endlessly

17. **A.** NO CHANGE
    B. and parodied
    C. and it was parodied
    D. it was parodied

18. **F.** NO CHANGE
    G. went missing and was stolen
    H. had been stolen, remaining missing
    J. was missing

19. Which of the following alternatives to the underlined portion would NOT be acceptable?
    A. this was
    B. which was
    C. evidently
    D. DELETE the underlined portion.

20. Given that all the choices are true, which one provides the most specific information about Perrugia's methods?
    F. NO CHANGE
    G. Perrugia somehow managed to evade detection
    H. just as he would eventually tell his grandchildren, Perrugia remained in the museum
    J. disguised in a smock, Perrugia walked around looking busy

21. Which of the following alternatives to the underlined portion would LEAST be acceptable?
    A. from
    B. off of
    C. from of
    D. from off

22. **F.** NO CHANGE
    G. Although he would find
    H. Just before he found
    J. Finding

1 ■ ■ ■ ■ ■ ■ ■ ■ 1

Perrugia wasn't the only one in the Louvre that day who had a plan. [23] Many workers passed the empty space on the wall where they knew the *Mona Lisa* usually hung, but since restorations were taking place all day, just assumed that the museum's prized possession was being touched up or reframed as quickly as possible. [24] When it was discovered that the painting was gone, a massive manhunt began. Theorizing that a radical young artist might have stolen it as a publicity stunt, [25] police even arrested and questioned such figures as Pablo Picasso and surrealist poet Guillaume Apollinaire.

Perrugia hid the painting in his apartment and waited. As time passed, the search lost momentum and the feared masterwork was gone forever. [26]

Fortunately, Perrugia was motivated [27] for the crime led to its recovery: he felt that the *Mona Lisa* belonged in da Vinci's native Italy, from whence [28] it had been stolen by Napoleon a century earlier. In 1913, he smuggled it there and offered it to the director of the Uffizi Gallery in Florence. Perrugia expected a hero's welcome and a reward for his patriotic crime, but gallery personnel stalled him while police were called, and he was arrested.

23. Given that all the choices are true, which one most effectively introduces the paragraph?
    - **A.** NO CHANGE
    - **B.** There's no record of how long it took for the lock to be repaired, if it ever was.
    - **C.** The staff of the Louvre did not immediately realize that a theft had occurred.
    - **D.** The Louvre had seen its share of troubles since it was first constructed as a fortress in the twelfth century.

24. **F.** NO CHANGE
    - **G.** in private.
    - **H.** by Italian artisans.
    - **J.** automatically.

25. Which of the following alternatives to the underlined portion would be LEAST acceptable?
    - **A.** out of ignorance
    - **B.** as a form of protest
    - **C.** to make a point
    - **D.** as some pretentious prank

26. **F.** NO CHANGE
    - **G.** gone masterwork was forever feared.
    - **H.** masterwork was feared gone forever.
    - **J.** masterwork was forever feared gone.

27. **A.** NO CHANGE
    - **B.** the motivation had
    - **C.** Perrugia being motivated
    - **D.** Perrugia's motivation

28. **F.** NO CHANGE
    - **G.** after which
    - **H.** into there
    - **J.** whereas

Practice Test 3

1 ■ ■ ■ ■ ■ ■ ■ ■ 1

Still, a lot of good came out of the business after all: [29] the *Mona Lisa* was exhibited all over Italy for months before being returned to the Louvre, and as for Vincenzo Perrugia himself, the Italian courts took his patriotism (and the popularity of his crime in Italy) into consideration, and for the theft of the most priceless portable object on the face of the earth, he served only a few months in jail!

29. The writer would like to begin the final sentence with a phrase that indicates Perrugia might not have been as crazy as he seems. Given that all the choices are true, which one best accomplishes the writer's goal?

A. NO CHANGE
B. Still, his expectations were not entirely off-base:
C. Curiously, it was the last time he ever felt the need to steal anything:
D. Curiously, a war between France and Italy was only a few short years away:

Question 30 asks about the preceding passage as a whole.

30. Suppose the writer's goal had been to write a brief essay explaining the background, execution, and aftermath of a famous crime. Would this essay accomplish that goal?

F. Yes, because it establishes that everyone knew about the theft at the time, even though some people don't nowadays.
G. Yes, because it presents a sufficiently complete picture of Perrugia's theft of the *Mona Lisa*.
H. No, because it tells us virtually nothing about why the *Mona Lisa* is so important.
J. No, because it clearly states that Perrugia's punishment was not nearly harsh enough.

Passage III

The following paragraphs may or may not be in the most logical order. Each paragraph is numbered in brackets, and question 45 will ask you to choose where Paragraph 1 should most logically be placed.

Whom Are You Calling a Barbarian?

(1)

His enemies dubbed [31] "The Scourge of God." His name is synonymous to [32] cruelty, mercilessness, and barbarism of all kinds. But has history really been fair

31. **A.** NO CHANGE
B. dubbed him
C. dubbed to him
D. dubbed him for

32. **F.** NO CHANGE
G. of
H. as
J. with

Practice Test 3

to the fifth-century king and military leader known to us as Attila the Hun? <u>It is modern historians who agree</u> [33] that it has not. Traditional views of this period in Europe have been based on Roman sources, which even at their best are still biased against Attila, and at worst contain outright lies. [34]

(2)

The Huns were not the nomadic tribe of brutes that popular culture has often portrayed them as being. At the time of Attila's birth in <u>406, the</u> [35] Huns were a vast and efficiently run nation stretching all the way from <u>Asias central seas</u> [36] to the west of what is now Germany, <u>and this was</u> [37] far larger and less fragmented than the Western Roman Empire then was. And unlike aristocratic Roman society, the Hun world was a meritocracy with little to no <u>separation because of class division</u> [38]. At least a few sources who had lived in both societies said that they preferred the Hun civilization to the Roman.

33. **A.** NO CHANGE
    B. It is agreed by modern historians
    C. Modern historians had finally agreed
    D. Modern historians agree

34. If the writer were to delete the preceding sentence, the paragraph would primarily lose information that:
    F. demonstrates that Roman historians were typically less honest than were historians from other cultures.
    G. proves that modern Europe is more indebted to Rome for its culture than to any other ancient society.
    H. explains the reasons behind the long-standing negative opinion of Attila.
    J. explains which myths about Attila were invented by the Romans.

35. **A.** NO CHANGE
    B. 406, and the
    C. 406; the
    D. 406. The

36. **F.** NO CHANGE
    G. Asia's central seas
    H. Asias central sea's
    J. Asias' central sea's

37. **A.** NO CHANGE
    B. this was
    C. which was
    D. DELETE the underlined portion.

38. **F.** NO CHANGE
    G. class division
    H. people being separated by class division
    J. unfair class division keeping people apart

Practice Test 3

Yes, the Huns had beards and wore furs, but this was only common sense: it was much colder where they lived than it was in Rome. [39]

(3)

Attila became king upon the death of his uncle in 434 and coexisting peacefully [40] with Western Rome for the first part of his reign. Roman armies in what is now France recruited soldiers from Hun lands with Attila's permission, and the two empires traded freely and even extradited criminals to each other. The trouble started in 450, when Honoria, the sister of the emperor, offered herself in marriage to Attila in an attempt to escape an arranged union with a much older senator. Valentinian, her brother, tried to deny that the offer was genuine, but Attila was understandably unwilling to pass up a chance to unite his royal line with that of Rome [41] and create the greatest empire in history. Rome was so frightened by this prospect that they aligned themselves with the Visigoths—formerly the common enemy of both the Huns, and Rome further insulted Attila. [42] Hun forces entered Italy in 452, and sacked several cities, but were forced to turn back before reaching the capital, as a famine prevented the army from obtaining sufficient food. Attila died in his native lands a year later, supposedly after partying too hard at a feast.

39. At this point, the writer is considering adding the following true statement:

    The Vikings wore even more furs and had even longer beards, and they sailed to America 500 years before Columbus!

    Should the writer make this addition?

    A. Yes, because it provides a much-needed additional example for the same point.
    B. Yes, because this little-known fact should be provided to people whenever possible.
    C. No, because it distracts the reader from the main focus of the essay.
    D. No, because the essay does not explain whether the Huns and Vikings got along.

40. **F.** NO CHANGE
    G. coexists in peace
    H. coexisted peacefully
    J. peaceful coexistence

41. **A.** NO CHANGE
    B. with they're own
    C. with Rome's one
    D. plus the Roman one

42. **F.** NO CHANGE
    G. Huns and Rome's, who had further insulted Attila.
    H. Huns and Rome—further insulting Attila.
    J. Huns everywhere. Rome thus insulted Attila further.

1 ■ ■ ■ ■ ■ ■ ■ ■ 1

(4)

Contrary to popular belief, neither Attila nor any Hun commander ever sacked Rome (the Visigoths took the city in 410, and the Vandals in 454, but neither nation was aligned or even friendly with the Huns). Although his tactics were brutal by modern standards, <u>they were</u> [43] no more so than those of any military leader from that time, the "civilized" Romans included. Attila may be known as a monster in the West, but is revered as a national hero in much of Eastern Europe to this day. <u>Should you visit that part of the world, you will be amazed at how often you see his name!</u> [44] [45]

43. **A.** NO CHANGE
B. but they were
C. since they were
D. it was

44. Given that all of the following statements are true, which one provides the most relevant and specific information?
F. NO CHANGE
G. There is almost certainly at least one giant statue of him there!
H. In Budapest, there are more than ten "Attila Streets!"
J. Of course, the map of Eastern Europe is now very different from the one most Americans remember from school!

Question 45 asks about the preceding passage as a whole.

45. For the sake of logic and coherence, Paragraph 1 should be placed:
A. where it is now.
B. after Paragraph 2.
C. after Paragraph 3.
D. after Paragraph 4.

Passage IV

The Christmas Truce

<u>When it started</u> [46] with the assassination of an Austrian nobleman in the summer of 1914, and by the end of that year all Europe was scarred by trenches full of soldiers and pits full of poison gas.

46. **F.** NO CHANGE
G. Since it started
H. Although it started
J. It started

Practice Test 3

GO ON TO THE NEXT PAGE.

Tanks and warplanes made their first appearances. [47] Old-fashioned commanders accustomed to valiant charges on horseback sent countless waves of young men to instant death in the face of another new invention, the machine gun. The Great War, or World War I as it would come to be called, was the deadliest conflict the Western World had ever seen. [48] But out of its horror came one of the most reassuring accounts of the essential goodness of the human spirit.

On Christmas Eve of 1914, near the town of Ypres, Belgium, German, [49] and English forces had fought to a standstill from their opposed trenches. Both sides had sent miners to dig tunnels toward the enemy line. Underground, [50] each unit could hear the sounds of the other's [51] digging getting closer, and knew that the tunnels would soon meet and a firefight would erupt in the darkness at point-blank range.

At that moment, every soldier must have thought that he was about to die. [52] Recognizing the melodies, the men in the other tunnel responded, singing along in their own language. The singing picked up above ground, where the armies lit candles visible to the enemy at the edges of their trenches. The fighting ceased, and slowly, some individuals even dared to cross No Man's Land

47. Which of the following alternatives to the underlined portion would be LEAST acceptable?
   A. were first put into use.
   B. were first introduced.
   C. were used in combat for the first time.
   D. reared their ugly heads.

48. The writer wishes to finish this sentence with a phrase that emphasizes the human cost of the war. Which of the following true statements best achieves that goal?
   F. NO CHANGE
   G. was the first modern war, involving horrors beyond description.
   H. led directly to the deadly Spanish Flu epidemic.
   J. is the only major war where the inhuman weapon of mustard gas was used.

49. A. NO CHANGE
   B. Ypres, Belgium, German
   C. Ypres, Belgium German
   D. Ypres, Belgium, and German

50. Which of the following alternatives to the underlined portion would NOT be acceptable?
   F. NO CHANGE
   G. line, underground,
   H. line; underground
   J. line: underground

51. A. NO CHANGE
   B. others
   C. others'
   D. other is

52. Given that all the choices are true, which one would be the best transition between the first and last parts of the paragrah?
   F. NO CHANGE
   G. you could have cut the tension with a knife.
   H. soldiers from one side began singing Christmas carols.
   J. no soldier in the tunnels had ever been more scared in his life.

1 ■ ■ ■ ■ ■ ■ ■ ■ ■ 1

and meet enemy soldiers in the middle, where they exchanged [53] food and drink from their respective homelands.

When word of the Christmas Truce got out, the high command on both sides were furious [54] and ordered the fighting to resume. When Christmas 1915 approached again [55], they took steps to ensure that such things would not happen, ordering artillery bombardments on Christmas Eve and Christmas Day to make No Man's Land uncrossable. The commanders in the trenches had to follow orders, on pain of court martial. But as the generals [56] had never specified coordinates for the mandatory bombardments, entrenched officers in several locations came up with the idea of ordering wildly inaccurate shelling, allowing gift-giving between enemy combatants once again. For example, [57] in one location English and German soldiers even organized a soccer game in the middle of the battlefield.

By the time World War I ended in 1918, 16 million people had been killed in battle, three world powers had ceased to exist altogether, and nothing discernible had been accomplished. The devastation ended up leading directly to the existence of both the Soviet Union and Nazi Germany. [58] Just about the only good thing that came out of it was the story of a few young men who couldn't understand or comprehend [59] each other's languages but still decided that they would rather play soccer than fight.

53. Which of the following alternatives to the underlined portion would NOT be acceptable?
- **A.** middle. There, they exchanged
- **B.** middle to exchange
- **C.** middle they exchanged
- **D.** middle, exchanging

54. **F.** NO CHANGE
- **G.** both sides, they were furious
- **H.** both sides furiously
- **J.** both sides was furious

55. The best placement for the underlined portion would be:
- **A.** were it is now.
- **B.** after the word *they*.
- **C.** after the word *happen*.
- **D.** after the word *bombardments*.

56. **F.** NO CHANGE
- **G.** when the generals
- **H.** that the generals
- **J.** the generals

57. **A.** NO CHANGE
- **B.** In addition,
- **C.** Meanwhile,
- **D.** On the other hand,

58. If the writer were to delete the underlined sentence, the paragraph would primarily lose:
- **F.** an example of how World War I shaped the major conflicts of the twentieth century.
- **G.** the answer to a question posed at the beginning of the essay.
- **H.** an example of pure speculation on the part of the writer.
- **J.** some minor details unrelated to the main point.

59. **A.** NO CHANGE
- **B.** understand nor comprehend
- **C.** understandably comprehend
- **D.** understand

GO ON TO THE NEXT PAGE.

Question 60 asks about the preceding passage as a whole.

60. Suppose the writer had intended to write a brief essay focusing on acts of protest within the armed forces during wars. Would this essay fulfill that goal?

F. Yes, because the Christmas Truce is the most famous battlefield protest of all time.
G. Yes, because the Christmas Truce was spontaneous in origin, rather than being planned in advance.
H. No, because it only discusses examples of soldiers acting in protest from one war.
J. No, because American troops had not yet entered World War I at the time of the Christmas Truce.

Passage V

Genius at the Last Minute

He was born in Oregon in 1954, the son of a schoolteacher mother <u>and his father had grown up</u> [61] in a Mennonite community. He <u>never liked or excelled in school,</u> [62] and chose to attend a "hippie college" in Washington State that had been founded only five years earlier and didn't even give grades.

He stayed in college for five years, <u>and</u> [63] writing articles and drawing cartoons for the campus paper.

<u>After graduation,</u> [64] he moved to Los Angeles to try to become a writer, but couldn't catch a break and wandered through a series of jobs: busing tables, washing dishes, and even working at a sewage

61. **A.** NO CHANGE
B. and father grew up
C. and whose father grew up
D. and a father who'd grown up

62. Which of the following alternatives to the underlined portion would NOT be acceptable?
F. never liked school or excelled in it,
G. neither liked nor excelled in school,
H. disliked school, which he didn't excel in it,
J. disliked and failed to excel in school,

63. **A.** NO CHANGE
B. where
C. in which
D. DELETE the underlined portion.

64. **F.** NO CHANGE
G. Although after graduation,
H. After graduation, when
J. After graduation, however,

1 ■ ■ ■ ■ ■ ■ ■ ■ 1

treatment plant. Finally, he ended up working in a record store, a job he was able to stand. [66]

To amuse himself and make a little extra money, he drew comic books about how miserable he was in Los Angeles and sold photocopies of them in the store.

The comics were sarcastic black-and-white doodles featuring a family of odd-looking, dysfunctional rabbits, became popular with neighborhood artists and intellectuals, and soon he was getting paid to draw a daily strip featuring his odd rabbits for a local alternative newspaper. (The paper also gave him a music column, but he lost that after admitting that he just made up the names of all the bands and albums he reviewed as a joke.)

The rabbit strip, called *Life in Hell*, came to the attention of a successful producer, who contacted the thirty-one-year-old cartoonist about the possibility to do animated shorts for television. The artist was thrilled, but while waiting in the lobby of the producer's building before his big meeting, he had a series of terrifying thoughts. What if the television series bombed and ruined the reputation of his beloved comic?

65. Which of the following alternatives to the underlined portion would NOT be acceptable?
- **A.** at
- **B.** of
- **C.** for
- **D.** the register in

66. At this point, the writer is considering adding the following true statement:

The name of the store was Licorice Pizza.

Should the writer make this addition?
- **F.** Yes, because it helps explain why he was able to stand the job.
- **G.** Yes, because otherwise readers will wonder which store it was.
- **H.** No, because it is a minor detail that disrupts the flow of the paragraph.
- **J.** No, because many readers will not believe that this was really the store's name.

67.
- **A.** NO CHANGE
- **B.** comics, sarcastic
- **C.** sarcastically comic
- **D.** sarcastic comic's

68. Which of the following alternatives to the underlined portion would NOT be acceptable?
- **F.** he
- **G.** he had
- **H.** that he had
- **J.** because he had

69.
- **A.** NO CHANGE
- **B.** producer then contacted
- **C.** producer, and contacted
- **D.** producer contacted

70.
- **F.** NO CHANGE
- **G.** of doing
- **H.** he could do
- **J.** that this would do

Practice Test 3

GO ON TO THE NEXT PAGE.

Or what if he had to give up the rights to the characters, and no longer had any control over how they were used?

Crazy stuff happens to young artists all the time. [71] So just before being called into the meeting, he quickly drew another group of characters and named them after his own family: he used the real names of his parents and two little sisters, but invented another for the sarcastic, academically unmotivated male child, thinking that using his own name would give away [72] how little work he had put into the idea. To the animator's great relief, the producer loved the hurriedly created new characters. Their first animated short debuted in 1987, and by the end of 1989 they had their own half-hour show.

By now, you may have guessed that the cartoonist's name, Matt Groening, [73] and that the family he invented off the top of his head in that lobby is now known to the whole world as *The Simpsons.* The cartoon in which they star [74] has become the longest-running sitcom in TV history, as well as one of the most beloved, by viewers and critics alike. Although it may not happen every day, don't [75] ever let anyone tell you that a work of genius was never done at the last minute.

71. Which of the following sentences makes for the best transition between the first and second parts of the paragraph?
    A. NO CHANGE
    B. At times like this, he wished he were still at college in Washington.
    C. It was probably silly for him to be worrying so much.
    D. He wanted the TV gig badly, but didn't want to risk losing *Life in Hell*.

72. Which of the following alternatives to the underlined portion would be LEAST acceptable?
    F. betray
    G. evince
    H. mask
    J. tip the producer off to

73. **A.** NO CHANGE
    B. name was Matt Groening
    C. name, was Matt Groening
    D. name, Matt Groening

74. **F.** NO CHANGE
    G. cartoon which they star in
    H. cartoon, which they star in,
    J. cartoon they star in which

75. **A.** NO CHANGE
    B. day, but don't
    C. day; don't
    D. day, don't people

STOP

If there is still time remaining, check your answers to this section.

2 △ △ △ △ △ △ △ △ 2

MATHEMATICS TEST

60 MINUTES—60 QUESTIONS

Directions: Solve each problem, choose the correct answer, and then fill in the corresponding oval on your answer document.

Do not linger over problems that take too much time. Solve as many as you can; then return to the others in the time you have left for this test.

You are permitted to use a calculator on this test. You may use your calculator for any problems you choose, but some of the problems may best be done without using a calculator.

Note: Unless otherwise stated, all of the following should be assumed.

1. Illustrative figures are NOT necessarily drawn to scale.
2. Geometric figures lie in a plane.
3. The word *line* indicates a straight line.
4. The word *average* indicates arithmetic mean.

DO YOUR FIGURING HERE.

1. If $3x - 5 = 7$, then $3x = ?$

 A. $\frac{2}{3}$
 B. $\frac{4}{3}$
 C. 4
 D. $\frac{22}{3}$
 E. 12

2. What is the complement of 70°?

 F. 10°
 G. 20°
 H. 30°
 J. 80°
 K. 110°

3. 70 is 10% of what number?

 A. 7
 B. 63
 C. 77
 D. 700
 E. 7,000

Practice Test 3

GO ON TO THE NEXT PAGE.

DO YOUR FIGURING HERE.

4. The sum of three consecutive integers is 99. What is the value of the greatest of the three integers?

   F. 32
   G. 33
   H. 34
   J. 35
   K. 36

5. What is the area of the figure below?

   A. 54 in^2
   B. 90 in^2
   C. 108 in^2
   D. 135 in^2
   E. 180 in^2

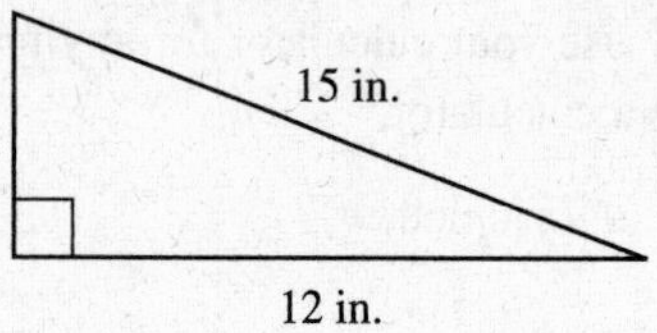

6. Last week Dyson earned \$8 per hour working at the local grocery store. This week his boss gave him a 10% raise. If he works 20 hours this week, what will his gross income be before taxes?

   F. \$160
   G. \$162
   H. \$174
   J. \$176
   K. \$180

7. Which of the following inequalities is equivalent to $3 - 4(x + 7) < 19$?

   A. $x > \frac{9}{2}$
   B. $x < \frac{9}{2}$
   C. $x < -11$
   D. $x > -11$
   E. $x < 11$

8. Which of the following is equivalent to $3\sqrt{300} - 5\sqrt{75}$?

   F. $-2\sqrt{225}$
   G. $5\sqrt{3}$
   H. $15\sqrt{3}$
   J. $2\sqrt{225}$
   K. $15\sqrt{225}$

9. $|-2 + 3^2| - |-2 - 3^2| = ?$

   A. −24
   B. −4
   C. 0
   D. 18
   E. 26

DO YOUR FIGURING HERE.

10. For triangle ABC, $m\angle A = 75°$ and $m\angle B = 36°$. Which segment of triangle ABC is the longest?

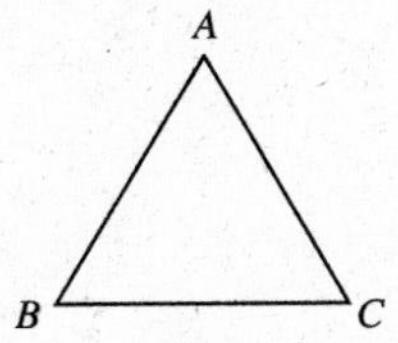

F. AB
G. BC
H. AC
J. AB and AC are both the longest sides.
K. Not enough information

11. Which of the following is a factor of $3x^2 + x - 4$?

A. $(x + 2)$
B. $(x - 2)$
C. $(3x - 4)$
D. $(x + 1)$
E. $(x - 1)$

12. Which of the following equations passes through the point (–3, 5)?

F. $y = -2x - 3$
G. $y = -4x + 5$
H. $y = -x + 2$
J. $y = 4x + 5$
K. $y = 5x + 9$

13. If $f(x) = \frac{-x^2 + 4}{x}$, then $f(-2) = ?$

A. –4
B. –1
C. 0
D. 6
E. 10

14. Which of the following equations is parallel to $y = -\frac{3}{4}x + 2$ in the standard (x, y) coordinate plane?

F. $y = -\frac{3}{4}x$
G. $y = \frac{4}{3}x + 2$
H. $y = -\frac{4}{3}x + 2$
J. $y = \frac{3}{4}x + 2$
K. $x = -\frac{3}{4}y + 2$

2 △ △ △ △ △ △ △ △ 2

DO YOUR FIGURING HERE.

15. An aquarium has exactly two types of fish: goldfish and angelfish. If the ratio of goldfish to angelfish is 2:5 and there are 25 angelfish in the aquarium, how many total fish are in the aquarium?

A. 7
B. 32
C. 35
D. 50
E. 125

16. Three different lines in the same plane can intersect at how many points?

F. 1
G. 1 or 2
H. 1 or 3
J. 1, 2, or 3
K. 0, 1, 2, or 3

17. If $-1 < a < 0$, $-4 < b < -3$, and $c = a - b$, then which of the following statements is true?

A. $c < a$
B. $c < b$
C. $c < a + b$
D. $c < 0$
E. $c > 0$

18. What is the slope between the points (–2, 5) and (0, 8)?

F. $-\frac{3}{2}$

G. $-\frac{2}{3}$

H. $\frac{7}{8}$

J. $\frac{8}{7}$

K. $\frac{3}{2}$

19. Rosemary and Caroline are baking cupcakes for a party. They are working from a recipe that will make 32 cupcakes. The recipe requires $2\frac{1}{2}$ cups of sugar to make 1 full batch. If they need to make 250 cupcakes for the party, which of the following amounts is the LEAST amount of sugar they need to make all 250 cupcakes?

A. 5 cups
B. 10 cups
C. 15 cups
D. 20 cups
E. 25 cups

2 △ △ △ △ △ △ △ △ 2

DO YOUR FIGURING HERE.

20. For the following triangle, $\measuredangle B$ is a right angle, $BC = 8, AC = 17$, what is the value of sin (C) ?

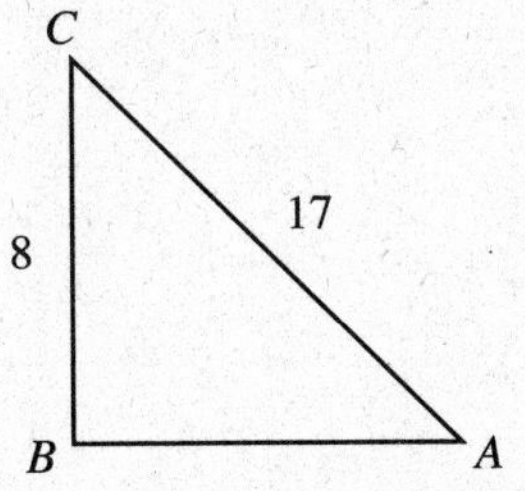

F. $\frac{8}{17}$

G. $\frac{15}{17}$

H. $\frac{\sqrt{353}}{17}$

J. $\frac{17}{15}$

K. $\frac{17}{8}$

21. If $5^3 \cdot 5^{-7} = \frac{1}{5^x}$, then x = ?

A. –21
B. –4
C. 4
D. 7
E. 21

22. In the figure below, $m\angle WYZ = 28°$ and $\overline{YM}$ bisects $\angle ZYX$. Which of the following is the measure of $\angle XYM$?

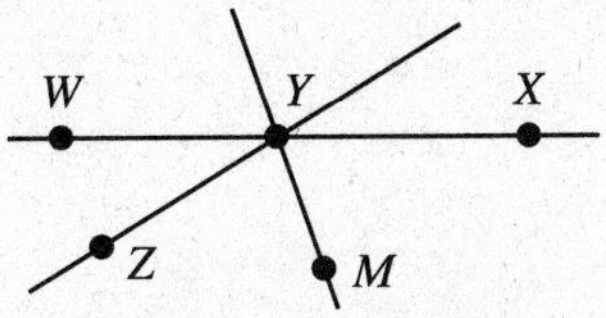

F. 76°
G. 78°
H. 84°
J. 90°
K. 152°

23. In the figure below, $\overline{AC}$ is a diameter of the circle and $m\angle BAC = 35°$. Find the measure of arc $\widehat{AB}$.

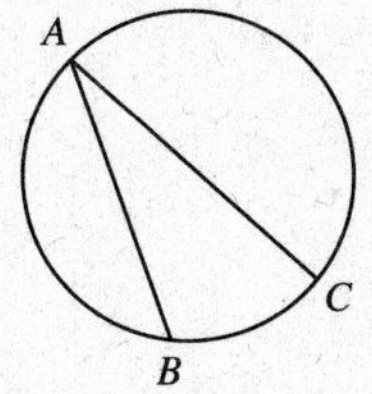

A. 35°
B. 60°
C. 70°
D. 90°
E. 110°

24. Which of the following is the greatest common factor of $36m^4n^3p^5$ and $24m^2n$?

F. $6m^2n$
G. $6m^4n^3p^5$
H. $12m^2n$
J. $12m^2np^5$
K. $72m^2n$

2 △ △ △ △ △ △ △ △ 2

DO YOUR FIGURING HERE.

25. Dave drove 144 miles to see his favorite band in concert. The drive to the concert took exactly 3 hours. On the drive home, Dave drove 10 miles per hour faster than he drove to the concert. Approximately how long did the return trip take?

    A. 2.2 hours
    B. 2.5 hours
    C. 2.7 hours
    D. 2.9 hours
    E. 3 hours

26. What value of x will satisfy the following matrix equation?

$$\begin{bmatrix} 23y^2 & 13z \\ 2x-1 & -15w^3 \end{bmatrix} + \begin{bmatrix} -7 & 10 \\ -4x-2 & 13 \end{bmatrix} = \begin{bmatrix} 16 & 23 \\ 12 & -2 \end{bmatrix}$$

    F. –7.5
    G. –3.5
    H. 1
    J. 6.5
    K. 13

27. Paxton leaves his house at noon heading due east for 4 miles. He then turns and heads directly south for 6 miles until he reaches the marina. What is the straight-line distance from Paxton's house to the marina?

    A. $2\sqrt{2}$
    B. 7
    C. $2\sqrt{13}$
    D. 10
    E. $4\sqrt{13}$

28. Which of the following is an expression for the area of the triangle below?

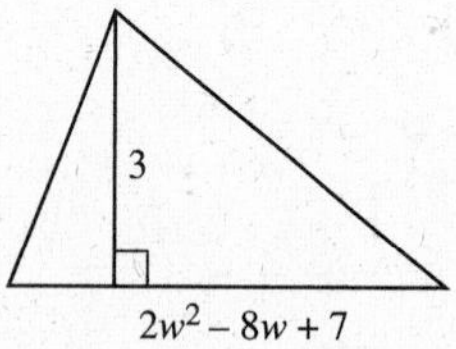

    F. $2w^2 - 8w + 10$
    G. $\dfrac{6w^2 - 24w + 21}{2}$
    H. $6w^2 - 24w + 21$
    J. $12w^2 - 48w + 42$
    K. $(2w - 7)(w + 3)$

29. What is the difference in the measure of one interior angle and one exterior angle of a regular decagon?

    A. 36°
    B. 64°
    C. 108°
    D. 144°
    E. 180°

2 △ △ △ △ △ △ △ △ 2

DO YOUR FIGURING HERE.

30. For $\triangle ABC$, $AB = 15$, $AC = 17$, $\measuredangle B$ is a right angle. What is the value of $\tan(A) - \cos(C)$?

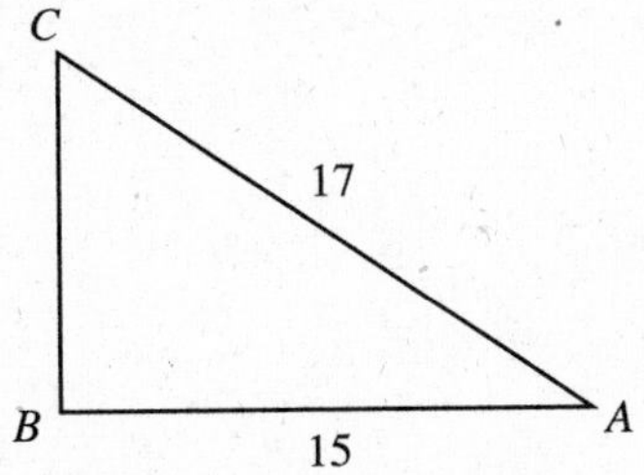

F. $-\frac{89}{255}$
G. $-\frac{16}{255}$
H. 0
J. $\frac{16}{255}$
K. $\frac{89}{255}$

31. If $\forall$ is defined for all real numbers x and y by $x \forall y = (x + y)(x - y)$, then $1\forall(2\forall 2) = ?$

A. 0
B. 1
C. 3
D. 4
E. 5

32. Sophie has played 6 games of soccer scoring 0, 1, 3, 2, 4, and 1 goals respectively in those games. For game 7, which of the following values will NOT yield a median of 2 goals scored?

F. 1 goal
G. 2 goals
H. 3 goals
J. 4 goals
K. 5 goals

33. What is the center of the circle with equation $(x + 7)^2 + (y - 5)^2 = 121$?

A. $(-7, -5)$
B. $(-7, 5)$
C. $(7, -5)$
D. $(7, 5)$
E. $(5, 11)$

34. Given the equation $3x - 7y = 21$, what is the equation in slope-intercept form?

F. $y = -\frac{3}{7}x + 3$
G. $y = -\frac{7}{3}x + 3$
H. $y = -\frac{3}{7}x - 3$
J. $y = \frac{3}{7}x + 3$
K. $y = \frac{3}{7}x - 3$

Practice Test 3

GO ON TO THE NEXT PAGE.

2 △ △ △ △ △ △ △ △ 2

DO YOUR FIGURING HERE.

35. In the graph below, line m is parallel to line n. Find the value of a.

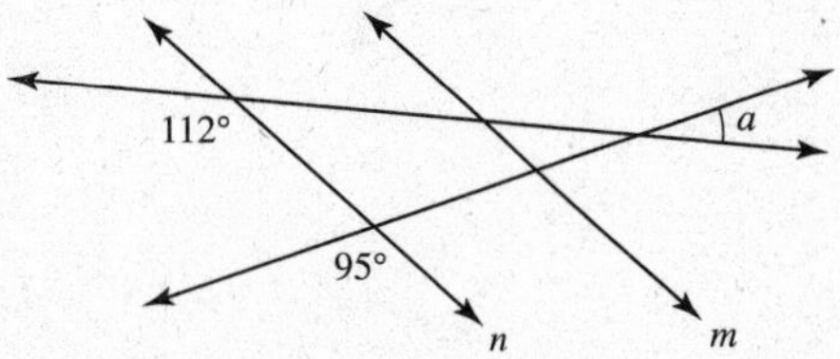

A. 17°
B. 68°
C. 85°
D. 95°
E. 112°

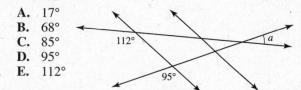

36. Which of the following is the set of solutions to the inequality $-\frac{2}{3}x + 5 < -\frac{1}{3}(2x + 9)$?

F. $x < 6$
G. $x > -6$
H. $x > 6$
J. There is no solution.
K. The set of all real numbers

37. Given the equation $-\frac{3}{5}x + 6y = 18$, which of the following equations is perpendicular to the given equation?

A. $y = \frac{1}{10}x + 2$
B. $y = \frac{5}{3}x + 7$
C. $y = \frac{3}{5}x + 5$
D. $y = -10x + 1$
E. $y = 10x + 18$

38. Dustin is in a 40-foot air traffic control tower at the local airport. He spots a plane that has just landed and using his protractor measures the angle of depression from the top of the tower to the landed plane to be 12°. How far from the base of the control tower is the plane?

F. $\frac{\tan(12°)}{40}$
G. $\frac{40}{\tan(12°)}$
H. $\frac{\sin(12°)}{40}$
J. $\frac{40}{\sin(12°)}$
K. $\frac{\cos(12°)}{40}$

2 △ △ △ △ △ △ △ △ 2

DO YOUR FIGURING HERE.

39. For what values of x is the function $\sqrt{x-5}$ undefined in the real number system?

A. $x = 0$
B. $x = 5$
C. $x = -5$
D. $x < 5$
E. $x > 5$

40. In the standard (x, y) coordinate plane, what are the coordinates of point A after the graph is reflected over the line $x = 7$?

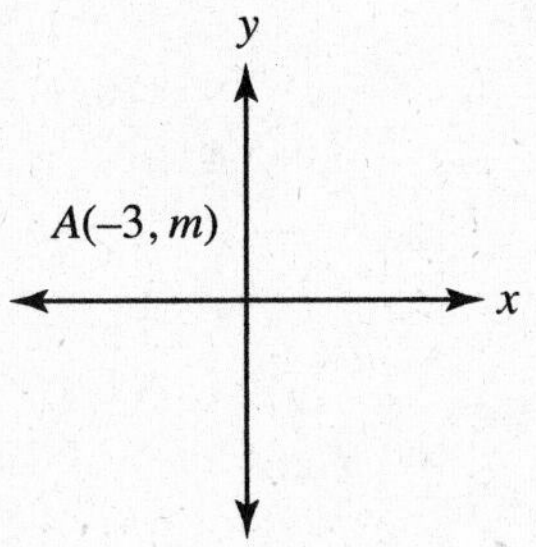

F. $(3, m)$
G. $(-3, -m)$
H. $(10, m)$
J. $(15, m)$
K. $(17, m)$

41. Given line segment AB with $A(-3, 2)$ and $B(5, 8)$, which of the following is the length of AB?

A. $\sqrt{34}$
B. $2\sqrt{10}$
C. 10
D. $9\sqrt{2}$
E. $\sqrt{170}$

42. Given similar rectangles *QUAD* and *RECT*, the ratio of sides *QU* to *RE* is 1:4. If the area of *QUAD* is 12, what is the area of *RECT?*

F. 0.75
G. 3
H. 12
J. 48
K. 192

Practice Test 3

GO ON TO THE NEXT PAGE.

2 △ △ △ △ △ △ △ △ 2

DO YOUR FIGURING HERE.

Use the following table to answer questions 43–44.

Forty students were asked to name their favorite pet. The following table lists the results.

Dog	16
Cat	15
Bird	9

43. Erick wants to make a circle graph from the given information. What would be the central angle for the dog piece of the graph?

A. 16°
B. 135°
C. 144°
D. 154°
E. 180°

44. When Erick recounted the votes later, he realized 3 of the votes that had actually been cast for cats got recorded as votes for dogs. What is the difference between the original percent of votes cast for cats and the corrected percent of votes for cats?

F. 2.5%
G. 7.5%
H. 15%
J. 37.5%
K. 45%

45. A parking lot downtown charges x dollars for the first hour and y dollars for each hour after the first. If Daniel parks in the lot for h hours where $h > 6$, which of the following equations represents P, the amount Daniel has to pay to park in the lot?

A. $P = h(x + y)$
B. $P = x + yh$
C. $P = y + x(h - 1)$
D. $P = xh + y(h - 1)$
E. $P = x + y(h - 1)$

46. Let $y = \frac{2x}{3z}$. What happens to the value of z as both x and y are doubled?

F. z remains the same
G. z doubles
H. z decreases by $\frac{1}{2}$
J. z quadruples
K. z decreases by a factor of $\frac{1}{4}$

2 △ △ △ △ △ △ △ △ 2

DO YOUR FIGURING HERE.

47. If $\frac{w^6t^5}{m^9} > 0$, then which of the following is true?

A. $w > 0$
B. $t > 0$
C. $m > 0$
D. $wt > 0$
E. $tm > 0$

48. Which of the following is equivalent to $2\log(x) + \frac{1}{2}\log(y) - 4\log(z)$?

F. $\log\left(2x + \frac{1}{2}y - 4z\right)$

G. $\log\left(x^2z^4\sqrt{y}\right)$

H. $\log\left(\frac{x^2\sqrt{y}}{z^4}\right)$

J. $\log\left(\frac{xy}{4z}\right)$

K. $\log\left(2x^2yz\right)$

49. Given the following table, find $f(g(2))$:

X	f(x)	g(x)
1	–5	0
2	–10	3
3	–15	6
4	–20	9

A. –15
B. –10
C. 0
D. 3
E. 6

50. The number of fish, p, a small pond can sustain varies inversely with the square root of the amount of predators, q, in the pond. If a pond with 49 predators can sustain a population of 800 fish, how many fish could a pond with 100 predators sustain?

F. 560
G. 600
H. 650
J. 1,600
K. 2,000

Practice Test 3

GO ON TO THE NEXT PAGE.

2 △ △ △ △ △ △ △ △ 2

DO YOUR FIGURING HERE.

51. Points $P(1, 1)$ and $Q(x, x^2)$ lie in the standard (x, y) coordinate plane. Which of the following is an expression for the slope between points P and Q when $x > 5$?

    A. 0
    B. $\frac{x^2+1}{x+1}$
    C. $x + 1$
    D. $\frac{x+1}{x^2+1}$
    E. Undefined

52. Which of the following expressions is equivalent to $\frac{3 \cdot 3^{2x-5}}{3^{x+1}}$?

    F. 3^{x-7}
    G. 3^{x-5}
    H. 3^{x-3}
    J. 3^{x-1}
    K. 1

53. What fraction is located exactly halfway between $\frac{3}{8}$ and $\frac{4}{5}$ on the standard number line?

    A. $\frac{15}{40}$
    B. $\frac{17}{40}$
    C. $\frac{1}{2}$
    D. $\frac{7}{13}$
    E. $\frac{47}{80}$

54. Mike has taken 4 tests in algebra so far. His average after 4 tests is 85%. If he has not received a grade lower than 80% on any tests, what is the highest possible score Mike could have achieved on one test?

    F. 96%
    G. 97%
    H. 98%
    J. 99%
    K. 100%

55. Given $|x - 3| > x - 3$, what is the solution set for the inequality?

    A. $x > 3$
    B. $x < 3$
    C. $x > 0$
    D. $x < 0$
    E. All real numbers

2 △ △ △ △ △ △ △ △ 2

DO YOUR FIGURING HERE.

56. For $i^2 = -1$, which of the following is equivalent to $\frac{i+7}{i-5} \cdot i$?

F. -1

G. $\frac{6}{13} - \frac{17}{13}i$

H. $\frac{6}{13} + \frac{17}{13}i$

J. $-\frac{1}{2} - \frac{3}{2}i$

K. $\frac{1}{2} + \frac{3}{2}i$

57. One square inch on the average pizza contains 50 calories. Alex bakes a 12″ diameter pizza and cuts it into 8 equal slices. If his dad eats 3 slices and Alex only eats 2, approximately how many more calories did Alex's dad eat than he did?

A. 100
B. 700
C. 1,400
D. 2,100
E. 2,200

58. Given $\tan(\theta) = v$ where $0° \leq \theta \leq 90°$, which of the following could be an expression for $\cos(\theta)$?

F. $\frac{v}{\sqrt{1+v^2}}$

G. $\frac{\sqrt{1+v^2}}{v}$

H. $\frac{1}{\sqrt{1+v^2}}$

J. $\sqrt{1-v^2}$

K. $\frac{\sqrt{1-v^2}}{v}$

59. Lisa, Carl, Max, Jenny, and Andy go to watch a movie and all sit next to each other in the same aisle. Andy must sit at either end of the group, but everyone else can sit anywhere within the group. How many possible seating arrangements are there?

A. 15
B. 48
C. 56
D. 92
E. 120

Practice Test 3

GO ON TO THE NEXT PAGE.

2 △ △ △ △ △ △ △ △ 2

DO YOUR FIGURING HERE.

60. In the standard (x, y) coordinate plane, points (m, n) and $(m - 2, n + \frac{2}{g})$ lie on the graph of the equation $y = \frac{1}{3}x - t$, where $t > 1$. What is the value of g?

F. -3

G. $-\frac{1}{4}$

H. 1

J. $\frac{7}{5}$

K. $\frac{123}{5}$

STOP

If there is still time remaining, check your answers to this section.

Turn page for the Reading Test

READING TEST

35 MINUTES—40 QUESTIONS

Directions: There are four passages in this test. Each passage is followed by several questions. After reading a passage, choose the best answer to each question and fill in the corresponding oval on your answer document. You may refer to the passages as often as necessary.

Passage I—Prose Fiction

This passage is adapted from the short story "A&P" by John Updike (© 1961 by John Updike).

In walks these three girls in nothing but bathing suits. I'm in the third check-out slot, with my back to the door, so I don't see them until they're over by the bread. The store's pretty empty, so there was nothing much to do except lean on the register and wait for the girls to show up again. After a while they come around out of the far aisle, around the light bulbs. Queenie puts down the jar and I take it into my fingers icy cold. Kingfish Fancy Herring Snacks in Pure Sour Cream: 49¢.

Then everybody's luck begins to run out. Lengel comes in from the lot and is about to scuttle into that door marked MANAGER behind which he hides all day when the girls touch his eye. Lengel's pretty dreary, teaches Sunday school and the rest, but he doesn't miss that much. He comes over and says, "Girls, this isn't the beach."

Queenie blushes, though maybe it's just a brush of sunburn I was noticing for the first time. "My mother asked me to pick up a jar of herring snacks." Her voice kind of startled me, the way voices do when you see the people first, coming out so flat yet kind of tony, too, the way it ticked over "pick up" and "snacks." All of a sudden I slid right down her voice into her living room. Her father and the other men were standing around in bow ties and the women were in sandals picking up herring snacks on toothpicks off a big plate and they were all holding drinks the color of water with olives and sprigs of mint in them.

"That's all right," Lengel said. "But this isn't the beach." His repeating this struck me as funny, as if it had just occurred to him. He didn't like my smiling—as I say he doesn't miss much—but he concentrates on giving the girls that sad Sunday-school-superintendent stare.

Queenie's blush is no sunburn now, and the plump one in plaid pipes up, "We just came in for the one thing."

"That makes no difference," Lengel tells her, and I could see from the way his eyes went that he hadn't noticed she was wearing a two-piece before. "We want you decently dressed when you come in here."

"We are decent," Queenie says suddenly, getting sore now that she remembers her place, a place from which the crowd that runs the A&P must look pretty crummy. Fancy Herring Snacks flashed in her very blue eyes.

"Girls, I don't want to argue with you. After this come in here with your shoulders covered. It's our policy." He turns his back. I could feel in the silence everybody getting nervous, most of all Lengel, who asks me, "Sammy, have you rung up this purchase?"

I thought and said "No." I go through the punches, 4, 9, GROC, TOT—it's more complicated than you think. I uncrease the bill and pass a half and a penny into her narrow pink palm, and nestle the herrings in a bag and hand it over, all the time thinking.

The girls, and who'd blame them, are in a hurry to get out, so I say "I quit" to Lengel quick enough for them to hear, hoping they'll stop and watch me, their unsuspected hero. They keep right on going; the door flies open and they flicker across the lot to their car, leaving me with Lengel and a kink in his eyebrow.

"Did you say something, Sammy?"

"I said I quit."

"I thought you did."

"You didn't have to embarrass them."

"It was they who were embarrassing us. I don't think you know what you're saying," Lengel said.

"I know you don't," I said. "But I do." I pull the bow at the back of my apron and start shrugging it off my shoulders. A couple customers that had been heading for

3 [redacted] 3

my slot begin to knock against each other, like scared pigs in a chute.

Lengel sighs and begins to look very patient and old and gray. He's been a friend of my parents for years. "Sammy, you don't want to do this to your Mom and Dad," he tells me. It's true, I don't. But it seems to me that once you begin a gesture it's fatal not to go through with it. I fold the apron, "Sammy" stitched in red on the pocket, and put it on the counter, and drop the bow tie on top of it. "You'll feel this for the rest of your life," Lengel says, and I know that's true too, but remembering how he made that pretty girl blush makes me so scrunchy inside. One advantage to this scene taking place in summer, I can follow this up with a clean exit, there's no fumbling around getting your coat and galoshes, I just saunter into the electric eye in my white shirt that my mother ironed the night before, and the door heaves itself open, and outside the sunshine is skating around on the asphalt.

I look around for my girls, but they're gone. There wasn't anybody but some young married screaming with her children about some candy they didn't get. Looking back in the big windows, I could see Lengel in my place, checking the sheep through. His face was dark gray and his back stiff, as if he'd just had an injection of iron, and my stomach kind of fell as I felt how hard the world was going to be to me hereafter.

1. The point of view from which the passage is told is best described as that of a (an):
   - **A.** young man relating a significant event in his life.
   - **B.** young man explaining to his parents why he has quit his job.
   - **C.** adult describing exactly what he should have done differently at a turning point in his life.
   - **D.** adolescent boy imagining what his life might be like in the future.

2. The passage contains recurring references to all of the following EXCEPT:
   - **F.** the narrator's family.
   - **G.** the other customers.
   - **H.** supermarket chains.
   - **J.** the girls' attire.

3. The first three paragraphs (lines 1–27) establish all of the following about the narrator EXCEPT that he:
   - **A.** is fascinated by the girls.
   - **B.** is new at his job.
   - **C.** dislikes his manager.
   - **D.** feels socially inferior to Queenie.

4. It can reasonably be inferred from the passage that the narrator aspires to be seen as:
   - **F.** romantic and poetic.
   - **G.** intellectual but rebellious.
   - **H.** tough but cultured.
   - **J.** principled and heroic.

5. Based on the narrator's account, life in his hometown is characterized by all of the following EXCEPT:
   - **A.** a tendency toward conformity.
   - **B.** an awareness of class hierarchy.
   - **C.** a mistrust of organized religion.
   - **D.** people knowing one another's business.

6. According to the narrator, which of the following articles of his clothing is the property of the store?
   - **F.** His shirt
   - **G.** His coat
   - **H.** His bow tie
   - **J.** His galoshes

7. When the narrator refers to Queenie "getting sore now that she remembers her place" (lines 39–40), he is most likely referring to the fact that she is:
   - **A.** much younger than Lengel and himself.
   - **B.** backed up by her two friends.
   - **C.** a stranger to this town.
   - **D.** wealthier than Lengel and himself.

8. Details in the passage most strongly suggest that the narrator's decision to quit ended up seeming most admirable from the point of view of:
   - **F.** himself.
   - **G.** the manager.
   - **H.** his parents.
   - **J.** Queenie.

9. The narrator indicates that Lengel the manager is extremely:
   - **A.** forgiving.
   - **B.** observant.
   - **C.** skeptical.
   - **D.** philosophical.

10. According to the passage, the narrator's decision to quit is most strongly motivated by his desire to:
    - **F.** impress the girls.
    - **G.** rebel against his parents.
    - **H.** get out of his hometown.
    - **J.** finally stand up to Lengel.

GO ON TO THE NEXT PAGE.

Passage II—Social Science

This passage is adapted from the essay "Into the Heart of India's Bone Trade" by Scott Carney, which appeared on NPR online in 2007.

Medical students across the world rely on anatomical models to become informed doctors. What many don't realize is that a large number of these models are stolen from graves in Calcutta, India.

For 200 years, the city has been the center of a shadowy network of bone traders who snatch up skeletons in order to sell them to universities and hospitals abroad. In colonial times, British doctors hired thieves to dig up bodies from Indian cemeteries. Despite changes in laws, a similar process is going strong today.

Throughout parts of Calcutta, many of the cemeteries have been empty for generations. "When I die, when I'm gone, my body will also be stolen," says Mohammad Jinnah Vishwas, a farmer who lives in the village of Amdanga. "Before we didn't understand where all the bones were going, now we know that they were taken by criminals."

A legal multimillion-dollar business throughout the 1970s, the export of human remains was banned by India in 1986 following rumors that traders were murdering people for their bones. The new law pushed most of the major companies out of business.

"It is kind of a sad situation because [my father] loved the business so much, and he saw it drift away from him," says Craig Kilgore, whose family founded Kilgore International, which at one point was the principal supplier of bones to the United States.

At least one organization, however, has managed to survive underground. Most prominently, a firm called Young Brothers—located conveniently between the city's biggest morgue and largest cemetery—has excelled in the black market. It has taken a bold approach—advertising its bone selection in catalogues and going to extreme measures to maintain its supply, according to a former clerk who requested anonymity for fear of retaliation.

"They took the bodies from the river, from the graveyard and from the hospital. More than 5,000 dead bodies I have seen," she says.

In 2001, Javed Ahmed Khan, Calcutta's health department chief, started receiving complaints about Young Brothers. The main storefront, neighbors said, was emitting a stench so horrible that it could be detected several blocks away. Neighbors also reported that they had seen bones drying on the roof and skeletons boiling in massive tubs.

A raid against the business, led by Khan, confirmed suspicions. "I went inside and saw two rooms full of human skeletons. There were huge bowls where skeletons were dipped to remove the fats and all that," Khan says.

In addition to three truckloads of bones, Khan said, he found invoices for shipments headed to the United States, Europe and Singapore. Despite the evidence, the owner of Young Brothers was released just a few days later.

"We won the case," says Vinesh Aron, the proprietor of Young Brothers. He denied a request to be interviewed, but when asked whether skeletons were recovered from his building, he said, "Those were all export materials." This answer hits on the hollowness of the rules governing the bones trade. Under the law, any bones being exported are technically "illegal"—but the question for police is often whether they are illegal enough to bother prosecuting.

That became evident again in May, when police intercepted a massive cache of human remains along a well-established smuggling route. The bleached white bones from over 100 people could have fetched around $70,000 had they made it to the United States. Whether the goods will ever be submitted as evidence in court is unclear.

"It depends on the seriousness that society places on it," says Rajeev Kuman, director inspector general of police in Calcutta. Kuman says he doesn't have enough resources to enforce the law. The fact that it's legal to import the bones into the United States and Europe, and that the "victims" are already dead, only serves to make the situation that much murkier.

Few retailers in the United States possess a steady supply of human bones. Those that do often purchase them through a chain of middlemen that spans the globe. The longer the chain, the easier it is to avoid considering the nature of that primary link.

11. Which of the following assumptions would be most critical for a reader to accept in order to agree fully with the author's claims in the passage?
    - **A.** The root of the problem lies within the attitudes of Indian law enforcement.
    - **B.** Local superstitions are keeping the illegal Indian bone market in business.
    - **C.** The situation in India is no different than in any other Asian nation.
    - **D.** Matters will not improve until American bone buyers insist upon greater accountability.

12. In the context of the passage, the statement "The longer the chain, the easier it is to avoid considering the nature of that primary link" (lines 78–79) most nearly suggests that:
    - **F.** American bone buyers have become complacent because they do not have to deal directly with criminals.
    - **G.** the general public does not believe that medical skeletons are made of real human bones.
    - **H.** larger criminal enterprises are harder to stop than smaller ones.
    - **J.** the bigger the bones, the more money criminals are able to get for them.

13. It can most reasonably be inferred from the passage that regarding the Indian bone trade, the author feels:
    - **A.** anger that the American media refuse to report on the problem.
    - **B.** fear that the criminals behind the enterprise will target him for exposing them.
    - **C.** sympathy for the people living in the conditions that are perpetuating the problem.
    - **D.** skepticism of whether the problem is really as widespread as people say.

14. The main purpose of the sixth paragraph (lines 27–34) is to:
    - **F.** establish that location is the primary factor determining which criminal enterprises will be more successful than others.
    - **G.** demonstrate the extreme boldness with which some bone-trafficking organizations operate.
    - **H.** convince the reader that the word of the former clerk can be trusted.
    - **J.** confirm the reader's suspicions that Young Brothers has been involved in illegal bone trafficking.

15. The main function of the eleventh paragraph (lines 52–60) is to:
    - **A.** establish that even flagrant violators of the bone laws will not necessarily end up convicted.
    - **B.** explain that Young Brothers had not been involved in illegal activity after all.
    - **C.** shift the question of blame to local police.
    - **D.** complain that American media have difficulty penetrating the veil of silence concerning Indian bone trafficking.

16. The passage notes all of the following as major contributors to the problem of illegal bone trafficking EXCEPT the:
    - **F.** power and influence of the criminals.
    - **G.** unfeasibility of prosecution.
    - **H.** frequent unreliability of witnesses.
    - **J.** willful ignorance of the American market.

17. The passage indicates that Calcutta law enforcement would do more about illegal bone trafficking if:
    - **A.** they were permitted to use the sort of weaponry necessary to win a fight with the traffickers.
    - **B.** they were better able to trust their own officers.
    - **C.** the cemeteries from which the bones were stolen lay inside their jurisdiction.
    - **D.** the public placed enough importance on the issue for the government to properly fund prosecution.

18. The passage implies that the skeletal remains of a single human might be worth approximately:
    - **F.** \$100
    - **G.** \$200
    - **H.** \$700
    - **J.** \$70,000

19. The passage implies that all of the following people oppose illegal bone trafficking EXCEPT:
    - **A.** Craig Kilgore.
    - **B.** Vinesh Aron.
    - **C.** Javed Ahmed Khan.
    - **D.** Mohammad Jinnah Vishwas.

20. The passage implies that the "catalogues" mentioned in line 32 would most likely be sent to:
    - **F.** medical students.
    - **G.** other criminals.
    - **H.** American media outlets.
    - **J.** superstitious locals.

Practice Test 3

Passage III—Humanities

This passage A is adapted from Mary Shelley's introduction to the 1831 second edition of her 1819 novel *Frankenstein*. Passage B is adapted from *Frankenstein* itself.

Passage A by Mary Shelley

The Publishers of the Standard Novels, in selecting "Frankenstein" for one of their series, expressed a wish that I should furnish them with some account of the origin of the story. I shall thus give a general answer to the question so frequently asked me—How I, then a young girl, came to think of and to dilate upon so very hideous an idea?

It is not singular that, as the daughter of two persons of literary celebrity, I should very early in life have thought of writing. As a child I scribbled, and my favourite pastime was to "write stories." Still I had a dearer pleasure than this, which was the formation of castles in the air—the indulging in waking dreams, which had for their subject the formation of a succession of imaginary incidents. My dreams were at once more fantastic and agreeable than my writings. In the latter I was a close imitator—rather doing as others had done than putting down the suggestions of my own mind. What I wrote was intended for other eyes, but my dreams were all my own.

I did not make myself the heroine of my tales. Life appeared to me too commonplace as regarded myself. I could not figure that romantic woes or wonderful events would ever be my lot, but I was not confined to my own identity, and I could people the hours with creations far more interesting to me than my own sensations.

After this my life became busier, and reality stood in place of fiction. My husband was very anxious that I should prove myself worthy of my parentage and enroll myself on the page of fame. He was forever inciting me to obtain literary reputation, which even on my own part I cared for then, though since I have become infinitely indifferent to it.

I thought and pondered—vainly. I felt that blank incapability of invention which is the greatest misery of authorship. *Have you thought of a story?* I was asked each morning, and each morning I was forced to reply with a mortifying negative.

When I placed my head on my pillow, I did not sleep, nor could I be said to think. My imagination, unbidden, possessed and guided me. I saw the pale student of unhallowed arts kneeling beside the thing he had put together. I saw the hideous phantasm of a man stretched out, and then, on the working of some powerful engine, show signs of life, and stir with an uneasy motion. His success would terrify the artist; he would rush away from his odious handiwork, horror-stricken. He would hope that, left to itself, the slight spark of life which he had communicated would fade. He sleeps; but he is awakened; the horrid thing stands at his bedside, opening his curtains, and looking on him with yellow, watery, but speculative eyes.

I opened mine in terror. Swift as light and as cheering was the idea that broke in upon me. "I have found it! What terrified me will terrify others; and I need only describe the spectre which had haunted my midnight pillow." On the morrow I announced that I had *thought of a story*.

And now, once again, I bid my hideous progeny go forth and prosper. I have an affection for it, for it was the offspring of happy days, when death and grief were but words, which found no true echo in my heart.

Passage B by Mary Shelley

It was on a dreary night of November that I beheld the accomplishment of my toils. With an anxiety that almost amounted to agony, I collected the instruments of life around me, that I might infuse a spark of being into the lifeless thing that lay at my feet. The rain pattered dismally against the panes, and my candle was nearly burnt out, when, by the glimmer of the half-extinguished light, I saw the dull yellow eye of the creature open; it breathed hard, and a convulsive motion agitated its limbs.

How can I describe my emotions at this catastrophe, or how delineate the wretch whom with such infinite pains and care I had endeavoured to form? His limbs were in proportion, and I had selected his features as beautiful. Beautiful! Great God! His yellow skin scarcely covered the work of muscles and arteries beneath; his hair was of a lustrous black, and flowing; his teeth of a pearly whiteness; but these luxuriances only formed a more horrid contrast with his watery eyes, that seemed almost of the same colour as the dun-white sockets in which they were set, his shrivelled complexion and straight black lips.

I had worked hard for nearly two years, for the sole purpose of infusing life into an inanimate body. I had desired it with an ardour that far exceeded moderation; but now that I had finished, the beauty of the dream vanished, and breathless horror and disgust filled my heart. Unable to endure the aspect of the being I had created, I rushed out of the room and continued a long time traversing my bed-chamber, unable to compose my mind. I slept, but I was disturbed by the wildest dreams. I thought I saw Elizabeth, in the bloom of health, walking in the streets of Ingolstadt. Delighted and surprised, I embraced her, but as I imprinted the first kiss on her lips, her features appeared to change, and I thought that I held the corpse of my dead mother in my arms. I started from my sleep with horror when, by the dim and yellow light of the moon, as it forced its way through the window shutters, I beheld the wretch—the miserable monster whom I had created.

Questions 21–25 ask about Passage A.

21. When Shelley writes "once again, I bid my hideous progeny go forth and prosper" (lines 55–56), she most nearly means that:

 A. she is launching the new edition of her most famous novel into the world, as she did with the first.
 B. she is prone to daydreaming about earlier times in her life when she was happier.
 C. she feels confident that the new edition will make more money than the first did, regardless of what the critics say.
 D. she is reluctant to publish the story but has no choice.

22. Passage A indicates that Shelley came to consider her earliest attempts at writing to be:

 F. cynical attempts at widespread popularity.
 G. unwilling to confront death and grief.
 H. too unrealistic to be critically respected.
 J. inorganic and insufficiently personal.

23. Shelley's claim that "since I have become infinitely indifferent to it" (lines 30–31) is meant to suggest that, over the course of the previous decade, she has:

 A. learned to write well without being emotionally affected by her subject matter.
 B. become more interested in writing nonfiction than unrealistic fiction.
 C. come to care far less about getting famous for her writing.
 D. developed a method of expertly disguising her own literary voice.

24. In the sixth and seventh paragraphs of Passage A (lines 37–54), Shelley explains the genesis of her realization that:

 F. her own psyche could in fact be the wellspring of effective literature.
 G. a tale of horror would be the last sort of book anyone expected from her.
 H. her novel would sell better if she wrote from the point of view of a male protagonist.
 J. she had already thought of the perfect story many years ago, when she was a child.

25. In Passage A, Shelley implies that, in the years since she wrote the first edition of *Frankenstein*:

 A. she has been surprised by how dramatically the public's taste in novels has changed.
 B. she has experienced profound personal tragedy in her own real life for the first time.
 C. she has been somewhat annoyed by how frequently the book's message is misinterpreted.
 D. her relationship with her parents has become less stressful and more one of mutual respect.

Questions 26–27 ask about Passage B.

26. In the second paragraph of Passage B (lines 68–78), the narrator describes his creation in a manner that:

 F. emphasizes the exhaustive degree of biological knowledge and long process of trial-and-error that went into creating him.
 G. apologizes for the creature's bizarre appearance by attempting to explain it logically and dispassionately.
 H. ironically juxtaposes the glory of the scientific knowledge involved in his creation with the grotesque form of the creature itself.
 J. emphasizes the personal jealousy he feels regarding the creature's prodigious physical strength.

27. Within Passage B, the narrator's dream in lines 87-95 functions symbolically to represent the idea that:

 A. true love gradually becomes impossible for anyone who knows too much about science.
 B. though the narrator has literally created life, he has metaphorically created death.
 C. death is a natural and inevitable part of life that should be embraced rather than feared.
 D. family is ultimately more important than either work or wisdom.

Questions 28–30 ask about both passages.

28. Both Passage A and Passage B highlight Shelley's taste for presenting:

 F. contrasting points of view via the device of frame narrative.
 G. necessary information in a roundabout fashion, in order to build suspense.
 H. the concepts of both death and genius as mere illusions.
 J. the depths of the human imagination as the source of true horror.

29. Based on Shelley's description in Passage A of her writing process, which of the following methods is likely to depict a way in which she might have gone about composing Passage B?

 A. Trying to analyze and then imitate other novels that have been widely regarded as terrifying.
 B. Allowing herself to feel frightened and then writing in a way that puts the reader in her position.
 C. Doing research into the biological mechanisms that cause fear and logically discerning how best to activate them.
 D. Jotting down unstructured notes while half-asleep and then examining them in the morning.

GO ON TO THE NEXT PAGE.

30. Elsewhere in the essay from which Passage A is adapted, Shelley writes:

> Invention, it must be humbly admitted, does not consist in creating out of void, but out of chaos; the materials must, in the first place, be afforded: it can give form to dark, shapeless substances, but cannot bring into being the substance itself. Invention consists in the capacity of seizing on the capabilities of the subject, and in the power of moulding and fashioning ideas suggested to it.

How do these statements apply to both Shelley's approach to storytelling as depicted in Passage A and the narration of her character Victor Frankenstein provided in Passage B?

F. They suggest that Shelley considered the origins of both art and life itself to be mysterious, and the role of any "creator" to be that of a conduit for an external force.
G. They amount to a cynical admission that every artistic idea is ultimately a copy of another, and that every supposedly "original" idea is actually "monstrous."
H. They describe Shelley's conviction that the concept of "inspiration" is actually a lie, and that all true beauty is the result of a process that is messy and ugly.
J. They suggest Shelley's viewpoint that all artistic creation is actually an act of destruction because we can only find words for what is already dead in our hearts.

3 3

Passage IV—Natural Science

This passage is adapted from "Magnetic Attraction" by Robert L. Park, Prof. emeritus of Physics, U. of Maryland.

In the early 16th century, the power of lodestone (magnetite) to attract iron filings without touching them suggested great power. Paracelsus, the famous Swiss alchemist and physician, began using powdered lodestone in salves to promote healing. William Gilbert, however, physician to Queen Elizabeth I and father of the scientific study of magnetism, pointed out that the process of grinding the lodestone into powder destroyed the magnetism. Nevertheless, a century later, magnetic cures were introduced into England by Robert Fludd as a remedy for all disease. The patient was placed in the "boreal position" with the head north and the feet south during the treatment.

By far the most famous of the magnetizers was Franz Mesmer (1734–1815), who carried the technique from Vienna to Paris in 1778 and soon became the rage of Parisian society. Dressed in colorful robes, he would seat patients in a circle around a vat of "magnetized water." While Mesmer waved magnetic wands over them, the patients held iron rods protruding from the vat. He would later discover that the cure was just as effective if he left the magnets out and merely waved his hand. He called this "animal magnetism."

Benjamin Franklin, in Paris on a diplomatic assignment, suspected that Mesmer's patients did indeed benefit from the strange ritual because it kept them away from the bloodletting and purges of other Paris physicians. Those physicians bitterly resented Mesmer, an outsider who was attracting their most affluent patients. At the urging of the medical establishment, King Louis XVI appointed a royal commission to investigate his claims. This remarkable group included Franklin, then the world's greatest authority on electricity; Antoine Lavoisier, the founder of modern chemistry; and Joseph Guillotine, the physician whose famous invention would one day be used to sever the head of his friend Lavoisier.

The commissioners designed a series of ingenious tests in which some subjects were deceived into thinking they were receiving Mesmer's treatment when they were not, and others received the treatment but were led to believe they had not. The results established beyond any doubt that the effects were due solely to the power of suggestion. Their report, never surpassed for clarity or reason, destroyed Mesmer's reputation in France, and he returned to Vienna.

Nevertheless, magnetic therapy eventually crossed the Atlantic. Its most famous practitioner in the United States was Daniel Palmer, who in 1890 opened Palmer's School of Magnetic Cure in Davenport, Iowa. Like Mesmer, Palmer soon discovered that his patients recovered just as quickly if he omitted the magnets and merely "laid on hands." Thus was founded "chiropractic therapy," and the school became Palmer's College of Chiropractic.

In recent years, an enormous amount of research has been done on the effect of magnetic fields on the human body, driven not by magnetic therapy, but by safety considerations associated with the phenomenal growth in the use of magnetic resonance imaging (MRI) for medical diagnoses and research. MRI subjects the whole body to a magnetic field about a hundred times stronger than the localized field of even the most powerful therapy magnet. Happily, no ill-effects have been found from exposure to MRI fields. Indeed, there are almost no effects at all—just a few reports of faint sensory responses, such as a slight metallic taste and visual sensations of flashing lights if patients move their eyes too rapidly. The fact is that the stuff we're made of just isn't very magnetic.

That's why scientists were surprised two years ago when Dr. Carlos Vallbona at the Baylor College of Medicine in Houston reported results of a double-blind trial of magnets in the treatment of 50 patients suffering post-polio pain. Some of the patients were treated with commercial therapy magnets; others were treated with sham magnets. Seventy-six percent of those treated with real magnets reported a decrease in pain, while only 19 percent receiving the placebo felt an improvement. The most frequent claim, which Vallbona supports, is that magnets promote the flow of blood to the treated area.

It's easy to check. An excess of blood shows up as a flushing or reddening of the skin. That's why the skin turns red when you apply heat; blood is being diverted to the heated area to serve as a coolant. But you will discover that placing a magnet of any strength against your skin produces no reddening at all. There is no indication that Vallbona tried this.

The argument is that blood, because it contains iron, should be attracted by the magnets. The iron in hemoglobin, however, is not ferromagnetic. The hemoglobin molecule itself is very weakly paramagnetic, but the fluid that carries the red cells, consisting mostly of water, is diamagnetic—it is weakly repelled. Indeed, small animals have even been levitated in powerful magnetic fields.

As medical scams go, magnet therapy may not seem like a big deal. Magnets generally cost less than a visit to the doctor and they certainly do no harm. But magnet therapy can be dangerous if it leads people to forego needed medical treatment. Worse, it tends to reinforce a sort of upside-down view of how the world works, leaving people vulnerable to predatory quacks if they become seriously ill. It's like trying to find your way around San Francisco with a map of New York. That could be dangerous for someone who is really sick—or really lost.

31. One of the main ideas established by the passage is that:

A. Benjamin Franklin helped to start a feud between Franz Mesmer and other physicians.
B. English scientists did more than Swiss ones to develop the science of magnetic therapy.
C. if it hadn't been for Franz Mesmer, we wouldn't have MRI technology now.
D. the alleged benefits of magnetic therapy are dubious at best.

32. Which of the following did the most to turn public opinion against Mesmer's theories?

F. The execution of Lavoisier
G. Benjamin Franklin's writings on electricity
H. The findings of the royal commission
J. The urging of King Louis XVI

33. The main purpose of the fifth paragraph (lines 45–52) is to establish that:

A. poorly supported medical theories became popular in the United States despite the lack of evidence.
B. Mesmer's theories were in fact not sufficiently disproved after all.
C. The bodies of some people are more magnetic than those of others.
D. Daniel Palmer ended up being a more important scientist than Franz Mesmer.

34. The passage states that, on the whole, human blood is actually:

F. ferromagnetic.
G. repelled by magnetic fields.
H. predominantly composed of iron.
J. capable of levitating small animals.

35. The passage notes that the MRI:

A. was invented in 1890.
B. is used primarily to treat post-polio pain.
C. promotes the flow of blood.
D. is about 100 times stronger than a therapy magnet.

36. As it is used in line 75, the word *placebo* most nearly means:

F. phony treatment.
G. powerful magnet.
H. traditional cure.
J. psychological boost.

37. As it is used in line 98, the word *quacks* most nearly means:

A. theories.
B. treatments.
C. dishonest therapists.
D. animal-borne diseases.

38. The passage indicates that skin turns red when exposed to heat because:

F. heat is absorbed and stored in the skin.
G. one function of blood is cooling hot skin.
H. hemoglobin is very weakly magnetic.
J. humans are not very magnetic.

39. The passage most strongly emphasizes that the process of bloodletting was:

A. an important step in the development of magnet therapy.
B. still popular in France long after it had ceased to be popular in America.
C. harmful enough to make magnet therapy appear beneficial.
D. indirectly involved with the discovery of hemoglobin.

40. According to the passage, the only legitimate experiment that involved magnet therapy was conducted by:

F. Benjamin Franklin.
G. Daniel Palmer.
H. William Gilbert.
J. Carlos Vallbona.

STOP

If there is still time remaining, check your answers to this section.

SCIENCE TEST

35 MINUTES—40 QUESTIONS

Directions: There are seven passages in this test. Each passage is followed by several questions. After reading a passage, choose the best answer to each question and fill in the corresponding oval on your answer document. You may refer to the passages as often as necessary.

You are NOT permitted to use a calculator on this test.

Passage I

Tornado intensity is commonly estimated by analyzing damage to structures and then correlating it with the wind speed required to produce such destruction. This method is essential to assigning tornadoes specific values on the *Fujita Scale* (F scale) of tornado intensity (see Figure 1).

Damage f scale		Little Damage	Minor Damage	Roof Gone	Walls Collapse	Blown Down	Blown Away
		f 0	f 1	f 2	f 3	f 4	f 5
Windspeed F scale (m/s)		17 m/s – 32	32 – 50	50 – 70	70 – 92	92 – 116	116 – 142
Windspeed F scale		F 0	F 1	F 2	F 3	F 4	F 5
Windspeed F scale (mph)		40 mph – 73	73 – 113	113 – 158	158 – 207	207 – 261	261 – 319
To convert f scale into F scale, add the appropriate number							
Weak Outbuilding	–3	f 3	f 4	f 5	f 5	f 5	f 5
Strong Outbuilding	–2	f 2	f 3	f 4	f 5	f 5	f 5
Weak Framehouse	–1	f 1	f 2	f 3	f 4	f 5	f 5
Strong Framehouse	0	F 0	F 1	F 2	F 3	F 4	F 5
Brick Structure	+1	-	f 0	f 1	f 2	f 3	f 4
Concrete Building	+2	-	-	f 0	f 1	f 2	f 3

Figure 1

A tornado is formed when the following occurs: (1) warm, moist air rises into cool, dry air; (2) when the barrier is breached, a bulge of warm, moist air expands and condenses to form a cloud; (3) as air moves upward, the resulting instability creates a spiral of air called a *mesocyclone*; (4) cold air moves downward and rain falls as the cloud becomes a *supercell*; (5) cool, moist air from rain cycles back into a cloud, forming a spinning wall-cloud; and (6) horizontal spiraling wind "tubes" are pushed upward by warm, moist air, forming a tornado. (See Figure 2.)

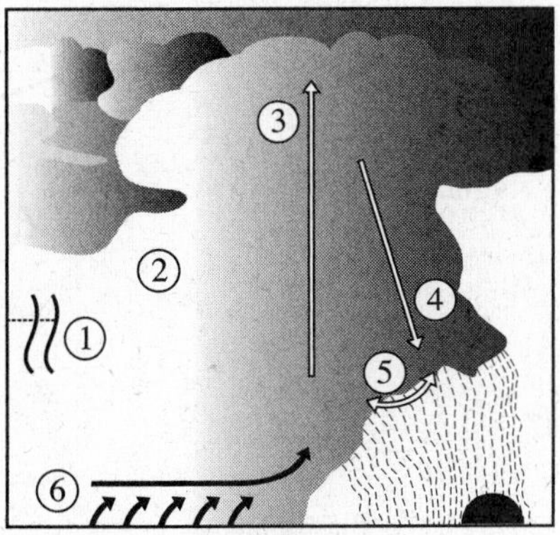

Figure 2

GO ON TO THE NEXT PAGE.

4 ○ ○ ○ ○ ○ ○ ○ ○ 4

The United States has the most tornadoes of any country, and most of these tornadoes form in an area of the central United States known as "Tornado Alley." Figure 3 displays a geographical (state-by-state) breakdown of the occurrence of tornadoes in the United States in 2005.

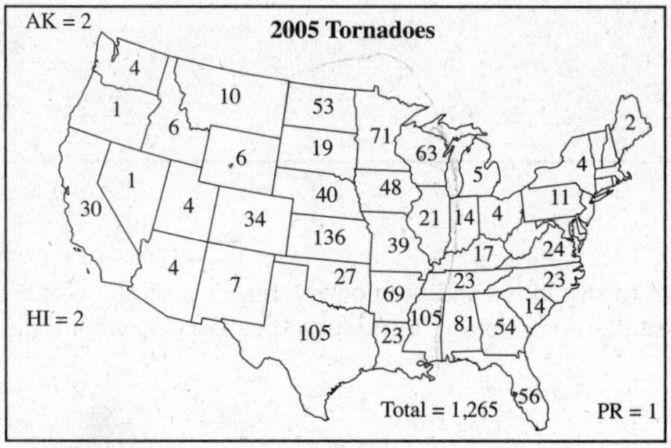

Figure 3

1. In Figure 2, the tornado is labeled with which number?

   A. 1
   B. 3
   C. 5
   D. 6

2. A tornado with an intensity of F4 on the Fujita Scale could have winds of which of the following speeds?

   F. 70 mph
   G. 155 mph
   H. 190 mph
   J. 210 mph

3. Which of the following does NOT precede the formation of a mesocyclone?

   A. Warm air flowing upward
   B. Cool air forming a spinning wall-cloud
   C. Cloud formation
   D. Moist air condensing

4. Based on the data provided in Figure 3, which of the following states can be inferred to be part of "Tornado Alley?"

   F. Texas
   G. Florida
   H. Michigan
   J. Washington

5. If the wind speed of a tornado was unknown, but it was observed that several brick buildings in the area sustained minor damage, what value would the tornado be assigned on the F scale?

   A. F0
   B. F1
   C. F2
   D. F3

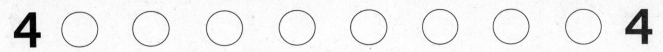

Passage II

Acid deposition delivers acids and acidifying compounds to the Earth's surface. Once on the surface, they move through soil, vegetation, and surface waters and, in turn, set off a cascade of adverse ecological effects. Acid deposition occurs in three forms: wet deposition, which falls as rain, snow, sleet, and hail; dry deposition, which includes particles, gases, and vapor; and cloud or fog deposition, which occurs at high altitudes and in coastal areas. Acid deposition is comprised of sulfuric acid, nitric acid, and ammonium derived from sulfur dioxide (SO_2), nitrogen oxides (NO_x), and ammonia (NH_3). Sulfuric and nitric acid lower the pH of rain, snow, soil, lakes, and streams.

Table 1

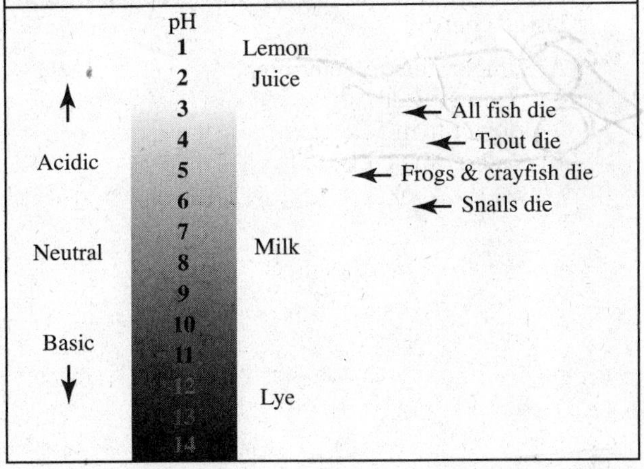

Study 1

A specially designed collection bucket was used to gather rain samples. The collector opened automatically during wet weather, allowing the precipitation to fall into the collection bucket, and then closed as soon as the precipitation stopped. The sample was then taken to a laboratory, where it was weighed and its acidity was measured. Finally, the concentrations of important inorganic chemicals found in the precipitation were analyzed. The results are shown in Table 2.

Table 2

Sample	pH	Cl (mg/L)	Mg (mg/L)	Na (mg/L)	NH_3 (mg/L)
1	5.41	0.02	0.002	0.010	0.01
2	5.28	0.09	0.009	0.029	0.05
3	5.43	0.15	0.008	0.084	0.03
4	5.16	0.08	0.006	0.038	0.01
5	5.45	0.00	0.002	0.003	0.00

Study 2

Another study was done to compare the average pH of precipitation across various months. The same procedure was used as in Study 1, and the results are shown in Table 3.

Table 3

Month	Average pH	Precipitation (cm)
Jan	4.58	8.45
Feb	4.77	8.20
Mar	4.90	7.01
Apr	5.16	17.12
May	4.81	11.48
Jun	4.68	51.67
Jul	4.79	9.24
Aug	4.18	23.52
Sep	4.92	42.26
Oct	4.34	9.74
Nov	4.89	11.76
Dec	4.91	4.67

4 ○ ○ ○ ○ ○ ○ ○ ○ 4

6. It is known that precipitation with a higher concentration of chlorine (Cl) does more damage to bodies of water than precipitation with a lower concentration of Cl. Based on this information, which sample tested in Study 1 would cause the most harm to rivers?

F. Sample 1
G. Sample 2
H. Sample 3
J. Sample 4

7. Based on the results of Study 2, it can be concluded that the deposition is least acidic during which season?

A. Spring
B. Summer
C. Fall
D. Winter

8. Based on the results of Study 1, which of the following can be concluded about the relationship between sodium (Na) concentration and the acidity of deposition?

F. The lower the concentration of Na, the more basic the precipitation.
G. The higher the concentration of Na, the more basic the precipitation.
H. The higher the concentration of Na, the more acidic the precipitation.
J. There is no correlation between the concentration of Na and acidity of the precipitation.

9. During which of the following months should there be the *least* concern for the health of frogs?

A. January
B. April
C. August
D. September

10. The precipitation collected in Study 1 is an example of which type of acid deposition?

F. Wet deposition
G. Dry deposition
H. Cloud deposition
J. Fog deposition

11. If the collection bucket used in Study 1 had been rinsed with sulfuric acid before collecting sample number 2, the resulting pH measurement would have been:

A. impossible to determine.
B. exactly 5.28.
C. lower than 5.28.
D. higher than 5.28.

Passage III

Students crystallized an impure, solid compound. First, they added just enough hot solvent to dissolve the compound. They then allowed the hot solution to cool, whereupon crystals began to form. Finally, the solution was placed in an ice bath to complete the crystallization process (see Figures 1 and 2). Figure 3 illustrates the progression of crystallization.

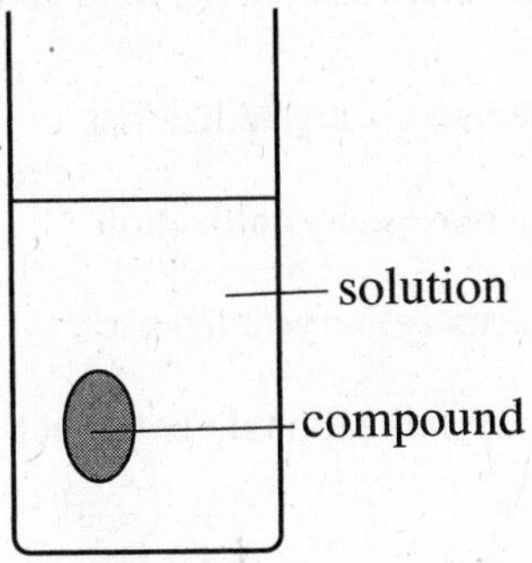

Figure 1

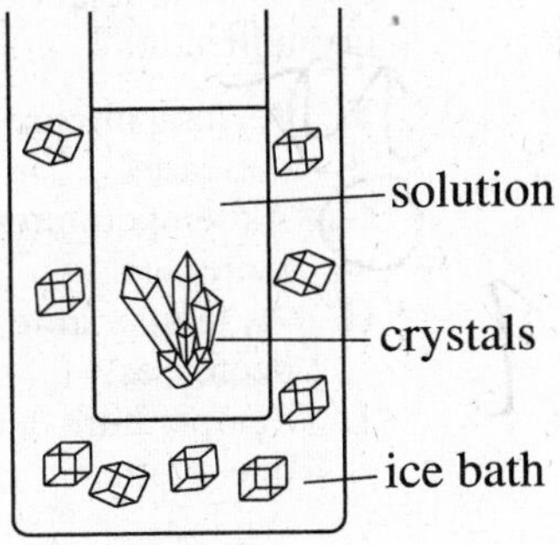

Figure 2

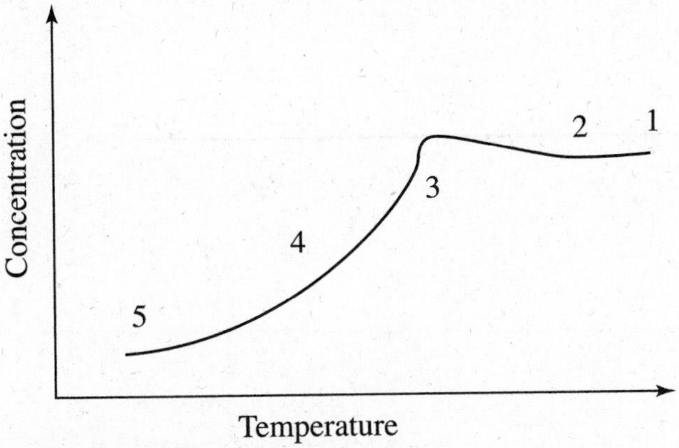

1 Solution added, undersaturated
2 Solution cools to saturation
3 Concentration decreases with crystal growth
4 Crystal growth during main cooling cycle
5 Supersaturated

Figure 3

Solubility (the amount of solute that will dissolve in a specific solvent) and crystallization are directly related. Since crystallization cannot begin until the solution becomes saturated, the faster a compound dissolves, the more quickly it can begin to form into crystals.

Study 1

Students tested the solubility of four different substances. The temperature was measured in °C, and water was used as the solvent. The results of the study are displayed in Figure 4.

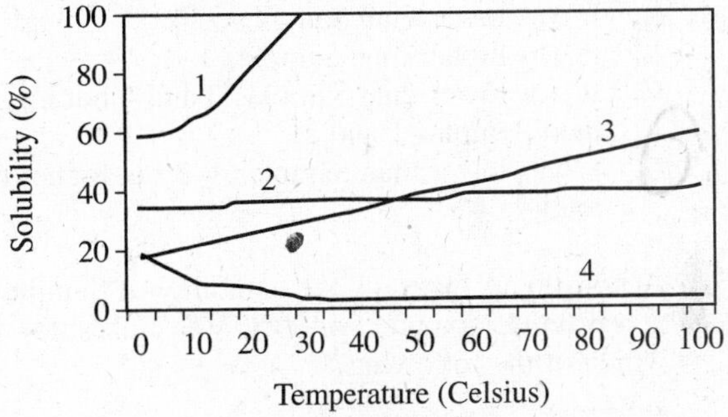

Figure 4

GO ON TO THE NEXT PAGE.

4 ○ ○ ○ ○ ○ ○ ○ ○ 4

12. In a solution of 60°C water, which sample from Study 1 would begin the crystallization process first?
    F. Sample 1
    G. Sample 2
    H. Sample 3
    J. Sample 4

13. A fifth sample was tested for solubility under the same conditions as in Study 1. The solubility at 30°C was 20%. How did the solubility of Sample 5 compare with that of Samples 1–4?
    A. It was lower than Samples 1–4.
    B. It was higher than Samples 1–4.
    C. It was lower than Samples 3 and 4 but higher than Samples 1 and 2.
    D. It was lower than Samples 1–3 but higher than Sample 4.

14. According to Figure 4, the solubility of Sample 1 at a water temperature of 30°C was closest to which of the following?
    F. 20%
    G. 60%
    H. 80%
    J. 95%

15. Based on the information in the passage and Figure 3, the solution was most likely placed in an ice bath at which of the following points?
    A. 1
    B. 2
    C. 4
    D. 5

16. Based on Figure 3, which of the following best explains the relationship between temperature and crystallization?
    F. As temperature decreases, crystallization increases.
    G. As temperature increases, crystallization increases.
    H. As temperature decreases, crystallization decreases.
    J. Temperature and crystallization do not affect one another.

4 ○ ○ ○ ○ ○ ○ ○ ○ 4

Passage IV

Blood type is a hereditary trait. The type is established by the genes inherited from the mother and father. The ABO system is widely accepted as the best blood classification system. In the ABO system, there are four types of blood: A, B, AB, and O. The combination of inherited genes is known as the *genotype* and the actual blood type is known as the *phenotype*. The genes ensure that only the blood cells of the proper blood type remain in the body.

Table 1

		Father's Blood Type			
		A	**B**	**AB**	**O**
Mother's Blood Type	A	A or O	A, B, AB, or O	A, B, or AB	A or O
	B	A, B, AB, or O	B or O	A, B, or AB	B or O
	AB	A, B, or AB	A, B, or AB	A, B, or AB	A, B, or AB
	O	A or O	B or O	A or B	O

The Rh (+/–) factor is inherited separately from the blood type. It is possible to have the Rh+ phenotype yet still carry the recessive gene for Rh–. The Rh+ (R) is the dominant gene and Rh– (r) is recessive. Table 2 shows the Rh phenotypes resulting from the various genotypes inherited from parents.

Table 2

Genotype	Phenotype
R R	Rh +
R r	Rh +
r r	Rh –

The surface of every red blood cell is covered with proteins. Rh factor and blood type determine the proteins and the compatibility of donated blood as shown in Table 3.

Table 3

Type	Can Donate Blood To	Can Receive Blood From
A+	A+ AB+	A+ A– O+ O–
O+	O+ A+ B+ AB+	O+ O–
B+	B+ AB+	B+ B– O+ O–
AB+	AB+	Everyone
A–	A+ A– AB+ AB–	A– O–
O–	Everyone	O–
B–	B+ B– AB+ AB–	B– O–
AB–	AB+ AB–	AB– B– O–

GO ON TO THE NEXT PAGE.

17. According to Table 1, parents with blood types O and B can only produce offspring with which blood types?

A. B or O
B. A or B
C. A or O
D. A

18. Parents with which blood types could produce offspring with AB+ blood?

F. O+ and A−
G. A− and B+
H. AB− and AB−
J. B+ and B+

19. A person who can donate blood to anyone could have parents with which of the following blood types?

A. A+ and AB−
B. AB− and AB−
C. B− and B−
D. AB+ and AB+

20. List all of the blood types possible for the offspring of parents of blood types A+ and O+.

F. A+ or O+
G. A+, A−, O−, or O+
H. O− or O+
J. AB+, A−, or O−

21. The genes that determine blood type are also responsible for:

A. Rh factor.
B. controlling the types of cells in the blood.
C. controlling blood volume.
D. creating proteins on white blood cells.

4 ○ ○ ○ ○ ○ ○ ○ ○ 4

Passage V

In a study of the effects of Ritalin and Adderall on children with ADHD, subjects were given one of four possible doses of medication. Their behavior in social and academic settings was then monitored and rated. The four possible doses were placebo (P), Ritalin given once in the morning (R1), Ritalin given twice daily (R2), or Adderall given once in the morning (A1).

The results for each group were averaged. Figure 1 shows the average behavioral rating (on a scale of 0–15, with 0 meaning no undesirable behavior) at various time periods throughout the day. Figure 2 shows the percentage of children who demonstrated side effects at a moderate or severe level on at least one day.

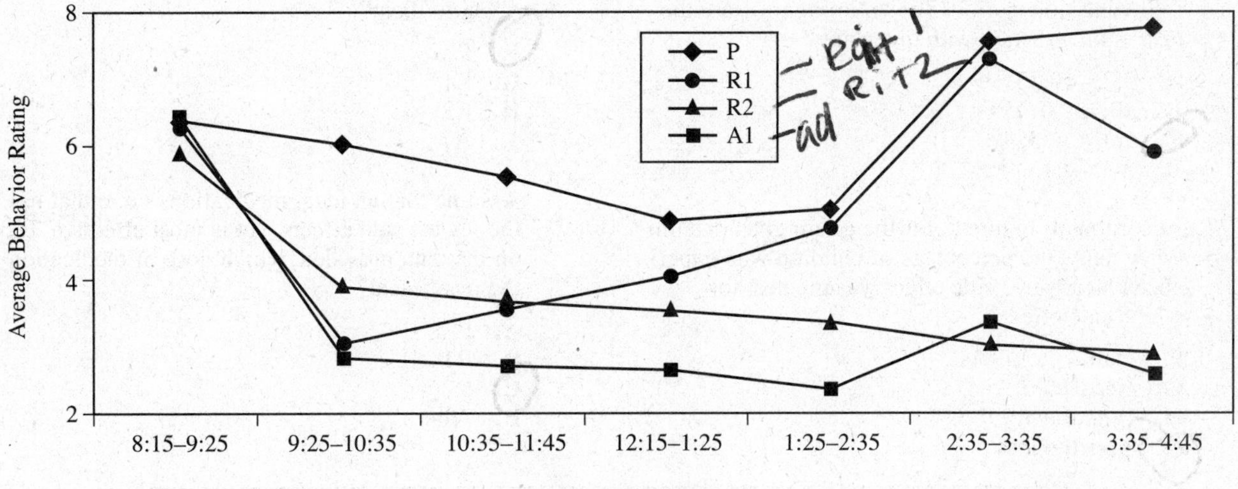

Figure 1

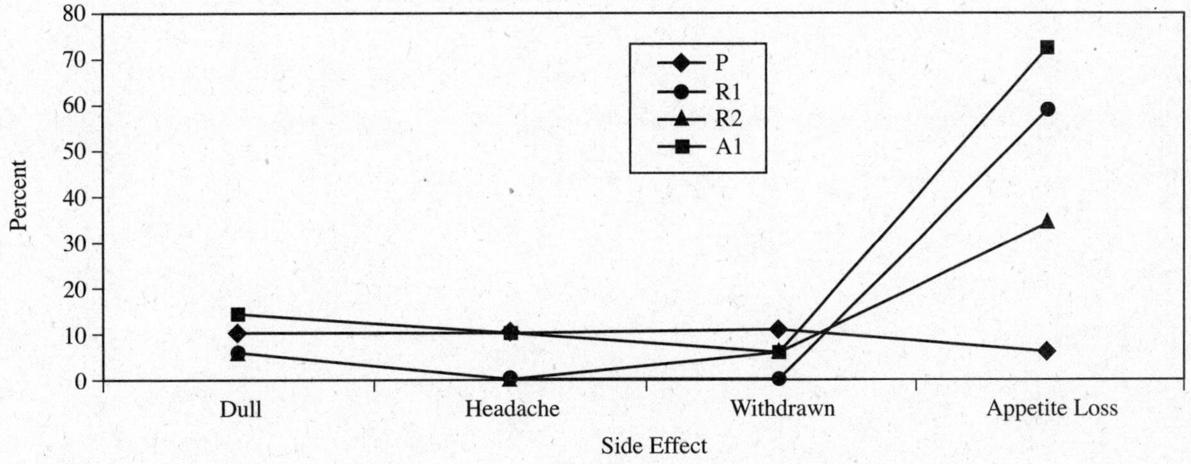

Figure 2

Practice Test 3

GO ON TO THE NEXT PAGE.

4 ○ ○ ○ ○ ○ ○ ○ ○ 4

22. Based on Figure 1, during which of the following time periods was the average behavior rating most similar for the four groups of children?

F. 8:15–9:25
G. 9:25–10:35
H. 10:35–11:45
J. 3:35–4:45

23. A scientist claimed that children given one dose of Adderall daily would exhibit fewer behavior problems than children given either one or two doses of Ritalin daily. During which of the following time periods shown in Figure 1 are the results *inconsistent* with this claim?

A. 9:25–10:35
B. 10:35–11:45
C. 2:35–3:35
D. 3:35–4:45

24. According to Figure 2, for the group given Ritalin twice daily, the percentage of children who experienced an adverse side effect was greatest for which side effect?

F. Dull
G. Headache
H. Withdrawn
J. Appetite loss

25. According to Figure 1, which dose of medication was the least successful in controlling children's behavior problems from 3:35–4:45?

A. P
B. R1
C. R2
D. A1

26. Suppose four groups of children were given one of the four possible medication regimens. Between 12:15 and 1:25, one group had a behavior rating of 5. Which medication regimen was most likely given to them?

F. P
G. R1
H. R2
J. A1

27. Assume that an ideal medication is one that has the fewest side effects, yet is most effective. Based on the data provided, which dose of medication is the most ideal?

A. P
B. R1
C. R2
D. A1

Practice Test 3

Passage VI

A solution consists of a solute dissolved in a solvent. For example, in a saltwater solution, the salt is the solute and the water is the solvent. Osmosis is the movement of solvent molecules across a barrier in order to equalize solution concentrations. When a saltwater solution is placed in a u-shaped tube with a selectively permeable barrier or semipermeable membrane, the phenomenon of osmotic pressure can be observed. Osmotic pressure is the pressure required to prevent the flow of a solvent across a barrier. In Figure 1, saltwater was poured in the right half of the tube and pure water was poured in the left half of the tube. As water passes from left to right in the figure below due to osmosis, the level of solution on the right rises. Eventually, the weight of the solution due to gravity becomes sufficient to prevent the further flow of water from right to left.

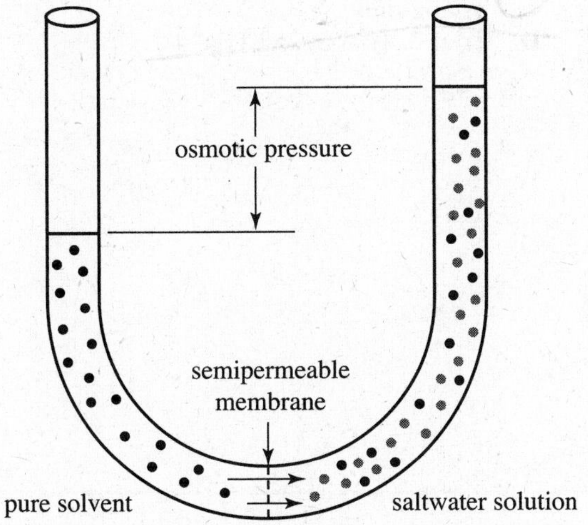

Figure 1

The following experiments were carried out to study how varying the molecular weight percentage of solvents and the temperature of solutions affects osmotic pressure. Table 1 shows the molecular weight percentages of the different solvents studied and Table 2 displays the temperatures of the various solutions used.

Table 1

Solution	Solution Concentration (% weight of solute)
1	5
2	10
3	15
4	20

Table 2

Trial	Temperature (°C)
1	20
2	30
3	40
4	50

Experiment 1

A 1000 ml u-shaped tube was fitted with a semipermeable membrane and 300 ml of solution was added on the right half and 300 ml of water was added on the left half. Table 1 shows the four solutions used in four separate trials of Experiment 1. The percent weight was measured by computing the ratio of the weight of the solute (salt) to the weight of the solution after dissolution. Every 5 seconds, the height of the solution on the right side of the tube was measured and recorded. Figure 2 shows the results of Experiment 1 recorded at 20°C.

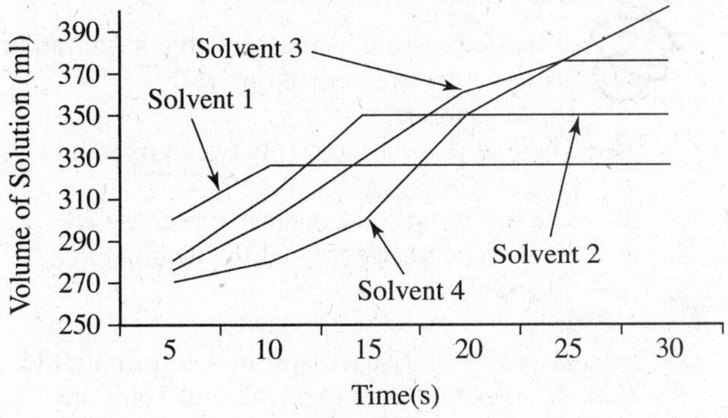

Figure 2

Experiment 2

Four more trials were performed but only the 10% solution was used. For each trial, the temperature was varied as shown in Table 2 and the results were graphed in Figure 3. In each trial, the height was measured 5 minutes after the water and solution were poured.

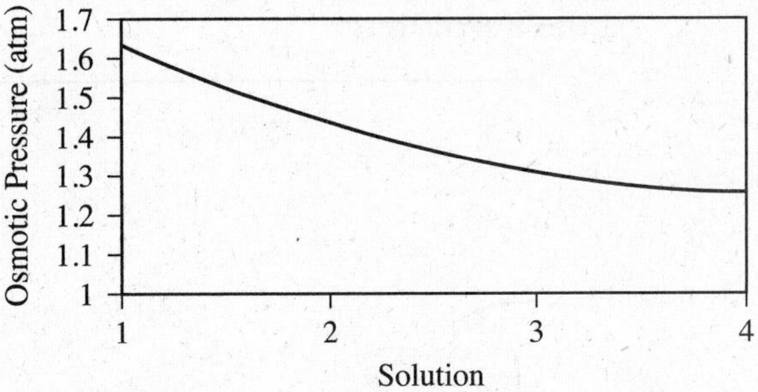

Figure 3

GO ON TO THE NEXT PAGE.

28. Based on Figure 2 and Table 2, which solution resulted in the greatest osmotic pressure after 30 seconds?

 F. Solution 1
 G. Solution 2
 H. Solution 3
 J. Solution 4

29. Based on the results of Experiment 2, what is the relationship between osmotic pressure and temperature?

 A. Osmotic pressure increases with an increase in temperature.
 B. Temperature and osmotic pressure are unrelated.
 C. Osmotic pressure decreases with an increase in temperature.
 D. Five minutes was insufficient time to allow the effects of osmotic pressure to be observed.

30. Based on Experiment 1, how does solution concentration affect osmotic pressure?

 F. Osmotic pressure increases with concentration.
 G. Osmotic pressure decreases with concentration.
 H. There is no relationship between osmotic pressure and concentration.
 J. The results were inconclusive because all solution heights were still fluctuating after 30 seconds.

31. Was Experiment 1 successful in determining the *relative* osmotic pressure of the four solutions tested?

 A. Yes. There is a clear difference in osmotic pressure between the four solutions with Solution 1 having the greatest osmotic pressure.
 B. Yes. There is a clear difference in osmotic pressure between the four solutions with Solution 4 having the greatest osmotic pressure.
 C. No. All osmotic pressures were too similar to make any determination.
 D. No. All solution heights were still fluctuating after 30 seconds.

32. *Reverse osmosis* occurs when the solvent flows from a solution of *higher* concentration to a solution of *lower* concentration. In Experiments 1 and 2, reverse osmosis can be observed by pouring more solution in the right side of the tube. Assuming the pressure required for reverse osmosis occurs at twice the osmotic pressure, approximately at what pressure would a 30° solution have to reach for reverse osmosis to occur?

 F. 0.7 atm
 G. 1.2 atm
 H. 2.8 atm
 J. 3.2 atm

33. Data in Figure 2 is consistent with which of the following trials?

 A. Trial 1 and Trial 3
 B. Trial 1 only
 C. Trial 2 only
 D. Trial 2, Trial 3, and Trial 4

Practice Test 3

Passage VII

Students studying mirrors and reflection were given the following information:

There is a definite relationship between image characteristics and the distance an object is placed with regard to a concave mirror (see Figure 1). If an object is located beyond the center of curvature (C), its reflected image will be inverted (upside down) and smaller than the object itself. If an object is located precisely at C, the image will also be located at C; it will appear inverted and true to the object's actual size. When the object is placed between C and the focal length (F), the image will be inverted and larger than the object. When the object is located precisely at F, no image is formed whatsoever. Lastly, if an object is placed between F and the mirror, its image will appear upright and larger than the object.

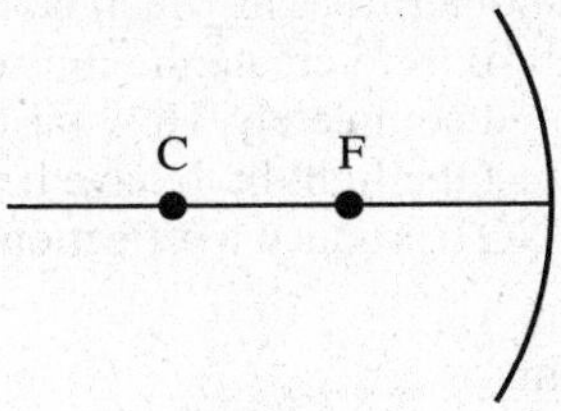

Figure 1

Given no further information, the students were asked to explain how the following magic trick is performed:

A famous Chinese magician conducts a classic magic trick utilizing a concave mirror with a focal length (F) of 1.6 m and a center of curvature (C) of 2.2 m. He is able to utilize the mirror in such a manner as to produce an image of a light bulb at the same location and of the same size as the actual light bulb itself.

Student 1

The light bulb must have been placed exactly 1.6 m in front of the mirror, creating a perfect reflection. The image would thus be in the same location as the light bulb, have the same dimensions as the light bulb, and be an upright image.

Student 2

The light bulb must have been placed exactly 2.2 m in front of the mirror. The image would then be in the same location and have the same dimensions as the actual light bulb, although it would be inverted.

Practice Test 3

34. The students disagreed about which aspect of the light bulb's image?

    F. Its size
    G. Its location
    H. Its orientation
    J. Its shape

35. The two explanations were similar to each other in that both explanations:

    A. assumed that the image was upright.
    B. assumed that the exact positioning of the light bulb was important.
    C. correctly interpreted the information provided by the teacher.
    D. incorrectly interpreted the information provided by the teacher.

36. Placing the light bulb in front of the mirror at which of the following distances would have resulted in an upright image?

    F. 1.0 m
    G. 1.6 m
    H. 2.2 m
    J. 2.6 m

37. Did Student 2 provide an adequate explanation of the magic trick?

    A. No. Student 2's explanation included an image that was upside down.
    B. No. if the light bulb were placed at 2.2 m, it would not have produced an image.
    C. Yes. 2.2 m is the center of curvature. Placing an object at C results in an image of the same size in the same place.
    D. Yes. The magician specified that the image was inverted; Student 2 was the only student to account for this.

38. All of the following statements concerning concave mirror reflections are true EXCEPT:

    F. an object placed anywhere in front of C (closer to the mirror) will produce a reflected image that is larger than the actual object.
    G. an object placed anywhere in front of F (closer to the mirror) will produce an upright reflection.
    H. an object placed anywhere beyond F (farther from the mirror) will produce an inverted reflection.
    J. the only possible way to produce a reflected image equal in size to the actual object is to place the object precisely at C.

39. The teacher posed another question to the students. The students were told that the magician performed another trick in which he relocated the light bulb so as to create the illusion that it had disappeared completely. How far in front of the mirror must the light bulb have been placed in order to NOT produce a reflection?

    A. 1.3 m
    B. 1.6 m
    C. 2.0 m
    D. 2.2 m

40. Assume that Student 2's explanation is correct. If the magician wanted to create an image of the light bulb that was smaller than the light bulb itself, at which of the following distances in front of the mirror could he place the light bulb?

    F. 1.6 m
    G. 2.0 m
    H. 2.2 m
    J. 2.5 m

STOP

If there is still time remaining, check your answers to this section.

WRITING PROMPT

Directions: This is a test of your writing skills. You will have thirty (30) minutes to write an essay in English. Before you begin planning and writing your essay, read the writing prompt below carefully to understand exactly what you are being asked to do. Your essay will be evaluated on the evidence it provides of your ability to express judgments by taking a position on the issue in the writing prompt; to maintain a focus on the topic throughout the essay; to develop a position by using logical reasoning and by supporting your ideas; to organize ideas in a logical way; and to use language clearly and effectively according to the conventions of standard written English.

You may use the unlined page to plan your essay. This page will not be scored. You must write your essay in pencil on the lined pages provided. Your writing on those lined pages will be scored. You may not need all the pages, but to ensure you have enough room to finish, do NOT skip lines. You may write corrections or additions neatly between the lines of your essay, but do NOT write in the margins of the lined pages. Illegible essays cannot be scored, so you must write (or print) clearly.

If you finish before time is called, you may review your work. Lay your pencil down immediately when time is called.

Childhood obesity is on the rise. In an effort to promote healthier eating habits, a number of schools have chosen to remove candy and soda from vending machines and to ban bake sales during school hours. Many oppose this ban because the money from the machines and from bake sales had been used to fund extracurricular activities. In your opinion, should schools take these measures to promote healthier eating habits?

In your essay, take a position on this question. You may write about either one of the two points of view given, or you may present a different point of view on this question. Use specific reasons and examples to support your position.

Use this page to *plan* your essay.

Begin WRITING TEST here.

If you need more space, continue on the next page.

WRITING TEST

Practice Test 3

Answer Key

PRACTICE TEST 3

English Test

1. D	16. G	31. B	46. J	61. D
2. F	17. B	32. J	47. D	62. H
3. C	18. F	33. D	48. F	63. D
4. J	19. A	34. H	49. B	64. F
5. B	20. J	35. A	50. G	65. B
6. H	21. C	36. G	51. A	66. H
7. D	22. J	37. D	52. H	67. B
8. J	23. C	38. G	53. C	68. J
9. A	24. G	39. C	54. J	69. A
10. H	25. A	40. H	55. C	70. G
11. B	26. H	41. A	56. F	71. D
12. F	27. D	42. H	57. B	72. H
13. A	28. F	43. A	58. F	73. B
14. H	29. B	44. H	59. D	74. F
15. C	30. G	45. A	60. H	75. A

Math Test

1. E	13. C	25. B	37. D	49. A
2. G	14. F	26. F	38. G	50. F
3. D	15. C	27. C	39. D	51. C
4. H	16. K	28. G	40. K	52. G
5. A	17. E	29. C	41. C	53. E
6. J	18. K	30. J	42. K	54. K
7. D	19. D	31. B	43. C	55. B
8. G	20. G	32. F	44. G	56. G
9. B	21. C	33. B	45. E	57. B
10. G	22. F	34. K	46. F	58. H
11. E	23. E	35. A	47. E	59. B
12. H	24. H	36. J	48. H	60. F

Answer Key

PRACTICE TEST 3

Reading Test

1. A	9. B	17. D	25. B	33. A
2. H	10. F	18. H	26. H	34. G
3. B	11. D	19. B	27. B	35. D
4. J	12. F	20. F	28. J	36. F
5. C	13. C	21. A	29. B	37. C
6. H	14. G	22. J	30. F	38. G
7. D	15. A	23. C	31. D	39. C
8. F	16. H	24. F	32. H	40. J

Science Test

1. D	9. B	17. A	25. A	33. B
2. J	10. F	18. G	26. F	34. H
3. B	11. C	19. C	27. C	35. B
4. F	12. F	20. G	28. J	36. F
5. B	13. D	21. B	29. C	37. C
6. H	14. J	22. F	30. F	38. F
7. A	15. C	23. C	31. B	39. B
8. J	16. F	24. J	32. H	40. J

HOW TO SCORE YOUR PRACTICE TEST

Step 1: Add up the number correct for each section and write that number in the blank under the Raw Score column on the Score Conversion Table. (Your goal is to get more questions correct on each subsequent practice test.)

Step 2: Using the Score Conversion Chart, find your scale score for each section and write it down. Then add up all four sections and divide by 4 to find your overall composite score. (Composite scores are rounded up at .5 or higher.)

Score Conversion Table

Section	Raw Score	Scaled Score
English	(out of 75)	____ / 36
Math	(out of 60)	____ / 36
Reading	(out of 40)	____ / 36
Science	(out of 40)	____ / 36
		Add and divide by 4
Overall Composite =		____ / 36

Score Conversion Chart

	Number Correct				
ACT Score*	English Section	Mathematics Section	Reading Section	Science Section	ACT Score*
36	75	60	40	40	**36**
35	74	59	39	39	**35**
34	73	58	38	38	**34**
33	72	57	37	—	**33**
32	71	56	36	37	**32**
31	70	54–55	35	36	**31**
30	69	53	34	35	**30**
29	67–68	51–52	33	34	**29**
28	65–66	49–50	32	33	**28**
27	64	46–48	31	31–32	**27**
26	62–63	44–45	30	30	**26**
25	60–61	41–43	29	28–29	**25**
24	58–59	39–40	27–28	25–27	**24**
23	55–57	37–38	25–26	24	**23**
22	53–54	35–36	23–24	22–23	**22**
21	50–52	33–34	22	20–21	**21**
20	47–49	31–32	21	18–19	**20**
19	44–46	28–30	19–20	17	**19**
18	42–43	25–27	18	15–16	**18**
17	40–41	22–24	17	14	**17**

Continued

Score Conversion Chart *(Continued)*

ACT Score*	Number Correct English Section	Mathematics Section	Reading Section	Science Section	ACT Score*
16	37–39	19–21	16	13	**16**
15	34–36	15–17	15	12	**15**
14	31–33	11–14	13–14	11	**14**
13	29–30	09–10	12	10	**13**
12	27–28	07–08	10–11	09	**12**
11	25–26	06	08–09	08	**11**
10	23–24	05	07	07	**10**
9	21–22	04	06	05–06	**9**
8	18–20	03	05	—	**8**
7	15–17	—	—	04	**7**
6	12–14	02	04	03	**6**
5	09–11	—	03	02	**5**
4	07–08	01	02	—	**4**
3	05–06	—	—	01	**3**
2	03–04	—	01	—	**2**
1	00–02	00	00	00	**1**

**These scores are based on student trials rather than national norms.*

SCORING YOUR ESSAY

As mentioned earlier in this text, two readers will evaluate your essay and each person will then assign it a score from 1 to 6. If, by chance, these two scorers disagree by more than 1 point, a third reader will step in and resolve the discrepancy. Performance on the essay will not affect your English, math, reading, science, or composite scores. You will receive two additional scores on your score sheet—a combined English/writing score (1–36) and a writing test subscore (1–12). Neither of these scores will affect your composite score!

The sample essay that follows reflects higher-level writing. It meets the criteria that ACT has put forth for essays that demonstrate effective writing skills.

- It takes a definite position.
- It addresses and expands on the counterargument.
- It has details that support the topic sentences and is well organized.
- It is not repetitive, and while there may be errors, they do not interfere with the competence of the essay.
- It is consistent and well balanced.
- The essay has a clear introduction and a conclusion that is not just a summary but ends with a significant thought.
- The vocabulary demonstrates good use of language and the sentence structure is varied.

Answer Explanations: English Test

1. **(D)** In the phrase *both critics and fans have agreed*, two groups of people (*critics* and *fans*) are both doing the same thing—that is, both nouns are performing the same verb. Therefore, you don't need a comma before *and*. As for what they have agreed on, in the extended phrase *both critics and fans have agreed that no individual is due more credit than Chuck Berry,* there is also no need for a comma. The relative pronoun *that* introduces essential information (as opposed to *which*, which introduces nonessential or "extra" information). You do not need a comma in front of it (but you do in front of *which*).

2. **(F)** The phrase *singer, songwriter, and guitarist* refers to a single individual (Chuck Berry), and this is the noun phrase performing the verb in question. Choice F is the only one of the options with a singular verb (*was*). The other choices all have plural verbs. There is an added prepositional phrase trick: since *behind* is a preposition, *behind such rock classics as "Maybelline" and "Johnny B. Goode"* is a prepositional phrase that must be skipped over when determining agreement.

3. **(C)** The surrounding sentence informs us that there were multiple *inductees* into the Rock and Roll Hall of Fame in 1986, of whom Chuck Berry was one. Thus, we need the verb/preposition pairing *was among* (equivalent to "was one of" or "was part of").

4. **(J)** Since the sentence would be grammatically correct without the name *Johnnie Johnson*, the name is therefore set off with commas. The relative pronoun *who* is necessary after the comma because without it the subordinate clause would have no subject (just read the sentence without the name and you will see it sounds very wrong without *who*).

5. **(B)** The sentence is a question beginning with *Could*. You would not say *Could [blank] is?* but rather *Could [blank] be?* and so the choice with *be* is correct.

6. **(H)** *Unthinkable* means "nearly impossible to believe," and thus best emphasizes how shocking the allegations were. It is the most "extreme" of the four terms given as options.

7. **(D)** *Corroborate* means to support the validity of something. Therefore, the least acceptable choice is (D) dispute.

8. **(J)** The fact that Chuck Berry joined Johnson's band at the last minute when another member happened to get sick on the night Johnson's band was playing Berry's town was a very lucky coincidence from Berry's perspective, and emphasizes how easily his life could have gone a completely different way.

9. **(A)** The subordinating conjunction *although* is like a version of *but* that goes elsewhere in the sentence (you can see how the sentence would also work if you got rid of *although* but put a *but* after the comma). The ACT English often tries to trick you with *although* because it is a conjunction that can go at the beginning of the first of two independent clauses, instead of just at the beginning of the second. Here, it is the only one of the four choices that results in a complete correct sentence that means what you want it to mean.

10. **(H)** The noun performing the underlined verb is *hits*, and so the verb needs to be plural. *Were* is the only choice that is both plural and makes grammatical sense in context. This is a classic prepositional phrase trick: the prepositional phrase *after his 1963 release* needs to be skipped over when determining agreement.

11. **(B)** The sentence establishes that Springsteen's comment was made *years earlier*, and so *had remarked* is the only one of the choices that is grammatically correct and means what you want it to mean.

12. **(F)** Information establishing that Berry had been in trouble with the law several times and cheated other partners is absolutely relevant to a passage exploring the question of whether he also cheated Johnnie Johnson.

13. **(A)** The fact that Johnson was unaware that he was entitled to more money than he was paid for the recording sessions is information relevant to the question of why he didn't speak up at the time, which is exactly the question this paragraph is addressing.

14. **(H)** What the sentence means to say is that too much time had elapsed between the time that the songs were composed and the time of the lawsuit, and so the option beginning with *since* is the appropriate choice.

15. **(C)** The passage deals only with a specific set of allegations made against Chuck Berry, and not with any other celebrities, much less with celebrities in general. (The fact that the passage deals only with one example and not an entire category is a <u>very</u> common answer on ACT English final "Suppose the Author..." questions!)

16. **(G)** The first thing to notice is that this sentence has more than one underlined portion; you must always be aware when this is the case, because the answers to both questions will affect each other (though there will never be more than one correct combination of answers). Since the part of the sentence before the comma is an independent clause, the part after it must either be a dependent clause or an independent clause with a conjunction. Choice G, *endlessly*, creates a grammatically correct "afterthought clause," a dependent descriptive clause preceded by a comma.

17. **(B)** The string of verbs constitutes a list, and so you need an *and* before the last of them: *endlessly admired, analyzed, and parodied* (either a comma or no comma before the *and* that precedes the last item in a list is acceptable; the ACT English will **never** test you on this directly).

18. **(F)** This option results in two independent clauses separated by a comma + *and*, forming a correct sentence that means what you want it to mean.

19. **(A)** Replacing the underlined portion with *this was* would result in a comma splice, and so this is the choice that is NOT acceptable.

20. **(J)** Choice J informs us that Perrugia disguised himself as one of the workers and walked around the museum pretending to work, and so it is the only one of the choices that provides specific information about how Perrugia avoided detection in the museum for so long.

21. **(C)** All of the other prepositions or combinations of prepositions are appropriate in context (although some are less formal than others), but *from of* is utter nonsense, and so it is the option that is LEAST acceptable.

22. **(J)** Because the subsequent clause is an independent one, the first clause of the sentence needs to be a dependent one. *Finding* is the only option that results in a sentence that is not a comma splice and means what you want to say.

23. **(C)** Since the subsequent sentence explains why people took so long to notice that the *Mona Lisa* had been stolen, the best opening sentence is the one that introduces this idea, even if some of the others relate to the end of the previous paragraph. (With questions about introductory sentences on the ACT English, it is always best to read a few sentences ahead and pick the sentence that best introduces the ones after it, rather than basing your answer on the previous paragraph!)

24. **(G)** Although all of the options result in complete correct sentences, only *in private* explains why no one was alarmed by the *Mona Lisa*'s absence (they assumed it was being worked on by museum staff in another room).

25. **(A)** Since it is inconceivable that another artist could be unaware of the *Mona Lisa*'s fame and importance, *out of ignorance* makes no sense as an explanation for an artist's motivation for stealing it, and so it is the choice that is the LEAST acceptable. The other three choices are so similar that they are essentially different ways of saying the same thing. (It is always a good idea to look for "which of these things is not like the other" on NOT and LEAST questions!)

26. **(H)** The *masterwork was feared gone forever* is the only one of the choices that makes sense and says what you mean to say. If it sounds strange, this may be because it is a situation where *to be* may be omitted, which you might not be used to hearing. The sentence means that the masterwork was feared to be gone forever.

27. **(D)** Since the verb of this independent clause is *led*, what goes in the underlined part needs to be a noun phrase performing that verb. *Perrugia's motivation* is the only noun phrase that forms a concise, correct sentence.

28. **(F)** Although you may not be used to seeing the formal phrase *from whence*, you should still understand from context that the painting was stolen *from* Italy, and that the other choices make no sense.

29. **(B)** The phrase *his expectations were not entirely off-base* is a way of saying that the things he believed were partially accurate, which is a paraphrase of the phrase *Perrugia might not have been as crazy as he seems* from the question.

30. **(G)** The passage does in fact explain the background, execution, and aftermath of a famous crime and this is all the question asks for. The explanation in choice G, the second of the *Yes* options, simply restates the demands of the question.

31. **(B)** *Dubbed* is a transitive verb that means *called* or *named*. So just as you would have to say *his enemies called him* or *his enemies named him*, you have to say *his enemies dubbed him*.

32. **(J)** Preposition usage in English is largely idiomatic. The phrase is *synonymous with* because that is simply what we say. It is one of those things that you just have to know from reading a lot. (Preposition-choice questions are becoming more common on the ACT English, so make sure to make an effort to start noticing such things!)

33. **(D)** Although all four choices are correct complete sentences, the other three choices are awkward and/or unnecessarily complex. *Modern historians agree* is the simplest and most succinct way to put it. (On style questions, always pick the simplest way of putting something as long as it makes a correct sentence, unless the question is specifically asking for something more complex, such as "the most detailed description.")

34. **(H)** The sentence says that most people's ideas about Attila come from Roman writers, and that these writers were unfair to him. Choice H is basically a paraphrase or summary of this.

35. **(A)** *At the time of Attila's birth in 406* is a dependent introductory clause, and so is followed by a comma. Although the rest of the sentence is long, and contains other underlined portions that should be double-checked alongside this answer, this introductory phrase could not constitute an independent clause no matter what. (Remember, when you see that two of the other choices are a semicolon and a period, this means they cancel each other out and the right answer must be a comma!)

36. **(G)** How many *Asias* are we talking about? One. And does it possess anything? Yes (the *central seas*). How many *seas* are we talking about? More than one. And do they possess anything? No. And so we need the singular possessive *Asia's* and the plural nonpossessive *seas*. It is as simple as that.

37. **(D)** Deleting the underlined portion makes the rest of the sentence into a succinct and grammatically correct "afterthought clause" describing the aforementioned *nation*.

38. **(G)** Simply saying *class division* concisely communicates the same information, whereas the other three choices are wordy and redundant.

39. **(C)** The Vikings, how they dressed, and when they sailed to America are all irrelevant to Attila, and distract the reader from the main idea.

40. **(H)** What we need here is the past tense verb *coexisted* and the modifying adverb *peacefully*.

41. **(A)** *That* is a pronoun standing in for the idea of Rome's royal line, and so the phrase *to unite his royal line* with that of Rome is correct.

42. **(H)** *Formerly the common enemy of both the Huns and Rome* is an appositive clause containing extra information, and is here set off with dashes (setting it off with commas would also be correct, but is not an option). The sentence then picks up with *further insulting Attila*, which grammatically matches up with the part of the sentence before the appositive. (On the ACT English, dashes usually come in pairs, so when you see a dash earlier in the sentence, expect the underlined part to contain the second one!)

43. **(A)** The presence of *Although* turns the first clause into a dependent one, and so the remainder of the sentence needs to be an independent clause. And since the noun being replaced here is *tactics*, the pronoun and verb need to be plural.

44. **(H)** The question asks for *relevant and specific information*, and only choice H provides a concrete example supporting the idea of Attila's high esteem in contemporary Eastern Europe.

45. **(A)** Paragraph 1 begins by building suspense about the identity of its subject, who is still a mystery until the third sentence (which also explains who Attila is). All this indicates that paragraph 1 is definitely supposed to come first. (If a paragraph had been in the wrong place the whole time, then something probably would have sounded "off" while you were reading the passage; if nothing did, then the paragraphs were probably in the right order!)

46. **(J)** The subsequent clause begins with a conjunction, which means that this first clause needs to be an independent one. *It started* is the only one of the choices that accomplishes this.

47. **(D)** *First reared their ugly heads* does not make sense in context, whereas the other three choices all indicate the first time. Hence D is the least acceptable.

48. **(F)** The question asks for a phrase that *emphasizes the human cost of the war* (in other words, something about how many people died). Only choice F, which explains that more people died in World War I than in any war in Western history, does this.

49. **(B)** There must be a comma between *Ypres* and *Belgium*, separating the name of the city from the name of the country. There must also be a comma after *Belgium*, since this is where the appositive phrase beginning with the word *near* ends. Since both German and English forces are performing the verb *had fought*, there should not be a comma between *German* and *and*.

50. **(G)** Merely inserting a comma between *line* and *underground* would create a comma splice, and so this is the choice that is NOT acceptable.

51. **(A)** The phrase *each other* is tricky when it comes to possession. There are two armies, but relative to each army there is only one other, and so we need the singular possessive *other's: each army could hear the sound of the other's digging.* (Because *digging* is a gerund, it takes a possessive.)

52. **(H)** Although every choice seems fine if you don't read ahead, the subsequent sentence makes reference to melodies being recognized and someone's singing being responded to. Therefore, what we need here is a sentence establishing that someone was singing, and only choice H accomplishes this. (Always read ahead a little before answering "What sentence/phrase should go here?" questions!)

53. **(C)** This results in a run-on sentence (with the second of two independent clauses beginning at the word *they*), whereas the other three choices all result in grammatically correct sentences. Hence, it is the one that is NOT acceptable.

54. **(J)** Though it refers to a group of people, the phrase *high command* itself is singular, and so takes the singular verb *was*. This is a classic prepositional phrase trick: the prepositional phrase *on both sides* must be skipped over. (Though more than one high command is involved, the phrase itself is still singular.)

55. **(C)** Logically, the word *again* would have to modify something that already took place at least once. Since the truce was the thing that already took place, *again* should follow *happen* (since the noun phrase *such things* refers to the truce and is performing the verb *happen*).

56. **(F)** What we need preceding *the generals* is a word meaning "since" or "because." Of the choices, only *as* accomplishes this.

57. **(B)** Although every choice would result in a grammatically correct sentence, only the introductory phrase *in addition* accurately describes the information that follows, whereas the other three choices do not make sense in context.

58. **(F)** If neither Nazi Germany nor the Soviet Union would have existed if it hadn't been for World War I, then this phrase explains how WWI indirectly led to both World War II and the Cold War, the major conflicts of the twentieth century.

59. **(D)** The word *understand* by itself is all that is necessary. The other choices are all either redundant or grammatically incorrect. (When three choices are several words long and the fourth choice is one word, the fourth choice is almost always correct, as long as it results in a complete sentence!)

60. **(H)** The passage does not discuss protests within the armed forces in general, but only one individual famous instance of this. (The fact that the passage only discusses one specific example, rather than a larger phenomenon in general is a <u>very</u> common answer to "Suppose the Author..." questions on the ACT English!)

61. **(D)** The descriptive phrase *the son of* needs to extend in parallel ways to the phrases *a mother* and *a father*; both nouns need to function as objects of the preposition *of*. Only choice D accomplishes this.

62. **(H)** This incorrectly attempts to link two independent clauses with the relative pronoun *which* as though it were a conjunction. Hence, it is the choice that is NOT acceptable.

63. **(D)** Deleting the underlined portion makes the second half into a dependent descriptive clause that adds more information to the initial independent clause.

64. **(F)** The sentence (before the list that follows the colon) is two independent clauses separated by a comma and a conjunction. Only the introductory prepositional phrase *After graduation* preserves the first half of the sentence as an independent clause and refrains from adding any unnecessary elements.

65. **(B)** Preposition usage is largely idiomatic, and in certain situations more than one preposition (or phrase involving a preposition) could be correct. In this case, every choice would be acceptable besides *of*. Hence, choice B is the one that is NOT acceptable.

66. **(H)** The name of the store is not important, and so this is a minor detail that interrupts the flow of the paragraph.

67. **(B)** Reading the entire sentence reveals that the main verb is *became*, which is being performed by the noun *comics*, and that therefore everything between them should be a descriptive appositive phrase set off with commas.

68. **(J)** Either including or omitting the word *that* is acceptable, and either including or omitting the word *had* is acceptable (with varying degrees of formality). Inserting the word *because* in addition to *after admitting*, however, is grammatically incorrect, and so choice J is the option that is NOT acceptable.

69. **(A)** *Strip* is the subject of the sentence, and *came* is the main verb. The word *producer* should end the initial independent clause, followed by a comma and a dependent clause beginning with the relative pronoun *who*.

70. **(G)** Preposition usage in English is largely idiomatic. The phrase *the possibility of doing* is correct simply because it is what we say. There are some other phrases that could also be correct here, but none of the other three options are. It is one of those things that you just have to know from reading a lot. (Preposition-choice questions are becoming more common on the ACT English, so make sure you start noticing such things!)

71. **(D)** Only this phrase both summarizes his concerns and explains his motivation for what he does next, thereby linking the two halves of the paragraph. Any of the other choices might well be true, but they are not sufficiently explanatory at this point in the passage.

72. **(H)** What we need here is a word or phrase meaning "give away" (in the sense of *reveal*, like with a secret). All the other choices mean "give away," but *mask* means "conceal," which is the opposite. Hence, it is the one that is LEAST acceptable.

73. **(B)** What is needed here is an independent clause subordinated to the relative pronoun *that*, and only *the cartoonist's name was Matt Groening* (uninterrupted by a comma) accomplishes this.

74. **(F)** The prepositional phrase *in which they star* adds important information to the noun *cartoon*, and does not need to be set off with any commas.

75. **(A)** The first clause is a dependent one beginning with *Although*, and so the part of the sentence after the comma needs to be an independent clause. (The conjunction *Although* is like a *but* that goes at the beginning of the first clause instead of the beginning of the second, and so the ACT English often tries to fool you using *although*!)

Answer Explanations: Math Test

1. **(E)** If you add 5 to both sides, you get $3x = 12$.
2. **(G)** Complementary angles are two angles whose sum is 90°: 70°+ 20° = 90°; therefore the complement of 70 is 20.
3. **(D)** You can set up an equation using the words of the problem to get $70 = .10(x)$. Solve for x by dividing both sides of the equation by .10 to get $x = 700$.
4. **(H)** You can find the three consecutive integers by either guessing and using your calculator, or you can set up an equation if that is what you prefer. Either way you will find the three consecutive integers whose sum is 99 are 32, 33, and 34. The greatest of these integers is 34.
5. **(A)** To find the area of a triangle use the formula $A = \frac{1}{2}\, b \cdot h$. To find the height of this triangle, either use the Pythagorean Theorem, or realize this is a 9-12-15 right triangle so the height must be 9. Now that we know the height, substitute into the area formula to get $A = \frac{1}{2}(12)(9) = 54$.
6. **(J)** If he gets a 10% raise, his new pay will be $8 + (.10)(8) = \$8.80$. If he works 20 hours he will make $20(8.80) = \$176$.
7. **(D)** First subtract 3 from both sides to get $-4(x + 7) < 16$, then distribute to get $-4x - 28 < 16$. Now add 28 to both sides: $-4x < 44$. Finally divide both sides by -4, but don't forget to switch the inequality to get $x > -11$.
8. **(G)** You could solve this problem using your calculator to get a decimal approximation, then plug the answers into your calculator to get a similar decimal approximation. For those who prefer to do it the algebra way: $3\sqrt{300} - 5\sqrt{75} \to 3\sqrt{100 \cdot 3} - 5\sqrt{25 \cdot 3} \to 3 \cdot 10\sqrt{3} - 5 \cdot 5\sqrt{3} \to 30\sqrt{3} - 25\sqrt{3}$. Subtract to get $5\sqrt{3}$.
9. **(B)** $|-2 + 3^2| - |-2 - 3^2| = |7| - |-11| = 7 - 11 = -4$.
10. **(G)** The longest side of a triangle is always opposite the largest angle in the triangle. To find the missing angle C use the fact that the sum of the three angles of a triangle is 180° to get 180 – 75 – 36 = 69°. Since angle A is 75°, it is the largest of the three angles and therefore the side opposite, BC, is the longest side.
11. **(E)** $3x^2 + x - 4$ can be factored using a "guess and check" approach to get $(x - 1)(3x + 4)$ making the factors $(x - 1)$ and $(3x + 4)$.
12. **(H)** Substituting $(-3, 5)$ into the equation gives $5 = -(-3) + 2 \to 5 = 5$. Since this is a true statement, the equation $y = -x + 2$ passes through the point.
13. **(C)** Substituting -2 for x into the equation gives $\frac{-(-2)^2 + 4}{-2}$. Simplifying using order of operations yields $\frac{-4 + 4}{-2} \to \frac{0}{-2} = 0$.
14. **(F)** Two lines are parallel if they have the same slope. The given equation is in slope-intercept form, $y = mx + b$ where m is the slope. In this equation, the slope is $-\frac{3}{4}$. The only answer that has the same slope is $y = -\frac{3}{4}x$.
15. **(C)** You can set up a proportion to find the number of goldfish: $\frac{2}{5} = \frac{x}{25}$. Cross multiply and solve for x to get $x = 10$, the number of goldfish. However, the question asks how many TOTAL fish, so add 10 + 25 = 35 fish.
16. **(K)** The 3 lines could be parallel yielding no points of intersection, they could all intersect at the same point giving 1 point of intersection, or 2 lines could be parallel with the third crossing the other 2 giving 2 points of intersection, and finally the 3 lines could intersect to form a triangle making 3 points of intersection. See the diagram below.

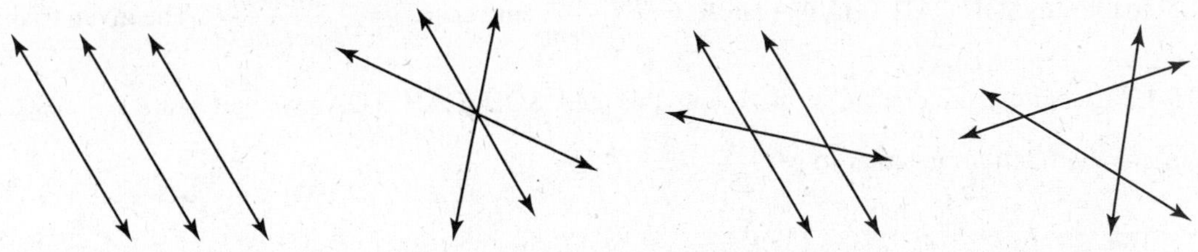

17. **(E)** Since $c = a - b$, and b is negative, its value actually gets added to a because subtracting a negative number is the same as adding a positive. When b is added to a the result will always be a positive number. Testing some numbers in the range of a and b will help lead you to the right answer.

18. **(K)** To find the slope between 2 points use the slope formula $\frac{y_2 - y_1}{x_2 - x_1}$ to get $\frac{8 - 5}{0 - (-2)}$. Simplify to get $\frac{3}{2}$. Always be careful and check your signs when using the slope formula; it is easy to make an integer error.

19. **(D)** Setting up a proportion to solve for how much sugar they need gives $\frac{2\frac{1}{2}}{32} = \frac{x}{250}$. Cross multiply and solve for x to get $x \approx 19.5$, which rounds to 20.

20. **(G)** Recall that the $\sin(C) = \frac{opposite}{hypotenuse}$. To find the side opposite angle C, either do the Pythagorean Theorem, or memorize your special 8-15-17 right triangle. Calculating AB gives $8^2 + x^2 = 17^2 \rightarrow x = 15$. Now using the above fact, $\sin(C) = \frac{15}{17}$.

21. **(C)** Using the laws of exponents we get $5^3 \cdot 5^{-7} = 5^{3 + (-7)} = 5^{-4}$. Recall that a negative exponent just means take the reciprocal of the base to get $5^{-4} = \frac{1}{5^4}$. Therefore, $x = 4$.

22. **(F)** WYX is a straight line making it 180°. Since $\angle WYZ = 28°$, the remaining angle ZYX must equal $180 - 28 = 152$. YM bisects angle ZYX making each angle $\frac{152}{2} = 76°$.

23. **(E)** Recall that an angle that lies on a circle is exactly $\frac{1}{2}$ of its intercepted arc, making arc $BC = 2(35) = 70$. Since AC is a diameter of the circle, the total arc from A to C measures 180°. To find arc AB take $180 - 70 = 110°$.

24. **(H)** To find the greatest common factor of two numbers, first find the largest number that divides into both 24 and 36. Testing various numbers gives 12 as the GCF. To find the GCF of two like variables, always take the smallest power. The GCF of m^4 and m^2 is m^2 because it is the smaller power. Doing this for n and p as well gives the answer $12m^2n$.

25. **(B)** Using the formula $d = r \cdot t$, we can solve to see how fast Dave was initially driving: $144 = r \cdot 3 \rightarrow r = 48$. Dave then speeds up 10 mph so he is now traveling 58 mph on the return trip. To calculate the time, use $d = r \cdot t$ again to get $144 = 58 \cdot t \rightarrow t \approx 2.5$.

26. **(F)** In matrix addition, you add elements in the same position to get the sum. Therefore, $(2x - 1) + (-4x - 2) = 12$. Solve the equation to get $-2x - 3 = 12 \rightarrow x = -7.5$.

27. **(C)** Connecting the dots of the path Paxton took will form a right triangle where the 4 miles and the 6 miles make up the legs of the triangle. To find the hypotenuse, use the Pythagorean Theorem to get $4^2 + 6^2 = c^2 \rightarrow c = \sqrt{52}$. Simplify to get $\sqrt{52} = \sqrt{4 \cdot 13} = 2\sqrt{13}$.

28. **(G)** Use the formula $A = \frac{1}{2} b \cdot h$ to find the area of the triangle to get $= \frac{1}{2}(2w^2 - 8w + 7)(3) = \frac{6w^2 - 24w + 21}{2}$.

29. **(C)** To find an interior angle of a regular polygon, use the formula $\frac{(n - 2)(180)}{n}$. Substituting 10 for n we get $\frac{(10 - 2)(180)}{10} = 144$. Exterior angles of a polygon are always supplementary to interior angles, making each exterior angle $180 - 144 = 36$. Now, find the difference between 144 and 36 to get $144 - 36 = 108°$.

30. **(J)** Recall from SOH CAH TOA that $\tan(A) = \frac{opposite}{adjacent}$ and $\cos(C) = \frac{adjacent}{hypotenuse}$. The given triangle is a special 8-15-17 triangle, therefore $BC = 8$. Using this and SOH CAH TOA, we get $\tan(A) - \cos(C) = \frac{8}{15} - \frac{8}{17}$. Combine the fractions together to get $\frac{16}{255}$.

31. **(B)** To evaluate $1 \vee (2 \vee 2)$ begin inside the parentheses. To evaluate $2 \vee 2$, substitute 2 into the given equation for both x and y to get $(x + y)(x - y) = (2 + 2)(2 - 2) = 0$. Therefore, the original problem becomes $1 \vee 0$. Evaluate this expression by plugging $x = 1$ and $y = 0$ to get $(1 + 0)(1 - 0) = 1$.

32. **(F)** If she scores just 1 goal in game 7, her overall goals scored would be 0, 1, 1, 1, 2, 3, 4. The median (middle number) in that set is 1, not 2.

33. **(B)** Recall the standard form of a circle $(x - h)^2 + (y - k)^2 = r^2$ where h and k represent the center of the circle. To find the center, take the opposite of each number after the x and y. For this problem, the opposite of positive 7 and negative 5 gives a center of $(-7, 5)$.

34. **(K)** Solving for y gives $3x - 7y = 21 \rightarrow -7y = -3x + 21 \rightarrow y = \frac{3}{7}x - 3$.

35. **(A)** Using supplementary angles, parallel lines, triangles, and vertical angles you can arrive at the correct answer. See the diagram below for help.

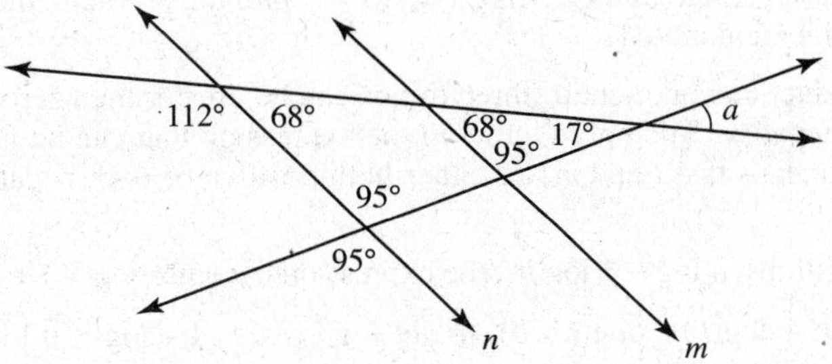

36. **(J)** First distribute in the inequality to get $-\frac{2}{3}x + 5 < -\frac{2}{3}x - 3$. Now we add $\frac{2}{3}x$ to both sides to get $5 < -3$. Since the x's dropped out of the inequality and the resulting statement is false, there is no solution.

37. **(D)** First solve the given equation for y to get $6y = \frac{3}{5}x + 18 \rightarrow y = \frac{1}{10}x + 3$. Therefore, the slope of the given equation is $\frac{1}{10}$ so the slope perpendicular to it is -10. The only answer with a slope of -10 is choice D.

38. **(G)** To start this problem, draw and label a diagram. If the angle of depression from the control tower to the plane is 12°, then the angle of elevation from the plane to the tower is also 12°. Let x be the distance from the plane to the tower, then use $\tan(12) = \frac{40}{x}$. Solve for x to get $x \cdot \tan(12) = 40 \rightarrow x = \frac{40}{\tan(12)}$.

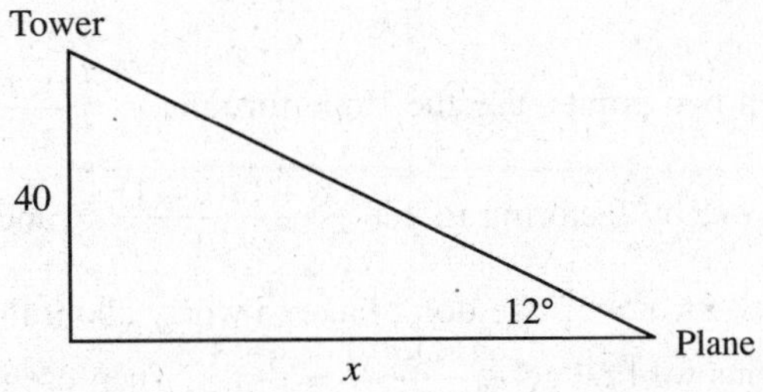

39. **(D)** A square root function is undefined in the real number system whenever the expression under the radical is less than zero. Set $x - 5 < 0$ and solve to get $x < 5$.

40. **(K)** The distance from $(-3, m)$ to the line $x = 7$ is $7 - (-3) = 10$ units. When reflected over the line, the point will move from its location 10 units left of $x = 7$ to its new location 10 units right of $x = 7$. The only point that is 10 units to the right of $x = 7$ is $(17, m)$.

41. **(C)** Using the distance formula $d = \sqrt{(x_2 - x_1)^2 + (y_2 - y_1)^2}$ we get $d = \sqrt{(5 - (-3))^2 + (8 - 2)^2} = \sqrt{64 + 36} = \sqrt{100} = 10$.

42. **(K)** If the ratio of the sides of the two rectangles is 1:4, the ratio of the areas is $(1{:}4)^2 = 1{:}16$. Set up a proportion to get $\frac{1}{16} = \frac{12}{x}$. Solve to get $x = 192$.

43. **(C)** Using the fact that a circle has 360° and that dogs got 16 out of 40 total votes, we can set up a proportion to get $\frac{16}{40} = \frac{x}{360}$. Solve for x to get $x = 144$.

44. **(G)** The original percent of votes cast for cats is $\frac{15}{40} \cdot 100 = 37.5\%$. After the 3 miscalculated votes are added to the cats, we now get a percent of: $\frac{18}{40} \cdot 100 = 45\%$. The difference in these two percents is 7.5%.

45. **(E)** For the first hour Daniel pays x dollars, so he pays $1(x)$ for the first hour. After the first hour, he pays y dollars for the remaining $h - 1$ hours, so he pays $y(h - 1)$. Add the expressions for the first hour and the remaining hours to get $P = x + y(h - 1)$.

46. **(F)** First, solve for z to get $3z \cdot y = 2x \rightarrow z = \frac{2x}{3y}$. Now to find out what happens as x and y are doubled, substitute $2x$ and $2y$ in place of them to get $\frac{2(2x)}{3(2y)}$. Simplify to get $\frac{2x}{3y}$, which is the same expression as what z originally started as. You could also substitute numbers like $x = 1, y = 1$ into the problem, then plug in $x = 2, y = 2$ to see what happens to z when x and y are doubled.

47. **(E)** The only way a product and quotient of three things can be greater than zero is if all factors are positive, or if exactly two factors are negative. The only factors in the expression that can be negative are t^5 and m^9 because w^6 is always positive. This means that t and m are either both positive or both negative. Either way the product $t \cdot m$ would be positive.

48. **(H)** Using a law of logarithms, $a \log b = \log b^a$, the expression becomes $\log(x^2) + \log(\sqrt{y}) - \log(z^4)$. Now, use the law of logarithms, $\log(a) + \log(b) = \log(a \cdot b)$, to get $\log(x^2 \cdot \sqrt{y}) - \log(z^4)$. Finally, use the law of logarithms, $\log(a) - \log(b) = \log\left(\frac{a}{b}\right)$ to get $\log\left(\frac{x^2\sqrt{y}}{z^4}\right)$.

49. **(A)** To evaluate $f(g(2))$ start inside the parentheses by finding $g(2)$. To find $g(2)$ from the table, look where $x = 2$, and read $g(x) = 3$, therefore $g(2) = 3$. Now, evaluate $f(3)$ using the table the same way to get $f(3) = -15$.

50. **(F)** The problem states that p varies inversely with the square root of q, meaning we can set up an equation $p = \frac{k}{\sqrt{q}}$ where k is a constant. Using the initial criteria $q = 49$ and $p = 800$, we get $800 = \frac{k}{\sqrt{49}}$. Solving for k gives $800 = \frac{k}{7} \rightarrow k = 5600$. Now that we know the constant, use it and the fact that there are 100 predators to get $p = \frac{5600}{\sqrt{100}} = 560$.

51. **(C)** To find the slope between two points, use the slope formula $m = \frac{y_2 - y_1}{x_2 - x_1}$ and substitute in the points to get $\frac{x^2 - 1}{x - 1}$. Now simplify the answer by factoring to get $\frac{(x + 1)(x - 1)}{x - 1}$. Cancel like factors to get $x + 1$, as long as $x \neq 1$. Since the problem states "for $x > 5$," we don't have to worry about this hole.

52. **(G)** Using the laws of exponents we first get $\frac{3^1 \cdot 3^{2x-5}}{3^{x+1}} = \frac{3^{2x-4}}{3^{x+1}}$. Then use the law of exponents to divide and get $3^{2x-4-(x+1)} = 3^{x-5}$.

53. **(E)** A good way to find a number that is halfway between two numbers is to find the average of those two numbers. To find the average of $\frac{3}{8}$ and $\frac{4}{5}$, add them up and divide by 2. A calculator can be handy for this step, or you can do it by hand. Either way, you should get $\frac{47}{80}$.

54. **(K)** For Mike to achieve the highest grade on one test, we want the other 3 tests to be as low as possible. The problem states that he never scored lower than 80%, so assume he scored an 80 on each of his first 3 tests and let x be the score on his fourth test. Set up an equation to find x using the fact that his average is an 85: $\frac{3(80) + x}{4} = 85$. Solve for x to get $x = 100$.

55. **(B)** To solve an absolute value inequality, split the problem into two inequalities without an absolute value. The first inequality stays exactly as the problem was written but without the absolute value bars: $x - 3 > x - 3$. Solving this inequality yields $-3 > -3$, which has no solution. The other inequality we get from splitting up the absolute value is $x - 3 < -(x - 3)$. Solve this inequality to get $x < 3$.

56. **(G)** Multiplying $\frac{i+7}{i-5} \cdot \frac{i}{1}$ gives $\frac{i^2+7i}{i-5}$. Recall that $i^2 = -1$; therefore, the expression becomes $\frac{-1+7i}{i-5}$.

Now multiply the top and bottom of the fraction by $i + 5$ to get $\frac{-1+7i}{i-5} \cdot \frac{i+5}{i+5} = \frac{-i-5+7i^2+35i}{i^2-25}$. Simplify to get $\frac{34i-12}{-26}$. Divide the top and bottom by 2 to get $\frac{-6+17i}{-13} \rightarrow \frac{6}{13} - \frac{17}{13}i$.

57. **(B)** First calculate the area of the pizza by using the formula $A = \pi r^2$ to get $A \approx 113.1$. If each square inch contains 50 calories, there is a total of $113.1 \cdot 50 = 5{,}655$ calories. Alex's dad eats 3 out of 8 slices, or in other words, $\frac{3}{8}$ of the pizza, which is $\frac{3}{8}(5{,}655) = 2{,}120$ calories. Alex eats two slices or $\frac{2}{8}(5{,}655) = 1{,}414$ calories. Subtract Alex's calories from his dad's to get $2120 - 1414 \approx 700$ calories.

58. **(H)** Start by drawing a right triangle with unknown angle θ as seen in the diagram below. Since $\tan(\theta) = v$ then we know the $\frac{\textit{opposite}}{\textit{adjacent}}$ from angle θ is $\frac{v}{1}$. Now find the missing side using the Pythagorean Theorem to get it: $\sqrt{1^2+v^2}$. Now using SOH CAH TOA, $\cos(\theta) = \frac{\textit{adjacent}}{\textit{hypotenuse}} = \frac{1}{\sqrt{1+v^2}}$.

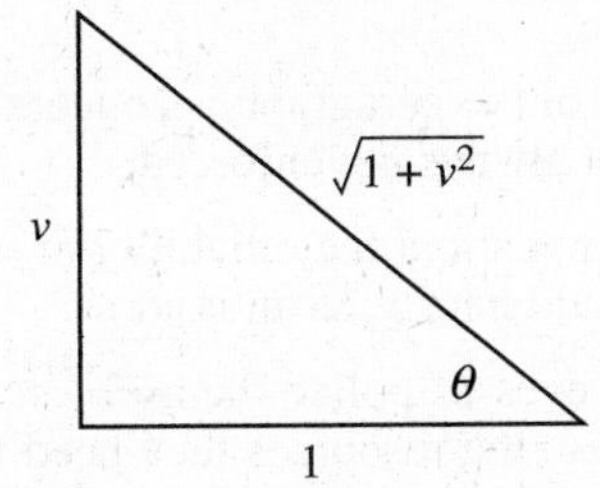

59. **(B)** Andy only has two possible places to sit, but the other four people can sit anywhere. Starting with just the arrangements for the other 4 people, we get $4 \cdot 3 \cdot 2 \cdot 1 = 24$ possible seating arrangements for them. Then multiply the answer by 2 for the two possible choices for Andy to get $2 \cdot 24 = 48$ total arrangements.

60. **(F)** If the two points lie on the graph of the equation, then their slope must equal $\frac{1}{3}$, which is the slope of the equation. Using the slope formula and setting it equal to $\frac{1}{3}$, we get $\frac{n+\frac{2}{g}-n}{m-2-m} = \frac{1}{3}$. Simplify the numerator and denominator to get $\frac{\frac{2}{g}}{-2} = \frac{1}{3}$. Keep simplifying to get $\frac{-1}{g} = \frac{1}{3}$. Solve to get $g = -3$.

Answer Explanations: Reading Test

1. **(A)** As is often the case on the Fiction section, the broadest answer is the correct one here. The passage sounds like a young man talking, and "relating a significant event" is so open-ended that there's really no way for it to be wrong. (If nothing is wrong, then it's right!)

2. **(H)** Although the story takes place in a supermarket, specific supermarket chains are never mentioned aside from line 41, and no other chain is mentioned besides the one in which the story is set.

3. **(B)** Although it's strongly implied that Sammy is young, there's no real indication that he is new at his job. He could easily have worked there for years.

4. **(J)** Sammy mentions thinking of himself as a hero in line 56, and his decision to quit is a stand on principle (if a minor and foolish one).

5. **(C)** Although Sammy makes jokes about Lengel being a Sunday-school teacher in lines 13–14 and 32, there is no indication that the locals in general are mistrustful of organized religion.

6. **(H)** The fact that Sammy turns in his bow tie after quitting (lines 75–77) establishes that it is the store's property.

7. **(D)** The reason that *the crowd that runs the A&P must look pretty crummy* to Queenie is that she is richer than they are, as implied in lines 16–27.

8. **(F)** There is never any indication that anyone besides Sammy finds his decision to quit admirable. Even Sammy himself barely feels this way by the end.

9. **(B)** We are told twice that Lengel "doesn't miss that much" (lines 14 and 30–31).

10. **(F)** Sammy explicitly states in lines 53–56 that he quit solely to try and impress the girls.

11. **(D)** The final paragraph, about how "a chain of middlemen" makes it easier for buyers to avoid considering where the bones come from, places blame on the fact that the bone buyers in other nations turn a blind eye to criminal practices.

12. **(F)** The "long chain" is the chain that separates Western buyers from the criminals who actually first obtain and prepare the bones. Western buyers are able to ignore the root problem or plead ignorance because they never have to deal directly with the criminals.

13. **(C)** All of the quotations that the author selected for use emphasize the horrifying environment and the fear and powerlessness of the people. The dominant emotion of the piece is sympathy for the people caught up in all of this.

14. **(G)** The paragraph emphasizes the fact that Young Brothers acquires bones openly from every conceivable location and even goes so far as to advertise despite the fact that their business is nominally illegal. The point here is the flagrancy of the enterprise.

15. **(A)** After the quote from Aron, the rest of the paragraph is concerned with explaining that, for various reasons, the laws concerning bone trafficking do not always get enforced.

16. **(H)** The passage never mentions anything about the reliability of witnesses (indeed, it implies that very few cases ever come to trial, and so witnesses would hardly be an issue).

17. **(D)** Lines 68–74 establish that, in the eyes of police themselves, they are powerless until society decides that it cares enough about the issue to give them the resources they need to enforce the law.

18. **(H)** Lines 64–65 state that the "bones from over 100 people could have fetched around $70,000," which works out to $700 per skeleton.

19. **(B)** Vinesh Aron is the owner of Young Brothers (lines 52–53), a bone-trafficking organization, and so would not oppose bone trafficking.

20. **(F)** It is established in lines 1–2 that the buyers of the bones are medical students. Therefore, they would be the audience for the catalogues.

21. **(A)** Passage A is adapted from Mary Shelley's introduction to a later edition of her famous novel, and so "once again" (i.e., for the second time) she is offering her "progeny" (a synonym for "offspring," as she is metaphorically the "parent" of the book) to the public.

22. **(J)** The second and third paragraphs of Passage A draw explicit contrast between Shelley's early attempts at writing and her personal fantasies. She states that only her fantasies were personal, whereas her early writing consisted of mechanical attempts to copy others.

23. **(C)** The antecedent of "it" in the sentence in question is "literary reputation"—i.e., getting famous for writing.

24. **(F)** The key phrase here is "what terrified me will terrify others." Shelley's epiphany was that the dreams and fantasies she had previously kept to herself had in fact been the key to success all along.

25. **(B)** Shelley closes her introduction by stating that her novel was originally written in "happy times, when death and grief were but words"—i.e., that although she was writing about horrible things, she had not yet experienced them, but now has. (Her husband, three of their children, and several of their close friends had all died in the interim.)

26. **(H)** In the paragraph in question, Victor Frankenstein begins by alluding to his meticulous scientific process, but then describes his emotional horror at seeing the result of that process come to life.

27. **(B)** Victor Frankenstein's quest was to create life, and he has done so, but the dream about his fiancée turning into his dead mother implies and foreshadows to the reader that the eventual results will be exactly the opposite.

28. **(J)** Shelley's autobiographical introduction describes her famous novel as being the product of a dream, and Victor Frankenstein's narration establishes that his aversion to his creation is an emotional reaction, rather than being the product of anything the Creature actually does (at least, not yet...).

29. **(B)** As with Question #24, the key phrase here is "what terrified me will terrify others." Mary Shelley's grand realization was that her own personal imagination and psychology was the key to creating a work of genius.

30. **(F)** Mary Shelley (a great self-promoter, no matter how much she claimed not to care for fame) is clearly drawing an explicit comparison between her "creation" of the *Frankenstein* story and Victor Frankenstein's creation of the Monster. The "idea that broke in" in Passage A and the "spark of being" in Passage B are analogous to each other—in both cases, the creator merely harnesses a mysterious energy that originates elsewhere.
31. **(D)** The passage as a whole is concerned with the history of magnetic therapy and how there has never been any credible evidence to support it. (As is frequently the case with "main point" questions, the broadest answer is the correct one!)
32. **(H)** Lines 36–44 explain that the findings of Franklin's commission made Mesmer so unpopular that he had to flee France in disgrace.
33. **(A)** The paragraph begins with "Nevertheless" (i.e., "despite all this") and goes on to explain that the same discredited practices took hold in the United States, eventually developing into a new pseudomedical practice of dubious value.
34. **(G)** Lines 87–93 explain that human blood is actually diamagnetic, that is, repelled by magnets.
35. **(D)** Lines 58–62 state that an MRI field is about a hundred times stronger than a powerful therapy magnet. (The trick here is that 100 is written as a numeral in the answer choice, but written out as a word in the passage, so people who are scanning the passage quickly for a numeral will not see it.)
36. **(F)** A *placebo* is a fake treatment given to some patients in a medical experiment in order to rule out the psychological effect—in this case, the "sham magnets" of line 73.
37. **(C)** The *predatory quacks* of line 98 are dishonest therapists. A *quack* is a doctor who believes (or pretends to believe) in false treatments.
38. **(G)** Lines 78–82 explain that skin gets red when it's heated because blood is being diverted to the area to act as a coolant.
39. **(C)** Lines 23–26 describe Benjamin Franklin correctly figuring out that magnet therapy only appeared to help because it was keeping patients away from the harmful treatments practiced by many other doctors at that time.
40. **(J)** Lines 67–77 describe an experiment conducted by Carlos Vallbona in which magnet therapy appeared to have beneficial effects, though no one knows why.

Answer Explanations: Science Test

1. **(D)** The tornado in Figure 2 is represented by the number 6. The paragraph above Figure 2 explains this (it is logical that the sixth and *final* step in the explanation would be the one that involves the tornado, since the paragraph is an explanation of how tornadoes are formed).
2. **(J)** The F4 box in Figure 1 (fifth box over, second one down) includes wind speeds from 207 to 261 mph.
3. **(B)** In the paragraph above Figure 2, a mesocyclone is formed in step 3. Since a spinning wall-cloud is formed in step 5, this would be the one that does NOT precede the formation of a mesocyclone.
4. **(F)** The paragraph above Figure 3 explains that "Tornado Alley" is in the central United States, and that the number over each state represents its number of tornadoes in 2005. Texas had 105 (higher than any of the other choices) and is in the central United States.
5. **(B)** The intersection box of the horizontal "Brick Structure" row and the vertical "Minor Damage" column says f0. The key within Figure 1 explains that the f scale (lower case) must then be *converted* into the F scale (upper case), and f0 + 1 = F1.
6. **(H)** The sample with the highest concentration of chlorine in Table 2 (the table in Study 1) is Sample 3, with a concentration of 0.15 mg/L.
7. **(A)** In Table 3 (the table in Study 2), the highest grouping of numbers in the "Average pH" column occurs during the spring months: April, May, and March or June. (Remember that acidity is indicated by *low* pH, and so the *least* acidic deposition would be represented by the *highest* numbers.) Spring is still the right answer even though there are other individual high numbers in other months, and regardless of whether you count March or June as the third spring month.
8. **(J)** The order of the samples by acidity, from lowest pH to highest, is 4, 2, 1, 3, 5. The order of the samples by sodium concentration, from lowest to highest, is 5, 1, 2, 4, 3. The orders are neither the same as nor the reverse of each other, and therefore there is no correlation, neither a positive nor an inverse. (Remember that when the last

choice is "no correlation" or "no relationship" or "date not included" or something weird like that, that is *probably* the answer, so test that one first!)

9. **(B)** The pH is highest in the month of April. Table 1 shows that frogs die at around a pH of 5. Clearly, the lower the pH, the greater the health risks for all animals. There is no definitive level but the question specifies *least* concerned. April is the best answer given the other three choices.

10. **(F)** The introductory paragraph above Table 1 explains that *wet deposition* refers to rain, snow, sleet, and hail. The paragraph in Study 1 explains that the samples in Study 2 were collected in the form of rain, and therefore they are examples of *wet deposition*.

11. **(C)** The introductory paragraph explains that sulfuric acid lowers the pH of rain. Since the samples in Table 2 were collected from rain, the pH of Sample 2 would necessarily be lower than its current pH of 5.28 had it been contaminated with sulfuric acid.

12. **(F)** The paragraph above Study 1 explains that crystallization cannot begin until the solution becomes saturated. Substance 1 in Figure 4 hits the top of the graph (i.e., is completely dissolved) at around 35°C, and so it would be more than ready to begin crystallization at 60°C.

13. **(D)** The point in Figure 4 representing the intersection of 20% solubility (vertical axis) and 30°C (horizontal axis) is below the lines representing Samples 1–3, but above the line representing Sample 4.

14. **(J)** This is a simple "Go Up, Hit Line, Go Over." A line drawn straight upward from the hash mark representing 30°C on the horizontal axis of Figure 4 would hit the line representing Sample 1 somewhere just below the top of the graph—that is, at around 95% solubility.

15. **(C)** As described in Figure 3, point 4 is described as the "main cooling cycle." The main cooling cycle implies the addition of an ice bath because of the description of the crystallization process in the opening paragraph. The opening paragraph indicates the solution is placed in an ice bath *after* crystallization. An argument might be made that the ice bath was introduced at point 3 but this is not a choice. Clearly, 4 would be the best choice given the information.

16. **(F)** The information in Figure 3 (as well as the explanation in the introductory paragraph) clearly indicates that crystallization is the result of cooling: as temperature decreases, crystallization increases.

17. **(A)** As shown in Table 1, parents with blood types of O and B can only produce offspring with O or B blood as well. Whether the mother is O or B, whether the father is O or B, the results are the same.

18. **(G)** As Tables 1 and 2 make clear, to produce a child with blood type AB+, at least one parent must have a blood type with A in it (A or AB), at least one parent must have a blood type with B in it (B or AB), and at least one parent must be Rh+. The only one of the choices that has an A, a B, and a + in it is choice G.

19. **(C)** Table 3 shows that the "universal donor" is type O–. Table 1 shows that a child with type O blood could not possibly have a parent who has type AB blood (i.e., *neither* parent can be AB). When both parents have B– blood, B– or O– offspring will be produced.

20. **(G)** Parents with blood types A and O can produce either A or O offspring (Table 1). The Rh factor could be + OR – because both parents could carry the recessive gene for Rh–.

21. **(B)** In the opening paragraph, the passage clearly states, "The genes ensure that only the blood cells of the proper blood type remain in the body"—that is, they control the types of cells in the blood.

22. **(F)** All this question wants you to do is find the point at which the four lines in Figure 1 are the closest to one another. That would be the starting point, which represents 8:15–9:25.

23. **(C)** The text explains that lower numbers on the behavioral scale indicate better behavior, so all this question is asking you to do is find the point (out of the choices) where the line representing the Adderall kids (the one with the squares) is *not* the *lowest*. (Even if you didn't get that, choice C is still the only one of the choices where the line representing the Adderall kids is in a *different* place relative to the other four lines—when in doubt, pick the odd one out.)

24. **(J)** All this question wants you to do is find the point in Figure 2 where the line representing the double-dose Ritalin kids (the one with the triangles) is highest, which is over "appetite loss" (as it is for all the lines except the one representing the placebo kids).

25. **(A)** The text explains that lower numbers on the behavioral scale indicate better behavior, so all this question wants you to do is find the line in Figure 1 that is highest at the 3:35–4:45 mark, and it is the one representing the placebo kids (the one with the diamonds).

26. **(F)** According to the legend for Figure 1, the group with a 5 behavior rating corresponds to P—placebo.

27. **(C)** In Figure 1, the effectiveness order of the medications from most to least effective is A1, R2, R1. In Figure 2, the side-effects order of the medications from fewest to most is R1, R2, A1. The medication choice that "splits the difference" is R2.

28. **(J)** All this question wants you to do is find which line in Figure 2 is the highest at the 30-second mark. The lines stop before the 30-second mark, but it is still clear from extrapolation that the line representing Solvent 4 would be highest (it is continuing to rise when the other three have leveled off).

29. **(C)** Table 2 shows that Solutions 1–4 progressively increase in temperature. Figure 3 shows that osmotic pressure decreases as the number of the solution used rises. Therefore, as temperature increases, osmotic pressure decreases.

30. **(F)** Table 1 indicates that Solvents 1–4 progressively increase in terms of molecular weight percentage. Figure 2 shows that the solutions finish passing through the semipermeable membrane (i.e., the lines representing them level off) in the same order. Therefore, the lower the molecular weight percentage of a solvent, the more quickly the solution passes through a membrane.

31. **(B)** The line in Figure 2 that represents Solvent 4 has the greatest osmotic pressure.

32. **(H)** Table 2 indicates that the 30°C solution is Solution 2. In Figure 3, the height of the line above the Solution 2 hash mark is about 1.4 atm. Double this, and the answer choice that is closest is 2.8 atm.

33. **(B)** Experiment 1 indicates in the paragraph that the Figure 2 results are shown as recorded at the 20° trial, which according to Table 2 is Trial 1.

34. **(H)** Student 1 closes by specifying that the image would be upright, whereas Student 2 closes by specifying that the image would be inverted. Therefore, the students disagree about the image's orientation.

35. **(B)** The fact that both students open by specifying the distance between the object and the mirror, and then base their theories on it, shows that both know that the exact positioning of the light bulb is important.

36. **(F)** The teacher's information specifies that an object must be between F and the mirror to appear upright, and the description of the magic trick specifies that F lies 1.6 m from the mirror. Therefore, an object 1.0 m away would produce an upright image.

37. **(C)** Student 2's explanation is perfectly accurate. The teacher's information specifies that an object at C will produce an exact but inverted image. (It is often the case on the ACT Science that remembering earlier questions in a passage can help you answer later ones!)

38. **(F)** This is not true because F is in front of C, and an object at F will produce no image at all (although an object at any point between C and the mirror *aside from F* will indeed produce a larger image).

39. **(B)** The teacher's information states that an object at F will produce no reflection, and the description of the magic trick states that F is 1.6 m away.

40. **(J)** The teacher's information states that objects placed beyond C will produce reflections smaller than the objects themselves. The description of the magic trick states that C is 2.2 m away. Therefore, an object at 2.5 m away will produce a reflection smaller than itself.

Writing Sample

I am on the side of leaving the vending machines in school, but before I explain, let me stress that I take the issue of childhood obesity very seriously. I make a big effort to eat right and keep in shape myself, and it bothers me that the rest of the world thinks of Americans as being out-of-shape and lazy. Nevertheless, I think we need to leave the machines and bake sales alone because the school and the student body need the money that those things bring in. I don't want to end up with an outdated computer or rusty athletic equipment because someone made an impulsive decision to get rid of the vending machines. Furthermore, bake sales provide money not for the school, but for the various grades and organizations to fund things like prom or that trip where the Physics Club goes to Six Flags and does equations about the kinetic energy of the roller coasters. People have a tendency to complain about things and demand for them to be changed without first thinking through all of the possible consequences of the change.

Many students might say that schools should keep the vending machines but put healthy snacks in them. Why aren't I saying that? Because while studying science I learned things about nutrition and realize that one of the reasons that current snacks are unhealthy is because they have preservatives in them, and that the reason you put preservatives in food is so the food won't go bad if it is going to be sitting someplace for a long time, for example inside a vending machine. If there were healthy food in the machine, then kids would have to buy it all that day before it went bad, and that's not going to happen. Besides, the vending-machine company probably doesn't have enough staff to come to every school every morning with a bunch of fresh fruit or other snacks without preservatives. All this would result in is a massive waste of food.

On the other hand, if students have easy access to junk food, particularly when they are at school and stressed out, they will buy it. What the school should do instead is make more of an effort to put snacks in the machines that are slightly healthier, but still tasty enough that kids will actually buy them and the school won't lose money. For example, they could have those potato chips that are baked instead of fried, and juice instead of soda. The school might even make more money that way than it does now, because the snacks would still appeal to the masses, but now health conscious students will buy more snacks from the machines. At the same time, schools should stress physical fitness and exercise. All kids need exercise whether they are athletic or not. A few bags of chips wouldn't matter if kids were running around outside like they did once upon a time, instead of playing video games and surfing the internet indoors all day long. Junk food has always been around in one form or another, but kids twenty years ago were nowhere near as out-of-shape as they are today. Why? Because they played outside all the time. It is unnatural for a rambunctious, growing kid to be indoors all day with a computer.

I would love to be able to say that there are easy answers to the problem of childhood obesity, but the truth is, there are not. People are very sensitive about their bodies, and you risk hurt feelings by even discussing the issue at all. But silence is not our friend here, because our modern-day sedentary culture needs to change. Once upon a time, American kids had a reputation for being rough-and-tumble and outdoorsy. Could you imagine Huckleberry Finn parked on the couch all day playing Playstation and eating Twinkies? No. But nowadays, American kids are seen as lazy. If Huck Finn were alive today, his raft probably wouldn't be able to keep him afloat, if he even had the energy to build it in the first place. The problem is that the current generation's culture doesn't make being in good shape a high priority, so schools need to play a part in changing the culture. Moving a few vending machines around is not the answer, but, getting some of those chemical-laden Frankenfoods out of them and replacing them with some snacks that kids will still buy but which have ingredients on the package that they can actually pronounce is a good start.

Answer Sheet

PRACTICE TEST 4

Directions: Mark one answer only for each question. Make the mark dark. Erase completely any mark made in error. (Additional or stray marks will be counted as mistakes.)

English Test

1 Ⓐ Ⓑ Ⓒ Ⓓ	21 Ⓐ Ⓑ Ⓒ Ⓓ	41 Ⓐ Ⓑ Ⓒ Ⓓ	61 Ⓐ Ⓑ Ⓒ Ⓓ
2 Ⓕ Ⓖ Ⓗ Ⓙ	22 Ⓕ Ⓖ Ⓗ Ⓙ	42 Ⓕ Ⓖ Ⓗ Ⓙ	62 Ⓕ Ⓖ Ⓗ Ⓙ
3 Ⓐ Ⓑ Ⓒ Ⓓ	23 Ⓐ Ⓑ Ⓒ Ⓓ	43 Ⓐ Ⓑ Ⓒ Ⓓ	63 Ⓐ Ⓑ Ⓒ Ⓓ
4 Ⓕ Ⓖ Ⓗ Ⓙ	24 Ⓕ Ⓖ Ⓗ Ⓙ	44 Ⓕ Ⓖ Ⓗ Ⓙ	64 Ⓕ Ⓖ Ⓗ Ⓙ
5 Ⓐ Ⓑ Ⓒ Ⓓ	25 Ⓐ Ⓑ Ⓒ Ⓓ	45 Ⓐ Ⓑ Ⓒ Ⓓ	65 Ⓐ Ⓑ Ⓒ Ⓓ
6 Ⓕ Ⓖ Ⓗ Ⓙ	26 Ⓕ Ⓖ Ⓗ Ⓙ	46 Ⓕ Ⓖ Ⓗ Ⓙ	66 Ⓕ Ⓖ Ⓗ Ⓙ
7 Ⓐ Ⓑ Ⓒ Ⓓ	27 Ⓐ Ⓑ Ⓒ Ⓓ	47 Ⓐ Ⓑ Ⓒ Ⓓ	67 Ⓐ Ⓑ Ⓒ Ⓓ
8 Ⓕ Ⓖ Ⓗ Ⓙ	28 Ⓕ Ⓖ Ⓗ Ⓙ	48 Ⓕ Ⓖ Ⓗ Ⓙ	68 Ⓕ Ⓖ Ⓗ Ⓙ
9 Ⓐ Ⓑ Ⓒ Ⓓ	29 Ⓐ Ⓑ Ⓒ Ⓓ	49 Ⓐ Ⓑ Ⓒ Ⓓ	69 Ⓐ Ⓑ Ⓒ Ⓓ
10 Ⓕ Ⓖ Ⓗ Ⓙ	30 Ⓕ Ⓖ Ⓗ Ⓙ	50 Ⓕ Ⓖ Ⓗ Ⓙ	70 Ⓕ Ⓖ Ⓗ Ⓙ
11 Ⓐ Ⓑ Ⓒ Ⓓ	31 Ⓐ Ⓑ Ⓒ Ⓓ	51 Ⓐ Ⓑ Ⓒ Ⓓ	71 Ⓐ Ⓑ Ⓒ Ⓓ
12 Ⓕ Ⓖ Ⓗ Ⓙ	32 Ⓕ Ⓖ Ⓗ Ⓙ	52 Ⓕ Ⓖ Ⓗ Ⓙ	72 Ⓕ Ⓖ Ⓗ Ⓙ
13 Ⓐ Ⓑ Ⓒ Ⓓ	33 Ⓐ Ⓑ Ⓒ Ⓓ	53 Ⓐ Ⓑ Ⓒ Ⓓ	73 Ⓐ Ⓑ Ⓒ Ⓓ
14 Ⓕ Ⓖ Ⓗ Ⓙ	34 Ⓕ Ⓖ Ⓗ Ⓙ	54 Ⓕ Ⓖ Ⓗ Ⓙ	74 Ⓕ Ⓖ Ⓗ Ⓙ
15 Ⓐ Ⓑ Ⓒ Ⓓ	35 Ⓐ Ⓑ Ⓒ Ⓓ	55 Ⓐ Ⓑ Ⓒ Ⓓ	75 Ⓐ Ⓑ Ⓒ Ⓓ
16 Ⓕ Ⓖ Ⓗ Ⓙ	36 Ⓕ Ⓖ Ⓗ Ⓙ	56 Ⓕ Ⓖ Ⓗ Ⓙ	
17 Ⓐ Ⓑ Ⓒ Ⓓ	37 Ⓐ Ⓑ Ⓒ Ⓓ	57 Ⓐ Ⓑ Ⓒ Ⓓ	
18 Ⓕ Ⓖ Ⓗ Ⓙ	38 Ⓕ Ⓖ Ⓗ Ⓙ	58 Ⓕ Ⓖ Ⓗ Ⓙ	
19 Ⓐ Ⓑ Ⓒ Ⓓ	39 Ⓐ Ⓑ Ⓒ Ⓓ	59 Ⓐ Ⓑ Ⓒ Ⓓ	
20 Ⓕ Ⓖ Ⓗ Ⓙ	40 Ⓕ Ⓖ Ⓗ Ⓙ	60 Ⓕ Ⓖ Ⓗ Ⓙ	

Math Test

1 Ⓐ Ⓑ Ⓒ Ⓓ Ⓔ	16 Ⓕ Ⓖ Ⓗ Ⓙ Ⓚ	31 Ⓐ Ⓑ Ⓒ Ⓓ Ⓔ	46 Ⓕ Ⓖ Ⓗ Ⓙ Ⓚ
2 Ⓕ Ⓖ Ⓗ Ⓙ Ⓚ	17 Ⓐ Ⓑ Ⓒ Ⓓ Ⓔ	32 Ⓕ Ⓖ Ⓗ Ⓙ Ⓚ	47 Ⓐ Ⓑ Ⓒ Ⓓ Ⓔ
3 Ⓐ Ⓑ Ⓒ Ⓓ Ⓔ	18 Ⓕ Ⓖ Ⓗ Ⓙ Ⓚ	33 Ⓐ Ⓑ Ⓒ Ⓓ Ⓔ	48 Ⓕ Ⓖ Ⓗ Ⓙ Ⓚ
4 Ⓕ Ⓖ Ⓗ Ⓙ Ⓚ	19 Ⓐ Ⓑ Ⓒ Ⓓ Ⓔ	34 Ⓕ Ⓖ Ⓗ Ⓙ Ⓚ	49 Ⓐ Ⓑ Ⓒ Ⓓ Ⓔ
5 Ⓐ Ⓑ Ⓒ Ⓓ Ⓔ	20 Ⓕ Ⓖ Ⓗ Ⓙ Ⓚ	35 Ⓐ Ⓑ Ⓒ Ⓓ Ⓔ	50 Ⓕ Ⓖ Ⓗ Ⓙ Ⓚ
6 Ⓕ Ⓖ Ⓗ Ⓙ Ⓚ	21 Ⓐ Ⓑ Ⓒ Ⓓ Ⓔ	36 Ⓕ Ⓖ Ⓗ Ⓙ Ⓚ	51 Ⓐ Ⓑ Ⓒ Ⓓ Ⓔ
7 Ⓐ Ⓑ Ⓒ Ⓓ Ⓔ	22 Ⓕ Ⓖ Ⓗ Ⓙ Ⓚ	37 Ⓐ Ⓑ Ⓒ Ⓓ Ⓔ	52 Ⓕ Ⓖ Ⓗ Ⓙ Ⓚ
8 Ⓕ Ⓖ Ⓗ Ⓙ Ⓚ	23 Ⓐ Ⓑ Ⓒ Ⓓ Ⓔ	38 Ⓕ Ⓖ Ⓗ Ⓙ Ⓚ	53 Ⓐ Ⓑ Ⓒ Ⓓ Ⓔ
9 Ⓐ Ⓑ Ⓒ Ⓓ Ⓔ	24 Ⓕ Ⓖ Ⓗ Ⓙ Ⓚ	39 Ⓐ Ⓑ Ⓒ Ⓓ Ⓔ	54 Ⓕ Ⓖ Ⓗ Ⓙ Ⓚ
10 Ⓕ Ⓖ Ⓗ Ⓙ Ⓚ	25 Ⓐ Ⓑ Ⓒ Ⓓ Ⓔ	40 Ⓕ Ⓖ Ⓗ Ⓙ Ⓚ	55 Ⓐ Ⓑ Ⓒ Ⓓ Ⓔ
11 Ⓐ Ⓑ Ⓒ Ⓓ Ⓔ	26 Ⓕ Ⓖ Ⓗ Ⓙ Ⓚ	41 Ⓐ Ⓑ Ⓒ Ⓓ Ⓔ	56 Ⓕ Ⓖ Ⓗ Ⓙ Ⓚ
12 Ⓕ Ⓖ Ⓗ Ⓙ Ⓚ	27 Ⓐ Ⓑ Ⓒ Ⓓ Ⓔ	42 Ⓕ Ⓖ Ⓗ Ⓙ Ⓚ	57 Ⓐ Ⓑ Ⓒ Ⓓ Ⓔ
13 Ⓐ Ⓑ Ⓒ Ⓓ Ⓔ	28 Ⓕ Ⓖ Ⓗ Ⓙ Ⓚ	43 Ⓐ Ⓑ Ⓒ Ⓓ Ⓔ	58 Ⓕ Ⓖ Ⓗ Ⓙ Ⓚ
14 Ⓕ Ⓖ Ⓗ Ⓙ Ⓚ	29 Ⓐ Ⓑ Ⓒ Ⓓ Ⓔ	44 Ⓕ Ⓖ Ⓗ Ⓙ Ⓚ	59 Ⓐ Ⓑ Ⓒ Ⓓ Ⓔ
15 Ⓐ Ⓑ Ⓒ Ⓓ Ⓔ	30 Ⓕ Ⓖ Ⓗ Ⓙ Ⓚ	45 Ⓐ Ⓑ Ⓒ Ⓓ Ⓔ	60 Ⓕ Ⓖ Ⓗ Ⓙ Ⓚ

Answer Sheet

PRACTICE TEST 4

Reading Test

1 Ⓐ Ⓑ Ⓒ Ⓓ	11 Ⓐ Ⓑ Ⓒ Ⓓ	21 Ⓐ Ⓑ Ⓒ Ⓓ	31 Ⓐ Ⓑ Ⓒ Ⓓ
2 Ⓕ Ⓖ Ⓗ Ⓙ	12 Ⓕ Ⓖ Ⓗ Ⓙ	22 Ⓕ Ⓖ Ⓗ Ⓙ	32 Ⓕ Ⓖ Ⓗ Ⓙ
3 Ⓐ Ⓑ Ⓒ Ⓓ	13 Ⓐ Ⓑ Ⓒ Ⓓ	23 Ⓐ Ⓑ Ⓒ Ⓓ	33 Ⓐ Ⓑ Ⓒ Ⓓ
4 Ⓕ Ⓖ Ⓗ Ⓙ	14 Ⓕ Ⓖ Ⓗ Ⓙ	24 Ⓕ Ⓖ Ⓗ Ⓙ	34 Ⓕ Ⓖ Ⓗ Ⓙ
5 Ⓐ Ⓑ Ⓒ Ⓓ	15 Ⓐ Ⓑ Ⓒ Ⓓ	25 Ⓐ Ⓑ Ⓒ Ⓓ	35 Ⓐ Ⓑ Ⓒ Ⓓ
6 Ⓕ Ⓖ Ⓗ Ⓙ	16 Ⓕ Ⓖ Ⓗ Ⓙ	26 Ⓕ Ⓖ Ⓗ Ⓙ	36 Ⓕ Ⓖ Ⓗ Ⓙ
7 Ⓐ Ⓑ Ⓒ Ⓓ	17 Ⓐ Ⓑ Ⓒ Ⓓ	27 Ⓐ Ⓑ Ⓒ Ⓓ	37 Ⓐ Ⓑ Ⓒ Ⓓ
8 Ⓕ Ⓖ Ⓗ Ⓙ	18 Ⓕ Ⓖ Ⓗ Ⓙ	28 Ⓕ Ⓖ Ⓗ Ⓙ	38 Ⓕ Ⓖ Ⓗ Ⓙ
9 Ⓐ Ⓑ Ⓒ Ⓓ	19 Ⓐ Ⓑ Ⓒ Ⓓ	29 Ⓐ Ⓑ Ⓒ Ⓓ	39 Ⓐ Ⓑ Ⓒ Ⓓ
10 Ⓕ Ⓖ Ⓗ Ⓙ	20 Ⓕ Ⓖ Ⓗ Ⓙ	30 Ⓕ Ⓖ Ⓗ Ⓙ	40 Ⓕ Ⓖ Ⓗ Ⓙ

Science Test

1 Ⓐ Ⓑ Ⓒ Ⓓ	11 Ⓐ Ⓑ Ⓒ Ⓓ	21 Ⓐ Ⓑ Ⓒ Ⓓ	31 Ⓐ Ⓑ Ⓒ Ⓓ
2 Ⓕ Ⓖ Ⓗ Ⓙ	12 Ⓕ Ⓖ Ⓗ Ⓙ	22 Ⓕ Ⓖ Ⓗ Ⓙ	32 Ⓕ Ⓖ Ⓗ Ⓙ
3 Ⓐ Ⓑ Ⓒ Ⓓ	13 Ⓐ Ⓑ Ⓒ Ⓓ	23 Ⓐ Ⓑ Ⓒ Ⓓ	33 Ⓐ Ⓑ Ⓒ Ⓓ
4 Ⓕ Ⓖ Ⓗ Ⓙ	14 Ⓕ Ⓖ Ⓗ Ⓙ	24 Ⓕ Ⓖ Ⓗ Ⓙ	34 Ⓕ Ⓖ Ⓗ Ⓙ
5 Ⓐ Ⓑ Ⓒ Ⓓ	15 Ⓐ Ⓑ Ⓒ Ⓓ	25 Ⓐ Ⓑ Ⓒ Ⓓ	35 Ⓐ Ⓑ Ⓒ Ⓓ
6 Ⓕ Ⓖ Ⓗ Ⓙ	16 Ⓕ Ⓖ Ⓗ Ⓙ	26 Ⓕ Ⓖ Ⓗ Ⓙ	36 Ⓕ Ⓖ Ⓗ Ⓙ
7 Ⓐ Ⓑ Ⓒ Ⓓ	17 Ⓐ Ⓑ Ⓒ Ⓓ	27 Ⓐ Ⓑ Ⓒ Ⓓ	37 Ⓐ Ⓑ Ⓒ Ⓓ
8 Ⓕ Ⓖ Ⓗ Ⓙ	18 Ⓕ Ⓖ Ⓗ Ⓙ	28 Ⓕ Ⓖ Ⓗ Ⓙ	38 Ⓕ Ⓖ Ⓗ Ⓙ
9 Ⓐ Ⓑ Ⓒ Ⓓ	19 Ⓐ Ⓑ Ⓒ Ⓓ	29 Ⓐ Ⓑ Ⓒ Ⓓ	39 Ⓐ Ⓑ Ⓒ Ⓓ
10 Ⓕ Ⓖ Ⓗ Ⓙ	20 Ⓕ Ⓖ Ⓗ Ⓙ	30 Ⓕ Ⓖ Ⓗ Ⓙ	40 Ⓕ Ⓖ Ⓗ Ⓙ

Practice Test 4

ENGLISH TEST

45 MINUTES—75 QUESTIONS

Directions: In the five passages that follow, certain words and phrases are underlined and numbered. In the right-hand column, you will find alternatives for the underlined part. In most cases, you are to choose the one that best expresses the idea, makes the statement appropriate for standard written English, or is worded most consistently with the style and tone of the passage as a whole. If you think the original version is best, choose "NO CHANGE." In some cases, you will find in the right-hand column a question about the underlined part. You are to choose the best answer to the question.

You will also find questions about a section of the passage, or about the passage as a whole. These questions do not refer to an underlined portion of the passage, but rather are identified by a number or numbers in a box.

For each question, choose the alternative you consider best and fill in the corresponding oval on your answer document. Read each passage through once before you begin to answer the questions that accompany it. For many of the questions, you must read several sentences beyond the question to determine the answer. Be sure that you have read far enough ahead each time you choose an alternative.

Passage I

When Third Was Second

People often say that you're "throwing your vote away," by voting for [1] a third-party candidate. It's true that no presidential candidate who didn't represent one of the two major parties always win [2] an election, but there have been a few elections in living memory where a third-party candidate would win [3] a few states. And although most people don't realize it, there [4] has been one presidential election in American history where a third-party candidate came in second.

1. **A.** NO CHANGE
   B. say, that you're "throwing your vote away," by voting for
   C. say, that you're "throwing your vote away" by voting, for
   D. say that you're "throwing your vote away" by voting for

2. **F.** NO CHANGE
   G. has ever won
   H. was winning
   J. were winning

3. **A.** NO CHANGE
   B. has won
   C. have won
   D. would have won

4. **F.** NO CHANGE
   G. so there
   H. but there
   J. however, there

<u>Born and raised on Long Island,</u> [5] Theodore Roosevelt ascended to the presidency upon the assassination of President William McKinley in 1901 (only 42 at the time, he remains the youngest president ever). Despite early concerns about his youth and <u>temperament, Roosevelt, or "Teddy"</u> [6] as the public affectionately nicknamed him—soon became immensely popular, <u>steered</u> [7] the Republican Party in a progressive new direction that emphasized nature conservation and opposition to corporate power. After finishing what had begun as McKinley's term, Roosevelt ran for reelection in 1904, winning in the biggest landslide since James Monroe's unopposed candidacy of 1820 <u>and becoming the first "accidental" president to win an election in his own right.</u> [8]

Since this had never <u>occurred before, it raised</u> [9] an interesting question: the custom (though not yet the law) was for presidents to limit themselves to two terms, so did the term of McKinley's that Roosevelt completed count as the first of two, or could he run again in 1908? Roosevelt settled the question himself by stepping aside and endorsing <u>Secretary of War William Howard Taft</u> [10] for the Republican nomination; with the beloved Teddy's endorsement, Taft won easily. After the election, Roosevelt left for an extended African safari, motivated by a desire both to pursue his

5. Which of the following phrases best introduces the paragraph?
   A. NO CHANGE
   B. Although sickly in his youth,
   C. As the sitting vice president,
   D. One of the four presidents depicted on Mount Rushmore,

6. **F.** NO CHANGE
   G. temperament, Roosevelt or "Teddy,"
   H. temperament, Roosevelt—or "Teddy"
   J. temperament. Roosevelt, or "Teddy"

7. **A.** NO CHANGE
   B. had steered
   C. to steer
   D. steering

8. If the writer were to delete the underlined portion, the paragraph would primarily lose:
   F. an explanation of what made Teddy Roosevelt so popular.
   G. information vital to the rest of the essay.
   H. a reminder that the United States was still young in Roosevelt's day.
   J. an interesting but unnecessary piece of trivia.

9. **A.** NO CHANGE
   B. occurred, before it raised
   C. occurred before, and it raised
   D. occurred before and raised

10. **F.** NO CHANGE
    G. Secretary of War, William Howard Taft
    H. Secretary of War William Howard Taft,
    J. Secretary of War, William Howard Taft,

lifelong interest in nature and then (11) to stay out of the spotlight and let President Taft be his own man.

But when Teddy returned to find that Taft had abandoned many of the policies he'd established and rendered the Republican Party more conservative, he changed his tune, announcing his intention to run for a third—or second, depending on your point of view—term in 1912. But the party bosses declined to wrest the nomination from the incumbent Taft and hand it to Roosevelt already had (12) his chance in 1908, and so Teddy was compelled to form his own party, which he dubbed the Progressive Party. [13]

Lots of people are aware that Teddy Roosevelt ran for another term on the Bull Moose ticket, but what many don't know is that he almost won, finishing second with a respectable 88 electoral votes. [14] The 1912 victory went to Woodrow Wilson—who, thanks to the divided Republicans, became only the second Democrat to win the White House since the Civil War—and poor Taft became the only major-party candidate in American history ever to finish third, winning only two states.

11. **A.** NO CHANGE
    B. both
    C. not
    D. DELETE the underlined portion.

12. **F.** NO CHANGE
    G. Roosevelt has
    H. Roosevelt, who would have
    J. Roosevelt, who had already had

13. Given that all the following statements are true, which one, if added here, would most effectively conclude this paragraph and introduce the following one?
    A. Roosevelt's friend and admirer Robert LaFollette would later win Wisconsin in 1924 on the Progressive ticket.
    B. But it became known by a nickname derived from a famous quip of Roosevelt's about his physical fitness: the Bull Moose Party.
    C. Roosevelt's rhetoric would now become more anticorporate than ever before.
    D. Even today, many left-wing thinkers prefer the term *progressive* to *liberal*.

14. At this point, the writer is considering adding the following true statement:

    Many people also don't realize that the famous incident when Roosevelt finished his entire speech after surviving an assassination attempt was in 1912.

    Should the writer make this addition here?
    F. Yes, because it corrects a common misconception.
    G. Yes, because the essay should contain as many facts about Roosevelt as possible.
    H. No, because the sentence does not explain who shot Roosevelt or why.
    J. No, because the information is unessential and disrupts the flow of the paragraph.

Question 15 asks about the preceding passage as a whole.

15. Suppose the author had intended to write a brief essay about the ways in which the major events in Teddy Roosevelt's life influenced his political beliefs. Would this essay fulfill that goal?
   A. Yes, because it explains Roosevelt's reasons both for leaving the country in 1908 and for running again in 1912.
   B. Yes, because the rift in the Republican Party is explained in sufficient detail.
   C. No, because nothing about Roosevelt's childhood is mentioned in the essay.
   D. No, because the essay does not make explicit connections between Roosevelt's personal life and his policy positions.

Passage II

The Medal on Her

The Congressional Medal of Honor is the United States' highest military decoration, awarded[16] for gallantry above and beyond the call of duty. Its recipients are respected, which[17] a buck private who wears the Medal of Honor will be saluted by a general. The decoration is presented personally by the president, but the requirements for winning involve such great personal danger that nearly half the time it is received posthumously. Since its inception in 1862, the Medal of Honor has been awarded to 3,448 people, but only[18] one of them was a woman.

Mary Edwards Walker, being born[19] on a farm in Oswego, New York, in 1832. The youngest of five

16. **F.** NO CHANGE
   G. decoration, and awarded
   H. decoration, it is awarded
   J. decoration. To be awarded

17. **A.** NO CHANGE
   B. respecting which
   C. respected, in which
   D. so respected that

18. Which of the following alternatives to the underlined portion would NOT be acceptable?
   F. people, only
   G. people; only
   H. people: only
   J. people. Only

19. **A.** NO CHANGE
   B. Walker, born
   C. Walker was born
   D. Walker had been born

daughters, <u>she also had one younger brother,</u> [20] and throughout her life would occasionally be arrested for impersonating a man. After saving money from working as a schoolteacher, <u>and put herself</u> [21] through Syracuse Medical College, graduating in 1855 as the only woman in her class. She and her husband Albert opened a clinic, but <u>because</u> [22] women doctors were an odd thing in those days, business was poor.

A fervent opponent of slavery, Mary offered her services as a battlefield surgeon to the Union Army when the Civil War broke out, but because of her gender was only allowed to practice as a nurse. She applied her skills at battles like First Bull Run, Fredericksburg, and <u>Chickamauga, occasionally</u> [23] working as a surgeon when one was needed, despite her official status. <u>It was Chickamauga that won fame for General George Thomas, known as the "Rock of Chickamauga."</u> [24] In September 1863, Mary Walker was officially commissioned as the first female U.S. Army surgeon. After bravely crossing battle lines to tend to injured civilians, she was captured by Confederate forces in April 1864, charged with espionage, and held as a POW for four months. After the war, she <u>recommended</u> [25] the Medal of Honor by both of the famous generals William T. Sherman and George Henry Thomas, and received it from President Andrew Johnson in November 1865.

20. Given that all the choices are true, which one provides the most specific and relevant information?
    - **F.** NO CHANGE
    - **G.** she became accustomed to wearing male clothing from performing farmwork,
    - **H.** Mary had a rebellious streak,
    - **J.** Mary naturally felt as if she had something to prove,

21.
    - **A.** NO CHANGE
    - **B.** putting herself
    - **C.** she put herself
    - **D.** DELETE the underlined portion.

22. Which of the following alternatives to the underlined portion would NOT be acceptable?
    - **F.** as
    - **G.** since
    - **H.** although
    - **J.** seeing as how

23.
    - **A.** NO CHANGE
    - **B.** Chickamauga, and occasionally
    - **C.** Chickamauga; occasionally
    - **D.** Chickamauga. Occasionally

24. Given that all the choices are true, which one would be the best transition between the first and last parts of the paragraph?
    - **F.** NO CHANGE
    - **G.** But as the war dragged on and the Army became more desperate, it also became less concerned with tradition.
    - **H.** Thankfully, Walker was not at Antietam, regarded by most historians as the most gruesome battle of the war.
    - **J.** At this time, it was still very much unclear whether the South's attempt at secession would succeed.

25.
    - **A.** NO CHANGE
    - **B.** received recommendation
    - **C.** had recommendation to
    - **D.** was recommended for

1 ■ ■ ■ ■ ■ ■ ■ ■ 1

Walker then devoted herself to [26] the cause of feminism, becoming an early leader in the struggle of American women for the right to vote and authoring [27] two books on the subject. Sadly, she fell out of favor with other prominent feminists over differences of opinion on strategy, and was increasingly ignored. Mary's story took an even sadder turn in 1917, when Congress revised the standards for the Medal of Honor, stipulating that it could only be won for actions taken in combat. The government ordered her to return her medal, but Mary refused, continually wore [28] it until her death in 1919. The United States finally granted women the right to vote just one year later. In accordance with her wishes, Mary Edwards Walker was buried in a man's suit instead of a dress. [29]

26. Which of the following alternatives to the underlined portion would be LEAST acceptable?
    - **F.** threw her considerable energies into
    - **G.** portrayed herself as supporting
    - **H.** turned her attention to
    - **J.** adopted

27. **A.** NO CHANGE
    - **B.** women, for the right to vote and authoring
    - **C.** women for the right to vote, and authoring
    - **D.** women, for the right to vote, and authoring

28. **F.** NO CHANGE
    - **G.** continued wearing
    - **H.** continued to wear
    - **J.** continuing to wear

29. The writer would like to end the essay with a sentence that emphasizes Walker's unique place in U.S. military history. Given that all the choices are true, which one best accomplishes the writer's goal?
    - **A.** NO CHANGE
    - **B.** A 20-cent stamp was issued in Mary Edwards Walker's honor in 1982.
    - **C.** The Whitman-Walker clinic in Washington, D.C., is named in honor of Mary Edwards Walker and the poet Walt Whitman.
    - **D.** Mary Edwards Walker's Medal of Honor was officially restored by President Carter in 1977.

Question 30 asks about the preceding passage as a whole.

30. Suppose the writer's goal had been to write a brief essay concerning the importance of Mary Edwards Walker, with an emphasis on her military significance. Would this essay accomplish that goal?
    - **F.** Yes, because it describes her major accomplishments, with a specific focus on the Medal of Honor.
    - **G.** Yes, because it begins by mentioning that she is the only woman ever to receive the Medal of Honor.
    - **H.** No, because it tells us virtually nothing about Mary Walker's family life.
    - **J.** No, because it explicitly mentions that she never served in actual combat.

Passage III

The following paragraphs may or may not be in the most logical order. Each paragraph is numbered in brackets, and question 45 will ask you to choose where Paragraph 4 should most logically be placed.

Mystery at the Roof of the World

[1]

Many trustworthy people swear, in which they saw it with their own eyes. (31) On the other hand, hard physical evidence, has been notoriously difficult to come by. (32) Does the mysterious Himalayan creature known as the Yeti really exist? We may be closer than ever to an answer.

[2]

After sightings, the most common pieces of Yeti evidence are footprints. (33) But footprints left in the snow or mud of such a frigid habitat are largely unreliable, as they are distorted by repeated cycles of freezing and thawing. [34] Some of the clearer tracks have turned out to be hoaxes, others still were determined to have been made by Himalayan Brown Bears. (35) Still, biologists have examined several that appear to have been made by a five-toed biped that is neither a human nor any known species of ape that exists. (36)

31. A. NO CHANGE
B. have sworn that
C. to swear that
D. who had sworn

32. F. NO CHANGE
G. evidence; has
H. evidence and has
J. evidence has

33. A. NO CHANGE
B. evidence is
C. evidence was
D. evidence had

34. If the writer were to delete the preceding sentence, the paragraph would primarily lose information that:
F. explains a common obstacle to Yeti research.
G. reveals why law enforcement officials consider footprints useless.
H. suggests a possible method that Yetis developed for concealing their existence.
J. exposes how most of the Yeti hoaxes have been perpetrated.

35. A. NO CHANGE
B. hoaxes others
C. hoaxes, as others
D. hoaxes. Others

36. F. NO CHANGE
G. ever.
H. in the world.
J. DELETE the underlined portion and end the sentence with a period.

GO ON TO THE NEXT PAGE.

[3]

In the 1950s, it became known that a few remote Buddhist monastery's[37] were in possession of relics claimed they were[38] real body parts from Yeti. A supposed Yeti scalp was examined, but was determined to have been taken from the shoulder of an antelope. A more bizarre story is that of the "Pangboche Hand." Supposedly the[39] bones of a Yeti forelimb, it was examined by adventurer Tom Slick in 1959, but the monks would not let it be removed for further testing. Slick covertly stole two finger bones from the hand, replacing them with human bones, and escaped with them into India. From there, the bones were smuggled by the famous actor Jimmy Stewart into London, where testing suggested that they were fossils from a Neanderthal. [40] In 1991, however, further testing with more advanced equipment determined that they were "near human," but from an unknown creature.

[4]

The creature, most often described as a tall, hairy biped, has for centuries been regarded with a mix of fear and reverence by the Tibetans and Nepalese. Westerners first became acquainted with him in 1832, a[41] British explorer publicized the eyewitness accounts of his guides. The most sensational, and memorable name for[42] the beast was coined in 1921 by journalist Henry

37. **A.** NO CHANGE
B. monasteries
C. monasterie's
D. monasteries'

38. **F.** NO CHANGE
G. that were
H. to be
J. as literally

39. **A.** NO CHANGE
B. The
C. Supposedly, the
D. Supposedly these

40. At this point, the writer is considering adding the following true statement:

> Obviously, Jimmy Stewart was just about the last person anyone could imagine smuggling stolen Yeti bones.

Should the writer make this addition?

F. Yes, because it is vital to know how the bones got to London without detection.
G. Yes, because it provides the essay with much-needed comic relief.
H. No, because it fails to explain why no one would suspect Stewart.
J. No, because it is an unnecessary flourish that disrupts the flow of the paragraph.

41. **A.** NO CHANGE
B. in 1832 which a
C. in 1832, when a
D. in 1832 when, a

42. **F.** NO CHANGE
G. sensational, and memorable name, for
H. sensational and a memorable name for
J. sensational—and memorable—name for

1 ■ ■ ■ ■ ■ ■ ■ ■ ■ 1

Newman after interviewing the members of an Everest expedition: "abominable snowman." Although still used informally, this term has fallen out of favor with serious investigators, as the vast majority of those who lend credence to Yeti tales believe that it is simply some unclassified species of ape, rather than a monster or anything supernatural.

[5]

Though the North American "Bigfoot" is popularly thought to be related to the Yeti, most researchers consider the Yeti's existence much more likely. [43] A 2007 investigation by an American TV program obtained a hair sample that testing revealed belonged to "an unknown primate." And just last year, the team of Japanese adventurer Yoshiteru Takahashi claiming [44] to have seen a Yeti in 2003, ventured into the Himalayas, determined to capture the furry fellow on film at last. Maybe they will find nothing, or maybe one day soon your favorite show will be interrupted by a special news bulletin announcing "We bring you… the Yeti!"

43. Given that all of the choices are true, which of the following statements would most effectively introduce the paragraph?

A. NO CHANGE
B. Officially, the Yeti is what's known as a "cryptid," or animal that is rumored to exist but is still undiscovered.
C. The 2004 discovery of extinct hominid *Homo floresiensis* brought renewed interest in the Yeti and exciting new finds.
D. Supposedly, Nazi troops on maneuvers in Asia shot a Yeti, but any records of this were lost at the end of World War II.

44. **F.** NO CHANGE
G. Takahashi claimed
H. Takahashi that claimed
J. Takahashi, who claims

Question 45 asks about the preceding passage as a whole.

45. For the sake of logic and coherence, Paragraph 4 should be placed:

A. where it is now.
B. after Paragraph 1.
C. after Paragraph 2.
D. after Paragraph 5.

Passage IV

The Pirate Queen

Legends of female pirate Anne Bonny are still[46] popular today. As piracy was a male-dominated occupation, to say the least, her[47] story has fascinated generations of feminists and pirate enthusiasts alike. Everyone wants to believe that her deeds were as fabulous as our collective imagination makes them, but the truth is that, although we know Bonny existed and spent some time on a pirate ship, we're not sure what became of the ship.[48]

The famous pirate queen is said to have been born Anne Cormac, the daughter of a successful lawyer,[49] around 1700 in Kinsale, in the south of Ireland. Supposedly disowned by her family as a teenager after stabbing another girl in the gut with a table knife, the beautifully redhead[50] is said then to have eloped to the Bahamas with a sailor named James Bonny, after burning down her family's[51] estate in vengeance. But aside from the fact that she arrived in Nassau, Bahamas, as the wife of James Bonny, none of the other information including[52] the identity of her family—can be verified, and may all just be romantic wishful thinking done after the fact.

It is known that, while living in Nassau, she became romantically involved with the pirate "Calico Jack" Rackham (there are records of her having been

46. **F.** NO CHANGE
G. is still
H. to still be
J. might still be

47. Which of the following alternatives to the underlined portion would be LEAST acceptable?
A. occupation for people then, her
B. occupation, as well as a deadly one, her
C. occupation (to put it mildly), her
D. occupation, her

48. The writer wishes to finish this sentence with a phrase that emphasizes the lack of information about Anne Bonny. Which of the following true statements best achieves that goal?
F. NO CHANGE
G. fewer people spend time thinking about her than you may imagine.
H. accounts of her life rely heavily on speculation.
J. the number of books that have been written about her is anyone's guess.

49. Which of the following best emphasizes the surprising nature of Anne's supposed origins?
A. NO CHANGE
B. which is a very common name in Ireland,
C. her parents' first and only girl,
D. neither a very large nor a very small baby,

50. **F.** NO CHANGE
G. redheaded beauty
H. redheaded, beautiful
J. beautiful and redheaded

51. **A.** NO CHANGE
B. familys
C. families
D. families'

52. **F.** NO CHANGE
G. information, including
H. information—including
J. information: including

1 ■ ■ ■ ■ ■ ■ ■ ■ 1

charged with adultery by Bonny) and sailed off with him on his ship, the *Revenge*. Their endeavors were successful over the next few years [53], with the *Revenge* taking several ships. We know that Anne Bonny's name appeared on lists of wanted pirates, but how prominent she was among the crew is disputable. [54] She apparently participated in the fighting when there was fighting doing [55] (less often than people imagine, as most ships overtaken by pirates surrendered immediately), but contrary to popular belief, she never captained her own ship or commanded her own crew.

The pirates of the *Revenge* were captured in port by authorities in 1720 supposedly [56] while all but Bonny and the one other female in the crew, Mary Read, were drunk, forcing the two women to fight alone (likely another embellishment). Every pirate was hanged aside from Bonny and Read, who both claimed to be pregnant and were because of this therefore [57] spared. Read subsequently died in prison of a fever, but there is no reliable record of what became of Anne Bonny. She may have been executed after delivering her baby—if she really was pregnant—or she may have convinced the law was [58] a prisoner on Rackham's ship and been

53. The best placement for the underlined portion would be:
   A. where it is now.
   B. after the word *were.*
   C. after the word *Revenge*.
   D. after the word *ships* (and before the period).

54. Given that all the choices are true, which one would be the best transition between the first and last parts of the paragraph?
   F. NO CHANGE
   G. In those days, the richest ships tended not to be equipped with heavy gunnery.
   H. Most pirate ships were democracies, and the captain was elected by the crew.
   J. The idea that Anne disguised herself as a man before the crew is actually a myth.

55. **A.** NO CHANGE
   B. a fight broke out
   C. was fighting to be done
   D. were any

56. **F.** NO CHANGE
   G. 1720, supposedly
   H. 1720; supposedly
   J. 1720 although supposedly,

57. **A.** NO CHANGE
   B. for this reason accordingly
   C. because of this reason
   D. therefore

58. **F.** NO CHANGE
   G. if she were
   H. once she was
   J. that she had been

GO ON TO THE NEXT PAGE.

released. Another theory holds that she was secretly ransomed by her father and lived to a ripe old age in South Carolina. [59] We'll probably never know any more about the story of Anne Bonny than we already do, but as with King Arthur, Robin Hood, or the many other larger-than-life figures whose legends have little basis in fact, this will surely not stop people from telling it.

59. If the writer were to delete the underlined sentence, the paragraph would primarily lose:
   - A. hard evidence that Anne Bonny spent considerable time in America.
   - B. additional evidence of the many varied accounts concerning Anne Bonny.
   - C. a suggestion that the earlier account of her family in Ireland was true.
   - D. an argument that people prefer happy endings to depressing ones.

Question 60 asks about the preceding passage as a whole.

60. Suppose the writer had intended to write a brief essay about women who lead lives of crime. Would this essay fulfill that goal?
   - F. Yes, because it establishes that Bonny definitely broke the law numerous times.
   - G. Yes, because Anne Bonny is a role model for female thieves the world over.
   - H. No, because it focuses only on Anne Bonny, and not female criminals in general.
   - J. No, because it strongly suggests that Bonny was merely the sidekick of a male pirate.

Passage V

Most Historically Inaccurate Movie Ever?

Mel Gibson's *Braveheart* won the Academy Award for Best Picture of 1995, took in over $200 million at the box office, and is still acclaimed by action fans to contain [61] some of the best battle scenes ever put on film. But how "historical" is this historical epic? Fans are often disappointed to learn that aside from the fact that the [62] major characters really existed, the film is nearly entirely fiction.

Yes, there was a historical William Wallace who led Scottish troops during [63] the First War of Scottish Independence in the late thirteenth century. But rather than the rustic commoner depicted in Gibson's film, he

61. A. NO CHANGE
   B. fans as containing
   C. fans that it contains
   D. fans, in which contains

62. F. NO CHANGE
   G. that aside from the fact, that the
   H. that, aside from the fact that the
   J. that aside from the fact that, the

63. A. NO CHANGE
   B. Wallace, who led Scottish troops, during
   C. Wallace who led Scottish troops, during
   D. Wallace, and who led Scottish troops during

was a nobleman a knight and, landowner. [64] It's documented that Wallace entered the war with his murder of an English sheriff in 1297, but the reason for [65] this event is unknown. The movie follows a famous poem [66] in attributing Wallace's anger to the murder of his wife, but there's no evidence that this wife even existed, much less executed [67] by the English. Older accounts claim that Wallace had already been an outlaw for years after killing five English soldiers who tried to steal his catch after a fishing trip; still others [68] allege that the trouble started when a teenage Wallace killed an English noble's son who bullied him at boarding school.

Clearly, the writers chose the tales about Wallace best suited to the hero of a blockbuster film: a formerly peaceful farmer avenging the death of his one true love is a [69] more sympathetic underdog than a private-school kid who psychotically overreacts to a bit of teasing. The same impulse led the writers to take further liberties with their depiction not only of Wallace, but the Scots generally are [70] presented as far too primitive in relation to the English. The facepaint Wallace wears into battle

64. **F.** NO CHANGE
G. a nobleman; a knight and landowner.
H. a nobleman—a knight, and landowner.
J. a nobleman: a knight and landowner.

65. Which of the following alternatives to the underlined portion would NOT be acceptable?

A. explanation for
B. cause of
C. impetus for
D. story to

66. At this point, the writer is considering adding the following true parenthetical information:

(composed 200 years later)

Should the writer make this addition?

F. Yes, because it suggests that the account is probably inaccurate.
G. Yes, because it suggests that the poem is probably written in modern English.
H. No, because it neglects to mention the identity of the poet.
J. No, because the date that a work of literature was composed never matters.

67. **A.** NO CHANGE
B. was executed
C. being executed
D. to be executed

68. Which of the following alternatives to the underlined portion would NOT be acceptable?

F. trip; others
G. trip, and still others
H. trip; while others
J. trip, while still others

69. Which of the following alternatives to the underlined portion would be LEAST acceptable?

A. has a
B. works as a
C. makes for a
D. would be seen as a

70. **F.** NO CHANGE
G. Wallace and the Scots generally are
H. Wallace; the Scots generally, who are
J. Wallace, but of the Scots generally, who are

was actually characteristic of the Picts were a tribe that lived in Scotland over a thousand years earlier and battled the Romans. By Wallace's time, the Scots were fighting in chain-mail and armor, and would have been visually indistinguishable from the English. The stereotypical plaids on *Braveheart*'s Scots', however, are anachronistic in a different way: kilts were not worn in battle until 400 years *later*.

The script plays fast and loose with people too: King Edward outlived Wallace by years, Princess Isabella was a young girl at the time and still in France, and Andrew de Moray, who was an equally important Scottish commander who fought beside Wallace, is omitted entirely. But *Braveheart*'s most troubling inaccuracy by far it is depiction of Robert the Bruce as a coward who betrays Wallace to the English. Not only did the historical Bruce never betray Wallace, but he barely knew him, and was far more instrumental in the eventual Scottish victory. In fact, the nickname "Braveheart" itself was historically not used for William Wallace at all, but rather for Robert the Bruce!

71. **A.** NO CHANGE
B. Picts, having been a
C. Picts, and also a
D. Picts, a

72. Which of the following alternatives to the underlined portion would be LEAST acceptable?
F. fought
G. had fought
H. would have fought
J. did their fighting

73. **A.** NO CHANGE
B. *Bravehearts* Scots,
C. *Braveheart*'s Scots,
D. *Bravehearts* Scots',

74. **F.** NO CHANGE
G. it is the
H. is its
J. is it's

75. **A.** NO CHANGE
B. betrayed
C. did betray
D. would have betrayed

STOP

If there is still time remaining, check your answers to this section.

MATHEMATICS TEST

60 MINUTES—60 QUESTIONS

Directions: Solve each problem, choose the correct answer, and then fill in the corresponding oval on your answer document.

Do not linger over problems that take too much time. Solve as many as you can; then return to the others in the time you have left for this test.

You are permitted to use a calculator on this test. You may use your calculator for any problems you choose, but some of the problems may best be done without using a calculator.

Note: Unless otherwise stated, all of the following should be assumed.

1. Illustrative figures are NOT necessarily drawn to scale.
2. Geometric figures lie in a plane.
3. The word *line* indicates a straight line.
4. The word *average* indicates arithmetic mean.

DO YOUR FIGURING HERE.

1. A rectangle is four times as long as it is wide. If the width of the rectangle is 4.5 cm, what is the rectangle's area, in square centimeters?

   A. 17
   B. 18
   C. 45
   D. 72
   E. 81

2. A bubble gum machine has 120 red, blue, yellow, and green gumballs in it. If 30 are yellow, 32 are red, and 28 are green, what is the probability that the next gumball out of the machine is NOT blue?

   F. $\frac{1}{4}$
   G. $\frac{3}{4}$
   H. 25%
   J. 1:4
   K. 2:1

3. Which of the following is equivalent to $4 \text{ x } 10^{-5}$?

   A. –2,000,000
   B. –400,000
   C. 0.00002
   D. 0.00004
   E. 0.000004

2 △ △ △ △ △ △ △ △ 2

DO YOUR FIGURING HERE.

4. If a 25-foot ladder leans against a building and the base of the ladder is 15 feet from the bottom of the building, at what height does the top of the ladder touch the building?

F. 10 ft.
G. 18 ft.
H. 20 ft.
J. 30 ft.
K. 40 ft.

5. Which of the following is equivalent to $\sqrt{96}$?

A. $4\sqrt{6}$

B. $6\sqrt{4}$

C. $8\sqrt{6}$

D. $8\sqrt{12}$

E. $16\sqrt{6}$

6. What is the perimeter of a square with an area of 49?

F. 7
G. 14
H. 20
J. 28
K. 49

7. What is the slope of the line $4y = -2x + 4$?

A. -2

B. $-\frac{1}{2}$

C. 1
D. 2
E. 4

8. What is the slope of any line perpendicular to the line $5x - 4y = -12$ in the standard (x, y) coordinate plane?

F. -4

G. $-\frac{5}{4}$

H. $-\frac{4}{5}$

J. $\frac{4}{5}$

K. $\frac{5}{4}$

2 △ △ △ △ △ △ △ △ 2

DO YOUR FIGURING HERE.

9. Given $\triangle XYZ$ with the angle measures shown below, and that point P lies on $\overline{XZ}$, what is m $\angle XYZ$?

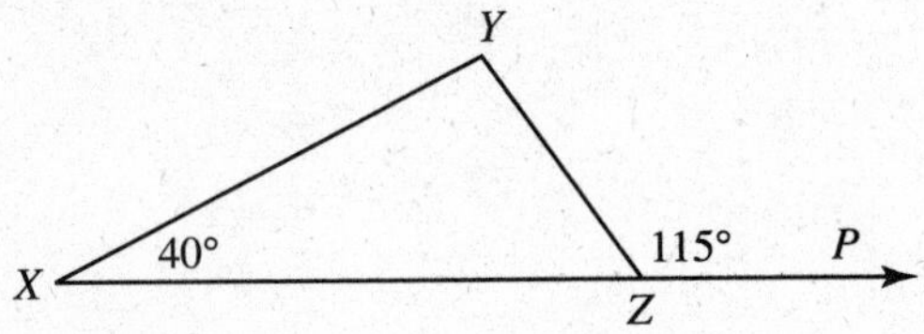

A. 25°
B. 65°
C. 75°
D. 85°
E. 140°

10. What is the area of a circle with a radius of 6?

F. 8π
G. 12π
H. 16π
J. 32π
K. 36π

11. Bette's 2 pieces of bacon and 1 egg cost \$2.10. Jed's 3 pieces of bacon and 2 eggs cost \$3.45. How much does 1 egg cost?

A. 45 cents
B. 50 cents
C. 60 cents
D. 70 cents
E. 75 cents

12. M, N, and x are all integers greater than 1. Given that $\frac{M}{24} + \frac{N}{108} = \frac{9M + 2N}{x}$, what must x equal?

F. 11
G. 12
H. 132
J. 216
K. 2,592

13. If $\angle Y$ is the vertex of isosceles $\triangle XYZ$ (shown below), what is the value of a?

A. 16°
B. 17°
C. 34°
D. 36°
E. 39°

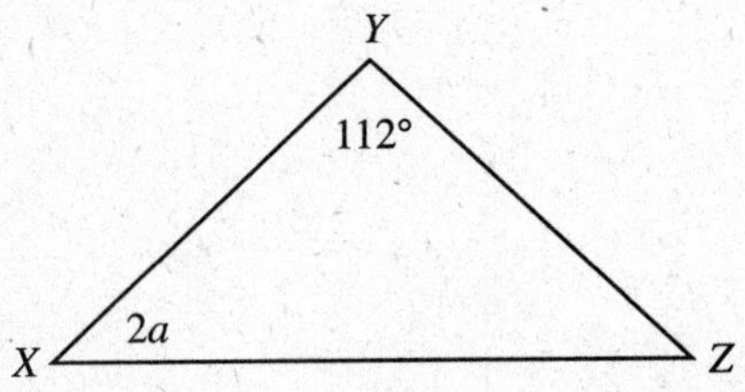

2 △ △ △ △ △ △ △ △ 2

DO YOUR FIGURING HERE

14. A function f is defined by $f(x) = -3x^2 + 4x$. What is the value of $f(4)$?

    F. –40
    G. –32
    H. 32
    J. 52
    K. 136

15. In the figure below, $\overline{MQ}$ intersects $\overline{PS}$ at point R, m $\angle TRS = 25°$, and $\angle QRT$ is a right angle. What is the measure of $\angle MRP$?

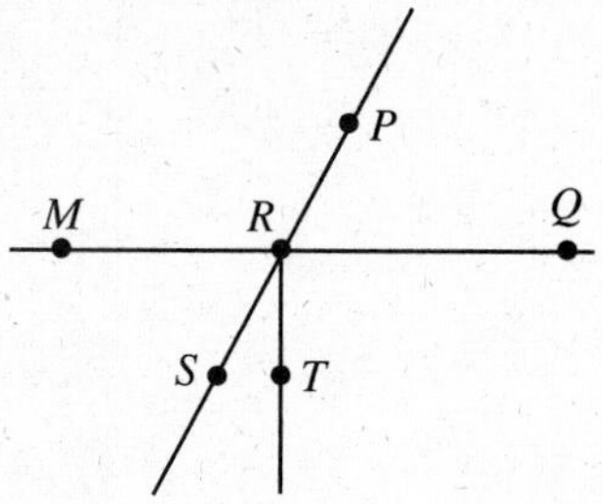

    A. 75°
    B. 90°
    C. 105°
    D. 115°
    E. 165°

16. In $\triangle ABC$ below, what is tan $\angle A$?

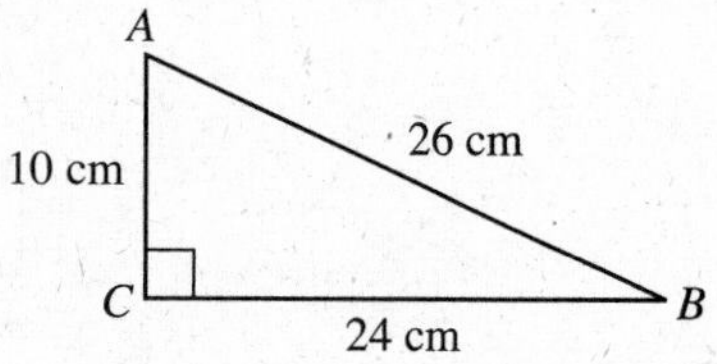

    F. $\frac{5}{13}$
    G. $\frac{5}{12}$
    H. $\frac{12}{13}$
    J. $\frac{12}{5}$
    K. $\frac{13}{5}$

17. Jenna wants to serve a large pot of soup to 25 people by 1:15 P.M. If it takes her 7 minutes to assemble the ingredients, 20 minutes to cut up the vegetables, and $2\frac{1}{2}$ hours to cook the soup on the stove, what is the latest time that Jenna could begin her meal preparation?

    A. 9:53 A.M.
    B. 9:58 A.M.
    C. 10:18 A.M.
    D. 10:21 A.M.
    E. 10:28 A.M.

2 △ △ △ △ △ △ △ △ 2

DO YOUR FIGURING HERE.

18. Hiram's garden contains 45 tomato plants, 15 watermelon plants, and 120 lettuce plants. There are no other plants in Hiram's garden. Approximately what percent of the garden is occupied by watermelon plants?

F. 0.12%
G. 8.3%
H. 12%
J. 15%
K. 83%

19. What is the additive inverse of the polynomial $5x^3 - 4x^2 + 6x - 9$?

A. $-5x^3 + 4x^2 - 6x - 9$
B. $-5x^3 + 4x^2 - 6x + 9$
C. $5x^3 - 4x^2 + 6x - 9$
D. $-9 + 6x - 4x^2 + 5x^3$
E. $9 - 6x - 4x^2 + 5x^3$

20. In the standard (x, y) coordinate plane, if $\overline{AB}$ has endpoint A at $(-2, 4)$ and midpoint M at $(3, 9)$, where is endpoint B located?

F. (0.5, 6.5)
G. (6.5, 0.5)
H. (7, 1)
J. (8, 14)
K. (14, 8)

21. Which of the following, if any, is equivalent to the inequality $|x| + 4 < 7$?

A. $x < -3$ and $x > 3$
B. $x < -3$ or $x > 3$
C. $-3 < x < 3$
D. $-3 > x$ and $3 < x$
E. None of these.

22. What is the sum of the interior angles of pentagon ⬠$LMNPR$?

F. 180°
G. 540°
H. 600°
J. 720°
K. 900°

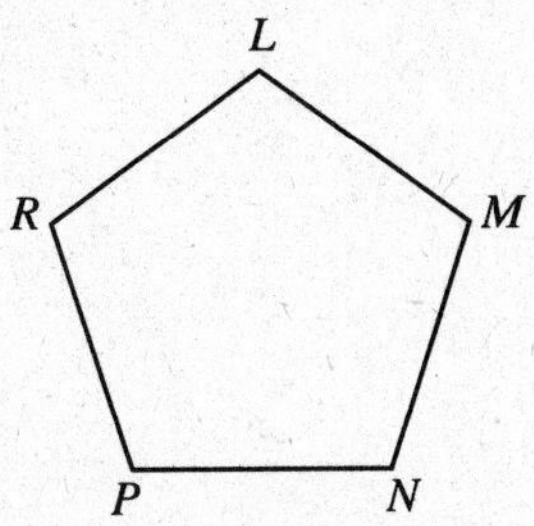

23. Which of the following values of n makes the statement $n^{1/2} = 4$ true?

A. 16
B. 8
C. 4
D. 2
E. $\frac{1}{8}$

GO ON TO THE NEXT PAGE.

2 △ △ △ △ △ △ △ △ 2

DO YOUR FIGURING HERE.

24. If a and b can be any two real numbers such that $b < -6$ and $3a - b = 21$, which of the following is a solution set for a?

F. $a \leq 9$
G. $a \leq 5$
H. $a < 5$
J. $a \geq 9$
K. $a \geq -5$

25. Darcy used a 12-m piece of rope to tie her dog to a tree while she mowed her front yard. The dog could only walk in a semicircle because the tree was located directly next to the house (see diagram below). Assuming 3.14 for π, how much area, in square meters, could the dog cover?

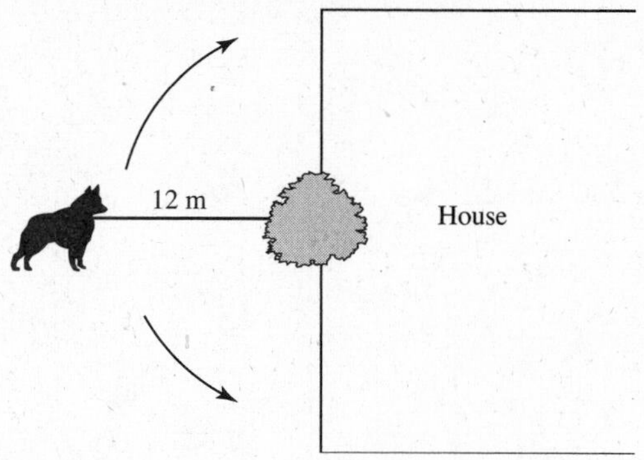

A. 57
B. 75
C. 113
D. 226
E. 452

26. For $3x \neq 2y$, the polynomial expression $\frac{24x^2 - 7xy - 6y^2}{3x - 2y}$ is equivalent to which of the following?

F. $2x - 3y$
G. $2x - 12y$
H. $3x - 2y$
J. $8x - 3y$
K. $8x + 3y$

27. Jose recently opened a new business. He projects that his profit will be $25,000 for the first year, and will increase by 7% over the next 8 years. Which of the following best describes the sequence formed by his annual profits?

A. Geometric with a common ratio of 0.07
B. Geometric with a common ratio of 1.07
C. Geometric with a common ratio of 1.7
D. Arithmetic with a common difference of 25.07
E. Arithmetic with a common difference of 25,000

2 △ △ △ △ △ △ △ △ 2

DO YOUR FIGURING HERE.

28. The trapezoid shown below in the standard (x, y) coordinate plane has vertices as marked. What is the area of the trapezoid in square units?

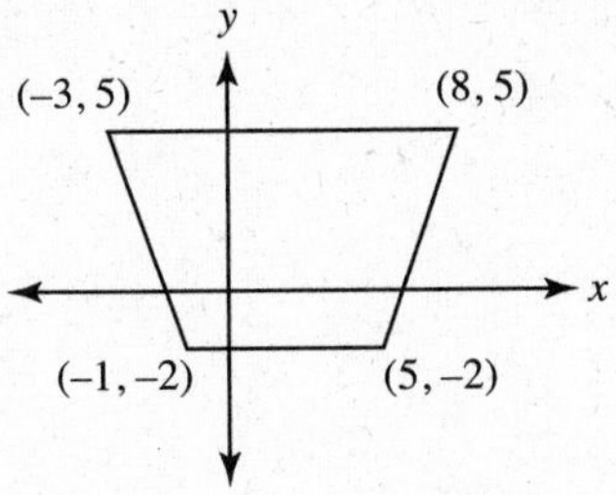

F. 49.5
G. 59.5
H. 66
J. 99
K. 119

29. What is the greatest common factor of the terms $12x^4y^2$ and $6xy^3$?

A. $6xy^2$
B. $6x^4y^2$
C. $6x^4y^3$
D. $12xy^2$
E. $12x^4y^3$

30. In the figure below, M is the midpoint of $\overline{NP}$ and $\triangle LMP$ is equilateral. If $NP = 8$, what is the length of $\overline{LN}$?

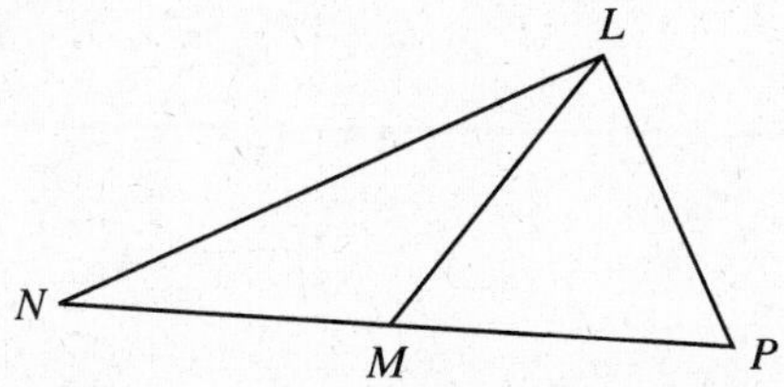

F. 4
G. $4\sqrt{2}$
H. $4\sqrt{3}$
J. 8
K. $8\sqrt{3}$

31. The formula for converting Celsius temperature to Fahrenheit temperature is $F = \frac{9}{5}C + 32$. If the current temperature is 122° Fahrenheit, what is the temperature in Celsius?

A. 50°
B. 59.7°
C. 65.5°
D. 162°
E. 277.2°

2 △ △ △ △ △ △ △ △ 2

DO YOUR FIGURING HERE.

32. If a ratio is selected at random from the set $\left\{\frac{1}{3}, \frac{3}{5}, \frac{3}{7}, \frac{5}{7}, \frac{5}{9}\right\}$, what is the probability that the ratio is greater than $\frac{1}{2}$?

F. $\frac{1}{5}$
G. $\frac{2}{5}$
H. $\frac{3}{5}$
J. $\frac{2}{3}$
K. $\frac{4}{5}$

33. Gertrude's Diner offers three different types of salads, two soups, four vegetable sides, five main dishes, and three desserts. If a customer can choose a salad **OR** a soup along with one main dish, one vegetable side, and one dessert, how many different meal combinations are possible?

A. 17
B. 19
C. 300
D. 360
E. 21,600

34. As shown below, $\triangle ABC$ has vertices at points A (1, 1), B (7, 2), and C (3, 4). If $\triangle ABC$ was reflected about the origin to form a new triangle, $\triangle A'B'C'$, which of the following correctly lists the coordinates of points A', B', and C', respectively?

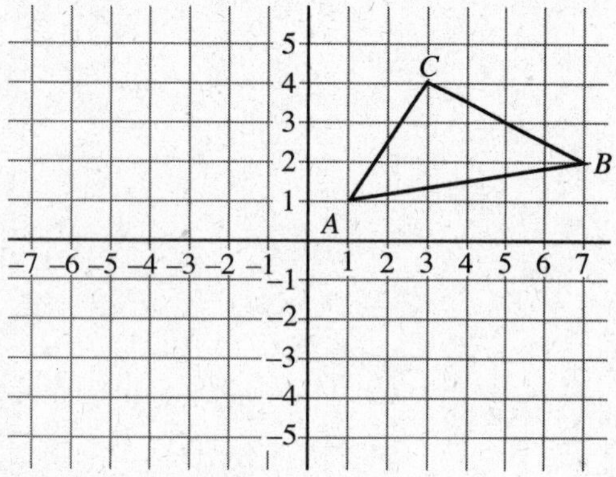

F. (1, 1); (2, 7); (4, 3)
G. (−1, 1); (−7, 2); (−4, 3)
H. (−1, −1);(−7, −2);(−3, −4)
J. (−1, −1); (−2, −7);(−3, −4)
K. (1, −1); (7, −2); (3, −4)

2 △ △ △ △ △ △ △ △ 2

DO YOUR FIGURING HERE.

35. A military tank is 228 meters due north of its target. The commander's jeep is due west of the tank and 247 meters north/northwest of its target. Which of the following gives the distance, in meters, between the tank and the jeep?

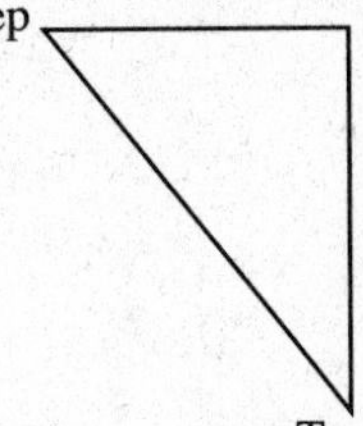

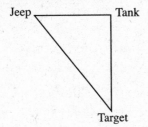

A. 19
B. 95
C. 190
D. 475
E. 9,025

36. What is the matrix product of $[x\ 2x\ 3x] \cdot \begin{bmatrix} 6 \\ 0 \\ -2 \end{bmatrix}$?

F. $[6x\ \ 0\ \ -6x]$
G. $[-6x\ \ 0\ \ 6x]$
H. $\begin{bmatrix} 6x & 12x & 18x \\ 0 & 0 & 0 \\ -2x & -4x & -6x \end{bmatrix}$
J. $[\,0\,]$
K. $\begin{bmatrix} 6x & 0 & -2x \\ 12x & 0 & -4x \\ 18x & 0 & -6x \end{bmatrix}$

37. Which of the following expresses the number of meters an athlete must travel in a 6-lap race around a circular track with a diameter of X meters?

A. $6\pi X^2$
B. $3\pi X^2$
C. $\frac{3}{2}\pi X^2$
D. $6\pi X$
E. $3\pi X$

38. For all real numbers m and n such that the product of m and 4 is n, which of the following expressions represents the sum of m and 4 in terms of n ?

F. $n + 4$
G. $4n + 4$
H. $4(n + 4)$
J. $\frac{n+4}{4}$
K. $\frac{n}{4} + 4$

GO ON TO THE NEXT PAGE.

2 △ △ △ △ △ △ △ △ 2

DO YOUR FIGURING HERE.

39. As shown below, rectangle *KLMN* is divided into 3 large squares (each labeled R) that measure x centimeters on a side, 12 small squares (each labeled S) that measure y centimeters on a side, and 13 rectangles (each labeled P). What is the total area, in square centimeters, of rectangle *KLMN*?

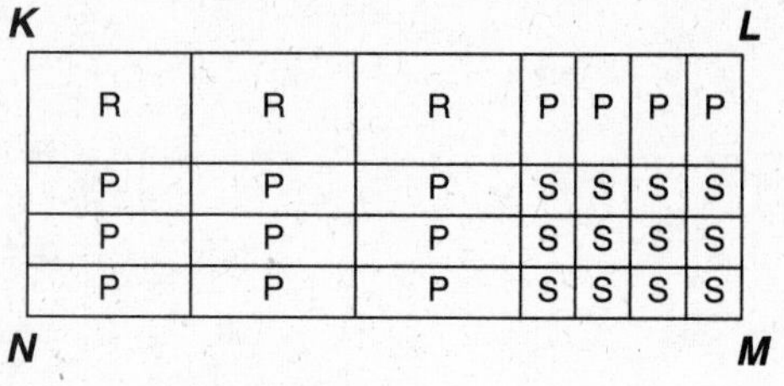

A. $3x + 4xy + 9yx + 12y$
B. $12x + 4xy + 9yx + 3y$
C. $3x^2 + 13xy + 12y^2$
D. $12x^2 + 13xy + 3y^2$
E. $3x^3 + 13xy + 12y^{12}$

40. For some real number D, the graph of the line $y = (D - 3)x + 7$ in the standard (x, y) coordinate plane passes through the point $(-5, 2)$. What is the slope of this line?

F. -3
G. -2
H. 0
J. 1
K. 4

41. When graphed in the standard (x, y) coordinate plane, the lines $x = -6$ and $y = 2x - 4$ intersect at what point?

A. $(-16, -6)$
B. $(-6, -16)$
C. $(-6, 8)$
D. $(-6, 16)$
E. $(8, -6)$

42. In $\triangle LMP$, shown below, $\overline{LN}$ is the perpendicular bisector of $\overline{PM}$, $\cos \angle LMP = 0.4$, and $\overline{PM} = 24$ inches. How many inches long is $\overline{LM}$?

F. 9.6
G. 30
H. 40
J. 48
K. 60

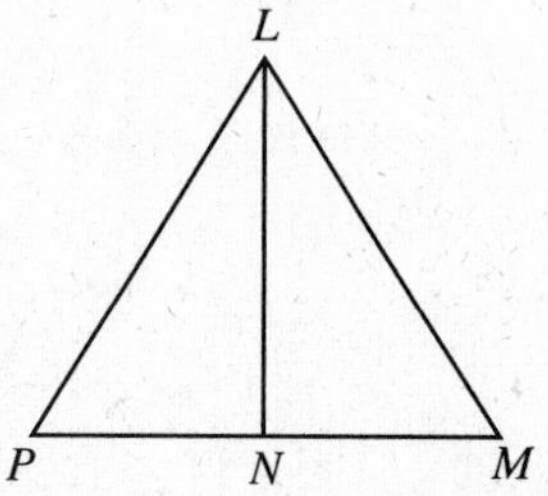

2 △ △ △ △ △ △ △ 2

DO YOUR FIGURING HERE.

43. A music instructor charges \$30 per lesson, plus an additional fee for violin rental. The charge for the violin varies directly with the square root of the time the violin is used. If a lesson plus 25 minutes of violin rental costs \$65, how much would it cost for a lesson plus 81 minutes of violin rental?

A. \$ 93
B. \$105
C. \$111
D. \$141
E. \$146

44. The figure below shows a small square inside of a larger square. The smaller square has sides 3 inches long, and the area of the shaded region is 16 square inches. What is the length, in inches, of one side of the larger square?

F. 4
G. $\sqrt{19}$
H. 5
J. $\sqrt{28}$
K. 25

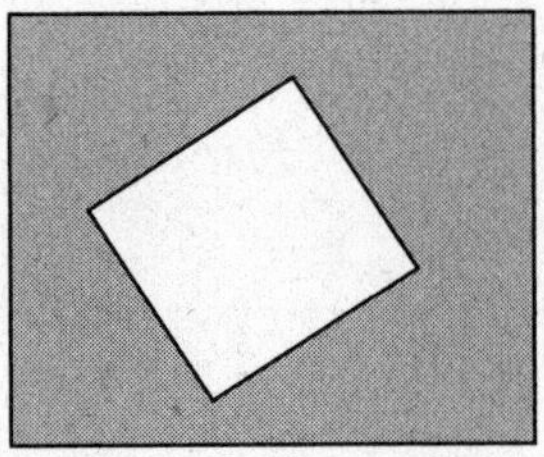

45. The quadrants of the standard (x, y) coordinate plane are labeled in the figure below. For each value of θ, let $x = \cos\theta$ and $y = \sin\theta$. Whenever $(\sin\theta)\left(\frac{1}{\cos\theta}\right) < 0$, the points (x, y) on the unit circle can lie in which of the following quadrants?

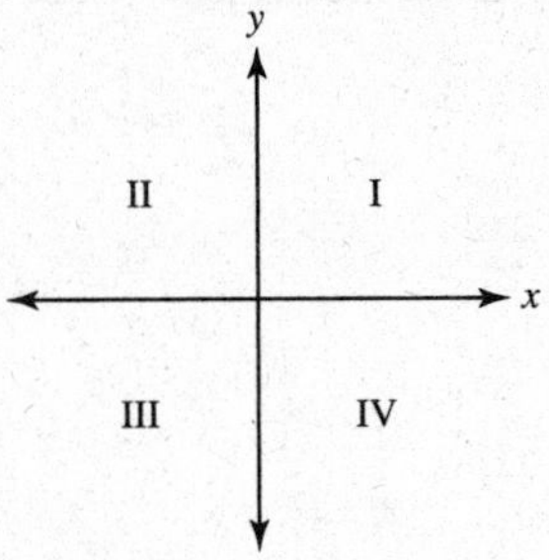

A. III only
B. IV only
C. I and III only
D. II and III only
E. II and IV only

46. For $i^2 = -1$, $(3 - i)^2 = ?$

F. 16
G. $2i$
H. $4i$
J. $10 - 6i$
K. $8 - 6i$

GO ON TO THE NEXT PAGE.

DO YOUR FIGURING HERE.

47. The volume of a sphere is determined by the equation $\frac{4}{3}\pi r^3$, where r is the radius of the sphere. In a given model of the solar system, all of the planets are perfect spheres. If the radius of Mars is exactly 4 times greater than the radius of Venus, how many times the volume of Venus is the volume of Mars?

A. 81
B. 64
C. 16
D. 12
E. 4

48. Which of the following is equivalent to $\sqrt[3]{16r^6}$?

F. $4r^3$
G. $4r^4$
H. $8r^3$
J. $8r^4$
K. $32r^{12}$

49. If 2 is a solution of the equation $x^2 + kx + 12 = 0$, what does k equal?

A. –12
B. –8
C. –2
D. 6
E. 8

50. In the standard (x, y) coordinate plane, the center of the circle shown below lies on the y-axis at $y = 3$. If the circle is also tangent to the x-axis, then what is the equation of the circle?

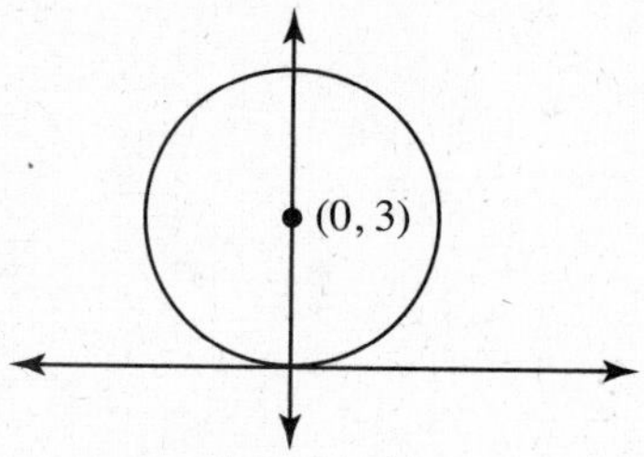

F. $x^2 + (y - 3)^2 = 6$
G. $x^2 + (y - 3)^2 = 9$
H. $x^2 + (y + 3)^2 = 9$
J. $(x - 3)^2 + y^2 = 6$
K. $(x + 3)^2 + y^2 = 9$

2 △ △ △ △ △ △ △ △ 2

DO YOUR FIGURING HERE.

51. Which of the following equations summarizes the data listed below?

x	−2	−1	0	1	2
y	−8	−5	−2	1	4

A. $y = -2x - 2$
B. $y = 2x - 4$
C. $y = 2x + 3$
D. $y = 3x - 2$
E. $y = 3x + 2$

52. The law of sines states that for any triangle, the ratio between the sine of an angle and the length of the side opposite that angle is the same for all of the interior angles in the triangle. In $\triangle XYZ$ shown below, $\overline{ZX} = 22$ cm, $\angle Z = 32°$, and $\angle Y = 44°$. What is the length of $\overline{ZY}$?

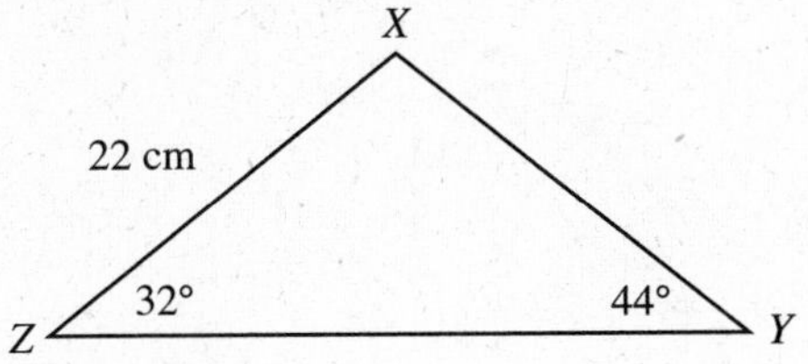

F. $\dfrac{22(\sin 104°)}{\sin 32°}$

G. $\dfrac{\sin 32°(\sin 104°)}{\sin 44°}$

H. $\dfrac{22(\sin 32°)}{\sin 104°}$

J. $\dfrac{22(\sin 104°)}{\sin 44°}$

K. $\dfrac{22(\sin 44°)}{\sin 104°}$

GO ON TO THE NEXT PAGE.

2 △ △ △ △ △ △ △ △ 2

DO YOUR FIGURING HERE.

53. Which of the following is the graph of the equation $3x - 2y = 6$?

A.

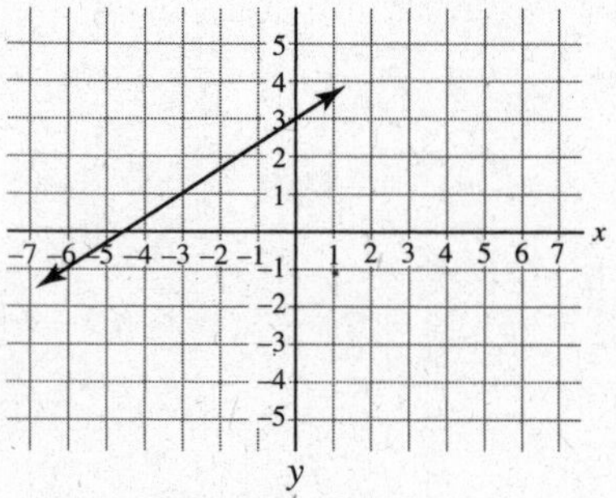

B.

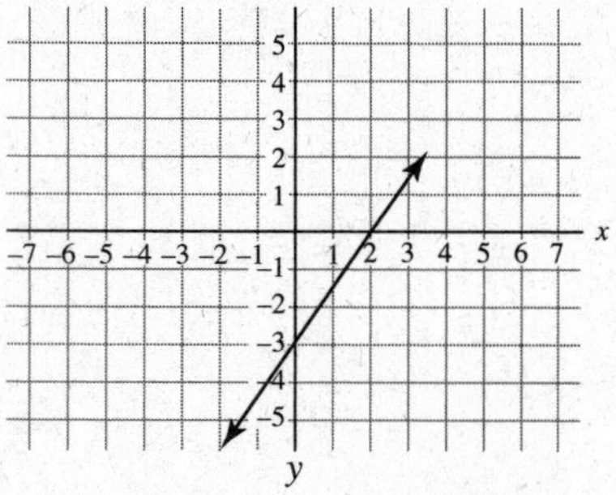

C.

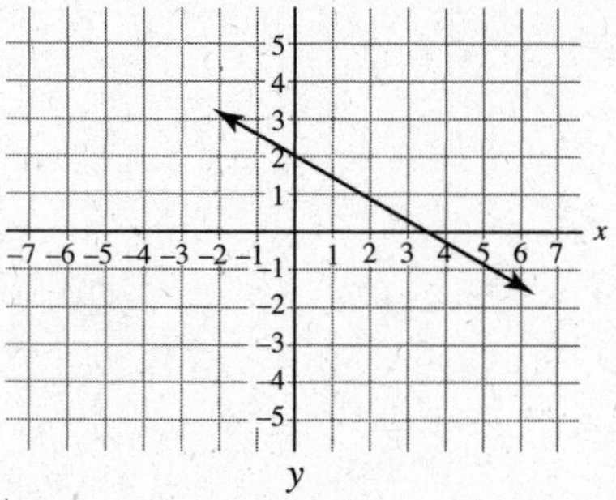

D.

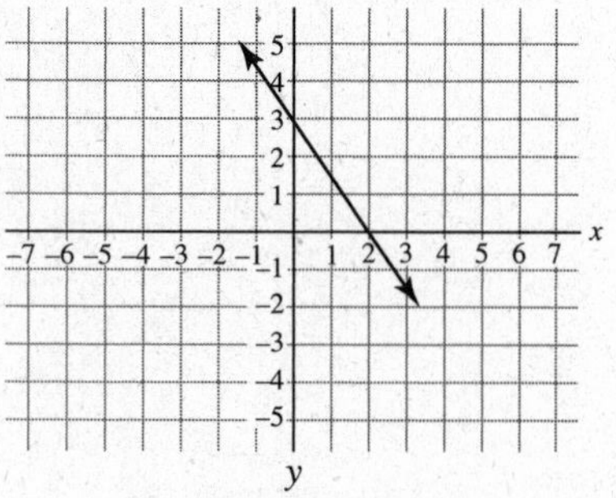

E.

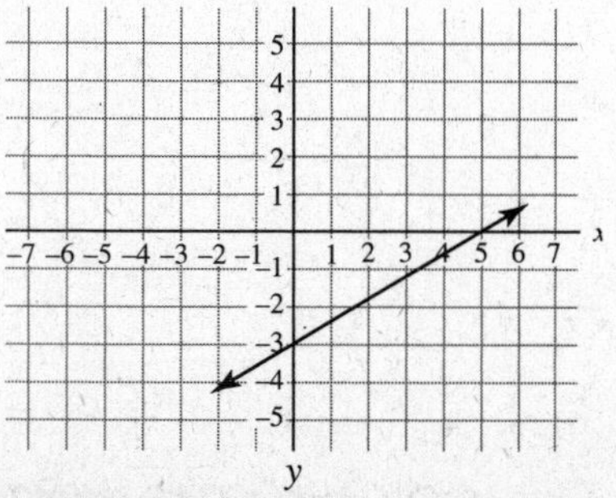

DO YOUR FIGURING HERE.

54. For $\sqrt{(3)(7)} \cdot \sqrt{(m)(n)} \cdot \sqrt{(7)(5)}$ to be an integer, with m and n representing positive prime numbers, the sum of $m + n$ must equal which of the following?

 F. 8
 G. 10
 H. 12
 J. 15
 K. 21

55. Cam is going into business selling umbrellas. He pays $25,000 for a building and machinery, and each umbrella costs $4.00 to manufacture. If Cam sells x umbrellas for $6.50 each, which of the following equations best represents his net profit in dollars?

 A. $10.50x - 25{,}000$
 B. $6.50x - 25{,}000$
 C. $4.00x + 25{,}000$
 D. $4.00x - 25{,}000$
 E. $2.50x - 25{,}000$

56. In the circle shown below, O lies on the center of the circle and on chords $\overline{LN}$ and $\overline{MP}$. The measure of $\widehat{PN} = 100°$. Which of the following statements is NOT true?

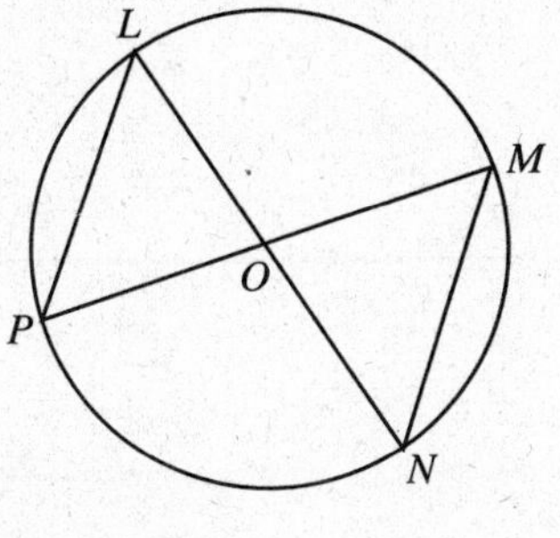

 F. $m\angle PLN = 50°$
 G. $m\angle POL = 80°$
 H. $\angle PON \cong \angle NOM$
 J. $\angle POL \cong \angle NOM$
 K. $\overline{LP} \parallel \overline{MN}$

57. For all real numbers m and n, when is the equation $|m - n| = |m + n|$ true?

 A. Never
 B. Always
 C. Only when $m = n$
 D. Only when $m = 0$ and $n = 0$
 E. Only when $m = 0$ or $n = 0$

2 △ △ △ △ △ △ △ △ 2

DO YOUR FIGURING HERE.

58. What is the value of $\log_4 16$?

F. 2
G. 4
H. 12
J. 20
K. 64

59. Television screen sizes are measured on the diagonal. Joshua bought a new television with a 24-inch screen and gave his old 21-inch television to his younger brother. If Joshua is watching a soccer ball that appears to be 4 inches in diameter on his new screen, how long does the diameter of the same ball, to the nearest tenth of an inch, appear to his brother watching on the smaller screen?

A. 3
B. 3.5
C. 4.6
D. 3π
E. 3.5π

60. When $0° < x < 90°$, which of the following is NOT equal to $\tan x$?

F. $\dfrac{\sin x}{\cos x}$
G. $(\sin^2 x + \cos^2 x)(\tan x)$
H. $\dfrac{\sec x}{\csc x}$
J. $\dfrac{(\sin^2 x + \cos^2 x)}{\cot x}$
K. $\dfrac{\cos x}{\sin x}$

STOP

If there is still time remaining, check your answers to this section.

Turn page for the Reading Test

3 3

READING TEST

35 MINUTES—40 QUESTIONS

Directions: There are four passages in this test. Each passage is followed by several questions. After reading a passage, choose the best answer to each question and fill in the corresponding oval on your answer document. You may refer to the passages as often as necessary.

Passage 1—Prose Fiction

Title: THE STORIES OF EVA LUNA
Author/Editor: Isabel Allende, translated from the Spanish by Margaret Sayers Peden
ISBN: 9780689121029 / 9780684873596 / 9780743217187
Selection: pp. 9–12 of "Two Words"—as submitted.

She went by the name of Belisa Crepusculario, not because she had been baptized with that name or given it by her mother, but because she herself had searched until she found the poetry of "beauty" and "twilight" and cloaked herself in it. She made her living selling words. She journeyed through the country from the high cold mountains to the burning coasts, stopping at fairs and in markets where she set up four poles covered by a canvas awning under which she took refuge from the sun and rain to minister to her customers. She did not have to peddle her merchandise because from having wandered far and near, everyone knew who she was. Some people waited for her from one year to the next, and when she appeared in the village with her bundle beneath her arm, they would form a line in front of her stall. Her prices were fair. For five centavos she delivered verses from memory, for seven she improved the quality of dreams, for nine she wrote love letters, for twelve she invented insults for irreconcilable enemies. She also sold stories, not fantasies but long, true stories she recited at one telling, never skipping a word.

This is how she carried news from one town to another. People paid her to add a line or two: our son was born, so-and-so died, our children got married, the crops burned in the field. Wherever she went a small crowd gathered around to listen as she began to speak. They learned about each others' doings, about distant relatives, about what was going on in the civil war. To anyone who paid her fifty centavos in trade, she gave the gift of a secret word to drive away melancholy. It was not the same word for everyone, naturally, because that would have been collective deceit. Each person received his or her own word, with the assurance that no one else would use it that way in this universe or Beyond.

Belisa Crepusculario had been born into a family so poor they did not even have names to give their children. She came into the world and grew up in an inhospitable land where some years the rains became avalanches of water that bore everything away before them and others when not a drop fell from the sky and the sun swelled to fill the horizon and the world became a desert. Until she was twelve, Belisa had no occupation or virtue other than having withstood hunger and the exhaustion of centuries. During one interminable drought, it fell to her to bury four younger brothers and sisters; when she realized that her turn was next, she decided to set out across the plains in the direction of the sea, in hopes that she might trick death along the way. The land was eroded, split with deep cracks, strewn with rocks, fossils of trees and thorny bushes, and skeletons of animals bleached by the sun.

From time to time she ran into families who, like her, were heading south, following the mirage of water. Some had begun their march carrying their belongings on their back or in small carts, but they could barely move their own bones, and after a while they had to abandon their possessions. They dragged themselves along painfully, their skin turned to lizard hide and their eyes burned by the reverberating glare. Belisa greeted them with a wave as she passed, but she did not stop, because she had no strength to waste in acts of compassion. Many people fell by the wayside, but she was so stubborn that she survived to cross through that hell and at long last reach the first trickles of water, fine, almost invisible threads that fed spindly vegetation and farther down widened into small streams and marshes.

Belisa Crepusculario saved her life and in the process accidentally discovered writing. In a village near the coast, the wind blew a page of newspaper at her feet. She picked up the brittle yellow paper and stood a long while looking at it, unable to determine its purpose, until curiosity overcame her shyness. She walked over to a man who was washing his horse in the muddy pool where she had quenched her thirst.

"What is this?" she asked.

"The sports page of the newspaper," the man replied, concealing his surprise at her ignorance. The answer astounded the girl, but she did not want to seem rude, so she merely inquired about the significance of the fly tracks scattered across the page. "Those are words, child. Here it says that Fulgencio Barba knocked out El Negro Tizano in the third round."

That was the day Belisa Crepusculario found out that words make their way in the world without a master, and that anyone with a little cleverness can appropriate them and do business with them. From that moment on, she worked at that profession, and was never tempted by any other. At the beginning, she offered her merchandise unaware that words can be written outside of newspapers. When she learned otherwise, she calculated the infinite possibilities of her trade and with her savings paid a priest twenty pesos to teach her to read and write; with her three remaining coins she bought a dictionary. She poured over it from *A* to *Z* and then threw it into the sea, because it was not her intention to defraud her customers with packaged words.

1. The main character of the passage can best be described as a (an):
   - **A.** shrewd businesswoman who becomes wealthy through her skills.
   - **B.** strong young woman who inadvertently discovers her destiny.
   - **C.** fearless explorer who sets off in search of new lands and experiences.
   - **D.** investigative journalist driven to right injustices.

2. The main purpose of the fourth paragraph (lines 52–66) is to:
   - **F.** establish that Belisa is primarily concerned about herself, rather than others.
   - **G.** demonstrate that Belisa is smarter than most of the other people from her hometown
   - **H.** acquaint the reader with the hardships Belisa saw others endure as she sought to save herself.
   - **J.** establish that the story takes place in the distant past, rather than the present day.

3. The main purpose of the last paragraph (lines 83–96) is to:
   - **A.** establish Belisa's originality in a fanciful manner.
   - **B.** contrast Belisa's approach to helping people with that of organized religion.
   - **C.** imply that early in her career Belisa was not very sensible about money.
   - **D.** demonstrate that Belisa has a very powerful memory.

4. In the passage, the exchange in lines 75–83 is most likely included to indicate that:
   - **F.** senseless violence is celebrated in Belisa's culture.
   - **G.** people are dismissive of Belisa because of her gender and age.
   - **H.** Belisa does not see in the same way that normal people do.
   - **J.** though imaginatively described, the world of this story is essentially real life.

5. Information in the passage indicates that Belisa's dream is to provide people with something:
   - **A.** useful and honest.
   - **B.** valuable but ephemeral.
   - **C.** secret and exciting.
   - **D.** false but comforting.

6. In the context of the passage, the statement in lines 1–5 most nearly means that:
   - **F.** the name Belisa goes by is not her real one.
   - **G.** Belisa never knew her real mother.
   - **H.** Belisa picked her own name based on words she liked.
   - **J.** Belisa's name has something to do with the fact that her family was not religious.

7. The passage mentions Belisa performing all of the following tasks EXCEPT:
   - **A.** carrying news.
   - **B.** exposing lies.
   - **C.** preventing sadness.
   - **D.** reciting poetry.

8. As it is used in line 44, the word *interminable* most nearly means:
   - **F.** very short.
   - **G.** unexpected.
   - **H.** illusory.
   - **J.** very long.

GO ON TO THE NEXT PAGE.

9. The passage makes clear that Belisa began working with words in order to:

   A. help her people.
   B. earn an income.
   C. discover her identity.
   D. avenge her family.

10. As it is used in line 65, the word *spindly* most nearly means:

   F. dead.
   G. thorny.
   H. very thin.
   J. poisonous.

Passage II—Social Science

This passage is adapted from the essay "The Basement Boys" by George F. Will (© 2010 George F. Will).

Current economic hardships have had what is called in constitutional law a "disparate impact:" The crisis has not afflicted everyone equally. Although women are a majority of the workforce, perhaps as many as 80 percent of jobs lost were held by men. This injury to men is particularly unfortunate because it may exacerbate, and be exacerbated by, a culture of immaturity among the many young men who are reluctant to grow up.

Increasingly, they are defecting from the meritocracy. Women now receive almost 58 percent of bachelor's degrees. This is why many colleges admit men with qualifications inferior to those of women applicants—which is one reason men have higher dropout rates. The Pew Research Center reports that 28 percent of wives between ages 30 and 44 have more education than their husbands, whereas only 19 percent of husbands in the same age group have more education than their wives. Twenty-three percent of men with some college education earn less than their wives. In law, medical, and doctoral programs, women are majorities or, if trends continue, will be.

In 1956, the median age of men marrying was 22.5. But between 1980 and 2004, the percentage of men reaching age 40 without marrying increased from 6 to 16.5. A recent study found that 55 percent of men 18 to 24 are living in their parents' homes, as are 13 percent of men 25 to 34, compared to 8 percent of women.

Mike Stivic, a.k.a. "Meathead,“ the liberal graduate student in *All in the Family*, reflected society's belief in the cultural superiority of youth, but he was a leading indicator of something else: He lived in his father-in-law Archie Bunker's home. What are today's "basement boys" doing down there? Perhaps watching *Friends* and *Seinfeld* reruns about a culture of extended youth utterly unlike the world of young adults in previous generations.

Gary Cross, a Penn State University historian, wonders, "Where have all the men gone?" His book, *Men to Boys: The Making of Modern Immaturity*, argues that "the culture of the boy-men today is less a life stage than a lifestyle." If you wonder what has become of manliness, he says, note the differences between Cary Grant and Hugh Grant, the former, dapper and debonair, the latter, a perpetually befuddled boy.

Permissive parenting, Cross says, made children less submissive, and the decline of deference coincided with the rise of consumer and media cultures celebrating the indefinite retention of the tastes and habits of childhood. The opening of careers to talented women has coincided with the attenuation of male role models in popular culture: In 1959, there were 27 Westerns on prime-time television glamorizing male responsibility.

Cross says the large-scale entry of women into the workforce made many men feel marginalized, especially when men were simultaneously bombarded by new parenting theories, which cast fathers as their children's pals, or worse: In 1945, *Parents* magazine said a father should "keep yourself huggable" but show a son the "respect" owed a "business associate." All this led to "ambiguity and confusion about what fathers were to do in the postwar home and, even more, about what it meant to grow up male."

Although Cross, an aging academic boomer, was a student leftist, he believes that 1960s radicalism became "a retreat into childish tantrums" symptomatic "of how permissive parents infantilized the boomer generation." And the boomers' children? Consider the television commercials for the restaurant chain called Dave & Buster's, which seems to be, ironically, a Chuck E. Cheese's for adults—a place for young adults, especially men, to drink beer and play electronic games and exemplify youth not as a stage of life but as a perpetual refuge from adulthood.

At the 2006 Super Bowl, the Rolling Stones sang "Satisfaction," a song older than the Super Bowl. At this year‘s game, another long-of-tooth act, the Who, continued the commerce of catering to baby boomers' limitless appetite for nostalgia. "My generation's obsession with youth and its memories," Cross writes, "stands out in the history of human vanity." Last November, when Tiger Woods's misadventures became public, his agent said: "Let's please give the kid a break." The kid was then 33. He is now 34 but, no doubt, still a kid. The puerile anthem of a current Pepsi commercial is drearily prophetic: "Forever young."

11. The main purpose of the passage is to:
   A. argue that institutions like higher education have become biased against males.
   B. address a supposed lack of maturity in contemporary males.
   C. question whether women are really smarter than men.
   D. examine the evolution of male role models in popular culture.

12. It is reasonable to infer from the passage that the author is basing many of his assertions on:
   F. data about the lifestyles of twentysomethings.
   G. psychologists' opinions on parenting.
   H. the economic successes of businesses like Dave & Buster's.
   J. TV ratings and record sales.

13. Information in the passage suggests that Gary Cross's theories conflict with the idea that:
   A. movies have gotten less popular with men over the last half-century or so.
   B. fathers are more involved in parenting now than ever before.
   C. there are more children's shows on TV now than there used to be.
   D. less strict parenting encourages people to succeed.

14. Which of the following questions is NOT directly answered by the passage?
   F. Which gender receives a majority of bachelor's degrees?
   G. What percent of women 18–24 are living in their parents' homes?
   H. Who wrote *Men to Boys: The Making of Modern Immaturity*?
   J. What percentage of men with some college education earn less than their wives?

15. According to the passage, the supposed problem that the author addresses began with:
   A. the current economic recession.
   B. TV and films of the 1970s.
   C. post-WWII parenting advice.
   D. the popular music of the 1960s.

16. Which of the following best summarizes the fourth paragraph (lines 27–34)?
   F. Youth culture was more celebrated in the 1970s than it is now.
   G. TV both reflects and reinforces a cult of perpetual adolescence.
   H. Popular TV shows have changed very little in the last 40 years.
   J. Offspring who still live at home should not be unsupervised, no matter their age.

17. The passage makes specific reference to all of the following professions EXCEPT:
   A. historian.
   B. actor.
   C. writer.
   D. professional athlete.

18. It is most reasonable to assume that Gary Cross views the behavior of his generation as a (an):
   F. immature attempt to regain the past.
   G. method for forgetting the difficulties of childhood.
   H. obsession to become superstars of their generation.
   J. desire to start a successful business in this economy.

19. As it is used in line 48, the word *attenuation* most nearly means:
   A. weakening.
   B. popularity.
   C. openness.
   D. tradition.

20. According to the passage, the choice of recent Super Bowl halftime acts reflects:
   F. bias against female musicians.
   G. fear of controversy.
   H. a desire to please the greatest possible number of viewers.
   J. an unhealthy obsession with youth.

GO ON TO THE NEXT PAGE.

Passage III—Humanities

This passage is adapted from the essay "Can Poetry Matter?" by Dana Gioia (© 1991 by Dana Gioia).

American poetry now belongs to a subculture. No longer part of the mainstream of artistic and intellectual life, it has become the specialized occupation of a relatively small and isolated group. Little of the frenetic activity it generates ever reaches outside that closed group. As a class poets are not without cultural status. Like priests in a town of agnostics, they still command a certain residual prestige. But as individual artists they are almost invisible.

What makes the situation of contemporary poets particularly surprising is that it comes at a moment of unprecedented expansion for the art. There have never before been so many new books of poetry published, so many anthologies or literary magazines. Never has it been so easy to earn a living as a poet. There are now several thousand college-level jobs in teaching creative writing, and many more at the primary and secondary levels. One also finds a complex network of public subvention for poets, funded by federal, state, and local agencies, augmented by private support in the form of foundation fellowships, prizes, and subsidized retreats. There has also never before been so much published criticism about contemporary poetry; it fills dozens of literary newsletters and scholarly journals.

The proliferation of new poetry and poetry programs is astounding by any historical measure. Just under a thousand new collections of verse are published each year, in addition to a myriad of new poems printed in magazines both small and large. No one knows how many poetry readings take place each year, but surely the total must run into the tens of thousands. And there are now about 200 graduate creative-writing programs in the United States, and more than a thousand undergraduate ones. With an average of ten poetry students in each graduate section, these programs alone will produce about 20,000 accredited professional poets over the next decade. From such statistics an observer might easily conclude that we live in the golden age of American poetry.

But the poetry boom has been a distressingly confined phenomenon. Decades of public and private funding have created a large professional class for the production and reception of new poetry comprising legions of teachers, graduate students, editors, publishers, and administrators. Based mostly in universities, these groups have gradually become the primary audience for contemporary verse.

Consequently, the energy of American poetry, which was once directed outward, is now increasingly focused inward. Reputations are made and rewards distributed within the poetry subculture. A "famous" poet now means someone famous only to other poets. But there are enough poets to make that local fame relatively meaningful. Not long ago, "only poets read poetry" was meant as damning criticism. Now it is a proven marketing strategy.

Over the past half century, as American poetry's specialist audience has steadily expanded, its general readership has declined. Moreover, the engines that have driven poetry's institutional success—the explosion of academic writing programs, the proliferation of subsidized magazines and presses, the emergence of a creative-writing career track, and the migration of American literary culture to the university—have unwittingly contributed to its disappearance from public view.

To the average reader, the proposition that poetry's audience has declined may seem self-evident. It is symptomatic of the art's current isolation that within the subculture such notions are often rejected. Poetry boosters offer impressive recitations of the numerical growth of publications, programs, and professorships. Given the bullish statistics on poetry's material expansion, how does one demonstrate that its intellectual and spiritual influence has eroded? One cannot easily marshal numbers, but to any candid observer the evidence throughout the world of ideas and letters seems inescapable.

One can see a microcosm of poetry's current position by studying its coverage in *The New York Times*. Virtually never reviewed in the daily edition, new poetry is intermittently discussed in the Sunday *Book Review*, but almost always in group reviews where three books are briefly considered together. Whereas a new novel or biography is reviewed on or around its publication date, a new collection by an important poet might wait up to a year for a notice. Or it might never be reviewed at all.

Poetry reviewing is no better anywhere else, and generally it is much worse. *The New York Times* only reflects the opinion that although there is a great deal of poetry around, none of it matters very much to readers, publishers, or advertisers—to anyone, that is, except other poets. For most newspapers and magazines, poetry has become a literary commodity intended less to be read than to be noted with approval. Most editors run poems and poetry reviews the way a prosperous Montana rancher might keep a few buffalo around—not to eat the endangered creatures but to display them for tradition's sake.

21. Which of the following quotations best expresses the main idea of the piece?

A. "As a class poets are not without cultural status." (line 6)
B. "Never has it been so easy to earn a living as a poet." (lines 14–15)
C. "From such statistics an observer might easily conclude that we live in the golden age of American poetry." (lines 37–38)
D. "Consequently, the energy of American poetry, which was once directed outward, is now increasingly focused inward." (lines 47–49)

22. It can most reasonably be inferred that the narrator makes mention of all the energy and institutions devoted to poetry in order to:

F. heighten the irony of the fact that no one reads it except other poets.
G. prevent accusations that he is arguing for increased government funding.
H. prove that all the alarmism is unwarranted.
J. establish that poetry could only have advanced to this degree in a capitalist society.

23. It can reasonably be inferred that the writer's biggest disagreement is with the:

A. "accredited professional poets" in line 36.
B. "average reader" in line 64.
C. "poetry boosters" in line 67.
D. editors of *The New York Times*.

24. The writer's statement in lines 57–63 most nearly means that he feels poetry:

F. has become too mechanical.
G. has alienated itself from the people.
H. is the domain of the overeducated.
J. requires far too much funding to be useful.

25. As it is used in line 8, the word *residual* most nearly means:

A. phony.
B. obligatory.
C. comical.
D. leftover.

26. As it is used in line 54, the phrase *proven marketing strategy* most nearly means:

F. something poets have accepted and allowed to influence their writing.
G. a way to make money that many poets have discovered.
H. something that is unnecessarily pitting poets against one another.
J. the best way the author can think of to promote poetry to a general readership.

27. The writer implies that those operating within the machinery of academia:

A. have deliberately caused poetry's decline.
B. are in denial about poetry's decline.
C. are employing outdated methods of bringing poetry to the people.
D. do not trust the people to appreciate poetry.

28. The metaphor in lines 91–94 is intended to support the idea that many editors view poetry as something that:

F. needs to be preserved as a link to America's literary past.
G. cannot be interfered with, since so few people write it anymore.
H. lends an air of authenticity by its presence, but is practically useless.
J. will be stronger as an industry in a decade's time than it is now.

29. When the writer states "Never has it been so easy to earn a living as a poet" (lines 14–15), he most likely means a living that would take the form of:

A. living off of royalties.
B. writing far more criticism than poetry.
C. making money off of other poets.
D. using poetry as a springboard to a professorship.

30. That narrator implies that poetry has suffered because the work many contemporary poets produce is motivated by a desire for:

F. money.
G. professional advancement.
H. fame.
J. shock value.

Passage IV–Natural Science

This passage is adapted from "Feces, Bite Marks Flesh Out Giant Dino-Eating Crocs" by Brian Handwekr (© 2010 *National Geographic*).

Rock-hard feces and oddly bitten bones are helping to flesh out one of the biggest crocs of prehistory. As long as a stretch limo, *Deinosuchus*—"terrible crocodile"—likely prowled shallow waters and hunted dinosaurs its own size, the evidence suggests. Paleontologists announced their conclusions after analyzing pieces of 79-million-year-old fossilized dung, or coprolites, that appear to be the first known droppings from *Deinosuchus.* The discoveries offer the newest insights into the lives of the giant crocs, which roamed much of what is now the United States and northern Mexico.

Sand and shell fragments in the droppings, found within the last few years near a Georgia stream, suggest the croc preferred estuaries, where, at least in Georgia—home to a great concentration of *Deinosuchus* remains—it probably dined mostly on sea turtles. Despite the Georgia *Deinosuchus*'s relatively docile prey, "we're pretty sure it was the apex predator in this region," said Samantha Harrell of Columbus State University in Georgia, who presented her research March 17 at a Geological Society of America meeting in Baltimore.

The team also found a fossilized shark tooth embedded in the outside of a coprolite. But because the tooth bears no signs of having been digested, the team suspects a shark left the tooth behind when scavenging on *Deinosuchus* droppings. What the researchers *didn't* find in the feces are bone or other bits of undigested animals. "That's actually good," Harrell said, "because both modern and ancient crocs have digestive juices that eat up bone, horns, teeth, and just about everything else"—so the "empty" dung supports the idea that the feces are from a croc.

Outside Georgia, *Deinosuchus* apparently took on slightly more challenging prey, according to older bite-mark evidence, which Columbus State paleontologist David R. Schwimmer presented alongside Harrell at the meeting. *Deinosuchus* tooth impressions in the bones of their prey tell the tale of titanic battles in which the 29-foot crocs took down dinosaurs their own size—including the *T. rex* relatives *Appalachiosaurus montgomeriensis* and *Albertosaurus.*

"One of the marks shows signs that the bone was healed, which means that the animal survived the bite," Schwimmer said. "That proves that at least this one specimen was obviously a predator and not scavenging." Schwimmer first noticed strange, dimpled, egg-shaped indentations in Georgia sea turtle fossils. Later he saw similar marks in dinosaur bones in Big Bend National Park in Texas and in the New Jersey State Museum. "I realized these bites were from something with really powerful jaws and lots of teeth," he said. "And it was pretty obvious that this big, blunt-toothed croc was the source. There was nothing else I've found that could create blunt bite marks like these."

Tooth marks, though, can show us only part of the picture, said Stephanie Drumheller, an expert on ancient crocodile bites. "Modern crocodilians"—crocodiles, alligators, and related extinct forms—"are more than capable of swallowing smaller prey whole and disarticulating larger animals into bite-sized pieces," leaving little evidence behind, said Drumheller, a Ph.D. candidate in geoscience at the University of Iowa. "We can infer that a giant like *Deinosuchus* would be capable of even more destructive feeding behaviors."

The bite-mark evidence that does exist, though, raises a question: Why would a croc capable of taking down big, meaty dinosaurs waste its energy on turtles? In a word: location. Modern crocs, which hunt a wide range of prey, eat whatever's available in their areas. The same factor may have determined whether *Deinosuchus* individuals feasted largely on turtles or dinosaurs or other prey, Drumheller said.

North America-born *Deinosuchus* also underscores that giant crocs arose at different places and times, said University of Chicago paleontologist Paul Sereno, who discovered 110-million-year-old *Sarcosuchus imperator*—aka SuperCroc—in Niger. "In *Deinosuchus,* and independently in SuperCroc, we have two lineages, one older than the other, that prove crocodile bodies grew to a gargantuan size—to dinosaur size," said Sereno, a National Geographic Society explorer-in-residence.

Deinosuchus, which lived just before the close of the Cretaceous period, is more closely related to modern croc lineages than SuperCroc—yet still faded to extinction. What happened to these prehistoric leviathans? A fully grown giant male croc likely would have had to commandeer miles of river territory to regularly find enough prey to sustain itself, Sereno explained. So space constraints likely kept population numbers low—making the giant crocs vulnerable to extinction in tough times. "It appears that every once in a while the right conditions arise for giant crocs," Sereno said. "But they usually don't last."

31. The main idea of the passage is that:

    A. giant crocodiles probably still exist.
    B. ancient giant crocodiles hunted dinosaurs.
    C. dinosaurs were actually a type of crocodile.
    D. all crocodiles will eventually go extinct.

32. Which of the following phrases most accurately describes how crocodilian feeding habits are described in the passage?

    F. Destructive but mindless
    G. Uniform and predatory
    H. Voracious but cowardly
    J. Varied and opportunistic

33. The passage most strongly supports which of the following inferences about crocodilian size?

    A. Crocodilians tend to grow as large as conditions permit them to.
    B. Freshwater crocodilians are able to grow larger than saltwater ones.
    C. Crocodilians always grow large enough to ensure that they are the local apex predator.
    D. It will never again be possible for crododilians to grow as large as *Deinosuchus.*

34. Which of the following is NOT mentioned in the passage as a habitat of *Deinosuchus*?

    F. Georgia
    G. Mexico
    H. Niger
    J. Texas

35. The main purpose of the third paragraph (lines 22–32) is to:

    A. argue that ancient crocodiles preyed on sharks.
    B. argue that sharks preyed on ancient crocodiles.
    C. establish that the dung in question is crocodilian in origin.
    D. suggest that *Deinosuchus* may not always have been carnivorous.

36. According to the passage, one major similarity between *Deinosuchus* and modern crocodilians is their:

    F. teeth.
    G. diet.
    H. range.
    J. digestive processes.

37. As it is used in line 78, the word *lineages* most nearly means:

    A. habits.
    B. bloodlines.
    C. behaviors.
    D. imitators.

38. According to the passage, the best evidence that *Deinosuchus* preyed on dinosaurs was obtained from:

    F. bones.
    G. dung.
    H. teeth.
    J. eggs.

39. Based on the passage, it can reasonably be inferred that a crocodilian species whose main food source dries up will:

    A. immediately starve to extinction.
    B. begin eating something else.
    C. decrease in size.
    D. decrease its range.

40. Based on the passage, the existence of giant crocodilians can best be described as:

    F. ideal.
    G. unavoidable.
    H. destructive.
    J. anomalous.

STOP

If there is still time remaining, check your answers to this section.

SCIENCE TEST

35 MINUTES—40 QUESTIONS

Directions: There are seven passages in this test. Each passage is followed by several questions. After reading a passage, choose the best answer to each question and fill in the corresponding oval on your answer document. You may refer to the passages as often as necessary.

You are NOT permitted to use a calculator on this test.

Passage I

Friction is the force that resists movement when two surfaces are in contact and is represented by F_f. The *coefficient of friction* (COF, symbolized by μ) is a quantity used to measure the force of friction based on the normal force (F_N). There are two COF's for a given surface-to-surface contact: static COF (μ_s) and kinetic COF (μ_k). μ_s is used for objects at rest and μ_k is used for objects in motion. The normal force is an upward force, perpendicular to the surface the object is either resting on or moving on.

The basic equation for calculating the coefficient of friction is:

$$\mu = \frac{F_f}{F_N}.$$

Figure 1 is a diagram of a block resting on an inclined plane. The forces shown are defined above. F_G represents the force of gravity.

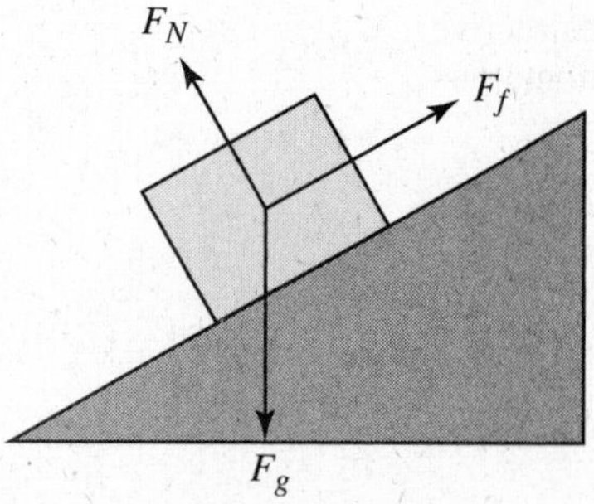

Figure 1

Scientists performed an experiment using several different materials to determine μ_s and μ_k for each pair of materials. Figures 2 and 3 show the results.

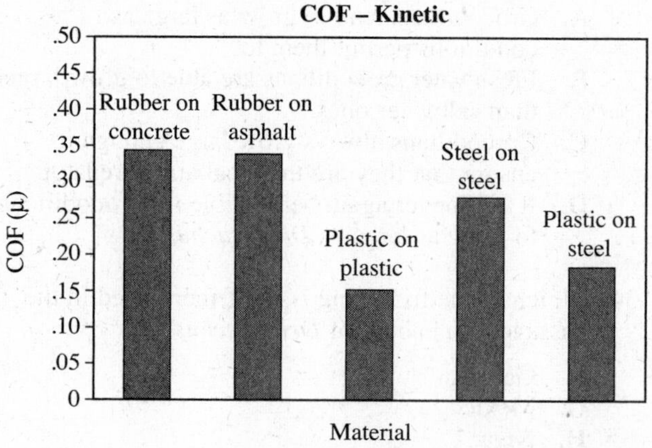

Figure 2

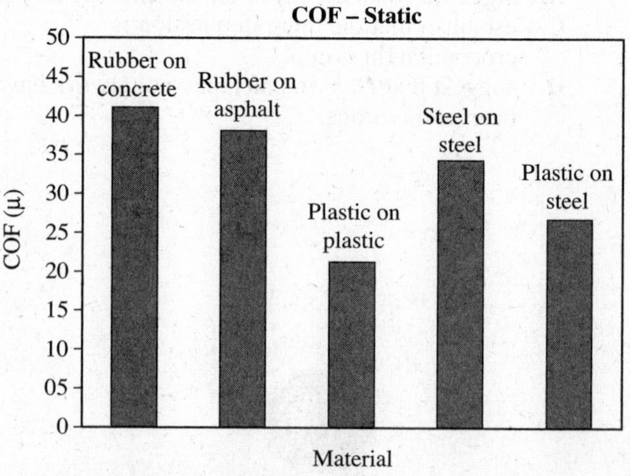

Figure 3

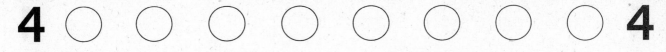

4 ○ ○ ○ ○ ○ ○ ○ ○ 4

1. Based on the results of the experiment, which combination of materials has the largest static COF?

   A. Plastic on plastic
   B. Plastic on steel
   C. Rubber on concrete
   D. Rubber on asphalt

2. A comparison of the COFs given in Figure 2 shows that, relative to the COF for rubber on concrete, the COF for plastic on plastic is approximately:

   F. 1/100 as high.
   G. 1/2 as high.
   H. 2 times as high.
   J. 10 times as high.

3. Which of the following ranks the materials used in the experiment from lowest static COF to highest static COF?

   A. Plastic on plastic, steel on steel, plastic on steel, rubber on asphalt, rubber on concrete
   B. Rubber on concrete, rubber on asphalt, steel on steel, plastic on steel, plastic on plastic
   C. Plastic on steel, plastic on plastic, rubber on asphalt, rubber on concrete, steel on steel
   D. Plastic on plastic, plastic on steel, steel on steel, rubber on asphalt, rubber on concrete

4. A student theorized that the higher the static COF for a material, the higher the kinetic COF would be. Do the results of the experiment support this theory?

   F. Yes. The materials with the highest static COF also had the highest kinetic COF.
   G. Yes. Plastic on steel had both the highest static COF and the highest kinetic COF.
   H. No. Plastic on plastic had both the lowest static COF and the lowest kinetic COF.
   J. No. There is no relationship between static COF and kinetic COF for any of the materials.

5. According to Figures 1, 2, and 3, which block would most likely slide down the incline the fastest?

   A. A steel block on a steel incline
   B. A plastic block on a plastic incline
   C. A rubber block on a concrete incline
   D. A plastic block on a steel incline

GO ON TO THE NEXT PAGE.

Passage II

The main source of the world's energy for the last century has been fossil fuels. To use fossil fuels, we must be able to locate and recover them at affordable costs, convert them to usable forms, and use them without wasting them or harming the environment.

Experiment 1

Scientists set out to determine the energy potential of various fossil fuels. They burned 1 ton of each of 5 different fuel varieties, and measured the energy produced. Table 1 shows the energy content of various fossil fuels.

Table 1

Fuel	Energy Content (Btu/Ton)
Coal	25,000,000
Crude oil	37,000,000
Gasoline	38,000,000
Natural gas	47,000,000
Peat	3,500,000

Experiment 2

Students completed an experiment to measure the heat energy obtained from natural gas, using water, a Fahrenheit thermometer, and a Bunsen burner (see Figure 1). They filled a beaker with enough water to weigh 1 pound (approximately 450 mL). They recorded the temperature of the water, then lit the Bunsen burner and stirred the water continuously. They took several measurements of the water's temperature, at 5-minute intervals. The results of the experiment are displayed in Table 2.

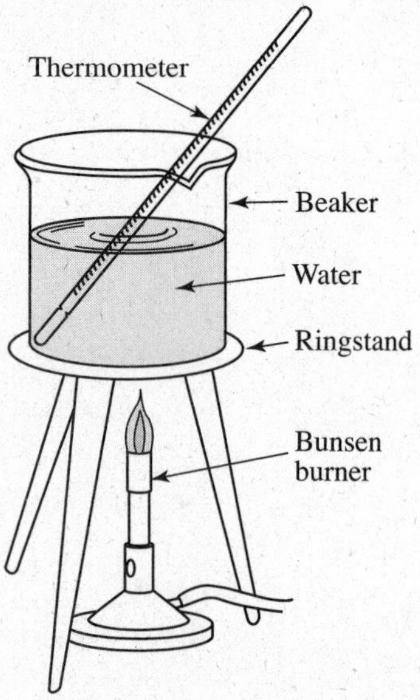

Figure 1

Table 2

Time (m)	Water Temperature (°F)
0	67°
5	92°
10	117°
15	142°

Each type of fossil fuel releases a different amount of energy. This energy is measured in a variety of units. Table 3 provides a conversion chart for energy units.

Table 3

1 Btu =	.252 kilocalorie .000293 kilowatt-hour
1 kilocalorie =	3.97 Btus .0012 kilowatt-hour
1 kilowatt-hour =	3,413 Btus 860 kilocalories
1 barrel of oil =	5,600,000 Btus 1,410,579 kilocalories 1,640.8 kilowatt-hours

4 ○ ○ ○ ○ ○ ○ ○ ○ 4

6. According to the results of Experiment 1, which of the following ranks the different types of fossil fuels in order of energy potential, from the most Btus/ton to the least?

   F. Peat, coal, crude oil, gasoline, natural gas
   G. Natural gas, gasoline, crude oil, coal, peat
   H. Gasoline, crude oil, peat, coal, natural gas
   J. Natural gas, crude oil, peat, gasoline, coal

7. If 1 Btu is the amount of heat needed to raise the temperature of 1 pound of water 1° Fahrenheit, then how many Btus of natural gas were used during the first 5 minutes of Experiment 2?

   A. 92
   B. 67
   C. 50
   D. 25

8. The main purpose of Experiment 2 was to:

   F. determine the amount of energy natural gas creates.
   G. compare various fossil fuels to see which one produces the most energy.
   H. see how long it would take to heat water to 100° F.
   J. calculate how much water is necessary to burn 25 Btus of natural gas.

9. If Experiment 2 had been repeated using gasoline to heat the water instead of natural gas, the temperature of the water after 10 minutes would most likely have been closest to which of the following?

   A. 40° F
   B. 99° F
   C. 117° F
   D. 180° F

10. According to the data in Table 3, which unit of energy is equivalent to the most Btus?

    F. 1 kilowatt-hour
    G. 1 kilocalorie
    H. 1 barrel of oil
    J. 10,000 Btus

11. Based on the results of Experiment 2, if temperature had continued to be measured for 5 more minutes, what would the temperature of the water have most likely been at the next measurement?

    A. 85° F
    B. 142° F
    C. 167° F
    D. 200° F

GO ON TO THE NEXT PAGE.

Passage III

The growth of tumor cells in a culture depends on the amount of nutrients in the culture. Cell production can be determined by counting the number of cells. The effects of various concentrations of glucose and calcium on the growth of three different cell types were tested. Each culture dish began the test with 0.5 million cells, to which was added a solution containing known concentrations of either glucose or calcium. The results after three days are shown in Figures 1 and 2.

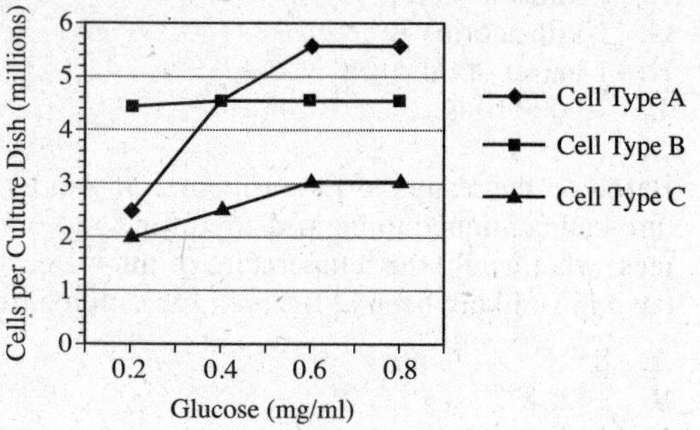

Figure 1

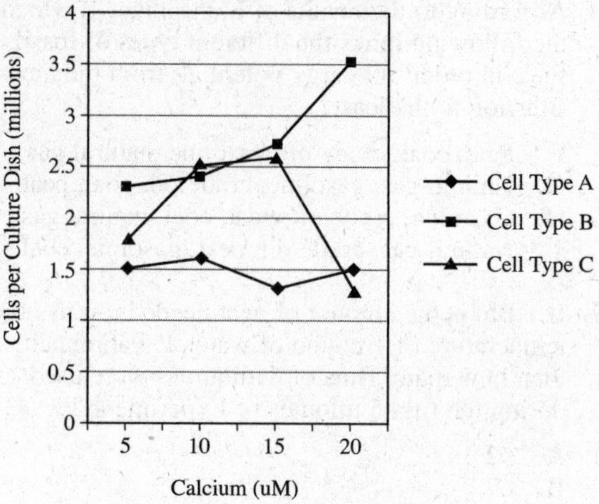

Figure 2

4 ○ ○ ○ ○ ○ ○ ○ ○ 4

12. Which of the following variables is represented by the *y*-axis of the graphs?
    - **F.** The number of cells per culture dish after three days
    - **G.** The concentration of glucose or calcium present in the solution after three days
    - **H.** The number of cells added to each culture dish on the first day
    - **J.** The concentration of glucose or calcium present in the solution on the first day

13. According to Figure 1, which cell type(s) produced the largest number of cells with a glucose concentration of 0.4 mg/ml?
    - **A.** Cell type A
    - **B.** Cell type B
    - **C.** Both cell types A and C
    - **D.** Both cell types A and B

14. Based on the trends in Figure 2, which of the following statements about cell behavior could you predict if 25 uM of calcium were introduced?
    - **F.** Cell type B would produce around 4 million cells.
    - **G.** Cell type A would produce around 2 million cells.
    - **H.** Cell type C would produce around 2.5 million cells.
    - **J.** Cell type C would produce around 0 million cells.

15. Based on the information in Figures 1 and 2, one would predict that the growth of cell type A would be greater than that of cell type C in solutions containing all of the following EXCEPT:
    - **A.** 0.2 mg/ml of glucose and 20 uM of calcium.
    - **B.** 0.2 mg/ml of glucose and 15 uM of calcium.
    - **C.** 0.4 mg/ml of glucose and 20 uM of calcium.
    - **D.** 0.6 mg/ml of glucose and 20 uM of calcium.

16. Based on the data in Figures 1 and 2, what can be concluded about the effectiveness of using glucose versus calcium to stimulate cell growth?
    - **F.** In all cell types, calcium is more effective than glucose at stimulating cell growth.
    - **G.** In all cell types, glucose is more effective than calcium at stimulating cell growth.
    - **H.** Calcium is more effective than glucose at stimulating cell growth in cell type B.
    - **J.** Glucose is more effective than calcium at stimulating cell growth in cell types A and C.

Passage IV

A science class studied the pH strength of acids and bases. The terms *strong* and *weak* indicate the ability of acid and base solutions to conduct electricity. Figure 1 displays the pH scale used to rank solutions as acidic or basic, and Table 1 provides an overview of what pH levels are considered *strong* and *weak* solutions.

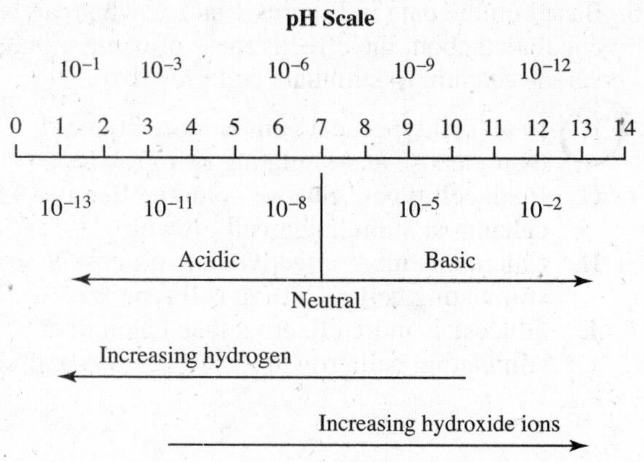

Figure 1

Table 1

Solution	pH
Strong acid	0–3
Weak acid	4–6
Neutral	7
Weak base	8–10
Strong base	11–14

Experiment 1

Students conducted an experiment to determine the conductivity of acid and base solutions, using a light bulb apparatus (see Figure 2). The light bulb circuit was incomplete. If the circuit is completed by a solution containing a large number of ions, the light bulb will glow brightly, indicating a strong ability to conduct electricity. If the circuit is completed by a solution containing a large number of molecules and either no ions or few ions, the solution does not conduct electricity or conducts it very weakly. Students tested the conductivity of several solutions; the results are reported in Table 2.

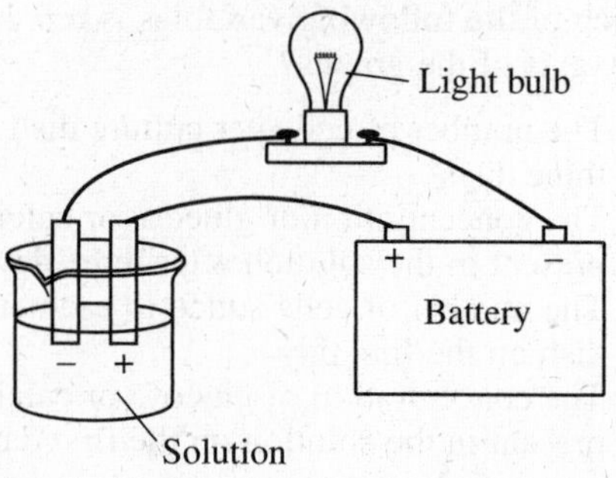

Figure 2

Table 2

Solution	Acid or Base	Light Bulb
H_2O	Neutral	No light
HCl	Acid	Bright
$HC_2H_3O_2$	Acid	Dim
H_2SO_4	Acid	Bright
H_2CO_3	Acid	Dim
NaOH	Base	Bright
KOH	Base	Bright
NH_4OH	Base	Dim

Experiment 2

Students mixed 50 mL of each chemical with 1 liter of water and then tested the pH of the solution. Table 3 displays the pH found for each chemical.

Table 3

Chemical	pH
HCl	0.86
$HC_2H_3O_2$	2.92
H_2SO_4	1.29
H_2CO_3	3.73
NaOH	13.1
KOH	11.2
NH_4OH	9.2

17. Based on the information presented in Figure 1 and Table 1, a solution with which pH would be the strongest base?

    A. 12.5
    B. 9.7
    C. 7
    D. 0.2

18. According to the results of Experiments 1 and 2, which of the following is true?

    F. The weaker the acid or base, the brighter the light bulb glowed.
    G. The lower the pH of the solution, the brighter the light bulb glowed.
    H. The stronger the acid or base, the brighter the light bulb glowed.
    J. The higher the pH of the solution, the brighter the light bulb glowed.

19. Based on the results of Experiment 2, KOH would be classified as:

    A. a strong acid.
    B. neutral.
    C. a strong base.
    D. a weak base.

20. According to the information presented in Figure 1 and Table 3, it can be concluded that which of the following acids contains the most hydrogen?

    F. H_2CO_3
    G. H_2SO_4
    H. $HC_2H_3O_2$
    J. HCl

21. Suppose the students decided to test the conductivity of an additional solution according to the procedures outlined in Experiment 1. They tested a solution of NaOCl, and they found that the solution caused the light bulb to glow brightly.
    The students would be correct in classifying the NaOCl solution as which of the following?

    A. A strong base
    B. A weak base
    C. A weak acid
    D. Cannot be determined from the given information

22. Based on Table 3, which of the following figures best represents the pH values for the 3 bases tested?

    F.

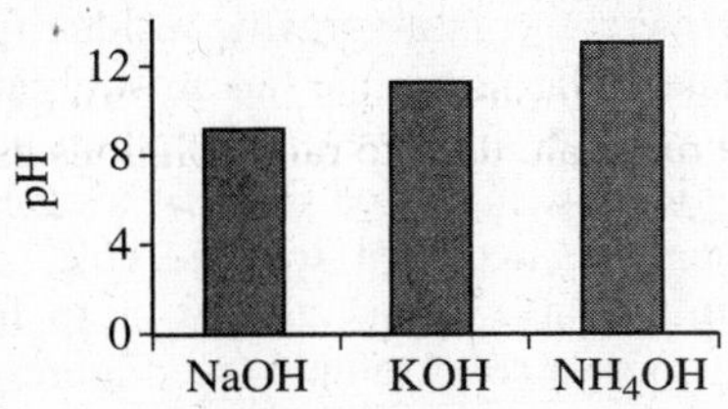

    G.

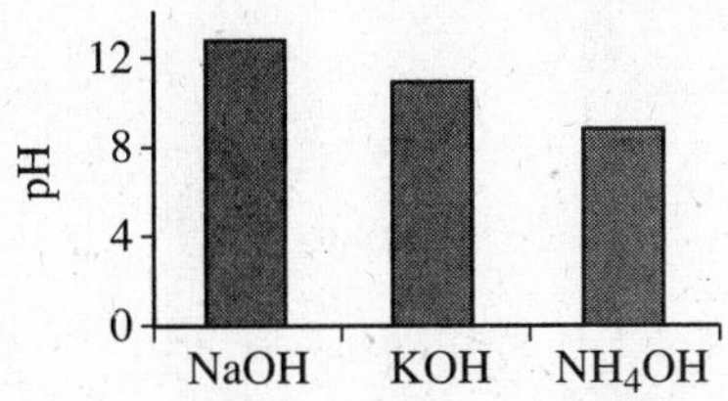

    H.

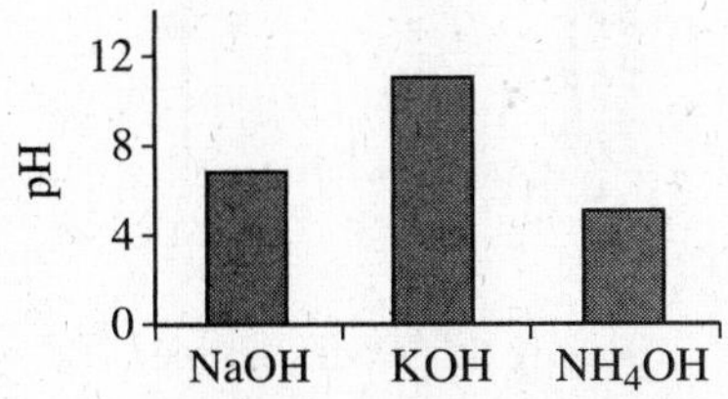

    J.

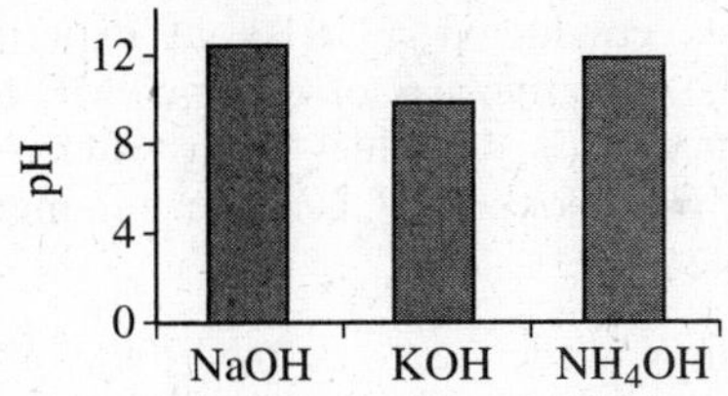

Passage V

Solid-phase microextraction (SPME) is a new technique for extracting volatile organic residue from sediment and water. The technique has several advantages (fast, simple, precise, sensitive), and requires no solvent. For this technique, a thin fused silica fiber coated with a stationary phase is exposed to a sample, either by immersion in a water or air sample or to headspace above an aqueous or solid sample (see Figure 1).

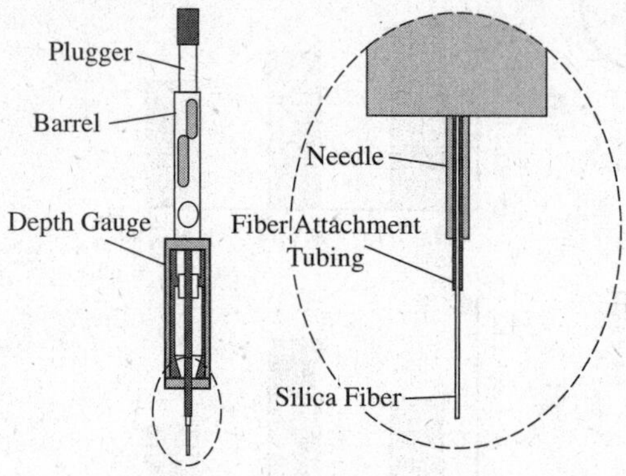

Figure 1: SPME device

Scientists conducted a series of experiments to determine the effectiveness of using SPME to extract white phosphorus (P_4) residues from water. All of the experiments were done using headspace immersion.

Experiment 1

To see how consistent SPME was, scientists conducted five trials using four different types of water (reagent grade, well, pond, salt marsh) at an aqueous concentration of 0.14 μg/L. Table 1 displays the results.

Table 1

	White Phosphorus Mass (pg)			
Trial	**Reagent**	**Well**	**Pond**	**Salt Marsh**
1	31.8	36.5	41.3	39.6
2	35.8	39.1	31.5	32.1
3	37.6	32.9	36.7	33.1
4	32.9	36.2	36.6	34.3
5	32.3	34.1	35.6	36.8
Mean	34.1	35.8	36.3	35.2

Experiment 2

Scientists varied the aqueous concentration and tested four different types of water using SPME, to see the effect on the mass of P_4 that could be extracted (see Figure 2).

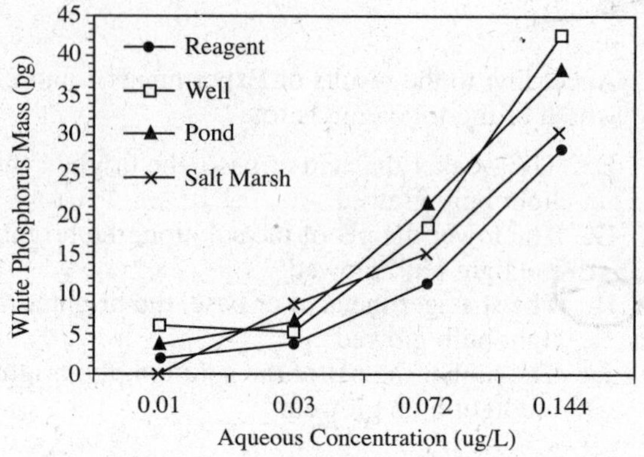

Figure 2

Experiment 3

To see if sonication had any effect on the results of SPME, scientists ran four trials, using four identical aqueous samples, at a concentration of 0.14 μg/L. The samples were analyzed using SPME by three methods: five minutes of sonication, ten minutes of sonication, and five minutes static. Table 2 displays the results.

Table 2

	White Phosphorus Mass (pg)		
Trial	**5-Min Sonic**	**10-Min Sonic**	**5-Min Static**
1	30.3	32.7	29.1
2	36.8	34.5	31.5
3	36.8	35.1	30.8
4	31.2	33.6	31.0

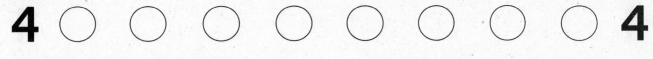

4 ○ ○ ○ ○ ○ ○ ○ ○ 4

23. According to Figure 2, as the aqueous concentration increased in the test done using salt marsh water, the white phosphorus mass:

    A. decreased, and then increased.
    B. increased and then decreased.
    C. increased.
    D. decreased.

24. Based on the results from Experiment 3, which trial resulted in the smallest amount of white phosphorus being extracted?

    F. Trial 2 after 5-minutes sonication
    G. Trial 3 after 5-minutes static
    H. Trial 1 after 5-minutes static
    J. Trial 4 after 10-minutes sonication

25. In order for the scientists to conduct these experiments, it was crucial for them to expose which part of the SPME device to the headspace above the water samples?

    A. The plugger
    B. The needle
    C. The barrel
    D. The silica fiber

26. A scientist theorized that more white phosphorus would be extracted from a sample if it were exposed to a longer period of sonication. Do the results from Experiment 3 support this theory?

    F. Yes, because in every trial more white phosphorus was extracted after 10-minutes sonication than after 5-minutes sonication.
    G. Yes, because in every trial more white phosphorus was extracted after 5-minutes sonication than after 5-minutes static.
    H. No, because in Trials 2 and 3 more white phosphorus was extracted after 5-minutes sonication than after 10-minutes sonication.
    J. No, because in all trials more white phosphorus was extracted after 5-minutes static than after 5-minutes sonication.

27. According to Table 1 the mean results demonstrate that the greatest amount of white phosphorus can be extracted from which type of water?

    A. Reagent
    B. Well
    C. Pond
    D. Salt marsh

28. Based on the results of Experiment 2, if SPME extraction was used on pond water with an aqueous concentration of 0.2 μg/L, it can be inferred that the amount of white phosphorus extracted would be closest to:

    F. 45 pg.
    G. 100 pg.
    H. 30 pg.
    J. 5 pg.

Passage VI

The melting point of a substance is the temperature at which the solid phase transitions to the liquid phase. When a substance melts, the attractive forces holding the molecules together are reduced sufficiently to allow the molecules to flow. The stronger the intermolecular forces in solid form, the higher the melting point will be.

The boiling point of a substance is the temperature at which the vapor pressure in the liquid phase equals the atmospheric temperature of its surroundings. When a substance boils, the substance transitions from a liquid phase to a gaseous phase and the intermolecular forces are completely severed. The stronger the attractive forces between the molecules in the liquid phase, the higher the boiling point will be.

Table 1 and Figure 1 show details of some of the elements from the third row of the periodic table.

Table 1

Classification	Name	# of Protons in Nucleus	Symbol
Metal	sodium	11	Na
	magnesium	12	Mg
	aluminum	13	Al
Semiconductor	silicon	14	Si
Nonmetal	phosphorus	15	P
	sulfur	16	S
	chlorine	17	Cl

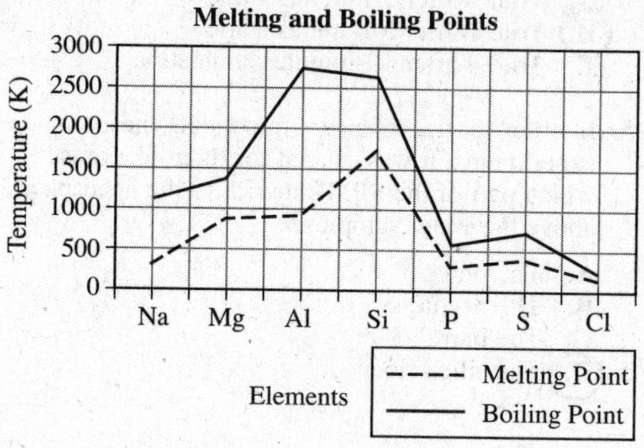

Figure 1

29. The melting point of silicon is closest to which temperature?

A. 700 K
B. 1200 K
C. 1700 K
D. 2200 K

30. Based on Table 1 and Figure 1, what can be concluded about the relationship between the number of protons in the nucleus and the attractive forces between molecules?

F. As the number of protons increase, the intermolecular forces increase.
G. As the number of protons increase, the intermolecular forces decrease.
H. As the number of protons increase, the intermolecular forces are unchanged.
J. There is no relationship between the number of protons and the intermolecular forces.

31. Based on Figure 1, what is the relationship between melting point (*MP*) and boiling point (*BP*)?

A. There is a direct relationship between melting point and boiling point and the constant of variation is roughly 2. The equation would be $MP \approx 2 \bullet (BP)$.
B. There is a direct relationship between melting point and boiling point and the constant of variation is roughly $\frac{1}{2}$. The equation would be $MP \approx \frac{1}{2} \bullet (BP)$.
C. There is an inverse relationship between melting point and boiling point and the constant of variation is roughly $1.5 \bullet 10^6$. The equation would be $(BP) \approx 1.5 \bullet 10^6$.
D. There is a direct relationship between melting point and boiling point but no constant of variation exists. When melting point increases, boiling point also increases but every element has a different numerical relationship.

32. Which element transitions from a liquid phase to a gaseous phase at 500 K?

F. P
G. Al
H. Mg
J. Na

33. Do Figure 1 and Table 1 support the conclusion that nonmetals have melting points and boiling points that are closer in temperature than the metals?

A. Yes. Phosphorus, sulfur, and chlorine all have melting points and boiling points that are less than 500 K apart. Sodium, magnesium, and aluminum have boiling points that are 500 K or more apart.
B. Yes. Phosphorus, sulfur, and chlorine all have melting points and boiling points that are less than 1000 K apart. Sodium, magnesium, and aluminum have boiling points that are more than 1000 K apart.
C. No. Silicon's melting point is 1000 K less than its boiling point. Magnesium's melting point is 500 K less than its boiling point.
D. No. There is no general relationship between melting points and boiling points and an element's classification as a metal or a nonmetal.

Passage VII

From 1971 to 2006, there was a dramatic reduction in the number of feral honeybees in the United States, and a significant, though somewhat gradual, decline in the number of colonies maintained by beekeepers. In early 2007 the rate of attrition reached new proportions, and the term *Colony Collapse Disorder (CCD)* was coined to describe this sudden decline. CCD is said to have occurred when a bee colony abruptly disappears, with little or no build-up of dead bees in or around the colonies. The cause or causes of the syndrome are not yet well understood. Proposed causes include environmental change-related stress, malnutrition, disease, and pests.

Study 1

In an attempt to quantify the degree and extent of losses experienced in the United States, scientists tracked beekeeping operations with various numbers of colonies between September 2006 and March 2007. For the sake of this study, a colony has encountered CCD when it loses at least 90% of its population in a period of 30 days. This loss must be accompanied by little or no trace of dead bees in or around the hive. Figure 1 displays the total losses experienced by all beekeeping operations.

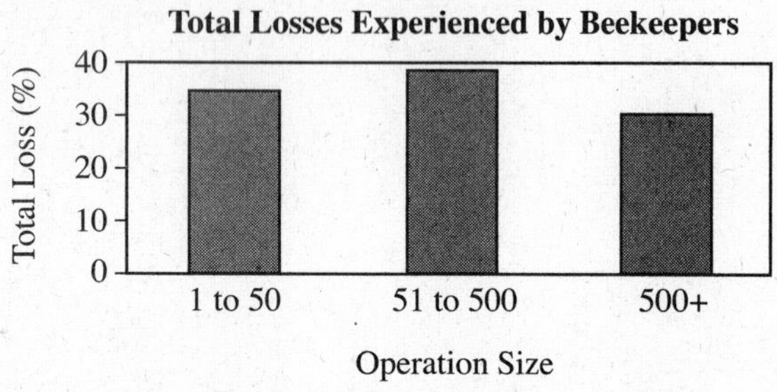

Figure 1

Study 2

Scientists studying CCD surveyed beekeepers whose hives have been affected by the disorder. The beekeepers were asked what they believe caused the CCD in their colonies. Table 1 displays the five most commonly suspected causes of CCD losses and the average percentage of loss experienced by operations of varying sizes due to each suspected cause. The scientists then surveyed beekeepers whose hives had collapsed for reasons unrelated to CCD, asking them the same question. Figure 2 compares the results from the scientists' two surveys, displaying the total loss experienced due to suspected causes of CCD and non-CCD losses, averaged for operations of all sizes.

Table 1

	Size		
Cause	**1 to 50**	**51 to 500**	**500+**
Starvation	40%	35%	7%
Weak in fall	16%	30%	0%
Weather	6%	15%	7%
Pests	8%	10%	43%
Queen death	12%	15%	7%

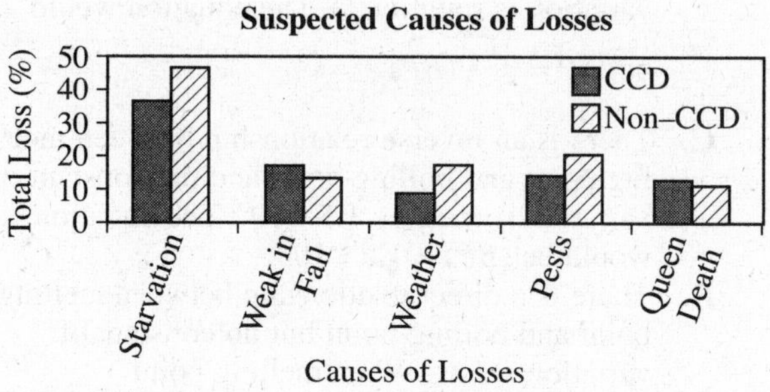

Figure 2

34. Beekeepers from operations of which size experienced the lowest total losses by percentage?

F. 1 to 50
G. 51 to 500
H. 500+
J. It cannot be determined from the data provided.

35. Based on the data in Figure 2, it can be determined that the least common suspected cause of CCD losses was:

A. starvation.
B. weak in fall.
C. weather.
D. queen death.

36. According to Study 2, for operations with between 1 and 50 colonies, what was the most common suspected cause of CCD losses?

F. Starvation
G. Weak in fall
H. Weather
J. Queen death

37. Prior to conducting the research, four scientists each proposed one of the following hypotheses. Which hypothesis is best supported by the results?

A. Environmental changes, including shifts in weather patterns, are the predominant causes of CCD-related loss.
B. An increase in pesticide-resistant pests is the main contributing factor to CCD loss at small beekeeping operations.
C. The larger a beekeeping operation, the higher the overall CCD loss will be.
D. A shortage of food sources, especially at smaller beekeeping operations, is leading to an increase in CCD loss.

38. Figure 2 indicates that, compared with the total loss for non-CCD, the total loss for CCD was higher for which of the following causes?

F. Starvation, weather, and pests
G. Weak in fall and queen death
H. Weak in fall and weather
J. Starvation and pests

39. A scientist theorized that the number of CCD losses would be higher than non-CCD losses for beekeeping operations of all sizes. Does the data support this theory?

A. Yes. For all causes the total loss was higher for CCD than for non-CCD.
B. Yes. Starvation was the most common cause of loss regardless of operation size.
C. No. For many of the causes there were more non-CCD losses than CCD losses.
D. No. Operations with 51 to 500 colonies experienced the greatest total loss.

40. Both Study 1 and Study 2 scientists gathered data directly from which of the following sources?

F. Feral honeybee colonies only
G. Feral honeybee colonies and non-CCD honeybee colonies
H. Non-CCD honeybee colonies only
J. CCD honeybee colonies and non-CCD honeybee colonies

STOP

If there is still time remaining, check your answers to this section.

WRITING PROMPT

Directions: This is a test of your writing skills. You will have thirty (30) minutes to write an essay in English. Before you begin planning and writing your essay, read the writing prompt below carefully to understand exactly what you are being asked to do. Your essay will be evaluated on the evidence it provides of your ability to express judgments by taking a position on the issue in the writing prompt; to maintain a focus on the topic throughout the essay; to develop a position by using logical reasoning and by supporting your ideas; to organize ideas in a logical way; and to use language clearly and effectively according to the conventions of standard written English.

You may use the unlined page to plan your essay. This page will not be scored. You must write your essay in pencil on the lined pages provided. Your writing on those lined pages will be scored. You may not need all the pages, but to ensure you have enough room to finish, do NOT skip lines. You may write corrections or additions neatly between the lines of your essay, but do NOT write in the margins of the lined pages. Illegible essays cannot be scored, so you must write (or print) clearly.

If you finish before time is called, you may review your work. Lay your pencil down immediately when time is called.

Many schools have instituted a policy requiring high school students to take at least one fine arts class (music, theater, dance, visual arts, etc.) in order to graduate. Some people think that this is a good rule because high school students would benefit from exposure to the fine arts. Other people think such a policy would not be appropriate because graduation requirements should only reflect core academic subjects, and this policy would punish students who are interested in subjects other than the fine arts. In your opinion, should high schools require that students take at least one fine arts class in order to graduate?

In your essay, take a position on this question. You may write about either one of the two points of view given, or you may present a different point of view on this question. Use specific reasons and examples to support your position.

Use this page to *plan* your essay.

Begin WRITING TEST here.

If you need more space, continue on the next page.

WRITING TEST

Answer Key

PRACTICE TEST 4

English Test

1. D	16. F	31. B	46. F	61. B
2. G	17. D	32. J	47. A	62. H
3. B	18. F	33. A	48. H	63. A
4. F	19. C	34. F	49. A	64. J
5. C	20. G	35. D	50. G	65. D
6. H	21. C	36. J	51. A	66. F
7. D	22. H	37. B	52. H	67. B
8. G	23. A	38. H	53. D	68. H
9. A	24. G	39. A	54. F	69. A
10. F	25. D	40. J	55. C	70. J
11. D	26. G	41. C	56. G	71. D
12. J	27. A	42. J	57. D	72. G
13. B	28. J	43. C	58. J	73. C
14. J	29. D	44. J	59. B	74. H
15. D	30. F	45. B	60. H	75. A

Math Test

1. E	13. B	25. D	37. D	49. B
2. G	14. G	26. K	38. K	50. G
3. D	15. D	27. B	39. C	51. D
4. H	16. J	28. G	40. J	52. J
5. A	17. C	29. A	41. B	53. B
6. J	18. G	30. H	42. G	54. F
7. B	19. B	31. A	43. A	55. E
8. H	20. J	32. H	44. H	56. H
9. C	21. C	33. C	45. E	57. E
10. K	22. G	34. H	46. K	58. F
11. C	23. A	35. B	47. B	59. B
12. J	24. H	36. J	48. F	60. K

Answer Key

PRACTICE TEST 4

Reading Test

1. B	9. B	17. C	25. D	33. A
2. H	10. H	18. F	26. F	34. H
3. A	11. B	19. A	27. B	35. C
4. J	12. F	20. J	28. H	36. J
5. A	13. D	21. D	29. D	37. B
6. H	14. G	22. F	30. G	38. F
7. B	15. C	23. C	31. B	39. B
8. J	16. G	24. G	32. J	40. J

Science Test

1. C	9. B	17. A	25. D	33. A
2. G	10. H	18. H	26. H	34. H
3. D	11. C	19. C	27. C	35. C
4. F	12. F	20. J	28. G	36. F
5. B	13. D	21. D	29. C	37. D
6. G	14. F	22. G	30. J	38. G
7. D	15. B	23. C	31. D	39. C
8. F	16. H	24. H	32. F	40. J

HOW TO SCORE YOUR PRACTICE TEST

Step 1: Add up the number correct for each section and write that number in the blank under the Raw Score column on the Score Conversion Table. (Your goal is to get more questions correct on each subsequent practice test.)

Step 2: Using the Score Conversion Chart, find your scale score for each section and write it down. Then add up all four sections and divide by 4 to find your overall composite score. (Composite scores are rounded up at .5 or higher.)

Score Conversion Table

Section	Raw Score	Scaled Score
English	(out of 75)	____ / 36
Math	(out of 60)	____ / 36
Reading	(out of 40)	____ / 36
Science	(out of 40)	____ / 36
		Add and divide by 4
Overall Composite =		____ / 36

Score Conversion Chart

	Number Correct				
ACT Score*	English Section	Mathematics Section	Reading Section	Science Section	ACT Score*
36	75	60	40	40	36
35	74	59	39	39	35
34	73	58	38	38	34
33	72	57	37	—	33
32	71	56	36	37	32
31	70	54–55	35	36	31
30	69	53	34	35	30
29	67–68	51–52	33	34	29
28	65–66	49–50	32	33	28
27	64	46–48	31	31–32	27
26	62–63	44–45	30	30	26
25	60–61	41–43	29	28–29	25
24	58–59	39–40	27–28	25–27	24
23	55–57	37–38	25–26	24	23
22	53–54	35–36	23–24	22–23	22
21	50–52	33–34	22	20–21	21
20	47–49	31–32	21	18–19	20
19	44–46	28–30	19–20	17	19
18	42–43	25–27	18	15–16	18
17	40–41	22–24	17	14	17

Continued

Score Conversion Chart *(Continued)*

ACT Score*	Number Correct English Section	Mathematics Section	Reading Section	Science Section	ACT Score*
16	37–39	19–21	16	13	16
15	34–36	15–17	15	12	15
14	31–33	11–14	13–14	11	14
13	29–30	09–10	12	10	13
12	27–28	07–08	10–11	09	12
11	25–26	06	08–09	08	11
10	23–24	05	07	07	10
9	21–22	04	06	05–06	9
8	18–20	03	05	—	8
7	15–17	—	—	04	7
6	12–14	02	04	03	6
5	09–11	—	03	02	5
4	07–08	01	02	—	4
3	05–06	—	—	01	3
2	03–04	—	01	—	2
1	00–02	00	00	00	1

**These scores are based on student trials rather than national norms.*

SCORING YOUR ESSAY

As mentioned earlier in this text, two readers will evaluate your essay and each person will then assign it a score from 1 to 6. If, by chance, these two scorers disagree by more than 1 point, a third reader will step in and resolve the discrepancy. Performance on the essay will not affect your English, math, reading, science, or composite scores. You will receive two additional scores on your score sheet—a combined English/writing score (1–36) and a writing test subscore (1–12). Neither of these scores will affect your composite score!

The sample essay that follows reflects higher-level writing. It meets the criteria that ACT has put forth for essays that demonstrate effective writing skills.

- It takes a definite position.
- It addresses and expands on the counterargument.
- It has details that support the topic sentences and is well organized.
- It is not repetitive, and while there may be errors, they do not interfere with the competence of the essay.
- It is consistent and well balanced.
- The essay has a clear introduction and a conclusion that is not just a summary but ends with a significant thought.
- The vocabulary demonstrates good use of language and the sentence structure is varied.

Answer Explanations: English Test

1. **(D)** Neither an essential "that" clause nor a prepositional phrase needs to be preceded by a comma, so the choice with no commas is correct here.
2. **(G)** Since the sentence concerns a *present* state of something *not having been done*, a negative version of the present perfect tense (i.e., transforming *candidate has won* into *no candidate has ever won*) is necessary. Even if you weren't aware of the factoid being discussed, this is still the only answer choice that results in a comprehensible and grammatically correct sentence.
3. **(B)** The singular present perfect form *has won* is appropriate here. (The regular past tense would also work, but is not one of the choices.)
4. **(F)** The first clause of the sentence is rendered dependent by the presence of *although*, and so the second clause must be independent; no conjunction is necessary. (The fact that the first clause also has *And* at the beginning is immaterial—the addition of *and* before *although* is merely a stylistic flourish here, and it's *although* that makes the difference.)
5. **(C)** All of the pieces of information concerning Teddy Roosevelt are both true and interesting, but the fact that he was vice president under McKinley is the one that is relevant to his ascending to the presidency in 1901.
6. **(H)** The clause about Roosevelt's nickname (from *or* to *him*) is set off from the rest of the sentence with a pair of dashes. (A pair of commas would also be correct, but is not one of the choices—and besides, a pair of dashes is preferable because the sentence is long, complex, and already contains a lot of other commas.)
7. **(D)** This choice correctly presents a dependent "afterthought" clause separated from the preceding independent clause by a comma. Since it concerns Roosevelt's ongoing actions at the time, the participial form of the initial verb (*steering*) is necessary.
8. **(G)** As the subsequent paragraph makes clear, the fact that an "accidental" president had never gone on to win an election before raised an important question about how to interpret the Constitution.
9. **(A)** This choice correctly presents an independent clause preceded by an introductory dependent clause, with the two separated by a comma.
10. **(F)** No commas are necessary, since the proper name *William Howard Taft* cannot be removed from the sentence (although it could if the definite article *the* preceded *Secretary of War*—the sentence would lack information, but it would be grammatically correct).
11. **(D)** Due to the presence of *both* and the rule of parallel phrasing, no word is necessary before the second infinitive ("*a desire both to pursue and to stay....*").
12. **(J)** The sentence concerns an event that was in the past relative to another point in the past, so the past perfect form is necessary: *Roosevelt had had his chance*. (Don't be confused by the fact that *had* is both the past tense of *have* and the "helper" verb form used to indicate the singular past perfect.)
13. **(B)** The information that "Bull Moose Party" is an alternate name for the Progressive Party is necessary in order to comprehend the subsequent paragraph.
14. **(J)** The paragraph is more about the election of 1912 itself, and so this fact disrupts the flow, interesting though it may be.
15. **(D)** The passage is more about Teddy Roosevelt's political career than his personal life, and it never addresses his reasons for adopting the positions he did.
16. **(F)** This choice correctly presents an independent clause followed by a dependent "afterthought" clause, with the two clauses separated by a comma.
17. **(D)** An essential *that* clause is correctly used here to indicate a matter of degree: "its recipients are *so* respected *that*...."
18. **(F)** This is a comma splice. All of the other choices are grammatically correct. (Remember, on "NOT acceptable" questions, the comma is frequently the odd one out!)
19. **(C)** This choice results in a complete, correct sentence that means what you want it to mean—a single independent clause in the past tense.
20. **(G)** Since it explains why Walker often wore male clothing, this is the only one of the choices that results in the rest of the sentence making sense.

21. **(C)** This is the only choice that results in an independent clause existing anywhere in the sentence.
22. **(H)** *Although* would mean "despite the fact that," rather than "due to the fact that," which is what you want to mean here (and what all the other choices mean).
23. **(A)** This choice correctly presents an independent clause followed by a dependent "afterthought" clause, with the two clauses separated by a comma (if the situation looks more complicated than that, it is due to the fact that the independent clause ends with items in a list, which are also separated by commas).
24. **(G)** In the previous part of the paragraph, Walker is officially only a nurse, because she is not allowed to be a doctor; in the subsequent part of the paragraph, she is made a doctor. This sentence needs to explain why the army changed its mind.
25. **(D)** We know that Walker ends up receiving the Medal of Honor, and the subsequent prepositional phrase begins with *by*—all this indicates that what we want to say here is that *Walker was recommended for the Medal of Honor by the generals* (i.e., the generals are doing the recommending, but the verb is assigned to Walker via the passive voice).
26. **(G)** Saying that Walker *portrayed herself as supporting* feminism would imply that she acted like she supported it more than actually supporting it.
27. **(A)** No comma is necessary before the prepositional phrase or before the conjunction, as the conjunction does not introduce an independent clause or complement.
28. **(J)** This choice correctly presents an independent clause followed by a dependent participial "afterthought" clause, with the two separated by a comma.
29. **(D)** Without the Medal of Honor, Walker no longer has a unique place in U.S. military history, and so the information that her medal was restored by President Carter is essential here.
30. **(F)** It is true that most of Walker's major accomplishments are covered by the passage, with a central focus on her receiving of the Medal of Honor—and this is basically just a paraphrase of exactly what the question asks for.
31. **(B)** The sentence correctly consists of an independent clause in the present perfect tense (*people have sworn*) augmented with an essential *that* clause. The present perfect is preferable because the sentence concerns the *current* state of something *already having been* done.
32. **(J)** There is no reason to insert anything between the subject phrase (*physical evidence*) and main verb (*has been*).
33. **(A)** This is the "prepositional phrase trick." The noun is the plural *pieces*, so the verb must be the plural *are*. The words *of Yeti evidence* constitute a prepositional phrase that must be "jumped."
34. **(F)** The fact that the climate tends to distort footprints is relevant because it constitutes an obstacle to Yeti research—that is, it is impossible to conclude anything from the prints.
35. **(D)** This choice correctly separates two independent clauses into two separate sentences.
36. **(J)** The sentence already clearly means what you want to say; all of the proposed additions are redundant.
37. **(B)** The sentence indicates more than one monastery, and they do not possess anything, so what we need here is the plural nonpossessive *monasteries*. (The question tries to trick you with the fact that the sentence says the monasteries are *in possession* of relics, but grammatically speaking the word *monasteries* does not possess any other noun.)
38. **(H)** Here, the passive voice is necessary because the identity of the people doing the claiming is unknown/irrelevant. The noun *relics* is modified by the passive verb form *claimed* + the infinitive *to be* + the adjective *real*. The monasteries had relics that were *claimed to be real* (by some people).
39. **(A)** This choice correctly presents an independent clause preceded by a dependent modifying clause, with the two separated by a comma.
40. **(J)** Although the idea of Jimmy Stewart assisting in international fake-Yeti-hand-based intrigue is certainly bizarre, the idea is already clearly bizarre enough without adding this sentence. Besides, the point is about the hand, not Stewart himself.
41. **(C)** A "linking word" of some kind is necessary between the two clauses, and since 1832 is a time, the relative adverb *when* (added to the beginning of the second clause, after the comma) is the appropriate choice.
42. **(J)** The phrase *and memorable* is set off with a pair of dashes for the sake of emphasis. (It would also be correct to have no punctuation around it at all, but that is not one of the choices.)
43. **(C)** This paragraph concerns very recent attempts to find the Yeti, and so it is best introduced with a factoid about recent biological discoveries.

44. **(J)** The clause *the team of Japanese adventurer Yoshiteru Takahashi ... ventured into the Himalayas* is interrupted by the "lift-out" clause *who claims to have seen a Yeti in 2003*, which offers extra information about Takahashi and is set off with a pair of commas.

45. **(B)** Paragraph 4 explains what the Yeti is, and so should come before everything except paragraph 1 (which obviously comes first, as it begins by building suspense before the subject is identified).

46. **(F)** This is the prepositional phrase trick again. The subject of the sentence is the plural *legends*, which agrees with the plural verb *are*, and the prepositional phrase *of female pirate Anne Bonny* must be "jumped." The rest of the paragraph makes clear that this sentence means to say that these legends *are* definitely popular, rather than that they *might* be.

47. **(A)** To say that *piracy was a male-dominated occupation for people then* is both redundant and awkward. *Then* is already implied by *was*, and *for people* is already implied by *occupation* (who has occupations besides people?).

48. **(H)** The fact that accounts of her life rely on *speculation* (educated guessing) is the only one of the choices that emphasizes the lack of information we have about Bonny, as the question requests.

49. **(A)** The fact that she was born to a fairly wealthy family is the only piece of information offered that would be surprising about someone who became a pirate.

50. **(G)** We need a subject noun here (to agree with the main verb *is*), and this choice gives us the noun *beauty*, modified by the adjective *redheaded*.

51. **(A)** There is one *family*, and it possesses the *estate*, so what we need here is the singular-possessive form *family's*.

52. **(H)** As the dash after *family* indicates, the phrase *including the identity of her family* is a "lift-out" clause containing extra information that should be set off with a pair of dashes (a pair of commas or parentheses would also work, but these are not choices).

53. **(D)** Although it is still possible to figure out what the sentence means no matter where this prepositional phrase appears, the most logical place for it is after *ships*, since this placement results in specific information about what exact actions were performed in what exact period of time: they took *several ships over the next few years*.

54. **(F)** The subsequent portion of the paragraph concerns Anne's exact rank and station among the crew (she fought, but was never in charge). Only this sentence sets up the question that is subsequently examined.

55. **(C)** Although it is the longest of the choices, only this one is grammatically correct. Anne participated in the fighting *when there was fighting to be done*. The end of the phrase describes a hypothetical imperative situation: *there was fighting* (that needed) *to be done*.

56. **(G)** This choice correctly presents an independent clause followed by a dependent clause containing additional information. Because the dependent clause begins with *supposedly*, it is preceded by a comma (it would not be if it just began with *while*).

57. **(D)** All that is needed is *therefore* (i.e., for this reason). All of the other choices are either redundant or prohibitively awkward.

58. **(J)** *Anne* (noun) *convinced* (verb) the *law* (direct object) *that she had been* a prisoner on Rackham's ship. The past perfect tense (*she had been*) is used because the idea takes place in the past relative to another moment in the past. All of the other choices are either grammatically incorrect or do not mean what you want them to mean.

59. **(B)** All this sentence does is provide yet another example of a legend about Anne Bonny that may or may not be true. (Don't be confused by the presence of the word *evidence*—the sentence is not evidence that the legend is true, but merely evidence that there are a lot of legends.)

60. **(H)** Anne Bonny is the only female criminal discussed in the passage, and so this would hardly constitute an essay about female criminals in general.

61. **(B)** The convention in a situation like this is to follow the verb with *as* and the participial form of the next verb: the film is *acclaimed as containing* good action scenes. This may sound hard, but think for a bit and you'll remember that you see this construction all the time (e.g., the source was *quoted as saying*). In situations like this, you have to trust in your instincts about what sounds right, even if you don't know why.

62. **(H)** The words from *aside* to *existed* constitute a "lift-out" clause containing extra information, and so this phrase is set off with a pair of commas. The rest of the sentence forms a single independent clause around it. (This question is tricky because it involves commas near *that*, but remember, the rule is that you don't need a comma before a *that* clause—you need a comma after *that* here because a "lift-out" clause *happens to* follow the word *that*.)

63. **(A)** The *who* clause here is an *essential* or *limiting* one, and so no commas are necessary. (In other words, it is the type of clause where you would use *that* instead of *which* if you were talking about an object, but since you are talking about a person here, you use *who*, but still with no comma.)

64. **(J)** Here, a colon is correctly used to divide an initial independent clause from a subsequent phrase that "emanates from" it. (The colon is an incredibly versatile punctuation mark, so the best rule is often that "It's the choice with the colon when the other three are wrong.")
65. **(D)** What we need here is a phrase synonymous with *reason for*, *explanation for*, and so on. The story uses an incorrect preposition.
66. **(F)** The fact that the first reference to Wallace's alleged murdered wife is in a poem composed 200 years later is highly relevant, as it strongly suggests that the story is made up (and the question of which stuff in *Braveheart* is made up is the point of the passage).
67. **(B)** We need the passive voice here: the wife *was executed* by the English. Although the passive voice is not usually preferred, it is necessitated here by the structure of the sentence, since we need the noun to extend to both verb phrases: there's no evidence that the wife *existed* (active voice) or *was executed* (passive voice).
68. **(H)** A semicolon here would separate two independent clauses, and so this choice is grammatically incorrect. The others are all fine.
69. **(A)** The character *is* an underdog (i.e., the David figure in a David-and-Goliath story); the character does not *have* an underdog (that would make the character and the underdog two different entities). The other choices are all fine.
70. **(J)** The phrase *not only* earlier in the sentence indicates that we need a *not only, but also* construction here. Only choice J is constructed in this manner (the word *also* does not appear, but it is implied).
71. **(D)** This choice correctly presents an independent clause followed by an explanatory "afterthought" clause, with the two separated by a comma.
72. **(G)** Saying *had fought* (past perfect tense) here would imply that by Wallace's time the Scots *had fought in the past* in armor (but didn't necessarily still do so), when what you mean to say was that they fought in armor *at* that time.
73. **(C)** The *Scots* do not possess anything in this sentence, but the film *Braveheart* grammatically possesses the Scots (i.e., they are the Scots *of* the movie *Braveheart*). So *Braveheart* needs to be possessive, but *Scots* does not.
74. **(H)** We need the third-person singular form of the verb *to be* and the possessive pronoun *its* (the one without the apostrophe): The film's most troubling inaccuracy *is its* depiction of Robert the Bruce.
75. **(A)** Although the sentence is in the past tense, and the subsequent verb *knew* is also in the past tense, the *not only did* construction means that we need the infinitive *betray*. The verb *did* is in the past tense, and *betray* is attached to it. You would say *He never betrayed*, but *Not only did he never betray, but he....*

Answer Explanations: Math Test

1. **(E)** The width is given as 4.5 cm and the length is given as four times the width, which is $4 \cdot 4.5 = 18$ cm. Using the area of a rectangle formula $A = L \cdot W$, we get $A = 4.5 \cdot 18 = 81$.
2. **(G)** Probability is calculated as the number of successful outcomes divided by the total possible outcomes. The number of gumballs that are NOT blue is 30 yellow + 32 red + 28 green = 90 gumballs. The formula becomes P(NOT blue) = $\frac{90}{120}$. Simplify the fraction to get $\frac{3}{4}$.
3. **(D)** 4×10^{-5} is scientific notation for 0.00004. Most calculators can perform scientific notation using the exponent key.
4. **(H)** The 25-foot ladder makes the hypotenuse of a right triangle (see diagram) with a base of 15 feet. Using the Pythagorean Theorem to find the missing side b, we get $(15)^2 + b^2 = 25^2$. Solving for b gives $225 + b^2 = 625 \rightarrow b^2 = 400$. Taking the square root of both sides yields $b = 20$ ft. Also, 15, 20, 25 is a Pythagorean triple (3, 4, 5).

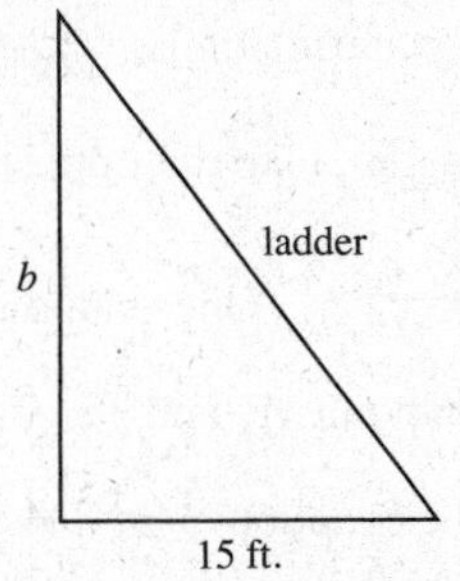

5. **(A)** $\sqrt{96} = \sqrt{16} \cdot \sqrt{6} = 4\sqrt{6}$.

6. **(J)** The formula for the area of a square is $A = s^2$. Plugging in 49 for the area yields $49 = s^2$. Taking the square root gives $s = 7$. The question asks for the perimeter of the square. To find the perimeter, use the formula $P = 4 \cdot s$. Plugging in 7 for s gives $P = 4 \cdot 7 = 28$.

7. **(B)** The slope of a line can be found using the formula $y = mx + b$ where m is the slope of the line and b is the y-intercept. To solve $4y = -2x + 4$ for y, divide both sides by 4 giving $\frac{4y}{4} = \frac{-2x}{4} + \frac{4}{4}$. Simplifying yields $y = -\frac{1}{2}x + 1$. The slope is the coefficient of x, which is $-\frac{1}{2}$.

8. **(H)** The slope of a line can be found using the formula $y = mx + b$ where m is the slope of the line and b is the y-intercept. To find the slope of $5x - 4y = -12$, first solve for y. This yields $y = \frac{5}{4}x + 3$ so the slope of the line is $\frac{5}{4}$.

   The slope of a perpendicular line can be found by taking the opposite reciprocal. The opposite reciprocal of $\frac{5}{4}$ is $-\frac{4}{5}$.

9. **(C)** The measure of $\angle XZY$ is supplementary to the measure of $\angle YZP$, which was given as 115. Calculating $\angle XZY$ yields $180 - 115 = 65$. The sum of the measures of the three angles of a triangle is 180, so to find $\angle XYZ$ take $180 - (40 + 65) = 180 - 105 = 75$.

10. **(K)** The area of a circle can be calculated by the formula $A = \pi r^2$. Plugging 6 in for the radius gives $A = \pi(6)^2 = 36\pi$.

11. **(C)** We can use the problem to set up 2 equations. Let B = the cost of a strip of bacon and E = the cost of one egg. The first sentence yields the equation $2B + E = \$2.10$. The second sentence yields the equation $3B + 2E = \$3.45$. Solving the first equation for E yields $E = 2.10 - 2B$. Substituting $2.10 - 2B$ into the second equation for E yields $3B + 2(2.10 - 2B) = 3.45$. Solving this equation for B gives $B = \$0.75$. However, the question asks for the price of an egg, so plugging 0.75 into the first equation for B and solving for E gives $E = .60$ or 60 cents.

12. **(J)** If you break down the problem, you are simply adding 2 fractions. Finding x requires finding a common denominator for the 2 fractions $\frac{M}{24}$ and $\frac{N}{108}$. A calculator can be used to test the LCD of 24 and 108 yielding 216. Therefore $x = 216$.

13. **(B)** ΔXYZ is an isosceles triangle with vertex Y meaning angles X and Z are congruent; therefore, angle Z has measure $2a$ as well. The sum of the 3 angles of a triangle is 180. Use this to set up the equation $112 + 2a + 2a = 180$. Solving for a gives $112 + 4a = 180 \rightarrow 4a = 68 \rightarrow a = 17$.

14. **(G)** $f(4) = -3(4)^2 + 4(4) = -48 + 16 = -32$.

15. **(D)** $\angle MRP$ is vertical to $\angle QRS$. Angle QRS is composed of 2 smaller angles, SRT and TRQ. $\angle SRT = 25°$ and $\angle TRQ = 90°$ making $\angle QRS = 25 + 90 = 115°$. Vertical angles are congruent, so $\angle MRP$ is equal to $\angle QRS$; therefore $\angle MRP = 115°$.

16. **(J)** Recall SOH CAH TOA from trigonometry, $\tan A = \frac{opposite}{adjacent}$. The side opposite angle A measures 24 cm and the adjacent side measures 10 cm. Dividing 24 by 10 and simplifying gives $\frac{24}{10} = \frac{12}{5}$. So $\tan A = \frac{12}{5}$.

17. **(C)** Jenna needs 2 hours 30 minutes to cook the soup, 7 minutes to assemble the ingredients, and 20 minutes to cut the vegetables. Adding these times together gives 2 hours 57 minutes. If she wants the meal ready at 1:15 P.M., she needs to start it 2 hours and 57 minutes before 1:15 P.M., which is 10:18 A.M. Checking your work gives 10:18 + 2 hours = 12:18 + 57 minutes = 1:15 P.M.

18. **(G)** The question asks what percent of the garden is occupied by watermelon. To find a percent, take the part of the garden that is occupied by watermelon divided by the total plants that occupy the garden. There are 45 + 15 + 120 = 180 total plants. The percent that is watermelon is $\frac{15}{180} = .08333$, which is approximately 8.3%.

19. **(B)** To find the additive inverse of an expression, take the opposite of each term. The opposite of $5x^3 - 4x^2 + 6x - 9$ is $-5x^3 + 4x^2 - 6x + 9$.

20. **(J)** The midpoint formula is $M = \left(\frac{x_1 + x_2}{2}, \frac{y_1 + y_2}{2}\right)$. One endpoint and the midpoint were given in the problem. Using (x, y) for endpoint B, $(-2, 4)$ for endpoint A, and $(3, 9)$ for midpoint M, we get the equation $(3, 9) = \left(\frac{-2+x}{2}, \frac{4+y}{2}\right)$. Solving for x and y, we get the equations $\frac{-2+x}{2} = 3$ and $\frac{4+y}{2} = 9$. Finish solving each equation to get $x = 8$ and $y = 14$; therefore the answer is $(8, 14)$.

21. **(C)** To solve an absolute value inequality, you must first isolate the absolute value. Subtracting 4 from both sides makes the inequality $|x| < 3$. This is equivalent to the compound sentence $x < 3$ "and" $x > -3$. This is equivalent to $-3 < x < 3$, so choice C is the correct answer.

22. **(G)** To find the sum of the interior angles of a polygon use the formula $(n - 2) \cdot 180$ where n represents the number of sides of the polygon. A pentagon has 5 sides so the formula becomes $(5 - 2) \cdot 180 = (3) \cdot 180 = 540°$.

23. **(A)** $n^{1/2}$ means the square root of n, so the equation becomes $\sqrt{n} = 4$. To solve a square root equation, square both sides of the equal sign to get $n = 16$. Another good way to solve this problem is by plugging the answers in for n and using your calculator. If you plug 16 in for n, you get $16^{1/2} = 4$.

24. **(H)** The problem states that $b < -6$ and $3a - b = 21$. Solving for b in the second equation, $b = 3a - 21$. Next, substitute $3a - 21$ in for b in the original inequality yielding $3a - 21 < -6$. Solve for a, $a < 5$.

25. **(D)** The path the dog can walk forms a semicircle of radius 12 blocked on the right side by the house. To find the area of a semicircle use the formula $A = \frac{1}{2}\pi r^2$. Plugging 12 in for the radius and 3.14 for pi, we get $A = \frac{1}{2}(3.14)(12)^2 = \frac{1}{2}(3.14)(144) = 226.08$, which would round to about 226 meters.

26. **(K)** If you factor the numerator it becomes $\frac{(3x-2y)(8x+3y)}{(3x-2y)}$. Canceling the like factors in the numerator and denominator, the fraction becomes $\frac{\cancel{(3x-2y)}(8x+3y)}{\cancel{(3x-2y)}} = 8x + 3y$.

27. **(B)** Jose's profit the first year will be \$25,000, and next year's profit can be found by taking $25{,}000 + 0.07(25{,}000) = \$26{,}750$. A geometric sequence is a sequence with a common ratio. The ratio of the profit for the second year to the first year is $26{,}750/25{,}000 = 1.07$. Therefore, choices A and C are both incorrect. Because the difference between the second year's profit and the first year's is $26{,}750 - 25{,}000 = 1{,}750$, neither answer choice D nor E is correct.

28. **(G)** The area of a trapezoid can be calculated by the formula $A = \frac{1}{2}h(b_1 + b_2)$. To find the height, base 1, and base 2 we count the coordinates on the graph. The height of the trapezoid goes from the y-coordinate -2 up to the y-coordinate 5; this is a difference of $h = 5 - (-2) = 7$. The lower base goes from x-coordinate -1 to x-coordinate 5, which makes $b_1 = 5 - (-1) = 6$. The upper base goes from x-coordinate -3 to x-coordinate 8, which makes $b_2 = 8 - (-3) = 11$. Plugging these numbers into the formula gives $A = \frac{1}{2}(7)(6+11) = \frac{1}{2}(7)(17) = 59.5$.

29. **(A)** To find the GCF of two terms, first find the GCF of the numbers 12 and 6. The largest factor that goes into both 12 and 6 is 6. The GCF of variables is the smallest exponent both terms share. For x, the first term has x^4 and the second term has x^1. The smallest exponent is 1. Using the same method to find the GCF of the y's gives y^2. Therefore, the GCF is $6xy^2$.

30. **(H)** After labeling the given information, $NM = MP = PL = ML = 4$. Since $\triangle LMP$ is equilateral, angles LMP and LPM equal 60°. Because $\angle LMP = 60°$, $\angle LMN = 180 - 60 = 120°$. Since $\triangle LMN$ is isosceles, angles LNM and MLN each equal $180 - 120 = \frac{60}{2} = 30°$. Finally, since $\angle LNM = 30$ and $\angle LPM = 60$, $\triangle LNP$ is a 30°-60°-90° triangle with a hypotenuse of 8 and one leg of 4. Using 30°-60°-90° ratios side $LN = 4 \cdot \sqrt{3} = 4\sqrt{3}$.

31. **(A)** Plugging 122° in for F in the given formula gives $122 = \frac{9}{5}C + 32$. Subtracting 32 from both sides yields $90 = \frac{9}{5}C \rightarrow C = 50°$.

32. **(H)** To calculate probability, use the formula $P = \frac{\textit{number of successful outcomes}}{\textit{number of total outcomes}}$. The fractions greater than $\frac{1}{2}$ are $\frac{3}{5}$, $\frac{5}{7}$, and $\frac{5}{9}$ so the number of successful outcomes is 3. The total number of outcomes is 5 because there are 5 fractions. Therefore, the probability is 3 out of 5 or $\frac{3}{5}$.

33. **(C)** To calculate the total number of possible outcomes, multiply all of the choices together. This problem has one kicker in it: the word *or* implies when the customer first chooses a salad OR a soup, he or she has a total of $3 + 2 = 5$ choices for his or her first course. The customer then chooses a main dish (5 choices), a vegetable (4 choices), and a dessert (3 choices). Multiply all these choices together to get $5 \cdot 5 \cdot 4 \cdot 3 = 300$ total choices for his or her meal.

34. **(H)** Reflecting over the origin is the same thing as reflecting over the line $y = -x$. Reflecting $\triangle ABC$ over the line $y = -x$ puts $\triangle ABC$ in the third quadrant. The only two solutions that have all three points in the third quadrant are choices H and J so we can eliminate choices F, G, and K. Reflecting a point over the line $y = -x$ negates both the x- and the y-coordinate. Since the original points were $A(1, 1)$, $B(7, 2)$, and $C(3, 4)$, the negated points would be $(-1, -1)$, $(-7, -2)$, and $(-3, -4)$ making choice H the correct answer.

35. **(B)** Labeling the given information in the correct places gives the hypotenuse of the right triangle to be 247 and one of the legs to be 228. Use the Pythagorean Theorem to find the missing leg of a right triangle. Setting up the formula we get $a^2 + b^2 = c^2 \rightarrow x^2 + 228^2 = 247^2 \rightarrow x^2 + 51{,}984 = 61{,}009 \rightarrow x^2 = 9{,}025$. Taking the square root of both sides gives $x = 95$.

36. **(J)** To multiply two matrices first check the dimensions of each matrix. The first matrix has dimensions (1×3), the second matrix has dimensions (3×1). Multiplying a (1×3) matrix with a (3×1) yields a (1×1) matrix. The only matrix with dimensions (1×1) is choice J. You could also plug any number in for x in this problem, then use your calculator's matrix function, if your calculator has one, to perform matrix multiplication.

37. **(D)** To calculate the distance a person would have to run around a circular track use the formula $C = \pi d$. Using a diameter of X, one lap around the track would be $C = \pi d \rightarrow C = \pi X$. The problem asks how far the athlete would run in a 6-lap race. If each lap is πX meters, 6 laps would be $6 \cdot \pi X = 6\pi X$.

38. **(K)** Using the first sentence to set up an equation and solving for m, we get $m \cdot 4 = n \rightarrow 4m = n \rightarrow m = \frac{n}{4}$. We want to express the sum of m and 4 in terms of n. The sum of m and 4 is written as $m + 4$. Substituting $\frac{n}{4}$ in for m gives $\frac{n}{4} + 4$.

39. **(C)** We are given 3 squares labeled R with side length x. To find the area of a square use the formula $A = s^2$. Plugging x in for s we get $A = x^2$. Since there are 3 squares labeled R, their total area would be $3x^2$. Using similar logic we get 12 squares labeled S that have a total area of $12y^2$, and 13 rectangles each labeled P have a total area of $13xy$. Adding all these areas together we get $3x^2 + 13xy + 12y^2$.

40. **(J)** If the line $y = (D - 3)x + 7$ passes through the point $(-5, 2)$, we can plug $x = -5$ into the equation and $y = 2$, then solve for D. Plugging in these values and solving for D we get $2 = (D - 3)(-5) + 7 \rightarrow -5 = (D - 3)(-5) \rightarrow 1 = (D - 3) \rightarrow D = 4$. Now, the question asks for the slope of the line that is the coefficient of x. In this case, the coefficient of x is $(D - 3)$. Plugging in 4 for D we get the slope to equal $4 - 3 = 1$.

41. **(B)** The first equation states $x = -6$; plugging -6 into the second equation for x gives $y = 2(-6) - 4 \rightarrow y = -12 - 4 \rightarrow y = -16$. Therefore the point of intersection is $(-6, -16)$.

42. **(G)** $\cos M = 0.4 = \frac{2}{5}$. Recalling SOH-CAH-TOA, cosine is the ratio of the adjacent side to the hypotenuse of a right triangle. Since $PM = 24$ and LN is the perpendicular bisector of PM, $NM = 12$. Labeling LM as x, we can set up a proportion, $\frac{adjacent}{hypotenuse} = \frac{adjacent}{hypotenuse} \rightarrow \frac{2}{5} = \frac{12}{x}$. Cross multiplying and solving for x gives $2x = 5(12) \rightarrow 2x = 60 \rightarrow x = 30$.

43. **(A)** From the given information we can set up the formula $C = 30 + k\sqrt{t}$ where C represents how much the violinist charges, k is the constant of variation, and t is the time the violin is rented. Plugging in 25 minutes for time and \$65 for C, we can solve for k to get $65 = 30 + k\sqrt{25} \rightarrow 35 = k\sqrt{25} \rightarrow 35 = 5k \rightarrow k = 7$. Now that we know the constant of variation, plug 81 minutes in for t and solve for C to find the cost of renting the violin for 81 minutes. $C = 30 + 7\sqrt{81} \rightarrow C = 30 + 7(9) \rightarrow C = 30 + 63 \rightarrow C = 93$.

44. **(H)** The area of the shaded region can be found by subtracting the area of the smaller square from the area of the larger square. Labeling the sides of the larger square x and using the area of a square formula $A = s^2$ we get $A_{\text{shaded region}} = A_{\text{large square}} - A_{\text{small square}} \rightarrow 16 = x^2 - 3^2 \rightarrow 16 = x^2 - 9 \rightarrow 25 = x^2$. Taking the square root of both sides gives $x = 5$.

45. **(E)** Substituting $x = \cos\theta$ and $y = \sin\theta$ into the inequality $(\sin\theta)\left(\frac{1}{\cos\theta}\right) < 0$ gives $(y)\left(\frac{1}{x}\right) < 0$. The problem is asking when the product of y and $\left(\frac{1}{x}\right)$ is negative. The only way the product of 2 factors can be negative is if exactly 1 of them is negative. The quadrants where x and y have opposite signs are quadrants II and IV.

46. **(K)** $(3-i)^2 = (3-i)(3-i) = 9 - 3i - 3i + i^2 = 9 - 6i + i^2$. Recalling $i^2 = -1$, the problem becomes $9 - 6i + (-1) = 8 - 6i$. A helpful tip is that TI-83 and TI-84 graphing calculators have an i button above the decimal point. Plugging $(3-i)^2$ into your calculator will also give you $8 - 6i$.

47. **(B)** To find how many times larger Mars is than Venus we must first know the size of each planet. Let x = the radius of Venus, then the radius of Mars = 4 • radius of Venus = $4x$. Using the given formula, the volume of Venus is $V = \frac{4}{3}\pi x^3$ and the volume of Mars is $V = \frac{4}{3}\pi(4x)^3 = \frac{4}{3}\pi(64x^3) = \frac{256}{3}\pi x^3$. When dividing the volume of Mars by the volume of Venus, the π and x^3 cancel out, leaving $\dfrac{\frac{256}{3}}{\frac{4}{3}} = \frac{256}{3}\cdot\frac{3}{4} = 64$.

48. **(F)** $\sqrt[2]{16r^6} = \sqrt[2]{16}\cdot\sqrt[2]{r^6} = 4\cdot r^3 = 4r^3$.

49. **(B)** If 2 is a solution for x, we can plug 2 into the equation for x and solve for k. This gives $(2)^2 + k(2) + 12 = 0$. Solving for k gives $4 + 2k + 12 = 0 \rightarrow 2k = -16 \rightarrow k = -8$.

50. **(G)** The standard form of a circle is $(x-h)^2 + (y-k)^2 = r^2$ where (h, k) is the center of the circle and r is the radius. The center of this circle is (0, 3) and the radius is 3. Plugging these numbers in for h, k, and r, respectively, gives $(x-0)^2 + (y-3)^2 = 3^2$. Simplifying the equation gives $x^2 + (y-3)^2 = 9$.

51. **(D)** To find the equation of a line we calculate the slope and the y-intercept. The slope can be found by finding the change in y divided by the change in x. The slope of the line through the first two data points is $m = \frac{y2 - y1}{x2 - x1} = \frac{-5-(-8)}{-1-(-2)} = \frac{3}{1} = 3$. The y-intercept is the value of y when $x = 0$. The third data point is $(0, -2)$; therefore, -2 is the y-intercept. Plugging what we found into the formula $y = mx + b$, we get $y = 3x - 2$.

52. **(J)** The sum of the angles of a triangle equals 180°. Using this, angle $X = 180 - 32 - 44 = 104°$. Using the law of sines, we get $\frac{x}{\sin X} = \frac{y}{\sin Y} \rightarrow \frac{x}{\sin(104)} = \frac{22}{\sin(44)}$. Cross multiplying and solving for x gives $x\cdot\sin(44) = 22\cdot\sin(104) \rightarrow x = \frac{22\sin(104)}{\sin 44}$.

53. **(B)** In order to graph the equation $3x - 2y = 6$, we must first get it in $y = mx + b$ form. Solving for y in the equation gives $-2y = -3x + 6 \rightarrow y = \frac{3}{2}x - 3$ so the slope of the equation is $\frac{3}{2}$ and the y-intercept is -3. The only graphs that have a y-intercept of -3 are choices B and E. The slope of the line in choice E is $\frac{2}{3}$ and the slope of the line in choice B is $\frac{3}{2}$ making choice B correct.

54. **(F)** For $\sqrt{(3)(7)}\cdot\sqrt{(m)(n)}\cdot\sqrt{(7)(5)}$ to simplify to an integer, each factor under the radical must have a pair. So far, there are two 7's, one 3, one 5, an m, and an n. For 3 and 5 to each have a pair, m and n must be 3 and 5, respectively. Checking to make sure we have the correct m and n we get $\sqrt{(3)(7)}\cdot\sqrt{(3)(5)}\cdot\sqrt{(7)(5)} = \sqrt{(3)(7)(3)(5)(7)(5)} = \sqrt{11{,}025} = 105$, which is an integer; therefore, m and n equal 3 and 5, respectively. Now, answering the question asked gives $m + n = 3 + 5 = 8$.

55. **(E)** To calculate profit we use the formula profit equals revenue minus cost, or P = R – C. To calculate revenue, Cam makes \$6.50 per umbrella or R = $6.5x$ where x represents the number of umbrellas sold. To calculate cost, Cam has to pay a one-time cost of \$25,000 for the building and machinery along with \$4.00 per umbrella, making his total cost C = 25,000 + $4x$. Plugging these into the formula P = R – C we get $P = 6.5x - (25{,}000 + 4x) = 2.50x - 25{,}000$.

56. **(H)** The question asks which statement is NOT true. $\angle PON = \widehat{PN} = 100°$. $\overline{PM}$ is a diameter so $\widehat{PM} = 180°$. Therefore, $\widehat{MN} = 180 - 100 = 80°$. If $\widehat{MN} = 80°$, then $\angle NOM = 80°$. Since $\angle PON = 100°$, $\angle PON \neq \angle NOM$.

57. **(E)** The best way to solve this problem is to plug in clever numbers for m and n to eliminate wrong answers. Starting with $m = 1$ and $n = 1$, the equation becomes $|1-1| = |1+1| \rightarrow 0 = 2$, which is a false statement. This eliminates choices B and C. Now, plug in $m = 0$ and $n = 0$ and the equation becomes $|0-0| = |0+0| \rightarrow 0 = 0$, which is a true statement, eliminating choice A. Finally, plug in $m = 0$ and $n = 1$ to get $|0-1| = |0+1| \rightarrow |-1| = |1| \rightarrow 1 = 1$, which is a true statement. This eliminates choice D, leaving choice E as the correct answer.

58. **(F)** Using the change of base formula $\log_a b = \frac{\log b}{\log a}$ the expression becomes $\log_4 16 = \frac{\log 16}{\log 4}$. Now, plug $\frac{\log 16}{\log 4}$ into a calculator to get 2.

59. **(B)** Setting up a ratio of *new tv*: *old tv* we get $\frac{\textit{new screen}}{\textit{new diameter}} = \frac{\textit{old screen}}{\textit{old diameter}} = \frac{24}{4} = \frac{21}{x}$. Setting the cross products equal, the equation becomes $24x = 4(21)$. Solving for x gives $x = \frac{4(21)}{24} = 3.5$.

60. **(K)** $\tan x = \frac{\sin x}{\cos x}$, which is not equivalent to $\frac{\cos x}{\sin x}$.

Answer Explanations: Reading Test

1. **(B)** The *strong young woman* part is definitely true, and the *inadvertently discovers her destiny* part is so broad that it can't really be wrong. There is nothing in it to make it wrong, and therefore it is right.

2. **(H)** The entire paragraph definitely details *hardships* that Belisa *saw* as she sought to save herself, and since there is no way that this general answer can be wrong, there is no need to gamble on any of the more specific ones.

3. **(A)** As is so often the case on the Prose Fiction passage, the right answer is the most broad one. The passage definitely establishes Belisa's *originality*, and it is definitely written in a *fanciful* (which means "surreal" and "stylized") manner, and since that is basically all that choice A says, it can't be wrong. (Some of the other choices seem like they might be close to true, but choice A contains the aspects of them that are true!)

4. **(J)** A newspaper with a sports section that contains an article about a boxing match is the most "real-world" thing that appears in the passage. At other times, the reader is not sure whether this story takes place in some sort of fantasyland, like a fairy tale.

5. **(A)** We know that Belisa's services are *useful* because the first two paragraphs establish that she was in great demand and that people were excited and grateful to purchase her words. We know that it was a goal of Belisa's to be *honest* because line 32 mentions her wanting to avoid *deceit* and line 95 mentions her not wanting to *defraud* people. (When questions on the ACT Reading present choices of paired adjectives, the right answer is almost always one with *and* between them, rather than *but*!)

6. **(H)** The phrase *she herself had searched* implies that Belisa had named herself based on words she liked. (And it helps to know that words beginning with *bel-* indicate "beauty" in the Romance languages, and how *crepuscular* means "active at twilight!")

7. **(B)** Although Belisa is strongly opposed to dishonesty in her own personal business, the passage never says anything about her exposing the lies of others. She does all of the options EXCEPT this one.

8. **(J)** *Interminable* means "very long" or "endless" (think of how a *term* is "a set period of time," and *terminate* means "to end something").

9. **(B)** Lines 83–86 clearly state that Belisa's primary goal was to *make a living* (she knew she had to, somehow). Some of the other choices were eventually effects of her work, but not her primary motivation at first.

10. **(H)** *Spindly* means "very thin," and in context is by far the closest.

11. **(B)** The last sentence of the opening paragraph makes clear that the passage is primarily concerned with addressing a *culture of immaturity* among contemporary men. (When a question on the ACT Reading asks you for the main idea, it is always a good idea to reread the first and last sentences of the first and last paragraphs!)

12. **(F)** All of paragraphs 2 and 3 (lines 9–26) are devoted to statistics about areas in which young women are outperforming young men, and ways in which the young men of the past outperformed the young men of today. This information is the primary support for the existence of the phenomenon that the author is addressing, and subsequent paragraphs only contain examinations of possible contributing factors.

13. **(D)** The first sentence of paragraph 6 (lines 43–47) paraphrases Cross as saying that less strict parenting makes children *less* likely to succeed, not more.

14. **(G)** The last sentence of paragraph 3 (lines 24–26) tells us what percentage of men 25–34 live with their parents (13%), what percentage of women 25–34 live with their parents (8%), and what percentage of men 18–24 live with their parents (55%), but NOT what percentage of women 18–24 live with their parents.

15. **(C)** The author addresses several phenomena that he considers to be contributing factors, the earliest of which chronologically is the 1945 parenting advice mentioned in paragraph 7 (lines 51–55).

16. **(G)** In Paragraph 4 (lines 27–34), the author discusses the 1970s TV series *All in the Family* as an early indicator of the maturity crisis, and the 1990s TV shows *Friends* and *Seinfeld* as celebrating it.

17. **(C)** Even though the passage mentions books and magazine articles, it mentions no one who is primarily a *writer* by profession. The passage makes reference to all of the professions listed EXCEPT this one.

18. **(F)** In the final paragraph Gary Cross says "my generation's obsession with youth and its memories," which clearly infers that his generation wishes to bring back the past and keep it alive.

19. **(A)** Although *attenuation* is a hard word, it is clear from context that the author's point is about male role models becoming more scarce or less prominent, and the only one of the choices that comes close to this idea is *weakening*.

20. **(J)** Lines 71–75 explicitly link the baby boomer bands that have played recent Super Bowl halftime shows to an *unhealthy obsession with youth*. This is essentially a restatement or crystallization of the main idea of the passage. (The last question on the Social Science passage, like the first question, frequently asks for a summary of the main idea!)

21. **(D)** The main idea of the passage is that, since only people who write poetry themselves pay any attention to poetry, poets now write for a narrow audience of specialists. *[T]he energy of American poetry, which was once directed outward, is now increasingly focused inward* (lines 47–49) is a paraphrase of this.

22. **(F)** The energy and institutions devoted to poetry that the author highlights, mainly in paragraphs 2 and 3 (lines 10–38), are discussed in order to provide an ironic contrast to the fact that *the recent boom has been a distressingly confined phenomenon* (i.e., that no one reads poetry except other poets), as mentioned in the first sentence of paragraph 4 (lines 39–40).

23. **(C)** The "poetry boosters" mentioned in line 67 are the people who are denying that poetry is receiving less general attention than it used to, and so the author's main disagreement is with them.

24. **(G)** The sentence running in lines 55–63 closes by making reference to poetry's *disappearance from public view*, and saying that poetry *has alienated itself from the people* is a paraphrase of this.

25. **(D)** *Residual* most nearly means "leftover" (think of *residue*). The sentence implies that poets' prestige lingers from a time when poetry actually mattered, simply because of cultural tradition.

26. **(F)** At the conclusion of a paragraph about how established poets have a guaranteed audience of budding poets, the phrase *proven marketing strategy* functions as a quip about how poets now write primarily for an audience of other poets—that is, it is *something poets have accepted and allowed to influence their writing*.

27. **(B)** Paragraph 7 (lines 64–74) depicts academics as being in denial about the decline of poetry's influence and importance.

28. **(H)** The implication of the analogy is that journal editors publish poetry not because anyone wants to read it, but simply because traditionally a literary journal is "supposed to" have poetry (just as a ranch is "supposed to" have buffalo).

29. **(D)** The sentence subsequent to the one quoted explains that many university jobs teaching creative writing are available. The implication is that poets *earn a living* by becoming professors.

30. **(G)** The passage establishes that poets write for an audience of poetry students, and earn a living by teaching poetry in universities. This all logically adds up to the idea that contemporary poets write with *professional advancement* (i.e., in the field of teaching poetry) in mind.

31. **(B)** The second sentence of the passage establishes that it concerns the discovery of fossils from crocodiles so large that they preyed on dinosaurs. (You can also get a clue from looking above the passage at the title, which includes the phrase *Dino-Eating Crocs*!)

32. **(J)** Lines 68–69 state that crocodiles *hunt a wide range of prey* and *eat whatever's available in their areas*. Therefore, their eating habits are *varied* and *opportunistic*. (When questions on the ACT Reading present choices of paired adjectives, the right answer is <u>almost always</u> one with *and* between them, rather than *but*!)

33. **(A)** Lines 91–92 suggest that crocodiles can grow to enormous sizes when *the right conditions arise,* and lines 73–74 establish that disparate lineages of giant crocs have arisen in *different places and times*. This all logically adds up to the idea that *crocodilians tend to grow as large as conditions permit them to*.

34. **(H)** Line 77 states that SuperCroc, and not *Deinosuchus*, lived in Niger.

35. **(C)** Paragraph 3 (lines 22–32) mainly discusses the fact that no undigested material was present in the fossilized dung, and that, since crocodiles' digestive systems digest everything, this suggests a crocodilian source.

36. **(J)** Lines 28–32 state that *both modern and ancient crocs* have digestive systems that eat up everything.

37. **(B)** *Lineages* means "bloodlines" (i.e., "ancestry"). It is the word from the choices that makes the most sense when plugged into the sentence.

38. **(F)** Lines 37–39 and 46–53 explain that *Deinosuchus* bite marks were found in fossilized dinosaur bones.

Practice Test 4

39. **(B)** Line 69 states that crocs *eat whatever's available in their areas,* suggesting that a crocodilian whose main food source dries up will simply eat something else. The fact that the answer to question 32 was J should have given you a clue here. (It is often the case on the ACT Reading that getting one right answer can help you figure out one or more others!)

40. **(J)** Lines 88–93 explain that the conditions necessary for the existence of giant crocs occur very rarely. Thus, the existence of giant crocs is *anomalous*, which means "not typical."

Answer Explanations: Science Test

1. **(C)** Look in Figure 3, which represents Static COF and the bar representing "Rubber on concrete" is the highest—that's all you have to do here! The only slightly tricky thing is that in Figure 2 (the graph for Kinetic COF) the bars for "Rubber on concrete" and "Rubber on asphalt" appear to be nearly equal, so someone who looks in the wrong place first might waste a few seconds being confused. (When you see something that appears to make no sense, always immediately double-check the labels to make sure you're looking at the right graph!)
2. **(G)** Look at the numbers on the vertical axis in Figure 2 and you'll see that the "Rubber on concrete" bar is at about 0.7 and the "Plastic on plastic" bar is at about 0.3. That's roughly (though not exactly) half as high. (But even without the numbers, you can easily just eyeball it—look at how far off the other answer choices are!)
3. **(D)** All this question wants you to do is look at Figure 3 (Static COF) and put the bars in order from lowest to highest. The order in choice D is correct.
4. **(F)** Even though the bars for "Rubber on concrete" and "Rubber on asphalt" in Figure 2 look roughly even, the "Rubber on concrete" bar is actually slightly higher, and so the height order of the bars in both graphs is indeed the same. (And even if you couldn't perceive that it is slightly higher, look how wrong the other choices are!)
5. **(B)** All this question is asking is which bar is the lowest (in both graphs). The bars represent friction, and less friction equals more speed. The "Plastic on plastic" bar is lowest in both graphs.
6. **(G)** All this question wants you to do is look in Table 1 and put those substances in highest to lowest order going by the numbers next to them.
7. **(D)** The water was 67°F when they started and 92°F after 5 minutes, so it went up by 25°F, meaning that 25 Btus were used (the text above Table 2 establishes that one pound of water was used).
8. **(F)** The first sentence of the paragraph in Experiment 2 clearly says that the students are measuring the amount of energy natural gas creates.
9. **(B)** Exact math is not necessary on this question, just guesstimating. Experiment 2 tells us that natural gas will heat one pound of water to 117°F after 10 minutes, and Experiment 1 tells us that the Btu/ton produced by gasoline is about 4/5 of the Btu/ton produced by natural gas. So you know that the answer is going to be around 4/5 of 117°F (less, but not too much less). The only choice that works is 99°F (it's less, but more than half).
10. **(H)** Table 3 says that a barrel of oil equals 5,600,000 Btus. That's way more than any of the other choices.
11. **(C)** The temperature in Table 2 is going up by 25°F every 5 minutes, and $142 + 25 = 167$.
12. **(F)** The y-axis (vertical line) in Figures 1 and 2 indicate cells per culture dish (millions), and the last sentence in the paragraph indicates results after three days are shown in the graphs.
13. **(D)** The lines for cell types A and B intersect at 0.4 mg/ml; thus the best answer must have both cell types included.
14. **(F)** An extrapolation of the cell type B line to where it would intersect should 25 uM be placed on the data graph would yield 4 million cells per culture dish.
15. **(B)** The question is asking you to locate the instances listed that would yield cell type A to be above cell type C and then find the one time (EXCEPT) when cell type C would be above cell type A. Thus the glucose at 0.2 mg/ml does have cell type A above cell type C but the 15 uM of calcium has cell type C above cell type A and that is the exception the question would have us select.
16. **(H)** Cell type B in calcium indicates an increase, whereas cell type B in glucose indicates a plateau or leveling of growth. The question asks for growth. Glucose would result in growth and then stagnation. Thus, the statement of calcium being more effective is in line with what the data shows in this particular instance.
17. **(A)** As Figure 1 and Table 1 indicate (and as you may already have known from school), low pH means acid and high pH means base, so a solution with a pH of 12.5 would be the strongest base.

18. **(H)** We look at Table 2 to see which substances made the bulb glow brightest, and then look at Table 3 to see the pH levels of those substances. You will notice that both strong acids and strong bases make the bulb glow brightest (in other words, the farther the pH is from 7 in either direction, the better a conductor the substance is).

19. **(C)** Table 3 says that KOH has a pH of 11.2, and Table 2 says that it made the bulb glow brightly, meaning that it is a strong base.

20. **(J)** Figure 1 says that stronger acids have more hydrogen, and Table 3 says that HCl has a pH of 0.86, making it a stronger acid than the other choices, and meaning it therefore has more hydrogen.

21. **(D)** A substance that makes the bulb glow brightly could be either a strong acid or a strong base, so the answer can't be determined from the information in the passage. (If you happen to know that NaCOl is the chemical formula for bleach, which is a strong base, you should ignore that knowledge, since the question is asking about what you can tell from the passage!)

22. **(G)** All you have to do here is plot the pH values listed in Table 3 for these substances as a bar graph. Table 3 says that the pH values for NaOH, KOH, and NH_4OH are 13.1, 11.2, and 9.2, respectively, so the graph in choice G is correct.

23. **(C)** That is the relationship shown in Figure 2. The key shows that salt marsh water is represented by the line with the x markers. The *x*-axis represents the aqueous concentration. The line with x markers clearly increases steadily, showing a direct relationship between the aqueous concentration and the white phosphorus mass: as the concentration increases, so does the mass.

24. **(H)** This is correct because of the data presented in Table 2. Look for the smallest number in the table. It is 29.1, in the first row and the last column. Look at the column and row headings to determine the answer is Trial 1 after 5-minutes static.

25. **(D)** This is correct because of the information presented in the opening passage. The third sentence explains the SPME technique and states, "a thin fused silica fiber ... is exposed to a sample ...."

26. **(H)** This is correct because of the data presented in Table 2. In order for the scientist's theory to be supported by the data, the numbers in the third column, titled 10-Min Sonic, would need to be larger than the numbers in the second column, titled 5-Min Sonic. However, that is not the case. The numbers in the second column are larger than those in the third column for Trials 2 and 3, meaning that more white phosphorus was extracted after 5-minutes sonication for those two trials only.

27. **(C)** Choice C is correct because of the data presented in Table 1. The last row in the table displays the mean mass of white phosphorus extracted from each type of water. The largest number in this row is 36.3, in the column with the heading Pond.

28. **(G)** This is correct because of the data presented in Figure 2. The *x*-axis represents the aqueous concentration, but the graph only includes concentrations up to 0.14 g/L. To infer the amount of white phosphorus that would be extracted at a concentration of 0.2 g/L, the line that represents pond water needs to be traced farther to the right along the *x*-axis. The key shows that the line with the triangle marker represents pond water. Following this line to the right demonstrates that the white phosphorus mass would continue to increase as the aqueous concentration increases. Since the line increases at a steep slope, and 0.2 g/L is much larger than 0.14 μg/L, we can infer that the answer would be much larger than 45, making 100 pg the only reasonable answer.

29. **(C)** This is a simple "Go Up, Hit Line, Go Over" question. In Figure 1, go up from silicon, hit the melting-point line (the broken one—and also the one on the bottom, since obviously substances melt at a lower temperature than the one at which they boil), and go over from there to the vertical axis, which reads about halfway between 1500 K and 2000 K below 1000 K. Of the choices, only 1700 K is a logical answer.

30. **(J)** The proton numbers of the elements in Table 1 get progressively greater, whereas the lines for melting point and boiling point in Table 2 go up and then back down. Remember, the passage states that both melting point and boiling point trend higher as intermolecular forces increase. Since there is no relationship with melting point and/or boiling point, there can be no relationship with the intermolecular forces.

31. **(D)** The two lines in Figure 1 basically each go up and down when the other does, but not exactly—that is, the lines are not always parallel and therefore there is no constant that can relate the two quantities.

32. **(F)** "Transitions from a liquid phase to a gaseous phase" means boiling point. According to the solid line in Figure 1, the element that boils at 500 K is phosphorus.

33. **(A)** The lines in Figure 1 are closer together above the elements that Table 1 names as nonmetals than they are above the elements identified as metals, so the conclusion is correct.

34. **(H)** The bar representing 500+ size operations is the lowest in Figure 1, which represents total losses by percentage.

35. **(C)** The bar representing CCD losses (the dark one) due to weather is the lowest bar in Figure 2, which plots the data for suspected causes of losses.

36. **(F)** The bar representing CCD losses (the dark one) due to starvation is the highest bar in Figure 2, which plots the data for suspected causes of losses.

37. **(D)** In Table 1 (which plots only CCD losses) the largest loss percentages are due to starvation in the smaller operations.

38. **(G)** All this question wants you to do is identify the suspected causes in Figure 2 that have CCD bars (the dark ones) higher than non-CCD bars (the light ones). The two that do are weak in fall and queen death.

39. **(C)** For three of the suspected causes in Figure 2—starvation, weather, and pests—the non-CCD bars are higher than the CCD bars. It would help you here to remember the answer to question 38. (It is often the case on the ACT Science that remembering answers to earlier questions on a passage can help you on later ones!)

40. **(J)** The scientists surveyed beekeepers to study CCD. The results of both Studies 1 and 2 show numbers related to CCD. Obviously, the beekeepers also had some colonies that did not experience CCD.

Writing Sample

Some people think that a fine-arts requirement in high school is frivolous or unfair and that required classes should only reflect "core academic subjects," and not "punish" kids with no artistic talent. I am not just in favor of the idea of high-school students being required to take a fine arts class—I am enthusiastic about it. Fine arts classes can be valuable in later life, can enhance a GPA or open a student's eyes to something new and provide a much-needed diversion from the rigors of the academic day.

Some people oppose this idea because there is not even enough time in a school day to get in all of the academic information. While this may be true, just because they spend all day in academic subjects doesn't mean students are learning. Students learn best when they are engaged. Often, arts related subjects provide students with an enhancement to the core curriculum and have a broader appeal than one might realize. Teenagers have the radio on all day long, and all the magazines we read and movies we watch are designed by people who have training in visual arts like photography. Art class doesn't just mean painting or working with clay—we could be doing graphic design on computers, and learning skills that we can use in later life just as often as some of the other academics. For example, an engineer will use physics, but he might also use a graphics computer program to help him design the next great bridge or skyscraper.

Another objection that some people have raised is the idea that an arts requirement would punish students who are not interested in the arts. True, there are many students who do not wish to take an art class because they believe that you need talent to succeed in this type of class and that they will be punished by receiving a low grade, or even worse face embarrassment. First of all, math class punishes kids who are not interested in math (when you grade the math section of my exam, you will realize this includes me), but everyone still has to take that. Sure, not every student is interested in art or music, but it's arbitrary to say that music and art are less important. In my experience, art and music teachers do not grade based on talent but give extra points for effort. And usually these classes raise students' GPAs not lower it. If people are still really nervous about fine arts, then maybe they could make the art and music classes pass/fail instead of assigning letter grades. Or better yet, they could give students the *option* of choosing pass/fail or letter grades—that way the students who are comfortable with the arts can raise their GPA, but the other students don't have to be scared to try something new. If an art or music class is pass/fail, then you pretty much automatically pass unless you cut class all the time, and I hope we are all in agreement that students shouldn't be cutting class no matter what class it is.

Even if some people are nervous about requiring art and music, these classes are good for teenagers. I don't have the data in front of me, but I know there have been many studies about how learning music makes you good at other things too. It exercises a certain part of your brain, and you get better at learning or thinking about complex ideas. Even if it didn't make you smarter, a music or art class would still mellow you out and might be beneficial as a sort of therapy. High school is an incredibly stressful time in people's lives, and having 40 minutes a day to relax and paint a painting or jam on a bass guitar might calm everybody down a little. Plus, taking up art or music as a hobby might occupy a student's time even outside of school, so they are less likely to get involved with things like drugs or vandalism. I speak from experience when I tell you that once a teenager falls in love with a musical instrument like the guitar, there is nothing he'd rather do than rush home to play it.

So I hope you'll agree that there is no reason to fear a so-called "fine arts" requirement in high school. Music and art are at least as useful and job-related as any other subject; there are many simple ways to keep anybody's GPA from suffering, and more exposure to art would be beneficial to the mental health and long-term well-being of today's stressed-out modern teenager.

Answer Sheet

PRACTICE TEST 5

Directions: Mark one answer only for each question. Make the mark dark. Erase completely any mark made in error. (Additional or stray marks will be counted as mistakes.)

English Test

1 Ⓐ Ⓑ Ⓒ Ⓓ	21 Ⓐ Ⓑ Ⓒ Ⓓ	41 Ⓐ Ⓑ Ⓒ Ⓓ	61 Ⓐ Ⓑ Ⓒ Ⓓ
2 Ⓕ Ⓖ Ⓗ Ⓙ	22 Ⓕ Ⓖ Ⓗ Ⓙ	42 Ⓕ Ⓖ Ⓗ Ⓙ	62 Ⓕ Ⓖ Ⓗ Ⓙ
3 Ⓐ Ⓑ Ⓒ Ⓓ	23 Ⓐ Ⓑ Ⓒ Ⓓ	43 Ⓐ Ⓑ Ⓒ Ⓓ	63 Ⓐ Ⓑ Ⓒ Ⓓ
4 Ⓕ Ⓖ Ⓗ Ⓙ	24 Ⓕ Ⓖ Ⓗ Ⓙ	44 Ⓕ Ⓖ Ⓗ Ⓙ	64 Ⓕ Ⓖ Ⓗ Ⓙ
5 Ⓐ Ⓑ Ⓒ Ⓓ	25 Ⓐ Ⓑ Ⓒ Ⓓ	45 Ⓐ Ⓑ Ⓒ Ⓓ	65 Ⓐ Ⓑ Ⓒ Ⓓ
6 Ⓕ Ⓖ Ⓗ Ⓙ	26 Ⓕ Ⓖ Ⓗ Ⓙ	46 Ⓕ Ⓖ Ⓗ Ⓙ	66 Ⓕ Ⓖ Ⓗ Ⓙ
7 Ⓐ Ⓑ Ⓒ Ⓓ	27 Ⓐ Ⓑ Ⓒ Ⓓ	47 Ⓐ Ⓑ Ⓒ Ⓓ	67 Ⓐ Ⓑ Ⓒ Ⓓ
8 Ⓕ Ⓖ Ⓗ Ⓙ	28 Ⓕ Ⓖ Ⓗ Ⓙ	48 Ⓕ Ⓖ Ⓗ Ⓙ	68 Ⓕ Ⓖ Ⓗ Ⓙ
9 Ⓐ Ⓑ Ⓒ Ⓓ	29 Ⓐ Ⓑ Ⓒ Ⓓ	49 Ⓐ Ⓑ Ⓒ Ⓓ	69 Ⓐ Ⓑ Ⓒ Ⓓ
10 Ⓕ Ⓖ Ⓗ Ⓙ	30 Ⓕ Ⓖ Ⓗ Ⓙ	50 Ⓕ Ⓖ Ⓗ Ⓙ	70 Ⓕ Ⓖ Ⓗ Ⓙ
11 Ⓐ Ⓑ Ⓒ Ⓓ	31 Ⓐ Ⓑ Ⓒ Ⓓ	51 Ⓐ Ⓑ Ⓒ Ⓓ	71 Ⓐ Ⓑ Ⓒ Ⓓ
12 Ⓕ Ⓖ Ⓗ Ⓙ	32 Ⓕ Ⓖ Ⓗ Ⓙ	52 Ⓕ Ⓖ Ⓗ Ⓙ	72 Ⓕ Ⓖ Ⓗ Ⓙ
13 Ⓐ Ⓑ Ⓒ Ⓓ	33 Ⓐ Ⓑ Ⓒ Ⓓ	53 Ⓐ Ⓑ Ⓒ Ⓓ	73 Ⓐ Ⓑ Ⓒ Ⓓ
14 Ⓕ Ⓖ Ⓗ Ⓙ	34 Ⓕ Ⓖ Ⓗ Ⓙ	54 Ⓕ Ⓖ Ⓗ Ⓙ	74 Ⓕ Ⓖ Ⓗ Ⓙ
15 Ⓐ Ⓑ Ⓒ Ⓓ	35 Ⓐ Ⓑ Ⓒ Ⓓ	55 Ⓐ Ⓑ Ⓒ Ⓓ	75 Ⓐ Ⓑ Ⓒ Ⓓ
16 Ⓕ Ⓖ Ⓗ Ⓙ	36 Ⓕ Ⓖ Ⓗ Ⓙ	56 Ⓕ Ⓖ Ⓗ Ⓙ	
17 Ⓐ Ⓑ Ⓒ Ⓓ	37 Ⓐ Ⓑ Ⓒ Ⓓ	57 Ⓐ Ⓑ Ⓒ Ⓓ	
18 Ⓕ Ⓖ Ⓗ Ⓙ	38 Ⓕ Ⓖ Ⓗ Ⓙ	58 Ⓕ Ⓖ Ⓗ Ⓙ	
19 Ⓐ Ⓑ Ⓒ Ⓓ	39 Ⓐ Ⓑ Ⓒ Ⓓ	59 Ⓐ Ⓑ Ⓒ Ⓓ	
20 Ⓕ Ⓖ Ⓗ Ⓙ	40 Ⓕ Ⓖ Ⓗ Ⓙ	60 Ⓕ Ⓖ Ⓗ Ⓙ	

Math Test

1 Ⓐ Ⓑ Ⓒ Ⓓ Ⓔ	16 Ⓕ Ⓖ Ⓗ Ⓙ Ⓚ	31 Ⓐ Ⓑ Ⓒ Ⓓ Ⓔ	46 Ⓕ Ⓖ Ⓗ Ⓙ Ⓚ
2 Ⓕ Ⓖ Ⓗ Ⓙ Ⓚ	17 Ⓐ Ⓑ Ⓒ Ⓓ Ⓔ	32 Ⓕ Ⓖ Ⓗ Ⓙ Ⓚ	47 Ⓐ Ⓑ Ⓒ Ⓓ Ⓔ
3 Ⓐ Ⓑ Ⓒ Ⓓ Ⓔ	18 Ⓕ Ⓖ Ⓗ Ⓙ Ⓚ	33 Ⓐ Ⓑ Ⓒ Ⓓ Ⓔ	48 Ⓕ Ⓖ Ⓗ Ⓙ Ⓚ
4 Ⓕ Ⓖ Ⓗ Ⓙ Ⓚ	19 Ⓐ Ⓑ Ⓒ Ⓓ Ⓔ	34 Ⓕ Ⓖ Ⓗ Ⓙ Ⓚ	49 Ⓐ Ⓑ Ⓒ Ⓓ Ⓔ
5 Ⓐ Ⓑ Ⓒ Ⓓ Ⓔ	20 Ⓕ Ⓖ Ⓗ Ⓙ Ⓚ	35 Ⓐ Ⓑ Ⓒ Ⓓ Ⓔ	50 Ⓕ Ⓖ Ⓗ Ⓙ Ⓚ
6 Ⓕ Ⓖ Ⓗ Ⓙ Ⓚ	21 Ⓐ Ⓑ Ⓒ Ⓓ Ⓔ	36 Ⓕ Ⓖ Ⓗ Ⓙ Ⓚ	51 Ⓐ Ⓑ Ⓒ Ⓓ Ⓔ
7 Ⓐ Ⓑ Ⓒ Ⓓ Ⓔ	22 Ⓕ Ⓖ Ⓗ Ⓙ Ⓚ	37 Ⓐ Ⓑ Ⓒ Ⓓ Ⓔ	52 Ⓕ Ⓖ Ⓗ Ⓙ Ⓚ
8 Ⓕ Ⓖ Ⓗ Ⓙ Ⓚ	23 Ⓐ Ⓑ Ⓒ Ⓓ Ⓔ	38 Ⓕ Ⓖ Ⓗ Ⓙ Ⓚ	53 Ⓐ Ⓑ Ⓒ Ⓓ Ⓔ
9 Ⓐ Ⓑ Ⓒ Ⓓ Ⓔ	24 Ⓕ Ⓖ Ⓗ Ⓙ Ⓚ	39 Ⓐ Ⓑ Ⓒ Ⓓ Ⓔ	54 Ⓕ Ⓖ Ⓗ Ⓙ Ⓚ
10 Ⓕ Ⓖ Ⓗ Ⓙ Ⓚ	25 Ⓐ Ⓑ Ⓒ Ⓓ Ⓔ	40 Ⓕ Ⓖ Ⓗ Ⓙ Ⓚ	55 Ⓐ Ⓑ Ⓒ Ⓓ Ⓔ
11 Ⓐ Ⓑ Ⓒ Ⓓ Ⓔ	26 Ⓕ Ⓖ Ⓗ Ⓙ Ⓚ	41 Ⓐ Ⓑ Ⓒ Ⓓ Ⓔ	56 Ⓕ Ⓖ Ⓗ Ⓙ Ⓚ
12 Ⓕ Ⓖ Ⓗ Ⓙ Ⓚ	27 Ⓐ Ⓑ Ⓒ Ⓓ Ⓔ	42 Ⓕ Ⓖ Ⓗ Ⓙ Ⓚ	57 Ⓐ Ⓑ Ⓒ Ⓓ Ⓔ
13 Ⓐ Ⓑ Ⓒ Ⓓ Ⓔ	28 Ⓕ Ⓖ Ⓗ Ⓙ Ⓚ	43 Ⓐ Ⓑ Ⓒ Ⓓ Ⓔ	58 Ⓕ Ⓖ Ⓗ Ⓙ Ⓚ
14 Ⓕ Ⓖ Ⓗ Ⓙ Ⓚ	29 Ⓐ Ⓑ Ⓒ Ⓓ Ⓔ	44 Ⓕ Ⓖ Ⓗ Ⓙ Ⓚ	59 Ⓐ Ⓑ Ⓒ Ⓓ Ⓔ
15 Ⓐ Ⓑ Ⓒ Ⓓ Ⓔ	30 Ⓕ Ⓖ Ⓗ Ⓙ Ⓚ	45 Ⓐ Ⓑ Ⓒ Ⓓ Ⓔ	60 Ⓕ Ⓖ Ⓗ Ⓙ Ⓚ

Answer Sheet

PRACTICE TEST 5

Reading Test

1 Ⓐ Ⓑ Ⓒ Ⓓ	11 Ⓐ Ⓑ Ⓒ Ⓓ	21 Ⓐ Ⓑ Ⓒ Ⓓ	31 Ⓐ Ⓑ Ⓒ Ⓓ
2 Ⓕ Ⓖ Ⓗ Ⓙ	12 Ⓕ Ⓖ Ⓗ Ⓙ	22 Ⓕ Ⓖ Ⓗ Ⓙ	32 Ⓕ Ⓖ Ⓗ Ⓙ
3 Ⓐ Ⓑ Ⓒ Ⓓ	13 Ⓐ Ⓑ Ⓒ Ⓓ	23 Ⓐ Ⓑ Ⓒ Ⓓ	33 Ⓐ Ⓑ Ⓒ Ⓓ
4 Ⓕ Ⓖ Ⓗ Ⓙ	14 Ⓕ Ⓖ Ⓗ Ⓙ	24 Ⓕ Ⓖ Ⓗ Ⓙ	34 Ⓕ Ⓖ Ⓗ Ⓙ
5 Ⓐ Ⓑ Ⓒ Ⓓ	15 Ⓐ Ⓑ Ⓒ Ⓓ	25 Ⓐ Ⓑ Ⓒ Ⓓ	35 Ⓐ Ⓑ Ⓒ Ⓓ
6 Ⓕ Ⓖ Ⓗ Ⓙ	16 Ⓕ Ⓖ Ⓗ Ⓙ	26 Ⓕ Ⓖ Ⓗ Ⓙ	36 Ⓕ Ⓖ Ⓗ Ⓙ
7 Ⓐ Ⓑ Ⓒ Ⓓ	17 Ⓐ Ⓑ Ⓒ Ⓓ	27 Ⓐ Ⓑ Ⓒ Ⓓ	37 Ⓐ Ⓑ Ⓒ Ⓓ
8 Ⓕ Ⓖ Ⓗ Ⓙ	18 Ⓕ Ⓖ Ⓗ Ⓙ	28 Ⓕ Ⓖ Ⓗ Ⓙ	38 Ⓕ Ⓖ Ⓗ Ⓙ
9 Ⓐ Ⓑ Ⓒ Ⓓ	19 Ⓐ Ⓑ Ⓒ Ⓓ	29 Ⓐ Ⓑ Ⓒ Ⓓ	39 Ⓐ Ⓑ Ⓒ Ⓓ
10 Ⓕ Ⓖ Ⓗ Ⓙ	20 Ⓕ Ⓖ Ⓗ Ⓙ	30 Ⓕ Ⓖ Ⓗ Ⓙ	40 Ⓕ Ⓖ Ⓗ Ⓙ

Science Test

1 Ⓐ Ⓑ Ⓒ Ⓓ	11 Ⓐ Ⓑ Ⓒ Ⓓ	21 Ⓐ Ⓑ Ⓒ Ⓓ	31 Ⓐ Ⓑ Ⓒ Ⓓ
2 Ⓕ Ⓖ Ⓗ Ⓙ	12 Ⓕ Ⓖ Ⓗ Ⓙ	22 Ⓕ Ⓖ Ⓗ Ⓙ	32 Ⓕ Ⓖ Ⓗ Ⓙ
3 Ⓐ Ⓑ Ⓒ Ⓓ	13 Ⓐ Ⓑ Ⓒ Ⓓ	23 Ⓐ Ⓑ Ⓒ Ⓓ	33 Ⓐ Ⓑ Ⓒ Ⓓ
4 Ⓕ Ⓖ Ⓗ Ⓙ	14 Ⓕ Ⓖ Ⓗ Ⓙ	24 Ⓕ Ⓖ Ⓗ Ⓙ	34 Ⓕ Ⓖ Ⓗ Ⓙ
5 Ⓐ Ⓑ Ⓒ Ⓓ	15 Ⓐ Ⓑ Ⓒ Ⓓ	25 Ⓐ Ⓑ Ⓒ Ⓓ	35 Ⓐ Ⓑ Ⓒ Ⓓ
6 Ⓕ Ⓖ Ⓗ Ⓙ	16 Ⓕ Ⓖ Ⓗ Ⓙ	26 Ⓕ Ⓖ Ⓗ Ⓙ	36 Ⓕ Ⓖ Ⓗ Ⓙ
7 Ⓐ Ⓑ Ⓒ Ⓓ	17 Ⓐ Ⓑ Ⓒ Ⓓ	27 Ⓐ Ⓑ Ⓒ Ⓓ	37 Ⓐ Ⓑ Ⓒ Ⓓ
8 Ⓕ Ⓖ Ⓗ Ⓙ	18 Ⓕ Ⓖ Ⓗ Ⓙ	28 Ⓕ Ⓖ Ⓗ Ⓙ	38 Ⓕ Ⓖ Ⓗ Ⓙ
9 Ⓐ Ⓑ Ⓒ Ⓓ	19 Ⓐ Ⓑ Ⓒ Ⓓ	29 Ⓐ Ⓑ Ⓒ Ⓓ	39 Ⓐ Ⓑ Ⓒ Ⓓ
10 Ⓕ Ⓖ Ⓗ Ⓙ	20 Ⓕ Ⓖ Ⓗ Ⓙ	30 Ⓕ Ⓖ Ⓗ Ⓙ	40 Ⓕ Ⓖ Ⓗ Ⓙ

Practice Test 5

ENGLISH TEST

45 MINUTES—75 QUESTIONS

Directions: In the five passages that follow, certain words and phrases are underlined and numbered. In the right-hand column, you will find alternatives for each underlined part. In most cases, you are to choose the one that best expresses the idea, makes the statement appropriate for standard written English, or is worded most consistently with the style and tone of the passage as a whole. If you think the original version is best, choose "NO CHANGE." In some cases, you will find in the right-hand column a question about the underlined part. You are to choose the best answer to the question.

You will also find questions about a section of the passage, or about the passage as a whole. These questions do not refer to an underlined portion of the passage, but rather are identified by a number or numbers in a box.

For each question, choose the alternative you consider best and fill in the corresponding oval on your answer document. Read each passage through once before you begin to answer the questions that accompany it. For many of the questions, you must read several sentences beyond the question to determine the answer. Be sure that you have read far enough ahead each time you choose an alternative.

Passage I

A Never-Ending Battle

Not many people know it, but the character was originally a villain. Intending it as an allegory for the growing Nazi menace in Europe, in 1933 two teenage, Jewish-American science-fiction [1] fans—Jerry Siegel and Joe Shuster—concocted a story for a pulp magazine about an evil figure with strange mind-control powers bent [2] on world domination. No one took much notice.

As the political situation in Europe and the Great Depression in America both worsened, and after Siegel's father died during a robbery of his New York City clothing store; the [3] two boys became disenchanted with writing about a villain. They decided that what the world needed were uplifting stories about a hero who used his

1. A. NO CHANGE
   B. two, teenage Jewish-American, science-fiction
   C. two teenage, Jewish-American, science-fiction,
   D. two teenage Jewish-American science-fiction

2. F. NO CHANGE
   G. powers being bent
   H. powers, which bent
   J. powers were bent

3. A. NO CHANGE
   B. store, the
   C. store. The
   D. store, therefore the

GO ON TO THE NEXT PAGE.

1 ■ ■ ■ ■ ■ ■ ■ ■ ■ 1

abilities to protect societies'[4] downtrodden and defenseless, rather than by exploiting[5] them.

Over the next few years they revamped their creation along these lines altering his appearance[6] and attributes but retaining the original name: Superman.

An instant success from his first appearance in 1938, when[7] Superman gave rise to the concept of the superhero, which quickly became the dominant genre of the comic-book medium. Today, everyone knows that a superhero is someone with special powers and a flashy costume involving shorts over tights, a cape and a logo,[8] on the chest. But few stop to consider the complex and moving psychological underpinnings of this cultural phenomenon. [9] Although he became a powerful symbol of "the American way," Superman is, like Siegel and Shuster's parents, an immigrant: the last survivor of[10] his doomed home planet of Krypton. In addition to his refugee status, some of Superman's other distinguishing characteristics also reflect his creators[11] heritage. His Kryptonian name, Kal-El, is similar to the Hebrew for "voice of God," and there has even been speculation that the famous "S" insignia on Superman's chest is a

4. **F.** NO CHANGE
   G. societys
   H. society's
   J. societies

5. **A.** NO CHANGE
   B. from exploiting
   C. was exploiting
   D. to exploit

6. **F.** NO CHANGE
   G. Over the next few years, they revamped their creation along these lines, altering his appearance
   H. Over the next few years they revamped their creation along these lines, altering his appearance,
   J. Over the next few years, they revamped their creation, along these lines altering his appearance

7. **A.** NO CHANGE
   B. however
   C. after which
   D. DELETE the underlined portion.

8. **F.** NO CHANGE
   G. shorts, over tights, a cape and a logo
   H. shorts over tights, a cape, and a logo
   J. shorts over tights a cape and a logo

9. If the writer were to delete the preceding sentence, the passage would primarily lose:
   A. a logical transition into the following sentence.
   B. details supporting the claim that the story of the creation of Superman is a moving one.
   C. insight into why so few people stop to consider the ideas concerned.
   D. an explanation of the psychological underpinnings of the creation of superheroes.

10. **F.** NO CHANGE
    G. parents an immigrant, the last survivor of
    H. parents, an immigrant, the last survivor: of
    J. parents, an immigrant—the last survivor—of

11. **A.** NO CHANGE
    B. his creators'
    C. Superman's creators
    D. Supermans creators'

subtle portrayal by the yellow badges that Jews were forced to wear in Nazi Germany.

12. F. NO CHANGE
    G. reference to
    H. definition of
    J. symbol within

The "Man of Steel" himself is invulnerable, but the story of his creation involves a great deal of suffering: a boy's mourning for his father, a people fleeing murderous oppression, and the struggle of immigrant groups became "more American than the Americans." Now and for all time, Superman symbolizes humanity's hope that the great power possessed by some will use for the benefit of all. [15]

13. A. NO CHANGE
    B. have became
    C. to become
    D. had become

14. F. NO CHANGE
    G. some use
    H. some have used
    J. some will be used

Question 15 asks about the preceding passage as a whole.

15. Suppose the author had intended to write an essay about the ways in which popular entertainment has been inspired by tragedy. Would this essay fulfill that goal?
    A. Yes, because it explains how suffering, on both personal and grand scales, led inevitably to the popularity of superhero comics.
    B. Yes, because Superman has appeared in a wide variety of media besides comic books.
    C. No, because the essay deals primarily with one specific character.
    D. No, because superhero comics are a niche medium that is only popular with a select audience.

Passage II

Splat, You're Out

I'm not sure whose idea it was, but around the end of ninth grade, a bunch of guys from my class, myself included: started playing paintball.

16. F. NO CHANGE
    G. class, myself included started
    H. class—myself included—started
    J. class. Myself included, started

If your not familiar, its that game where two teams run around shooting at each other with gas-powered

17. A. NO CHANGE
    B. you're not familiar, it's
    C. your not familiar, it's
    D. you're not familiar, its

Practice Test 5

GO ON TO THE NEXT PAGE.

guns that fire little pellets of brightly colored paint: get hit with a pellet, and you're out.[18]

18. Which of the following alternatives to the underlined portion would NOT be acceptable?

- **F.** getting hit with a pellet means you're out.
- **G.** when a player is hit, they're out.
- **H.** a direct hit means that a player is out.
- **J.** you're out once you get hit, but only until the next game.

[1] The first thing I learned about paintball is that it's quite an investment. A decent gun at the time costs[19] about seventy-five dollars, but that wasn't the end of it. [2] Pads aren't necessary, because getting shot in the arm or leg doesn't hurt much, but you'd be a fool to play without a facemask, throatguard, and another piece of athletic equipment specific to male players.

19.
- **A.** NO CHANGE
- **B.** having cost
- **C.** costing
- **D.** cost

[3] You'll be sufficiently sick, after your first day too, to shell out for a suit of camouflage after—the odds are—getting spotted a mile away and immediately peppered.[20] [4] And of course, paintball means regular bike rides to the sporting-goods store to buy more ammunition and get your gas canister refilled.

20.
- **F.** NO CHANGE
- **G.** The odds are, to shell out for a suit of camouflage, you'll be sufficiently sick after your first day of getting spotted, a mile away too, and immediately peppered.
- **H.** To shell out for a suit of camouflage after your first day, the odds are you'll be sufficiently sick of getting spotted a mile away and immediately peppered too.
- **J.** After your first day, the odds are you'll be sufficiently sick of getting spotted a mile away and immediately peppered to shell out for a suit of camouflage too.

[5] A bunch of protective gear is required too. [21]

21. For the sake of logic and coherence, Sentence 5 should be placed:

- **A.** where it is now.
- **B.** before Sentence 4.
- **C.** after Sentence 1.
- **D.** after Sentence 2.

Nowadays, there are official paintball ranges you can pay to play on, but we just played in the woods behind Bobby's house.[22] It was the only location where we could be sure not to hit any homes, cars, or innocent bystanders, that[23] surely would have brought our paintball days to an abrupt end. We cleared brush to make paths, and dug pits and erected walls to make two

22. Which of the following choices best introduces the paragraph?

- **F.** NO CHANGE
- **G.** There weren't any official paintball ranges near us (at least, not that we knew of).
- **H.** There were a few different guys in our crew whose houses had back woods big enough to play in.
- **J.** What we needed now was a safe place to play.

23.
- **A.** NO CHANGE
- **B.** bystanders
- **C.** bystanders, whom
- **D.** bystanders; any such occurrence

1 ■ ■ ■ ■ ■ ■ ■ ■ 1

opposing forts. This was more yardwork than we would have done even if our parents had paid us, but no hardship was going to stand between the thrill [24] of sneaking up on a friend and shooting him in the butt with exploding pellets of neon goo.

Now and then, the memories of my heroism that summer still bring [25] a smile to my face. There was the time I discovered a secret trail up a hillside full of pricker-bushes and picked off three guys without their having [26] any idea where I was. Then there was the time I snuck a giant sheet of clear plexiglass into Bobby's woods, put it up between two trees, and tauntingly danced safely behind it while opponents wasted their ammo. Sure, it was cheating, but it was also hilarious. [27]

[1] I guess, one by one, everyone got a girlfriend and stopped coming out to the games. [2] After a year or two, he probably did the same. [3] I ended up selling my gun and all my gear to a kid a couple of grades younger. [4] I didn't exactly remember [28] why we stopped playing. [5] And I'd like to believe that, even now, that same equipment is still being used by some ninth grader he is [29] discovering the joy of squeezing the trigger on a paintball gun and hearing his shot followed by a loud pop and a swear word from his friend echoing through the woods. [30]

24. **F.** NO CHANGE
    G. our thrill
    H. us and the thrill
    J. ourselves, and the thrill

25. **A.** NO CHANGE
    B. brings
    C. brought
    D. have brought

26. **F.** NO CHANGE
    G. having
    H. him having
    J. DELETE the underlined portion.

27. The author is considering deleting the underlined sentence. Should the author make this deletion?
    A. Yes, because such specific information about the rules of paintball is unnecessary in this brief essay.
    B. Yes, because it contradicts information presented elsewhere in the essay.
    C. No, because it is a humorous way of establishing that the author and his friends did not take the game too seriously.
    D. No, because it is important for the reader to know that the author is someone who once cheated at paintball.

28. **F.** NO CHANGE
    G. don't exactly remember
    H. hadn't exactly remembered
    J. wouldn't remember exactly

29. **A.** NO CHANGE
    B. just
    C. and
    D. whose

30. The most logical order for the sentences in the final paragraph would be:
    F. NO CHANGE
    G. 4, 3, 5, 1, 2.
    H. 4, 1, 3, 2, 5.
    J. 3, 5, 4, 2, 1.

Practice Test 5

GO ON TO THE NEXT PAGE.

Passage III

The following paragraphs may or may not be in the most logical order. Each paragraph is numbered in brackets, and question 45 will ask you to choose where paragraph 3 should most logically be placed.

On the Borderline of History

[1]

The now-familiar story of King Arthur, complete with Merlin the wizard, and the magic sword Excalibur first appeared [31] in a fanciful history of England composed in the 12th century by a monk named Geoffrey of Monmouth. Since today we know that there are no such things as wizards or magic swords, and discount [32] this version of events, but there are earlier works that mention Arthur as well. His first appearance in a surviving text is in the *Historia Brittonum*, composed by a Welsh monk around the year 830. Since Arthur's famous victory's [33] are all supposed to have taken place over three hundred years prior, the fact that no source in all those intervening years mentions [34] him is suspicious. On the other hand, this was not a terribly literate age, and of the few histories that were composed we know, of which [35] many have been simply lost.

[2]

Most of the battles and people mentioned in the *Historia* can be historically verified, which seems to

31. **A.** NO CHANGE
    B. story, of King Arthur complete with Merlin the wizard and the magic sword Excalibur first appeared
    C. story of King Arthur, complete with Merlin the wizard and the magic sword Excalibur, first appeared
    D. story of King Arthur complete with Merlin the wizard and the magic sword Excalibur first appeared

32. **F.** NO CHANGE
    G. swords discounted
    H. swords, we had discounted
    J. swords, we must discount

33. **A.** NO CHANGE
    B. Arthur's famous victories
    C. Arthurs famous victories'
    D. Arthur's famous victories'

34. **F.** NO CHANGE
    G. mention
    H. have mentioned
    J. were mentioning

35. **A.** NO CHANGE
    B. composed, but
    C. composed, we know that
    D. composed. Unfortunately,

1 ■ ■ ■ ■ ■ ■ ■ ■ 1

support the historicity of Arthur. [36] And yet, the earlier texts that corroborate the accounts of the battles make no mention of him. Therefore, the *Historia* does not even call Arthur a king at all, but only a "war leader" who succeeding commands the Britons in several battles against the invading Saxons. This would seem an account sufficiently humble at least to persuade us that *someone* named "Arthur" was involved in British history at this time, if not for the fact that the deeds attributed to him are so obviously exaggerated, such as the claim that he killed 960 men single-handedly at the Battle of Badon.

[3]

Most of us can't even remember being young enough not to have heard of him. His name is inseparable from all our romantic ideas about knights and chivalry. A majority of people think of him as an actual historical figure. But did King Arthur really exist?

36. The author is considering adding the following sentence at the point indicated:

> Vortigern, for example, was widely written about prior to the 9th century.

Should the author make this addition?

- **F.** Yes, because without it the essay would contain no proof that the author has actually read any earlier texts.
- **G.** No, because it is information that most people already possess.
- **H.** Yes, because otherwise readers might assume that the author knows only about Arthur and no other famous kings.
- **J.** No, because it is a minor fact that interrupts the flow of the paragraph.

37. **A.** NO CHANGE
B. Although,
C. Meanwhile,
D. Curiously,

38. **F.** NO CHANGE
G. successfully commanded
H. successful command
J. succeed commanding

39. The author is considering deleting the underlined portion and ending the sentence after the word *exaggerated.*

Should the author make this deletion?

- **A.** Yes, because there is no point in including a claim that we know can't possibly be true.
- **B.** Yes, because the essay fails to explain the significance of the Battle of Badon.
- **C.** No, because it provides support for the claim that Arthur's deeds are clearly unrealistic.
- **D.** No, because it establishes that even battles this long ago had high casualty rates.

40. Which of the following alternatives to the underlined portion would NOT be acceptable?

- **F.** Many of them
- **G.** You probably
- **H.** The odds are that anyone you might ask
- **J.** Even today, people

Practice Test 5

GO ON TO THE NEXT PAGE.

It's possible, but there is less evidence to support this claim than most realize. [41]

41. **A.** NO CHANGE
B. claim then you might think
C. claim then there used to be
D. claim, and than most realize

[4]

Every such early reference to Arthur seeming strongly like [42] an insertion of popular legend into an otherwise historical text. The two most reliable accounts of first-millennium England are the [43] *Anglo-Saxon Chronicle* and Bede's *Ecclesiastical History*—make no mention of Arthur, though they do include accounts of the battles with which he was allegedly involved. Countless scholars have labored for year's hope [44] of proving Arthur's existence, only to meet with the frustration that caused archaeologist Nowell Myres to remark that "no figure on the borderline of history and mythology has wasted more of the historian's time." [45]

42. **F.** NO CHANGE
G. seems strongly to be
H. seemed strong until
J. seems strong, but

43. **A.** NO CHANGE
B. England, the
C. England except for the
D. England—the

44. **F.** NO CHANGE
G. years hoped
H. years in the hopes
J. years and hoping

Question 45 asks about the preceding passage as a whole.

45. For the sake of logic and coherence, Paragraph 3 should be placed:

A. where it is now.
B. before Paragraph 1.
C. after Paragraph 1.
D. after Paragraph 4.

Passage IV

A Van Full of Nerds

They say boys won't dance unless their lives depend on it [46], but in my case all it took was for this girl I had a major crush on to start a ballroom dance club near the end of our sophomore year in college, where we'd been for almost two years. [47] Since I'd been hearing for years about how impossible it is to get boys to

46. Which of the following alternatives to the underlined portion would NOT be acceptable?

F. until pigs fly
G. like the deserts miss the rain
H. for all the tea in China
J. even if you pay them

47. **A.** NO CHANGE
B. college, which was almost halfway over.
C. college, which we had just gotten used to.
D. college.

dance, I hypothesized that no guys would show up except total nerds who couldn't find any other way to interact with girls. Afterwards, this category included me as well, but I figured that maybe out of all the nerds I'd be the coolest one.

I made sure to wear comfortable shoes to the first meeting. So did lots of cool kids, and lots of people in between. Pretty much half the school showed up, actually. I wasn't the only one who had a crush on Emily, so I guess lots of other guys had the same idea. And as for the girls, well, they never need an excuse to dance. Guys and girls switched partners every few minutes until the instructor finally started to lead us through the basics of several dances that I'd heard of, but knew nothing about, like the foxtrot, rhumba, and cha-cha. Emily was way up at the front of the banquet hall somewhere, but the place was so packed that I would've needed a stepladder and binoculars to see her. For some reason, I bothered attending the next few meetings, and I noticed an odd insight: there were fewer popular kids there each time.

The funny thing about popular kids are terrified of doing anything that isn't popular. So when they noticed that there were also nerds at the meetings, they figured "Better safe than sorry" and stopped coming. Since I wasn't cool enough to have a reputation to worry about,

48\. **F.** NO CHANGE
G. dance, and
H. dance, so
J. dance. I

49\. **A.** NO CHANGE
B. Allegorically,
C. Apparently,
D. Although

50\. Which of the following sentences best introduces the paragraph?
F. NO CHANGE
G. Sure enough, lots of nerds showed up to the first meeting.
H. The first meeting was held in a banquet hall on the north end of campus.
J. I had so much going on that week that I nearly spaced on attending the first meeting.

51\. **A.** NO CHANGE
B. when an instructor appeared and guided us
C. as the instructor the club had hired led us
D. and, meanwhile, the instructor put us

52\. Given that all the choices are true, which one best expresses the author's feelings of distance from Emily?
F. NO CHANGE
G. in that vintage maroon dress that flared out whenever she spun around.
H. with that friend of hers who always pulled her away whenever I tried to talk to her.
J. probably dancing with that jerk who always wore soccer shorts, even in the winter.

53\. **A.** NO CHANGE
B. portrayal
C. aspect
D. phenomenon

54\. **F.** NO CHANGE
G. kids is
H. kids, who are
J. kids is that they're

1 ■ ■ ■ ■ ■ ■ ■ ■ ■ 1

I stuck things <u>out, and after</u> [55] a few weeks I was practically the most popular guy there (or at least, the least unpopular).

My plan to get closer to Emily would have worked perfectly if not for two <u>things, like the</u> [56] fact that sophomore year ended and I had to wait out the summer, and the fact that Emily had decided to take her junior year abroad and wasn't there anymore in the fall. But this disappointing turn of events <u>weren't my only problems:</u> [57] by this time, the club was ready to start attending ballroom dance competitions, and somehow, I was one of the best dancers and felt too guilty to quit!

For the rest of college, I spent one weekend a month driving to some stupid dance competition in a van full of nerds. If you're about to enter college yourself, heed my advice: never join a club for a girl, or at least make sure that she <u>first</u> [58] isn't about to disappear to France for a year.

Anyway, at least now, when <u>my friend got married, I'm</u> [59] the only guy at the wedding who knows how to dance.

<u>And I also know a lot of knock-knock jokes about math!</u> [60]

55. Which of the following alternatives to the underlined portion would NOT be acceptable?
    A. out, after
    B. out; after
    C. out: after
    D. out. After

56. **F.** NO CHANGE
    G. things, and the
    H. things: the
    J. things. Like the

57. **A.** NO CHANGE
    B. was suddenly the least of my problems:
    C. were surpassed by a bigger problem:
    D. is my only problem:

58. The best placement in the sentence for the underlined portion would be:
    F. where it is now.
    G. after the word *sure*.
    H. after the word *disappear*.
    J. after the word *France*.

59. **A.** NO CHANGE
    B. our friends got married, I was
    C. my friends were married, I was
    D. a friend gets married, I'm

60. The author is considering deleting this sentence and ending the essay with the previous one. Should the author make this deletion?
    F. Yes, because the sentence is sarcastic, and so far the essay has been utterly free of sarcasm.
    G. Yes, because it is unrelated to dance, and the essay is primarily a sociological one about ballroom dancing's recent resurgence in popularity.
    H. No, because it provides humorous insight into the author's experience of having to hang out with nerds.
    J. No, because the sentence is useless without specific examples of these jokes.

1 ■ ■ ■ ■ ■ ■ ■ ■ 1

Passage V

The Greatest

[1]

In Louisville Kentucky, in 1954 12-year-old (61) Cassius Clay's bike was stolen. Devastated, he vowed (62) to beat up the thief if he ever found him, and someone suggested that Cassius had taken (63) boxing lessons before making such boasts.

[2]

[1] It would not be the last time he would prove everyone wrong, but even bigger, greater struggles (64) lay ahead. [2] After winning a gold medal at the 1960 Olympics he turned pro, and stunned the sporting world, by defeating Sonny Liston for the heavyweight championship. (65) [3] He turned out to be a very gifted boxer, and decided to stick with the sport, working his way up through the amateur ranks. [4] Liston had been heavily favored, and Cassius's brashness; prior to the fight he'd (66) called himself "too fast" and "too pretty" to lose—had made people think he was in for a rude awakening. [67]

61. **A.** NO CHANGE
    B. Louisville Kentucky, in 1954, 12-year-old
    C. Louisville, Kentucky in 1954, 12-year-old
    D. Louisville, Kentucky, in 1954, 12-year-old

62. **F.** NO CHANGE
    G. Devastation vows
    H. Devastatedly vowing
    J. Devastated, and he vowed

63. **A.** NO CHANGE
    B. took
    C. would take
    D. had better take

64. **F.** NO CHANGE
    G. bigger struggles
    H. greater, more challenging struggles
    J. more challenges to overcome

65. **A.** NO CHANGE
    B. After winning a gold medal, at the 1960 Olympics he turned pro and stunned the sporting world, by defeating Sonny Liston for the heavyweight championship.
    C. After winning a gold medal at the 1960 Olympics, he turned pro and stunned the sporting world by defeating Sonny Liston, for the heavyweight championship.
    D. After winning a gold medal at the 1960 Olympics, he turned pro and stunned the sporting world by defeating Sonny Liston for the heavyweight championship.

66. **F.** NO CHANGE
    G. brashness prior to the fight, and
    H. brashness prior to the fight—he'd
    J. brashness: prior to the fight he'd

67. The most logical order for the sentences in Paragraph 2 would be:
    A. NO CHANGE
    B. 1, 3, 2, 4.
    C. 3, 2, 4, 1.
    D. 3, 1, 4, 2.

Practice Test 5

GO ON TO THE NEXT PAGE.

[3]

After the victory, Clay announced that he had converted to Islam, and changed his name to the one by which we know him[68] today: Muhammad Ali. In addition to defeating one challenger after another, Ali became active in the Black civil rights movement, which upset[69] many conservative boxing fans. In 1966, the U.S. government tried to draft Ali into service in the Vietnam War. Unsurprisingly, on[70] religious grounds, he refused to go, and was stripped of his title and imprisoned.

[4]

Released in 1970, another shot at the championship was soon in the works for Ali,[71] against the undefeated George Foreman. Foreman seemed invincible, and fans feared that Ali might be seriously hurt or even killed. Ali spent the beginning of the fight on the ropes, and seemed to be losing badly, but then his strategy became clear: after Foreman exhausted him,[72] Ali sprang to life, knocking out the younger fighter in the eighth round.

[5]

Ali retired in 1981, and was eventually diagnosed with Parkinson's disease, but the sporting world he'd once shocked now revered him.[73] He lit the Olympic flame before an adoring crowd in 1996, and *Sports Illustrated* magazine later named him "Sportsman of

68. **F.** NO CHANGE
G. one, which we know
H. one in which we know
J. one that we know of him

69. Which of the following alternatives to the underlined portion would be LEAST acceptable?
A. movement; this upset
B. movement, this choice upset
C. movement, thereby upsetting
D. movement, a decision that upset

70. **F.** NO CHANGE
G. Therefore, on
H. Although on
J. On

71. **A.** NO CHANGE
B. the championship would be Ali's again if he managed to win his bout
C. the boxing commission eventually granted Ali a chance to regain the championship: a match
D. Ali worked his way up to another shot at the championship,

72. **F.** NO CHANGE
G. exhausted,
H. when Foreman had exhausted himself,
J. quickly, before Foreman was exhausted,

73. **A.** NO CHANGE
B. finally shocking the sporting world into revering him
C. both shocking and revering the sporting world
D. which the sporting world first shocked, but then revered

the Century," for his combination of skill, bravery and magnetism. [74] Ali himself still prefers the familiar title he correctly predicted he would hold: "The Greatest of All Time." [75]

74. **F.** NO CHANGE
G. Century" for his combination of skill, bravery, and magnetism.
H. Century" for his combination, of skill, bravery and magnetism.
J. Century" for his combination of skill bravery and magnetism.

Question 75 asks about the preceding passage as a whole.

75. Suppose the author had intended to write an essay for boxing fans about what made Muhammad Ali such a successful boxer. Did this essay achieve that goal?
A. Yes, because it makes very clear that Ali is widely considered the greatest boxer of all time.
B. No, because it is more an essay for a general audience about Ali's cultural importance.
C. Yes, because the essay describes the strategy Ali used to win one very famous fight.
D. No, because the essay's style is much too flowery and verbose to appeal to boxing fans.

STOP

If there is still time remaining, check your answers to this section.

2 △ △ △ △ △ △ △ △ 2

MATHEMATICS TEST

60 MINUTES—60 QUESTIONS

Directions: Solve each problem, choose the correct answer, and then fill in the corresponding oval on your answer document.

Do not linger over problems that take too much time. Solve as many as you can; then return to the others in the time you have left for this test.

You are permitted to use a calculator on this test. You may use your calculator for any problems you choose, but some of the problems may best be done without using a calculator.

Note: Unless otherwise stated, all of the following should be assumed.

1. Illustrative figures are NOT necessarily drawn to scale.
2. Geometric figures lie in a plane.
3. The word *line* indicates a straight line.
4. The word *average* indicates arithmetic mean.

DO YOUR FIGURING HERE.

1. If $\frac{5x}{3} + 6 = 4$, then $x = ?$

   A. 6
   B. $\frac{6}{5}$
   C. 0
   D. $-\frac{6}{5}$
   E. –4

2. A Fahrenheit temperature F can be approximated by doubling the Celsius temperature C and adding 32. If the temperature outside is 18°C, what is the approximate temperature in Fahrenheit?

   F. 25°
   G. 41°
   H. 50°
   J. 68°
   K. 100°

3. Carol worked one summer and earned money that she spent on new clothes. After spending 65% of her money, Carol had $875 left. How much money did Carol earn for the summer?

   A. $1,625
   B. $2,500
   C. $3,375
   D. $4,125
   E. $7,375

2 △ △ △ △ △ △ △ △ 2

4. $(x^4)^{15}$ is equivalent to:

F. $60x$
G. $15x^4$
H. $15x^{11}$
J. x^{19}
K. x^{60}

DO YOUR FIGURING HERE.

5. Doris and Clyde volunteered to help paint their friend's apartment. Doris used $1\frac{3}{4}$ gallons of paint and Clyde used $2\frac{1}{2}$ gallons. If 5 gallons of paint were purchased, how many gallons were left?

A. $\frac{3}{4}$
B. $1\frac{3}{4}$
C. $3\frac{1}{4}$
D. $4\frac{1}{4}$
E. $4\frac{1}{2}$

6. The expression $(3p + 4)(5p - 6)$ is equivalent to:

F. $8p^2 - 24$
G. $8p^2 + 2p - 24$
H. $15p^2 - 24$
J. $15p^2 - 4p - 24$
K. $15p^2 + 2p - 24$

7. What is a possible equation for a line that is parallel to $4x - 3y = 6$?

A. $y = -\frac{4}{3}x + 2$
B. $y = \frac{3}{4}x - 2$
C. $y = -4x + 6$
D. $y = \frac{4}{3}x + 2$
E. $y = -\frac{3}{4}x - 2$

8. In an isosceles triangle, the measure of each of the base angles is one-third the measure of the vertex angle. What is the measure, in degrees, of each of the base angles?

F. 36°
G. 60°
H. 72°
J. 108°
K. 216°

Practice Test 5

DO YOUR FIGURING HERE.

9. What is the length, in feet, of the hypotenuse of a right triangle with legs that are 8 feet long and 9 feet long, respectively?

   A. $\sqrt{17}$
   B. $\sqrt{145}$
   C. 17
   D. 36
   E. 72

10. The lengths of the corresponding sides of 2 similar right triangles are in the ratio of 3:4. If the hypotenuse of the larger triangle is 6 inches long, how many inches long is the hypotenuse of the smaller triangle?

    F. 3.5
    G. 4
    H. 4.5
    J. 8
    K. 18

11. When Sara bought gas for her car 30 years ago, the price was 20% of today's price. If today's price is \$3.25, which of the following is closest to the price of a gallon of gas 30 years ago?

    A. \$3.05
    B. \$2.60
    C. \$1.30
    D. \$0.65
    E. \$0.60

12. To the nearest foot, what is the length of a diagonal of the top of a rectangular platform that is 14 feet wide and 15 feet long?

    F. 16
    G. 19
    H. 21
    J. 22
    K. 29

13. Which real number satisfies $(3^x)(9) = 27^2$?

    A. 1
    B. 3
    C. 4
    D. 4.5
    E. 8

2 △ △ △ △ △ △ △ △ 2

DO YOUR FIGURING HERE.

14. A rectangular room that is 3 feet longer than it is wide has an area of 54 square feet. How many feet long is the room?

F. 6
G. 9
H. 15
J. 18
K. 27

15. The perimeter of a parallelogram is 36 inches, and one side measures 6 inches. What are the lengths, in inches, of the other 3 sides?

A. 6, 6, 18
B. 6, 9, 9
C. 6, 12, 12
D. 6, 15, 15
E. Cannot be determined from the given information.

16. The average of 5 numbers is 7. If each of the numbers is decreased by 4, what is the average of the 5 new numbers?

F. 0.0
G. 1.0
H. 2.0
J. 3.0
K. 7.0

17. Julie works in a clothing store and gets a base salary of $48.00 plus a fixed amount for each item she sells per day. Yesterday she earned $68.00 because she sold 4 items. If Julie sells 3 more items today than yesterday, what will she earn for the day?

A. $51.00
B. $55.00
C. $63.00
D. $78.00
E. $83.00

18. If $\frac{6}{x} \geq \frac{1}{4}$, what is the largest possible value for x?

F. $\frac{2}{3}$
G. 1.5
H. 10
J. 24
K. 36

Practice Test 5

19. Starting at midnight, how many degrees has the hour hand of a clock moved when it gets to 8:00 A.M.?

A. 80°
B. 100°
C. 120°
D. 240°
E. 270°

DO YOUR FIGURING HERE.

20. An airplane has r rows of seats with $(s + d)$ seats in each row. Which of the following is an expression for the number of seats in the entire airplane?

F. $(r \cdot s) + d$
G. $(r \cdot s) + (r \cdot d)$
H. $s + (r \cdot d)$
J. $r \cdot s \cdot d$
K. $r + s + d$

21. Which nonnegative value of x makes the expression $\frac{1}{16 - x^2}$ undefined?

A. 256
B. 32
C. 16
D. 8
E. 4

22. A punch recipe calls for 3 parts fruit juice to 2 parts soda. In order to make 20 quarts of punch, how many quarts of fruit juice should be used?

F. 12
G. 9
H. 8
J. 6
K. 4

23. A line contains the points E, F, G, and H. Point F is between points E and G. Point H is between points G and F. Which of the following inequalities must be true about the lengths of these segments?

A. $FG < EF$
B. $GH < FG$
C. $FH < GH$
D. $GH < EF$
E. $FH < EF$

2 △ △ △ △ △ △ △ △ 2

DO YOUR FIGURING HERE.

24. What is the volume, in cubic centimeters, of a cone with a height of 9 centimeters and a base with a radius of 4 centimeters? (The volume of a cone is $\frac{\pi}{3}r^2h$, where r is the radius of the base of the cone and h is the height of the cone.)

F. 144π
G. 72π
H. 48π
J. 16π
K. 9π

25. One endpoint of a diameter of a circle with center (3, –4) has coordinates (5, –3) in the standard (x, y) plane. What are the coordinates of the other endpoint of that diameter?

A. (1, –5)
B. (1, 2)
C. (–1, 5)
D. $(3 + \sqrt{5}, -3 + \sqrt{5})$
E. $(3 - \sqrt{5}, -3 - \sqrt{5})$

26. At an airport, the planes take off from two airfields. One of the fields is capable of sending up a plane every 4 minutes. The other field is capable of sending up 5 planes every 10 minutes. At these rates, which of the following is the best estimate of the total number of minutes the two airfields would need to send up 15 planes?

F. 10
G. 12
H. 15
J. 18
K. 20

27. Which of the following expressions represents the product xy, if $x = 4a^3$ and $y = -3a^5 + b$?

A. $a^3 + b$
B. $a^5 + b$
C. $-12a^8 + 4a^3b$
D. $-12a^{15} + 4a^3b$
E. $-243a^{15} + 4a^3b$

Practice Test 5

DO YOUR FIGURING HERE.

28. Ann is wrapping a gift for her friend's shower. She wants to cut ribbon so that she can place it on the gift as shown in the picture below. What is the minimum length of the ribbon, in centimeters, that Ann would need to cut in order to wrap the box, assuming no overlap?

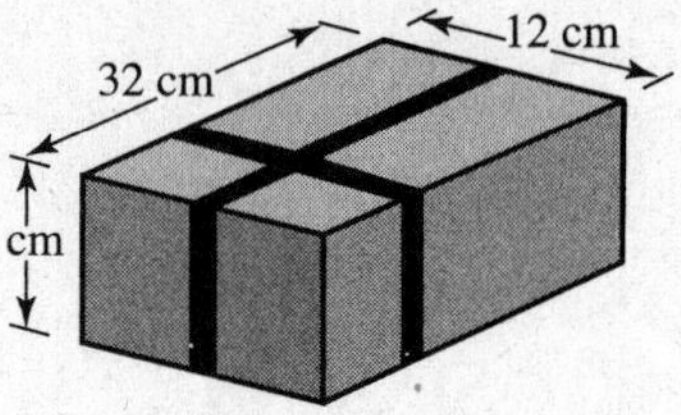

F. 52
G. 104
H. 120
J. 128
K. 3,072

29. For all nonzero x and y, $\dfrac{(9x^{-2}y^2)(-8x^2y^3)}{(4x^2y^4)} = ?$

A. $\dfrac{-9x^6y}{4}$
B. $\dfrac{x^2y^2}{18}$
C. $-18x^{-2}$
D. $-18x^{-2}y$
E. $-18x^2y^2$

30. What is the area in centimeters of the polygon below?

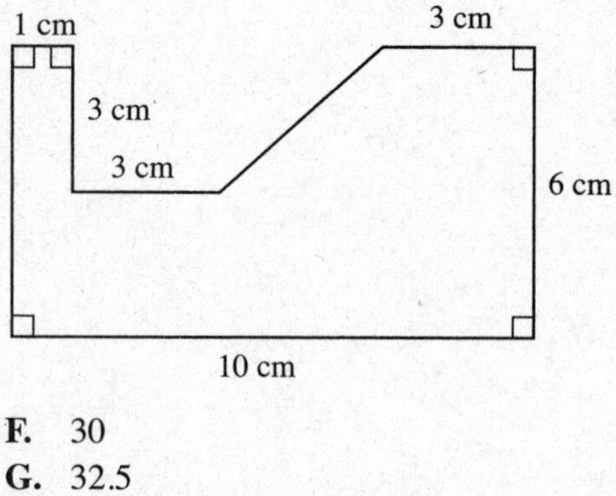

F. 30
G. 32.5
H. 35
J. 42
K. 46.5

2 △ △ △ △ △ △ △ △ 2

Use the figure below to answer questions 31–32.

DO YOUR FIGURING HERE.

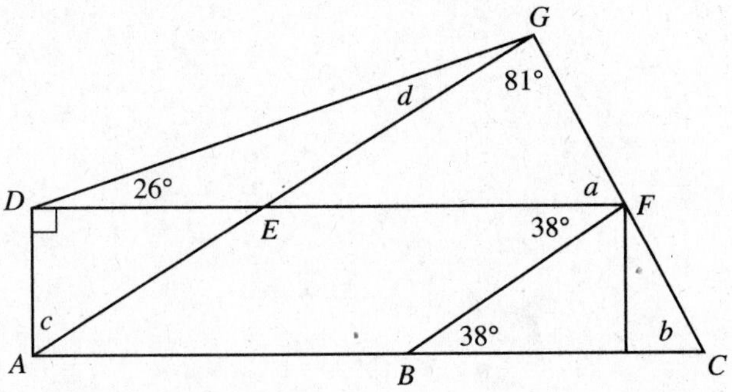

31. In the quadrilateral *ACGD*, *DF* ∥ *AC* and *AG* ∥ *BF*. What is the value of ∠*d*?

A. 9°
B. 12°
C. 21°
D. 26°
E. 38°

32. For triangle *EFG*, what is the value of ∠*a*?

F. 52°
G. 58°
H. 61°
J. 71°
K. 73°

33. A boat is anchored in a small lake with a rope that is 34 feet long. A wind blows the boat until the rope is taut and the water is 16 feet deep. Measuring across the bottom of the lake, how far has the boat moved from the anchor?

A. 30
B. 50
C. 60
D. 80
E. 120

Practice Test 5

GO ON TO THE NEXT PAGE.

2 △ △ △ △ △ △ △ △ 2

DO YOUR FIGURING HERE.

34. If a and b are real numbers and $\sqrt{3\left(\frac{a^2}{b}\right)} = 1$, then what must be true of the value of b?

F. b must be positive.
G. b must be negative.
H. b must equal $\frac{1}{3}$.
J. b must equal 3.
K. b may have any value.

35. In the figure below, ℓ_1 is parallel to ℓ_2, and ℓ_3 is parallel to ℓ_4. What is the value of $\angle b$?

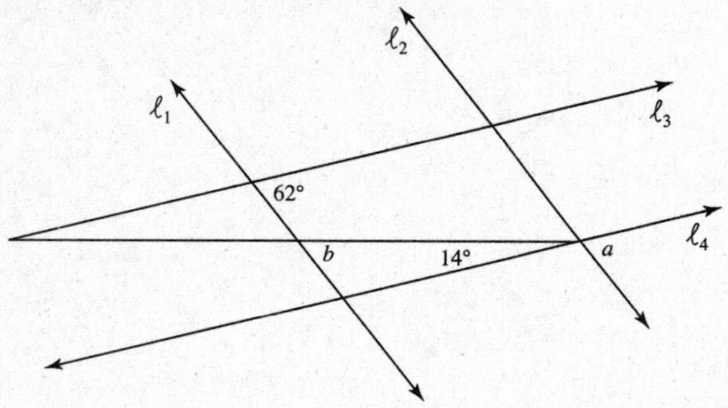

A. 44
B. 46
C. 48
D. 62
E. 132

36. If $0° \le x \le 90°$ and $\cos x = \frac{8}{17}$, then $\tan x = ?$

F. $\frac{8}{15}$
G. $\frac{15}{17}$
H. $\frac{17}{15}$
J. $\frac{15}{8}$
K. $\frac{17}{8}$

2 △ △ △ △ △ △ △ △ 2

37. In the figure, AD is a diameter of the circle with center O and $AO = 5$. What is the measure of arc BCD?

DO YOUR FIGURING HERE.

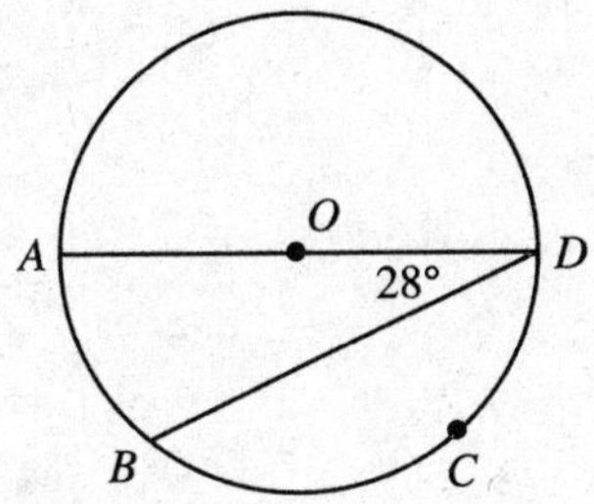

A. 56°
B. 116°
C. 120°
D. 124°
E. 128°

38. If $\sin \theta = \frac{1}{2}$ and $\cos \theta = \frac{\sqrt{3}}{2}$, then $\csc \theta = ?$

F. 2
G. $\sqrt{3}$
H. $\frac{2\sqrt{3}}{3}$
J. $\frac{2}{3}$
K. $\frac{\sqrt{3}}{3}$

39. Triangle PQR is equilateral. Find the sum of $a + b + c + d$.

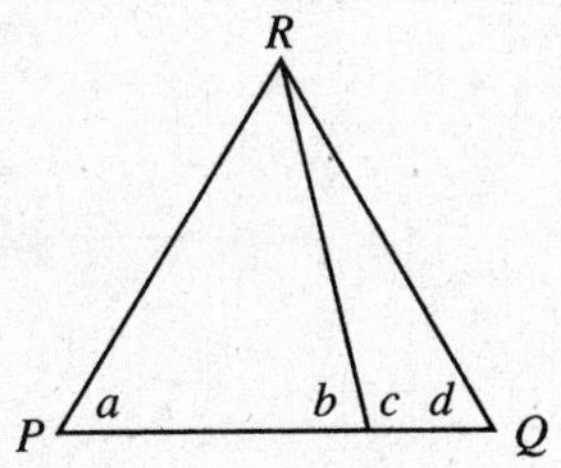

A. 180°
B. 210°
C. 240°
D. 270°
E. 300°

Practice Test 5

GO ON TO THE NEXT PAGE.

2 △ △ △ △ △ △ △ △ 2

40. If ⊕ is defined for all positive numbers a and b by $a \oplus b = \frac{ab}{a+b}$, then $8 \oplus 2 = ?$

DO YOUR FIGURING HERE.

F. $\frac{1}{2}$
G. $\frac{2}{3}$
H. $\frac{8}{9}$
J. 1
K. $\frac{8}{5}$

41. The measures of the lengths of the 3 sides of a triangle are prime numbers. If 2 of the sides are 5 and 23, how many different lengths are possible for the third side?

A. 1
B. 2
C. 9
D. More than 18 but less than 29
E. An infinite number

42. If a wheel on a stationary bike is 26 inches in diameter, and Mike pedals to make the wheel revolve 50 times, what would be the total distance that the wheel would travel if it weren't stationary?

F. 169π
G. 1,300
H. 676π
J. $1{,}300\pi$
K. $2{,}600\pi$

43. What is the equivalent of $(3i + 4)^2$?

A. $12i^2$
B. $9i^2 + 16$
C. $3i^2 + 24i + 16$
D. $7 + 24i$
E. $13 + 24i$

2 △ △ △ △ △ △ △ △ 2

44. Maureen wants to put an exercise wheel in her hamster's cage. The height of the cage is 22 inches, but there must be a 1-inch space above and below the wheel to allow for the wheel frame. What is the radius of the largest wheel that Maureen can place in the cage?

F. 5
G. $2\sqrt{5}$
H. 10
J. 11
K. 20

DO YOUR FIGURING HERE.

45. What is the sum of the first 15 multiples of 5?

A. 375
B. 560
C. 600
D. 750
E. 1,200

46. If $\frac{n!}{(n-1)!} = 5$, then $(n - 2)! = ?$

F. 6
G. 20
H. 30
J. 60
K. 120

47. At a local restaurant a customer can order a lunch special with the following choices: a salad **OR** 2 kinds of soup and a sandwich with 4 types of meat, 2 types of bread, and 3 types of cheese. How many different combinations could be made for the lunch special?

A. 11
B. 12
C. 48
D. 72
E. 96

48. What is the distance, in coordinate units, between the points $S(-\sqrt{2}, 7)$ and $T(-3\sqrt{2}, 9)$ in the standard (x, y) coordinate plane?

F. 2
G. 3
H. $2\sqrt{3}$
J. $4\sqrt{2}$
K. 6

2 △ △ △ △ △ △ △ △ 2

DO YOUR FIGURING HERE.

49. Which of the following expressions is equivalent to $\frac{a}{b}$ if all integers a, b, and c are positive?

A. $\frac{a \cdot c}{b \cdot c}$

B. $\frac{b \cdot a}{a \cdot b}$

C. $\frac{a \cdot a}{b \cdot b}$

D. $\frac{a + c}{b + c}$

E. $\frac{a - c}{b - c}$

50. The sum of twice a smaller number and three times a larger number is 49. The larger of the two numbers exceeds four times the smaller number by 7. If x is the smaller number, which equation below determines the correct value of x?

F. $2(4x + 7) + 3x = 49$

G. $2(4x - 7) + 3x = 49$

H. $(12x + 7) + 2x = 49$

J. $3(4x + 7) + 2x = 49$

K. $3(4x - 7) + 2x = 49$

51. If $x = 3t - 7$ and $y = 4 - t$, which of the following expresses y in terms of x?

A. $y = 5 - x$

B. $y = \frac{5 - x}{3}$

C. $y = 4 - x$

D. $y = 11 - 3x$

E. $y = \frac{19 - x}{3}$

52. Which of the following is an equation of the line that passes through the points (2, 4) and (–2, –12) in the standard (x, y) coordinate plane?

F. $y = 8$

G. $4x - y = 4$

H. $4x + y = -4$

J. $7x - 3y = 2$

K. $8x - 2y = 7$

53. If $f(x) = 7x^2 - 4x - 10$, then $f(-3) = ?$

A. 85

B. 65

C. 41

D. –1

E. –61

Practice Test 5

2 △ △ △ △ △ △ △ 2

DO YOUR FIGURING HERE.

54. How much larger, in degrees, is the measure of one angle in a regular 8-sided polygon than the measure of one angle in a regular 6-sided polygon? (The measure of each interior angle of a regular n-sided polygon is $\frac{(n-2)180}{n}$.)

F. 15°
G. 27°
H. 108°
J. 120°
K. 135°

55. Which of the following expressions is equivalent to $3\log_2 x + \frac{1}{3}\log_4 y - \log_2 z$ when x, y, and z are positive real numbers?

A. $\log_2 \frac{x^3 y}{z}$

B. $\log_2 \frac{z}{x^3} + \log_4\left(\frac{y}{3}\right)$

C. $\log_2\left(\frac{x^3}{z}\right) + \log_4\left(\sqrt[3]{y}\right)$

D. $\log_2(x - z) + \log_4\left(\sqrt[3]{y}\right)$

E. $3\log_2(x - z) + \log_4\left(\frac{y}{3}\right)$

56. For all $x > 10$, $\frac{(x^2 + 8x + 15)(x - 2)}{(x^2 + 3x - 10)(x + 3)} = ?$

F. $\frac{3}{2}$

G. $\frac{(x-2)}{(x+2)}$

H. $\frac{2(x-2)}{x+3}$

J. 1

K. $-\frac{3(x-2)}{x+3}$

57. If the amplitude of a trigonometric function is $\frac{1}{2}$ the nonnegative difference between the maximum and minimum values of the function, which of the following trigonometric functions has an amplitude of 3?

A. $\frac{1}{3}\cos x$

B. $\cos 3x$

C. $\sin \frac{1}{3} x$

D. $3 \tan x$

E. $3 \sin x$

Practice Test 5

GO ON TO THE NEXT PAGE.

58. If $90° < x < 180°$, which of the following equals $\sin x$, if $\tan x = -\frac{24}{7}$?

F. $\frac{-24}{25}$
G. $\frac{-7}{25}$
H. $\frac{7}{25}$
J. $\frac{7}{24}$
K. $\frac{24}{25}$

59. Which of the following is the factored form of the expression $12x^2 - x - 6$?

A. $(3x + 2)(4x - 3)$
B. $(3x - 2)(4x + 3)$
C. $(4x + 2)(3x - 3)$
D. $(6x + 1)(2x - 6)$
E. $(x - 2)(12x + 3)$

60. Harry has a bag containing jelly beans: 7 pink, 8 blue, and 9 orange. How many additional pink beans must be added to the 24 jelly beans already in the bag so that the probability of randomly drawing a pink jelly bean is $\frac{1}{2}$?

F. 1
G. 5
H. 7
J. 9
K. 10

DO YOUR FIGURING HERE.

STOP

If there is still time remaining, check your answers to this section.

Turn page for the Reading Test

READING TEST

35 MINUTES—40 QUESTIONS

Directions: There are four passages in this test. Each passage is followed by several questions. After reading a passage, choose the best answer to each question and fill in the corresponding oval on your answer document. You may refer to the passages as often as necessary.

Passage I—Prose Fiction

This passage is adapted from the short story "Pickman's Model" by H.P. Lovecraft (1927, Public Domain).

No, I don't know what's become of Pickman, and I don't like to guess. You might have surmised I had some inside information when I dropped him—and that's why I don't want to think where he's gone. Let the police find what they can—it won't be much, judging from the fact that they don't know yet of the old North End place he hired under the name of Peters. I'm not sure that I could find it again myself—not that I'd ever try, even in broad daylight!

Yes, I do know, or am afraid I know, why he maintained it. I'm coming to that. And I think you'll understand before I'm through why I don't tell the police. They would ask me to guide them, but I couldn't go back there even if I knew the way. There was something there—and now I can't use the subway or (and you may as well have your laugh at this, too) go down into cellars any more.

I should think you'd have known I didn't drop Pickman for the same silly reasons that Dr. Reid or Joe Minot or Rosworth did. Morbid art doesn't shock me, and when a man has the genius Pickman had I feel it an honour to know him, no matter what direction his work takes. Boston never had a greater painter than Richard Upton Pickman. I said it at first and I say it still, and I never swerved an inch, either, when he showed that "Ghoul Feeding." That, you remember, was when Minot cut him.

You know, it takes profound art and profound insight into Nature to turn out stuff like Pickman's. Any magazine-cover hack can splash paint around wildly and call it a nightmare or a Witches' Sabbath or a portrait of the devil, but only a great painter can make such a thing really scare or ring true. That's because only a real artist knows the actual anatomy of the terrible or the physiology of fear—the exact sort of lines and proportions that connect up with latent instincts or hereditary memories of fright, and the proper colour contrasts and lighting effects to stir the dormant sense of strangeness. I don't have to tell you why a Fuseli really brings a shiver while a cheap ghost-story frontispiece merely makes us laugh. There's something those fellows catch—beyond life—that they're able to make us catch for a second. Doré had it. Sime has it. Angarola of Chicago has it. And Pickman had it as no man ever had it before or—I hope to Heaven—ever will again.

Don't ask me what it is they see. You know, in ordinary art, there's all the difference in the world between the vital, breathing things drawn from Nature or models and the artificial truck that commercial small fry reel off in a bare studio by rule. Well, I should say that the really weird artist has a kind of vision which makes models, or summons up what amounts to actual scenes from the spectral world he lives in. Anyhow, he manages to turn out results that differ from the pretender's mince-pie dreams in just about the same way that the life painter's results differ from the concoctions of a correspondence-school cartoonist. If I had ever seen what Pickman saw—but no! Here, let's have a drink before we get any deeper. God, I wouldn't be alive if I'd ever seen what that man—if he was a man—saw!

You recall that Pickman's forte was faces. I don't believe anybody since Goya could put so much of sheer hell into a set of features or a twist of expression. And before Goya you have to go back to the mediaeval chaps who did the gargoyles and chimaeras on Notre Dame and Mont Saint-Michel. They believed all sorts of things—and maybe they saw all sorts of things, too, for the Middle Ages had some curious phases. I remember your asking Pickman yourself once, the year before you went away, wherever in thunder he got such ideas and visions. Wasn't that a nasty laugh he gave you? It was partly because of that laugh that Reid dropped him. Reid, you know, had just taken up comparative pathology, and was full of pompous "inside stuff" about the biological or evolutionary significance of this or that mental or physical symptom. He said Pickman repelled him more and more every day, and almost frightened him towards the

3 3

last—that the fellow's features and expression were slowly developing in a way he didn't like; in a way that wasn't human. He had a lot of talk about diet, and said Pickman must be abnormal and eccentric to the last degree. I suppose you told Reid, if you and he had any correspondence over it, that he'd let Pickman's paintings get on his nerves or harrow up his imagination. I know I told him that myself—then.

1. It can reasonably be inferred that which of the following events mentioned in the passage occurred first chronologically?
   A. Pickman disappears to a location unknown by the narrator.
   B. Pickman brings the narrator to see his room in the North End.
   C. Pickman composes the painting known as "Ghoul Feeding."
   D. Pickman is dropped from the narrator's art gallery.

2. Which of the following questions does the passage NOT directly answer?
   F. In what city do the events of the story take place?
   G. What is the name of the man that the narrator is talking to?
   H. Why did Joe Minot drop Pickman from his gallery?
   J. What strange fear did the narrator develop as a result of being shown Pickman's studio?

3. In the context of the passage, the main purpose of the first paragraph is to:
   A. establish Pickman as the central figure in some sort of mystery.
   B. provide ominous details about the crime that Pickman has committed.
   C. demonstrate that the narrator has always been a fearful and superstitious man.
   D. foreshadow the difficulties that the narrator will face in his search for Pickman's old studio.

4. In the fourth paragraph (lines 28–45), the narrator seems most impressed with Pickman's:
   F. willingness to depict controversial subjects without fear of controversy.
   G. quickness to learn from the traditions established by previous artists.
   H. knack for creating paintings that are both frightening and humorous.
   J. ability to tap into and understand the instincts of his audience.

5. The author provides information about all of the following aspects of Pickman's life EXCEPT the:
   A. sorts of subjects that he was in the habit of painting.
   B. amount of money that he had been making at the time of his disappearance.
   C. effect that his odd mannerisms could have on people who met him in person.
   D. secretive habits that surrounded his creative process.

6. The best summary of the fifth paragraph (lines 46–60) is that the narrator:
   F. believes that the minds of truly unique artists blur the distinctions between fantasy and reality.
   G. believes all artists to be equally strange, the good ones and bad ones alike.
   H. is furious with Pickman for refusing to divulge the secret of his genius.
   J. is secretly concerned that he doesn't really know all that much about art.

7. If the third paragraph (lines 18–27) were deleted, the passage would lose all of the following EXCEPT:
   A. the only reference to a title of one of Pickman's paintings.
   B. the narrator's opinion of his own open-mindedness compared with that of other gallery owners.
   C. information about which gallery owner was the first to drop Pickman.
   D. the only mention made of anyone's first name.

8. It can reasonably be inferred that the narrator's final break with Pickman was initiated by:
   F. Pickman's habit of upsetting the narrator's personal acquaintances.
   G. the narrator's having experienced something horrifying in Pickman's North End studio.
   H. Pickman's feelings of betrayal after the narrator dropped him due to public outcry.
   J. the narrator's discovery that Pickman was a fraud.

GO ON TO THE NEXT PAGE.

9. The word *dormant* (line 38) most nearly means:
   A. tired.
   B. harmless.
   C. impolite.
   D. subconscious.

10. The narrator indicates that before Reid dropped him, Pickman had been:
    F. rudely dismissive of people's inquiries into his creative process.
    G. completely mystified as to why other people found his work to be so upsetting.
    H. the most popular artist in town.
    J. more terrified than anyone else of his own dark secrets.

Passage II—Social Science

This passage is adapted from the essay "The Trouble with Bright Girls" by Heidi Grant Halvorson (©2011 by Heidi Grant Halvorson).

Successful women know only too well that in any male-dominated profession, we often find ourselves at a disadvantage. We are routinely underestimated, underutilized and even underpaid. Studies show that women need to perform at extraordinarily high levels just to appear moderately competent compared to our male coworkers.

But in my experience, smart and talented women rarely realize that one of the toughest hurdles they'll have to overcome lies within. Compared with our male colleagues, we judge our own abilities not only more harshly but fundamentally differently. Understanding why we do it is the first step to righting a terrible wrong. And to do that, we need to take a step back in time.

Chances are good that if you are a successful professional today, you were a pretty bright fifth grade girl. Psychologist Carol Dweck conducted a series of studies in the 1980s looking at how bright girls and boys in the fifth grade handled new, difficult and confusing material.

She found that bright girls, when given something to learn that was particularly foreign or complex, were quick to give up; the higher the girls' IQ, the more likely they were to throw in the towel. In fact, the straight-A girls showed the most helpless responses. Bright boys, on the other hand, saw the difficult material as a challenge, and found it energizing. They were more likely to redouble their efforts than give up.

Why does this happen? What makes smart girls less confident when they should be the most confident kids in the room? At the 5th-grade level, girls routinely outperform boys in every subject, including math and science. So there were no differences between these boys and girls in ability, nor in past history of success. The only difference was how bright boys and girls interpreted difficulty—what it meant to them when material seemed hard to learn. Bright girls were much quicker to doubt their ability, to lose confidence and to become less effective learners as a result.

Researchers have uncovered the reason for this difference in how difficulty is interpreted: more often than not, bright girls believe that their abilities are innate and unchangeable, while bright boys believe that they can develop ability through effort and practice.

How do girls and boys develop these different views? Most likely, it has to do with the kinds of feedback we get from parents and teachers as children. Girls, who develop self-control earlier and are better able to follow instructions, are often praised for their "goodness." When we do well in school, we are told that we are "so smart," "so clever," or "such a good student." This kind of praise implies that traits like smartness, cleverness and goodness are qualities you either have or you don't.

Boys, on the other hand, are a handful. Just trying to get boys to sit still and pay attention is a real challenge for any parent or teacher. As a result, boys are given feedback that emphasizes effort (e.g., "If you would just pay attention you could learn this," "If you would just try a little harder you could get it right"). The result: when learning something new is difficult, girls take it as a sign that they aren't "good" and "smart," and boys take it as a sign to try harder.

We continue to carry these beliefs, often unconsciously, around with us throughout our lives. And because bright girls are particularly likely to see their abilities as innate and unchangeable, they grow up to be women who are far too hard on themselves—women who will prematurely conclude that they don't have what it takes to succeed in a particular arena, and give up way too soon.

Even if every external disadvantage is removed—every inequality of opportunity, every chauvinistic stereotype, all the challenges we face balancing work and family—we would still have to deal with the fact that through our mistaken beliefs about our abilities, we may be our own worst enemy.

How often have you found yourself avoiding challenges and playing it safe, sticking to goals you knew would be easy for you to reach? Are there things you decided long ago that you could never be good at? Skills you believed you would never possess? If the list is a long one, you were probably one of the bright girls—and your belief that you are stuck being exactly as you are has done more to determine the course of your life than you probably ever imagined.

No matter the ability—whether it's intelligence, creativity, self-control, charm or athleticism—studies show them to be profoundly malleable. When it comes to mastering any skill, your experience, effort and persistence matter a lot. So if you were a bright girl, it's time to toss out your mistaken belief about how ability works, embrace the fact that you can always improve and reclaim the confidence that you lost so long ago.

11. The main idea of the passage is that:

A. educational methodology in our society is biased against girls, especially bright ones.
B. paradoxically, bright girls grow up to be far less confident in themselves than they should be.
C. because they mature faster, girls are better at following directions than boys are.
D. contrary to popular belief, there are actually no differences in how girls and boys learn.

12. The passage's tone is best described as:

F. bitter.
G. lighthearted.
H. sardonic.
J. analytical.

13. One of the main ideas of the seventh paragraph (lines 43–51) is that:

A. adults unintentionally contribute to the low confidence of bright girls.
B. bright boys at the elementary school level do not receive sufficient praise from adults.
C. most adults mistakenly believe that girls develop self-control earlier than boys.
D. adults should make more of an effort to praise all students, rather than just the bright ones.

14. According to the passage, which of the following factors does NOT contribute to eventual confidence problems in bright girls?

F. Their knowledge of the fact that adult women, even bright ones, are often underpaid
G. The fact that young girls tend to be better behaved than young boys are
H. A valuable approach to challenges that adults unintentionally instill only in boys
J. Bright girls believe their abilities are innate and are almost impossible to change

15. The passage best supports which of the following as a possible solution to the confidence problems of bright adult women?

A. Removing inequalities of opportunity and chauvinistic stereotypes
B. Encouraging women to reexamine their own views about the nature of ability
C. Refraining from informing children of their IQs until they are much older
D. Teaching boys to develop self-control earlier

16. As it is used in line 86, the phrase *profoundly malleable* most nearly means:

F. philosophically accurate.
G. significantly different.
H. extremely changeable.
J. inspirationally beneficial.

17. In the context of the passage, the statement in lines 7–9 most nearly means that:

A. the author believes that her experiences have made her uniquely qualified to address this subject matter.
B. smart women are harmed by the fact that they were not encouraged to participate in sports as young girls.
C. professional women often don't devote enough time to maintaining their emotional health.
D. many women don't realize that their own beliefs may be holding them back as much as the sexism of others.

18. The passage best supports which of the following claims about Carol Dweck's study?

F. It uncovered a problem in learning development unique to the smartest girls.
G. It found that IQ is a more accurate predictor of scholastic success in boys than in girls.
H. The methodology used to conduct the study was a great innovation for the time.
J. More recent research has uncovered possible flaws in its conclusions.

19. The passage mentions all of the following as differences between girls and boys EXCEPT:

    A. how fast they mature.
    B. how easy they are to control.
    C. which subjects they tend to excel at.
    D. the ways that adults talk to them.

20. According to the passage, success in overcoming challenges of all kinds is:

    F. determined very early in life.
    G. largely the result of self-image.
    H. completely unrelated to gender.
    J. completely unrelated to IQ.

Passage III—Humanities

This passage is adapted from the essay "Songwriters and Scientists Both Hope to Peer Over God's Shoulder, If Only for a Moment" by John Roderick (©2011 by John Roderick).

It's a popular adage that you should never decide to become a musician for the money. This is absolutely sane advice, as the vast majority of musicians don't make enough money to live on comfortably, and there is no retirement plan. The people who give this advice usually follow it by saying "You should only play music if you love it."

This is also good advice, but what does it mean? Everybody loves music. Do they mean that you should only play music if you love it like a psychopath and have no other interests? I mean, what good is music? It toys with emotions in a manner that, if a friend acted the same way, you would hate their guts. And far from bringing people together, most music is listened to now in solitude on headphones at the gym, or wherever. So why is it still so powerful? What does it do?

There are plenty of things about the universe that we know to be true. Energy equals mass times the speed of light squared. The speed of light in a vacuum is 186,000 miles per second. The quadratic formula is X equals negative B plus or minus the square root of B squared minus four times A times C, all divided by two times A. This is science, and it makes up the indisputable body of known fact that enables us to build computer networks, suspension bridges, predator drones, and mechanical bulls.

But outside this illuminated circle of understanding are vast dark places where other truths about the universe still live in shadow. What is gravity, exactly? Is there really such a thing as dark matter or dark energy, and if so, does it speak in a low, menacing voice? Do trees communicate telepathically with one another? Physicists and mathematicians working at the forefront of human discovery are leaning into these shadows and trying to expand the circle of light. Imagine how their hearts must soar when they develop a theory and see it proved, thrilled to be the first sentient creature to divine this aspect of the mechanics of the universe.

Musicians can feel the same exact thing. Some people might scoff at the comparison between some kid wearing white Ray-Bans and singing about how "love" is like "a flower" and a super-genius physicist peering into the darkness at the beginning of time, but both occupations are capable, in their greatest moments, of getting a brief glimpse over God's shoulder.

When John Lennon wrote "Imagine," he was standing at the center of 10,000 years of science, religion, music, and myth. That song is his Theory of Relativity, describing the universe of emotion and belief as surely as Einstein did time and space. Mathematicians roll their eyes, protesting that the touchy-feely realm of emotion cannot be compared to the certainty of math, but emotion cannot be inconsistent with math. Emotion is just another aspect of the universe about which some small portion of our understanding is illuminated while the vast majority waits in shadow.

Both music and science are keys and codes which describe and unlock connections, patterns, and truths that were formerly felt but never drawn. In the right hands, both science and song allow recipients to experience personally the revelation, the excitement of the moment of discovery, in their own minds.

Just as scientists build on the discoveries of those who've come before, so do songwriters. There's no chord change on Nirvana's *Nevermind* that hadn't been discovered and used hundreds of times before. But Nirvana combined this ribonucleic acid of rock to create music that reverberated with millions across languages and cultures instantaneously. It may still be difficult for us to determine exactly what universal truths are contained in "Smells Like Teen Spirit," but the results of the experiment are unequivocal.

It's impossible to consider this prospect without traipsing over into what sounds like hippie balderdash, but the principles of fractal geometry and of melody and rhythm converge somewhere out on the horizon, somewhere much closer to the Grand Unified Theory than we're able to connect at present. After all, music is math at its heart. But music transcends basic math just as string theory does. How can you mathematically account for Aretha Franklin's voice? How can you plot on a graph the effect of her voice on various listeners?

It's no mistake to consider music one of the sciences. Whatever your creed, the idea of glimpsing some small aspect of the universal clockwork is irresistible. Theoretical physics attempts to describe multiple universes and scales of large and small that we may never fully comprehend. Likewise, every day musicians deliver new information about the very real, tangible, formative realm of thinking and feeling. Our appreciation of music is the closest to practical philosophy most of us will experience.

21. The main purpose of the passage is to:

A. suggest that people who only pay attention to trivial things like pop music should try to learn about more important things like science.
B. argue that the mission of artists has more in common with the mission of the hard sciences than most realize.
C. analyze the ways in which both science and art have emerged from and been inspired by various religious traditions.
D. declare a personal belief that science and religion are not as incompatible as many seem to think, and that art reveals this.

22. The passage describes popular music as being all of the following EXCEPT:

F. usually completely original.
G. currently impossible to analyze mathematically.
H. occasionally silly at first glance.
J. a synthesis of emotional traditions.

23. Based on the passage, how should the assertion that artists and scientists are capable of "getting a brief glimpse over God's shoulder" (lines 42–43) be read?

A. Literally; both professions can reveal truths that a deity intended to remain mysterious.
B. Literally; both professions occasionally arrive at sound arguments for the existence of a deity.
C. Metaphorically; both professions are methods of arriving at answers about human existence.
D. Ironically; both scientists and artists tend to be less religious than the average person.

24. The passage most strongly implies that John Lennon viewed "Imagine" as:

F. more a work of science than a work of art.
G. a mission statement of personal philosophy.
H. the intersection of artistic and religious history.
J. a rebuke to skeptical mathematicians.

25. It can reasonably be inferred that the author believes Nirvana's "Smells Like Teen Spirit" is:

A. a work that is inarguably important, though it is impossible to say exactly why.
B. secretly a tribute to John Lennon's "Imagine."
C. a song that is unique in being accessible to listeners who do not understand English.
D. a piece of derivative songwriting that gets more attention than it probably deserves.

26. Through his comparison of music to a friend, the author reveals his belief that music:

F. is always there for us when we need it most.
G. cannot always be trusted to challenge us.
H. influences our beliefs in gentle ways.
J. is, in a sense, designed to be manipulative.

27. According to the passage, which of the following is part of an "indisputable body of known fact"?

A. The theory of relativity
B. The existence of dark matter
C. The formula used to calculate energy
D. The ribonucleic acid of rock

28. The statement in lines 75–80 most nearly means that:

F. one should be aware that referring to music as a science will sound silly to most people.
G. some other cultures understand the relationship between music and science much better than we.
H. geometry might end up being more accurate if we would allow it to be influenced by music.
J. in some way that we cannot comprehend, music and math are ultimately the same thing.

29. In the passage, the significance of mechanical bulls is that they are:

A. proof that scientific knowledge can be used to create fun and "cool" things.
B. the result of science, but associated with people who like a certain style of music.
C. far less important than things like computers, bridges, and military aircraft.
D. an example of something that would not work if our ideas about science were inaccurate.

30. As it is used in line 69, the word *unequivocal* most nearly means:

F. absolutely clear.
G. surprising to most people.
H. not yet possible to see.
J. difficult to express in words.

Passage IV—Natural Science

This passage is adapted from the article "Could Jupiter Moon Harbor Fish-Sized Life?" by Victoria Jaggerd (© 2009 by *National Geographic*).

Below its icy crust Jupiter's moon Europa is believed to host a global ocean a hundred miles deep, with no land at the surface. And the extraterrestrial ocean is currently being fed more than a hundred times more oxygen than previous models had suggested, according to provocative new research. That amount of oxygen would be enough to support more than just microscopic life-forms: at least three million tons of fishlike creatures could theoretically live and breathe on Europa, said study author Richard Greenberg of the University of Arizona. "There's nothing saying there is life there now," said Greenberg. "But we do know there are the physical conditions to support it."

Based on what we know about the Jovian moon, parts of Europa's seafloor should greatly resemble the environments around Earth's deep-ocean hydrothermal vents, said deep-sea molecular ecologist Timothy Shank. "I'd be shocked if no life existed on Europa," said Shank, of the Woods Hole Oceanographic Institution. Despite the promising new estimates, it's too early to do more than speculate about how Europan life might have evolved. A closer look—perhaps by a NASA orbiter now in development—will be needed to tell exactly how chemicals are distributed on Europa and how the moon's geologic history might have contributed to life's chances.

It wasn't until Galileo, the NASA spacecraft, reached the Jupiter system in 1995 that scientists were able to study the moon in detail. What the Galileo probe found was so exciting that NASA deliberately crashed the spacecraft into Jupiter in 2003 to prevent the craft from contaminating one of its own discoveries: the salty, subsurface ocean on Europa. Although the probe didn't see the ocean directly, scientists are pretty sure it's there, based on the age, composition, and structure of the moon's icy surface.

Europa, like the other planets and moons in our solar system, is more than four billion years old. But a relative lack of impact craters implies that the icy crust is just 50 million years old. "It's an entirely different surface now than it was at the time the dinosaurs went extinct on Earth," Greenberg said. Europa's smooth surface is marred only by dark, crisscrossing ridges that suggest the icy shell is being stretched and compressed by tidal forces.

"We're used to thinking of tides on Earth as something seen on the shore," Greenberg explained. But on a larger scale, gravity from the sun and moon constantly squishes and stretches Earth. Europa, which is about as big as our moon, also gets tidally stretched, not by the sun but by the gravity of massive Jupiter. The friction from all this tidal stretching probably heats Europa enough to maintain liquid water, Greenberg said.

The warmer ocean material may be oozing up through cracks in the ice and freezing on the surface at the same rate that older ice sinks and melts into the liquid interior. This cycle of "repaving" would explain the young look of the surface ice—and would open the door for oxygen at the surface to permeate the subsurface ocean. Oxygen is created when charged particles from Jupiter's magnetic field hit the ice. Given his estimates for the moon's rate of repaving, Greenberg thinks it would have taken one to two billion years for the first surface oxygen to reach the ocean below.

A few million years after the ice-repaving process had started, oxygen levels in Europan seas reached their current levels—which exceed levels in Earth's oceans—Greenberg speculates. This timeframe actually improves the chances that life as we know it took root on Europa. For starters, the most primitive life-forms need an absence of oxygen to form, Greenberg said. "Oxygen tends to cause other molecules to come apart," he said, so genetic material such as DNA can't freely assemble with oxygen present. "You need the delay so genetic material and structures can take shape," he said. "And then when oxygen arrives, organisms will at least have a fighting chance." Greenberg's generous estimate of oxygen in Europa's ocean—and the resulting speculation that fish-like creatures may exist there—depends on the surface repaving to have happened at a relatively stable rate, in this case, a complete renewal every 50 million years.

But planetary scientist Robert Pappalardo said the process may have been more intermittent, and therefore the oxygen level—and chance for fishlike life—lower. "Maybe 50 million years ago it was churning away, and now it's slowed down," said Pappalardo. Europa is gravitationally locked with its neighboring moon Io, which may be pushing and pulling on Europa in extreme cycles, resulting in periods of high and low tidal friction. If tidal activity on Europa comes in fits and starts, that would change the rates at which heat and nutrients from the rocky mantle become available, he said. "Say there are microbes down there," Pappalardo added. "What would it mean for their evolution if every hundred thousand years there was much more heat and chemicals? It might lead to much more hardy organisms"—but not necessarily complex life.

31. Based on the passage as a whole, the main factor that makes some scientists suspect Europan life is the:

A. high oxygen levels of its ocean.
B. unusual warmth of its ocean.
C. fact that NASA kept the Galileo probe from contaminating its ocean.
D. fact that its tidal activity comes in fits and starts.

32. In terms of the passage as a whole, the third paragraph (lines 27–36) mainly serves to:

F. provide evidence that, contrary to popular belief, NASA still does important work.
G. explain why the possibility of an ocean on Europa is so exciting.
H. demonstrate the level of control that NASA has over its exploratory craft.
J. emphasize both the importance and recentness of the discovery of Europa's ocean.

33. The passage suggests that compared to other bodies in our solar system, Europa has:

A. been the focus of much more scientific attention.
B. a unique system of tidal activity.
C. much more resilient microbes.
D. a surface formed much more recently.

34. Lines 71–77 primarily serve to illustrate the point that, to have resulted in advanced life, oxygen levels in Europa's ocean would need to:

F. exceed levels in Earth's oceans.
G. have slowed in the last 50 million years.
H. have risen gradually.
J. have been consistently high all along.

35. It can reasonably be inferred from the passage that which of the following bodies has the LEAST gravitational effect on Europa?

A. The sun
B. The Earth
C. Jupiter
D. Io

36. Which of the following is NOT mentioned in the passage as being something about which scientists are not yet sure?

F. Whether life of any kind exists on Europa
G. Whether Europa is gravitationally locked with Io
H. Whether Europa is warm enough for liquid water
J. Whether Europa's ocean even exists

37. As it is used in line 80, the word *stable* most nearly means:

A. regular.
B. sturdy.
C. average.
D. safe.

38. The main purpose of the final paragraph (lines 82–97) is to:

F. represent the viewpoint that any life on Europa is impossible.
G. explain the process by which microbes evolve into larger life forms.
H. explore the possibility that evolution on Europa works differently from how it does on Earth.
J. suggest that advanced life on Europa may be unlikely.

39. As it is used in line 90, the expression *in fits and starts* most nearly means:

A. unpredictably.
B. effectively.
C. intermittently.
D. dangerously.

40. It can most reasonably be inferred from the passage that tidal activity on any celestial body is due to:

F. the moon.
G. surface repaving.
H. the influence of other celestial bodies.
J. oxygen-rich liquid water.

STOP

If there is still time remaining, check your answers to this section.

SCIENCE TEST

35 MINUTES—40 QUESTIONS

Directions: **There are seven passages in this test. Each passage is followed by several questions. After reading a passage, choose the best answer to each question and fill in the corresponding oval on your answer document. You may refer to the passages as often as necessary.**

You are NOT permitted to use a calculator on this test.

Passage I

Radium-226 (^{226}Ra) activity is often elevated in bodies of water that have been augmented with groundwater. Samples were collected over a two-year period in order to study ^{226}Ra activity in Florida Marsh and Cypress wetlands. Figure 1 shows the average ^{226}Ra activity from surface sediment samples collected in 2002 and 2004. Cores were taken from shallow sediment (0 to 4 cm) in the wetlands and analyzed for ^{226}Ra activity. The activity, in disintegration per minute per gram (dpm/g), found in the Marsh and Cypress wetlands is displayed in Figures 2 and 3.

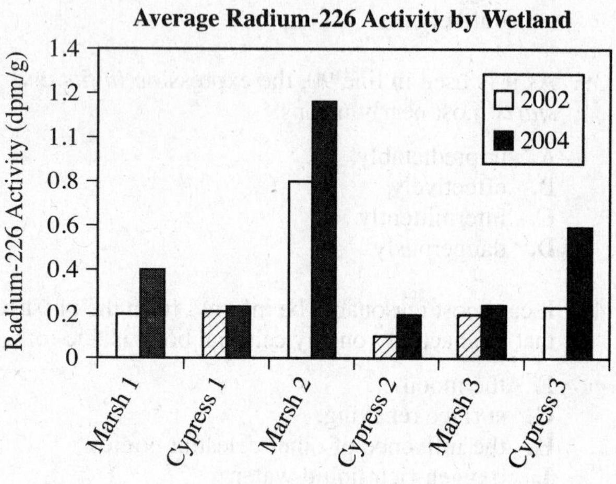

Figure 1

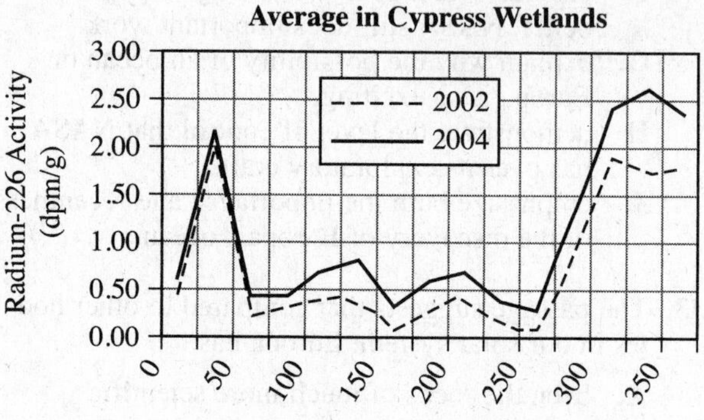

Figure 2

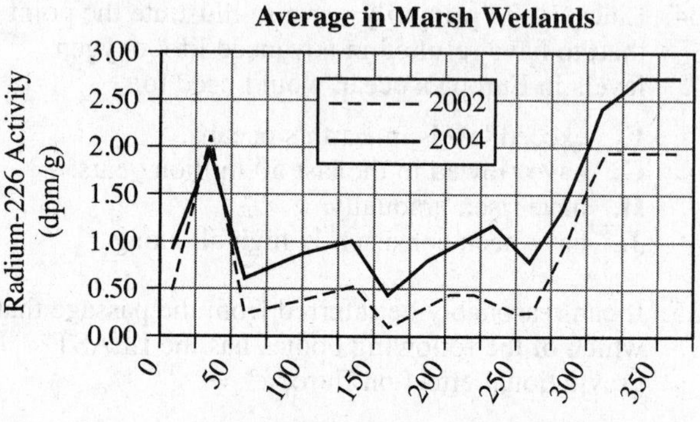

Figure 3

4 ○ ○ ○ ○ ○ ○ ○ ○ 4

1. According to Figure 2, the average radium-226 activity in Cypress wetlands in 2004 at a depth of 200 cm was closest to which of the following?

A. 0.30 dpm/g
B. 0.70 dpm/g
C. 1.00 dpm/g
D. 2.50 dpm/g

2. Based on the information in Figure 3, if the average radium-226 activity had been measured in Marsh wetlands at the depth of 400 cm in 2002, it most likely would have been closest to which of the following?

F. 2.75 dpm/g
G. 2.50 dpm/g
H. 2.00 dpm/g
J. 1.80 dpm/g

3. Which of the following is the most likely explanation for the difference in the average ^{226}Ra activity between 2002 and 2004?

A. In 2004 the wetlands were augmented with groundwater, which caused an increase in ^{226}Ra activity.
B. In 2002 the wetlands were augmented with groundwater, and in 2004, they were not. This resulted in more ^{226}Ra activity in 2004.
C. The amount of groundwater the wetlands were augmented with was higher in 2002 than in 2004.
D. In 2004 there was more rainfall than in 2002, which created a decrease in ^{226}Ra activity.

4. If the data in Figures 2 and 3 are typical of Cypress and Marsh wetlands, one would most likely make which of the following conclusions about the ^{226}Ra activity in a wetland?

F. ^{226}Ra activity is highest in wetlands in the top 50 cm of the sediment layer.
G. ^{226}Ra activity gets higher as the sediment gets deeper.
H. ^{226}Ra activity is highest in wetlands at around 325 cm below the top of the sediment.
J. Each year, the ^{226}Ra activity in wetlands will become less.

5. According to Figures 2 and 3, the ^{226}Ra activity increased between the depths of 200 and 250 cm for which wetlands?

A. Cypress wetlands in 2002
B. Cypress wetlands in 2004
C. Marsh wetlands in 2002
D. Marsh wetlands in 2004

Practice Test 5

Passage II

The balanced chemical equation for the dissociation of acetic acid in water is shown below:

$$CH_3COOH(aq) \rightleftharpoons CH_3COO^-(aq) + H^+(aq)$$

The reaction can proceed in either direction in order to maintain a constant value for the acid dissociation constant. Acetic acid is an acid because it contributes H^+ ions to the solution. The acid dissociation constant for the above reaction can be expressed as follows:

$$K_a = \frac{[H^+(aq)][CH_3COO^-(aq)]}{[CH_3COOH(aq)]}$$

$$K_a = 1.82 \cdot 10^{-5} \text{ at } 25$$

The expression [A] represents *the concentration of substance A in moles/liter*. One mole is $6.02 \cdot 10^{23}$ molecules.

Experiment 1

NaOH is a strong base because it dissociates readily in water and contributes OH^- ions to the water. A 1 M solution of NaOH, a strong base, is slowly added to a 100 ml, 2 M (M represents *molarity*, a measure of concentration in $\frac{moles}{liter}$) solution of acetic acid. The NaOH solution contributes OH^- ions to the mixture. An ion is a charged atom or molecule. The OH^- ions from the NaOH combine with the H^+ ions from the acetic acid to form water as shown below:

$$H^+(aq) + OH^-(aq) \rightarrow H_2O\ (l)$$

Various measurements were taken and the results are shown in Table 1 and graphed in Figure 1.
Note: $pH = -\log\ [H^+]$

Table 1

NaOH added (ml)	$[CH_3COO^-(aq)]$ (moles/liter)	$[H^+(aq)]$ (moles/liter)	$[CH_3COOH(aq)]$ (moles/liter)	pH	K_a ($\cdot 10^{-5}$)
0	$6.0 \cdot 10^{-3}$	$6.0 \cdot 10^{-3}$	2	2.2	1.8
100	.45	$1.9 \cdot 10^{-5}$	.51	4.7	1.7
200	.68	$6.0 \cdot 10^{-10}$	$2.0 \cdot 10^{-5}$	9.3	2.0
300	.69	$5.0 \cdot 10^{-14}$	$2 \cdot 10^{-10}$	13.4	1.7
400	.69	$2.5 \cdot 10^{-14}$	$9 \cdot 10^{-10}$	13.5	1.9

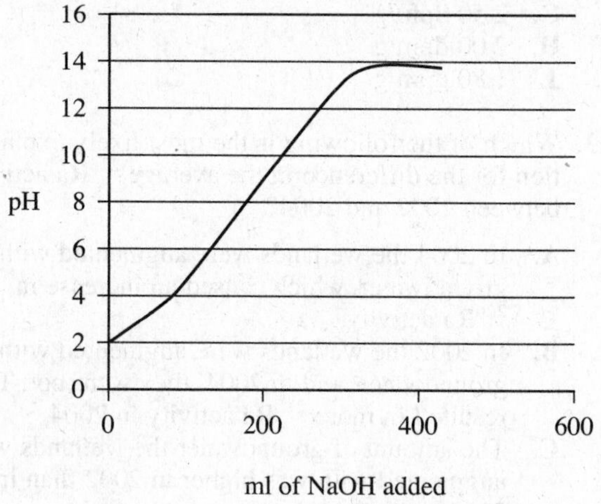

Figure 1

6. Using Table 1 and Figure 1, how much NaOH was added in order to increase the pH to 9.3?

   F. 0 ml
   G. 100 ml
   H. 200 ml
   J. 300 ml

7. If only 50 ml of NaOH had been added, what approximate value would the pH have been?

   A. 1.5
   B. 3.5
   C. 5.5
   D. 7.5

8. Using all the information in the passage, why did the concentration of $CH_3COOH(aq)$ continue to decrease while the concentration of $CH_3COO^-(aq)$ remained nearly unchanged?

   F. Looking at the K_a, [$CH_3COOH(aq)$] is in the denominator and [$CH_3COO^-(aq)$] is in the numerator. The system counteracts the decrease in [$H^+(aq)$] by dissociating more molecules of CH_3COOH.
   G. Looking at the K_a, [$CH_3COOH(aq)$] is in the denominator and [$CH_3COO^-(aq)$] is in the numerator. The system counteracts the increase in [$H^+(aq)$] by synthesizing more molecules of CH_3COOH.
   H. The NaOH produces Na^+ ions that must be combining with the CH_3COOH molecules in such a way that the concentration continues to decrease.
   J. Clearly, the data must be inaccurate. Looking at the balanced equation, for every molecule of acetic acid that dissociates, one CH_3COO^- ion must form and the [$CH_3COO^-(aq)$] should have continued to increase.

9. What would be the effect on the results if 100 ml of 1 M acetic acid was used instead of 100 ml of 2 M?

   A. The decreased concentration of acetic acid will decrease acidity and increase the initial pH.
   B. The decreased concentration of acetic acid will decrease acidity and decrease the initial pH.
   C. The increased concentration of acetic acid will increase acidity and increase the initial pH.
   D. The increased concentration of acetic acid will increase acidity and decrease the initial pH.

10. How could you lower the pH back to 2.2?

    F. Adding enough NaOH will eventually lower the pH because the cycle will repeat.
    G. Adding enough water will dilute the base and lower the pH.
    H. Evaporating some of the water will increase the concentration of H^+ ions sufficiently to lower the pH.
    J. Adding a sufficient amount of acetic acid will add H^+ ions and lower the pH.

11. What is true about the relationship between [$H^+(aq)$] and pH?

    A. There is an inverse relationship; as [$H^+(aq)$] decreases, the pH increases.
    B. There is a direct relationship; as [$H^+(aq)$] decreases, the pH decreases.
    C. The relationship is complex. Because the concentrations are so small, the pH jumps after 200 ml of NaOH is added because small quantities of H^+ ions increase the pH greatly, whereas large quantities of H^+ ions have little effect.
    D. There is no relationship between [$H^+(aq)$] and pH.

4 ○ ○ ○ ○ ○ ○ ○ ○ 4

Passage III

Air permeability is defined as the ability of soil to transmit air through interconnected air-filled pores under an imposed air pressure gradient. Air permeability is a function of volumetric water content, porosity, pore size distribution, and pore geometry. Scientists used a soil corer air permeameter (SCAP) to digitally measure the *flow rates* of air through desert soil under low-pressure gradients. The SCAP measured air permeability both in situ, with the instrument inserted in the soil and ex situ, after the soil corer had been removed from the soil. Figures 1 and 2 display the results of field testing conducted at two of the four sites in Arizona, over the course of three months. The porosity of the soil at each site is displayed in Figure 3. Figure 4 shows the relationship between the air pressure used and the flow rate of the air for each site.

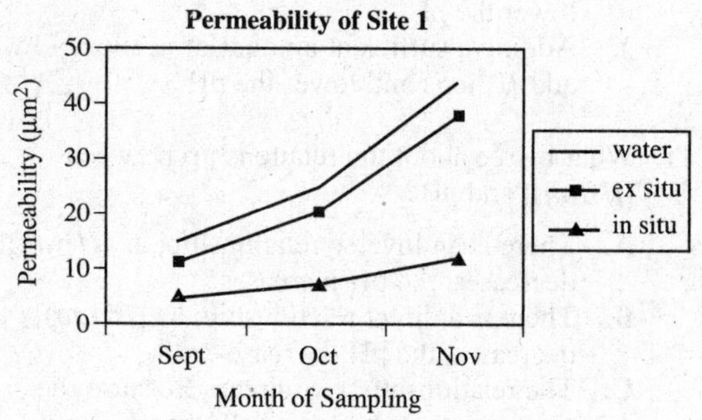

Figure 1

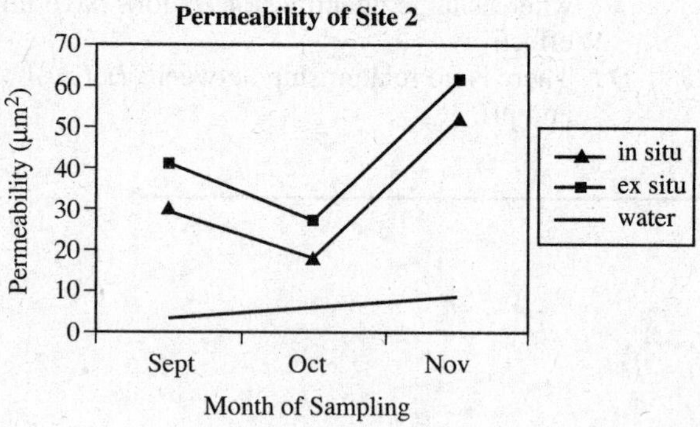

Figure 2

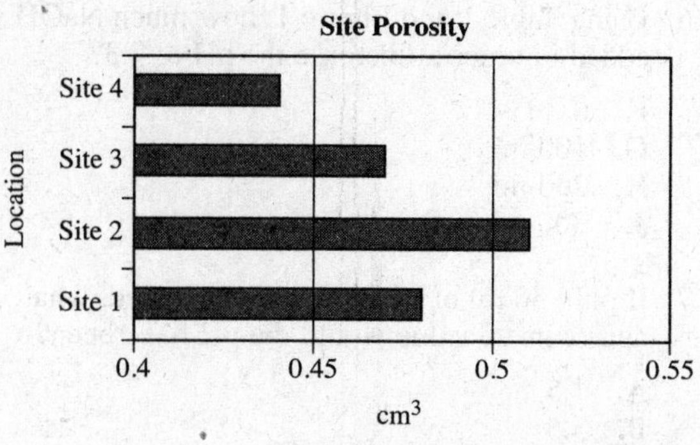

Figure 3

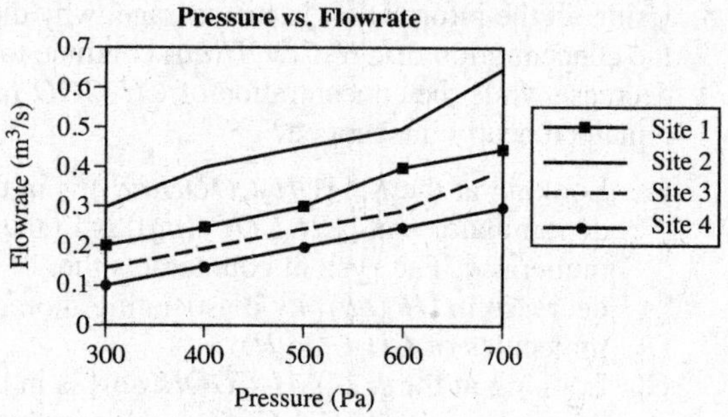

Figure 4

4 ○ ○ ○ ○ ○ ○ ○ ○ 4

12. According to Figure 2, the air permeability measured ex situ in October was closest to which of the following?

   F. 5 μm^2
   G. 15 μm^2
   H. 20 μm^2
   J. 30 μm^2

13. Based on Figure 4, if the air permeability had been tested at Site 1 using 800 Pa, the flow rate would most likely have been closest to which of the following?

   A. 0.5 m^3/s
   B. 0.6 m^3/s
   C. 0.4 m^3/s
   D. 0.3 m^3/s

14. Which of the following is the most likely explanation for the difference in air permeability at Site 1 versus Site 2?

   F. The overall air permeability is higher at Site 1 due to the lower porosity of the soil.
   G. The overall air permeability is higher at Site 2 due to the higher porosity of the soil.
   H. The overall air permeability at Site 2 is higher because less pressure was used when testing the soil.
   J. The overall air permeability at Site 2 is higher because more pressure was used when testing the soil.

15. If the data in Figures 1 and 2 is typical of air permeability measurements, one would most likely make which of the following conclusions about air permeability in situ versus ex situ?

   A. The permeability will always be higher ex situ than in situ.
   B. The permeability will always be lower ex situ than in situ.
   C. Water permeability is higher than air permeability in situ and ex situ.
   D. At high pressures, air permeability is greater in situ than ex situ.

16. According to Figure 1, which of the following statements is most accurate regarding permeability during the month of November?

   F. Permeability was lower than in previous months.
   G. Permeability was highest for air measured while the SCAP was still inserted in the ground.
   H. Permeability was highest for air measured after the SCAP had removed a core from the soil.
   J. Permeability was highest for water.

Practice Test 5

Passage IV

Scientists studying sucrose examined oranges and lemons to determine how the two fruits form and synthesize sucrose. Studies were conducted both on extractions from the fruits and on small, intact fruits.

Study 1

Mature lemon and orange fruits were obtained and then juiced by hand. Formation of fructose was determined using two portions of the fruits: the juice, and the particulate sediment. The results are shown in Table 1.

Table 1—Formation of Sucrose by Fructose Reaction

Preparation	Sucrose Synthesized (μmoles)
Oranges	
Juice	0.12
Particulate sediment	0.9
Lemons	
Juice	0.4
Particulate sediment	0.17

Study 2

Scientists found lemons of varying ages from the same fruit grove. Each piece of fruit was cut into sections, and various tissue samples were isolated for testing. The three tissue types tested were the *flavedo* (colored, outer layer of the peel), the *albedo* (white peel layer), and the *vesicle* (fleshy part of the fruit). The results of the formation of sucrose in lemons are shown in Figure 1.

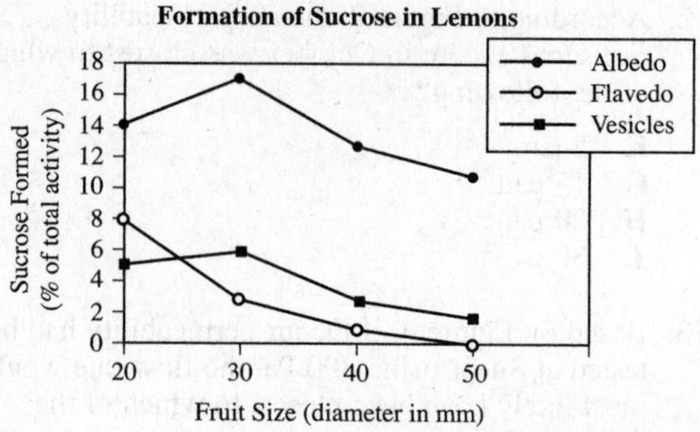

Figure 1

Study 3

Whole fruits (each weighing approximately 5 g) were tested and then cut into sections to measure sucrose activity in the various tissues. Figure 2 displays the results.

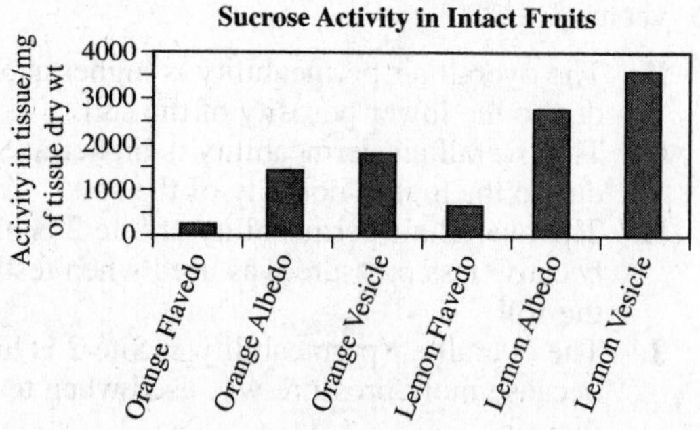

Figure 2

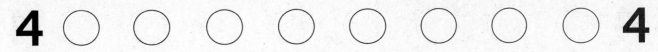

4 ○ ○ ○ ○ ○ ○ ○ ○ 4

17. Based on Figure 1, which type of lemon tissue forms the most sucrose?

A. The albedo tissue in a large lemon
B. The albedo tissue in a small lemon
C. The flavedo tissue in a large lemon
D. The vesicles in a small lemon

18. According to the results of Study 2, as fruit size increased, the sucrose found in the vesicles:

F. increased only.
G. increased, then decreased.
H. decreased only.
J. decreased, then increased.

19. Based on the results of Study 3, the largest difference in sucrose activity was found in:

A. oranges between the flavedo tissue and the albedo tissue.
B. oranges between the albedo tissue and the vesicle tissue.
C. lemons between the flavedo tissue and the vesicle tissue.
D. lemons between the flavedo tissue and the albedo tissue.

20. Based on the results of Study 1, which of the following is most accurate about the formation of sucrose?

F. Orange juice is more effective at forming sucrose than lemon juice.
G. Orange juice is less effective at forming sucrose than lemon juice.
H. Lemon juice and orange juice are equally effective at forming sucrose.
J. Lemon juice forms less sucrose than lemon particulate sediment.

21. Assume Study 2 was repeated using oranges instead of lemons. Based on the information presented in Figures 1 and 2, and assuming that the fruits used in Study 3 were 30 mm in diameter, which of the following would most likely be the sucrose formation (as a percent of total activity) in the albedo tissue of the oranges?

A. 0
B. 3
C.. 9
D. 20

22. Based on the results of Study 2, which statement most accurately summarizes the formation of sucrose in lemons?

F. The fleshy part of the lemon formed the majority of the sucrose.
G. The colored outer layer of the peel does not form any sucrose.
H. The part of the lemon that forms the most sucrose is dependent on the size of the lemon.
J. More sucrose is formed in the white peel layer of a lemon than anywhere else.

Passage V

Two experiments were performed to study Newton's laws of motion using air track gliders. The friction between the gliders and the air track is nearly zero. Each glider has a spring attached on each end.

Experiment 1

Two identical gliders were placed on an air track as shown in Figure 1. The gliders' springs were then compressed completely together along with the gliders and released. When the gliders were pushed apart by their springs, the data in Table 1 was recorded. The zero position was recorded as the far-left point where Glider 1 is shown in Figure 1.

Table 1

Time (seconds)	Glider 1 Position (m)	Glider 2 Position (m)
0	.75	.80
.5	.71	.85
1	.62	.94
1.5	.50	1.07
2	.38	1.20
2.5	.24	1.32

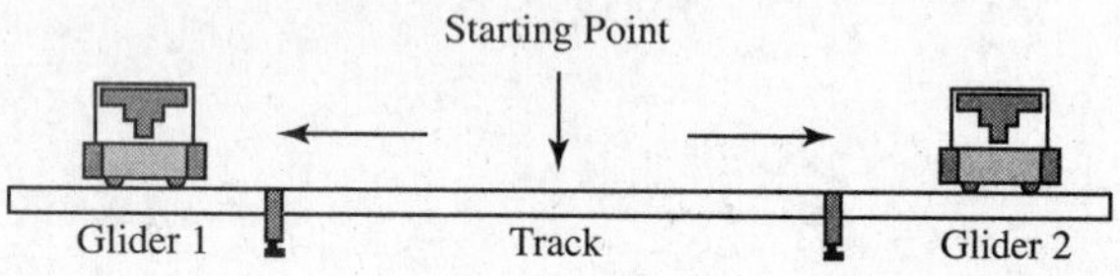

Figure 1

Experiment 2

The same experiment was performed but Glider 3 was a double-weight glider in the first trial. In the second trial, Glider 4, a triple-weight glider, was tested.

Table 2

Time (seconds)	Glider 1 Position (m)	Glider 3 Position (m)	Glider 1 Position (m)	Glider 4 Position (m)
0	.75	.80	.75	.80
.5	.70	.82	.71	.82
1.0	.61	.87	.63	.84
1.5	.48	.93	.50	.86
2.0	.35	.99	.36	.91
2.5	.21	1.04	.22	.95

The velocity for each trial was calculated and the ratio of Glider 1 to the other glider was graphed and shown in Figure 2.

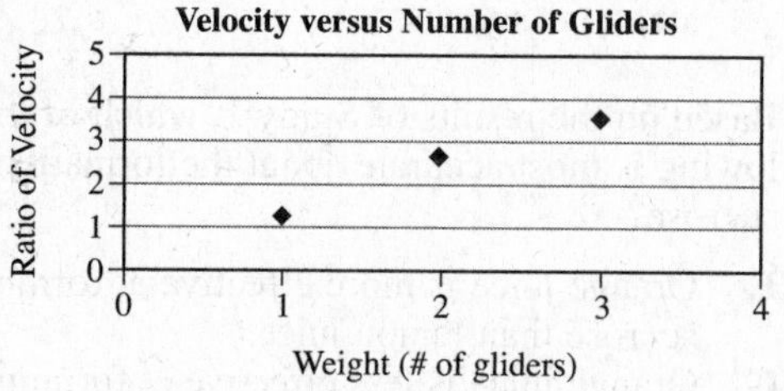

Figure 2

23. Suppose another trial was run with Glider 1 and a Glider 4 that weighs 4 times Glider 1. The ratio of the velocities would be closest to what number?

A. 1
B. 2
C. 3
D. 4

24. In Experiment 1, how many times a second did the experimenters record the position of the gliders?

F. Once per second
G. Twice per second
H. Three times per second
J. Four times per second

25. Based on Tables 1 and 2, how did the total distance traveled by both gliders vary against the weight of the gliders?

	Total Distance	Total Weight
A.	Decreased	Increased
B.	Increased	Decreased
C.	Increased	Increased
D.	Unchanged	Increased

26. Based on Table 2, how far had Glider 4 traveled after 1.5 seconds?

F. .02 m
G. .06 m
H. .80 m
J. .86 m

27. What distance was separating the gliders before they were released in each experiment?

A. 0 m
B. .02 m
C. .05 m
D. .08 m

Practice Test 5

GO ON TO THE NEXT PAGE.

Passage VI

Since carbon is essential to life on Earth, understanding the global carbon cycle can provide valuable information. Through the process of photosynthesis, plants on land or algae living in water convert carbon dioxide into organic products. Through the process of respiration, organisms convert these organic compounds into energy and release carbon dioxide. Figure 1 displays the global carbon cycle.

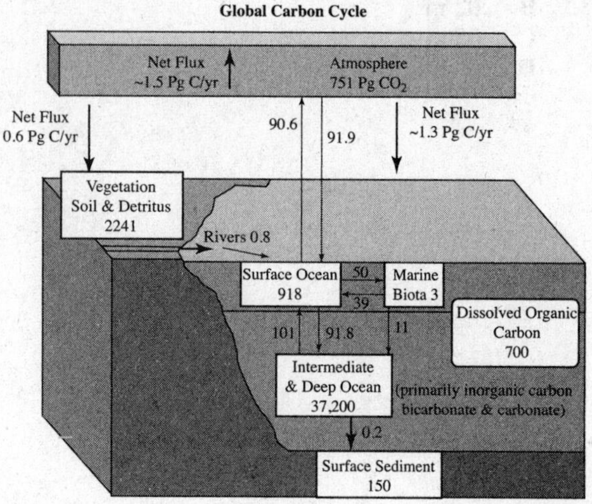

Figure 1

A significant amount of carbon is released through the burning of fossil fuels. Some of this carbon is stored in the atmosphere, while a significant portion is stored in ocean waters and sediments. Carbon in the ocean is described as dissolved inorganic carbon, particulate inorganic carbon, particulate organic carbon (POC), and dissolved organic carbon (DOC). Particulates are defined as those larger than 0.2 micrometers, whereas dissolved matter is that smaller than 0.2 micrometers (see Figure 2).

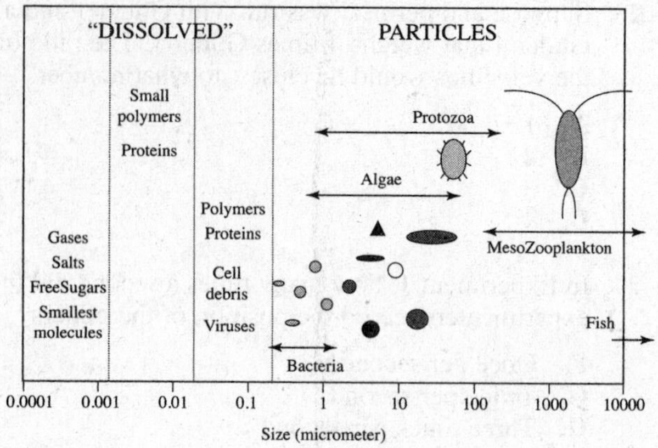

Figure 2

Chromophoric dissolved organic matter (CDOM) is the colored portion of DOC. It is colored because it intensely absorbs violet and blue light. Figure 3 displays DOC and CDOM absorption in the tropical North Atlantic Ocean.

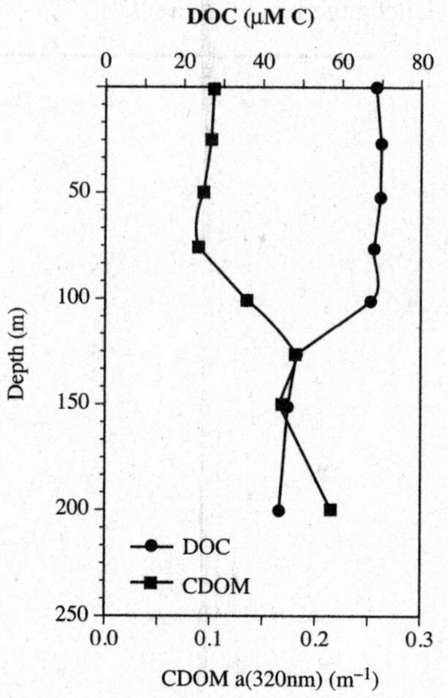

Figure 3

4 ○ ○ ○ ○ ○ ○ ○ ○ 4

28. Based on Figure 1, how much carbon is transmitted from the ocean to the atmosphere?
    - **F.** 91.9 Pg C/yr
    - **G.** 90.6 Pg C/yr
    - **H.** 918 Pg C/yr
    - **J.** 700 Pg C/yr

29. According to Figure 2, which of the following is NOT considered a dissolved carbon?
    - **A.** Proteins
    - **B.** Salts
    - **C.** Algae
    - **D.** Viruses

30. Based on Figure 3, which of the following statements best describes the relationship between ocean depth and amount of DOC?
    - **F.** As the ocean depth increased, the amount of DOC remained fairly constant, then decreased steadily, then began to increase again.
    - **G.** As the ocean depth increased, the amount of DOC steadily decreased.
    - **H.** As the ocean depth increased, the amount of DOC remained fairly constant, then decreased steadily, then became fairly constant again.
    - **J.** As the ocean depth increased, the amount of DOC steadily increased.

31. Suppose a fragment of organic carbon was found in the ocean and measured approximately 0.01 micrometers. It would mostly likely be featured in Figure 2 by which of the following?
    - **A.** Gases
    - **B.** Protozoa
    - **C.** Bacteria
    - **D.** Small polymers

32. At an ocean depth of 100 m, there is approximately how much CDOM, according to Figure 3?
    - **F.** 0.25
    - **G.** 0.12
    - **H.** 40
    - **J.** 70

33. Which of the following fragments, if found in the ocean, would be described as dissolved inorganic carbon?
    - **A.** Bacteria
    - **B.** Protozoa
    - **C.** Viruses
    - **D.** Polymers

4 ○ ○ ○ ○ ○ ○ ○ ○ 4

Passage VII

Three substances have been shown to inhibit respiration in various organisms: hydrocyanic acid, hydrogen sulfide, and carbon monoxide. An experiment was conducted to determine the effect that each of these substances has on the respiration of the green alga *Chlorella*. Figure 1 shows the results.

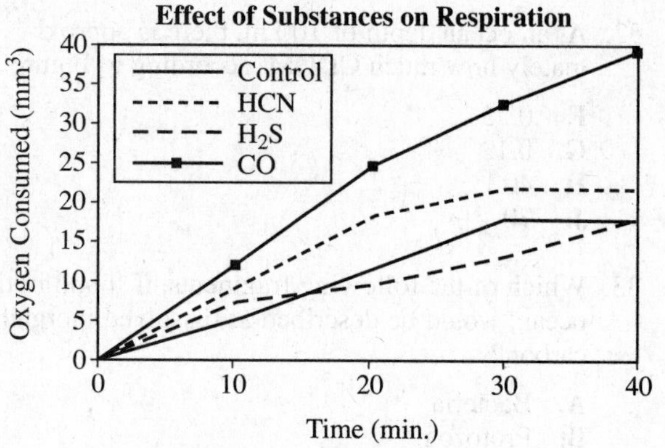

Figure 1

Researcher 1 argued that glucose would have a contradictory effect on the alga, so that if the *Chlorella* were suspended in a solution containing 1 percent glucose, there would be less of an effect on respiration. Figure 2 displays the results of the experiment.

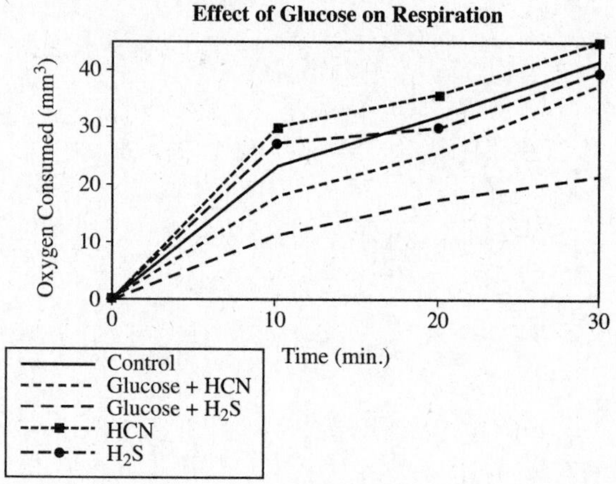

Figure 2

Researcher 2 hypothesized that light may play an active part in respiration of *Chlorella*, so an experiment was done to measure the effect of successive periods of light and darkness on the respiration of cells suspended in carbon monoxide and in nitrogen. The results are shown in Figure 3.

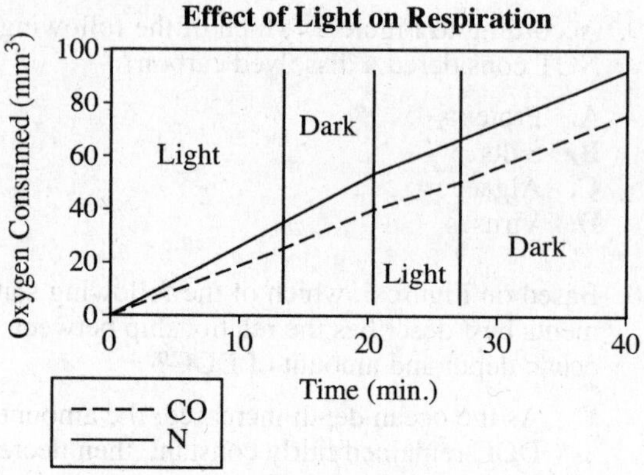

Figure 3

Practice Test 5

34. The theories of the two researchers are similar in that both researchers believe that:

F. glucose will increase the respiration of *Chlorella*.
G. HCN and H_2S have no effect on the respiration of *Chlorella*.
H. an additional factor will have an effect on the respiration of *Chlorella*.
J. CO and N also affect the respiration of *Chlorella*.

35. According to Figure 1, *Chlorella* would typically consume about how much oxygen after half an hour?

A. 10 mm^3
B. 18 mm^3
C. 22 mm^3
D. 35 mm^3

36. If Researcher 1 was correct about the effect of glucose on the respiration of *Chlorella*, then based on the information in Figure 2, Researcher 1 would most likely predict that *Chlorella* suspended in a solution containing 2 percent glucose and HCN would consume how much oxygen after 20 minutes?

F. 15 mm^3
G. 25 mm^3
H. 30 mm^3
J. 40 mm^3

37. Does the data in Figure 3 support Researcher 2's hypothesis?

A. Yes. It shows that light is necessary for the respiration of *Chlorella*.
B. Yes. It shows that equal respiration occurs in the darkness and in light.
C. No. More respiration of *Chlorella* occurred in the darkness.
D. No. Varying the amount of light did not yield significantly different rates of respiration.

38. Suppose a third researcher studied the effect of glucose and CO on the respiration of *Chlorella*, using the same conditions and methods as Researcher 1. After 20 minutes the results showed that the sample suspended in CO had consumed 50 mm^3 of oxygen, while the sample suspended in a mixture of CO and glucose had consumed 60 mm^3 of oxygen. How would this experiment most likely affect the researchers' viewpoints?

F. It would weaken Researcher 2's viewpoint only.
G. It would weaken Researcher 1's viewpoint only.
H. It would strengthen both researchers' viewpoints.
J. It would have no effect on either researcher's viewpoint.

39. According to Figure 2, which substance had the LEAST effect on respiration of *Chlorella* after 30 minutes?

A. HCN
B. H_2S
C. Glucose + HCN
D. Glucose + H_2S

40. According to Researcher 2, experiment findings indicate the following is FALSE regarding the relationship between *Chlorella* cells suspended in carbon monoxide and *Chlorella* cells suspended in nitrogen EXCEPT:

F. *Chlorella* cells suspended in carbon monoxide consume more oxygen.
G. *Chlorella* cells suspended in nitrogen consume less oxygen.
H. *Chlorella* cells suspended in carbon monoxide and nitrogen consume the same amount of oxygen.
J. *Chlorella* cells suspended in nitrogen consume more oxygen.

Practice Test 5

STOP

If there is still time remaining, check your answers to this section.

WRITING PROMPT

Directions: This is a test of your writing skills. You will have thirty (30) minutes to write an essay in English. Before you begin planning and writing your essay, read the writing prompt below carefully to understand exactly what you are being asked to do. Your essay will be evaluated on the evidence it provides of your ability to express judgments by taking a position on the issue in the writing prompt; to maintain a focus on the topic throughout the essay; to develop a position by using logical reasoning and by supporting your ideas; to organize ideas in a logical way; and to use language clearly and effectively according to the conventions of standard written English.

You may use the unlined page to plan your essay. This page will not be scored. You must write your essay in pencil on the lined pages provided. Your writing on those lined pages will be scored. You may not need all the pages, but to ensure you have enough room to finish, do NOT skip lines. You may write corrections or additions neatly between the lines of your essay, but do NOT write in the margins of the lined pages. Illegible essays cannot be scored, so you must write (or print) clearly.

If you finish before time is called, you may review your work. Lay your pencil down immediately when time is called.

The mayor of your city is trying to decide if a 7:00 PM curfew for children under the age of 16 is needed. What do you think? Write a persuasive essay to the mayor describing your position on this issue.

In your essay, take a position on this question. You may write about either one of the two points of view given, or you may present a different point of view on this question. Use specific reasons and examples to support your position.

Use this page to *plan* your essay.

Begin WRITING TEST here.

If you need more space, continue on the next page.

WRITING TEST

Practice Test 5

Answer Key

PRACTICE TEST 5

English Test

1. D	16. H	31. C	46. G	61. C
2. F	17. B	32. J	47. D	62. F
3. B	18. G	33. B	48. F	63. D
4. H	19. D	34. F	49. C	64. G
5. D	20. J	35. C	50. G	65. D
6. G	21. D	36. J	51. C	66. H
7. D	22. F	37. D	52. F	67. C
8. H	23. D	38. G	53. D	68. F
9. A	24. H	39. C	54. J	69. B
10. F	25. A	40. F	55. A	70. J
11. B	26. F	41. A	56. H	71. D
12. G	27. C	42. G	57. B	72. H
13. C	28. G	43. D	58. G	73. A
14. J	29. B	44. H	59. D	74. G
15. C	30. H	45. B	60. H	75. B

Math Test

1. D	13. C	25. A	37. D	49. A
2. J	14. G	26. K	38. F	50. J
3. B	15. C	27. C	39. E	51. B
4. K	16. J	28. H	40. K	52. G
5. A	17. E	29. D	41. B	53. B
6. K	18. J	30. K	42. J	54. F
7. D	19. D	31. B	43. D	55. C
8. F	20. G	32. H	44. H	56. J
9. B	21. E	33. A	45. C	57. E
10. H	22. F	34. F	46. F	58. K
11. D	23. B	35. C	47. D	59. A
12. H	24. H	36. J	48. H	60. K

Answer Key
PRACTICE TEST 5

Reading Test

1. C	9. D	17. D	25. A	33. D
2. G	10. F	18. F	26. J	34. H
3. A	11. B	19. C	27. C	35. B
4. J	12. J	20. G	28. J	36. G
5. B	13. A	21. B	29. D	37. A
6. F	14. F	22. F	30. F	38. J
7. C	15. B	23. C	31. A	39. C
8. G	16. H	24. G	32. J	40. H

Science Test

1. B	9. A	17. B	25. A	33. D
2. H	10. J	18. G	26. G	34. H
3. A	11. A	19. C	27. C	35. B
4. H	12. J	20. G	28. G	36. F
5. D	13. A	21. C	29. C	37. D
6. H	14. G	22. J	30. H	38. G
7. B	15. A	23. D	31. D	39. B
8. F	16. J	24. G	32. G	40. J

HOW TO SCORE YOUR PRACTICE TEST

Step 1: Add up the number correct for each section and write that number in the blank under the Raw Score column on the Score Conversion Table. (Your goal is to get more questions correct on each subsequent practice test.)

Step 2: Using the Score Conversion Chart, find your scale score for each section and write it down. Then add up all four sections and divide by 4 to find your overall composite score. (Composite scores are rounded up at .5 or higher.)

Score Conversion Table

Section	Raw Score	Scaled Score
English	(out of 75)	____ / 36
Math	(out of 60)	____ / 36
Reading	(out of 40)	____ / 36
Science	(out of 40)	____ / 36
		Add and divide by 4
Overall Composite =		____ / 36

Score Conversion Chart

	Number Correct				
ACT Score*	English Section	Mathematics Section	Reading Section	Science Section	ACT Score*
36	75	60	40	40	**36**
35	74	59	39	39	**35**
34	73	58	38	38	**34**
33	72	57	37	—	**33**
32	71	56	36	37	**32**
31	70	54–55	35	36	**31**
30	69	53	34	35	**30**
29	67–68	51–52	33	34	**29**
28	65–66	49–50	32	33	**28**
27	64	46–48	31	31–32	**27**
26	62–63	44–45	30	30	**26**
25	60–61	41–43	29	28–29	**25**
24	58–59	39–40	27–28	25–27	**24**
23	55–57	37–38	25–26	24	**23**
22	53–54	35–36	23–24	22–23	**22**
21	50–52	33–34	22	20–21	**21**
20	47–49	31–32	21	18–19	**20**
19	44–46	28–30	19–20	17	**19**
18	42–43	25–27	18	15–16	**18**
17	40–41	22–24	17	14	**17**

Continued

Score Conversion Chart *(Continued)*

ACT Score*	Number Correct: English Section	Mathematics Section	Reading Section	Science Section	ACT Score*
16	37–39	19–21	16	13	16
15	34–36	15–17	15	12	15
14	31–33	11–14	13–14	11	14
13	29–30	09–10	12	10	13
12	27–28	07–08	10–11	09	12
11	25–26	06	08–09	08	11
10	23–24	05	07	07	10
9	21–22	04	06	05–06	9
8	18–20	03	05	—	8
7	15–17	—	—	04	7
6	12–14	02	04	03	6
5	09–11	—	03	02	5
4	07–08	01	02	—	4
3	05–06	—	—	01	3
2	03–04	—	01	—	2
1	00–02	00	00	00	1

*These scores are based on student trials rather than national norms.

SCORING YOUR ESSAY

As mentioned earlier in this text, two readers will evaluate your essay and each person will then assign it a score from 1 to 6. If, by chance, these two scorers disagree by more than 1 point, a third reader will step in and resolve the discrepancy. Performance on the essay will not affect your English, math, reading, science, or composite scores. You will receive two additional scores on your score sheet—a combined English/writing score (1–36) and a writing test subscore (1–12). Neither of these scores will affect your composite score!

The sample essay that follows reflects higher-level writing. It meets the criteria that ACT has put forth for essays that demonstrate effective writing skills.

- It takes a definite position.
- It addresses and expands on the counterargument.
- It has details that support the topic sentences and is well organized.
- It is not repetitive, and while there may be errors, they do not interfere with the competence of the essay.
- It is consistent and well balanced.
- The essay has a clear introduction and a conclusion that is not just a summary but ends with a significant thought.
- The vocabulary demonstrates good use of language and the sentence structure is varied.

Answer Explanations: English Test

1. **(D)** Even though there are a bunch of adjectives here, the right answer is the one with no commas, because the adjectives are not the kind you would separate with commas. Don't panic! It's not that hard, and in fact you already knew this. If you wrote "The three young French girls," would you use commas anywhere in there? No, right? This is because the adjectives concern *number*, *age*, and *nationality/ethnicity*. This makes them feel like they are part of the noun idea, and so even though they are adjectives, we don't use commas the same way we would if we were writing "The nice, funny, pretty girls." The other tricky part here is "science-fiction fans," because you have to realize that that entire phrase is the noun idea, not just "fans." I know this sounds complicated, but I bet you still *felt like* the answer with no commas was right, and if you missed this one it was probably because you second-guessed your instincts.
2. **(F)** The noun controlling the verb *bent* is *figure,* not *powers*. There is an implied "who is" there: "an evil figure with strange mind-control powers *who is* bent on world domination." If you are unfamiliar with the expression "bent on," it means something like "obsessed with" or "determined to achieve."
3. **(B)** Only what comes after the punctuation mark is an independent clause, and the two clauses before it are dependent ones beginning with *as* and *after*, so you need a comma. It is a huge clue that two of the other choices are a semicolon and a period: if one of those is right, the other one is too, so when you see that, odds are they cancel each other out and the answer is the one with the comma.
4. **(H)** How many societies are we talking about? One. And does it possess something here? Yes (the downtrodden and defenseless). This means we need the singular possessive: *society's*. It is just that simple. (Okay, maybe it seems tricky because when you say *society* you are talking about a bunch of people, so it may feel plural, but the bottom line is that *society* is still a singular word!)
5. **(D)** The relevant rule here is parallel phrasing. Earlier in the sentence we see "who used his abilities to protect," and then right before the underlined part we see "rather than." So the verb in the underlined part needs to be in the infinitive tense, just like "to protect," giving us "to exploit." *To protect rather than to exploit.*
6. **(G)** "They revamped their creation along these lines" is the core independent clause of the sentence. What comes before it is an introductory dependent clause followed by a comma, and what comes after it is an afterthought clause preceded by a comma.
7. **(D)** You've got three clauses here, so at least one of them has to be an independent clause. The first and third clauses aren't, so the middle one has to be, which means you have to get rid of *when*. This question is an excellent example of why you always have to read the entire sentence.
8. **(H)** The idea here is commas separating items in a list, but the items are all more than one word long. All you need to do is group the words correctly and put the commas in the appropriate places: *shorts over tights* is one idea, *a cape* is one idea, and *a logo on the chest* is one idea, so the commas separate those things. Be aware that whether you have a comma before the *and* that precedes the last item in a list does not matter (either way is correct). A question on the ACT will never ask you about that (some choices here have a comma before the *and* while others do not, but the wrong choices are all wrong for other reasons).
9. **(A)** As with many style questions, this is a case of "the simplest explanation is probably the correct one." Is the sentence a logical transition into the following paragraph? Yes, because the next paragraph begins to discuss the psychological underpinnings of the creation of Superman. If choice A can't be wrong, then it must be right. The subsequent choices are tempting because they sound more complex, but this is only a trick that the test plays on us: something that sounds harder isn't necessarily right, even though the pressure of the test can make us feel this way.
10. **(F)** The comma after *parents* completes the appositive clause that was begun before the underlined part, and then the colon after *immigrant* properly introduces an explanatory clause. The phrase "like Siegel and Shuster's parents" is extra information that has been dropped into the middle of the independent clause "Superman is an immigrant," and so it must be set off with commas.
11. **(B)** How many creators are we talking about? Two. And do they possess something here? Yes (their heritage). This means we need the plural possessive. It is just that simple. The question also *appears to be* asking you to choose between *his* and *Superman's*, but this part doesn't matter: either is correct as long as *Superman's* is possessive.
12. **(G)** A *reference* is a word or idea that calls up the memory of another idea, and the preposition used with *reference* would be *to*.
13. **(C)** The full verb phrase is *struggle to become*, and this is interrupted by the prepositional phrase *of immigrant groups* to signal whose struggle it was.

14. **(J)** *Power* is the noun here, and *will be used* is the verb. *Possessed by some* is extra information concerning the power. To determine agreement, all you need to do is ignore the words *possessed by some* and see what sounds right or makes sense: "The power will be used for the benefit of all."

15. **(C)** The essay deals only with how the creation of Superman was inspired by tragedy, and does not discuss even one other example of popular entertainment, much less popular entertainment in general. The Yes/No questions that often end ACT English passages frequently use variations of this same trick, so watch out for it.

16. **(H)** The clause is "a bunch of guys from my class started playing paintball," and the additional information "myself included" is inserted into that clause. It needs to be set off with two of the same punctuation mark, and choice H, with two commas, is the only choice that does so.

17. **(B)** We need the word *you're* (the contraction for "you are") and the word *it's* (the contraction for "it is"), and choice B is the one that has both. *Your* and *its* are both possessive pronouns, and would be wrong here. (It can be hard to remember this, because apostrophes usually indicate possession, but not with pronouns.) Whenever you're not sure in a situation like this, just substitute *you are* or *it is* for the word and see whether it makes sense.

18. **(G)** This answer uses *they're* ("they are"), which is plural, to replace the antecedent *a player*, which is singular. Even though we often use *they* as a gender-neutral singular pronoun when speaking, remember that it is technically grammatically wrong, and therefore wrong on the test! The other trick here is that choice G is the shortest alternative, and we are used to longer choices being wrong due to awkwardness or inefficiency. But whether a choice is grammatically right or wrong is always more important!

19. **(D)** The sentence is in the past tense, and so we need the past-tense form *cost*. This is a tricky one because, although the story takes place in the past, some of the phrases near this sentence state ongoing truths, and so are in the present tense, like "it's quite an investment" or "Pads aren't necessary." The clues are that this sentence contains the phrase *at the time* before the underlined part and the word *wasn't* after it, both of which clearly indicate past tense. Correct answers to verb-tense questions on the ACT usually involve simpler tenses, as opposed to more complex ones.

20. **(J)** This answer contains a single, comprehensible independent clause, preceded by the introductory dependent clause "after your first day." All of the other choices involve chopping up and rearranging this sentence into nonsensical variations on it. With questions like this one, which involve rearranging an entire long sentence, look for the "smoothest" answer, or the one that sounds the most like everyday speech (it is frequently the last choice, but not always).

21. **(D)** Since the sentence "A bunch of protective gear is required too" introduces the topic of protective gear, it should come before the parts that talk about such equipment. But the sentence ends with the word *too*, which indicates that it comes after some other requirement was stated.

22. **(F)** Although all the choices concern finding a place to play, the beginning of the following sentence implies that a specific location ("It was the only...") has already been chosen. Only choice F settles on a specific location.

23. **(D)** This is the only grammatically correct choice, as it creates two independent clauses and separates them appropriately with a semicolon. It may sound wordy, but the other three choices are grammatically wrong.

24. **(H)** Since the underlined part is preceded by *stand between*, you know you need two things. The test tries to trick you with the *and* that occurs later in the sentence, but that is just part of the prepositional phrase (*of* and everything after it) that adds more information about the nature of *the thrill*. Choice H has two things and uses the correct *us* with no comma.

25. **(A)** The sentence is in the present tense (it talks about the *memories* of the past, not the past itself), and the noun performing the verb here is *memories*, which is plural, and so you need *bring*. This is the prepositional phrase trick: the words *of my heroism that summer* are extra information that can be taken out, so you have to jump over them. Someone who doesn't notice this could be fooled by the word *heroism* or the word *summer*, which are both singular.

26. **(F)** We need the plural possessive here. *Their having* might sound weird, but since *having* is a gerund, it takes a possessive pronoun. In speech, you would probably be more likely to say "without *them* having any idea," but this is a test.

27. **(C)** When a sentence should be deleted, it is usually obvious. The underlined sentence is funny, consistent with the author's voice and the mood of the essay, and relevant to the action at this point. There is no reason to get rid of it.

28. **(G)** The author here is speaking in the present tense about the past. He *currently* does not remember why they stopped playing.

29. **(B)** This is the only choice that creates a correct sentence that means what you want it to say.

30. **(H)** This is the sentence order that establishes a clear narrative in which each sentence makes sense after the one before it. The biggest clues are that sentence 5 seems like it should be last, sentence 4 seems like it should be first, and sentence 2 should come right after sentence 3. Only choice H satisfies all these requirements.

31. **(C)** The core independent clause is "The now-familiar story of King Arthur first appeared in a fanciful history," and this clause is being interrupted with the extra information "complete with Merlin the wizard and the magic sword Excalibur," so the extra information must be set off with commas. The test is trying to trick you by using an appositive clause that contains the word *and*, which makes you want to put a comma before it, but don't be fooled! The *story* is *complete* with both of those things (the *wizard* and the *sword*), so no comma is necessary.

32. **(J)** This is the only choice that makes the middle clause into an independent one in the present tense.

33. **(B)** How many Arthurs are we talking about? One. And does he possess something? Yes ("famous victories"). How many victories are we talking about? More than one. And do they possess anything? No. So we need the singular possessive *Arthur's* and the plural nonpossessive *victories*. It is just that simple.

34. **(F)** The noun performing the verb is *source*, which is singular, and so we need the form *mentions*. This is the prepositional phrase trick: you have to jump over the extra information "in all those intervening years" (even though *years*, which is plural, comes right before the verb, it is not the relevant noun). The tense changes are just a red herring to confuse you; the only issue here is singular versus plural, so don't even worry about what tenses the wrong answers are in.

35. **(C)** This sentence is two independent clauses joined by a comma and conjunction, and so everything after the central *and* must constitute an independent clause. Choice C is the only choice that accomplishes this.

36. **(J)** The aside about Vortigern is unnecessary. The preceding assertion is not disputable to a point where other examples need to be listed, and the selection of Vortigern out of all the historical figures mentioned in the *Historia Brittonum* is irrelevant and distracting.

37. **(D)** The sentence contains information that is surprising and suspicious, and so *Curiously* would be the proper introductory word.

38. **(G)** This answer contains the past-tense verb *commanded* and modifies it with the adverb *successfully*.

39. **(C)** The example of the impossible deeds attributed to Arthur at Badon provides needed support for the preceding claim that the *Historia Brittonum*'s claims are *obviously exaggerated*.

40. **(F)** The underlined phrase needs to convey some idea of "the average person" or "people in general." *Many of them* implies some specific group of people, which doesn't work here, so choice F is the one that would NOT be acceptable.

41. **(A)** Since the issue is comparison, we need *than* (with an *a*), and choice A is the only one that has *than* and forms a complete correct sentence.

42. **(G)** This is the only one of the choices that forms a complete correct sentence.

43. **(D)** The sentence contains an explanatory appositive clause set off with a pair of dashes, and only choice D inserts a dash between *England* and *the* to match the one between *History* and *make*.

44. **(H)** This is the only choice that correctly finishes the initial independent clause ("Countless scholars have labored for years") with the nonpossessive plural *years* and goes on to correctly augment it with a prepositional phrase ("in the hopes of proving Arthur's existence").

45. **(B)** Paragraph 3 is clearly supposed to be the first paragraph of the essay, as it opens by being suspenseful about the subject's identity, and closes by posing the direct question *Did King Arthur really exist?* which we would expect to come at the beginning.

46. **(G)** The acceptable choices are all designed to indicate that boys will only dance under extreme circumstances, if at all. Choice G, *like the deserts miss the rain,* is a completely unrelated simile describing loneliness, and hence it is NOT acceptable.

47. **(D)** All of the other choices contain information that is either redundant or unnecessary. There is no reason not to simply end the sentence at the word *college*. (When the last choice is just a single word and all the other choices feature that word plus more information, the choice with just the single word is almost always correct!)

48. **(F)** The inclusion of the word *Since* at the beginning of the sentence makes the first clause a dependent one, and so the second clause must be an independent one that is a part of the same sentence. This is a common trick, and usually involves the words *since* and *although*.

49. **(C)** The introductory word *Apparently* indicates that the narrator has realized that the joke he made in the previous sentence applies to him too.

50. **(G)** The two subsequent sentences are about how many people, and what kinds of people, attended the first meeting, and so the paragraph is best introduced by a sentence that also concerns this. The sentence immediately following clearly refers to the content of choice G.

51. **(C)** The sentence is meant to communicate that the dancers switched partners at the same time that they were being guided by the instructor, and only choice C does so in a grammatically correct and sensible way.

52. **(F)** Although all four choices are eloquent and vivid ideas appropriate to the essay and consistent with the authorial voice, the question specifically asks for the one that best expresses the narrator's *feelings of distance* from Emily, and choice F is the only one about distance. (Even when it seems obvious what you are supposed to do, always read the little directions above a style question, as they frequently give very big hints.)

53. **(D)** What is needed here is a word meaning something like "development" or "series of events," and *phenomenon* is by far the closest of the four choices.

54. **(J)** The noun performing the verb in the underlined part is *thing*, not *kids*, which is part of the prepositional phrase *about popular kids*. (It is the prepositional phrase trick once again.) Choice J is the only one that results in a complete correct sentence.

55. **(A)** This would result in a comma splice, and thus is the only choice that is NOT acceptable. Every other option would form one or two complete sentences. (When you see that options like a semicolon, a colon, or a period and a new sentence form two or more of the other choices, you know that the one with the comma and no conjunction is wrong!)

56. **(H)** Though it frequently does, a colon doesn't have to precede an independent clause. It can also precede things like a list, a quotation, or an explanation. In this case, an independent clause referencing *two things* ends with a colon, which is then correctly followed by a list of what the two things were.

57. **(B)** This is the prepositional phrase trick again. The noun performing the verb here is *turn*, not *events*, and so we need a singular verb. Choice B is the only option that has a singular verb and means what you want it to mean.

58. **(G)** The order implied in the advice the sentence is trying to give is that you should make sure before joining a club that the girl you like isn't going to subsequently go to France. Only choice G, which places *first* after the verb phrase *make sure*, achieves this.

59. **(D)** The sentence is supposed to imply an ongoing condition, and so should be in the present tense. Choice D is the only option that creates a correct sentence in the present tense.

60. **(H)** Although deleting the underlined sentence and ending the essay with the previous one might also be acceptable, you have to look at the explanations. Choice H states that the underlined sentence *provides humorous insight into the author's experience of having to hang out with nerds,* which is true, and the other three choices say things that are not true. Even if you think the essay works better with the other ending, none of the choices gives a valid reason for deleting this one.

61. **(C)** Commas are required to separate the name of the city from the name of the state and to separate the introductory dependent clause from the main independent clause, and so commas go after *Louisville* and after *1954*, and nowhere else.

62. **(F)** This is the only option that results in a complete correct sentence that means what you want it to mean. (Since the second half of the sentence, starting at *someone*, is an independent clause preceded by a comma and conjunction, you know the entire sentence before that comma needs to be an independent clause too!)

63. **(D)** The person means that Cassius should take boxing lessons (in the immediate future) if he plans to beat someone up (at a later point in the future). Even though *had* is the past tense of *have*, the idiomatic construction *had better* is used to give advice about the future. (*You'd better* is a contraction of *You had better*.)

64. **(G)** The brief and to-the-point *bigger struggles* is the only one of the four choices that is not redundant.

65. **(D)** This includes the necessary comma after the introductory dependent clause, and does not include any unnecessary additional commas.

66. **(H)** The phrase *he'd called himself "too fast" and "too pretty" to lose* is an appositive clause that interrupts the main independent clause. The dash between *lose* and *had* shows that the clause is set off with dashes, and so the correct answer is the one that places a complementary dash between *fight* and *he'd*.

67. **(C)** Turning out to be gifted and deciding to stick with boxing would obviously come before the Olympics, which would come before turning pro and winning the heavyweight championship, which would come before an explanation of why this was so surprising, which would come before foreshadowing of the next paragraph. So the correct sentence order is 3, 2, 4, 1.

68. **(F)** *The one by which we know him* is a more proper way of saying *the one we know him by*.

69. **(B)** This choice contains a comma splice. There are two sentences connected by just a comma, which is incorrect.

Practice Test 5

70. **(J)** There is no real need to begin the sentence with an introductory word, and in any case all of the options that include introductory words are clearly wrong. (When three options begin with an introductory or transition word and one does not, the one that does not is almost always correct!)

71. **(D)** Since the sentence begins with the dependent descriptive clause *Released in 1970* followed by a comma, the noun idea after the comma has to be the person or thing that was released in 1970, or it results in a misplaced modifier. Muhammad Ali was the person released in 1970 here, and choice D is the only one that begins with *Ali*.

72. **(H)** The sentence needs to mean that it was Foreman who was exhausted, and that Ali sprang to life after this. Only choice H successfully communicates both.

73. **(A)** The sentence means to say that the sporting world was shocked by Ali in the past, but reveres him now.

74. **(G)** Commas are unnecessary before the prepositional phrases beginning with *for* and *of*, but commas are necessary to separate the items in the list: *skill, bravery, and magnetism*. (Whether or not there is a comma before the final *and* when separating items in a list is immaterial; either way is acceptable, and no question will ever come down to this rule.)

75. **(B)** The essay is not a technical one for boxing fans about what made Ali successful as a boxer; it is an essay for a general audience about Ali's cultural importance. It contains very little analysis of what went on in the ring, and discusses many things that went on outside the ring. (On questions like this, the choices that imply the passage is aimed at any type of audience other than *a general audience* are almost always wrong!)

Answer Explanations: Math Test

1. **(D)** Solving the equation for x gives $\frac{5x}{3} + 6 - 6 = 4 - 6 \rightarrow \frac{5x}{3} = -2 \rightarrow \frac{3}{5} \cdot \frac{5x}{3} = \frac{3}{5} \cdot \frac{-2}{1} \rightarrow x = \frac{-6}{5}$.

2. **(J)** Converting "doubling the Celsius temperature C and adding 32" can be written as an algebraic expression $2 \cdot C + 32$. Plugging in 18° for C gives $2 \cdot 18 + 32 = 36 + 32 = 68°$.

3. **(B)** If Carol spent 65% of her money, she had 100% – 65% = 35% remaining. Setting up a proportion using 35% remaining and $875 remaining gives $\frac{35}{100} = \frac{875}{x}$. Cross multiplying and solving for x gives $35x = 87{,}500 \rightarrow x = \$2{,}500$.

4. **(K)** The power rule for exponents is $(x^a)^b = x^{a \cdot b}$. Applying this rule, the expression becomes $(x^4)^{15} = x^{4 \cdot 15} = x^{60}$.

5. **(A)** Together Doris and Clyde used $1\frac{3}{4} + 2\frac{1}{2} = 4\frac{1}{4}$ gallons of paint. To find the amount of paint remaining, subtract this answer from the total amount of paint to get $5 - 4\frac{1}{4} = \frac{3}{4}$ gallon left.

6. **(K)** Distributing (FOIL) the given expression gives $(3p + 4)(5p - 6) = 15p^2 - 18p + 20p - 24$. Combine like terms to get $15p^2 + 2p - 24$.

7. **(D)** Getting the equation in slope-intercept form by solving for y gives $4x - 3y = 6 \rightarrow -3y = -4x + 6 \rightarrow y = \frac{4}{3}x - 2$. The slope of the line is $\frac{4}{3}$, and recall for two lines to be parallel they must have the same slope. The only answer choice with a slope of $\frac{4}{3}$ is D.

8. **(F)** Let x equal the vertex angle, then each of the base angles would be $\frac{1}{3}x$. The sum of the three angles of a triangle equals 180° so set up the equation: $x + \frac{1}{3}x + \frac{1}{3}x = 180$. Solve for x to get $\frac{5}{3}x = 180 \rightarrow x = 108$. Since the vertex equals 108°, each base angle equals $\frac{1}{3}(108) = 36°$.

9. **(B)** To find the missing side of a right triangle use the Pythagorean Theorem: $a^2 + b^2 = c^2 \rightarrow 8^2 + 9^2 = c^2 \rightarrow 145 = c^2 \rightarrow c = \sqrt{145}$.

10. **(H)** Setting up a ratio for the corresponding parts of the triangles gives $\frac{3}{4} = \frac{x}{6}$. Cross multiply and solve for x to get $18 = 4x \rightarrow x = 4.5$.

11. **(D)** Using the phrase "the price was 20% of today's," we can write the equation $x = .20(\$3.25) = \$0.65$.

12. **(H)** The diagonal of a rectangle divides the rectangle into two right triangles with legs formed by the length and width of the rectangle. Setting up the Pythagorean Theorem to find the hypotenuse we get $a^2 + b^2 = c^2 \rightarrow 14^2 + 15^2 = c^2 \rightarrow 421 = c^2$. Taking the square root, we get $c = \sqrt{421} \approx 20.5$. The closest given answer is 21.

13. **(C)** Solving the equation gives $3^x \cdot 9 = 729 \rightarrow 3^x = 81$. Since $3^4 = 81$, $x = 4$. Another way you could solve this problem is using your calculator and plugging the answers in for x until you find one that makes the left side of the equation equal the right.

14. **(G)** Setting up expressions from the given information we get x = width and $x + 3$ = length. Use the area formula of a rectangle: $A = L \cdot W$ to set up the equation $54 = (x + 3)(x)$. Distribute and put in standard form to get $54 = x^2 + 3x \rightarrow x^2 + 3x - 54 = 0$. Factor to get $(x + 9)(x - 6) = 0$; therefore $x = -9$ and $x = 6$. Since the width of a rectangle cannot be negative, the only answer left is $x = 6$. The question asks for the length of the rectangle, which is $6 + 3 = 9$.

15. **(C)** Opposite sides of a parallelogram are congruent. Since one side measures 6, the opposite side also measures 6 leaving $36 - 6 - 6 = 24$ inches for the remaining two sides. Dividing by 2, we get each of the remaining two sides to equal 12 inches. Therefore the three sides have measures: 6, 12, 12.

16. **(J)** If each of the five numbers was decreased by 4, the average would also be decreased by 4 making it $7 - 4 = 3$.

17. **(E)** Setting up an equation for Julie's overall salary we get *salary* = *base salary* + *amount for sales* $\rightarrow S = 48 + (k)(i)$ where S is her salary, k is the amount she makes per sale, and i is the number of items she sells. Substituting the values from the problem the equation becomes $68 = 48 + (k)(4)$. Solving for k gives $k = 5$. If Julie sells 4 more items today than yesterday, that is a total of $3 + 4 = 7$ items. Using the formula again we get $S = 48 + (5)(7) = \$83$.

18. **(J)** Sometimes the easiest way to solve a problem is to plug in answers. Substitute in answers to find the largest number that will make a true statement. Trying 24 we get $\frac{6}{24} \geq \frac{1}{4}$, which simplifies to $\frac{1}{4} \geq \frac{1}{4}$, which is a true statement. Therefore, 24 is the correct answer.

19. **(D)** There are 12 hours on a clock; set up a proportion to get $\frac{hours}{total\ hours} = \frac{degrees}{total\ degrees} \rightarrow \frac{8}{12} = \frac{x}{360}$. Cross multiply and solve for x to get $2880 = 12x \rightarrow x = 240°$.

20. **(G)** To find the total number of seats on the airplane we multiply the number of rows by the number of seats in each row to get $r \cdot (s + d)$. Since this answer is not one of the choices, distribute to get $(r \cdot s) + (r \cdot d)$.

21. **(E)** A rational expression is undefined when the denominator equals zero. To find the value that makes the denominator equal zero set the denominator equal to zero and solve the equation: $16 - x^2 = 0 \rightarrow x^2 = 16 \rightarrow x = 4$.

22. **(F)** Mixing 3 quarts juice to 2 quarts soda would make 5 quarts punch. According to the problem we need 20 quarts of punch, which is $5 \cdot 4$. Multiplying each of the other dimensions by 4 we get $3 \cdot 4 = 12$ quarts juice and $2 \cdot 4 = 8$ quarts soda. We are asked how much juice we need: 12 quarts.

23. **(B)** Point H is between F and G meaning $GH < FG$. Choice B is correct.

24. **(H)** Using the formula given with $h = 9$ and $r = 4$ we get $V = \frac{\pi}{3} \cdot 4^2 \cdot 9 = \frac{\pi}{3} \cdot 144 = 48\pi$.

25. **(A)** The midpoint formula is *midpoint* $= \left(\frac{x_1 + x_2}{2}, \frac{y_1 + y_2}{2}\right)$. Remember, the center of the circle is the midpoint of any diameter of the circle. Substituting $(3, -4)$ for the midpoint, $(5, -3)$ for (x_1, y_1), and (x, y) for (x_2, y_2) we get $(3, -4) = \left(\frac{5 + x}{2}, \frac{-3 + y}{2}\right)$. Solve for x to get $3 = \frac{5 + x}{2} \rightarrow 6 = 5 + x \rightarrow x = 1$. Solving for y the same way gives $-4 = \frac{-3 + y}{2} \rightarrow -8 = -3 + y \rightarrow y = -5$. Therefore, the other endpoint lies at $(1, -5)$.

26. **(K)** Set up a proportion for each of the choices to get, for 20 minutes, airport 1 sends up $\frac{1}{4} = \frac{x}{20}$ and airport 2 sends up $\frac{5}{10} = \frac{y}{20}$. Solve for x and y to get $4x = 20 \rightarrow x = 5$ and $100 = 10y \rightarrow y = 10$. Therefore, the total number of planes sent up in 20 minutes is $5 + 10 = 15$ planes.

27. **(C)** $xy = (4a^3)(-3a^5 + b)$. Distribute and use the laws of exponents to get $4a^3 \cdot (-3a^5) + 4a^3 \cdot b = -12a^8 + 4a^3b$.

28. **(H)** To find the length of ribbon, add the length of ribbon needed for each side of the box. The top needs $32 + 12 = 44$ cm. All 4 sides each need 8 cm for a total of $8 \cdot 4 = 32$ cm. The bottom needs $32 + 12 = 44$ cm. Add the top, bottom, and all 4 sides together to get $44 + 32 + 44 = 120$ cm.

29. **(D)** Starting with the multiplication rule of exponents the expression becomes $\frac{-72x^0 y^5}{4x^2 y^4}$. Now use the division rule of exponents to get $-18x^{-2}y$.

30. **(K)** We draw two strategic lines to divide the shape into two rectangles and a trapezoid. The area of the small rectangle is $A = L \cdot W = 1 \cdot 6 = 6$. The area of the larger rectangle is $A = L \cdot W = 9 \cdot 3 = 27$. The area of the trapezoid is $A = \frac{1}{2}h(b_1 + b_2) = \frac{1}{2}(3)(3 + 6)$. Simplify to get $(1.5)(9) = 13.5$. Add all the areas together to get $6 + 27 + 13.5 = 46.5$.

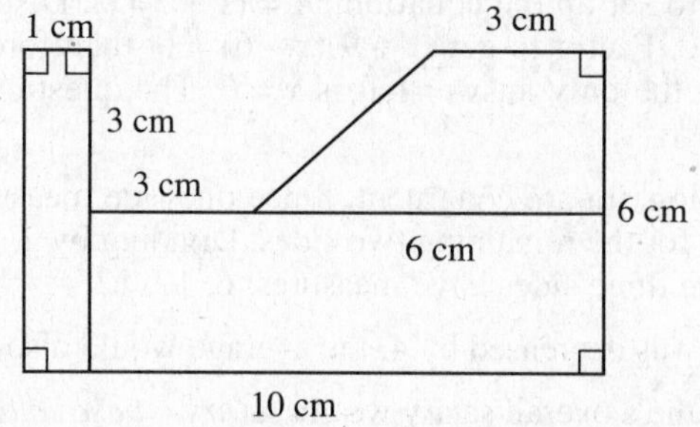

31. **(B)** *ABFE* is a parallelogram; therefore $\angle ABF \cong \angle AEF = 142°$ making $\angle DEG = 142°$ because it is vertical to $\angle AEF$. Looking at $\triangle DEG$, we know two angles, so we calculate the missing angle d to get $d = 180 - (26 + 142) = 180 - 168 = 12°$.

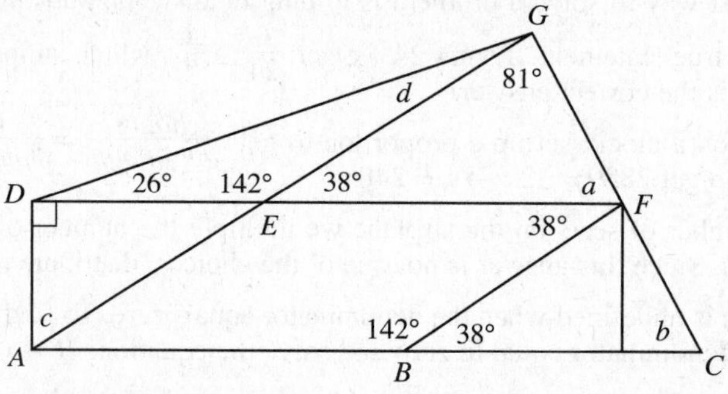

32. **(H)** Looking at $\triangle GEF$, we know two of the angles so we can find the missing angle a by calculating $a = 180 - (38 + 81) = 180 - 119 = 61°$.

33. **(A)** Making a sketch from the information gives the following right triangle. Find the missing side using the Pythagorean Theorem to get $x^2 + 16^2 = 34^2 \rightarrow x^2 = 900 \rightarrow x = 30$.

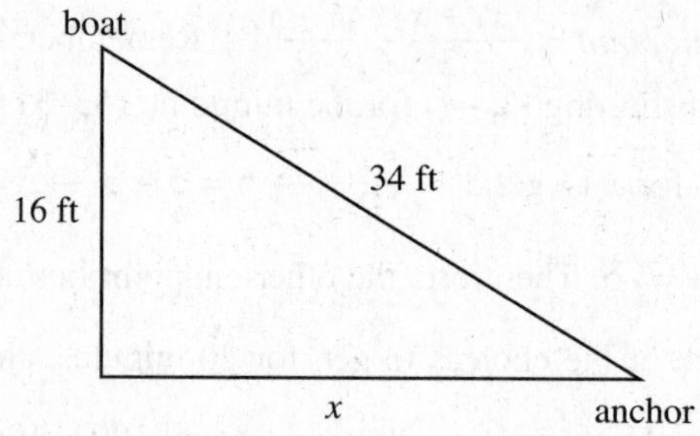

34. **(F)** You cannot evaluate the square root of a negative expression. Since a^2 is always positive, b must also be positive; otherwise the quotient $\frac{a^2}{b}$ would be negative.

Practice Test 5

35. **(C)** Same-side interior angles are supplementary making it 180 – 62 = 118°. Now we have the measure of two angles of a triangle; find the third angle, *b*: 180 – (118 + 14) = 48°.

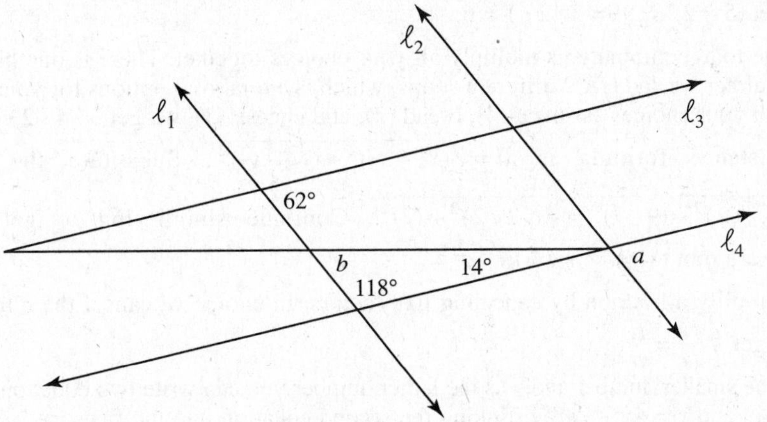

36. **(J)** Recall $\cos x = \dfrac{adjacent}{hypotenuse}$ and $\tan x = \dfrac{opposite}{adjacent}$. Find the opposite side using the Pythagorean Theorem: $8^2 + x^2 = 17^2 \rightarrow x = 15$. Therefore, $\tan x = \dfrac{opposite}{adjacent} = \dfrac{15}{8}$.

37. **(D)** $\overline{AD}$ is a diameter of the circle meaning $\widehat{ABD} = 180°$. Since angle *ADB* is 28°, arc $\widehat{AB} = 2 \cdot 28 = 56°$. Finally, $\widehat{BCD} = 180 - 56 = 124°$.

38. **(F)** $\csc\theta = \dfrac{1}{\sin\theta} = \dfrac{1}{\frac{1}{2}} = \dfrac{2}{1} = 2$.

39. **(E)** *b* and *c* form a linear pair; therefore *b* + *c* = 180. Since △*PQR* is an equilateral, *a* and *d* each measure 60°. The sum of *a* + *b* + *c* + *d* = 60 + (180) + 60 = 300°.

40. **(K)** $8 \oplus 2 = \dfrac{8 \cdot 2}{8+2} = \dfrac{16}{10} = \dfrac{8}{5}$.

41. **(B)** Using the triangle inequality theorem, we know the length of the third side of the triangle is between 23 – 5 = 18 and 23 + 5 = 28. Between 18 and 28 there are exactly two prime numbers, 19 and 23. Therefore, the answer is 2.

42. **(J)** To find the total distance traveled after 50 revolutions we find the circumference of the wheel and multiply that answer by 50. Calculating, we get $C = \pi d = 26\pi$. Multiplying by 50 we get $26\pi \cdot 50 = 1{,}300\pi$.

43. **(D)** $(3i + 4)^2 = (3i + 4)(3i + 4) = 9i^2 + 12i + 12i + 16$. Recalling $i^2 = -1$ we get $9(-1) + 24i + 16 = 7 + 24i$.

44. **(H)** From the diagram we can tell the diameter of the wheel is 20 inches. If the diameter is 20 inches, the radius is $\frac{1}{2}(20) = 10$ inches.

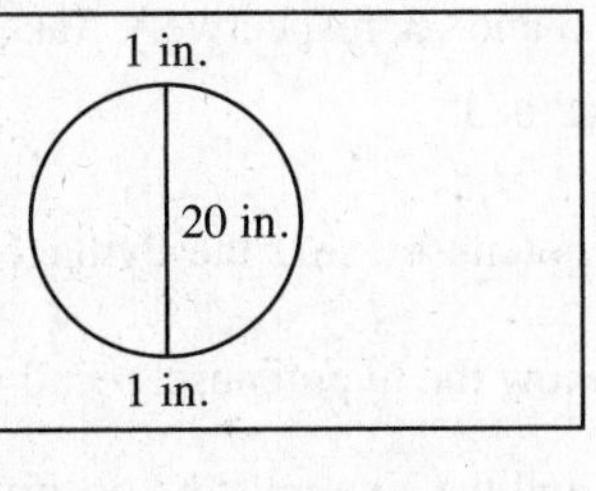

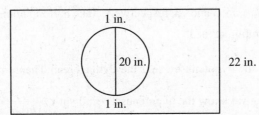

45. **(C)** To find the sum of an arithmetic sequence we use the formula $sum = \dfrac{n(s_0 + s_n)}{2}$ where *n* is the number of numbers in the sequence, s_0 is the first number in the sequence, and s_n is the last number in the sequence. We know $n = 15$, $s_0 = 5$, but we still need to calculate the 15th multiple of 5. Take $5 \cdot 15 = 75$ so $s_n = 75$. Now substitute everything into the equation to get $sum = \dfrac{15(5 + 75)}{2} = \dfrac{1200}{2} = 600$. If you do not have these formulas memorized and you had enough time, you could find the sum by listing the first 15 multiples of 5 and adding them together with a calculator. It takes more time, but it is just as effective.

Practice Test 5

46. **(F)** $\frac{n!}{(n-1)!} = \frac{n \cdot (n-1)!}{(n-1)!} = 5$. Canceling like factors we get $n = 5$. Now that we know n, plug it in to the given expression to get $(5 - 2)! = 3! = 3 \cdot 2 \cdot 1 = 6$.

47. **(D)** To calculate total combinations multiply all your choices together. There is one hitch in this problem: your first decision is either 1 salad OR 2 different soups, which is a total of 3 options for your first choice. Multiplying this number with your choices for meat (4), bread (2), and cheese (3), we get $3 \cdot 4 \cdot 2 \cdot 3 = 72$.

48. **(H)** The distance formula is $d = \sqrt{(x_2 - x_1)^2 + (y_2 - y_1)^2}$. Substitute the given points to get $d = \sqrt{(-3\sqrt{2} - (-\sqrt{2}))^2 + (9 - 7)^2} = \sqrt{(-2\sqrt{2})^2 + (2)^2}$. Continue simplifying to get $d = \sqrt{(4 \cdot 2) + 4} = \sqrt{12}$. Simplify the square root to get $d = \sqrt{4} \cdot \sqrt{3} = 2\sqrt{3}$.

49. **(A)** You can simplify a fraction by canceling like factors. In choice A, cancel the c in both the numerator and denominator to get $\frac{a \cdot c}{b \cdot c} = \frac{a}{b}$.

50. **(J)** Using x as the smaller number and y as the larger number you can write two equations from the given information: $2x + 3y = 49$ and $y = 4x + 7$. Substituting the second equation into the first one we get $2x + 3(4x + 7) = 49$, which is equivalent to choice J.

51. **(B)** To express y in terms of x first solve the x equation for t to get $x = 3t - 7 \rightarrow t = \frac{x+7}{3}$. Substitute into the second equation to get $y = 4 - \left(\frac{x+7}{3}\right)$. Simplify to get $y = \frac{12}{3} - \frac{x+7}{3} = \frac{5-x}{3}$.

52. **(G)** To write the equation of the line we use the formula $y - y_1 = m(x - x_1)$ where m is the slope of the line and (x_1, y_1) is any point on the line. First calculate m to get $m = \frac{y_2 - y_1}{x_2 - x_1} = \frac{-12 - 4}{-2 - 2} = 4$. Now, substitute m and point (2, 4) into the formula above to get $y - 4 = 4(x - 2)$. Rewrite the equation in standard form to get $y - 4 = 4x - 8 \rightarrow 4x - y = 4$.

53. **(B)** $f(-3) = 7(-3)^2 - 4(-3) - 10 = 63 + 12 - 10 = 65$.

54. **(F)** Using the given formula, the measure of an angle of a regular octagon equals $\frac{(8-2) \cdot 180}{8} = 135°$ and a hexagon equals $\frac{(6-2) \cdot 180}{6} = 120°$. Calculate the difference to get $135 - 120 = 15°$.

55. **(C)** To condense a logarithm expression we use the three properties of logs: $a \cdot \log b = \log b^a$, $\log(a \cdot b) = \log a + \log b$, and $\log \frac{a}{b} = \log a - \log b$. Using the first property the expression becomes $\log_2 x^3 + \log_4 y^{\frac{1}{3}} - \log_2 z$. Now use the third property to get $\log_2\left(\frac{x^3}{z}\right) + \log_4(\sqrt[3]{y})$. You cannot combine the remaining two logs together because they have different bases.

56. **(J)** Factoring the numerator and denominator yields $\frac{(x+5)(x+3)(x-2)}{(x+5)(x-2)(x+3)}$. Canceling like factors we get $\frac{\cancel{(x+5)(x+3)(x-2)}}{\cancel{(x+5)(x-2)(x+3)}} = 1$.

57. **(E)** The max and min of 3 sin x are 3 and -3, respectively. Take half the nonnegative difference to get $\frac{1}{2}(3 - (-3)) = \frac{1}{2}(6) = 3$. Therefore, the amplitude is 3.

58. **(K)** $\tan x = \frac{\textit{opposite}}{\textit{adjacent}}$. Find the hypotenuse using the Pythagorean Theorem to get $(-24)^2 + (7)^2 = \textit{hypotenuse}^2 \rightarrow \textit{hypotenuse} = 25$. Now that we know the hypotenuse, recall $\sin x = \frac{\textit{opposite}}{\textit{hypotenuse}} = \frac{24}{25}$. Because $90° < x < 180°$, the angle is in the second quadrant and the sine must be positive.

59. **(A)** Checking each of the solutions using FOIL gives $(3x + 2)(4x - 3) = 12x^2 - 9x + 8x - 6 = 12x^2 - x - 6$.

60. **(K)** To calculate probability we use the formula $= \frac{\textit{number of successful outcomes}}{\textit{total number of outcomes}}$. Since we are adding pink jelly beans, both the number of successful outcomes and total outcomes are increased by x. Therefore, the formula becomes $P = \frac{7+x}{24+x}$. Substitute 0.5 in for P, the probability, and solve for x to get $0.5 = \frac{7+x}{24+x} \rightarrow 12 + 0.5x = 7 + x \rightarrow 5 = 0.5x \rightarrow x = 10$. So we must add 10 pink jelly beans to get a probability of $\frac{1}{2}$.

Answer Explanations: Reading Test

1. **(C)** Lines 24–27 establish that the narrator didn't drop Pickman because of "Ghoul Feeding," even though another gallery owner did. The opening paragraph implies that the narrator dropped Pickman because of something he saw in Pickman's secret studio, and obviously Pickman didn't disappear until *after* that. Therefore, the composition of "Ghoul Feeding" predates the other three events.
2. **(G)** The narrator's friend, to whom he relates the story, is never identified by name.
3. **(A)** The first paragraph's references to Pickman's unknown whereabouts, the fact that the police are searching for him, his rental of a secret studio, and the narrator's refusal to try to find it again all serve to establish Pickman as the central figure in a spooky mystery.
4. **(J)** In lines 33–38, the narrator credits Pickman with an uncanny ability to exploit deep, primal responses in his audience. This is most evident in the choices of the terms *latent instincts* and *hereditary memories* (lines 36–37).
5. **(B)** Although it is implied that Pickman was notably successful for a while, nothing about the amount of money he made is ever mentioned.
6. **(F)** In the fifth paragraph, particularly in lines 50–53, the narrator expounds upon his theory that the *really weird artist* is great as a result of living partly in a *spectral world* (i.e., the artist's own unusually powerful imagination).
7. **(C)** The passage never conclusively establishes which gallery owner was the first to drop Pickman, in the third paragraph or anywhere else.
8. **(G)** The first two paragraphs strongly imply that the *inside information* (line 3) that prompted the narrator's final break with Pickman was obtained during his visit to Pickman's secret studio, especially in phrases like *or am afraid I know* (line 10) and *[t]here was something there* (lines 14–15).
9. **(D)** In the context of other phrases like *latent instincts* (line 36) and *hereditary memories* (lines 36–37), it is clear that *dormant* is intended to mean "subconscious" here.
10. **(F)** Lines 68–71 depict Pickman being rudely and disturbingly dismissive of people's inquiries into his creative process.
11. **(B)** The main idea is not always explicitly stated in the first paragraph. Here, it is slowly developed over the course of the first five paragraphs, before being explicitly stated in lines 35–37. Going by the last paragraph—the other place to look on "main idea" questions—would have been a good idea here: lines 86–91 make it very clear that the main idea concerns bright girls losing confidence.
12. **(J)** When you saw this question, you were probably thinking that there isn't really a tone at all, and that the passage is just presenting facts and theories without any emotion. Well, exactly—that should have been a clue that the passage is *analytical* in nature.
13. **(A)** The first sentence of the seventh paragraph asks a question, and the second answers it: *it has to do with the kinds of feedback we get from parents and teachers* (lines 44–45). The rest of the paragraph gives examples to support that assertion and explains what the problem with those comments is.
14. **(F)** Although the idea that adult women are underpaid may seem like a key idea here because it is mentioned in the first paragraph, it is actually unrelated to the *causes* of the issue being discussed. There is no indication in the passage that young girls are even aware that adult women are underpaid. The other three choices, however, are all closely related to one another and presented as possible causes of the problem.
15. **(B)** The final paragraph—specifically the final sentence of the final paragraph—posits that the solution is for bright women to reexamine their beliefs about ability.
16. **(H)** The subsequent sentence emphasizes *skill*, *experience*, *effort*, and *persistence* (line 87), so it should have been clear that *profoundly malleable* means "extremely changeable."
17. **(D)** The sentence in question asserts that one of women's biggest obstacles *lies within*—that is, within their own beliefs about themselves.
18. **(F)** Lines 19–22 explicitly state that Carol Dweck's study uncovered an odd confidence problem unique to bright girls. (The fact that *Carol Dweck* is the antecedent of *she* is established by the previous sentence.)
19. **(C)** Lines 29–30 state that, at the elementary school level, girls outperform boys at *every* subject, and so which subjects girls and boys excel at is not presented as a *difference* between them in the passage.

20. **(G)** The final paragraph explains that success can be achieved with persistence, and that persistence is the result of believing in yourself.

21. **(B)** The author is arguing a similarity between music and science. This is first established in line 37 (in relation to the previous paragraph), and explicitly stated as the thesis in lines 54–56.

22. **(F)** In lines 61–63, the author establishes his position that popular music can be brilliant despite being largely derivative of previous popular music.

23. **(C)** The previous phrase, concerning a super-genius physicist, and the subsequent paragraph, about the emotional power of John Lennon's "Imagine," involve people unlocking truths about the universe and human experience in it. There is nothing literal about a deity or supernatural being in this area (or anywhere in the passage), and so it is clear that "God" here is a metaphor.

24. **(G)** The sixth paragraph—particularly in lines 46–48, which compare Lennon's "Imagine" to Einstein's theory of relativity—figures the song as Lennon's personal masterpiece of ethical and emotional philosophy.

25. **(A)** In lines 63–69, the author says that even though we cannot scientifically describe why "Smells Like Teen Spirit" was so important, we cannot deny that for some reason it was ("the results of the experiment are unequivocal").

26. **(J)** In lines 10–12, the author states that music *toys with emotions in a manner that, if a friend acted the same way, you would hate their guts*—that is, that music is designed to be emotionally manipulative.

27. **(C)** The phrase *indisputable body of known fact* is used in lines 22–23 to describe those aspects of science that are solidly mathematically verifiable. One example he gives (lines 17–18) is the formula used to calculate energy. The tricky part is that the formula is written out in words instead of symbols or numerals, and so it might not immediately jump out at someone who is scanning the passage for symbols and numerals (watch out for that trick—the ACT Reading uses it often!).

28. **(J)** When the author says that the principles of geometry and music converge somewhere out on the horizon, he means that somehow the "rules" of music must be governed by basic math in some way that we have not yet figured out. (The grand unified theory is a still hypothetical idea about a concept or realization that will unite all the sciences into one.)

29. **(D)** The author isn't judging mechanical bulls (line 24) or the people who ride them. He just names them as one example in a list of things that we have been able to build as a result of mastering certain aspects of science. (It is worth noting that all of the other choices are "bigger" than this one—this answer can be right by itself, but the others can't be true without this one *also* being true.)

30. **(F)** The previous sentence establishes that "Smells Like Teen Spirit" was a phenomenally successful song. The author says here that, although we don't know from a scientific standpoint what it is that *makes* a song successful, we know for a fact that successful songs *are* successful. This fact is *inarguable*, or *unequivocal*, or *absolutely clear*.

31. **(A)** Lines 6–11 explicitly state that it is the oxygen levels of Europa's ocean that would theoretically make advanced life possible.

32. **(J)** The fact that Europa's ocean was only discovered in the last decade or so, and that NASA was excited enough by this to destroy a valuable spacecraft, is the point of the paragraph—this is a *recent* and *exciting* discovery (this helps establish why the reader should care).

33. **(D)** Lines 38–40 state that Europa's icy crust is startlingly new.

34. **(H)** *You need the delay*, Greenberg says, because the building blocks of life can't form in the presence of too much oxygen, but subsequent advanced life wouldn't survive without it. Oxygen levels would need to have risen gradually.

35. **(B)** There's no reason why a small, faraway planet would exert gravitational influence on the moon of a much larger planet.

36. **(G)** Lines 86–89 state it as a fact that Europa and Io are gravitationally locked.

37. **(A)** If a *stable* rate involves *a complete renewal every 50 million years*, then in this context *stable* must mean "regular."

38. **(J)** In the final paragraph, Pappalardo offers some scenarios under which advanced life might not exist on Europa after all. He doesn't prove that it *definitely* doesn't, but establishes that it *may* be *unlikely*.

39. **(C)** If the process of surface repaving happened in *extreme cycles*, resulting in *high and low periods of activity*, then it's clear that *fits and starts* means "intermittently" (see the use of *intermittent* in line 83).

40. **(H)** The explanation of tidal activity in lines 46–53 makes it clear that tides on a body with water are affected by other celestial bodies in the vicinity.

Answer Explanations: Science Test

1. **(B)** This question is a classic "Go Up, Hit Line, Go Over." Go to Figure 2 (being careful to notice that the labels are below the figures, so you don't accidentally look at Figure 3), find 200 cm on the *x*-axis (the horizontal line), look up to the solid line representing 2004, and see how high up it is on the *y*-axis (the vertical line) at that point. It is a little less than halfway between 0.50 and 1.00, making 0.70 the closest answer by far.
2. **(H)** This is a simple "extrapolation" question, meaning that you have to guess about a value not pictured on the graph based on the way that the data are trending. Though the dotted line in Figure 3 representing 2002 stops at 350 cm, around 315 cm it appears to level off at 2.00 dpm/g, meaning that if the line were to continue, the radium-226 activity at 400 cm below the top of the sediment would almost certainly be 2.00 dpm/g.
3. **(A)** The first sentence of the introductory paragraph states that "^{226}Ra activity is often elevated in bodies of water that have been augmented with groundwater." We know that there was more ^{226}Ra activity in 2004 than in 2002, so therefore, the wetlands were probably augmented with groundwater in 2004.
4. **(H)** A question that begins "If the data are typical…" is simply asking you to identify which one of the choices is true of all the given figures. In this case, it is true that both Figure 2 and Figure 3 show ^{226}Ra activity peaking somewhere around 325 cm below the top of the sediment in both 2002 and 2004. (Though ^{226}Ra activity does not peak at exactly 325 cm below the top of the sediment in all four lines, choice H is still clearly much better than the other three.)
5. **(D)** The question is simply asking: in which of the four lines contained in Figures 2 and 3 were ^{226}Ra levels higher at 250 cm below the top of the sediment than they were at 200 cm below the top of the sediment? This is only the case with the solid line (representing 2004) in Figure 3 (representing marshes), and so the answer is "Marsh wetlands in 2004."
6. **(H)** The row in Table 1 that corresponds to a pH of 9.3 corresponds to 200 ml NaOH.
7. **(B)** A 3.5 pH intersects the graph at about 50 ml. You could also use the table to see that 3.5 falls between 2.2 and 4.7. Clearly, a 3.5 pH would result from somewhere between 0 and 100 ml of NaOH added.
8. **(F)** The reasoning is correct. The OH^- ions from NaOH will combine with OH^+ ions to form water. The trend in the table is lower and lower concentrations of OH^+ and CH_3COOH and higher concentrations of CH_3COO^-. The only way to counteract the decrease in H^+ ions and keep the K_a a constant is to reduce the denominator or increase the numerator. Since the two quantities are interrelated, $[CH_3COOH(aq)]$ decreases while $[CH_3COO^-(aq)]$ increases. It only appears that $[CH_3COO^-(aq)]$ is unchanged because the orders of magnitudes of the two quantities are drastically different after 200 ml NaOH have been added. The increase in $[CH_3COO^-(aq)]$ is not noticeable.
9. **(A)** The figure and the table support this choice. A lower initial concentration of acetic acid will lower the concentration of H^+ ions, which lowers acidity. The lower $[H^+(aq)]$ would correspond to higher pH based on all the data.
10. **(J)** The presence of acetic acid and H^+ is what made the pH 2.2 in the first place. As the $[H^+(aq)]$ decreased, the pH increased.
11. **(A)** As the $[H^+(aq)]$ decreases going down the table, the pH increases consistently.
12. **(J)** This is a simple "Go Up, Hit Line, Go Over." Starting from October in the *x*-axis (horizontal) of Figure 2, the line representing ex situ permeability (the one with squares on it) is roughly as high as 30 on the *y*-axis (vertical).
13. **(A)** This is an "extrapolation" question, meaning that you have to guess about a value not pictured on the graph based on the way the data are trending. The Site 1 line (squares) in Figure 4 appears to rise roughly 0.1 m^3/s for every 100 Pa of pressure, and at that rate would have been at around 0.5 m^3/s by 800 Pa.
14. **(G)** This question just asks you to compare the data in the figures and paragraph and then pick the answer that presents true statements as indicated by that data. Figure 3 indicates that soil porosity is highest at Site 2, as choice G suggests, and Figure 4 indicates that flow rate is highest at Site 2, another indicator that choice G is a good bet.
15. **(A)** This is an "If the data are typical…" question, asking you to select which of the choices is true based on what has been observed. In both Figure 1 and Figure 2, air permeability is higher ex situ than it is in situ. (This is to be expected, since the paragraph explains that *in situ* means that the instrument is buried in the dirt, and *ex situ* means that it is not!)
16. **(J)** In Figure 1, permeability was highest for water during all the months, including November.

17. **(B)** Although no official distinction between a "small" lemon and a "large" lemon is given, the lemons on the left-hand side of the *x*-axis (horizontal) in Figure 1 are smaller than those on the right-hand side, and the highest peak (representing greater sucrose formation) of any line occurs in the albedo tissue line (dark circles) on the left-hand side.

18. **(G)** The line representing sucrose production in the vesicles goes up between the diameters of 20 and 30 mm, and then down between 30 and 50 mm: in other words, the sucrose production increases and then decreases.

19. **(C)** The question is simply asking you to look at Figure 2 and compare the length of the bars to determine which of the four answer choices represents the greatest difference in bar height. Of the four answer choices, the greatest difference is between flavedo tissue and vesicle tissue in lemons.

20. **(G)** In Table 1, the number representing sucrose formed from orange juice (0.12) is lower than the number representing sucrose formed from lemon juice (0.4).

21. **(C)** By comparing the appropriate bars in Figure 2, we see that sucrose production in albedo tissue of oranges is roughly half that of albedo tissue in lemons. Since Figure 1 indicates that sucrose production in the albedo tissue of a 30-mm lemon is around 17, we can intuit that sucrose production in an orange of the same size would be roughly half that, and 9 is the only one of the choices that is anywhere close to half of 17.

22. **(J)** The paragraph at the beginning of Study 2 explains that *albedo* is just the name for the "white peel layer" of a fruit, and according to Figure 2 it is indeed true that more sucrose is formed in the albedo tissue of a lemon than in any other part.

23. **(D)** This is an "extrapolation" question in which you are required to guess about an unknown value based on the way the available data are trending. In Figure 2, we can see that the ratio of velocity is always a value higher than the number of gliders, and by increasing amounts: with one glider it is a bit above 1, with two gliders it is about halfway above 2, and then with three gliders it is more than halfway above 3 and almost to 4. At that rate, with four gliders it would definitely be closer to 5 than to 4 but 4 is clearly the best answer.

24. **(G)** The students record the gliders' positions every 0.5 seconds, which works out to 2 times per second $\left(\frac{1}{.5\text{ sec}} = 2\right)$.

25. **(A)** The total distance decreased as the weights of the gliders increased. When Glider 4 (triple weight) was used, the total distance was .53 + .15 = .68 m. When Glider 2 was used (single weight), the total distance was .51 + .52 = 1.03 m.

26. **(G)** The distance traveled was the Glider 4 position at $t = 1.5$ sec – the position at time $t = 0$ sec .86 m – .80 m = .06 m.

27. **(C)** Comparisons of the positions of the gliders at $t = 0$ was identical in each case: .80 m – .75 m = .05 m.

28. **(G)** The arrows in Figure 1 show how much carbon is transmitted in the global carbon cycle. There is an arrow at the top of the figure, in the center, which illustrates carbon being transmitted from the ocean to the atmosphere, and the number next to the arrow is 90.6.

29. **(C)** This is correct because of the data presented in Figure 2. The right side of the figure is labeled Particles, and the left side of the figure is labeled Dissolved, with the line dividing them at 0.2 micrometers. Algae is the only type of carbon listed that is on the right side of the figure, making it the only type of carbon that is NOT a dissolved carbon.

30. **(H)** This is correct because of the information presented in Figure 3. The *y*-axis represents ocean depth and the *x*-axis on the top of the figure represents DOC. The key identifies the line with circular markers as the one for DOC. Trace the line representing DOC down to determine what happens as the depth increases. It goes straight down for a while, remaining constant, then it moves to the left, decreasing the amount of DOC. Then it becomes fairly consistent again.

31. **(D)** This is correct because of the information presented in Figure 2. The line at the bottom of the figure represents the size of the carbon fragments. The third dash from the left is labeled 0.01. Trace your finger up from that dash to find that two types of dissolved carbon are listed: small polymers and proteins, making choice D the correct answer.

32. **(G)** This is correct because of the data presented in Figure 3. The *y*-axis represents ocean depth. The key shows that the line with the square markers represents CDOM. The *x*-axis on the bottom of the figure represents CDOM. Find the dash on the *y*-axis labeled 100 and trace your finger over to the line with the square markers. Then trace your finger down to the *x*-axis to find that 0.12 is the best answer.

33. **(D)** Figure 2 displays which types of carbon fragments are considered dissolved and which are particles. Organic matter is living, whereas inorganic matter is not. Polymers are not living, so they are inorganic carbon, and they are displayed on the left side of Figure 2, under the heading Dissolved.

34. **(H)** The second paragraph begins by stating that Researcher 1 expected glucose to have an effect on alga respiration, and the third paragraph begins by stating that Researcher 2 expected light to have an effect.

35. **(B)** For this question it is necessary either to know or to intuit that *control* is the term for the version of a scientific experiment in which nothing has been altered, and that is run so that the experimenters can have something to compare the results of the experiments in which something has been altered. Other than that, it is a standard "Go Up, Hit Line, Go Over" question. The solid line in Figure 1 representing the control (*Chlorella* to which nothing has been added) is at around 18 mm^3 on the *y*-axis (vertical) after 30 minutes.

36. **(F)** Researcher 1 predicted in the paragraph that the addition of glucose would inhibit respiration even further, and Figure 1 shows that the lines representing HCN and H_2S plus glucose are indeed lower than the lines representing HCN and H_2S alone (so Researcher 1 was right). The question asks what effect a solution with 2 percent glucose would have, and since the paragraph established that the previous solutions contained 1 percent glucose, that is twice as much. Twice as much glucose should drop the lines down to roughly half their current levels. The dotted line representing glucose + HCN is currently at around 28 mm^3 after 20 minutes, and so 15 mm^3 would be around half as much (although it is not exactly half as much, 15 mm^3 is the only one of the choices that is substantially lower at all).

37. **(D)** Neither of the lines representing *Chlorella* respiration altered direction as a response to the presence or absence of light, and this did not support Researcher 2's hypothesis.

38. **(G)** Researcher 1 hypothesized that the addition of glucose would result in the *Chlorella* consuming less oxygen, and so an experiment in which the addition of glucose causes *Chlorella* to consume more would weaken his viewpoint.

39. **(B)** The substance that had the least effect would be whatever substance is represented by the line that is closest to the solid control line. After 30 minutes, the line that is closest to the control line is the dotted line with circles on it, which represents H_2S.

40. **(J)** In Figure 3, the solid line representing nitrogen is higher than the dotted line representing carbon monoxide. Therefore, it is true that *Chlorella* cells suspended in nitrogen consume more oxygen than cells suspended in carbon monoxide (in other words, all of the choices are <u>false except</u> for that one).

Writing Sample

Mr. Mayor, I know that even as I write this there are people putting pressure on you to put into effect a 7pm curfew for people under 16 years of age. I know that I'm not old enough to vote, and that it's only natural that a politician who has to worry about reelection would pay more attention to people who can. But I'm writing to you anyway, in the hopes that you will listen to reason and do the right thing—namely, refuse to pass this absurd curfew. First of all, don't you think 7pm is a little extreme? I am against curfews as a general rule, but I think even most people who are in favor of them would agree that midnight or thereabouts is a bit more reasonable. I also think that this law would be discriminatory against teenagers. Who says that someone out after 7pm is necessarily up to no good, just because he or she is under 16? Finally, and most importantly, this law would be an enormous waste of the time and energy of our police force, who should really have their eyes open for more important things.

I could understand their point of view if people were arguing for a midnight curfew. After all, most parents have house curfews that are earlier than that anyway, so things wouldn't be any different for most teenagers. The law would just be giving a little support to what parents already want anyway. In the case of someone under 16 who is out after midnight, I have serious doubts about the parenting skills of that kid's parents, so maybe at that point it is society's business and there is a compelling reason to bring the law into it. But 7pm? We are talking about 16-year olds, not 6-year olds. Just think of all the perfectly wholesome teenage activities that involve being out after 7:00. A pair of junior-high students on their first date would not be getting out of the movie until after 7:00. In the summertime, it is not even dark yet at 7:00, so why should a baseball game be cut short before it has a chance to be bathed in the sunset? You wouldn't want to be responsible for shooing American boys off of the baseball field, would you? And speaking of America, what about the 4th of July? Would everyone under 16 have to go home before they light off the fireworks?

Though I am over 16 now, I was under 16 not so long ago, and so I am still rather offended by the implication that someone under 16 who is out after 7:00 must be up to something nefarious. When I was much younger, I used to spend the evenings watching TV with my grandparents, who lived just a ways down the block. I got my first job at age 15, and often didn't get out of work until after 7:00. Why should there be a law preventing kids from spending time with their families or having jobs? You might say that there would be exceptions for things like that, as long as the kids go straight home, but just think of how complicated that will all be to enforce. How could a kid prove that he was at a relative's, or at work? And why should kids have to go straight home anyway. Sometimes, at that first job, I'd get out around 8:00 and ride my bike to my friend's house to watch a movie or play video games before heading home. What is so terrible about that? People might say that kids under 16 should just see their friends before 7:00, but while that might be all well and good for wealthy kids who don't have jobs, it is terribly unfair to kids who work after school or during the summer.

Finally, and perhaps most importantly, just think of what a headache this rule would be for police. Instead of being able to drive around looking for real crimes and real criminals, now they would have to pull over and check the ID of every kid they see on the street after 7:00. And if the kid turns out to be under 16, what then? Do the cops have to waste more time driving the kid home? This would take up so much police time and attention, I honestly think criminals from other cities would start moving here because we would have the most distracted police force in the nation. Criminals could even take advantage of the curfew directly. If someone wants to break into a house and not get caught, all they would have to do is hire a kid to walk down the street outside the house, so then if cops drove by they would see the kid and have to go hassle him instead of noticing the burglar. I'm just some kid and I thought of that plan right away, so imagine how easy it would be for a professional criminal to think of. I'm sure the police agree with me here, Mr. Mayor, so if you are still worried about the voters calling for a curfew, just tell them the police think it's a bad idea and that should calm them down.

I think I've presented some pretty solid reasons why a 7pm curfew is a terrible idea. First, 7:00 is so ridiculously early that it would interfere with too many perfectly innocent childhood activities to list here. Secondly, the assumption that any kid out in the evenings must be up to no good is unfounded, not to mention an offensive stereotype about young people. Most importantly, enforcing this law would involve such a drain on law-enforcement resources that there would almost definitely be a spike in crime—and if you think voters will be mad that you rejected their curfew idea, that's nothing compared to how mad they will be when the crime rate doubles. And just to give you some friendly advice, Mr. Mayor, although the kids who would be affected by this curfew aren't old enough to vote yet, they will be in a few years, and if you think they are all just going to forget about that time you passed a law that wrecked their lives, you are sorely mistaken. I support your other policies, and so do most of the young people I know. Don't throw away all that goodwill just for the sake of some draconian curfew.

Answer Sheet

PRACTICE TEST 6

Directions: Mark one answer only for each question. Make the mark dark. Erase completely any mark made in error. (Additional or stray marks will be counted as mistakes.)

English Test

1 Ⓐ Ⓑ Ⓒ Ⓓ	21 Ⓐ Ⓑ Ⓒ Ⓓ	41 Ⓐ Ⓑ Ⓒ Ⓓ	61 Ⓐ Ⓑ Ⓒ Ⓓ
2 Ⓕ Ⓖ Ⓗ Ⓙ	22 Ⓕ Ⓖ Ⓗ Ⓙ	42 Ⓕ Ⓖ Ⓗ Ⓙ	62 Ⓕ Ⓖ Ⓗ Ⓙ
3 Ⓐ Ⓑ Ⓒ Ⓓ	23 Ⓐ Ⓑ Ⓒ Ⓓ	43 Ⓐ Ⓑ Ⓒ Ⓓ	63 Ⓐ Ⓑ Ⓒ Ⓓ
4 Ⓕ Ⓖ Ⓗ Ⓙ	24 Ⓕ Ⓖ Ⓗ Ⓙ	44 Ⓕ Ⓖ Ⓗ Ⓙ	64 Ⓕ Ⓖ Ⓗ Ⓙ
5 Ⓐ Ⓑ Ⓒ Ⓓ	25 Ⓐ Ⓑ Ⓒ Ⓓ	45 Ⓐ Ⓑ Ⓒ Ⓓ	65 Ⓐ Ⓑ Ⓒ Ⓓ
6 Ⓕ Ⓖ Ⓗ Ⓙ	26 Ⓕ Ⓖ Ⓗ Ⓙ	46 Ⓕ Ⓖ Ⓗ Ⓙ	66 Ⓕ Ⓖ Ⓗ Ⓙ
7 Ⓐ Ⓑ Ⓒ Ⓓ	27 Ⓐ Ⓑ Ⓒ Ⓓ	47 Ⓐ Ⓑ Ⓒ Ⓓ	67 Ⓐ Ⓑ Ⓒ Ⓓ
8 Ⓕ Ⓖ Ⓗ Ⓙ	28 Ⓕ Ⓖ Ⓗ Ⓙ	48 Ⓕ Ⓖ Ⓗ Ⓙ	68 Ⓕ Ⓖ Ⓗ Ⓙ
9 Ⓐ Ⓑ Ⓒ Ⓓ	29 Ⓐ Ⓑ Ⓒ Ⓓ	49 Ⓐ Ⓑ Ⓒ Ⓓ	69 Ⓐ Ⓑ Ⓒ Ⓓ
10 Ⓕ Ⓖ Ⓗ Ⓙ	30 Ⓕ Ⓖ Ⓗ Ⓙ	50 Ⓕ Ⓖ Ⓗ Ⓙ	70 Ⓕ Ⓖ Ⓗ Ⓙ
11 Ⓐ Ⓑ Ⓒ Ⓓ	31 Ⓐ Ⓑ Ⓒ Ⓓ	51 Ⓐ Ⓑ Ⓒ Ⓓ	71 Ⓐ Ⓑ Ⓒ Ⓓ
12 Ⓕ Ⓖ Ⓗ Ⓙ	32 Ⓕ Ⓖ Ⓗ Ⓙ	52 Ⓕ Ⓖ Ⓗ Ⓙ	72 Ⓕ Ⓖ Ⓗ Ⓙ
13 Ⓐ Ⓑ Ⓒ Ⓓ	33 Ⓐ Ⓑ Ⓒ Ⓓ	53 Ⓐ Ⓑ Ⓒ Ⓓ	73 Ⓐ Ⓑ Ⓒ Ⓓ
14 Ⓕ Ⓖ Ⓗ Ⓙ	34 Ⓕ Ⓖ Ⓗ Ⓙ	54 Ⓕ Ⓖ Ⓗ Ⓙ	74 Ⓕ Ⓖ Ⓗ Ⓙ
15 Ⓐ Ⓑ Ⓒ Ⓓ	35 Ⓐ Ⓑ Ⓒ Ⓓ	55 Ⓐ Ⓑ Ⓒ Ⓓ	75 Ⓐ Ⓑ Ⓒ Ⓓ
16 Ⓕ Ⓖ Ⓗ Ⓙ	36 Ⓕ Ⓖ Ⓗ Ⓙ	56 Ⓕ Ⓖ Ⓗ Ⓙ	
17 Ⓐ Ⓑ Ⓒ Ⓓ	37 Ⓐ Ⓑ Ⓒ Ⓓ	57 Ⓐ Ⓑ Ⓒ Ⓓ	
18 Ⓕ Ⓖ Ⓗ Ⓙ	38 Ⓕ Ⓖ Ⓗ Ⓙ	58 Ⓕ Ⓖ Ⓗ Ⓙ	
19 Ⓐ Ⓑ Ⓒ Ⓓ	39 Ⓐ Ⓑ Ⓒ Ⓓ	59 Ⓐ Ⓑ Ⓒ Ⓓ	
20 Ⓕ Ⓖ Ⓗ Ⓙ	40 Ⓕ Ⓖ Ⓗ Ⓙ	60 Ⓕ Ⓖ Ⓗ Ⓙ	

Math Test

1 Ⓐ Ⓑ Ⓒ Ⓓ Ⓔ	16 Ⓕ Ⓖ Ⓗ Ⓙ Ⓚ	31 Ⓐ Ⓑ Ⓒ Ⓓ Ⓔ	46 Ⓕ Ⓖ Ⓗ Ⓙ Ⓚ
2 Ⓕ Ⓖ Ⓗ Ⓙ Ⓚ	17 Ⓐ Ⓑ Ⓒ Ⓓ Ⓔ	32 Ⓕ Ⓖ Ⓗ Ⓙ Ⓚ	47 Ⓐ Ⓑ Ⓒ Ⓓ Ⓔ
3 Ⓐ Ⓑ Ⓒ Ⓓ Ⓔ	18 Ⓕ Ⓖ Ⓗ Ⓙ Ⓚ	33 Ⓐ Ⓑ Ⓒ Ⓓ Ⓔ	48 Ⓕ Ⓖ Ⓗ Ⓙ Ⓚ
4 Ⓕ Ⓖ Ⓗ Ⓙ Ⓚ	19 Ⓐ Ⓑ Ⓒ Ⓓ Ⓔ	34 Ⓕ Ⓖ Ⓗ Ⓙ Ⓚ	49 Ⓐ Ⓑ Ⓒ Ⓓ Ⓔ
5 Ⓐ Ⓑ Ⓒ Ⓓ Ⓔ	20 Ⓕ Ⓖ Ⓗ Ⓙ Ⓚ	35 Ⓐ Ⓑ Ⓒ Ⓓ Ⓔ	50 Ⓕ Ⓖ Ⓗ Ⓙ Ⓚ
6 Ⓕ Ⓖ Ⓗ Ⓙ Ⓚ	21 Ⓐ Ⓑ Ⓒ Ⓓ Ⓔ	36 Ⓕ Ⓖ Ⓗ Ⓙ Ⓚ	51 Ⓐ Ⓑ Ⓒ Ⓓ Ⓔ
7 Ⓐ Ⓑ Ⓒ Ⓓ Ⓔ	22 Ⓕ Ⓖ Ⓗ Ⓙ Ⓚ	37 Ⓐ Ⓑ Ⓒ Ⓓ Ⓔ	52 Ⓕ Ⓖ Ⓗ Ⓙ Ⓚ
8 Ⓕ Ⓖ Ⓗ Ⓙ Ⓚ	23 Ⓐ Ⓑ Ⓒ Ⓓ Ⓔ	38 Ⓕ Ⓖ Ⓗ Ⓙ Ⓚ	53 Ⓐ Ⓑ Ⓒ Ⓓ Ⓔ
9 Ⓐ Ⓑ Ⓒ Ⓓ Ⓔ	24 Ⓕ Ⓖ Ⓗ Ⓙ Ⓚ	39 Ⓐ Ⓑ Ⓒ Ⓓ Ⓔ	54 Ⓕ Ⓖ Ⓗ Ⓙ Ⓚ
10 Ⓕ Ⓖ Ⓗ Ⓙ Ⓚ	25 Ⓐ Ⓑ Ⓒ Ⓓ Ⓔ	40 Ⓕ Ⓖ Ⓗ Ⓙ Ⓚ	55 Ⓐ Ⓑ Ⓒ Ⓓ Ⓔ
11 Ⓐ Ⓑ Ⓒ Ⓓ Ⓔ	26 Ⓕ Ⓖ Ⓗ Ⓙ Ⓚ	41 Ⓐ Ⓑ Ⓒ Ⓓ Ⓔ	56 Ⓕ Ⓖ Ⓗ Ⓙ Ⓚ
12 Ⓕ Ⓖ Ⓗ Ⓙ Ⓚ	27 Ⓐ Ⓑ Ⓒ Ⓓ Ⓔ	42 Ⓕ Ⓖ Ⓗ Ⓙ Ⓚ	57 Ⓐ Ⓑ Ⓒ Ⓓ Ⓔ
13 Ⓐ Ⓑ Ⓒ Ⓓ Ⓔ	28 Ⓕ Ⓖ Ⓗ Ⓙ Ⓚ	43 Ⓐ Ⓑ Ⓒ Ⓓ Ⓔ	58 Ⓕ Ⓖ Ⓗ Ⓙ Ⓚ
14 Ⓕ Ⓖ Ⓗ Ⓙ Ⓚ	29 Ⓐ Ⓑ Ⓒ Ⓓ Ⓔ	44 Ⓕ Ⓖ Ⓗ Ⓙ Ⓚ	59 Ⓐ Ⓑ Ⓒ Ⓓ Ⓔ
15 Ⓐ Ⓑ Ⓒ Ⓓ Ⓔ	30 Ⓕ Ⓖ Ⓗ Ⓙ Ⓚ	45 Ⓐ Ⓑ Ⓒ Ⓓ Ⓔ	60 Ⓕ Ⓖ Ⓗ Ⓙ Ⓚ

Answer Sheet
PRACTICE TEST 6

Reading Test

1 A B C D	11 A B C D	21 A B C D	31 A B C D
2 F G H J	12 F G H J	22 F G H J	32 F G H J
3 A B C D	13 A B C D	23 A B C D	33 A B C D
4 F G H J	14 F G H J	24 F G H J	34 F G H J
5 A B C D	15 A B C D	25 A B C D	35 A B C D
6 F G H J	16 F G H J	26 F G H J	36 F G H J
7 A B C D	17 A B C D	27 A B C D	37 A B C D
8 F G H J	18 F G H J	28 F G H J	38 F G H J
9 A B C D	19 A B C D	29 A B C D	39 A B C D
10 F G H J	20 F G H J	30 F G H J	40 F G H J

Science Test

1 A B C D	11 A B C D	21 A B C D	31 A B C D
2 F G H J	12 F G H J	22 F G H J	32 F G H J
3 A B C D	13 A B C D	23 A B C D	33 A B C D
4 F G H J	14 F G H J	24 F G H J	34 F G H J
5 A B C D	15 A B C D	25 A B C D	35 A B C D
6 F G H J	16 F G H J	26 F G H J	36 F G H J
7 A B C D	17 A B C D	27 A B C D	37 A B C D
8 F G H J	18 F G H J	28 F G H J	38 F G H J
9 A B C D	19 A B C D	29 A B C D	39 A B C D
10 F G H J	20 F G H J	30 F G H J	40 F G H J

Practice Test 6

ENGLISH TEST

45 MINUTES—75 QUESTIONS

Directions: In the five passages that follow, certain words and phrases are underlined and numbered. In the right-hand column, you will find alternatives for the underlined part. In most cases, you are to choose the one that best expresses the idea, makes the statement appropriate for standard written English, or is worded most consistently with the style and tone of the passage as a whole. If you think the original version is best, choose "NO CHANGE." In some cases, you will find in the right-hand column a question about the underlined part. You are to choose the best answer to the question.

You will also find questions about a section of the passage, or about the passage as a whole. These questions do not refer to an underlined portion of the passage, but rather are identified by a number or numbers in a box.

For each question, choose the alternative you consider best and fill in the corresponding oval on your answer document. Read each passage through once before you begin to answer the questions that accompany it. For many of the questions, you must read several sentences beyond the question to determine the answer. Be sure that you have read far enough ahead each time you choose an alternative.

Passage I

How Romantic!

When you hear the word *romantic*, you probably think to[1] "chick flick" movies and Valentine's Day, but the time in history known as the Romantic Period was a lot more exciting than that. In Europe in the late eighteenth and early nineteenth centuries, communities of writers, painters, and musicians begins feeling[2] stifled by the rationality and orderliness of the Age of Enlightenment, and started producing work that emphasized uncontrollable emotion and the dark side of Nature.

1. **A.** NO CHANGE
   B. in
   C. of
   D. like

2. **F.** NO CHANGE
   G. feeling
   H. has felt
   J. had begun to feel

Practice Test 6

GO ON TO THE NEXT PAGE.

Most people think of classical music as "relaxing," but the stirring urgently with compositions [3] of Romantic musicians like Beethoven and Wagner are anything but, and would come to influence rock and roll music over a century later. In the visual arts, painters like Henry Fuseli and Eugène Delacroix created disturbing, chaotic works emphasizing struggle, fear, and loneliness that inspired [4] today's horror and "goth" imagery.

3. A. NO CHANGE
   B. stirring, urgent compositions
   C. compositions stirring in their urgency
   D. urgent compositions that stirred

4. F. NO CHANGE
   G. loneliness inspired
   H. loneliness, in which inspired
   J. loneliness; inspired

But [5] the movement is most closely associated with literature, and indeed Romanticism radically changed people's ideas not only of the function of literature, but also of what writers themselves would be [6] like. Previously, most famous writers had been educated aristocrats who wrote complex works about human society, but the reflective nature poems of William Wordsworth and the short, sad life of the brilliant, struggling commoner John Keats have much more in common with how we think of poetry and poets today. [7]

5. Which of the following alternatives to the underlined portion would NOT be acceptable?
   A. However,
   B. Meanwhile,
   C. Still,
   D. Today,

6. F. NO CHANGE
   G. would have been
   H. to be
   J. are

7. If the writer were to delete the phrase "brilliant, struggling commoner" in the preceding sentence and replace it with "masterful sonneteer," the paragraph would primarily lose:
   A. a link between Keats and the contemporary idea of the starving artist.
   B. support for the idea that Keats was actually more talented than Wordsworth.
   C. an explanation of what made the work of Keats so original and groundbreaking.
   D. proof that "John Keats" was Keats's real name, rather than a pseudonym he used when writing.

Perhaps Romanticism's most influential innovation was the "Byronic hero," named for the central figures in the works of rebellious English poet Lord Byron.

He defined [8] a supremely gifted individual troubled by a dark past, torn between good and evil, and plagued by tragic love affairs, the figure of the Byronic hero is everywhere in pop culture even today,

8. F. NO CHANGE
   G. Having defined
   H. Defined as
   J. Defining

1 ■ ■ ■ ■ ■ ■ ■ ■ 1

from *Star Wars'* Anakin Skywalker, to *X-Men*'s Wolverine, to *Twilight*'s brooding vampire Edward Cullen. [9]

The Romantic Movement was largely unconcerned with [10] science. Researchers turned their attention away from the microscope and toward the dynamic forces of electricity and magnetism. [A] The fascination with nature inspired the new science of biology. [B] And the emphasis on mystery and human behavior led to the beginnings of what would eventually become psychology. [C] Since [11] most artistic movements fade into history, becoming [12] of interest mainly to academics, the ideals and aesthetics of Romanticism have remained popular and continue to influence mainstream culture to this day, whether people know it or not. [D] The writers of the Romantic Period are studied more frequently in college courses than any others, with the exception of Shakespeare. [13] [14]

9. If the writer were to delete the underlined portion (ending the sentence with a period after *today*), the paragraph would primarily lose:
   - **A.** an explanation of why Byronic heroes are so appealing.
   - **B.** proof of the fact that Byronic heroes are more suited to film than to literature.
   - **C.** support for the assertion that all Byronic heroes are male.
   - **D.** some examples of current fictional Byronic heroes.

10. **F.** NO CHANGE
    G. took a long time to penetrate the realm of
    H. tried to warn humanity about
    J. even had an influence on

11. **A.** NO CHANGE
    B. While
    C. Because
    D. However,

12. **F.** NO CHANGE
    G. became
    H. and became
    J. to have become

13. Given that all the choices are true, which one best serves to conclude the passage with an emphasis on how Romanticism has widely affected popular culture?
    - **A.** NO CHANGE
    - **B.** In the 1970s, bands like Rush and Led Zeppelin made frequent reference to "Kubla Khan," a poem by Samuel Taylor Coleridge.
    - **C.** If it hadn't been for a certain few artists who lived 200 years ago, then today we probably wouldn't have rock music, horror movies, or superheroes.
    - **D.** Most people aren't aware of this, but James Dean's middle name was "Byron!"

14. If the writer were to divide this paragraph into two, the most logical place to begin the new paragraph would be at point:
    - **F.** A.
    - **G.** B.
    - **H.** C.
    - **J.** D.

GO ON TO THE NEXT PAGE.

Question 15 asks about the preceding passage as a whole.

15. Suppose the writer's goal had been to write a brief essay about the ways in which pop culture is greatly influenced by high culture. Would this essay accomplish that goal?
   A. Yes, because it contains many examples of mass entertainment derived from principles in great art.
   B. Yes, because it establishes that Romanticism has been more influential than other artistic movements.
   C. No, because it contains no examples of Romanticism's influence on pop culture.
   D. No, because it concerns only Romanticism, and also describes its influence on things besides pop culture.

Passage II

My Favorite Place

Whenever someone asks me what my favorite place on earth is, I have trouble to decide [16] between two candidates: the American Museum of Natural History and the Bronx Zoo. Of course, there are a lot of obvious similarities between the two—they are both in New York City, and they both appeal to people who are interested in animals—but there are a lot of important differences too, at least to me there are. [17]

Obviously, the zoo is outdoors, and the animals in it are alive, which is nice for them. [18] Being at the zoo *feels* different: it's hot, there are bees and screaming kids everywhere, and the smell of the city mixes with the smells of animals and snack food. It's just so full of life

16. **F.** NO CHANGE
   G. and decide
   H. about deciding
   J. deciding

17. **A.** NO CHANGE
   B. they are different.
   C. it would seem.
   D. DELETE the underlined portion and end the sentence with a period.

18. Which choice most logically supports the first part of this sentence?
   F. NO CHANGE
   G. but those aren't the differences I'm talking about.
   H. and most of them are mammals, like you and me.
   J. which is a relief, since so many are endangered species.

and exciting. Even as a kid, that place was [19] way more exciting than going to a rollercoaster park or sporting event. To this day, nothing fills me with joy and energy quite like a day at the zoo.

19. **A.** NO CHANGE
B. the zoo was
C. I found it
D. would you believe it was

The museum, on the other hand, makes me feel more like what I imagine other people must feel like in church. [20] It's just so dark and cool and quiet, and its [21] high ceilings and long echoes always fill me with a feeling of deep reverence, [22] though I'm not exactly sure toward what. Unlike the zoo, which is always changing, the museum is basically the same every time you go. The same animals have been frozen [23] in the same positions in their clear tombs since my grandfather was little, and even when the scientific information on the plaques beside them gets outdated, the staff sometimes doesn't bother to change it. And of course, every trip ends with the dinosaurs on the top floor, their fossilized bones older than anything you're ever likely to see.

20. Given that all the choices are true, which one provides material most relevant to what follows in this paragraph?
F. NO CHANGE
G. The museum, on the other hand, makes me just as happy and just as hungry.
H. People don't realize it, but the museum hasn't always been in its present location.
J. I can't possibly express how the museum makes me feel, so I'm not even going to try.

21. **A.** NO CHANGE
B. with its
C. although its
D. because its

22. Which of the following alternatives to the underlined portion would be **LEAST** acceptable
F. respect
G. veneration
H. awe
J. grandeur

23. Which of the following alternatives to the underlined portion would NOT be acceptable?
A. animals have frozen
B. mounted animals have been
C. animals have been there
D. mounted animals have been frozen

I can remember going from each other [24] to both places often as a child, but even those trips were different. I would go to the zoo in the summer on a car trip, along with my whole family, but the museum was a special wintertime thing between my father and me,

24. The best placement for the underlined portion would be:
F. where it is now.
G. after the word *places*.
H. after the word *trips*.
J. after the word *different*.

1 ■ ■ ■ ■ ■ ■ ■ ■ 1

and the two of us would take the <u>train, which</u> [25] was exciting in itself—rather than drive. [26]

I've lived all over the country, but I've tried to visit both places at least once every year for my whole life. I'm a little scared that the museum will change in the future from the way I remember it being, and even more scared that some of my favorite <u>friends'</u> [27] from the zoo, like tigers and rhinos, will go extinct during my lifetime. But <u>I never fail to notice</u> [28] how fascinated all the kids always are at both places; it reminds me that, at least when we're young, we all love animals and learning. [29]

25. **A.** NO CHANGE
B. train
C. train—which
D. train. This

26. At this point, the writer is considering adding the following true statement: "I've never understood why, but trains are the only form of transportation I don't get sick on."
Should the writer make this addition here?
F. Yes, because it provides a further link between his love for the museum and his love of trains.
G. Yes, because it provides information that will become necessary later.
H. No, because it would distract readers from the main focus of this paragraph.
J. No, because the writer never discusses getting sick on any of the various other forms of transportation.

27. **A.** NO CHANGE
B. friends
C. friend's
D. friends's

28. Which choice most effectively expresses the writer's great reverence for the zoo and museum?
F. NO CHANGE
G. I almost can't believe
H. I always tell my friends about
J. I'm also reassured and inspired by

29. Which of the following sentences, if added here, would most effectively express one of the main ideas of the essay?
A. Although the zoo and museum are both fun, the real reason I love them is that they give me hope, as I look at the children's faces.
B. It's funny, but I am annoyed by kids pretty much everywhere else.
C. When I was a kid, the zoo had elephant rides, but nowadays they only have camel rides.
D. People always have trouble choosing between the zoo and the museum. I wonder why.

1 ■ ■ ■ ■ ■ ■ ■ ■ 1

Passage III

The Other Golf

[1]

All my life, I've been terrible at sports. I couldn't hit a baseball to save my life, or sink a basketball either, and I don't even want to talk about football. I used to think I'd never be able to experience the joy that more athletically gifted people derive from a sunny Sunday spent out on their field of choice. [30] All that changed when I went to college and learned about disc golf, and now I finally have an answer when someone asks me what one of my favorite sports <u>are</u>.[31]

[2]

Affectionately known as a "non-sport"—that is, a sport for people who don't like <u>sports:</u>[32] disc golf is very similar to regular golf, but instead of hitting balls with a club, players throw weighted flying discs at basketlike targets. Just like in traditional "ball golf," you start from a tee, and the object is to get your disc in the hole in the fewest number of shots. Disc-golf courses are similar to those of traditional golf in that <u>course's</u>[33] normally have 18 holes, some of which are harder than <u>others, all with</u>[34] unique combinations of traditional golf obstacles like trees, bushes, and ponds.

30. The author is thinking about deleting the previous sentence. Should it be deleted or kept?
   - **F.** Kept, because it supports the theme of the opening paragraph with memorable imagery.
   - **G.** Kept, because it is the only place that the author mentions being bad at traditional sports.
   - **H.** Deleted, because it contradicts information presented elsewhere in the opening paragraph.
   - **J.** Deleted, because not all sports are played outdoors.

31. **A.** NO CHANGE
   B. is
   C. were
   D. have been

32. **F.** NO CHANGE
   G. sports,
   H. sports;
   J. sports—

33. **A.** NO CHANGE
   B. courses'
   C. courses's
   D. courses

34. Which of the following alternatives to the underlined portion would NOT be acceptable?
   - **F.** others, and all have
   - **G.** others; all have
   - **H.** others; all with
   - **J.** others, and all of which have

Practice Test 6

1 ■ ■ ■ ■ ■ ■ ■ ■ 1

[3]

Disc golf is sometimes mistakenly referred to as [35] "Frisbee golf," but the discs used are actually very different from Frisbees: they're weighted and have tapered edges, and so can be thrown much farther with much greater accuracy. [36] There are even different kinds of discs, designed for different types of shots: drivers for distance, putters to land safely in the basket, and "trick" discs that curve to get around obstacles.

[4]

Despite the game's "non-sport" reputation, because [37] it takes skill and practice to get good at throwing a disc accurately. The people, who play in professional disc-golf tournaments, [38] have obviously spent a lot of time getting good enough making [39] those amazing shots. Currently, the #1 ranked disc golfer in the world is David Feldberg. [40] Most people who play disc golf are so laid-back that the game is more about being pleasantly surprised in that [41] you make a good shot than embarrassed when you make a bad one.

35. A. NO CHANGE
B. referred, to as
C. referred to, as
D. referred to as,

36. At this point, the author is thinking of adding the following true statement: True Frisbees were invented much earlier, in 1957.
Should the writer make this addition here?
F. Yes, because it emphasizes the degree to which times have changed since the days of Frisbees.
G. Yes, because the information is crucial to an understanding of the evolution of disc golf.
H. No, because the sentence does not explain what qualifies as a "true" Frisbee.
J. No, because it is of little relevance to this paragraph and stalls its development.

37. A. NO CHANGE
B. although
C. therefore
D. DELETE the underlined portion.

38. F. NO CHANGE
G. people who play in professional disc-golf tournaments
H. people, who play in professional disc-golf tournaments
J. people who play in professional disc-golf tournaments,

39. A. NO CHANGE
B. they made
C. to make
D. at making

40. Which choice provides the most logical and effective transition to the rest of this paragraph?
F. NO CHANGE
G. There are videos on YouTube of people making the craziest shots you've ever seen!
H. But it doesn't take much time at all to become good enough to have fun with your friends.
J. The biggest teams tournament is held every year in Austin, Texas.

41. A. NO CHANGE
B. when
C. before
D. whereas

1 ■ ■ ■ ■ ■ ■ ■ ■ 1

[5]

Although such a claim is hard to prove, disc golf is commonly referred to as the fastest-growing sport in the world. <u>It wasn't invented until the 1970s, but there are now over 3,000 courses in the United States.</u> [42] Most of them are located in public parks and are free to play on. The discs can be found at almost any sporting-goods store, and a quick Internet search will <u>inform</u> [43] you about courses in your area. So if <u>there's</u> [44] someone who thought you'd never be good at sports, what are you waiting for?

42. Given that all the choices are true, which one provides the best support for the statement in the preceding sentence?

F. NO CHANGE
G. Before disc golf got so popular, people used to say the same thing about kickboxing.
H. Designing a disc-golf course doesn't exactly take a rocket scientist.
J. There was even an episode of *Seinfeld* where George plays disc golf.

43. Which of the following alternatives to the underlined portion would be **LEAST** acceptable:

A. persuade
B. acquaint
C. teach
D. enlighten

44. **F.** NO CHANGE
G. your
H. one is
J. you're

Question 45 asks about the preceding passage as a whole.

45. While reviewing notes for this essay, the writer comes across some information and incorporates it into the following sentence:

> The "two-meter rule" dictates that a disc stuck in a tree more than this high off the ground is a one-stroke penalty.

If the writer were to include this sentence in the essay, the most logical place to add it would be after the last sentence in paragraph:

A. 2.
B. 3.
C. 4.
D. 5.

Practice Test 6

GO ON TO THE NEXT PAGE.

Passage IV

The Best Party

Here in the United States, we're politically [46] comedians can sometimes seem to understand things better than politician's [47] do, people often jokingly suggest that comedians should run for office. But just this year, the small European island nation of Iceland went even further: it actually elected a stand-up comedian the mayor of its capital city of Reykjavik, and the political party he founded as a prank now controls more than a third of the seats on the City Council.

Comedian and film actor Jon Gnarr [48] was already well known to Icelanders. In 2008, after the collapse [49] devastated Iceland's economy, he started a web site for a fictitious political party that he called the "Best Party" and began writing blogs satirizing the nation's policies. When the web site became unexpectedly popular, Gnarr began at actually staffing [50] the Best Party, mostly with people from the punk and alternative music scenes he has long been close to (Gnarr's wife is best friends with Iceland's most famous musician, the [51] eccentric singer Björk).

Gnarr's 2010 campaign for mayor of Reykjavik—which is only one city, but over a third [52] of Iceland's population—was hardly a serious one. His campaign promises included free towels, more polar bears at the zoo, and a Disneyland at the airport. Still, the humorous

46. **F.** NO CHANGE
G. were political
H. we're political
J. where political

47. **A.** NO CHANGE
B. politicians'
C. our politicians
D. some politicians'

48. **F.** NO CHANGE
G. actor, Jon Gnarr
H. actor Jon Gnarr,
J. actor, Jon Gnarr,

49. **A.** NO CHANGE
B. a severe banking collapse
C. a banking collapse that severely affected the financial sector
D. it

50. **F.** NO CHANGE
G. by actually staffing
H. to actually staff
J. by which to staff

51. **A.** NO CHANGE
B. musician; the
C. musician being
D. musician is

52. **F.** NO CHANGE
G. home
H. it is a third
J. home to over a third

platform highlighted [53] serious issues: polar bears have recently been showing up in Iceland, where they did not live before, because of global warming. [54]

[1] Though Gnarr did not expect to win, he has high hopes for his time in office. [2] Constant political shake-ups have ejected Reykjavik's last several mayors from office sooner than expected, and he hopes to be the first of the twenty-first century to serve out a full four-year term. [3] Gnarr says his surprise political career has given him "the greatest sense of contentment" of anything he's ever worked on in his career [55]. [4] This would be an impressive feat for someone who dropped out of school at age 16 and identifies himself as an anarchist, but the comedian has apparently gotten serious. [56]

[57] It is the world's oldest parliamentary democracy, having had an elected legislature since 930 A.D. In 1117, it became the first European country to outlaw the slave trade. And in 2009, the people of Iceland elected Johanna Sigurthardottir as prime minister, making her the world's

53. Which of the following alternatives to the underlined portion would NOT be acceptable?
    - **A.** recommended
    - **B.** mirrored
    - **C.** called attention to
    - **D.** called to mind

54. The writer is considering deleting the phrase "where they did not live before, because of global warming" from the preceding sentence (and ending it with a period after "Iceland"). Should this phrase be kept or deleted?
    - **F.** Kept, because it proves that global warming will affect everyone.
    - **G.** Kept, because it explains why the presence of polar bears is a "serious issue."
    - **H.** Deleted, because there are some people who don't believe in global warming.
    - **J.** Deleted, because the majority of people like polar bears and would love to have more of them around.

55.
    - **A.** NO CHANGE
    - **B.** the whole time.
    - **C.** so far in his life.
    - **D.** DELETE the underlined portion and end the sentence with a period.

56. For the sake of the logic and coherence of this paragraph, Sentence 4 should be placed:
    - **F.** where it is now.
    - **G.** before Sentence 1.
    - **H.** after Sentence 1.
    - **J.** after Sentence 2.

57. Given that all of the following statements are true, which one, if added here, would most clearly and effectively introduce the main subject of this paragraph?
    - **A.** Genetically speaking, Iceland has the peculiar distinction of being home to the highest percentage of green-eyed people of any nation.
    - **B.** All Icelandic schoolchildren learn to read the *Old Icelandic Sagas* in the original, which would be like if all American kids could understand *Beowulf*!
    - **C.** Though it may not be a country you hear about much, Iceland has often been ahead of the curve in political matters.
    - **D.** Though Iceland and Greenland are right next to each other, Iceland counts as part of Europe, whereas Greenland counts as part of North America.

GO ON TO THE NEXT PAGE.

first openly gay head of state. So is they're[58] election of a comedian mayor and his satirical party a sign of things to come? Only time will tell.

58. F. NO CHANGE
G. their
H. there
J. his or her

Question 59 asks about the preceding passage as a whole.

59. Suppose the writer's goal had been to write a brief essay focusing on the unique political history of Iceland. Would this essay accomplish that goal?
A. Yes, because it provides information about several key figures in Iceland's government.
B. Yes, because it mentions several of the important political events in Icelandic history.
C. No, because it primarily concerns Jon Gnarr and the 2010 Reykjavik mayoral election.
D. No, because it only mentions Iceland, so readers have no basis for deciding whether its politics are unique.

Passage V

The End of Trivia?

Ever since the 1960s, when trivia was popularized as a pastime by the invention of collegiate Quizbowl and the premiere of the beloved quiz show *Jeopardy!,* bars and restaurants all over the country has attracted[60] patrons with quiz nights, during which[61] patrons form teams with friends or strangers and compete for prizes of food, beverages, or even cash. Of course, the environment is much less formally[62] than on a game show: instead of using buzzers, players sit with their teams and write down answers to the questions a bar employee asks over a microphone, then turn in their sheets to be scored at the end of the night. But now that nearly everyone carries a phone or some other portable device with Internet

60. F. NO CHANGE
G. attracted
H. had attracted
J. have been attracting

61. A. NO CHANGE
B. nights that
C. nights; where
D. nights, and these

62. F. NO CHANGE
G. less formal
H. less formality
J. fewer formalities

access, trivia [63] cheating has become nearly impossible to control.

Ironically, [64] trivia questions involve information that is obscure but interesting, such as "Who is the only president to have also served as chief justice of the Supreme Court?" (the answer is William Howard Taft) or "What was the first animated film to receive an Academy Award nomination for Best Picture?" (the answer is *Beauty and the Beast*). In a pub-quiz setting, and talking [65] the possible answers over with your friends is half the fun. When people first began carrying cell phones, players sometimes called friends during games, but even then, you still could of had [66] a friend who knew the answer, because [67] it wasn't that much of a problem.

But phones with Internet access are a different story: if cheating on those continues to not be looked out for [68] by the pub's staff, then every team will know the answer to every question! But stopping this is very hard indeed: someone typing into a tiny phone under the table is tough to spot in a big bar, and if a player sneaks into the bathroom to cheat with a phone, then stopping [69] him or her is impossible!

Some quiz nights have chosen to trust in the honor system, with moderators simply not caring whether people cheat or not. [70] Other venues have tried to develop "cheat-proof" questions, like playing very short clips from pop songs or projecting celebrity yearbook

63. **A.** NO CHANGE
B. access; trivia
C. access, and trivia
D. access. Therefore, trivia

64. **F.** NO CHANGE
G. Predictably,
H. Lamentably,
J. Traditionally,

65. **A.** NO CHANGE
B. setting, talking
C. sitting to talk
D. sit, and talk

66. **F.** NO CHANGE
G. would have had
H. had to have
J. can had

67. **A.** NO CHANGE
B. so
C. since
D. DELETE the underlined portion.

68. **F.** NO CHANGE
G. doesn't get itself regulated
H. wouldn't be put an end to
J. is not adequately policed

69. **A.** NO CHANGE
B. phone then stopping
C. phone, than stopping
D. phone than stopping

70. Given that all the choices are true, which one most effectively concludes the sentence by offering specific examples of what the sentence begins by discussing?
F. NO CHANGE
G. stationing staff at every table as observers.
H. begging patrons not to use their phones and encouraging teams to turn in cheaters.
J. deliberately holding events in buildings where phones don't get reception.

GO ON TO THE NEXT PAGE.

pictures onto a screen and asking players to <u>identify them all by name.</u> [71] But trivia purists often balk at such <u>practices,</u> [72] identifying yearbook pictures or drum fills, they argue, is not true trivia. True trivia concerns bits of information … but every bit of information can be looked up on a portable device! [73]

<u>In a few years, phones will probably be able to identify songs and pictures too, but even this is not the biggest threat to the great sport of pub quiz.</u> [74] The biggest threat is that future generations raised on technology <u>in the first place</u> [75] that can instantly summon up any factoid at the push of a button will have no motivation to memorize them, and hence no interest in trivia!

71. **A.** NO CHANGE
    B. identify them.
    C. identify the ones.
    D. identify.

72. **F.** NO CHANGE
    G. practices;
    H. practices; therefore,
    J. practices, when they are

73. The writer is considering deleting the portion of the preceding sentence that follows the ellipses (and replacing the ellipses with a period). If the writer were to make this deletion, the paragraph would primarily lose:
    A. unnecessary information that constitutes a digression from the main idea of the passage.
    B. an identification of a problem that the writer has just realized and mentions nowhere else.
    C. an explanation of the conflict between modern technology and traditional notions about trivia.
    D. an argument that trivia buffs should purchase gadgets with Internet access.

74. Given that all of the choices are true, which one makes for the most effective transition into this paragraph from the preceding one?
    F. NO CHANGE
    G. Sometimes patrons who aren't even playing yell out the answers, but this is not the biggest threat to pub quizzes.
    H. Cell phones are also hazardous when people talk on them while driving, but this is not the biggest threat they pose.
    J. The biggest threat to pub quizzes is something I am going to tell you about right now.

75. The best placement for the underlined portion would be:
    A. where it is now.
    B. after the word *generations*.
    C. after the word *factoid.*
    D. after the word *trivia* (and before the exclamation point).

STOP

If there is still time remaining, check your answers to this section.

2 △ △ △ △ △ △ △ △ 2

MATHEMATICS TEST

60 MINUTES—60 QUESTIONS

Directions: Solve each problem, choose the correct answer, and then fill in the corresponding oval on your answer document.

Do not linger over problems that take too much time. Solve as many as you can; then return to the others in the time you have left for this test.

You are permitted to use a calculator on this test. You may use your calculator for any problems you choose, but some of the problems may best be done without using a calculator.

Note: Unless otherwise stated, all of the following should be assumed.

1. Illustrative figures are NOT necessarily drawn to scale.
2. Geometric figures lie in a plane.
3. The word *line* indicates a straight line.
4. The word *average* indicates arithmetic mean.

DO YOUR FIGURING HERE.

1. Last week Kylie spent the following amounts of time doing homework. Sunday: $1\frac{3}{4}$ hours, Monday: $1\frac{1}{2}$ hours, Tuesday: 3 hours, Wednesday: $2\frac{1}{3}$ hours, Thursday: $1\frac{1}{2}$ hours. What was the median number of hours Kylie spent doing homework last week?

   A. 3
   B. $2\frac{1}{3}$
   C. $2\frac{1}{60}$
   D. $1\frac{3}{4}$
   E. $1\frac{1}{2}$

2. What is $(-2x^5)^4$ equivalent to?

   F. $-16x^9$
   G. $-2x^9$
   H. $-2x^{20}$
   J. $2x^{20}$
   K. $16x^{20}$

Practice Test 6

2 △ △ △ △ △ △ △ △ 2

DO YOUR FIGURING HERE.

3. So far Parveen has earned the following scores on four 100-point tests this grading period: 85, 83, 91, and 94. What score must Parveen earn on the fifth and last 100-point test of the grading period to earn an average grade of exactly 90 for the 5 tests?

   A. 85
   B. 87
   C. 89
   D. 97
   E. 99

4. If $x = -3$ and $y = 2$, then $2x^2 - 5xy + y^2 = ?$

   F. -44
   G. 16
   H. 27
   J. 52
   K. 70

5. What is the solution set for the inequality $2x - 3 < 5x + 6$?

   A. $x < -3$
   B. $x = -3$
   C. $x > -3$
   D. $x < 4$
   E. $x > 5$

6. In regular hexagon *ABCDEF*, *CD* = 12 cm. What is the length of $\overline{BE}$ in cm?

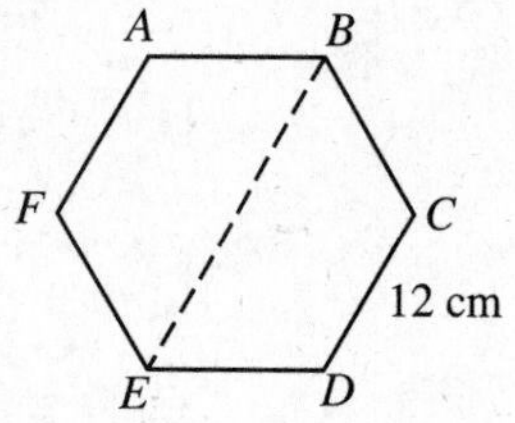

   F. 12
   G. $12 + 2\sqrt{b}$
   H. $12 + 4\sqrt{2}$
   J. 24
   K. 72

7. If 18% of a given number is 63, then what is 45% of the given number?

   A. 126
   B. 157.5
   C. 189
   D. 220.5
   E. 350

8. What is $(x^3 - 4x^2 + 5) - (3x^3 + 6x^2 - 9)$ equivalent to?

   F. $-2x^3 - 10x^2 + 14$
   G. $4x^3 + 2x^2 - 4$
   H. $-2x^6 - 10x^4 + 14$
   J. $-2x^3 + 2x^2 - 4$
   K. $-2x^3 - 10x^2 - 4$

2 △ △ △ △ △ △ △ △ 2

DO YOUR FIGURING HERE.

9. In the diagram, B, C, and D are collinear. The measures of $\measuredangle A$ and $\measuredangle ABC$ are 56° and 69°, respectively. The measure of $\measuredangle ACD$ = ?

   A. 55°
   B. 111°
   C. 115°
   D. 121°
   E. 125°

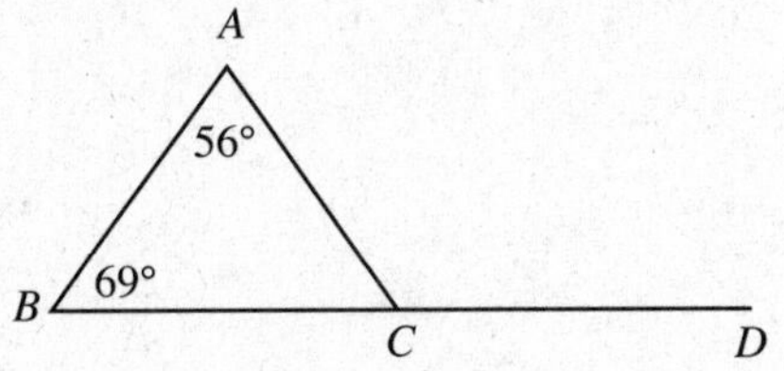

10. What is the expression $(5x - 4y)(3x + y)$ equivalent to?

   F. $15x^2 - 17xy - 4y^2$
   G. $15x^2 - 7xy + 4y^2$
   H. $15x^2 - 7xy - 4y^2$
   J. $15x + 7xy - 4y$
   K. $8x^2 - 7xy - 4y^2$

11. What value of x makes the equation $8x - 2(x - 5) = 2x - 20$ true?

   A. $-7\frac{1}{2}$
   B. $-2\frac{1}{2}$
   C. $-1\frac{1}{4}$
   D. 1
   E. $1\frac{2}{3}$

12. When $-3 \le x \le 3$, $|x - 3| + |3 + x| = ?$

   F. 3
   G. 6
   H. $2x - 6$
   J. $2x$
   K. $2x + 6$

13. The figure shows quadrilateral $ABCD$ with angles measured as marked. What is the measure of $\measuredangle C$?

   A. 120°
   B. 115°
   C. 105°
   D. 100°
   E. 80°

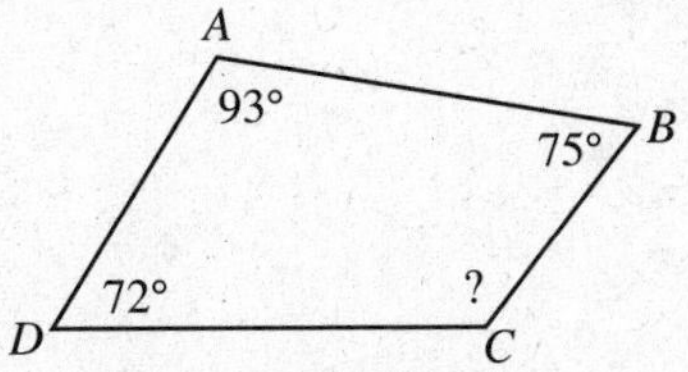

14. A tank currently holds 5,000 gallons of water. Each gallon of water weighs about 8 pounds. About how many pounds does the water in the tank weigh?

   F. 625
   G. 4,000
   H. 4,992
   J. 5,008
   K. 40,000

GO ON TO THE NEXT PAGE.

2 △ △ △ △ △ △ △ △ 2

DO YOUR FIGURING HERE.

15. A 3-pound bag of oranges costs \$1.99 at Yong's Grocery. A 3-pound bag of the same type of oranges costs \$2.17 at Pat's Pantry. How much cheaper, per pound, are the Yong's Grocery oranges than Pat's Pantry oranges?

    A. \$0.02
    B. \$0.04
    C. \$0.06
    D. \$0.18
    E. \$1.00

16. Graeme is going to replace his kitchen floor that is 12 feet by 16 feet. He will use tiles that are 8 inches by 8 inches. How many tiles will Graeme need?

    F. 3
    G. 24
    H. 36
    J. 360
    K. 432

17. Five patients arrived at a doctor's office about the same time. The nurse decided to call them in to see the doctor in random order. In how many different orders can these 5 patients be called?

    A. 4
    B. 5
    C. 25
    D. 120
    E. 3,125

18. What is the *y*-intercept of the line in the standard (*x*, *y*) coordinate plane that goes through the points (–3, 2) and (3, 6)?

    F. 0
    G. 2
    H. 4
    J. 6
    K. 8

19. In the diagram, $\overleftrightarrow{AB}$ is parallel to $\overleftrightarrow{CD}$. The measure of $\measuredangle PCD = 37°$ and the measure of $\measuredangle BPD$ is 40°. What is the measure of $\measuredangle CPD$?

    A. 100°
    B. 103°
    C. 106°
    D. 140°
    E. CANNOT be determined.

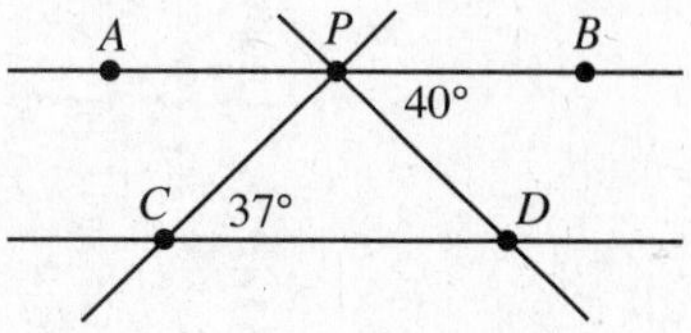

2 △ △ △ △ △ △ △ △ 2

DO YOUR FIGURING HERE.

20. What is the slope of the line $2x - 3y + 7 = 0$?

F. $-\frac{7}{3}$
G. $-\frac{2}{3}$
H. $\frac{2}{3}$
J. $\frac{3}{2}$
K. 2

21. In $\triangle PQR$, shown, what is the $\cos\measuredangle R$?

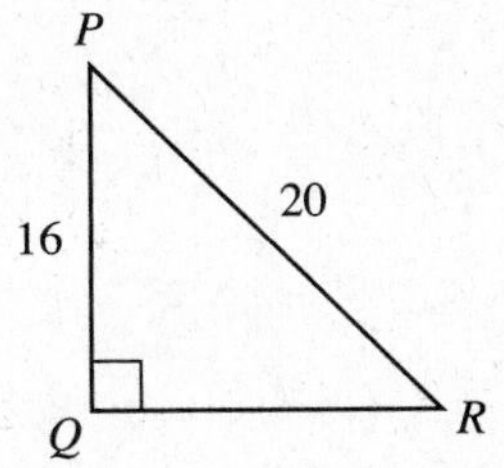

A. $\frac{12}{20}$
B. $\frac{12}{16}$
C. $\frac{16}{20}$
D. $\frac{16}{12}$
E. $\frac{\sqrt{656}}{20}$

22. If $x \neq -2$ or 3, what is $\frac{x^2 + x - 12}{x^2 - x - 6}$ equivalent to?

F. −2
G. 2
H. $\frac{x-4}{x-2}$
J. $\frac{x+4}{x+2}$
K. 0

23. In a certain year, Lincoln Middle School had an enrollment of exactly 1,000 students. The following year, the enrollment increased by 5%. In the third year, the enrollment decreased by 2% of what the enrollment was in the second year. What was the enrollment for the third year?

A. 1,030
B. 1,029
C. 990
D. 980
E. 971

24. Zinc, tin, and copper are used in the ratio of 2:3:4, respectively, in making a certain type of engine. If each engine weighs 63 ounces, how many ounces of tin are in each engine?

F. 7
G. 9
H. 14
J. 21
K. 28

Practice Test 6

GO ON TO THE NEXT PAGE.

2 △ △ △ △ △ △ △ △ 2

DO YOUR FIGURING HERE.

25. Driving home from school Joan spotted her brother Andrew and picked him up after he'd walked $\frac{1}{2}$ of the way home. A while later they saw younger brother Bill and picked him up after he'd walked $\frac{2}{3}$ of the way home from the same school. If they live $4\frac{1}{2}$ miles from school, how many miles farther than Andrew had Bill walked?

 A. $\frac{3}{8}$
 B. $\frac{1}{2}$
 C. $\frac{2}{3}$
 D. $\frac{3}{4}$
 E. $1\frac{1}{2}$

26. What positive value of k would make the lines below parallel in the (x, y) coordinate plane?
 $kx + 2y = 6$
 $32x + ky = 18$

 F. 0
 G. 3
 H. 6
 J. 8
 K. 12

27. In the standard (x, y) coordinate plane what is the distance between the points $(-2, 1)$ and $(4, -7)$?

 A. $\sqrt{28}$
 B. $\sqrt{40}$
 C. $\sqrt{68}$
 D. 10
 E. 14

28. In the diagram, circle P is inscribed in square $ABCD$. If the area of square $ABCD$ is 36 square feet, then what is the area of circle P in square feet?

 F. 9π
 G. 12π
 H. 36π
 J. 324π
 K. $1,296\pi$

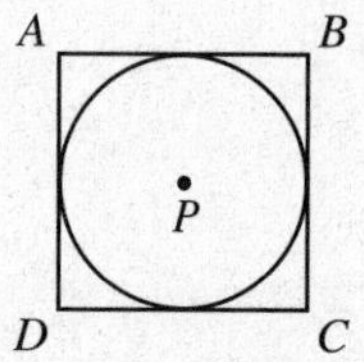

DO YOUR FIGURING HERE.

29. What are the solutions of the polynomial equation $2x^2 - 5x = 12$?

   A. –4 or 1.5
   B. –4 or –3
   C. –1.5 or 4
   D. 1.5 or 4
   E. 4 or 6

30. For what positive values of x is it true that $x^2 < 2x < x + 4$?

   F. No positive values
   G. Only positive values < 2
   H. Only positive values between 2 and 4
   J. Only positive values > 4
   K. All positive values

31. In the figure all angles are right angles and each dimension given is in inches. What is the perimeter of the figure in inches?

   A. 21
   B. 35
   C. 36
   D. 54
   E. 72

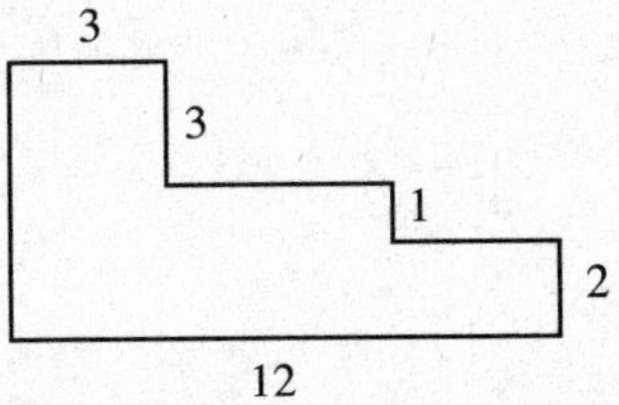

32. Which of the following graphs represents the solution set of the inequality $|x| > 2$ on the real number line?

F.
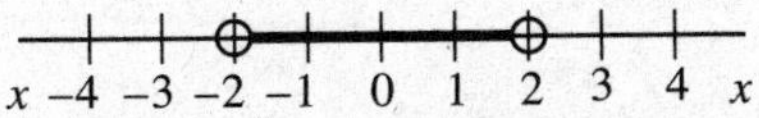

G.
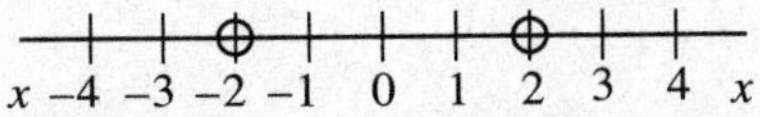

H.
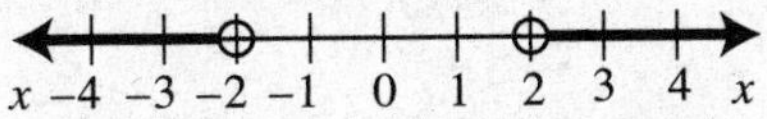

J.
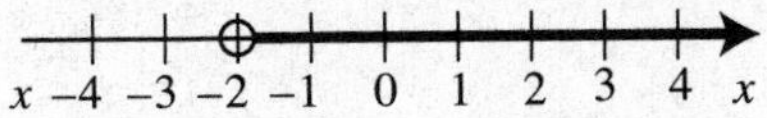

K.
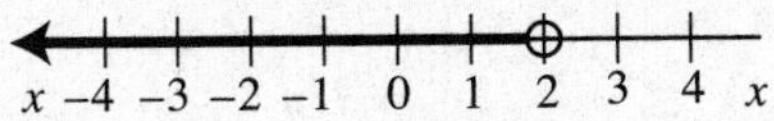

GO ON TO THE NEXT PAGE.

DO YOUR FIGURING HERE.

33. In a game, 100 marbles numbered 0–99 are placed into a box. A player draws 1 marble at random from the box. Without replacing the first marble, the player draws a second marble at random. If both marbles drawn have the same tens digit (that is, both are numbered 0–9 or 10–19 or 20–29, etc.), the player is a winner. If the first marble drawn is numbered 56, what is the probability that Terry will be a winner on the next draw?

A. $\frac{1}{8}$
B. $\frac{1}{9}$
C. $\frac{1}{10}$
D. $\frac{1}{11}$
E. $\frac{1}{99}$

34. In the diagram $\overline{AE}$ intersects $\overline{BD}$ at C and $\overline{AB}$ is parallel to $\overline{DE}$. Which of the following statements must be true?

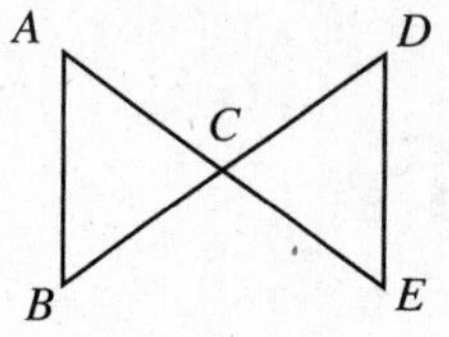

F. $\measuredangle A$ is congruent to $\measuredangle D$.
G. $\triangle ACB$ is congruent to $\triangle ECD$.
H. $\overline{AC}$ is congruent to $\overline{EC}$.
J. $\triangle ACB$ is similar to $\triangle ECD$.
K. $\measuredangle ACB$ is congruent to $\measuredangle CED$.

35. At the same time that a 6-foot man has a 4-foot shadow, a flag pole has a 14-foot shadow. What is the height of the flag pole, in feet?

A. $9\frac{1}{3}$
B. 12
C. 16
D. 21
E. 28

36. The formula for surface area of a right circular cylinder is $A = 2\pi r(r + h)$ where A is surface area, r = radius of the cylinder, and h is the height of the cylinder. Then h = ?

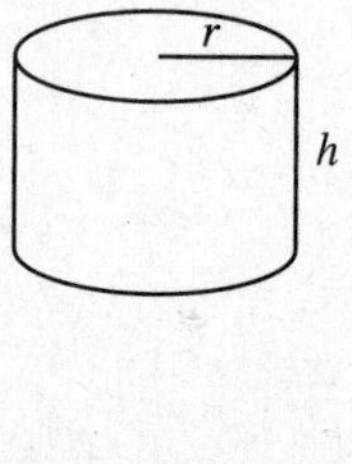

F. $A - 2\pi r - r$
G. $\frac{A - 2\pi r}{r}$
H. $\frac{A}{2\pi r} - r$
J. $\frac{A}{2\pi r} + r$
K. $\frac{A}{2\pi r^2}$

Practice Test 6

2 △ △ △ △ △ △ △ △ 2

Use the following information to answer questions 37 and 38.

DO YOUR FIGURING HERE.

Employees of We-Bug-U sell merchandise by telephone. Employees are offered 2 different pay options. Option A offers employees \$8.00 per hour plus a commission equal to 10% of their sales. Option B offers \$11.00 per hour with no commission. Each employee must choose one of these options at the beginning of each pay period.

37. Juanita, an employee of We-Bug-U, worked for 6 hours and earned \$68.00 for the 6-hour period. What was the amount of her sales for the 6-hour period?

A. \$20.00
B. \$80.00
C. \$100.00
D. \$200.00
E. \$400.00

38. Romeo and Juliet (both employees of We-Bug-U) each worked 15 hours and had sales of \$400.00. Romeo chose Option A while Juliet chose Option B. Which employee made more money and how much more?

F. Romeo: \$5.00 more
G. Juliet: \$5.00 more
H. They earned the same amount.
J. Juliet: \$25.00 more
K. Romeo: \$355.00 more

39. The width of a rectangle is 27 feet and the length is 36 feet. What is the length of a diagonal of the rectangle in feet?

A. 63
B. 54
C. 45
D. 42
E. 36

40. The vertices of a parallelogram in the coordinate plane are (3, 3), (7, 3), (8, 8), and (4, 8). What is the area of this parallelogram?

F. 10
G. $2\sqrt{26}$
H. 16
J. 20
K. $4\sqrt{26}$

Practice Test 6

GO ON TO THE NEXT PAGE.

2 △ △ △ △ △ △ △ △ 2

DO YOUR FIGURING HERE.

41. The point (–1, 1) is the midpoint of the line segment in the standard (*x*, *y*) coordinate plane joining the point (1, 6) and the point (*a*, *b*). Which of the following is (*a*, *b*)?
    A. (–2, 3)
    B. (–3, –4)
    C. (0, 3.5)
    D. (3, 11)
    E. (2, 5)

42. The first term of the geometric sequence below is 27. What is the twelfth term? 27, 9, 3....
    F. $\frac{1}{3^7}$
    G. $\frac{1}{3^8}$
    H. $\frac{1}{3^{10}}$
    J. $\frac{1}{3^{11}}$
    K. $\frac{1}{3^{12}}$

43. In $\triangle ABC$, $AB = AC = 14$. Which of these values could NOT be the length of the third side, $\overline{BC}$?
    A. 5
    B. 7
    C. 14
    D. 16
    E. 28

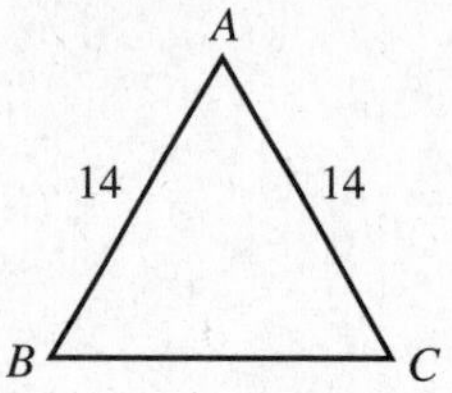

44. If $4^{3x+1} = 8^{x+2}$, then x = ?
    F. $\frac{1}{2}$
    G. $\frac{3}{4}$
    H. $\frac{4}{3}$
    J. 3
    K. None of these

45. If $f(x) = x^2$ and $g(x) = 2x - 1$, then $f(g(x))$ = ?
    A. $4x^2 - 4x + 1$
    B. $4x^2 + 1$
    C. $2x^2 - 1$
    D. $x^2 - 1$
    E. $4x^2 + 4x + 1$

2 △ △ △ △ △ △ △ △ 2

46. In the diagram B, D, and C are collinear. $\measuredangle B = 30°$ and $\measuredangle C = 45°$. $\overline{AD}$ is perpendicular to $\overline{BC}$ and $\overline{AD} = 6$. What is the perimeter of $\triangle ABC$ to the nearest tenth?

F. 29.9
G. 30
H. 32.5
J. 34.4
K. 36.9

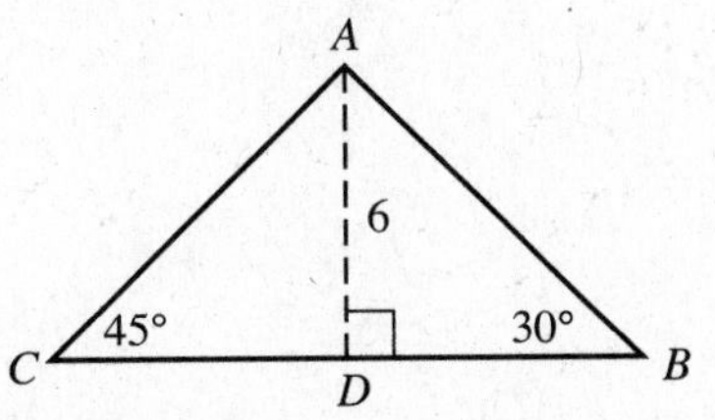

47. Quadrilateral $ABCD$ is a trapezoid with $\overline{AB}$ parallel to $\overline{CD}$. $\overline{AE}$ and $\overline{BF}$ are perpendicular to $\overline{CD}$. $AB = 6$, $CD = 12$, and $AE = 4$. What is the sum of the areas of $\triangle AED$ and $\triangle BFC$?

A. 12
B. 24
C. 36
D. 48
E. 120

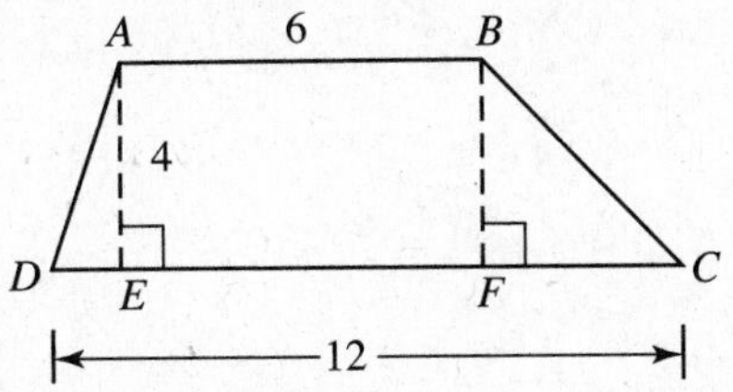

48. $(2 - 3i)^2 = ?$ [Note: $i = \sqrt{-1}$]

F. -5
G. 13
H. $-5 - 6i$
J. $-5 - 12i$
K. $-5 + 12i$

49. How many prime numbers are there between 50 and 70?

A. 4
B. 5
C. 6
D. 7
E. 8

50. If $(x + 2)$ is a factor of $3x^2 - 13x + k$, what is the value of k?

F. -38
G. -14
H. -2
J. 14
K. 38

DO YOUR FIGURING HERE.

DO YOUR FIGURING HERE.

51. If the radius of a sphere is tripled, the volume of the resulting sphere is how many times the volume of the original sphere?

[The volume of a sphere = $\frac{4\pi r^3}{3}$]

A. 1
B. 3
C. 9
D. 27
E. 81

52. If $f(x) = x^2 - 2x + 4$, then $f(t + 2) = ?$

F. $t^2 - 2t + 4$
G. $t^2 - 2t$
H. $t^2 + 2t + 8$
J. $t^2 + 6t + 12$
K. $t^2 + 2t + 4$

53. In the circle illustrated, the radius is 8 feet. The measure of central angle *AOB* is 60°. What is the length, in feet, of arc *AB*?

A. $\frac{4\pi}{3}$

B. $\frac{8\pi}{3}$

C. $\frac{32\pi}{3}$

D. 16π

E. 24π

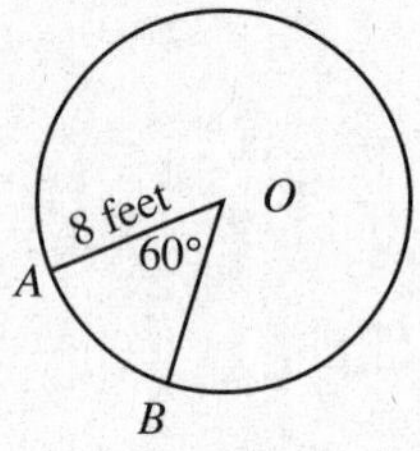

54. If $x = 4y + 2$, what is $y + 6$ in terms of x?

F. $x + 4$

G. $x + 6$

H. $\frac{x + 22}{4}$

J. $\frac{x + 2}{4} + 6$

K. $\frac{x - 4}{2} + 6$

2 △ △ △ △ △ △ △ 2

DO YOUR FIGURING HERE.

55. If $\sin\theta = \frac{5}{7}$, $\frac{\pi}{2} < \theta < \pi$, then $\cos\theta$ = ?

A. $-\frac{7}{2\sqrt{6}}$

B. $-\frac{2\sqrt{6}}{5}$

C. $-\frac{2\sqrt{6}}{7}$

D. $\frac{2\sqrt{6}}{7}$

E. $\frac{2\sqrt{6}}{5}$

56. If $\log_b x = g$ and $\log_b y = p$, then $\log_b\left(\frac{x}{y^3}\right)$ = ?

F. $\frac{g}{p^3}$

G. gp^3

H. $g - p$

J. $g + 3p$

K. $g - 3p$

57. The measures of ∡A and ∡B are 35° and 44°, respectively. The length of $\overline{AB}$ is 12 miles. Which of the following expressions, if any, gives the approximate distance, in miles, of side $\overline{AC}$?

[Note: The law of sines states that the ratio between the length of the side opposite an angle and the sine of that angle is the same for all interior angles in the same triangle.]

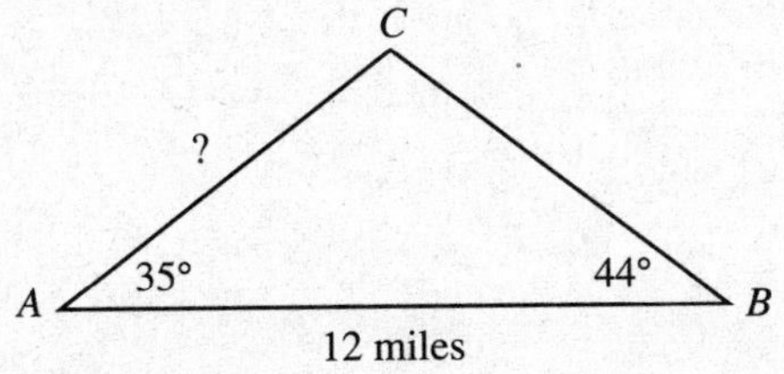

A. The distance cannot be approximated without more information.

B. $\sqrt{35^2 + 44^2}$

C. $\frac{12\cos 44°}{\cos 101°}$

D. 12 tan 44°

E. $\frac{12\sin 44°}{\sin 101°}$

Practice Test 6

GO ON TO THE NEXT PAGE.

58. When $-2 \leq x \leq 5$ and $-3 \leq y \leq 3$, what is the maximum possible value for $x - y$?

F. –5
G. –2
H. 1
J. 2
K. 8

59. For how many different integers b (consider positive integers, negative integers, and zero) does $x^2 + bx + 20$ factor into linear factors with integer coefficients?

A. 1
B. 2
C. 3
D. 4
E. 6

60. M and N are prime numbers. If $\sqrt{21(M)(N)(5)(7)}$ is a rational number, then $(M)(N) = ?$

F. 8
G. 15
H. 21
J. 35
K. 735

DO YOUR FIGURING HERE

STOP

If there is still time remaining, check your answers to this section.

Turn page for the Reading Test

READING TEST

35 MINUTES—40 QUESTIONS

Directions: There are four passages in this test. Each passage is followed by several questions. After reading a passage, choose the best answer to each question and fill in the corresponding oval on your answer document. You may refer to the passages as often as necessary.

Passage 1—Prose Fiction

This passage is adapted from the short story "Bernice Bobs Her Hair" by F. Scott Fitzgerald (© 1922 by F. Scott Fitzgerald).

When Marjorie and Bernice reached home at half after midnight they said good night at the top of the stairs. Though cousins, they were not intimates. Bernice all through this parent-arranged visit had rather longed to exchange those confidences flavored with giggles and tears that she considered an indispensable factor in all feminine intercourse. But in this respect she found Marjorie rather cold; felt somehow the same difficulty in talking to her that she had in talking to men. Marjorie never giggled, was never frightened, seldom embarrassed, and in fact had very few of the qualities which Bernice considered appropriately and blessedly feminine.

Bernice wondered for the hundredth time why she never had any attention when she was away from home. That her family were the wealthiest in Eau Claire; that her mother entertained tremendously, gave little dinners for her daughter before all dances and bought her a car of her own to drive round in, never occurred to her as factors in her home-town social success. Like most girls, she had been brought up on novels in which the female was beloved because of certain mysterious womanly qualities always mentioned but never displayed.

Bernice felt a vague pain that she was not at present engaged in being popular. She knew that even in Eau Claire other girls with less position and less pulchritude were given a much bigger rush. She attributed this to something subtly unscrupulous in those girls. It had never worried her, and if it had her mother would have assured her that the other girls cheapened themselves and that men really respected girls like Bernice.

She turned out the light in her bathroom, and on an impulse decided to go in and chat for a moment with her Aunt Josephine, whose light was still on. Her soft slippers bore her noiselessly down the carpeted hall, but hearing voices inside she stopped near the partly opened door. Then she caught her own name, and without any definite intention of eavesdropping lingered—and the thread of the conversation going on inside pierced her consciousness sharply as if it had been drawn through with a needle.

"She's absolutely hopeless!" It was Marjorie's voice. "Oh, I know what you're going to say! So many people have told you how pretty and sweet she is, and how she can cook! What of it? She has a bum time. Men don't like her."

"What's a little cheap popularity?" Mrs. Harvey sounded annoyed.

"It's everything when you're eighteen," said Marjorie emphatically. "I've done my best. I've been polite and I've made men dance with her, but they just won't stand being bored. When I think of that gorgeous coloring wasted on such a ninny, and think what Martha Carey could do with it—oh!"

"There's no courtesy these days." Mrs. Harvey's voice implied that modern situations were too much for her. When she was a girl all young ladies who belonged to nice families had glorious times.

"Well," said Marjorie, "no girl can permanently bolster up a lame-duck visitor, because these days it's every girl for herself. I've tried to drop her hints about clothes and things, and she's been furious—given me the funniest looks. I'll bet she consoles herself by thinking that she's very virtuous and that I'm too fickle and will come to a bad end. All unpopular girls think that way. Sour grapes! Sarah Hopkins refers to Genevieve and Roberta and me as gardenia girls! I'll bet she'd give ten years of

Practice Test 6

her life and her European education to be a gardenia girl and have three or four men in love with her and be cut in on every few feet at dances."

"It seems to me," interrupted Mrs. Harvey rather wearily, "that you ought to be able to do something for Bernice. I know she's not very vivacious."

Marjorie groaned. "Vivacious! Good grief! I've never heard her say anything to a boy except that it's hot or the floor's crowded or that she's going to school in New York next year. Sometimes she asks them what kind of car they have and tells them the kind she has. Thrilling!"

Mrs. Harvey yawned. Marjorie considered whether or not convincing her mother was worth the trouble. People over forty can seldom be permanently convinced of anything. At eighteen our convictions are hills from which we look; at forty-five they are caves in which we hide. Having decided this, Marjorie said good night. When she came out into the hall it was quite empty.

1. The events in the passage are described primarily from the point of view of a narrator who presents:
   A. the inner thoughts and feelings of Bernice exclusively.
   B. the inner thoughts and feelings of Bernice primarily, but also occasionally Marjorie.
   C. little insight into any character's thoughts or feelings except through dialogue.
   D. primarily Marjorie's point of view, with educated guesses about how Bernice feels.

2. The passage supports all of the following statements about Bernice's home life in Eau Claire EXCEPT that:
   F. her mother writes novels for a living.
   G. she will no longer live there next year.
   H. she owns her own car.
   J. it is easier for less attractive girls to be popular there.

3. Which of the following questions is NOT answered by the passage?
   A. Whose idea was it for Bernice to come and stay with Marjorie?
   B. What does Marjorie suspect that Bernice thinks of her?
   C. In what city do the events of the story take place?
   D. What is Mrs. Harvey's first name?

4. One of the main ideas of the second paragraph (lines 14–24) is that:
   F. Bernice's family has more money than does Marjorie's, though Marjorie's is better known.
   G. Bernice is the only girl in her hometown with a car, and Marjorie is jealous of this.
   H. Bernice prefers to read novels written by women, a trait Marjorie finds dull and embarrassing.
   J. Bernice does not understand why socializing is so much harder here than it is at home.

5. According to the passage, all of the following are true of people's attitudes toward Marjorie EXCEPT:
   A. Bernice's parents consider her a bad influence.
   B. Sarah Hopkins considers her shallow.
   C. Bernice finds her aloof and inscrutable.
   D. her mother is often dismissive of her ideas.

6. In the passage, the statement that it is difficult to convince people over forty of anything is best described as the opinion of:
   F. Marjorie, formed based on her mother's advice.
   G. Marjorie, formed in response to her mother's behavior.
   H. the narrator, in contrast to what Marjorie thinks.
   J. the narrator, offered as an explanation of why Mrs. Harvey disapproves of Bernice.

7. The passage indicates that Bernice's primary response to the conversation she overhears is to:
   A. feel relief that other people have noticed the difficulties she is having.
   B. feel betrayed at being discussed this way by her lifelong friend Marjorie.
   C. say nothing and formulate a plan for revenge.
   D. feel hurt that she was talked about behind her back.

8. According to the passage, as a young woman, Mrs. Harvey saw the youth culture of her day as being:
   F. less concerned with material things.
   G. more respectful of its elders.
   H. easier for the right kind of girls to negotiate.
   J. interested in other activities besides dancing.

9. The passage indicates that, compared with Bernice, Marjorie finds her friend Martha Carey to be:
   A. more personable but less pretty.
   B. prettier but less personable.
   C. a better dancer but less intelligent.
   D. equally intelligent but wittier.

10. That Marjorie is cold and hard to get along with is:
   F. a reputation Bernice had heard about even before meeting her.
   G. an impression Bernice got from comparing her to an ideal.
   H. probably an act Marjorie puts on in an effort to be intimidating and desirable.
   J. something Bernice never suspected until overhearing her conversation with her mother.

Passage II—Social Science

This passage is adapted from "Music Piracy," which appeared on UKEssays.com., February 2009.

In the future, the only way musicians will make money is by playing live. New federal legislation says universities must agree to provide not just deterrents but also "alternatives" to peer-to-peer piracy, such as paying monthly subscription fees to the music industry for their students, on penalty of losing all financial aid.

When record companies appeared, the services they provided were necessary in order for people to listen to recorded music. Making and selling records was a major undertaking. At that time, making recorded music available to the masses required significant capital and investments, which in turn required a legal structure that would provide stable profits and return on the required investment. The music industry used to provide people with tools that were essential to listen to recorded music. The difference between that time and our day is that record companies now charge people for permission to use tools they already have that the record companies did not provide—that in fact people paid someone else for—yet the legal structure that developed during the time when those services were useful remains. The legal structure says if you don't pay, you are breaking the law.

In our day, there is no need of publishers, distributors, and in most cases manufacturers. Modern technology allows people to burn CDs at home or publish their own records using the internet, distributing the material across the web digitally.

The problem of piracy has been rising for the past ten years, and the numbers of "pirates" is growing day by day. The reason is simple: user-friendly peer-to-peer software takes only a couple of minutes to set up and another minute to become familiar with all the features. In another ten minutes it is possible to find your favorite artist and download your favorite album. It's so convenient that it is becoming only a question of conscience whether to become a pirate.

It is becoming more and more difficult for the music industry to ignore the basic economics, technological progress, and the outdated legal structures of the industry such as unenforceable property rights (because it is impossible to sue everyone) and "zero" production costs (peer-to-peer and file sharing systems became way too popular). Music companies are still trying to charge for their music, but it's becoming more and more clear that as long as there is a free alternative (peer-to peer and other file sharing systems), the price of music and other media will have to fall.

Some artists have already started to accept the situation, and instead of fighting the "problems" have started to look for opportunities. Marginal production costs are zero, and with software applications, it doesn't cost anything to produce another digital copy that would be as good as the original; as soon as the first copy exists, anyone can create additional copies. Unless effective technical, legal or other artificial barriers to production can be created, simple economic theory dictates that zero marginal cost plus competition (the possibility that the consumer will create and spread another copy) results in a zero price, unless government creates artificial barriers to a free market.

In October 2007, Radiohead announced that their new album *In Rainbows* would be available to download free of charge. But the networks and file-sharing systems had grown even easier to use than what Radiohead was offering. Radiohead's only requirement was for downloaders to set up an account on their website, but according to the statistics, that turned out to be not "cheap" enough.

A new era is coming—the era of free music. Recorded music will become one of the marketing tools to get people to pay for live concerts, which will put emphasis on performance quality, resulting in cultural socialization and stronger musical communites. In countries like Brazil, people have already started to use the situation as an opportunity, doing huge amounts of remixes, resulting in new styles and music cultures like Techno Brega.

Record labels are going down, struggling to make profits from CD sales, and it appears that digital music selling is more reliable for revenue. Copyright and intellectual-property law have to be updated, and the CD-sales model has to be reinvented as the CD-promotional model in order to regain the value of a physical product with the emphasis now on live performances.

11. The passage's author most strongly implies that over time, record companies:
   - **A.** reported increased profits as production costs increasingly approached zero.
   - **B.** have taken positive steps to build stronger musical communities.
   - **C.** have broken the law by trying to sue everybody.
   - **D.** began feeling as if they had the right to charge people for the services of others.

12. According to the passage, the "new era" mentioned in line 71 will partly be characterized by:
   - **F.** increased governmental regulation of the record industry.
   - **G.** recorded music being used mainly to promote concerts.
   - **H.** increased popularity in the United States of foreign musical styles such as Techno Brega.
   - **J.** reinvention of the CD-sales model so that CD sales will become more profitable than ever.

13. As portrayed in the passage, so-called music "piracy" has been:
   - **A.** increased by the public's mastery of difficult computer software.
   - **B.** decreased by successful updating of intellectual-property laws.
   - **C.** increased by the user-friendliness of downloading sites and programs.
   - **D.** decreased by the record industry's appeals to conscience.

14. In the statement in lines 56–62, the author most strongly stresses:
   - **F.** his opinion that more government intervention in the matter is necessary.
   - **G.** the economic realities of where the record business is headed.
   - **H.** the suspicion that most consumers are distributing free music to their friends.
   - **J.** his distrust of the free market as it applies to the music business of today.

15. According to the passage, the reaction of record companies to the realities of the digital age has been to:
   - **A.** stubbornly demand unchanged profits in exchange for fewer provided services.
   - **B.** put more advertising money into the promotion of live performances.
   - **C.** start depicting themselves as an arm of the federal government.
   - **D.** look for opportunities in the "problems" and reform their business model.

16. The passage most strongly suggests that the author sees the modern music-consuming public as behaving:
   - **F.** dishonorably.
   - **G.** aggressively.
   - **H.** logically.
   - **J.** unimaginatively.

17. In lines 2–6, the author depicts an example of what he feels is:
   - **A.** young music pirates beginning to see themselves as a unified group with common interests.
   - **B.** record companies using their connections to influence legislation in illegal ways.
   - **C.** a commonsense move that will become normal in the near future.
   - **D.** the government passing responsibility for music piracy onto an institution not directly related to it.

18. The passage's author characterizes peer-to-peer filesharing technology as:
   - **F.** something that should be approached with caution, as it is still in its infancy.
   - **G.** something that will ultimately lead to increased creativity on the part of musicians.
   - **H.** something that the record companies should have more direct control over.
   - **J.** the most significant artistic development of the twenty-first century so far.

19. For the author, lines 82–86 mainly serve to support his earlier point that:
   - **A.** the CD will soon be a thing of the past.
   - **B.** most CDs will soon have data on them other than music.
   - **C.** CDs will continue to exist, but serve a different purpose.
   - **D.** CDs will soon only be manufactured by the consumers themselves.

20. Another cultural analyst discussing the controversy over peer-to-peer filesharing has this to say:

    We have to ask whether allowing or prohibiting filesharing would promote the greatest amount of happiness for the greatest amount of people. Thus, we have to examine how many people are affected by the prohibition or permission of filesharing.

    How does this account compare to that of the passage's author?

    F. Both agree that the record companies have been foolish to ignore the way things are headed.
    G. Both agree that the actions taken by music consumers have been predictable, if not necessarily morally correct.
    H. The second author feels that filesharing is a matter of individual conscience, whereas the author of the passage feels it should be up to the law to decide.
    J. The second author attempts to apply universal moral truths to the issue, whereas the author of the passage is more of a pragmatic realist.

Passage III—Humanities

This passage is adapted from the essay "Why TV Lost" by Paul Graham (© 2009 Paul Graham).

Moore's Law is a principle of computer hardware engineering stating that the number of transistors on an integrated circuit will double every two years.

About twenty years ago people noticed computers and TV were on a collision course and started to speculate about what they'd produce when they converged. We now know the answer: computers. It's clear now that even by using the word "convergence" we were giving TV too much credit. This won't be convergence so much as replacement. People may still watch things they call "TV shows," but they'll watch them mostly on computers.

What decided the contest for computers? Four forces, three of which one could have predicted, and one that would have been harder to. One predictable cause of victory is that the Internet is an open platform. Anyone can build whatever they want on it, and the market picks the winners. So innovation happens at hacker speeds instead of big-company speeds. The second is Moore's Law, which has worked its usual magic on Internet bandwidth. The third reason computers won is piracy. Users prefer it not just because it's free, but because it's more convenient. BitTorrent and YouTube have already trained a new generation of viewers that the place to watch shows is on a computer screen.

The somewhat more surprising force was one specific type of innovation: social applications. The average teenage kid has a pretty much infinite capacity for talking to their friends. But they can't physically be with them all the time. When I was in high school the solution was the telephone. Now it's social networks, multiplayer games, and various messaging applications. The way you reach them all is through a computer, which means every teenage kid wants a computer with an Internet connection, has an incentive to figure out how to use it, and spends countless hours in front of it.

After decades of running an IV drip right into their audience, people in the entertainment business had understandably come to think of them as rather passive. They thought they'd be able to dictate the way shows reached audiences. But they underestimated the force of their desire to connect with one another. Facebook killed TV. That is wildly oversimplified, of course, but probably as close to the truth as you can get in three words.

The TV networks already seem, grudgingly, to see where things are going, and have responded by putting their stuff, grudgingly, online. But they're still dragging their heels. They still seem to wish people would watch shows on TV instead, just as newspapers that put their stories online still seem to wish people would wait till the next morning and read them printed on paper. They should both just face the fact that the Internet is the primary medium.

They'd be in a better position if they'd done that earlier. When a new medium arises that's powerful enough to make incumbents nervous, then it's probably powerful enough to win, and the best thing they can do is jump in immediately. Whether they like it or not, big changes are coming, because the Internet dissolves the two cornerstones of broadcast media: synchronicity and locality. On the Internet, you don't have to send everyone the same signal, and you don't have to send it to them from a local source. People will watch what they want when they want it, and group themselves according to whatever shared interest they feel most strongly. Maybe their strongest shared interest will be their physical location, but I'm guessing not—which means local TV is probably dead. It was an artifact of limitations imposed by old technology. If someone were creating an Internet-based TV company from scratch now, they might have some plan for shows aimed at specific regions, but it wouldn't be a top priority.

TV networks will fight these trends, because they don't have sufficient flexibility to adapt to them. They're hemmed in by local affiliates in much the same way car companies are hemmed in by dealers and unions. Inevitably, the people running the networks will take the easy route and try to keep the old model running for a couple more years, just as the record labels have done.

The networks used to be gatekeepers. They distributed your work, and sold advertising on it. Now the people who produce a show can distribute it themselves. The main value networks supply now is ad sales, which will tend to put them in the position of service providers rather than publishers.

Shows will change even more. On the Internet there's no reason to keep their current format, or even the fact that they have a single format. Indeed, the more interesting sort of convergence that's coming is between shows and games. But on the question of what sort of entertainment gets distributed on the Internet in 20 years, I wouldn't dare to make any predictions, except that things will change a lot. We'll get whatever the most imaginative people can cook up.

That's why the Internet won.

21. The passage's author most strongly implies that over time, TV's hold over its audience grew:

A. stronger, because people group themselves according to shared interests.
B. weaker, due to the effects of Moore's Law on the content of Web programming.
C. stronger, because TV shows are always changing to better reflect the times.
D. weaker, because of limitations in the medium of TV and formats of TV shows.

22. According to the passage, which of the following is NOT an obvious predictable force that led to the supremacy of computers?

F. Facebook
G. The magic of Internet bandwidth
H. Free pirated content
J. The Internet's status as an open platform

23. As portrayed in the passage, the computer industry has benefited from the fact that teenagers are:

A. energetic and social.
B. adaptable but lazy.
C. friendly but shy.
D. trendy and easily amused.

24. In the statement in lines 64–67, the author most strongly stresses the:

F. idea that people should take more of an interest in their physical location.
G. fact that national news covers more important issues than local news.
H. fact that TV's self-image is based on the technological limitations of the past.
J. threat of local stations being outcompeted or bought up by national networks.

25. According to the passage, the reaction of TV networks to the Internet phenomenon has been to:

A. try to dissolve the cornerstones of the Internet.
B. rush to put all their content on the Internet, just as newspapers put their stories online.
C. put some of what they produce on the Web, but resist the change in spirit.
D. become hemmed in by local affiliates, in an effort to develop sufficient flexibility.

26. The passage most strongly suggests that the author sees traditional media outlets like TV and newspapers as exhibiting:

F. determined originality.
G. resentful stubbornness.
H. open hostility.
J. petulant solicitousness.

27. Lines 77–80 most nearly mean that the networks:

A. will try their best to converge with the record labels.
B. will wait for Web-based business models to make innovations and then buy them out.
C. are fighting among themselves about what their next step should be.
D. will squeeze as much life as possible out of their current business practices.

Practice Test 6

28. The passage's author characterizes the younger generation as being:

F. prohibitively ignorant of the rich histories of TV and newspapers.
G. soundly conditioned to the idea of computers meeting all their entertainment needs.
H. easily amused by culturally destructive habits like social networking.
J. unintentionally subversive of international commerce in the twenty-first century.

29. For the author, lines 68–72 mainly serve to support his earlier point that:

A. Internet writers still have fewer plans for shows than TV writers do.
B. Internet companies have done better market research than TV networks have.
C. programming aimed at specific regions is not what people really want.
D. Internet creators are true artists who have priorities other than making money.

30. Another cultural analyst discussing the relationship between TV and the Internet had this to say:

> The era of appointment-to-view TV is coming to an end. It will continue to exist for the simple reason that some things—like, say, a World Cup final—are best covered using a few-to-many technology. But it will lose its dominant position in the ecosystem.

How does this account compare to that of the passage's author?

F. Both agree that sooner or later the Internet will completely replace TV.
G. Both agree that the battle between TV and the Internet will go on forever.
H. This account suggests that TV's dominance will continue, whereas the passage does not.
J. This account concedes that TV is better suited to some things, whereas the passage does not.

Passage IV—Natural Science

This passage is adapted from "The Creepy Scientific Explanation Behind Ghost Sightings" by Jack Mendoza, which appeared on cracked.com (October, 2010).

There is simply no evidence that dead people wander aimlessly around old houses, and no known scientific principle that would make it possible, but a lot of people have seen ghosts. There are certain spots and buildings where separate, unrelated witnesses have reported ghosts, without having talked to each other or being aware of the area being "haunted."

It appears that science has stumbled across the reason for it. It has nothing to do with the supernatural, but the answer is almost as weird. While working in his robotics laboratory, Vladimir Gavreau noticed that one of his assistants was bleeding from the ears. Puzzled, Gavreau started researching the phenomenon, and soon realized that a vibrating pipe of the right length and girth can cause a number of unpleasant effects ranging from mild irritation to serious pain.

What he had discovered was infrasound. It's noise at a low enough frequency that you don't consciously hear it, but your ears still sense it. The process of receiving sensory input without your conscious mind understanding where it's coming from wreaks havoc with your emotions. Specifically, researchers found that sounds between 7 and 19 Hz could induce fear, dread or panic.

As an experiment, acoustic scientists sneaked in low-frequency sounds at a live concert. Most of the concertgoers had no idea what was going on. At the end of the experiment, 22 percent of the people involved reported feelings of unexplainable dread, chills and depression when infrasound was blasted into the crowd.

Why would it have this effect? It may be evolution. It doesn't take a mad-scientist device to create infrasound: nature creates this type of low-frequency vibration all the time. Volcanos, earthquakes, strong ocean waves and even winds hitting the hillside in just the right spot can create infrasound. Even animals can create it. The frequency of a tiger's roar is around 18 Hz. All the things that create the sound are huge, powerful and dangerous. Evolution might have taught us that this sound means bad news.

So now we have a phenomenon that occurs in nature, is invisible, is imperceptible on a conscious level, but can spontaneously make you feel irrational fear, even if you're sitting in an empty room. We've just described one of the first and primary signs of a "haunting"—unexplained feelings of fear or dread. But what about actual *sightings* of ghosts? For that we need to go to a researcher named Vic Tandy. In the engineering building where Tandy worked, cleaning staff as well as fellow researchers complained of feeling dread, depression and a strange feeling that someone was watching them. Every so often, the staff would see dark figures out of the corners of their eyes. After one particularly strange experience when a gray shape sat next to his desk for several minutes, Tandy was determined to figure out what was going on. After eliminating gas poisoning and rogue equipment, he realized that the ghostly apparitions seemed to almost always occur in a certain section of the lab. He also realized that if he put a metal sheet in a vice, it would spontaneously vibrate uncontrollably for no apparent reason.

Poltergeist? No, just infrasound. A silent exhaust fan was sending out low-frequency vibrations that bounced back and forth on the lab's walls until they formed a powerful wave at 18.9 Hz, right at the top of the panic range. According to a NASA study, it was powerful enough to resonate with the average human eyeball, causing "smeared" vision, a phenomenon where the eye vibrates just enough to register something static—say, the frame of your glasses or a speck of dust—as large, moving shapes. Once the fan was removed, the strange apparitions and feelings of fear disappeared.

Convinced that he had stumbled onto something, Tandy went on to test this explanation for ghostly apparitions in the cellar of a nearby "haunted" abbey. According to the locals, as soon as someone would step into the cellar they would freeze up, see strange gray ghosts and have to leave because of nausea. Vic discovered that the shape of the cellar and the hallway leading to it, as well as nearby factories, all contributed to making the haunted cellar a perfect resonating chamber. The vibrations created were exactly 18.9 Hz and were most powerful at the threshold of the cellar, where most people became sick and terrified.

So if you're ever troubled by strange noises in the middle of the night or you experience feelings of dread in your basement or attic or even if someone in your family sees a ghost.... Well, call the repair guy, because it might be caused by a malfunctioning ventilation fan.

31. The primary purpose of the passage is to:

A. suggest that the vast majority of ghost sightings have in fact been elaborate hoaxes.
B. explain why legends about supernatural experiences have gotten more numerous as technology advanced.
C. suggest that the myths associated with ghosts and hauntings are caused by an explainable phenomenon.
D. gently satirize the types of people who claim to have seen ghosts or believe in hauntings.

32. The main function of the fifth paragraph (lines 30–39) in relation to the passage as a whole is to:

F. explain that most people who reported supernatural experiences were probably actually hearing animals.
G. suggest that virtually anyone could successfully fake a haunting without a lot of elaborate equipment.
H. argue in favor of belief in evolution over belief in supernatural things like ghosts.
J. explain why humans would have evolved the responses that cause them to imagine ghosts.

33. The author uses the story of the concert experiment (lines 24–29) primarily to demonstrate that:

A. the feelings normally reported in conjunction with a "haunting" are replicable even in people who are not expecting to feel them.
B. the percentage of people who respond to infrasound goes down when they are exposed to it in large groups.
C. many reported supernatural experiences are probably the result of elaborate pranks.
D. the scientists who developed the infrasound theory of hauntings were irresponsible, and therefore further study is needed.

34. The scientific theories described in the passage would appear to explain all of the phenomena traditionally associated with ghosts and haunting EXCEPT:

F. sudden feelings of unease or panic.
G. information supposedly communicated by ghosts.
H. personal injury supposedly inflicted by ghosts.
J. distinct, moving visual apparitions.

35. According to the author, it's entirely possible that most of the people in history who reported seeing ghosts were actually:

A. making an honest mistake.
B. unusually superstitious, even for their time.
C. inventing stories to explain their inexplicable emotions.
D. knowledgeable about science.

36. According to the passage, Tandy discovered that the cause of ghost apparitions was the result of a (an):

F. animal's roar at 14 Hz.
G. powerful wind vibrating at 7 Hz.
H. ventilation fan vibrating at 12 Hz.
J. silent exhaust fan vibrating at 18 Hz.

37. As it is used in line 21, *havoc* most nearly means:
    - **A.** depression.
    - **B.** chaos.
    - **C.** misunderstanding.
    - **D.** surprise.

38. In the context of the passage, the phrase "bad news" most nearly represents something:
    - **F.** liable to cause depression and sadness.
    - **G.** incomprehensible to the human mind.
    - **H.** real and potentially dangerous.
    - **J.** imaginary and potentially frightening.

39. The passage indicates that Vladimir Gavreau was initially motivated by a desire to:
    - **A.** discover infrasound.
    - **B.** find a scientific explanation for ghost sightings.
    - **C.** investigate a specific physical ailment.
    - **D.** make his work with robotics more efficient.

40. Suppose a group of researchers wanted to construct a "haunted house." They would most likely need to make use of:
    - **F.** a device sending out vibrations at a certain frequency.
    - **G.** live animals.
    - **H.** rooms of a precise, predetermined shape.
    - **J.** both F and H.

STOP

If there is still time remaining, check your answers to this section.

Turn page for the Science Test

SCIENCE TEST

35 MINUTES—40 QUESTIONS

Directions: There are seven passages in this test. Each passage is followed by several questions. After reading a passage, choose the best answer to each question and fill in the corresponding oval on your answer document. You may refer to the passages as often as necessary.

You are NOT permitted to use a calculator on this test.

Passage I

A *catalyst* is a substance that speeds up a reaction, but is chemically unchanged at the end of the reaction. Catalysts can be divided into two main types—*heterogeneous* and *homogeneous*. In a heterogeneous reaction, the catalyst is in a different phase (such as solid, liquid, or gas) from the reactants. In a homogeneous reaction, the catalyst is in the same phase as the reactants. Most examples of heterogeneous catalysis go through the same stages (see Table 1).

Table 1

Stage	Description
1	One or more of the reactants are absorbed onto the surface of the catalyst.
2	There is some sort of interaction between the surface of the catalyst and the reactant molecules, which makes them more reactive.
3	The reaction happens.
4	The product molecules are desorbed, meaning that the product molecules break away.

Students did experiments to convert propanol to propene using alumina beads, and then to convert propene to propanol using a palladium catalyst.

Experiment 1

Two glass syringes were connected to an alumina-bead catalyst tube (see Figure 1). The 1 mL syringe was filled with 1 mL of propanol. Next, the apparatus was held above a burner's flame and the alumina-bead catalyst tube was gently heated while the liquid propanol was slowly introduced into the catalyst tube. The liquid flowed through the tube until it hit the hot region. Then it vaporized, reacted with the catalyst, and exited the catalyst tube as gaseous propene into the 60-mL receiver syringe. The procedure was repeated with various amounts of propanol and alumina beads and the amount of gaseous propene collected was recorded (see Table 2).

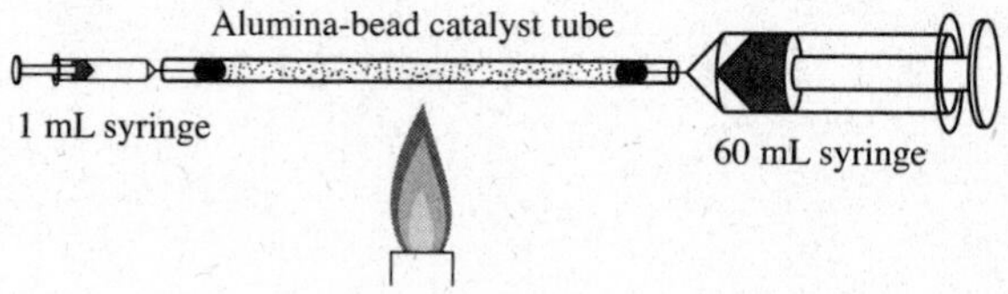

Figure 1

Table 2

Trial	Volume of Propanol (mL)	Volume of Alumina Beads (g)	Volume of Propene (mL)
1	1	1.75	58
2	1	1	49
3	0.5	1.75	28
4	0.75	1.75	45

Experiment 2

A reactant syringe was filled with equal volumes of hydrogen and propene. The reactant syringe and receiver syringe were connected to the catalyst tube filled with solid palladium as shown in Figure 2. Then the hydrogen-propene mixture was slowly passed over the catalyst, the reaction occurred, and the propane was collected in the receiver syringe. The procedure was repeated several times, varying the amount of time the reactant was passed over the catalyst. The results are shown in Table 3.

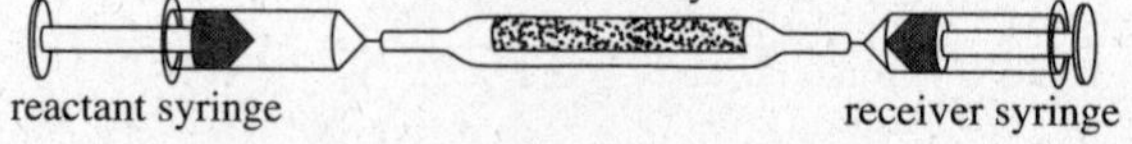

Figure 2

4 ○ ○ ○ ○ ○ ○ ○ ○ 4

Table 3

Trial	Volume of Hydrogen (mL)	Volume of Propene (mL)	Time Reactant Passed Over Catalyst(s)	Volume of Propane in Receiver Syringe (mL)
1	30	30	60	56
2	30	30	45	52
3	30	30	30	49
4	30	30	15	0

1. In Experiment 2, as the amount of time the reactant was passed over the catalyst decreased, the volume of propane created:

   A. increased only.
   B. decreased only.
   C. increased and then remained constant.
   D. decreased and then remained constant.

2. Which is the most likely explanation for why 0 mL of propane was produced in Trial 4 of Experiment 2?

   F. There was not enough volume of hydrogen and propene to create a reaction.
   G. Fifteen seconds was too long a time for the reactant to pass over the catalyst.
   H. There was not enough volume of palladium in the catalyst tube to create a reaction and produce propane.
   J. The reactant was not allowed enough time to interact with the catalyst; therefore no reaction occurred and no propane was produced.

3. What type of catalyst was used in Experiment 1?

   A. It cannot be determined from the information given.
   B. A liquid catalyst
   C. A heterogeneous catalyst
   D. A homogeneous catalyst

4. In Experiment 2, the hydrogen-propene mixture turns into propane at what stage of the catalysis?

   F. Stage 1
   G. Stage 2
   H. Stage 3
   J. Stage 4

5. Based on the data in Table 2, which two trials illustrate the effect that varying the volume of the catalyst has on the volume of propene produced?

   A. Trials 1 and 2
   B. Trials 1 and 3
   C. Trials 3 and 4
   D. Trials 2 and 4

6. Which of the following best describes what occurred to the plunger of the 60-mL syringe during Experiment 1? When propanol was injected into the catalyst tube, the distance between the end of the plunger and the syringe tip:

   F. decreased slowly over 30 seconds.
   G. increased immediately, and then decreased as the reaction occurred.
   H. remained in place until the reaction occurred, and then decreased.
   J. remained in place until the reaction occurred, and then increased.

Passage II

Table 1 lists two genes found in *Sesamum indicum* (sesame), the possible alleles of each gene, and the possible genotypes for each gene.

Table 1

Gene	Alleles	Genotypes
P	P, p	PP, Pp, pp
L	L, l	LL, Ll, ll

Table 2 lists various sesame genotypes and the phenotype associated with each genotype. Each gene affects only one of the phenotype traits listed.

Table 2

Genotype	Phenotype	
	Pod Number	Leaf Texture
PPLL	1	normal
PpLL	1	normal
ppLL	3	normal
ppLl	3	normal
PpLl	1	normal
PPLl	1	normal
PPll	1	wrinkled
Ppll	1	wrinkled
ppll	3	wrinkled

Table 3 lists four sesame plant crosses, the genotypes of the parents, and the percent of offspring that had each phenotype for the traits listed in Table 2. In each cross, each parent donated one allele to each offspring at each gene.

Table 3

Cross	Genotype of:		Offspring Phenotype	
	Female parent	Male parent	Pod number	Leaf texture
1	PpLL	ppll	50% 1 pod	50% normal
2	PpLl	Ppll	75% 1 pod	50% wrinkled
3	ppLl	ppLl	100% 3 pods	75% normal
4	PPLL	PPLL	100% 1 pod	100% normal

4 ○ ○ ○ ○ ○ ○ ○ ○ 4

7. Based on Table 2, which of the 2 genes affects leaf texture?

A. P
B. L
C. Neither
D. Both

8. Based on Table 2, a sesame plant with 2 recessive alleles for each of the 2 genes will have which of the following phenotypes?

F. 1 pod and normal leaves
G. 3 pods and normal leaves
H. 3 pods and wrinkled leaves
J. 1 pod and wrinkled leaves

9. Based on the information provided, all of the offspring of Cross 3 had 3 pods because each received:

A. allele p from its female parent and allele p from its male parent.
B. allele L from its female parent and allele l from its male parent.
C. allele l from its female parent and allele L from its male parent.
D. allele P from its female parent and allele P from its male parent.

10. In Cross 3, what percent of the offspring had genotype pp?

F. 0%
G. 25%
H. 50%
J. 100%

11. Based on the information provided, a sesame plant with 3 pods and normal leaves could have which of the following genotypes?

A. PPll
B. PPLL
C. ppll
D. ppLl

GO ON TO THE NEXT PAGE.

Passage III

To determine the effect of ambient ultraviolet radiation (UVR) on the *chlorophyll* production, growth rate, and cell death of Antarctic *phytoplankton*, scientists conducted experiments on phytoplankton communities exposed to natural levels of solar radiation.

Experiments were conducted during three different periods of time. Experiment 1 took place February 1–6, Experiment 2 February 7–12, and Experiment 3 February 13–20. A meteorological station automatically recorded solar radiation for the duration of the study (see Figure 1).

The experiments involved sampling surface seawater, placing them in bottles submersed in incubators, and exposing them to either natural solar radiation (UVR) or radiation filtered to exclude ultraviolet radiation (PAR).

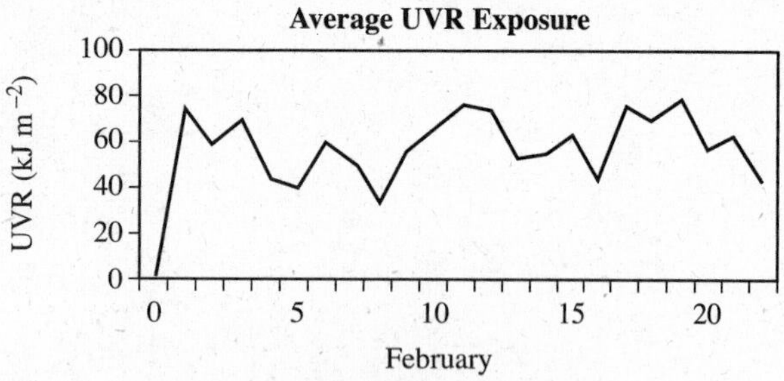

Figure 1

Every two days, duplicate samples were taken from each location to determine chlorophyll amounts and phytoplankton cell death (see Table 1 and Figure 2). Net population growth rates were calculated for *diatoms* and *flagellates* from the cell abundances obtained at the beginning and end of the experiments (see Figure 3).

Table 1

Amount of Chlorophyll per Experiment	Time (d)				
	0	2	4	6	8
1-UVR	0.8	1	1.3	1.4	–
1-PAR	0.8	1.2	1.5	17	–
2-UVR	0.7	0.9	1	1.2	–
2-PAR	0.7	1	4	15	–
3-UVR	0.2	1	1.3	2	4
3-PAR	0.2	1	3	10	24

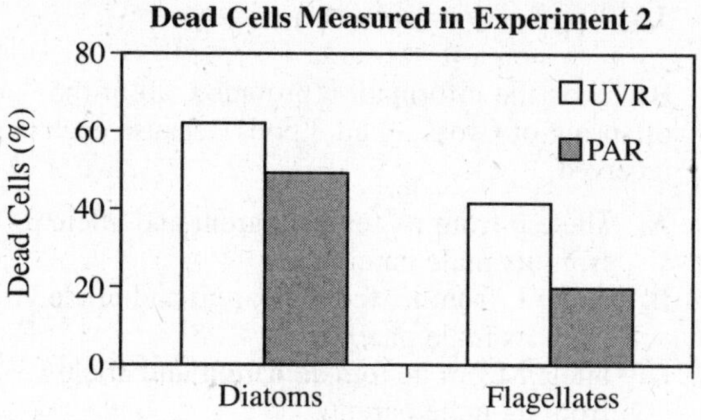

Figure 2

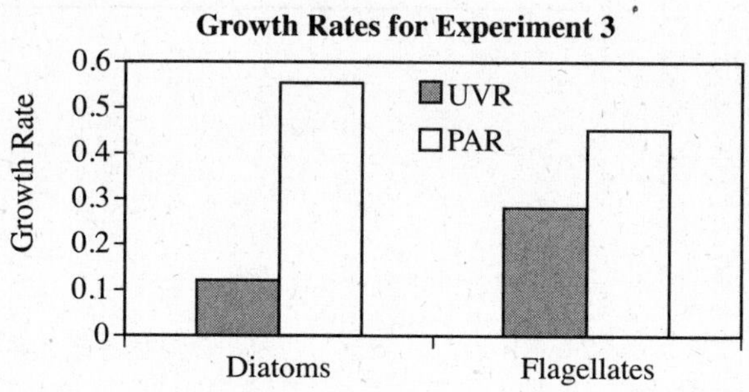

Figure 3

4 ○ ○ ○ ○ ○ ○ ○ ○ 4

12. Based on the data in Table 1, how much chlorophyll was measured in Experiment 3 for the sample exposed to UVR after 4 days?

F. 1
G. 1.3
H. 3
J. 4

13. Based on the information presented in Table 1, UVR seems to have what effect on the amount of chlorophyll measured?

A. UVR seems to inhibit the production of chlorophyll.
B. UVR seems to stimulate the production of chlorophyll.
C. UVR seems to have no effect on the production of chlorophyll.
D. It cannot be determined what the effect of UVR is on chlorophyll.

14. According to the data shown in Figure 3, which cells showed the least growth in Experiment 3?

F. Diatoms shielded from UVR
G. Diatoms exposed to UVR
H. Flagellates shielded from UVR
J. Flagellates exposed to UVR

15. Based on the information presented in Table 1, if Experiment 1 had been continued for another 2 days, the amount of chlorophyll measured in the samples that were not exposed to UVR would most likely be closest to what amount?

A. 0
B. 17
C. 3
D. 36

16. Based on the results displayed in Figure 2, it can be assumed that ultraviolet radiation (UVR) has what effect on the life of the diatoms and flagellates found in phytoplankton?

F. The presence of UVR leads to fewer dead diatoms and more dead flagellates.
G. The presence of UVR leads to more dead diatoms and fewer dead flagellates.
H. The presence of UVR leads to fewer dead cells for both diatoms and flagellates.
J. The presence of UVR leads to more dead cells for both diatoms and flagellates.

Passage IV

Ecological *indicators* are used to assess the condition of the environment, to provide early warning signals of changes in the environment, or to diagnose the cause of environmental problems. Some important criteria for selecting an indicator include:

1. The indicator should provide an accurate picture of what it is supposed to indicate, such as "ecosystem health."
2. The indicator should respond quickly to environmental changes.
3. The indicator should be easy to monitor.
4. The responses of the indicator in one or a few locations should indicate the state of the ecosystem in a larger area.

It has been suggested that seabirds are useful indicators. Two researchers discuss the effectiveness of using seabirds as indicators.

Researcher 1

Seabirds are valuable indicators because they are top predators in their ecosystem. Seabird populations and reproduction rates are regulated by prey abundance, and will therefore reflect environmentally induced changes in prey availability. The effects of reductions in prey resources, such as declining numbers of seabirds, are usually very rapid, due to the short food chain, which is another advantage.

A few species of small fishes are important species of the ecosystem, having a major effect on the ecosystem as a whole. Seabirds that eat mainly these key fish are good indicators of the ecosystem in general.

Additional demographic parameters that can easily be monitored in seabirds are population size, duration of foraging trips, and changes in body mass and offspring growth rate, all of which are useful environmental monitors.

Overall, seabirds are a cost-effective, useful, and meaningful indicator of environmental changes in ocean ecosystems.

Researcher 2

There are several reasons why seabirds may not be suitable as indicators of the impacts of environmental changes. First of all, not all marine ecosystems follow a top-down food chain. Some marine food webs are dynamic and can alternate between bottom-up and top-down. In addition, change in seabird numbers due to food scarcity usually has a lag of several months or even years. Because of this seabirds are not suitable as indicators of the food supply in all ecosystems.

In general, the effect of environmental change on seabird populations may take many years to become apparent. Its effect is complex and involves many physical and biological processes. This is a severe drawback to using seabirds as indicators. Another drawback is the handling effect. It is not fully understood what effect handling seabirds has on them. There is some evidence that bands placed on penguins to track them can reduce both breeding success and survival rates. With seabirds that are tagged and handled, it is difficult to be sure that observed effects are actually due to changes in the environment and not other factors.

The effect of environmental changes on seabirds is complex and it is not clear what the best way to monitor seabirds is. Therefore, seabirds are not a good choice for indicators.

17. Based on Researcher 1's discussion, demographic factors that can be easily monitored in seabirds include all of the following EXCEPT:

    A. population size.
    B. changes in offspring growth rate.
    C. mortality rates.
    D. length of foraging trips.

18. Sardines are plentiful in Chiriqui Bay, and their presence affects the entire ecosystem of the bay. Kingfisher birds eat mostly sardines and because their numbers are declining, scientists are concerned about the environmental health of Chiriqui Bay. Is this concern consistent with the viewpoint of Researcher 1?

    F. No, because Researcher 1 states that changes in the food chain are not adequate indicators of the environmental health of a body of water.
    G. No, because Researcher 1 states that only changes in body mass and offspring growth rate are valuable indicators of environmental changes.
    H. Yes, because Researcher 1 states that the effect of environmental changes on seabirds will be slow due to the short food chain in a marine ecosystem.
    J. Yes, because Researcher 1 states that seabirds that consume key fish in an ecosystem are valuable indicators of the ecosystem in general.

19. Which researcher believes that handling seabirds may affect the validity of the results gathered by monitoring them?

    A. Researcher 1, because that researcher states that changes in prey resources are very quick, and therefore results gathered will be valid.
    B. Researcher 1, because that researcher states that overall, seabirds are a useful indicator of environmental changes.
    C. Researcher 2, because that researcher states that placing bands on penguins has been shown to reduce their survival rates.
    D. Researcher 2, because that researcher states that it is clear that handling seabirds will always reduce their breeding rates.

20. A study found that within two months of an oil spill in a bay, there was a drastic reduction in the number of small forage fish found in the water, and that the number of seabirds in the area was drastically reduced as well. Which researcher would most likely use this study to support his or her viewpoint?

    F. Researcher 1, because it would demonstrate how quickly environmental changes impact prey resources and seabird behavior.
    G. Researcher 1, because it would demonstrate how important seabirds are for the overall ecosystem.
    H. Researcher 2, because it would demonstrate how quickly environmental changes impact prey resources and seabird behavior.
    J. Researcher 2, because it would demonstrate how important seabirds are for the overall ecosystem.

21. Based on Researcher 2's discussion, seabirds would not be effective indicators because they do not meet which criteria of a good indicator?

    A. Point 1 only
    B. Points 1 and 2 only
    C. Points 1, 2, and 3 only
    D. Points 2 and 3 only

4 ◯ ◯ ◯ ◯ ◯ ◯ ◯ ◯ 4

22. Which of the following graphs is most consistent with Researcher 1's view on the relationship between prey abundance and seabird population?

F.

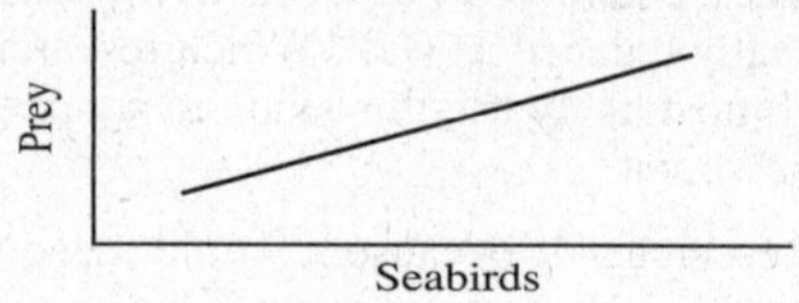

G.

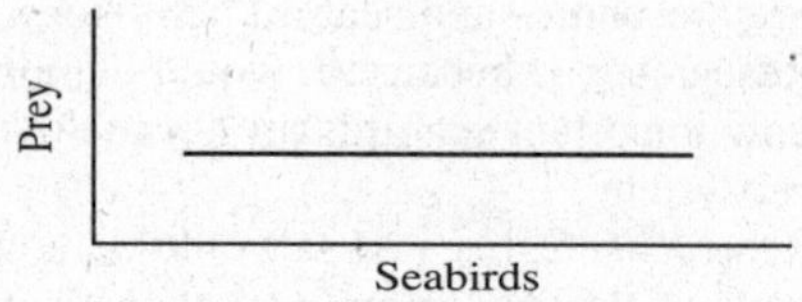

H.

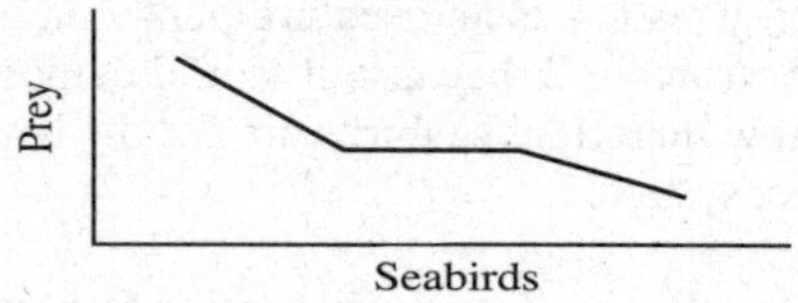

J.

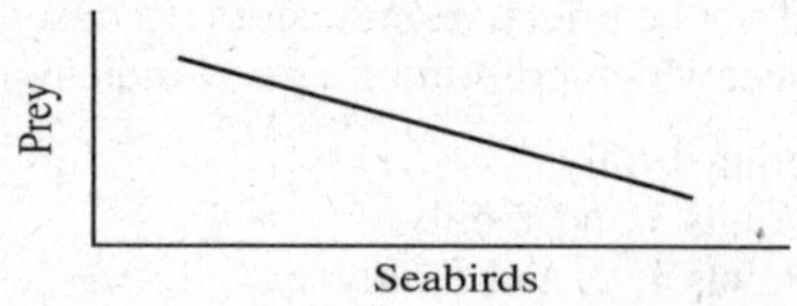

23. Researcher 2 cites all of the following as reasons why seabirds may not be suitable as indicators EXCEPT:

A. the impact of food scarcity on seabird numbers may not be apparent for several months or years.
B. it is not known how handling seabirds might impact them.
C. it is expensive to use seabirds as indicators.
D. it is uncertain how to best monitor seabirds.

Passage V

Scientists used gas chromatography to analyze benzene concentrations in fuel vapors. The results of the analysis are displayed in Table 1.

Samples from four different brands of fuel were collected, with each brand offering both leaded and unleaded versions of fuel. A portion of each sample was analyzed for benzene concentration in the liquid, while the rest of the sample was placed in a vial and prepared for vapor analysis. Each vial was put into an oven, heated, and the gas chromatograph detected the concentrations of benzene in the vapor. Figure 1 displays the oven temperature during the experiment.

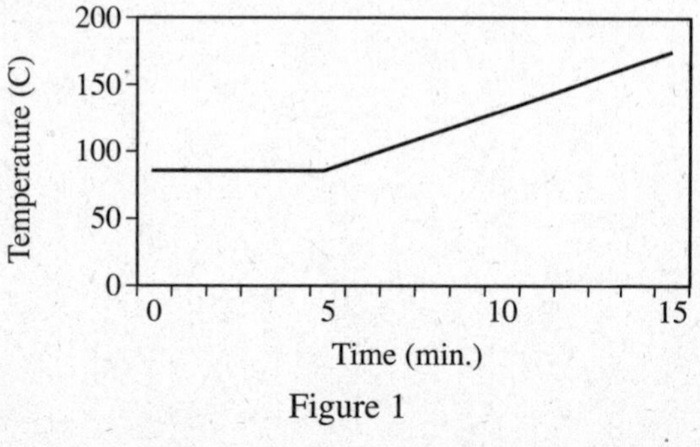

Figure 1

Table 1

Brand	Liquid (mg/l)	Vapor (mg/l)
A (leaded)	191	431
A (unleaded)	198	334
B (leaded)	176	447
B (unleaded)	271	414
C (leaded)	245	500
C (unleaded)	222	488
D (leaded)	197	513
D (unleaded)	264	350

A *gasohol* is a fuel blended with certain alcohols such as ethanol or methanol. Two of the fuels tested in this experiment (brands C and D) were gasohols. Figure 2 shows the average concentrations of benzene found in the liquid and vapor form of the leaded and unleaded fuels tested. Figure 3 compares the average concentrations of benzene found in gasohols and regular unleaded fuels.

4 ○ ○ ○ ○ ○ ○ ○ ○ 4

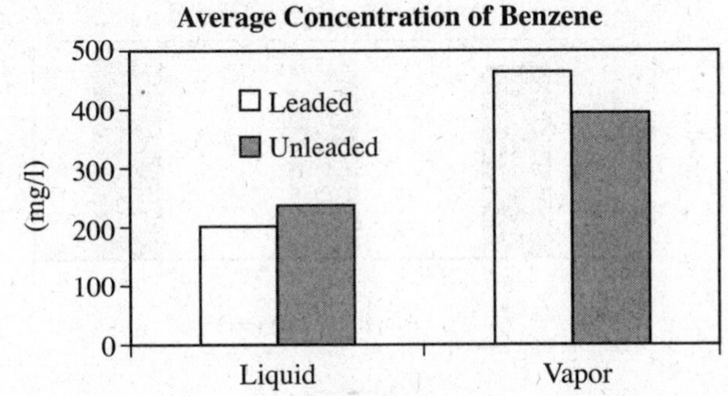

Figure 2

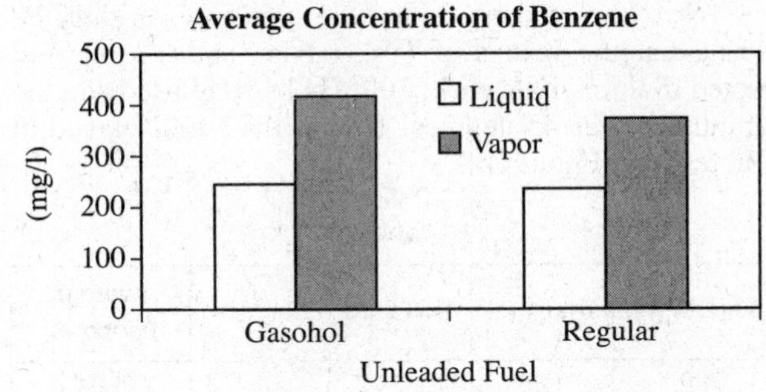

Figure 3

24. According to Figure 2, the average concentration of benzene found in the liquid form of leaded fuel was approximately:

F. 200 mg/l.
G. 240 mg/l.
H. 480 mg/l.
J. 400 mg/l.

25. Based on Figure 2, which type of fuel tested was found to contain the highest average concentration of benzene?

A. Liquid unleaded
B. Liquid leaded
C. Vapor leaded
D. Vapor unleaded

26. Suppose that during the experiment the samples of fuel had been kept in the oven for 20 minutes. Based on Figure 1, the temperature in the oven after 20 minutes would most likely have been:

F. less than 100°C.
G. between 100°C and 150°C.
H. between 150°C and 200°C.
J. greater than 200°C.

27. A scientist claimed that, in liquid form, a leaded fuel would emit more benzene than an unleaded fuel. Does the data in Table 1 support this claim?

A. Yes. For all fuel brands tested, the benzene levels were higher in the leaded fuel than in the unleaded fuel.
B. Yes. For all fuels tested, the amount of benzene found in the vapor form was higher than that found in the liquid form.
C. No. The amount of benzene found in the leaded fuel was only higher than the amount found in the unleaded fuel for one brand tested.
D. No. Only nongasohols emit more benzene in the leaded version of the fuel.

28. According to Figure 3, how did vaporizing the gasohol fuels affect the average concentration of benzene found in the fuel? In the gasohol fuels, the average concentration of benzene found in the liquid form of the gas was about:

F. two times the average concentration found in the vapor form.
G. one-half the average concentration found in the vapor form.
H. one-quarter the average concentration found in the vapor form.
J. the same as the average concentration found in the vapor form.

Passage VI

Students conducted experiments to determine what factors affect the *period* of a *pendulum.* A pendulum is a swinging weight, or bob, attached to a string (see Figure 1). When released from an angle, a pendulum will move back and forth. One complete back-and-forth movement is called a *period.*

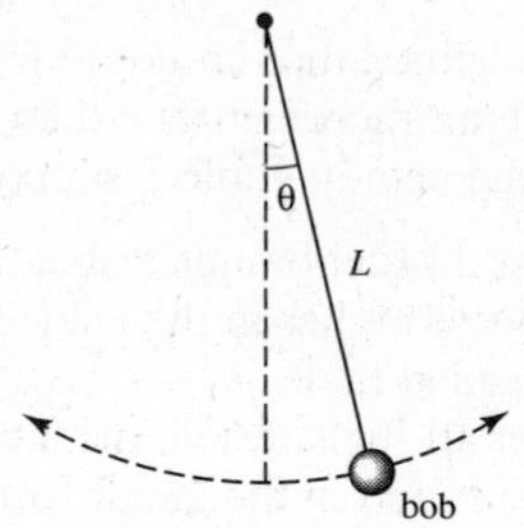

Figure 1

Three variables may affect the period of a pendulum: swing amplitude, measured as the angle at which the bob is released; the length of the string; and the mass of the bob. Students created pendulums by attaching a string to the ceiling and then tying a bob onto the other end of the string. They conducted three experiments. In each experiment all variables except the one tested were kept constant.

Experiment 1

In this experiment students varied the mass of the bob. Bobs of 20g, 100g, and 200g were tested for three trials each. The string length was 1m and the amplitude was 45 degrees. The results are shown in Table 1.

Table 1

Mass (g)	Trial 1 (s)	Trial 2 (s)	Trial 3 (s)	Average Period (s)
20	1.72	1.81	1.84	1.79
100	1.78	1.82	1.88	1.83
200	1.9	1.85	1.91	1.89

Experiment 2

The second variable tested was amplitude. Bobs were dropped from 15-, 45-, and 75-degree angles for three trials each. The string length was 1 m and the bobs used were 100 g. Figure 2 displays the average results.

Amplitude vs. Average Period

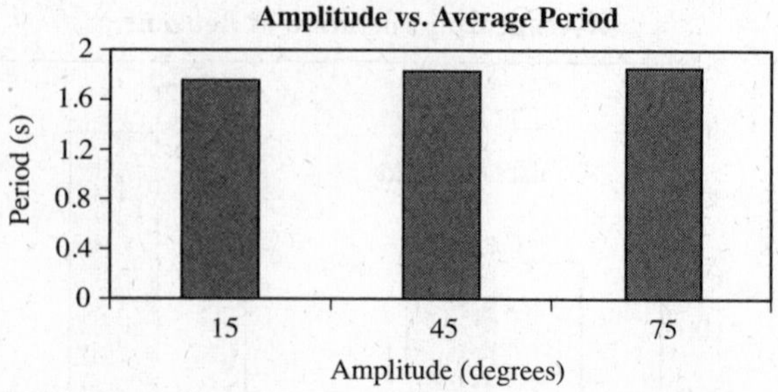

Figure 2

Experiment 3

Next the students tested the effect of varying the string length. Strings of 1 m, 0.6 m, and 0.3 m were tested in three trials each; 100 g bobs were used and the amplitude was 45 degrees. The results are displayed in Table 2 and Figure 3.

Table 2

Length (m)	Trial 1 (s)	Trial 2 (s)	Trial 3 (s)	Average Period (s)
1	1.85	1.84	1.84	1.84
0.6	1.44	1.44	1.47	1.45
0.3	0.97	1.06	1.06	1.03

Length vs. Average Period

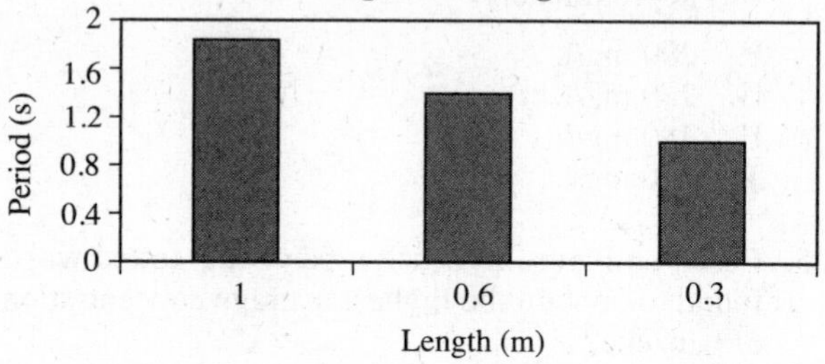

Figure 3

29. Based on the results of Experiment 1, the average period for a bob of 100 g was:

A. 1.79 s.
B. 1.83 s.
C. 1.89 s.
D. 1.91 s.

30. If an additional trial had been conducted in Experiment 3 with the length of the string being 0.8 m, the average period would most likely have been:

F. between 1.03–1.45
G. between 1.45–1.84
H. less than 1.45
J. greater than 1.84

31. For each trial in Experiment 1, as the mass of the bob increased, the time of the period:

A. stayed the same.
B. increased.
C. decreased.
D. increased and then decreased.

32. Based on the information presented in Figure 2, which of the following pendulums would have the longest average period? Assume that the string length and bob weight are equal.

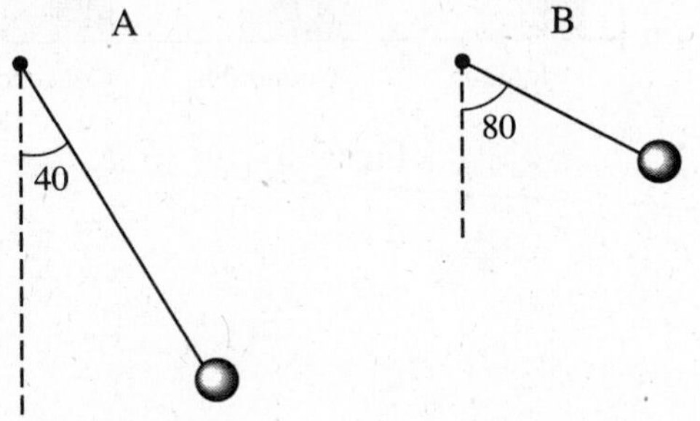

F. Pendulum A
G. Pendulum B
H. The average period would be about the same.
J. It is impossible to determine from the information given.

33. In Experiment 3, Trial 2, how long did it take the pendulum with the string length of 0.6 m to complete one back-and-forth movement?

A. 1.06 s
B. 1.44 s
C. 1.47 s
D. 1.84 s

34. Which of the following variables was NOT tested during the experiments conducted by the students?

F. Mass of the bob
G. Length of string
H. Size of bob
J. Swing amplitude

GO ON TO THE NEXT PAGE.

Passage VII

Scientists conducted a series of experiments to determine the effect of changes in temperature on the intertidal rocky shore crab, *Petrolisthes granulsus* (*P. granulosus*). Several fitness-related traits, such as body size and reproductive capacity in *P. granulosus* individuals from three sites were compared after the crabs were exposed to various temperatures. In addition, metabolic rate experiments were conducted to determine the energetic cost associated with crab exposure to high temperatures.

Table 1 displays the temperatures (°C) used in the experiments. Thermal category TC1 refers to the maximum temperature registered at each site, while TC2 refers to the average of maximum temperatures recorded every day. The Control thermal category is defined as the average temperature experienced by the crabs during the acclimation period.

Table 1

Thermal Category	Site		
	Iquique	Coquimbo	Concepcion
TC1	26	22	19
TC2	22	20	17
Control	16	16	16

Figure 1 displays the average size (cephalothorax length) of *P. granulosus* in the 3 populations, while Figure 2 displays the average egg volume in the 3 populations.

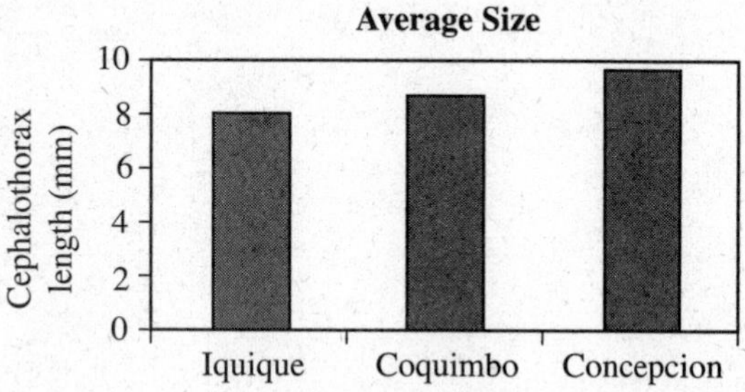

Figure 1

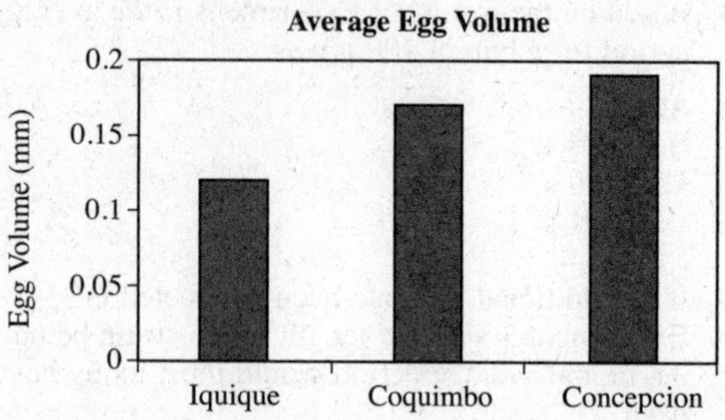

Figure 2

Figure 3 shows the average standard metabolic rates (SMR) of male crabs from the 3 populations exposed to 3 thermal categories.

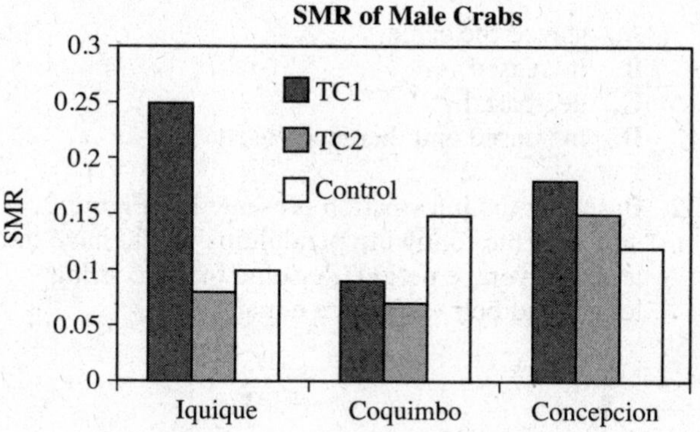

Figure 3

4 ○ ○ ○ ○ ○ ○ ○ ○ 4

35. According to Table 1, crabs from which site were exposed to the highest temperatures during the experiments?

    A. Iquique
    B. Coquimbo
    C. Concepcion
    D. Crabs at all of the locations were exposed to the same maximum temperatures.

36. Based on the information in Figure 2, the average eggs of crabs from the Coquimbo site were found to be closest to which size?

    F. 0.1 mm
    G. 0.17 mm
    H. 0.2 mm
    J. 0.25 mm

37. According to Figure 3, adult male crabs from which category were found to have the highest average standard metabolic rates?

    A. TC1 from Concepcion
    B. Control from Coquimbo
    C. TC1 from Iquique
    D. TC2 from Concepcion

38. Based on the information provided, which of the following best describes the effect that average maximum temperature has on the average size of the crabs?

    F. As the average maximum temperature increased, the average size of the crabs stayed the same.
    G. As the average maximum temperature increased, the average size of the crabs increased.
    H. As the average maximum temperature decreased, the average size of the crabs decreased.
    J. As the average maximum temperature decreased, the average size of the crabs increased.

39. Suppose the scientists had measured the average egg volume of crabs in the control groups. Based on the information in Table 1 and Figure 2, the average egg volume of crabs at the Concepcion site would have been closest to:

    A. 0.05 mm.
    B. 0.1 mm.
    C. 0.2 mm.
    D. 0.3 mm.

40. The scientists started this experiment with the theory that crabs exposed to higher temperatures would develop higher standard metabolic rates. Do the results of the experiment support this theory?

    F. Yes. The crabs at Iquique in the thermal category TC2 were exposed to the highest temperatures and were found to have the highest SMR.
    G. Yes. At all locations the crabs from thermal category TC1 were found to have the highest SMR.
    H. No. At all locations the crabs from thermal category TC1 were found to have the lowest SMR.
    J. No. The results were mixed. At two locations the crabs from thermal category TC1 were found to have the highest SMR, but at one location the crabs from the control group had the highest SMR.

STOP

If there is still time remaining, check your answers to this section.

WRITING PROMPT

Directions: This is a test of your writing skills. You will have thirty (30) minutes to write an essay in English. Before you begin planning and writing your essay, read the writing prompt below carefully to understand exactly what you are being asked to do. Your essay will be evaluated on the evidence it provides of your ability to express judgments by taking a position on the issue in the writing prompt; to maintain a focus on the topic throughout the essay; to develop a position by using logical reasoning and by supporting your ideas; to organize ideas in a logical way; and to use language clearly and effectively according to the conventions of standard written English.

You may use the unlined page to plan your essay. This page will not be scored. You must write your essay in pencil on the lined pages provided. Your writing on those lined pages will be scored. You may not need all the pages, but to ensure you have enough room to finish, do NOT skip lines. You may write corrections or additions neatly between the lines of your essay, but do NOT write in the margins of the lined pages. Illegible essays cannot be scored, so you must write (or print) clearly.

If you finish before time is called, you may review your work. Lay your pencil down immediately when time is called.

Many of the students who participate in high school extracurricular activities do not achieve good grades. Some educators believe that students should be held to a minimum grade standard in order to take part in these activities. Others believe this would be unfair and punish students who work hard but cannot achieve good grades.

In your essay, take a position on this question. You may write about either one of the two points of view given, or you may present a different point of view on this question. Use specific reasons and examples to support your position.

Use this page to *plan* your essay.

Begin WRITING TEST here.

If you need more space, continue on the next page.

WRITING TEST

Answer Key
PRACTICE TEST 6

English Test

1. C	16. J	31. B	46. J	61. A
2. J	17. D	32. J	47. C	62. G
3. B	18. G	33. D	48. F	63. A
4. F	19. C	34. H	49. B	64. J
5. B	20. F	35. A	50. H	65. B
6. J	21. A	36. J	51. A	66. H
7. A	22. J	37. D	52. J	67. B
8. H	23. A	38. G	53. A	68. J
9. D	24. J	39. C	54. G	69. A
10. J	25. C	40. H	55. D	70. H
11. B	26. H	41. B	56. J	71. B
12. F	27. B	42. F	57. C	72. G
13. C	28. J	43. A	58. G	73. C
14. H	29. A	44. J	59. C	74. F
15. D	30. F	45. A	60. J	75. D

Math Test

1. D	13. A	25. D	37. D	49. A
2. K	14. K	26. J	38. G	50. F
3. D	15. C	27. D	39. C	51. D
4. J	16. K	28. F	40. J	52. K
5. C	17. D	29. C	41. B	53. B
6. J	18. H	30. G	42. G	54. H
7. B	19. B	31. C	43. E	55. C
8. F	20. H	32. H	44. H	56. K
9. E	21. A	33. D	45. A	57. E
10. H	22. J	34. J	46. K	58. K
11. A	23. B	35. D	47. A	59. E
12. G	24. J	36. H	48. J	60. G

Answer Key

PRACTICE TEST 6

Reading Test

1. B	9. A	17. D	25. C	33. A
2. F	10. G	18. G	26. G	34. G
3. C	11. D	19. C	27. D	35. A
4. J	12. G	20. J	28. G	36. J
5. A	13. C	21. D	29. C	37. B
6. G	14. G	22. F	30. J	38. H
7. D	15. A	23. A	31. C	39. C
8. H	16. H	24. H	32. J	40. J

Science Test

1. B	9. A	17. C	25. C	33. B
2. J	10. J	18. J	26. J	34. H
3. C	11. D	19. C	27. C	35. A
4. H	12. G	20. F	28. G	36. G
5. A	13. A	21. C	29. B	37. C
6. J	14. G	22. F	30. G	38. J
7. B	15. D	23. C	31. B	39. C
8. H	16. J	24. F	32. H	40. J

HOW TO SCORE YOUR PRACTICE TEST

Step 1: Add up the number correct for each section and write that number in the blank under the Raw Score column on the Score Conversion Table. (Your goal is to get more questions correct on each subsequent practice test.)

Step 2: Using the Score Conversion Chart, find your scale score for each section and write it down. Then add up all four sections and divide by 4 to find your overall composite score. (Composite scores are rounded up at .5 or higher.)

Score Conversion Table

Section	Raw Score	Scaled Score
English	(out of 75)	____ / 36
Math	(out of 60)	____ / 36
Reading	(out of 40)	____ / 36
Science	(out of 40)	____ / 36
		Add and divide by 4
Overall Composite =		____ / 36

Score Conversion Chart

	Number Correct				
ACT Score*	English Section	Mathematics Section	Reading Section	Science Section	ACT Score*
36	75	60	40	40	**36**
35	74	59	39	39	**35**
34	73	58	38	38	**34**
33	72	57	37	—	**33**
32	71	56	36	37	**32**
31	70	54–55	35	36	**31**
30	69	53	34	35	**30**
29	67–68	51–52	33	34	**29**
28	65–66	49–50	32	33	**28**
27	64	46–48	31	31–32	**27**
26	62–63	44–45	30	30	**26**
25	60–61	41–43	29	28–29	**25**
24	58–59	39–40	27–28	25–27	**24**
23	55–57	37–38	25–26	24	**23**
22	53–54	35–36	23–24	22–23	**22**
21	50–52	33–34	22	20–21	**21**
20	47–49	31–32	21	18–19	**20**
19	44–46	28–30	19–20	17	**19**
18	42–43	25–27	18	15–16	**18**
17	40–41	22–24	17	14	**17**

Continued

Score Conversion Chart *(Continued)*

ACT Score*	Number Correct: English Section	Mathematics Section	Reading Section	Science Section	ACT Score*
16	37–39	19–21	16	13	**16**
15	34–36	15–17	15	12	**15**
14	31–33	11–14	13–14	11	**14**
13	29–30	09–10	12	10	**13**
12	27–28	07–08	10–11	09	**12**
11	25–26	06	08–09	08	**11**
10	23–24	05	07	07	**10**
9	21–22	04	06	05–06	**9**
8	18–20	03	05	—	**8**
7	15–17	—	—	04	**7**
6	12–14	02	04	03	**6**
5	09–11	—	03	02	**5**
4	07–08	01	02	—	**4**
3	05–06	—	—	01	**3**
2	03–04	—	01	—	**2**
1	00–02	00	00	00	**1**

**These scores are based on student trials rather than national norms.*

SCORING YOUR ESSAY

As mentioned earlier in this text, two readers will evaluate your essay and each person will then assign it a score from 1 to 6. If, by chance, these two scorers disagree by more than 1 point, a third reader will step in and resolve the discrepancy. Performance on the essay will not affect your English, math, reading, science, or composite scores. You will receive two additional scores on your score sheet—a combined English/writing score (1–36) and a writing test subscore (1–12). Neither of these scores will affect your composite score!

The sample essay that follows reflects higher-level writing. It meets the criteria that ACT has put forth for essays that demonstrate effective writing skills.

- It takes a definite position.
- It addresses and expands on the counterargument.
- It has details that support the topic sentences and is well organized.
- It is not repetitive, and while there may be errors, they do not interfere with the competence of the essay.
- It is consistent and well balanced.
- The essay has a clear introduction and a conclusion that is not just a summary but ends with a significant thought.
- The vocabulary demonstrates good use of language and the sentence structure is varied.

Answer Explanations: English Test

1. **(C)** Preposition usage in English is largely idiomatic. The phrase is *think of* because that is simply what we say (*think about* would also be correct, but is not one of the choices). It is one of those things that you just have to know from reading a lot. (Preposition-choice questions are becoming more common on the ACT English, so you should make an effort to start.)
2. **(J)** The subject of the sentence is the plural *communities*, and the communities in question lived over 200 years ago, and so the main verb phrase is *had begun to feel*, the past perfect form of *begin* followed by the infinitive form of *feel*. This verb form may seem complicated, but it is the only one of the choices that is both plural and in any kind of past tense, so it is obviously correct even if you don't understand the past perfect.
3. **(B)** The prepositional phrase of *Romantic musicians* that follows signifies possession, which indicates that we need a noun phrase here. The correct answer is *stirring, urgent compositions*—a noun preceded by two adjectives.
4. **(F)** The main idea that the artists *created works that inspired* is interrupted by the descriptive phrase *emphasizing struggle, fear, and loneliness*, which is placed after *works* (the noun it describes). Although the underlined words may not look correct, they are in the context of the sentence as a whole. (The ACT English will often place underlines at the most confusing possible place in a sentence!)
5. **(B)** What is needed here is a transition phrase indicating that *despite* everything that was just said about music and painting, Romanticism's most famous legacy is literature. All of the choices communicate this in one way or another EXCEPT for *Meanwhile*, which means "at the same time, but elsewhere," and so is nonsense in context.
6. **(J)** The sentence means to imply an ongoing condition, and so the correct phrase is *what writers themselves are like*. In other words, what is true of all writers as a general rule.
7. **(A)** The information communicated in the phrase *brilliant, struggling commoner* is that Keats was born poor and had to pull himself up using only his talent, rather than any advantages of birth. This links him with the stereotype of the "starving artist."
8. **(H)** This sentence opens with a long dependent descriptive phrase, and the main independent clause begins with the words *the figure*. The dependent clause is about the defining characteristics of the Byronic hero, and so opens with the phrase *defined as*.
9. **(D)** The three popular fictional characters mentioned in the underlined portion are specific examples of modern Byronic heroes, and so if the underlined portion were deleted, the sentence would lose examples.
10. **(J)** It is necessary to read ahead in order to answer this question correctly. The sentences following the one with the underlined portion describe the effects that Romanticism had on the sciences, and so *The Romantic movement even had an influence on science* is the correct choice.
11. **(B)** The sentence means to set up a contrast: most artistic movements fade into history, but Romanticism is still famous. The way to do this is to start the first clause with *While* (effectively a synonym for *although*).
12. **(F)** The extra descriptive phrase modifying *most artistic movements* correctly begins with *becoming*.
13. **(C)** The sentence that mentions rock music, horror movies, and superheroes best demonstrates how *wide* Romanticism's influence has been, because it touches upon three different popular genres.
14. **(H)** This long paragraph discusses Romanticism's influence on science in the first part, and the general popular legacy of Romanticism in the second part. The most logical place to divide it would be at point C—after the part about science, but before the part about its legacy.
15. **(D)** The influence of "high culture" in general is not the issue here, but only the influence of Romanticism specifically. Furthermore, not all of the passage is about influence on popular culture—some of it concerns influence on science, or on subsequent genres of art.
16. **(J)** The participial form *deciding* is what we need here: I *have trouble deciding* between.... There is no rule to be memorized on this one—this is simply the answer that would sound right to someone who is familiar with English prose.
17. **(D)** In order for the portion of the sentence after the second dash to end with an acceptable "afterthought" phrase rather than an unacceptable comma error, the part after the final comma must not constitute an independent clause. All of the other choices would add a subject and verb to the final phrase, and so we must DELETE the underlined portion.
18. **(G)** The first part of this sentence, taking its cue from the end of the previous paragraph, is introducing some of the *important differences*. The only answer that makes this clear is choice G.

19. **(C)** Since the introductory modifying phrase *Even as a kid* refers to the author, a noun referring to the author—in this case, the pronoun *I*—must immediately follow the comma in order to avoid creating a misplaced modifier.

20. **(F)** This paragraph goes on to describe the ways that the museum feels different from the zoo. The transition phrase *on the other hand* signals this, and the comparison of the museum with a church is supported by the description in the subsequent sentence.

21. **(A)** The conjunction *and* introduces the second independent clause connecting two ideas.

22. **(J)** Respect, veneration, and awe are all synonyms for reverence. Grandeur is not a synonym so it is the least acceptable.

23. **(A)** No matter which verb you pick, the idea is that the animals have been acted upon by humans, rather than having performed the action themselves. Therefore, the "odd one out" is *animals have frozen* (because the animals did not freeze in those positions themselves), which does NOT successfully communicate this idea, and in fact contradicts it.

24. **(J)** The phrase *from each other* modifies *different*; the trips were *different from each other*.

25. **(C)** The presence of the dash later in the sentence indicates that the *which* clause should be set off with a pair of dashes. There is no reason why *rather than drive* would be set off with a single dash.

26. **(H)** Neither the passage in general nor this paragraph in particular is about trains. An additional sentence about trains (rather than about the zoo, museum, or the author's memories of his family) would constitute a distracting tangent.

27. **(B)** All we need here is the plural form *friends*. Nothing is possessed by the friends, and so no apostrophe is necessary anywhere.

28. **(J)** The author saying that he is *reassured and inspired* most effectively captures his *reverence* (spiritually profound respect) for the museum.

29. **(A)** In the preceding sentence (among other places in the essay as a whole), the author is using the kids' fascination at the zoo and museum as evidence that the human race is essentially good. In other words, seeing this gives him hope.

30. **(F)** Although the sentence is not strictly necessary in order for the reader to know what is going on, it is an eloquent characterization of the author's problem that is both emotionally affecting and highly relevant to the subject of the passage. The passage would suffer if it were deleted.

31. **(B)** This is the infamous prepositional phrase trick. The noun that governs the verb is the singular *one*, not the plural *sports*. The word *sports* is part of the prepositional phrase *of my favorite sports*, which must be "jumped" so that the main noun and verb of the clause agree. The tense differences between the choices are a red herring—the only issue is singular versus plural.

32. **(J)** The dash that appears earlier in the sentence is a clue that we are dealing with a "lift-out" clause (explaining what "*non-sport*" means) set off with a pair of dashes. A single independent clause exists around it.

33. **(D)** What we need here is just the regular plural form *courses*. No possession is going on, and so no apostrophe is necessary. (Although the sentence says that the courses *have* 18 holes, which is a possessive idea, grammatically speaking the noun *courses* does not possess "18 holes;" the verb *have* does—watch out for this trick!)

34. **(H)** The part of the sentence after the semicolon does not constitute an independent clause. All of the other choices are grammatically correct, but NOT this one.

35. **(A)** No comma is necessary anywhere in this region of the sentence. It is a single independent clause with normal word order.

36. **(J)** The history of Frisbees would be an irrelevant distraction at this point, since the sport being discussed is not even played with Frisbees. All that is necessary is to point out that disc-golf discs are not Frisbees and move on.

37. **(D)** This is the only choice that results in a complete correct sentence that makes sense. It presents a dependent clause followed by a comma and an independent clause.

38. **(G)** This part of the sentence involves a limiting (or "essential") clause followed by a verb being performed by the people in that clause. No comma is necessary at any point. Although limiting and nonlimiting clauses about animals or things can be distinguished by the use of *that* (with no comma) versus *which* (with a comma), when the clause is about people you use *who* in either case, with the only difference being the absence or presence of a comma.

39. **(C)** The infinitive form is necessary here. The players are *good enough to make* the shots.

40. **(H)** The sentence that goes here needs to transition between talking about world-class players (like in the sentence before it) and talking about amateurs who play for fun (like in the sentence after it). Only choice H does so—the other three are all still about the pros.

41. **(B)** Due to the rule of parallel phrasing, we need a double *when* here: the game is more about being surprised *when* you make a good shot than embarrassed *when* you make a bad one.

42. **(F)** Of the choices, only this sentence provides actual statistics to indicate how popular disc golf has gotten in a specific amount of time.

43. **(A)** Three of the choices mean the same as inform: persuade does not. An Internet search will not persuade you about courses in your area.

44. **(J)** As the rest of the sentence indicates, the reader is being addressed: if *you're someone who thought you'd never be good at sports, what are you waiting for?*

45. **(A)** Paragraph 2 is the only paragraph that discusses the rules of disc golf, and since this sentence concerns a rule, that would be the logical place to add it.

46. **(J)** The *United States* is a place, so we need the relative pronoun *where*, and *comedians* is a noun, so it needs to be modified with the adjective *political*.

47. **(C)** What we need here is the plural form *politicians*. Nothing is being possessed, and so no apostrophe is necessary. The addition of *our* makes no difference one way or the other.

48. **(F)** The nouns being used as adjectives here, *comedian* and *film actor*, do not specify Gnarr's identity by themselves (there are lots of comedians and film actors). Because of this, the name "Jon Gnarr" could not be lifted out of the sentence, and so it is not set off with commas.

49. **(B)** The phrase *a severe banking collapse* is the only one of the choices that is neither ambiguous nor redundant.

50. **(H)** A past tense verb followed by another in the infinitive form is needed here: Gnarr *began to staff* the party. The addition of *actually* makes no difference one way or the other (it breaks a very old-fashioned rule about not "splitting" infinitives, but the other choices are all wrong for much more important reasons).

51. **(A)** This choice correctly presents an "afterthought" clause specifying Björk's identity preceded by a comma.

52. **(J)** The city of Reykjavik is *home to over a third* of Iceland's population (i.e., over one-third of Icelanders live there).

53. **(A)** What's needed here is a term indicating that Gnarr's platform reminded people about serious issues even though it was funny. All of the other choices accomplish this, but NOT *recommended*. Gnarr's platform did not *recommend* issues to people.

54. **(G)** Without this additional information, readers would not know that there are not normally polar bears in Iceland, or why their presence there now is a bad sign.

55. **(D)** The sentence is complete and clear if it ends with a period after the word *on*. All of the other choices are redundant.

56. **(J)** Since the sentence begins *This would be an impressive feat*, it logically needs to come after a reference to something that would be an impressive feat. Sentence 2 closes by mentioning that Gnarr has a chance to become the first mayor of Reykjavik this century to serve a full term—this is the only prospective "impressive feat" mentioned in the paragraph, so the sentence should be inserted after sentence 2.

57. **(C)** The paragraph goes on to discuss a few politically progressive landmarks in Icelandic history, and this sentence is the only one of the choices that introduces this theme ("ahead of the curve in political matters").

58. **(G)** What we need here is the possessive pronoun *their*. The people of Iceland elected a comedian mayor—it was *their* election of a comedian mayor.

59. **(C)** Although it contains some tidbits about Icelandic history, the passage as a whole is overwhelmingly concerned with Jon Gnarr and the 2010 Reykjavik mayoral election.

60. **(J)** This is the infamous prepositional phrase trick with an added element of verb-tense trickiness. The noun phrase that governs the underlined verb is *bars and restaurants*—not *country*, which is part of the prepositional phrase *all over the country* (though *all* itself is not a preposition, *all over* is an expression that functions as a preposition, with a definition similar to *throughout*). So the verb must be plural. And since the verb must also express an ongoing action, the present perfect continuous form *have been attracting* is necessary (even if you don't understand that tense, you should still be able to eliminate the other choices).

61. **(A)** This choice presents a comprehensible sentence that correctly consists of an independent clause followed by a comma and a dependent *which* clause.

62. **(G)** The choice in which an adverb modifies an adjective, *less formal*, is grammatically correct and makes sense in context.

63. **(A)** This choice correctly presents a dependent clause followed by a comma and an independent clause. It is worth noting that all three of the wrong answers are wrong for the same reason—they involve a semicolon, a comma + conjunction, and a period, all of which must separate two independent clauses. The comma is the "odd one out."

64. **(J)** Only *Traditionally*, which expresses the idea that trivia questions have worked a certain way for a long time, makes sense in context.

65. **(B)** This choice correctly consists of a dependent introductory clause followed by a comma and an independent clause.

66. **(H)** To get the answer from a friend, you *had to have* a friend who knew the answer. If you cut away "extra" words to get down to the core idea, the right answer just clearly sounds right.

67. **(B)** This clause states that people phoning friends wasn't that much of a problem, and the previous clause explains why. Therefore, the conjunction *so* is correct. *You still had to have a friend who knew, so* (i.e., "and for this reason") *it wasn't that much of a problem.*

68. **(J)** This is the only one of the choices that is not horribly awkward. If cheating *is not adequately policed*, the game will be ruined.

69. **(A)** We need the adverb *then*, which refers to chronological order. In an *if* ... *then* construction, the *if* clause and the *then* clause are separated with a comma.

70. **(H)** The *honor system* means that authorities are trusting people to police themselves. Only choice H describes such a situation.

71. **(B)** This is the only one of the choices that is neither redundant nor insufficiently specific.

72. **(G)** This choice correctly separates two independent clauses with a semicolon.

73. **(C)** The second part of the sentence is also necessary in order for the problem to be clear: trivia concerns knowledge, and all knowledge can now be looked up on cell phones.

74. **(F)** This choice provides a smooth transition from the previous subject (phone cheating) into the new problem that the author brings up at the end.

75. **(D)** What the sentence means to express is the possibility that, in the future, the issue of people cheating at trivia will be moot, because no one will even be interested in it *in the first place*—that is, this problem will *precede* the other one.

Answer Explanations: Math Test

1. **(D)** The median is the middle number when arranged in order from least to greatest: $1\frac{1}{2}, 1\frac{1}{2}, 1\frac{3}{4}, 2\frac{1}{3}, 3$.
2. **(K)** $\left(-2x^5\right)^4 = (-2)^4 x^{20}$.
3. **(D)** $\frac{85+83+91+94+x}{5} = 90 \Rightarrow \frac{353+x}{5} = 90 \Rightarrow 353 + x = 450 \Rightarrow x = 97$.
4. **(J)** $2(-3)^2 - 5(-3)(2) + (2)^2 = 2(9) + 30 + 4 = 18 + 30 + 4 = 52$.
5. **(C)** $2x - 3 < 5x + 6 \Rightarrow -3x < 9 \Rightarrow x > -3$. You need to change the inequality sign when dividing by a negative number.
6. **(J)** $\overline{BE}$ is twice the length of $\overline{CD}$ since the 6 triangles are equilateral.

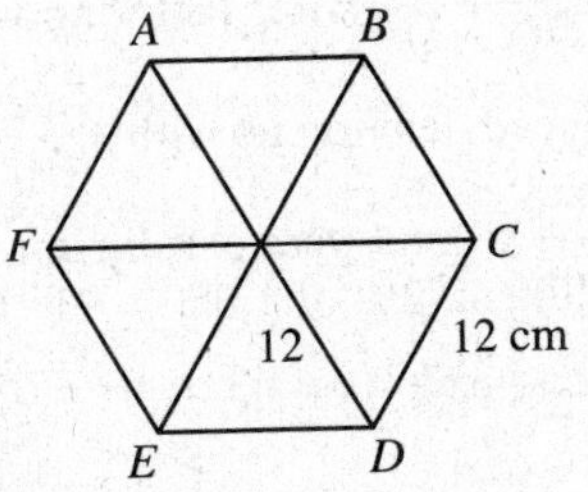

7. **(B)** This type of problem works well with proportions $\frac{18}{63} = \frac{45}{x} \Rightarrow 18x = 2835 \Rightarrow x = 157.5$.
8. **(F)** You need to distribute the "negative": $x^3 - 4x^2 + 5 - 3x^3 - 6x^2 + 9 = -2x^3 - 10x^2 + 14$.

9. **(E)** $\angle ACD$ is an exterior angle of $\triangle ABC$. Its measure equals the sum of the 2 remote interior angles: $55 + 69 = 125$ or $180 - 55 = 125$.

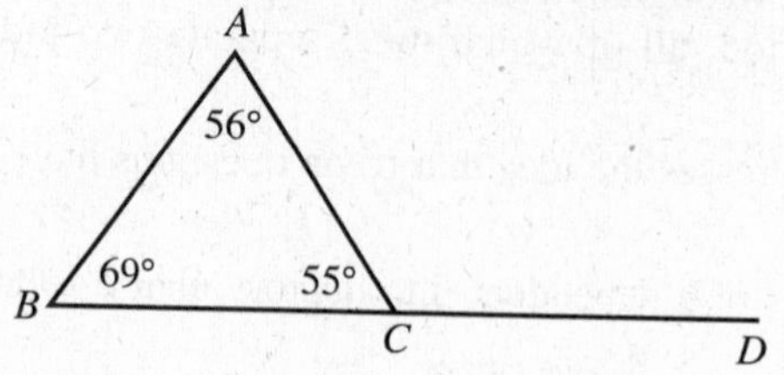

10. **(H)** The FOIL method applies to this equation: $(5x - 4y)(3x + y) = 15x^2 + 5xy - 12xy - 4y^2 = 15x^2 - 7xy - 4y^2$.

11. **(A)** $8x - 2(x - 5) = 2x - 20$; $8x - 2x + 10 = 2x - 20 \Rightarrow 4x = -30 \Rightarrow -7\frac{1}{2}$.

12. **(G)** When $-3 \le x \le 3$, then $x - 3 \le 0$ and $x + 3 \ge 0$. Therefore, $|x - 3| = -(x - 3)$ and $|x + 3| = x + 3 \Rightarrow |x - 3| + |3 + x| = -(x - 3) + 3 + x = 6$. You could also pick any number in the interval, for example, 0: $|0 - 3| + |3 + 0| = |-3| + |3| = 6$.

13. **(A)** The sum of the angles of a quadrilateral is $(4 - 2)180 = 360$. Therefore, $93 + 75 + 72 + x = 360$; $240 + x = 360$; $x = 120$.

14. **(K)** Each gallon of water weighs 8 pounds, so 5,000 gallons = 5,000(8) = 40,000 pounds.

15. **(C)** To find the price per pound, divide the price for 3 pounds by 3. To find how much cheaper, we subtract these values, $\frac{\$2.17}{3} - \frac{\$1.99}{3} = \$0.06$. Alternately, it costs \$0.18 more (2.17 – 1.99) for 3 pounds: $\frac{\$0.18}{3} = \$0.06$.

16. **(K)** In this problem there are different units of measure. It is imperative to have the same units. It is easier to change feet into inches since 1 foot = 12 inches. 12 feet = 12(12) = 144 inches, 16 feet = 12(16) = 192 inches. To cover the floor indicates area. Area of room = 144(192) = 27,648 square inches. Area of tile = 8(8) = 64 square inches. $27{,}648 \div 64 = 432$.

17. **(D)** This is a case in which order is important. Therefore, it is a "permutations" problem. The answer is found by finding the number of permutations of 5 things taken 5 at a time. Symbolically it is $_5P_5$. You can do this on your calculator. It equals 120. You can also solve this by making 5 spaces such as (5) (4) (3) (2) (1). The first space can be filled in 5 ways, the second in 4 ways, and so on. Then you multiply $5 \times 4 \times 3 \times 2 \times 1 = 120$.

18. **(H)** Once you graph the 2 points and draw a line, 4 is the only possible choice. Mathematically, find the slope $\frac{6 - 2}{3 - (-3)} = \frac{4}{6} = \frac{2}{3}$. Then from $y = mx + b$, $6 = \frac{2}{3}(3) + b \Rightarrow 6 = 2 + b$. So $b = 4$. $y = \frac{2}{3}x + 4$. The y-intercept is 4.

19. **(B)** Since $\overleftrightarrow{AB}$ is parallel to $\overleftrightarrow{CD}$, the measure of $\angle APC = 37°$, by alternate interior angles. Then $37 + 40 + y = 180$. So the measure of $\angle CPD = 103°$. Also could be done by seeing that the measure of $\angle PCD = 40°$ by alternate interior angles. Then the sum of the angles of a triangle is 180°.

20. **(H)** If we transform $2x - 3y + 7 = 0$ into $y = mx + b$ form, the slope will be the coefficient of x. You get $-3y = -2x - 7$ by subtraction. Then divide each term by (–3) to get $y = \frac{2}{3}x + \frac{7}{3}$. The slope is $\frac{2}{3}$.

21. **(A)** You need to use the Pythagorean Theorem: $(QR)^2 + 16^2 = 20°$; $(QR)^2 + 256 = 400$; $(QR)^2 = 144$; $QR = 12$. Then by using SOH CAH TOA, $\cos = \frac{\text{adj}}{\text{hyp.}}$. Thus, $\cos \angle R = \frac{12}{20}$. Also, 12,16,20 is a Pythagorean triple (3,4,5).

22. **(J)** This factors both polynomials: $\frac{(x + 4)(x - 3)}{(x + 2)(x - 3)}$. After factoring we can cancel common factors. So the $(x - 3)$ factor that is in top and bottom can be reduced, leaving us with $\frac{x + 4}{x + 2}$.

23. **(B)** 5% of 1,000 is 50: [.05(1,000)]. So the second-year enrollment was 1,000 + 50 = 1,050. For the third year it decreased by 2% of the second-year enrollment: 2% of 1,050 = 21; 1,050 – 21 = 1,029.

24. **(J)** If we rewrite 2:3:4 as $2x{:}3x{:}4x$, then $2x + 3x + 4x = 63 \Rightarrow 9x = 63 \Rightarrow x = 7$. Tin is the $3x$. Therefore, tin = 3(7) = 21. The ratio then is 14:21:28.

25. **(D)** Bill walked $\frac{2}{3}$ of $4\frac{1}{2} = 3$ miles. $3 - 2\frac{1}{4} = \frac{3}{4}$.

26. **(J)** For the lines to be parallel, the ratio of the x-coefficients has to equal the ratio of the y-coefficients, while the ratio of the constant terms must be different. If the ratio of the constant terms is not different, the two equations would represent the same line. Therefore, $\frac{k}{32} = \frac{2}{k} \Rightarrow k^2 = 64 \Rightarrow k = 8$ and $\frac{2}{k} \ne \frac{6}{18}$.

27. **(D)** Using the distance formula $\sqrt{(x_2 - x_1)^2 + (y_2 - y_1)^2}$, we get $\sqrt{(4 - -2)^2 + (-7 - 1)^2} = \sqrt{6^2 + (-8)^2} = \sqrt{36 + 64} = \sqrt{100} = 10$.

28. **(F)** The area of a square is s^2. We have $s^2 = 36$. Thus a side of the square is 6. And the diameter of the circle is 6. The radius is $\frac{1}{2}$ the diameter, so the radius equals 3. Area of a circle is πr^2. Therefore, the area of the circle $= \pi(3)^2 = 9\pi$. Also note that choices G, H, J, and K are all incorrect because these values are all greater than 36 and the area of the circle should be less than 36.

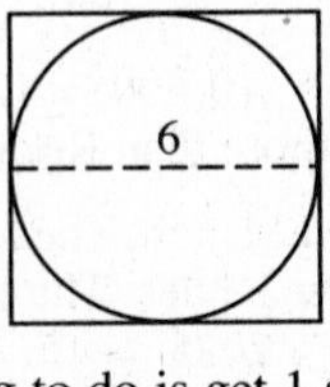

29. **(C)** This is a quadratic equation. The first thing to do is get 1 side of the equation equal to zero: $2x^2 - 5x - 12 = 0$. This factors to $(x - 4)(2x + 3) = 0$. Set each factor equal to zero: $x - 4 = 0 \Rightarrow x = 4$ and $2x + 3 = 0 \Rightarrow x = -1.5$. You could also use the quadratic formula $x = \frac{-b \pm \sqrt{b^2 - 4ac}}{2a}$, $a = 2$, $b = -5$, and $c = -12$; $x = \frac{5 \pm \sqrt{(-5)^2 - 4(2)(-12)}}{2(2)}$ $= \frac{5 \pm \sqrt{121}}{4} = \frac{5 \pm 11}{4}$. It would be easier if you had a program that would solve a quadratic equation on your calculator.

30. **(G)** You need to use the first part of the inequality and you have $x^2 < 2x$. Since x is positive we divide by x and get $x < 2$. The second half of the compound inequality yields $2x < x + 4 \Rightarrow x < 4$. Because this compound inequality represents an AND, the intersection of the two solutions is used and the final answer is $x < 2$.

31. **(C)** We can calculate the length of all but two of the segments. Call these two segments x and y. By adding the horizontal segments, we get $3 + x + y = 12 \Rightarrow x + y = 9$. Now the perimeter equals $6 + 3 + 3 + x + 1 + y + 2 + 12$. This yields $27 + (x + y) = 27 + 9 = 36$. The same answer would be obtained by making a rectangle and adding the perimeter of it. Note: it is not possible to get values for x and y, but we can find their sum.

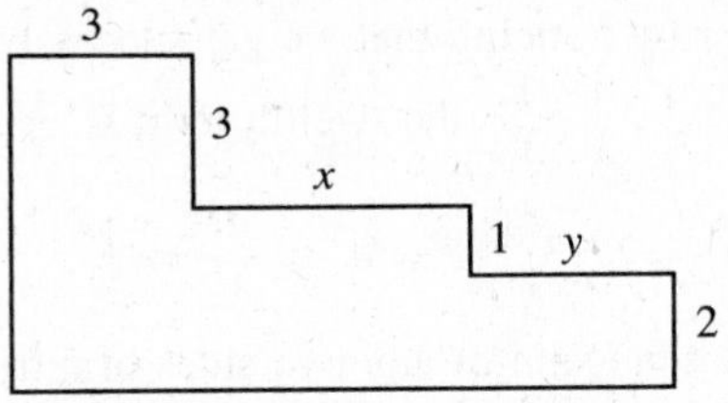

32. **(H)** The inequality $|x| > 2$ is equivalent to the compound inequality $x > 2$ OR $x < -2$. The correct answer is easily obtained by choosing numbers.

33. **(D)** After the first marble is drawn, there are 99 marbles left in the box. A winning marble must have a 5 in the tens digit. Originally, there were 10 marbles in the 50's but after the first was drawn, only 9 are left. Probability is $\frac{successes}{outcomes} = \frac{9}{99} = \frac{1}{11}$.

34. **(J)** Two triangles are similar if 2 corresponding angles are congruent. In this case, $\angle A$ must be congruent to $\angle E$, and $\angle B$ must be congruent to $\angle D$, by alternate interior angles. By vertical angles $\angle ACB$ is congruent to $\angle ECD$. Therefore, $\triangle ACB$ must be similar to $\triangle ECD$.

35. **(D)** These are similar triangles and the following proportion is true: $\frac{6}{x} = \frac{4}{14} \Rightarrow 4x = 84 \Rightarrow x = 21$ ft.

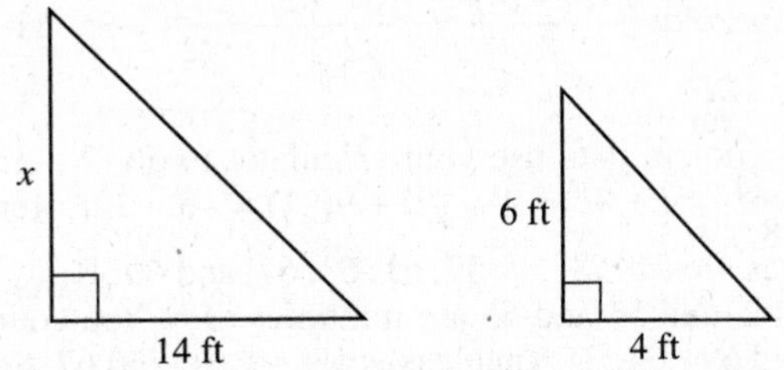

36. **(H)** Since we are multiplying by $2\pi r$ in $A = 2\pi r(r + h)$, we should divide by $2\pi r$. We get $\frac{A}{2\pi r} = \frac{2\pi r(r+h)}{2\pi r} \Rightarrow \frac{A}{2\pi r} = r + h$. Then subtract r from both sides and get $\frac{A}{2\pi r} - r = h$.

37. **(D)** Juanita must have Option A since 6 hours for Option B would be 6(11) = \$66. Under Option A, she would make 6(8) plus 10% of her sales. This gives the equation 6(8) + .10(sales) = 68 ⇒ .10(sales) = 20 ⇒ sales = $\frac{20}{.10}$ = \$200.

38. **(G)** Under Option A, Romeo would earn 15(8) + .10(400) = 120 + 40 = \$160. Under Option B, Juliette would earn 15(11) = \$165. Juliette makes 165 – 160 = \$5 more than Romeo.

39. **(C)** For a problem involving a rectangle, make a sketch. The rectangle has 4 right angles. When we draw the diagonal we make a right triangle in which we know 2 sides. The Pythagorean Theorem applies: $a^2 + b^2 = c^2$, so $27^2 + 36^2 = c^2 \Rightarrow 729 + 1296 = c^2 \Rightarrow c^2 = 2025$; $c = \sqrt{2025} = 45$. Also, 27, 36, 45 is a Pythagorean triple (3,4,5).

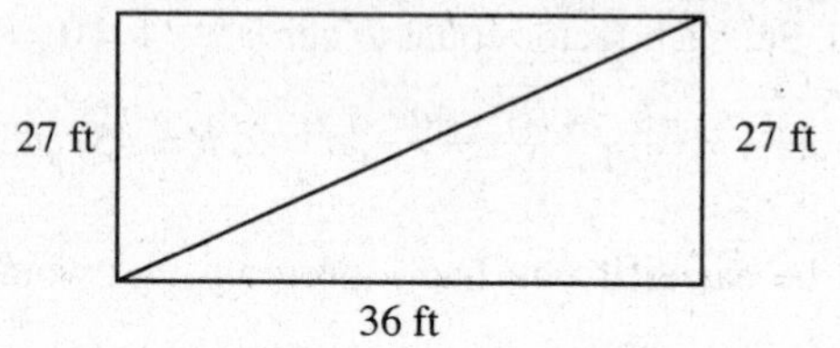

40. **(J)** When given coordinates of points, we graph them. The segment joining (3, 3) and (7, 3) is horizontal, so its length is 7 – 3 = 4. The height of the parallelogram is the distance between the 2 horizontal segments. That distance is 5. It is the distance from 3 to 8 on the *y*-axis. Area of a parallelogram = bh; $A = 4(5) = 20$.

41. **(B)** We use the midpoint formula to get this equation: $\left(\frac{a+1}{2}, \frac{b+6}{2}\right) = (-1, 1)$. Thus, $\frac{a+1}{2} = -1$ and $\frac{b+6}{2} = 1$ $\Rightarrow a + 1 = -2$ and $b + 6 = 2 \Rightarrow a = -3$ and $b = -4$.
Graph the points in the (x, y) plane. By your knowledge of what a midpoint is, you should see that the other endpoint has to be in quadrant III; (–3, –4) is the only choice that is in quadrant III.

42. **(G)** We could get the correct answer by noticing that we get successive terms by dividing by 3. Writing out 12 terms, 27, 9, 3, 1, $\frac{1}{3}, \frac{1}{3^2}, \frac{1}{3^3}, \frac{1}{3^4}, \frac{1}{3^5}, \frac{1}{3^6}, \frac{1}{3^7}, \frac{1}{3^8}$, the twelfth term is $\frac{1}{3^8}$. Using the formula for the *n*th term of a geometric sequence: $a_n = a_1 r^{n-1} \Rightarrow a_{12} = 27(3)^{(12-1)} \Rightarrow a_{12} = \frac{3^3}{3^{11}} = \frac{1}{3^8}$.

43. **(E)** The triangle inequality states that the sum of any two sides of a triangle must be greater than the third side. Since 14 + 14 = 28, the third side has to be less than 28.

44. **(H)** Both 4 and 8 are powers of 2 ($4 = 2^2$ and $8 = 2^3$, respectively); therefore, we can write both expressions as 2 to a power: $4^{3x+1} = (2^2)^{(3x+1)} = 2^{6x+2}$ and $8^{x+2} = (2^3)^{x+2} = 2^{3x+6}$. The equation can then be written as $2^{6x+2} = 2^{3x+6}$. Since the base (2) is the same, the exponents must be equal: $6x + 2 = 3x + 6$: $3x = 4$: $x = \frac{4}{3}$.

45. **(A)** $f(g(x))$ is equivalent to $f(2x - 1)$, which is equivalent to $(2x - 1)^2$. This is a FOIL problem: $(2x - 1)(2x - 1) = 4x^2 - 2x - 2x + 1 = 4x^2 - 4x + 1$.

46. **(K)** In the diagram, there is a 30°-60°-90° triangle and a 45°-45°-90° triangle. The ratio of sides in the 30°-60°-90° is $x : x\sqrt{3} : 2x$, so $BD = 6\sqrt{3}$ and $AB = 12$. The ratio of sides in the 45°-45°-90° is $x : x : x\sqrt{2}$, so $CD = 6$ and $AC = 6\sqrt{2}$. The perimeter is $6 + 6\sqrt{3} + 12 + 6\sqrt{2} \approx 36.9$.

47. **(A)** Subtracting the area of the rectangle *ABFE* from the area of the trapezoid *ABCD* gives the sum of the areas of $\triangle AED$ and $\triangle BFC$. Area of a trapezoid: $\frac{h(b_1 + b_2)}{2} = \frac{4(6+12)}{2} = \frac{72}{2} = 36$. The area of a rectangle: $bh = 6(4) = 24$. Subtracting the areas: 36 – 24 = 12.

48. **(J)** The easiest way to do this problem is to use your calculator to do $(2 - 3i)^2 = -5 - 12i$. Alternatively, do $(2 - 3i)(2 - 3i)$, which is FOIL: $4 - 6i - 6i + 9i^2 = 4 - 12i + 9(-1) = -5 - 12i$. Remember, $i^2 = -1$.

49. **(A)** The only possible candidates are 51, 53, 57, 59, 61, 63, 67, and 69. B, C, D, and E are incorrect because there are no even primes greater than 2, and 55 and 65 are multiples of 5. You counted too many prime numbers. 51 = 3(17), 57 = 3(19), 63 = 3(21), and 69 = 3(23). That leaves 53, 59, 61, and 67. So there are 4 prime numbers between 50 and 70.

50. **(F)** If $(x + 2)$ is a factor, then substituting -2 for x in $3x^2 - 13x + k$ must yield zero: $3(-2)^2 - 13(-2) + k = 0$; $3(4) + 26 + k = 0$: $k = -38$.

51. **(D)** Tripling the radius means the new radius is $3r$ and the new volume would be $\frac{4\pi}{3}(3r)^3 = \frac{4\pi}{3}(27r^3) = 27\left(\frac{4\pi r^3}{3}\right) = 27$ times the volume of the original sphere.

52. **(K)** If $f(x) = x^2 - 2x + 4$, then $f(t + 2) = (t + 2)^2 - 2(t + 2) + 4$ by substitution. This expression must be expanded and simplified: $(t + 2)^2 - 2(t + 2) + 4 = t^2 + 4t + 4 - 2t - 4 + 4$, which simplifies to $t^2 + 2t + 4$.

53. **(B)** The formula for arc length $= \frac{\textit{central angle}}{360}(2\pi r)$. In this case, arc length $\widehat{AB} = \frac{60}{360}(2\pi 8) = \frac{1}{6}(16\pi) = \frac{8\pi}{3}$.

54. **(H)** If $x = 4y + 2$, then $4y = x - 2$ and $y = \frac{x-2}{4}$, so $y + 6 = \frac{x-2}{4} + 6$. Find a common denominator and this becomes $\frac{x-2}{4} + \frac{24}{4} = \frac{x+22}{4}$.

55. **(C)** Since $\frac{\pi}{2} < \theta < \pi$, θ is in quadrant II. If we make a reference triangle in quadrant II, we get this triangle by using $\sin\theta = \frac{5}{7}$ and SOH CAH TOA. By the Pythagorean Theorem $a^2 + 5^2 = 7^2$, $a^2 = 24$, $a = \pm 2\sqrt{6}$. The x-coordinate is negative in quadrant II: $a = -2\sqrt{6}$. Then $\cos\theta = -\frac{2\sqrt{6}}{7}$.

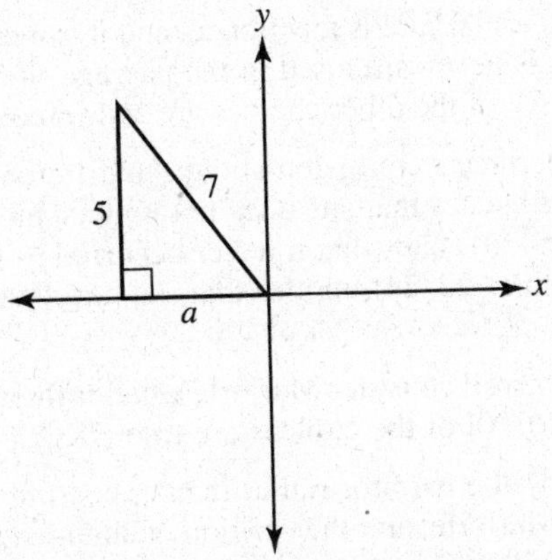

56. **(K)** There are 2 properties of logarithms that apply in this problem. They are:
1) The log of a quotient is the difference of logarithms.
2) The log of a number raised to an exponent (i.e., $\log a^b = b \cdot \log a$) is the product of the power and the log.

Applying these we get $\log_b\left(\frac{x}{y^3}\right) = \log_b x - \log_b y^3 = \log_b x - 3\log_b y$ and by substitution equals $g - 3p$.

57. **(E)** The third angle of the triangle is $180 - (35 + 44) = 101°$. Then by the law of sines: $\frac{12}{\sin 101°} = \frac{AC}{\sin 44°}$. At this point, we could eliminate choices A, B, C, and D comparing each to our equation. However, we can easily solve for AC by multiplying both sides of our equation by sin 44°. The result is $AC = \frac{12\sin 44°}{\sin 101°}$.

58. **(K)** This problem is an example of linear programming. However, we do not have to actually do linear programming. All we need to do is write 4 ordered pairs using combinations of smallest and largest possible values of x with smallest and largest possible values of y. These 4 ordered pairs are $(-2, -3)$, $(-2, 3)$, $(5, -3)$, and $(5, 3)$. Then evaluate $(x - y)$ for each. We get $-2 - (-3) = 1$, $-2 - 3 = 5$, $5 - (-3) = 8$, and $5 - 3 = 2$. The largest of these is 8, which is the maximum possible value.

59. **(E)** Listing all the possible factors of 20, we would be able to write linear factors of the form $(x+\ )(x+\ )$ or $(x-\ )(x-\ )$ since the coefficient of x^2 is 1. We could factor 20 as (1)(20), (2)(10), (4, 5), (−1)(−20), (−2, 10), and (−4, −5). Then the possible linear factors are

$(x + 1)(x + 20) = x^2 + 21x + 20$

$(x + 2)(x + 10) = x^2 + 12x + 20$

$(x + 4)(x + 5) = x^2 + 9x + 20$

$(x-1)(x-20) = x^2 - 21x + 20$

$(x-2)(x-10) = x^2 - 12x + 20$

$(x-4)(x-5) = x^2 - 9x + 20.$

So b could be any of these numbers $\{21, 12, 9, -21, -12, -9\}$. There are 6 possibilities. Thus the only possible choice is E. All of the other choices do not consider all possibilities.

60. **(G)** There are 2 important conditions. They are that M and N are prime numbers and that $\sqrt{21(M)(N)(5)(7)}$ is a rational number. If we factor 21 as (3)(7), we get $\sqrt{(3)(7)(M)(N)(5)(7)} = 7\sqrt{(3)(M)(N)(5)}$. Since $\sqrt{(3)(M)(N)(5)}$ must be rational, $(3)(M)(N)(5)$ has to be a perfect square. We are dealing with prime numbers. Therefore, $(M)(N) = 15$. The prime factorization of 15 is 3(5), which means M and N must be 3 and 5, in any order.

Answer Explanations: Reading Test

1. **(B)** Although the narrator mainly communicates the inner thoughts of Bernice, the last paragraph clearly conveys Marjorie's thoughts also.
2. **(F)** Although the passage mentions Bernice's having been "brought up on novels" (line 21), there is no indication that her mother was the author. All of the choices are true EXCEPT this one.
3. **(C)** Although Bernice's hometown of Eau Claire is mentioned, and it is mentioned that she will attend college in New York, the characters' current location is never disclosed in the passage (it is implied that this place is more sophisticated than Eau Claire, but that's all). All of the other choices are answered by the passage, but NOT this one.
4. **(J)** The second paragraph depicts Bernice's confusion about the difference in her levels of popularity here and at home. The first sentence (lines 14–15) states that she does not understand "why she never had any attention" elsewhere. The second sentence (lines 16–20) states that it never occurred to Bernice that her mother's help was a factor at home. And the third sentence (lines 20–24) implies that she has developed unrealistic expectations as a result of the books she reads.
5. **(A)** Although Bernice's parents *might* well consider Marjorie a bad influence *if* they knew what she was really like, the passage never implies that they do. All of the choices are true EXCEPT this one.
6. **(G)** Although the opinion is stated by the narrator rather than appearing in a line of Marjorie's dialogue, the last paragraph is "close third person" on Marjorie, and the opinion is intended to be taken as hers. The second and third sentences of the final paragraph are followed by "Having decided this, Marjorie..." (line 87), confirming that they were Marjorie's thoughts.
7. **(D)** The passage states (lines 40–43) that the conversation "pierced" Bernice as if she had been "drawn through with a needle," indicating that she was hurt emotionally by overhearing it.
8. **(H)** The passage establishes (lines 57–60) that Mrs. Harvey believes things have changed, and that in her day all well-bred or upper-class (ones from "nice families") girls "had glorious times."
9. **(A)** Marjorie states (lines 54–56) that Bernice has "gorgeous coloring" (i.e., she is pretty) but is a "ninny" (i.e., her personality is the problem), whereas her friend Martha could do more with such physical gifts if only she had them. The implication is that Martha's personality is superior to Bernice's.
10. **(G)** The first paragraph states that Bernice finds Marjorie to possess "very few of the qualities" that she considers "appropriately ... feminine" (lines 11–13). The second paragraph (lines 20–24) implies that Bernice's concept of appropriate femininity is based on fictional novels. In other words, she is comparing Marjorie to an unrealistic ideal.
11. **(D)** The author explains in paragraph 2 that most music is now obtained by consumers using software that was developed and sold by businesses external to the record companies, and yet the record companies still feel entitled to the same "cut" that they got back when they did all the work.
12. **(G)** The author sees the "CD-promotional model" mentioned in the last paragraph as the basis of a new system whereby music itself would be free, and record companies would make money from concerts.
13. **(C)** The author explains in paragraph 4 that peer-to-peer software is now so easy to use that there are no longer any technical obstacles to music piracy.

14. **(G)** In these lines, the author describes an economic reality: technological advances have led to a state where people can get music without paying for it unless the government stops them somehow.
15. **(A)** The opening paragraphs explain the ways in which the music industry has changed, and assert that record companies still expect to make just as much money even though they do less work.
16. **(H)** The author repeatedly asserts that consumers who download music for free are a natural consequence of the new technology, and so he sees these consumers as behaving *logically*.
17. **(D)** The first paragraph depicts the government "passing the buck," as it were, trying to make schools culpable for music piracy just because lots of music pirates go to school, even though music piracy is not the school's fault.
18. **(G)** In the closing paragraphs, the author details a few ways that musicians and remixers have gotten more creative as a result of the situation.
19. **(C)** The author closes by predicting that CDs will continue to exist, but for a different purpose: they will become free promotions for concerts, rather than a source of revenue.
20. **(J)** The second author examines filesharing as a moral issue in the light of older moral philosophy (in this case, Utilitarianism), while the author of the passage simply seems to think that you can't stop progress, so there is no use in philosophizing about it.
21. **(D)** The passage as a whole is about the Internet outcompeting TV (the title is "Why TV Lost," after all), so you know it's going to be one of the choices that begins with "weaker." Of those choices, only the assertion about TV's limitations is consistent with the passage. (Right answer + true statement.)
22. **(F)** Lines 10–35 allude to three predictable forces, and one that would have been "harder to" predict. The three predictable forces are outlined in the rest of paragraph 2. Paragraphs 3 and 4 then discuss the "somewhat more surprising" (line 24) force: *social applications* (for example, Facebook).
23. **(A)** Lines 25–28 address how important to teenagers socializing is, and lines 31–35 explain that this fact gives them the energy and motivation to learn a lot about computers very quickly. Therefore, the relevant traits are that teens are *energetic* and *social*.
24. **(H)** This section of the passage discusses how TV technology forces stations to tailor content to local concerns, and how this puts TV at a disadvantage compared with the Internet, where geographical location doesn't matter. The sentence immediately following in lines 66–68 is basically a paraphrase of the correct answer.
25. **(C)** Lines 45–53 explain that TV networks "grudgingly" put some shows online, but wish they didn't have to.
26. **(G)** Paragraphs 5, 6, and 7 (lines 45–80) discuss the attitudes of "old media" toward the changes brought by the Internet. They are portrayed as angrily resisting the new business models. Therefore, *resentful stubbornness* is correct.
27. **(D)** "Keep the old model running" is an automotive metaphor about patching up an old machine rather than caving in and buying a new one; choice D is basically a paraphrase of the sentence indicated.
28. **(G)** Lines 20–23 state that the younger generation is used to everything they're interested in being available on computers. It is worth noting that the other three answer choices are all *critical* of young people, whereas the passage and the right answer are not (young people expect to be criticized by adults, and so the wrong answers are playing on the expectations of the test takers).
29. **(C)** The last sentence of paragraph 6 echoes the main point it has been making: that the only reason TV shows are aimed at local audiences is because TV itself relies on broadcasting a limited signal from a local source, not because it was ever what people wanted.
30. **(J)** Whereas the passage suggests that the Internet will soon completely replace TV, which will essentially have no reason to exist anymore, the author of this excerpt points out that TV is better suited to some specific situations (like a live sporting event).
31. **(C)** The passage argues that virtually all of the phenomena traditionally associated with ghosts and hauntings are scientifically explainable.
32. **(J)** This paragraph explains why humans would have evolved a fear reponse to certain vibrations (because those vibrations are usually made by dangerous things).
33. **(A)** The concert experiment proves that humans will exhibit fear responses to infrasound even when they are not expecting to be scared (as someone who knowingly enters a reputedly haunted house might).

34. **(G)** The passage never addresses accounts of people who supposedly received information from ghosts.

35. **(A)** The passage implies that many of the people who have reported seeing ghosts were probably confused by infrasound and making an honest mistake.

36. **(J)** The passage in lines 61–62 explains that the cause of the sound was made by a silent exhaust fan.

37. **(B)** *Havoc* most nearly means "*chaos*." To "wreak havoc" on something is to throw it into chaos or extreme disarray.

38. **(H)** When the passage says that evolution taught us that these sounds represent "bad news," it means that they are frequently made by things that pose real dangers, like wild animals or storms.

39. **(C)** Gavreau's initial motivation was to figure out why his assistant's ear was suddenly bleeding. He didn't know at first that he was going to discover infrasound or that this would explain hauntings.

40. **(J)** For a good haunted house, you would need both vibrations in the infrasound "panic range" and a properly shaped room for them to bounce around in. It doesn't matter what is making the vibrations, as long as they are in the right range.

Answer Explanations: Science Test

1. **(B)** The fourth column in Table 3 lists the amount of time the reactant was passed over the catalyst. The fifth column lists the amount of propane collected for each trial. As the numbers in the fourth column get smaller, the numbers in the fifth column get smaller also.

2. **(J)** As stated in the first paragraph of text, a catalyst is a substance that speeds up a reaction. Since no propane was collected in Trial 4, we can assume the hydrogen and propene did not have enough time to interact with the catalyst and no reaction occurred.

3. **(C)** Paragraph 1 of the text states that a heterogeneous catalyst is when the catalyst is in a different phase from the reactants. In the description of Experiment 1, it is stated that the catalyst is made up of alumina beads and that the propanol is in a vapor phase when it reacts with the catalyst. Vapor and solid are two different phases, so it is a heterogeneous catalyst.

4. **(H)** Table 1 clearly states that Stage 3 is when the reaction occurs. The description of Experiment 2 states that the reaction occurs after the hydrogen-propene mixture passed over the catalyst, and then the propane was collected. Table 1 describes the four stages of catalysis.

5. **(A)** The volume of propanol was the same for each trial, whereas the volume of alumina beads was different. Look at Table 2. We know from reading the description of Experiment 1 that the catalyst is the alumina beads. The third column in Table 2 lists the volume of the catalyst used for each trial. The amounts would have to be different, while the volume of propanol used as reactant would have to be the same, to test the effect that varying the amount of catalyst has on the outcome.

6. **(J)** There was no reason for the plunger to move until the propene entered the syringe.

7. **(B)** When there are two recessive L alleles in the genotype, the leaf texture is wrinkled, so it can be determined that the L gene affects leaf texture.

8. **(H)** The last row in Table 2 lists the phenotypes for this genotype.

9. **(A)** The genotype would contain two recessive P alleles. Table 3 contains the data for the four different crosses performed. It can be determined from Table 2 that if a plant has 3 pods, the genotype is made up of two recessive P alleles.

10. **(J)** It can be determined from Table 2 that the genotype pp results in 3 pods. Table 3 shows that 100% of the offspring for Cross 3 had 3 pods, so 100% of the offspring must have the genotype pp.

11. **(D)** Table 2 displays all the possible genotypes and the associated phenotypes. There are only two rows where the phenotypes are 3 pods and normal leaves, and the associated genotypes listed are ppLL and ppLl. All other answers can be eliminated.

12. **(G)** Find Table 1. Look at the column labeled Am*ount of Chlorophyll per Experiment*. The bottom two rows are the data for Experiment 3. The sample exposed to UVR is labeled *3-UVR*. Follow that row until you come to the column with the heading *4*, for day 4. The amount of chlorophyll measured was 1.3.

13. **(A)** We compare the amounts of chlorophyll measured in Experiment 1 for the sample exposed to UVR and the sample not exposed to UVR, labeled PAR. For each measurement, the amount of chlorophyll found in the sample

exposed to UVR is either the same as, or lower than, the PAR sample. The same is true if you compare the data from Experiments 2 and 3. Therefore, it can be concluded that UVR exposure inhibits chlorophyll production.

14. **(G)** Look at Figure 3. The diatoms exposed to UVR are labeled UVR. The bars on the graph for UVR are gray. If you compare the two bars for diatoms, you will see that the UVR bar is much lower than the PAR bar. In fact, the UVR bar for diatoms is the lowest bar on the graph, making this the correct answer.
15. **(D)** The only experiment that continued for eight days was Experiment 3. If you look at the data from Experiment 3, you will see that the sample not exposed to UVR, labeled 3-PAR, measured more than twice the amount of chlorophyll on day 8 than on day 6. Assume Experiment 1 would produce similar results. On day 6 the sample 1-PAR measured 17 for chlorophyll. Day 8 would be more than double that amount, so 36 is the best answer.
16. **(J)** Look at Figure 2. According to the legend, the bars that show the number of dead cells found in the samples exposed to UVR are white. The white bars are higher for both diatoms and flagellates.
17. **(C)** Look at the section under the heading Researcher 1. The third paragraph lists the demographic parameters that can be monitored in seabirds. Mortality rates are not listed.
18. **(J)** Look at the section under the heading Researcher 1. The second paragraph makes this point.
19. **(C)** Look at the section under the heading Researcher 2. The second paragraph addresses this issue and mentions that placing bands on penguins has been shown to reduce both breeding success and survival rates.
20. **(F)** Look at the section under the heading Researcher 1. The last sentence of paragraph 1 supports this answer.
21. **(C)** The first paragraph of the passage discusses indicators, and there is a 4-point list of important criteria for an effective indicator. Researcher 2's views state that seabirds do not fit the first three criteria and do not address the fourth item in the list. Look at the section under the heading Researcher 2 to understand how his or her views are related to each point. Point 1—the last sentence of paragraph 1 explains why seabirds don't meet this criterion. Point 2—the first sentence of paragraph 2 explains why seabirds don't meet this criterion. Point 3—the first sentence of paragraph 3 explains why seabirds don't meet this criterion.
22. **(F)** When the amount of prey is low, so is the number of seabirds. Look at the section under the heading Researcher 1. The last sentence of paragraph 1 makes it clear that as there is less prey available, the seabird population will decline. This is a direct relationship and the graph to reflect that will be a diagonal line.
23. **(C)** Researcher 2 doesn't mention the cost associated with using seabirds as indicators. The last paragraph of Researcher 1's point of view states that "seabirds are…cost-effective."
24. **(F)** Look at Figure 2. The first set of columns is for liquid fuel, as the label shows. The white column represents leaded fuel, as the legend states. Follow the top of the white column over to the left, and you will see that it is at about the 200 mark on the *y*-axis.
25. **(C)** Look at Figure 2. The highest column represents the type of fuel found to have the highest average concentration of benzene. The third column is the highest. Looking down we see that it is labeled as a vapor, and the legend tells us that the white columns represent leaded fuel, so we can determine the highest average concentration of benzene was found in leaded vapor fuel.
26. **(J)** Look at Figure 1. Follow the line on the graph. After 5 minutes, the line steadily climbs up as time passes. It can be deduced that after 20 minutes the line would have continued to climb, meaning that the temperature would have continued to increase. Choice D is the only answer that reflects this outcome.
27. **(C)** Brand C is the only brand that had a higher concentration of benzene in the leaded fuel. Look at the data in Table 1. The second column lists the concentration of benzene found in the liquid form of the fuels. Compare the amounts found in each brand for leaded versus unleaded. Brand C is the only brand that had a higher concentration of benzene in the leaded fuel.
28. **(G)** Look at Figure 3. The first set of columns represents the gasohol fuels, according to the *x*-axis labels. The legend tells us that the white column represents the liquid form of the fuel, and the gray column represents the vapor form of the fuel. By looking at the relative heights of the columns, it can be determined that the white column is about half the size of the gray column.
29. **(B)** Look at Table 1. The second row displays the data for the bob with a mass of 100 g. The last column displays the average period. Follow the second row over to the last column to find the number 1.83.
30. **(G)** Look at Table 2. The longer the length of the string, the longer the average period; 1 m was the longest length of string tested, and the average period was 1.84 s. We can deduce that if the string was 0.8 m, then the average period would be less than 1.84 s and greater than 1.45 m.

31. **(B)** Look at Table 1. The first column shows the mass of the bob tested. As the column for each trial shows, as well as the average period, the larger the mass of the bob, the longer the period.

32. **(H)** Figure 2 displays the affect that changing the amplitude of the pendulum has on the average period. Each column in the figure is roughly the same size, meaning that regardless of the amplitude, the average period is about the same. We can deduce that pendulums A and B would have about the same average period.

33. **(B)** Look at Table 2. The third column displays the results for Trial 2. Look at the second row down that displays the results for the string with a length of 0.6 m. The table shows 1.44 s as the period recorded.

34. **(H)** Based on the information in the text preceding the explanation of the experiments, and the descriptions of the experiments and results displayed, it can be determined that the mass of the bob, the length of the string, and the swing amplitude were all varied.

35. **(A)** Look at Table 1 and find the largest number, which is 26. Follow the column up to find that the location is Iquique.

36. **(G)** Look at the middle column in Figure 2, which is labeled Coquimbo. Trace your finger to the left from the top of the bar to find that the average egg size is between 0.15 and 0.2 mm.

37. **(C)** Look at Figure 3. Find the tallest bar, which represents the average SMR. The bar on the left is the tallest and it is a solid black bar. The legend tells you this represents the TC1 thermal category. Now look down to find the label on the *x*-axis, which is Iquique.

38. **(J)** *Several things must be consulted to answer this question.* Table 1 contains the temperatures that the crabs were exposed to at each location. The text in paragraph 2 defines TC2 as the average maximum temperature, so you know you need to pay attention to the numbers in that row of the table. In addition, Figure 1 must be consulted because it contains information about the size of the crabs. Table 1 shows that crabs at Iquique were exposed to the highest average temperatures at 22, then Coquimbo at 20, and Concepcion at 17. Figure 1 shows that the average size of the crabs was smallest at Iquique, slightly larger at Coquimbo, and then largest at Concepcion.

39. **(C)** The information in Table 1 and Figure 2 needs to be analyzed to answer this question. Table 1 shows that the temperatures were highest at Iquique, then Coquimbo, and lowest at Concepcion. The control temperature was only 1° lower than the average maximum temperature at Concepcion. Using this information, and looking at Figure 2, it can be determined that at lower temperatures, the egg volume is greater. So, if scientists had measured the egg volume of crabs in the control groups, they would have most likely found larger sizes than at any of the sites measured.

40. **(J)** Look at the information in Table 1 and Figure 3 to answer this question. For both Iquique and Concepcion the black column in Figure 3 is the highest, but for Coquimbo the white column is the highest. So there is no clear relationship between temperature exposure and SMR.

Writing Sample

Recently, some people have suggested that students at this school should be required to maintain a certain minimum GPA in order to be allowed to participate in extracurricular activities. As a good student, you might assume I would be in favor of this plan. But in my opinion, this is one of those ideas that sounds great at first, but turns out to be built on many fallacies and false assumptions, as I will demonstrate in the ensuing paragraphs. First of all, extracurricular activities can foster a sense of school or team spirit, which has actually been shown to raise grades. Secondly, it's not actually the case that colleges will care more about GPA than extracurriculars in the case of every student. And finally, let's remember that extracurriculars are not just about fun—they can teach and hone skills just as important to a student's future as the classes do.

The reasoning that the people in favor of this rule are using seems logical enough. If a student is getting bad grades, then more time to study would help, and no extracurricular activities means more time to study, right? But I'm afraid it's not that simple. It's not enough just to have the extra time—a student has to be motivated to use that time well. And as any psychologist will tell you, a teenager is more motivated to excel when he or she feels like part of a team, rather than when they are all on their own. Whether we are talking about sports or one of the academic clubs, all extracurricular activities make students feel like they are part of a team, both as a member of their particular club and as a representative of our school in general. The importance of letting students participate in activities that they choose to do, as opposed to just the classes that they have to attend, cannot be overestimated. Passing this rule would involve tearing struggling students away from the only thing they like about coming to school. That's not how you motivate someone to study!

Now, let's remember why we care so much about students' GPAs. A high GPA is how you get into a good college, right? So by helping students raise their GPAs, we are helping them get into better colleges, thereby ensuring brighter futures. But not so fast! Once again, the logic seems airtight at first, but is a little oversimplified. It's not the case that colleges only care about GPA. They balance it with other things. Take the athletes for example, who are usually the ones people are the most worried about when they propose rules like this. Dropping out of sports in exchange for a slightly higher GPA might be a good idea for some of the athletes, but what about the stars? The kids who are really good at sports are going to get into top schools just based on their athletic skill, no matter what their GPA is, so kicking them off the teams just to turn their "C" average into a "C+" average would be the absolute worst thing anyone could do for them! And the same goes for a student in the orchestra who is amazing at his or her instrument, or a student in drama club with a lot of acting talent. I'm not making excuses for people who neglect their studies completely, but I think decisions like whether to drop out of extracurriculars should be made on an individual basis by the student and his or her parents. An across-the-board rule that treats every student the same runs the risk of hurting more students than it helps.

And of course, after college comes real life. We can't make the mistake of assuming that extracurriculars are only about fun and getting into college. Some extracurricular activities teach and hone skills that will be just as useful to students in the real world as the things they learn in class are. The things we learn in class are important, but we both know that most students aren't going to end up using trigonometry in their eventual careers. On the other hand, a student who is on the Yearbook Committee or school paper is learning about graphic design, photo editing, journalism, publishing, and the list goes on. Just from being in one club, a student can learn upwards of half a dozen marketable skills that they don't teach us in the normal classes. And since students get to choose which extracurriculars they are involved with based on what they're interested in, the odds that the skills they learn will be related to their eventual careers are much higher than with any individual class.

So, even though I have a high GPA and this rule would not affect me personally, I am still against it, simply because I think it is not in the best interests of the majority of students. It's questionable whether the extra time a student would gain from being kicked off the clubs would raise his or her grade in the first place. Even if a student's GPA did go up, the trade-off might not be worth it in the eyes of a college, depending on what else the student is good at. And finally, extracurriculars teach marketable skills to the same extent that the core classes do. If there are individual students who are on thin ice academically, then by all means the school should communicate with those students' parents to determine the best course of action. But as I have just shown, a "one size fits all" rule would be a terrible idea in this case. Thank you for your kind attention.

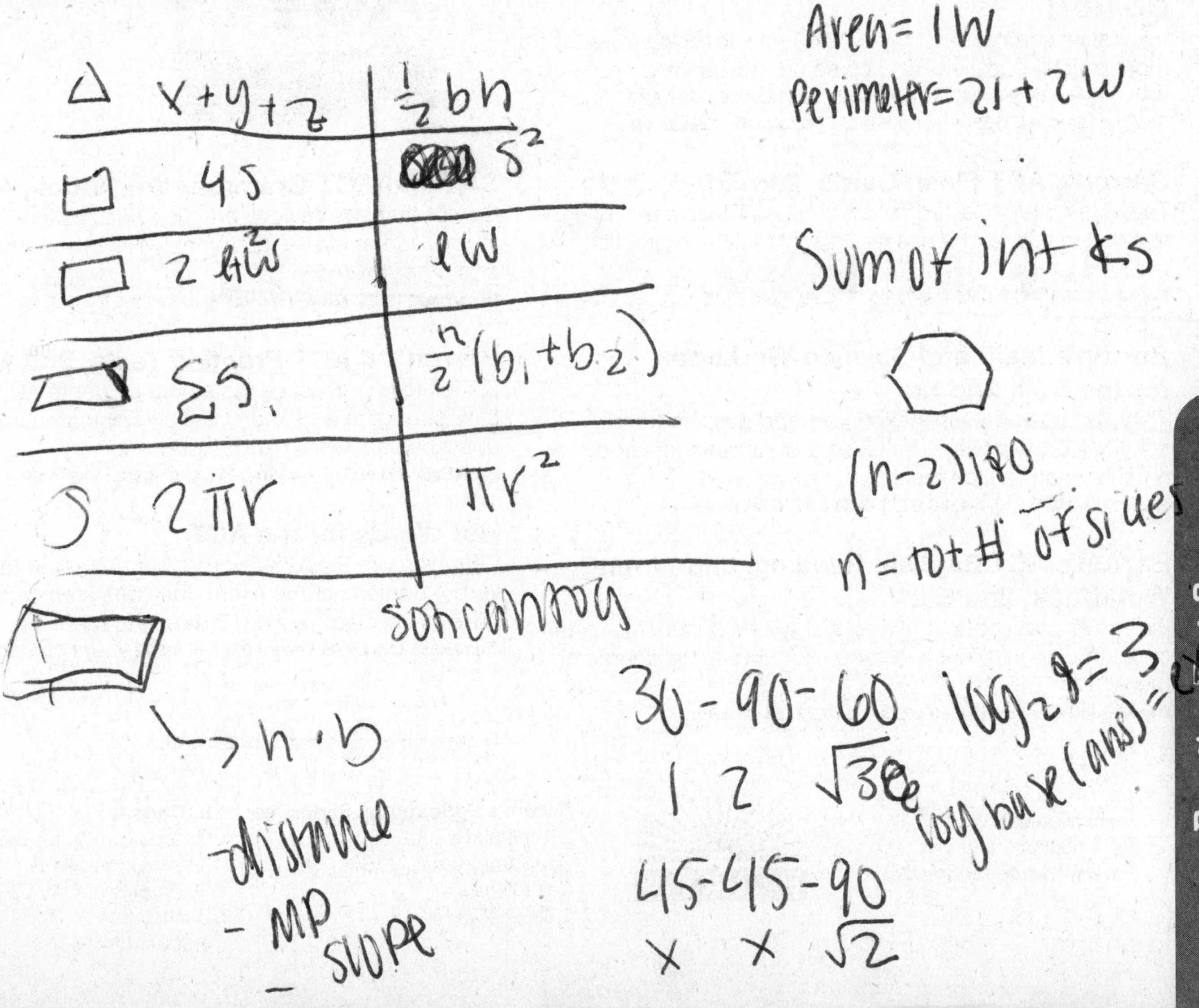

BARRON'S—The Leader in ACT Test Preparation!

STUDENTS' #1 CHOICE

Students preparing for the ACT college entrance exam will find plenty of help from Barron's. With a wide range of study tools—from manuals, flash cards, and CD-ROMs, to cutting-edge online and digital tools—Barron's has everything test-takers need to get the score they want. Why go anywhere else?

Barron's ACT, w/optional CD-ROM, 2nd Ed.
Four full-length model tests with questions answered and explained. An optional CD-ROM presents two additional tests.
Book: paperback, ISBN 978-1-4380-0796-0, $18.99, *Can$22.99*
Book with CD-ROM: ISBN 978-1-4380-7637-9, $29.99, *Can$35.99*

Pass Key to the ACT, 2nd Ed.
This shorter version of the ACT manual presents two full-length practice tests with all questions answered and explained.
Paperback, ISBN 978-1-4380-0800-4, $9.99, *Can$11.99*

Barron's ACT 36, 3rd Ed., w/optional CD-ROM
Innovative strategies show students how to tackle the ACT's most difficult questions and come up with winning answers.
Book: paperback, ISBN 978-1-4380-0625-3, $18.99, *Can$22.99*
Book w/CD-ROM: ISBN 978-1-4380-7567-9, $29.99, *Can$35.99*

Barron's ACT Flash Cards, 2nd Ed.
These test-prep flash cards cover all ACT test areas, offer test-taking tips, and present pertinent facts and practice problems.
Boxed set, ISBN 978-0-7641-6768-3, $16.99, *Can$19.99*

Barron's Math and Science Workbook for the ACT, 2nd Ed.
This workbook presents exercises and quizzes with solutions and answers. Includes a diagnostic test and a full-length practice test.
Paperback, ISBN 978-1-4380-0222-4, $14.99, *Can$16.99*

Barron's ACT English, Reading, and Writing Workbook, 2nd Ed.
Extensive practice and review that will help students excel on all three verbal sections and all four reading genres of the ACT.
Paperback, ISBN 978-1-4380-0223-1, $14.99, *Can$16.99*

SAT and ACT Grammar Workbook, 4th Ed.
Comprehensive review, practice quizzes, and exercises to sharpen students' grammar skills for the ACT, SAT, and other exams.
Paperback, ISBN 978-1-4380-0873-8, $14.99, *Can$17.99*

Barron's 6 ACT Practice Tests, 2nd Ed.
Six full-length practice tests help students determine their strengths and improve their weak areas. All questions answered and explained.
Paperback, ISBN 978-1-4380-0494-5, $14.99, *Can$16.99*

Hot Words for the ACT
Defines more than 250 words that appear in the verbal portions of the exam. Includes memory tips, review exercises, a word index, and more.
Paperback, ISBN 978-1-4380-0365-8, $9.99, *Can$11.50*

Prices subject to change without notice.

Available at your local book store or visit
www.barronseduc.com

BARRON'S

Barron's Educational Series, Inc.
250 Wireless Blvd.
Hauppauge, NY 11788
Call toll-free:
1-800-645-3476

In Canada:
Georgetown Book Warehouse
34 Armstrong Ave.
Georgetown, Ont. L7G 4R9
Call toll-free:
1-800-247-7160

(#164) R1/16